Visiting the Gardens of Europe

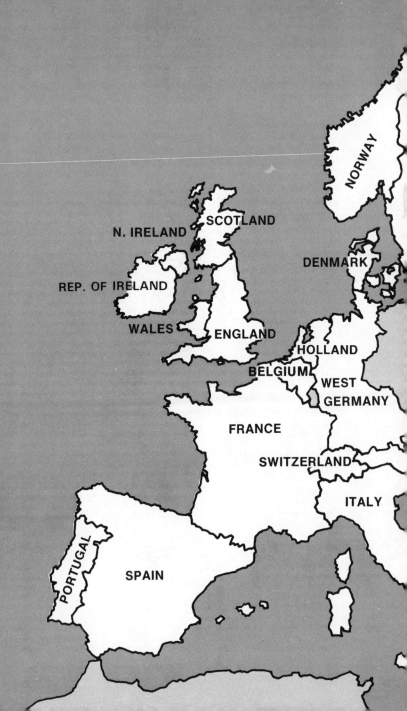

EUROPE

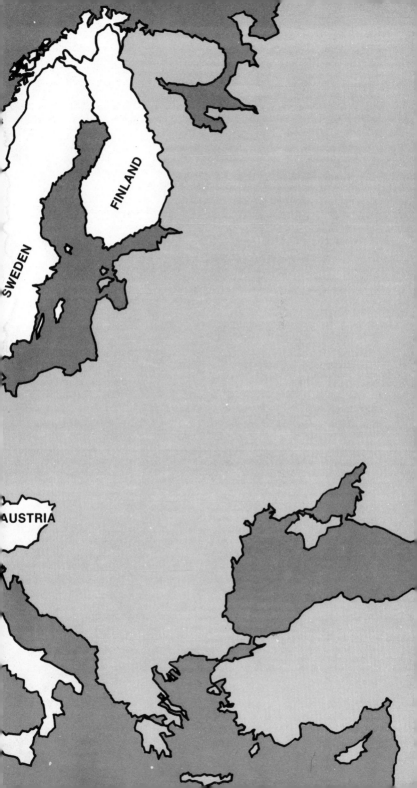

Visiting the Gardens of Europe

Harriet Bridgeman &

Elizabeth Drury

 Thomas Congdon Books   E.P. Dutton   New York

First American edition published 1979 by
E.P. Dutton, a Division of Elsevier-Dutton
Publishing Co., Inc., New York

For information contact: E.P. Dutton, 2 Park Avenue,
New York, N.Y. 10016

Library of Congress Catalog Card Number: 79-51562

ISBN: 0-525-04700-X

10 9 8 7 6 5 4 3 2 1

CONTENTS

This is a completely new venture: a handbook to the principal gardens in Western Europe that are open to the public permanently or regularly.

More than 1,000 gardens are described. They include botanical gardens, formal gardens, romantic, cottage and woodland gardens, landscape gardens, specialist gardens and arboreta, cloister gardens and patios and town parks. From Finland to Gibraltar, from near-sea level in Holland to high in the Alps and the Spanish sierras, a wide variety of geological and climatic conditions are represented.

The botanical gardens contain collections of plants that are often as remarkable for their curiosity as for their beauty. These are plant museums, displaying specimens of indigenous species and species brought back from intemperate climates and high altitudes by adventurous botanists. In botanical gardens, and in a small number of privately owned gardens, species on the verge of extinction are preserved, and scientific research is undertaken in the fields of nutrition and medicine.

Many of the great formal gardens were swept away with the late eighteenth-century fashion for the 'natural' garden, but those that remain are historically as important as the castles and palaces for which they were the setting. Magnificent rooms give on to terraces, parterres and avenues, to grounds ornamented with topiary, statuary, fountains and pools that were conceived as an extension to, and in the same spirit as, the high ordered interiors and façades.

A traditional English cottage garden is equally the manifestation of a particular way of life. There are few sights more pleasing than orderly rows of vegetables growing between beds of simple herbaceous plants and roses. Whereas a large house and estate might have a walled kitchen garden, an orchard, hothouses and beds of flowers for cutting, the cottager must make do with quarter of an acre or less to grow vegetables, fruit and flowers.

Cloister gardens and patios served a different purpose. Essentially tranquil places, they were often designed to appeal as much to the sense of smell and to the ear as to the eye. Woodland and landscape gardens, by contrast, need to be explored.

Although most of the gardens in the *Guide* are open regularly from spring to autumn, there are some that are particularly worth visiting at a specific moment in the year – for the spring bulbs, the rhododendrons and azaleas, the roses or for the autumn colour on the trees. We have tried to indicate this in describing the general character of each of the gardens. We have also in almost every instance given a brief account of the history of the garden. In some, sad cases there is more to say about the past than the present and it is to be hoped that the entrance charges exacted from visitors will contribute towards the gardens' upkeep or restoration.

There are maps of each country showing the geographical relation of one garden to another and to the principal towns. At the end of the book there is a list of useful addresses. These include the organizations in the British Isles that arrange for privately-owned gardens to be opened for charity. Gardens open under these schemes are beyond the scope of the *Guide*, with a few exceptions, since they are not accessible to the public permanently or regularly, but we recommend obtaining their information pamphlets and handbooks.

We acknowledge below the help given by owners and administrators, tourist boards and horticultural organizations and a number of knowledgeable individuals. We have made every attempt to give accurate descriptions and keep up to date with changes to the gardens and to their opening times.

The book will have many shortcomings. However, it is the first time that this information has been put together in one volume and the first time that some of the gardens and parks have appeared in a guide book of any kind. It is a response to the increasing demand for a comprehensive record of, and guide to, the gardens of Britain and Europe.

(1) Opening times. All times of opening are inclusive. Thus, May–Aug means 1 May–31 August and Mon–Fri includes Monday *and* Friday. 'Daily' on its own means that the garden is never closed.
(2) Entrance *Charge* or entrance *Free*
(3) Refreshments
(4) Other attractions at the same address and opening times
(5) Owner or administrator

GSO: Gardeners' Sunday Organization
NGS: National Gardens Scheme
SGS: Scottish Gardens Scheme

The material contained in this publication has been based on the most up-to-date information available at the time of going to press. Opening arrangements are, however, subject to annual alteration and visitors may be well advised to check opening times, the price of entry and other details by applying to the owner or administrator, or to the relevant tourist board.

When taking a party it is advisable to enquire what arrangements there are for parking and refreshments and whether there are reductions in the price of the tickets. It might also be necessary to check whether the garden or park is suitable for wheelchairs and whether dogs are allowed. Look out for notices when you get there, especially those asking visitors not to walk on the grass.

The intention is to update the *Guide* at intervals, altering the descriptions when changes have been made, adding information that has not been obtainable for this edition – such as the owners or administrators of the German gardens – and including other gardens that are open to the public on a permanent or regular basis. We would be pleased to receive your help in compiling future editions.

We would like to thank all the owners and administrators, or their representatives, of the gardens and parks included in the *Guide* who replied to the questionnaires sent to them, especially those who sent us detailed descriptions, booklets and photographs.

Our particular thanks are due to Isobyl la Croix, who worked so hard on the section on England. She sifted through more than 600 replies to the questionnaire, comparing their contents with published descriptions, and prepared entries for the *Guide*. We are grateful to Anthony Huxley for introducing us to her.

Monica Wyatt worked on the entries for France, Germany, Austria, Switzerland and Portugal and we are very grateful to her; and also to Elisabeth Cameron, Mary Cresswell-Turner, Iris Gollner, Jeanie Yorke, Paul Miles and Rosemary Williams.

We would also like to acknowledge the help given by the following individuals and organizations:

England: The National Trust and the Historic Houses Association
Scotland: Hilary Maclean and Eric Robson of the National Trust for Scotland
Northern Ireland: Lyn Gallagher of the National Trust and Ernest Sandford of the Northern Ireland Tourist Board
Republic of Ireland: The Historic Irish Tourist Houses and Gardens Association Ltd and Shevawn Lynam
France: The French Government Tourist Office in London; in France, the Sous-direction des Parcs, Jardins et Espaces Verts, the Association Française des Directeurs de Jardins et d'Espaces Verts Publics and the Association des Parcs Botaniques de France
Holland: Mrs Dra C. Taudin Chabot and the IONA Stichting for information derived from *IONA Tuinengids*
Belgium: René Pechère and Mme Anne van Marcke de Lummen of the organization Espaces Verts et Art des Jardins, in Brussels
Switzerland: Swiss National Tourist Office in London
Denmark: Martin Drury, Thetis Blacker, Peter Munk Plum, Count and Countess Möltke, Helle Halberg and Count and Countess Ahlefeldt-Laurvig-Bille; also the Danish Tourist Board in London
Portugal: Baroness Beck, Paul Miles and Mrs Lowndes Marques
Malta: Malta Government Tourist Office in London

Finally, we would like to express our thanks to the experts on gardens who advised on various aspects of the book and read the entries:

England: Fred Whitsey
France: Le Vicomte de Noailles, Mme Pierre Hottinguer and La Marquise de Ganay
Italy: Henry Cocker, Sir Harold Acton and Sir Paul Grey, KCMG

Spain: Dr Luis Riudor
Belgium: René Pechère
Norway: Knut Lønø
Denmark: Aage Gylling
Germany: Peter Menzel

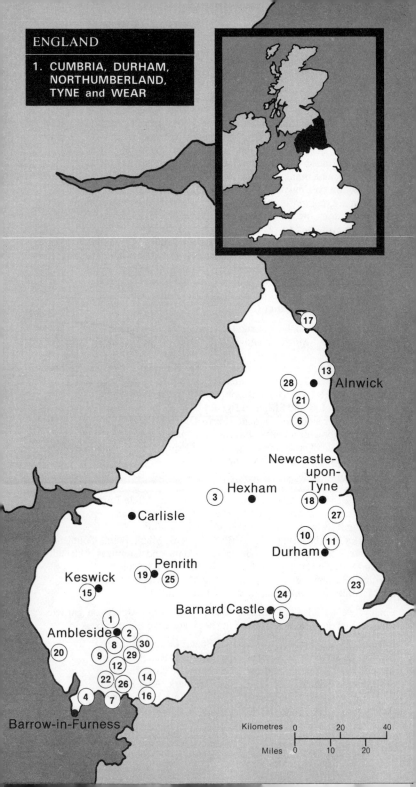

ENGLAND

1. CUMBRIA, DURHAM, NORTHUMBERLAND, TYNE and WEAR

17

13
Alnwick

28
21
6

Newcastle-upon-Tyne

3 Hexham

18

Carlisle

27

10 11
Durham

Penrith
19 25

23

Keswick
15

24
Barnard Castle
5

1
Ambleside
2
8 30
20
9 29
12
22 14
26
4 7 16

Barrow-in-Furness

Kilometres 0   20   40

Miles 0   10   20

Visiting the Gardens of Europe

Ambleside

Cumbria

1. Rydal Mount

The poet William Wordsworth, who lived here for 37 years, made the original garden from 4½ acres (1·8 ha) of fellside. It has been described as 'one of the most interesting small gardens to be found anywhere in England'. Terraces and rare trees and shrubs are set against a natural lakeland background. A notable feature is the Mound, a series of raised circles planted with shrubs, with a grassed sitting area at the top from which are fine views of the fells and Lake Windermere. The owner is the great great grand-daughter of the poet. Visit in May and June and in autumn.

(1) Mar–Oct: Daily 10–5.30; Nov–mid-Jan: Daily (except Wed) 10–12.30, 2–4
(2) Charge
(3) Café
[4] House and bookshop (same times)
(5) Mrs Mary Henderson

Ambleside

2. Stagshaw

The creation of this garden was begun in 1959 by the present owner. It is planted mainly with trees and shrubs, especially rhododendrons, azaleas and magnolias. There are fine views across Lake Windermere.

(1) Daily during daylight hours
(2) Collection box for specified charities
(3) C. H. D. Acland, Esq

Bardon Mill, nr Hexham

Northumberland

3. Vindolanda

Vindolanda, the site of a Roman settlement, covers an area of 22 acres (10 ha), including natural grassland, woodland and streams. The gardens surround the museum and contain many fine trees and flowering shrubs, including species and varieties of rhododendron, cornus, euonymus, weigela, cotoneaster and philadelphus.

(1) Daily. Mar: 10–5; Apr, Oct: 10–5.30; May, Jun, Sep: 10–6; Jul, Aug: 10–7.30; Nov–Feb: 10–4
(2) Charge
(3) Café
(4) Roman site; museum with archaeological finds on display; museum shop (same times)
(5) Vindolanda Trust

Bardsea, nr Ulverston

Cumbria

4. Conishead Priory

The original priory was founded during the 12th cent in the reign of Henry II, but the present building, designed by Philip Wyatt,

dates from 1821. The grounds cover 70 acres (32 ha) including a half-mile (0·8 km) stretch of beach, a tunnel leading to an artificial lake and a 'hermit's cave' in a hillside wood. The woodland contains many species of tree, such as wellingtonias, *Sequoiadendron giganteum*, and cedars of Lebanon; the gardens, which are cultivated using organic methods, include shrubberies, rose gardens and rock gardens.

(1) Sat and Sun 2–6
(2) Charge
(3) Refreshments
(4) Crafts and produce sometimes available
(5) Manjushri Institute

Barnard Castle

Durham

5. Bowes Museum

The house, built in 1869 in the style of a French château, is set in 20 acres (9 ha) of parkland. Around the museum are rockeries and formal flowerbeds; elsewhere a good selection of interesting trees and shrubs.

(1) Nov–Apr: Mon–Sat 10–4; Sun 2–4 (except 25 and 26 Dec and 1 Jan); May–Sep: Mon–Sat 10–5.30; Sun 2–5; Oct: Mon–Sat 10–5; Sun 2–5
(2) Charge
(3) Refreshments
(4) Museum (same times)
(5) Durham County Council

Cambo, nr Morpeth

Northumberland

6. Wallington Hall

The garden was largely the creation of Sir Walter Calverley Blackett, squire from 1728 to 1777, but it has been altered since, particularly by Sir George and Lady Trevelyan, who made the rustic terraces at the top of the garden in the late 19th and early 20th cents, and by the National Trust, which took it over in 1966. It has been described by Arthur Hellyer as 'one of the prettiest gardens in England'.

The grounds consist of 100 acres (40 ha) of amenity woodland and lakes, a stream flowing between rocky banks, a delightful walled garden made from the old kitchen garden during the 1760s and a conservatory containing large fuchsias. The many fine shrubs include a number of species roses.

(1) Daily
(2) Charge
(3) Café
(4) House and Information centre (Apr–Sep: Daily, except Tue, 1–6; Oct: Sat and Sun 2–5)
(5) National Trust

Cark-in-Cartmel

Cumbria

7. Holker Hall

Although parts of the house date from the 16th cent. the 22 acre (10 ha) garden, as it is now, is mainly Victorian. There are two small formal gardens, one set out with herbaceous borders and the other a rose garden approached through a pergola covered with many other climbers besides roses. The rest of the garden is informal, with many fine specimen trees, including *Magnolia campbellii*; the tulip-tree, *Liriodendron tulipifera*; yellow-wood, *Cladrastis lutea*; and winterbark, *Drimys winteri*, and large plantings of rhododendrons, both species and hybrids, such as *R. arboreum, R. ciliatum, R. discolor, R.* 'Fragrantissimum' (not often seen outside so far north) and the early-flowering *R. x Nobleanum*.

In spring naturalized daffodils make a good display. Beyond the garden, a deer park has herds of fallow, sika and red deer.

(*1*) *Easter Sun–Sep: Sun–Fri 11–6*
(*2*) *Charge*
(*3*) *Restaurant and café*
(*4*) *House; gift shop; children's farm; adventure playground (same times)*
(*5*) *Mr and Mrs Hugh Cavendish*

Clappersgate, nr Ambleside

Cumbria

8. White Craggs Rock Garden

This natural rock garden covering 3¼ acres (1·4 ha) was founded by Dr C. H. Hough in 1904. The steeply sloping site, with magnificent views across to Lake Windermere, is planted with rhododendrons, azaleas, heaths, alpines and a variety of rare shrubs.

(*1*) *Daily during daylight hours*
(*2*) *Collecting box*
(*3*) *Nursery garden (Mar–Oct: Mon–Fri 8–5; Sat and Sun 10–5; Nov–Feb: Mon–Fri 8–5)*
(*5*) *A. R. Aitchison, Esq*

Coniston

Cumbria

9. Brantwood

The garden at Brantwood, on the east shore of Lake Coniston, was created by the writer John Ruskin. He cleared the woodland to create vistas and make paths, and planted a number of exotic species, including western red cedar, *Thuja plicata*; Japanese maples, *Acer palmatum*, clumps of bamboo and the scented yellow Pontic azalea, *Rhododendron luteum*. In spring there are massed daffodils, followed by bluebells. The garden, which had become very overgrown, is now being cleared and 20 acres (9 ha) are on view. Visit in April and May.

(*1*) *Good Friday–Sep: Sun–Fri 11–5.30*
(*2*) *Charge*
(*4*) *John Ruskin Memorial Exhibition; nature trail*
(*5*) *Administrator: Derek Phippard, Esq*

Durham

10. St Aidan's College

The idea for the garden, which covers about 4 acres (1·6 ha), came from Sir Basil Spence, architect of the college, and was laid out in 1964–5 by Brian Hackett, now Professor of Landscape Architecture at Newcastle University. He took great care that the new buildings, sited on a hill to the south of the city, should be absorbed into the landscape, especially as seen from Durham, and with this end in view, groups of native forest trees, such as sycamore, oak, beech and wild cherry, were planted in a field to the north and east of the building; a fourth plantation of poplars was planted later, in order to screen the car park. The courtyard contains a collection of old-fashioned and species roses, mostly in shades of pink, including *Rosa moyesii, R. banksiae* 'Lutea', 'Rosa Mundi', 'Cardinal de Richelieu' and 'Prince Charles'. There are also beds of modern roses, such as 'Super Star' and 'Masquerade'. A pond with fish, lilies and marginal plants forms a focus of interest, and a steep bank by the drive has been planted as a rockery, with a good selection of winter, spring and summer flowering varieties of heather, amongst other plants.

Many plants have been donated by well-wishers, including a laburnum walk presented by the late Lady Reading. Raised beds near the front door contain early spring bulbs such as aconites, dwarf irises and narcissi and dog's tooth violets (erythronium species) and, elsewhere, there is a notable display of crocuses in flower from February to Easter. About 12,000 corms were planted by the first generation of students and these have become naturalized. A collection of clematis planted along one of the inner courtyard terraces was given by the Professor of Botany. Near the tennis court is a small area planted with rhododendrons and azaleas.

(*1*) *Daily during daylight hours*
(*2*) *Charge*
(*5*) *St Aidan's College*

Durham

11. University of Durham Botanic Garden

The gardens were moved to their present site in 1971; 21,000 trees have been planted within the past four years. It is hoped that it will be of use and interest to horticulturists, landscape architects, naturalists, conservationists, planners and teachers. The north section is devoted mainly to British and European species: plants of horticultural value and modern drug plants.

The south section is divided into two parts: the North American Collection has nine areas of woodland planted to represent the major dominant forest types of North America, while the Sino-Himalayan Collection, on a steep-sided valley with a stream running along its length and with acid soil, is to be planted with plant associations found in Nepal. The garden is still in the course of development.

(1) *Daily 9.30–4. Groups by appointment*
(2) *Free*
(5) *University of Durham*

Far Sawrey, nr Windermere

Cumbria

12. Tabramhill Gardens

The 3½ acre (1·4 ha) garden at the edge of Lake Windermere was planted by Geoffrey Yates, author of *Pocket Guide to Heather Gardening*, and contains the largest collection in the world of hardy heaths and heathers. As well as this, there are fine mature trees and many interesting shrubs and herbaceous plants. There is something in flower at all seasons of the year.

(1) *Mon–Fri 2–5; Sat and Public Holidays 10–5*
(2) *Donations to charity*
(4) *Nursery*
(5) *G. Yates, Esq*

Howick, nr Alnwick

Northumberland

13. Howick Hall

There are formal terraces near the late 18th-cent mansion house and raised beds for alpines, but principally it is an informal, woodland garden with large plantings of rhododendrons, azaleas, magnolias and other exotic species as well as herbaceous plants such as primulas, meconopsis and agapanthus.

(1) *Apr–Sep: Daily 2–7*
(2) *Charge*
(5) *Lord Howick of Glendale*

Kendal

Cumbria

14. Sizergh Castle

The lay-out of the park and garden has been greatly altered over the centuries: the lake is thought to have been created in the 17th or 18th cent, but was enlarged in 1926 and the previously steep, grassy slopes were replaced by terraces and steps. The main feature is the rock garden, constructed by T.R. Hayes & Son, also in 1926, on the site of an old orchard; a number of Japanese maples and conifers, including the Arolla pine, *Pinus cembra*; Bhutan pine, *P. wallichiana*, and umbrella pine, *Sciadopitys verticillata*, were planted at the same time. The rock garden, with streams and pools,

covers approx ¼ acre (0·1 ha) and contains a collection of almost 100 varieties of hardy ferns as well as dwarf conifers, gentians and other alpines. The south wall of the tower provides shelter for some not-too-hardy plants, such as *Osmanthus delavayi*, hebes, ceanothus and *Solanum crispum*. Elsewhere in the grounds are magnolias, tree peonies and shrub roses, underplanted with geraniums.

(1) *Apr–Sep: Wed and Sun 2–5.45; Jul–Aug: also Thu 2–5.45*
(2) *Charge*
(4) *House (same times)*
(5) *National Trust*

Keswick

Cumbria

15. Lingholm

The house, in a beautiful setting on the shores of Derwentwater, was built for Col J. F. Greenall in the 1870s by the architect Alfred Waterhouse; Beatrix Potter and her family used to stay here in the summer in the last years of the century. The gardens as they are now were developed in the early 1900s by a later owner, Col George Kemp, created Lord Rochdale; the terraces on the lake side of the house were built then.

The gardens have been steadily developed since the end of World War II and the woodland garden much improved, although the formal gardens have been reduced in size. There is a fine collection of rhododendrons and azaleas, both species and hybrid and mostly labelled, the season starting in March with *R. arboreum* var. *album* and finishing in August with the beautiful white scented flowers of the tree-like *R. auriculatum*. Other interesting trees include *Embothrium coccineum*, *Eucryphia glutinosa*, *Eucalyptus* species and *Magnolia acuminata*, the cucumber tree, and there are also camellias, a rose garden and interesting herbaceous plants such as gentians. Visit in April to June and early autumn.

(1) *Apr–Oct: Mon–Sat 10–5. Dogs on a lead only*
(2) *Charge (proportion to NGS and other charities)*
(4) *Plants for sale (Mon–Fri 9–5)*
(5) *Viscount Rochdale*

Levens, nr Kendal

Cumbria

16. Levens Hall

The oldest part of the house dates back to the 13th cent. The famous topiary garden was laid out in 1692 by Guillaume Beaumont who trained at Versailles under Le Nôtre and came to England to work for James II. Although the trees, yew and box, have grown and some were probably added or replaced in the 19th cent, the plan has never been altered. There are formal flower-beds edged with box, herbaceous borders, a beech circle and a beech walk. Besides the garden proper there is a landscaped park, traversed by the River Kent.

(1) Easter–late Sep: Daily 10–5
(2) Charge
(3) Licensed bar and café
(4) House and steam engine collection (Easter–late Sep: Tue–Thu, Sun and Public Holidays 2–5); Plant centre (same times as grounds)
(5) C. H. Bagot, Esq

Lindisfarne

Northumberland

17. Lindisfarne Castle

The original building on Holy Island, more a fort than a castle, is thought to date from the 16th cent. It fell into decay and was bought by Edward Hudson, the founder of the magazine, *Country Life*, in 1902, who commissioned the architect Sir Edwin Lutyens to convert it into a modern house. Gertrude Jekyll, who frequently worked with Lutyens, was brought in to design the garden. She made a small walled garden on a sheltered southern slope about 500 yds (457 m) from the castle; the original plans for this have recently been discovered and the plantings are being re-created as nearly as possible by the National Trust.

(1) Apr–Sep: Sat–Thu 11–1 (last admission 12.30), 2–5, when tides permit; it is not accessible 2 hours before and 4 hours after high tide
(2) Charge
(4) Castle (same times)
(5) National Trust

Newcastle upon Tyne

Tyne and Wear

18. Jesmond Dene

Jesmond Dene, which covers approx 84 acres (34 ha), was originally the private estate of Sir William Armstrong, inventor of the Armstrong gun, who landscaped it in the 1850s, making the broad carriageways and paths that remain today. In 1883 he presented it by deed of gift to Newcastle upon Tyne Corporation.

The Dene is planted with many exotic trees and shrubs and in late spring the display of rhododendrons is well known in the area. The park also contains Jesmond Dene waterfall and Jesmond Mill, the ruin of a 13th-cent flow mill. Late spring and summer are the best seasons to visit.

(1) Daily Sunrise–Sunset
(2) Free
(3) Restaurant
(4) St Mary's Chapel and Well

(5) Newcastle upon Tyne City Council, Recreation Dept

Penrith

Cumbria

19. Dalemain

The house is partly medieval and the garden was originally laid out in Elizabethan times. Part of the formal garden still remains with beds edged with clipped box and filled with spring and summer bedding. An Elizabethan summer house with mullioned windows and a pointed roof also remains; another summer house, built into an alcove in the garden wall and furnished with Chippendale seats, is early Georgian. Also at that period the parkland was landscaped and part of the River Eamont was dammed to form a lake in the style of 'Capability' Brown. There are some fine specimen trees, including a 200-year-old tulip-tree, *Liriodendron tulipifera*, a rare Grecian silver fir, *Abies cephalonica*, and some very old walnuts and Spanish chestnuts. Peonies are grown in the old vine border. There is a collection of old-fashioned and shrub roses, and the brilliant scarlet *Tropaeolum speciosum* climbs over the high yew hedge. The wild garden includes Turkey oaks, *Quercus cerris*, Douglas firs, *Pseudotsuga menziesii*, prunus species, lilacs, *Liquidambar styraciflua* and azaleas.

(1) Easter–Sep: Sat–Thu 2–5.15
(2) Charge
(3) Tea
(4) House; agricultural museum; Westmorland and Cumberland Yeomanry Regimental Museum; shop; garden centre (same times)
(5) Mr and Mrs Bryce McCosh

Ravenglass

Cumbria

20. Muncaster Castle

Although there has been a castle on the site since the 13th cent, the gardens as they now are were designed by Sir John Ramsden, Bt after World War I. Many species of rhododendron were already growing there when he inherited the estate in 1917 and he enlarged on these considerably, sponsoring expeditions to the Himalayas, so that now the collection of rhododendrons and azaleas ranks among the finest in the country. Magnificent views over the Esk Valley can be had from the terrace walk, and there are many other interesting trees and shrubs including *Eucryphia cordifolia*, *Podocarpus salignus*, *Nothofagus betuloides*, *N. antarctica*, *N. obliqua*, *Corokia virgata*, *Michelia doltsopa*, *Magnolia delavayi*, *Cercidiphyllum japonicum*, *Picea breweriana* and *Sciadopitys verticillata*.

(1) Good Friday–1st Sun in Oct: Sat–Thu noon–5
(2) Charge
(3) Café and restaurant

(4) Castle (Good Friday–1st Sun in Oct: Tue–Thu and Sun 2–5); Garden centre (Daily 8–5)
(5) Sir William Pennington-Ramsay, Bt

Rothbury

Northumberland

21. Cragside

The grounds of the house built by the Victorian architect Norman Shaw are extensive, covering over 900 acres (360 ha) on the south edge of Alnwick Moor. There are many fine trees and magnificent rhododendrons and azaleas, seen at their best in May and June.

(1) Apr–Sep: Daily 10.30–6; Oct: Sat and Sun 2–5
(2) Charge
(4) House (Apr–Sep: Daily, except Mon, but open Bank Holiday Mon and closed Tue following 1–6; Oct: Sat and Sun 2–5)
(5) National Trust

Rusland, nr Ulverston

Cumbria

22. Rusland Hall

Georgian house built in 1720 and set in 4 acres (1·6 ha) of grounds laid out in the manner of 'Capability' Brown. Ha-has were used so that the gardens appear to merge with the surrounding landscape. There are many fine specimen trees and in spring the valley is full of daffodils and bluebells. These are followed by flowering shrubs in May and June.

(1) Apr–Sep: Daily 11–6
(2) Charge
(4) House (same times)
(5) Mr and Mrs J. Birkby

Sedgefield

Durham

23. Hardwick Hall Country Park

The original gardens and park at Hardwick Hall, landscaped between 1754 and 1758 by James Paine, are now divided between several owners and most of the land is in agricultural use. 40 acres (16 ha) of the gardens are being developed by Durham County Council as a country park and an arboretum is being planted using as a basis the existing fine specimens of beech, yew, horse chestnut, birch and sycamore. Exotics from a variety of countries are joining them, including eucalyptus and nothofagus species, *Taxodium distichum*, the swamp cypress, and *Catalpa bignonioides*, the Indian bean-tree.

The serpentine lake, which was part of the original design, has been cleared and planted with aquatics. Kingfishers and wild ducks are regularly seen. Some of the original ornamental buildings survive but are in a dangerous condition.

(1) Daily
(2) Free
(5) Durham County Council

Staindrop, nr Darlington

Durham

24. Raby Castle

The castle is medieval; the park, which has two herds of deer, one red and one fallow, covers approx 270 acres (120 ha), but the gardens proper are approx 10 acres (4·5 ha) in extent. They date from c 1760 and were probably designed by Carr of York or by Paine, both of whom were architects working at Raby during this period. The gardens are divided by walls and two fine old yew hedges. On the south terrace is a white Ischia fig tree, believed to have been brought from Italy in c 1786. The conservatory is Victorian. Parts of the garden are at present being re-landscaped.

(1) Easter Sat–Easter Tue 2–5; April: Sun 2–5; May: Sun and Wed 2–5; Jun, Jul and Sep: Wed, Sat and Sun 2–5; Aug: Daily (except Fri) 2–5
(2) Charge
(3) Tea
(4) Castle (same times)
(5) Lord Barnard

Temple Sowerby

Cumbria

25. Acorn Bank Garden

The main feature of interest lies in the old walled kitchen garden which has been turned into a herb garden with the National Trust's extensive collection of medicinal and culinary herbs. Over 180 varieties are grown. Tender herbs and scented plants are grown in a small glasshouse. There is a fine collection of lead and bronze Medici vases and putti.

(1) Apr–Oct: Tue–Sun 10–5.30. No dogs
(2) Charge
(4) Plants and seeds of hardy herbs for sale
(5) National Trust

Ulverston

Cumbria

26. Graythwaite Hall

The 7 acre (3 ha) garden was originally designed in 1880–90 by the garden architect T. H. Mawson and, although some alterations have been made to the detail, the lay-out and landscaping are still of historical interest. The garden is planted largely with flowering shrubs, particularly rhododendrons and azaleas.

(1) Apr–Jun: Daily 10–6
(2) Charge
(5) Major M. E. M. Sandys

Washington, nr Sunderland

Durham

27. Washington Old Hall

The original house was built in the 12th cent of local sandstone by an ancestor of George Washington; in 1613 it was sold and partly demolished and the present house was built on the foundations. In 1936, it was condemned as unfit for habitation but was saved and restored by a local preservation committee. In 1955 it was officially opened by the American ambassador. Near the hall is a rose garden; two flights of steps lead to the lower garden, planted in 1971–2 with shrubs, old roses, irises, hollyhocks and other herbaceous perennials. A sundial was a gift from Walter Annenberg, American ambassador in London.

(1) *Mar–Oct: Daily (except Tue) 1–6 or Sunset; Nov–Feb: Sat and Sun 2–5 or Sunset*
(2) *Charge*
(5) *National Trust*

Whittingham, nr Alnwick

Northumberland

28. Callaly Castle

The 17th-cent mansion, with Georgian and Victorian additions, incorporates a 13th-cent pele tower. There are fine views across to the hills from the garden, which contains lawns, herbaceous borders, shrubs, woodland (mainly beech) and a chain of small lakes.

(1) *Late May–late Sep: Sat, Sun and Public Holidays 2.15–5.30*
(2) *Charge*
(3) *Tea (Sun and Public Holidays)*
(4) *Castle (same times)*
(5) *Major A. S. C. Browne*

Windermere

Cumbria

29. Brockhole (Lake District National Park Centre)

The 32 acre (12·8 ha) grounds were laid out by Thomas Mawson, a noted northern landscape gardener, at about the time the house was built, in 1900. A formal English garden, with lawns, terraces, clipped box and yew, herbaceous borders, bedding plants and wisteria on the house walls, gives way to shrubs and woodland and finally the lake shore. The rhododendrons and azaleas are at their best in May and June and the herbaceous borders are colourful in July and August.

(1) *Mid-March–mid-Nov: Daily 10–4.30*
(2) *Charge*
(3) *Café*

(4) *House, with audio-visual exhibitions on the Lake District; in summer films are shown with French, German and Dutch commentaries (same times)*
(5) *Lake District Planning Board*

Windermere

30. Holehird

The garden was founded in *c* 1870 by Mr Lee-Groves, then owner of the Holehird Estate. He helped to finance a number of plant-hunting expeditions with the result that many interesting specimens were sent back to Holehird. The garden became derelict but in 1969 the Lakeland Horticultural Society took over a large part of it and began the work of restoration which still continues. There is an interesting rock garden and many fine specimen trees including one of the handkerchief tree, *Davidia involucrata*, considered to be one of the finest in the British Isles.

(1) *Daily during daylight hours*
(2) *Free but donations towards upkeep are welcome*
(5) *Lakeland Horticultural Society*

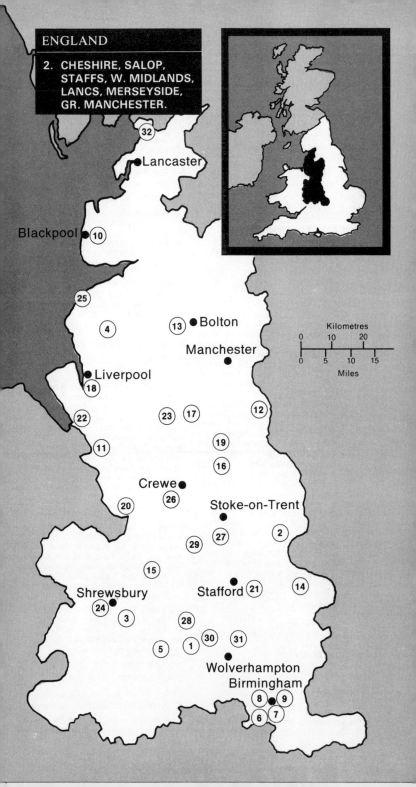

ENGLAND

2. CHESHIRE, SALOP, STAFFS, W. MIDLANDS, LANCS, MERSEYSIDE, GR. MANCHESTER.

(32)

● Lancaster

Blackpool (10)

(25)

(4)

(13) ● Bolton

● Manchester

● Liverpool

(18)

(23) (17)

(12)

(22)

(19)

(11)

(16)

Crewe ●

(26)

Stoke-on-Trent ●

(2)

(20)

(29)

(27)

(15)

Shrewsbury

Stafford (21)

(14)

(24)

(3)

(28)

(5)

(1) (30)

(31)

Wolverhampton ●

Birmingham

(8) ● (9)

(6) (7)

Kilometres

0   10   20

0   5   10   15

Miles

ENGLAND

Albrighton, Bowling Green Lane, nr Wolverhampton

Salop

1. David Austin Roses

The large rose garden was founded by the present owner and contains one of the most extensive collections of rare and unusual roses in Europe, including old roses, modern shrub roses, species and climbing roses as well as modern Hybrid Teas and floribundas. The commercial rose fields can also be viewed. Many new roses have been bred here, including 'Constance Spry', 'Wife of Bath', 'Chaucer' and 'Scintillation'.

(1) *Mon–Fri 9–4; Sat and Sun 2–4*
(2) *Free*
(4) *Nursery (same times)*
(5) *David S. H. Austin, Esq.*

Alton

Staffordshire

2. Alton Towers

The gardens were founded by Charles, 15th Earl of Shrewsbury, who succeeded to the property in 1787. In 1814, he started excavating lakes and pools and laying out gardens and terraces; he built the conservatories, the Gothic-style Chinese Temple and the Chinese Pagoda Fountain which sends up a 70 ft (21·3 m) high jet of water. His nephew John, who succeeded him and came to live at Alton in 1831, completed laying out the formal garden near the house, including Her Ladyship's Garden beside the chapel, the terraced garden near the conservatory and the Dutch Garden. Thousands of rhododendrons were planted, and there is a wide variety of roses.

The rock garden, on a steep and naturally rocky slope, is planted with heathers, azaleas, Japanese maples and dwarf conifers. Among notable trees in the grounds are a wellingtonia; several cedars, one of which was planted by Edward VII; magnolias; Judas trees, *Cercis siliquastrum*; tulip-trees, *Liriodendron tulipifera*; and a fern-leaved beech, *Fagus sylvatica heterophylla*. The grounds cover approx 500 acres (230 ha).

(1) *Good Friday–1st weekend in Oct: 9.30–Sunset*
(2) *Charge*
(3) *Restaurant and café*
(4) *Model railway and amusement park (same times)*
(5) *Alton Towers Ltd*

Atcham, nr Shrewsbury

Salop

3. Attingham Park

The house was designed for Noel Hill, later 1st Lord Berwick, by the architect George Stuart in 1782, encasing an older house. Further additions were made by John Nash in 1805, who also designed the entrance gates to the park. The 1,159 acre (464 ha) park was laid out and planted by Humphry Repton and remains little changed from what is described in his Red Book for Attingham of 1797–8. He built two weirs on the River Tern which runs through the park, widening it and creating a cascade.

(1) *Easter Mon–Sep: Tue–Thu, Sat, Sun and Public Holidays 2–5.30*
(2) *Charge*
(4) *House (same times)*
(5) *National Trust*

Aughton, nr Ormskirk

Lancashire

4. Cranford

An interesting example of a small garden planned specifically for ease of maintenance. It is planted mainly with trees and shrubs, including a wide range of maples, birches and cherries.

(1) *Apr–Oct: Daily 10–Sunset*
(2) *Collection box*
(5) *Theodore J. C. V. S. Taylor, Esq*

Benthall, nr Much Wenlock

Salop

5. Benthall Hall

The house is believed to date from the late 16th cent, and the exterior is largely unaltered apart from a 17th-cent wing. In 1860 the brothers George and Arthur Maw took over the tenancy. The former travelled widely in Europe, Asia Minor and North America and collected many plants, including *Chinodoxa luciliae*; he grew many alpines and bulbous plants, in particular species of crocus. *C. speciosus*, *C. pulchellus*, *C. nudiflorus*, *C. tomasinianus* and *C. vernus* are naturalized here, presumably relics of his plantings.

The terraces and rockeries were laid out by the architect Robert Bateman and his wife who lived here from 1890 to 1906. In recent years, the National Trust and Sir Paul and Lady Benthall have done much restoration work and new planting, including establishing a rose garden and shelter belts of trees to give protection from the north and east.

(1) *Easter Mon–Sep: Tue, Wed, Sat and Public Holidays 2–6*
(2) *Charge*
(4) *House (Public Holidays 2–6)*
(5) *National Trust*

Birmingham, Edgbaston

West Midlands

6. Birmingham Botanical Gardens

The gardens were founded by the Birmingham Botanical and Horticultural

Society to promote interest in botany, horticulture and aviculture and to exhibit the widest possible range of specimens; they were opened at the present site in 1832. Interesting features include a tropical house, with plants of economic importance; a rock garden (opened to the public in 1895); chronological and herbaceous beds, a rose garden and a collection of rhododendrons enclosed within a fine beech hedge.

(1) *Winter: Mon–Sat 9–4.30; Summer: Mon–Sat 9–8*
(2) *Charge*
(3) *Refreshments (Easter–Autumn)*
(4) *Aviaries; Market Garden with indoor and outdoor plants and local arts and crafts for sale*
(5) *Birmingham Botanical and Horticultural Society Ltd*

Birmingham
7. Grove Estate

The Grove Estate was conveyed to the city by G. W. Kenrick in 1934 and the Corporation took possession of the land upon the death of his brother Alderman W. Byng Kenrick in 1962. The 20 acre (9 ha) park includes sweeping lawns, herbaceous borders, rock gardens, azalea beds and an ornamental pool.

(1) *Daily Sunrise–Sunset*
(2) *Free*
(5) *City of Birmingham*

Birmingham
8. Lightwoods Park

Lightwoods Park was constructed in 1902 from 30 acres (12 ha) of woodland then threatened with destruction. A particular feature is the Shakespeare Garden, a walled garden which contains all the plants mentioned in the works of Shakespeare.

(1) *Daily Sunrise–Sunset*
(2) *Free*
(5) *City of Birmingham*

Birmingham
9. Queen's Park

The 10 acre (4·5 ha) park was opened to the public and presented to the Council to commemorate Queen Victoria's Diamond Jubilee. The most notable feature is the Garden for the Blind, constructed in 1953. Round two sides of the garden are raised borders, planted with fragrant plants, and on the other sides is a pergola covered with climbing, scented plants. There are small lawns and a raised pool with a fountain. Two fine copper beeches are surrounded by seats. A plan of the garden is embossed on metal, and the plants are labelled in braille.

(1) *Daily Sunrise–Sunset*
(2) *Free*
(5) *City of Birmingham*

Blackpool, West Park Drive
Lancashire
10. Stanley Park

The park covers 250 acres (113 ha) in all, including a 109 acre (44 ha) golf course. It was designed by Thomas Mawson and Sons (London and Lancaster) in the early 1920s and opened in 1926. It contains both formal and neo-classical features. There is a 4 acre (1·8 ha) woodland garden, a 22 acre (10 ha) ornamental lake, a circular Italian garden, a remembrance garden, a rose garden, a floral clock and carpet bedding, and conservatories divided into three sections – tropical, temperate and for seasonal massed displays.

(1) *Daily Sunrise–Sunset*
(2) *Free*
(3) *Café*
(4) *Model village*
(5) *Blackpool Borough Council*

Chester
Cheshire
11. Chester Zoological Gardens

The zoo was founded in 1931, when the area covered was 9 acres (4 ha), and was taken over by the North of England Zoological Society in 1934. As the acreage increased to the present approx 350 (140 ha), the gardens were designed by the present Director-Secretary, G. S. Mottishead, and P. W. Gallup, head gardener for 23 years until his retirement in 1976. About 80,000 plants are set out each year for spring and summer bedding; the former is at its best in mid-May and the latter from mid-August to the end of September. A fuchsia bed contains approx 600 plants of over 100 varieties, while over 14,000 roses, Hybrid Teas and floribundas, are planted in various parts of the grounds.

Plants are used in most of the indoor animal houses; most notable is the tropical house, which itself contains 1¾ acres (0·7 ha) of garden, including orchids, bougainvillea, hibiscus, hoya, citrus, bananas and palms. Over 80 different species of birds fly freely in the house.

(1) *Daily 9–Sunset*
(2) *Charge*
(3) *Restaurant*
(5) *North of England Zoological Society*

Disley
Greater Manchester
12. Lyme Park

The Elizabethan house, with a Palladian exterior by Giacomo Leoni, is surrounded by a deer park covering approx 1,320 acres (530 ha). The garden includes a stream and herbaceous borders and below the house terrace there is a formal area in the Dutch style, with parterres and seasonal bedding. A stone orangery dates from the early 19th cent.

(1) *Daily 8–Sunset*
(2) *Free*
(3) *Café*
(4) *House (April–Sep: Sun and Public Holidays 1–5.30; Tue–Sat 2–5; Mar and Oct: Sun 1–4; Tue–Sat conducted tours only at 2, 3 and 4)*
(5) *National Trust; leased to Stockport Metropolitan Borough Council*

Heaton, nr Bolton

Greater Manchester

13. Ravenhurst

The formal, Italian-style garden was designed by T. H. Mawson; there are terraces, lawns, two rose gardens, pergolas, herbaceous borders, a sunken garden, a water garden and many flowering shrubs including rhododendrons, both species and hybrid, and deciduous and evergreen azaleas.

(1) *May–Aug: Wed 10–4. Other times by appointment*
(2) *Charge (NGS)*
(5) *Mr and Mrs T. J. Arkwright*

Hoar Cross, nr Burton-on-Trent

Staffordshire

14. Hoar Cross Hall

The house was built in 1871 in Elizabethan style; the gardens were laid out at the same time in accordance with Bacon's essay *Of Gardens*. The main south lawn is terraced gently down to a series of smaller gardens; there is a water garden and yew-tree walks and a pair of wrought-iron gates by Robert Bakewell, the 18th-cent blacksmith. The grounds cover a total of 20 acres (9 ha), including an area of woodland.

(1) *Jun–1st Sun in Sep: Sun 2–6; Bank Holiday Mon and following Tue noon–7. Organized parties by arrangement*
(2) *Charge*
(3) *Tea*
(4) *House (same times)*
(5) *W. A. Bickerton-Jones, Esq*

Hodnet, nr Market Drayton

Salop

15. Hodnet Hall

The 60 acre (27 ha) gardens have extensive lawns, chains of lakes and mature forest trees forming a background for daffodils and other spring flowers, followed by rhododendrons, camellias, azaleas, laburnum and lilac. In summer, colour is provided by roses and herbaceous borders with peonies and astilbes among other plants. Later, hydrangeas and other late summer shrubs are in flower and in autumn there is a fine show of berries and coloured foliage.

(1) *Late Mar–late Sep: Sun and Public Holidays noon–6; Mon–Sat 2–5*
(2) *Charge*
(3) *Tea (Sun and Public Holidays; May–Aug: Daily)*
(4) *Garden centre (same times)*
(5) *A. E. H. Heber-Percy, Esq*

Kent Green, nr Congleton

Cheshire

16. Little Moreton Hall

The house, with moat and gatehouse, provides one of the finest remaining examples of 16th-cent half-timbering. The garden contains two mounds, often a feature of Tudor gardens, and a knot garden which has recently been laid out to a 17th-cent design.

(1) *Apr–Oct: Wed–Mon 2–6 or Sunset; Mar: Sat, Sun and Public Holidays 2–6 or Sunset*
(2) *Charge*
(4) *House (same times)*
(5) *National Trust*

Knutsford

Cheshire

17. Tatton Park

The present Regency house, built on the site of an older house, is surrounded by approx 1,000 acres (450 ha) of deer park and gardens, the former laid out by Humphry Repton in the 1790s. In the 1850s Sir Joseph Paxton was employed by the 1st Lord Egerton, and he laid out the terraces on the south front, with flights of steps and vases. A central fountain basin on the lower level is flanked by parterres. The orangery, designed by the architect L. W. Wyatt in 1818, contains orange and lemon trees and other exotic plants; a fernery to the west of this may have been designed by Paxton and from this a long herbaceous border leads to a small, walled rose garden and the Tower Garden. From here there is a choice of paths; the left-hand path leads to the Broad Walk past a pool with banks of azaleas to a classical temple, while the right-hand path leads through a glade of rhododendrons and bluebells to a Japanese garden with a Shinto temple imported from Japan and set on an island in a lake. The 4th and last Lord Egerton planted many rhododendrons, azaleas and other rare shrubs between 1940 and his death in 1958.

(1) *Garden. Early Apr–mid-May and early Sep–mid-Oct: Daily noon–5; mid-May–early Sep: Daily (except Sun and Public Holiday Mon) 1–6; Sun and Public Holiday Mon 11–6.30; mid-Oct–early Apr: Mon–Sat 1–4; Sun*

noon–4. Park. Daily 9–7, 8 or Sunset
if earlier
(2) *Charge*
(3) *Refreshments*
(4) *House (Daily, hours variable)*
(5) *National Trust*

Liverpool

Merseyside

18. City of Liverpool Botanic Gardens

The botanic gardens are now located at Harthill and Calderstones Park. Perhaps their most notable feature is the complex of 16 glasshouses, nine of which are propagation and growing houses while seven are display houses. These connect with the fernery, divided into two sections, temperate and tropical, and running parallel to the central corridor. This also contains plants from both temperate and tropical regions, including many species of the climber hoya and a number of passion flowers. The houses cater for tropical and warm temperate flowering plants; tropical foliage plants; bromeliads and orchid houses.

Outside, there is a rose garden with over 6,000 plants, including a collection of rose species and another of trees belonging to the family *Rosaceae*, such as cherries and sorbus. A shrub border is designed to give an all-year-round display of flower, foliage or berries. Rhododendrons and azaleas are underplanted with species of primula and meconopsis and other shade-loving plants and throughout the grounds there are many fine specimen trees. There is also an 'Old English' garden; a Japanese garden; a systematic garden with beds arranged in the supposed evolutionary sequence of the various families and a herb garden, designed as a reconstruction of the old Westminster physic garden in London.

(1) *Oct–Feb: Daily 2–4; Mar–Apr: Daily 2–5; May–Sep: Daily 2–7*
(2) *Charge*
(5) *City of Liverpool, Recreation and Open Spaces Dept*

Lower Withington, nr Macclesfield

Cheshire

19. Granada Arboretum

The arboretum was founded in 1972 by the University of Manchester, supported by grants from the Granada Foundation. The total area is 30 acres (12·5 ha) of which 10 acres (4 ha), containing some of the more rapidly growing trees and shrubs, are at present open to the public. Around the entrance are collections of alder and birch, including *Betula jacquemontii* which has a notably white bark; nearby is a group of cherries, such as *Prunus serrula*, also grown largely for their attractive bark. Opposite the entrance is a collection of pink

and red flowered species roses and their hybrids, such as *Rosa rugosa* and *R. moyesii* with, nearby, a group of different forms of the native beech and species of hazel. In the centre of the site are several small gardens, each enclosed by hedges showing the use of various hedging plants, formal and informal.

There are a number of collections of trees and shrubs suitable for use in small gardens, including species of sorbus, cotoneaster, chamaecyparis, spiraea, deutzia, potentilla, berberis and mahonia. A heath garden is planted to give colour all the year round, and there is a selection of trees that give good autumn colour, such as the scarlet oak, *Quercus coccinea*, *Parrotia persica* and species of rhus and amelanchier.

(1) *Easter–Oct: Daily 2–5.30*
(2) *Charge*
(3) *Refreshments*
(4) *Jodrell Bank Radio Telescope Concourse*
(5) *University of Manchester*

Malpas

Cheshire

20. Cholmondeley Castle

The gardens were probably laid out when the house was rebuilt by Sir Robert Smirke in the early 19th cent. Many of the fine specimen trees, such as a wellingtonia (*Sequoiadendron giganteum*), a swamp cypress (*Taxodium distichum*) and cedars – cedar of Lebanon and the blue Atlas cedar (*Cedrus atlantica glauca*) – date from this period.

In 1954 the Temple Garden was cleared and planted and the rock garden and waterfall rebuilt. In 1960 James Russell, the landscape gardener and plantsman, began the planting of hundreds of rhododendrons and azaleas, and other shrubs such as magnolias, camellias and cornus. The lake was cleared and water-lilies established, and water gardens were set out.

(1) *Easter–early Oct: Sun and Public Holidays 1–6*
(2) *Charge*
(3) *Tea*
(4) *Gift shop; farm with rare breeds of farm animals (same times)*
(5) *Marquess and Marchioness of Cholmondeley*

Milford, nr Stafford

Staffordshire

21. Shugborough

The house was built for William Anson, the foundations being laid in 1693; his son Thomas, who succeeded to the property in 1720, enlarged the house in the mid-18th cent and started to create the park landscape. He employed James 'Athenian' Stuart to build a variety of temples and monuments and of these the Triumphal Arch (1761) and Tower of the Winds (completed c 1765) are among the earliest buildings in England in the neo-Greek style. Other monuments in the garden include the Chinese House, probably the first of Thomas Anson's garden buildings, which was completed in 1747. There is a rose garden, and west of the house lie terraced lawns leading down to the river Sow, thought to have been designed in c 1855 by the landscape gardener W. A. Nesfield. South of the house, beside the river, is a wild garden.

(1) *Mid-March–late Oct: Tue–Fri 10.30–5.30; Sat, Sun and Public Holidays 2–6; late Oct–mid-Mar: Tue–Fri 10.30–4.30; 1st and 3rd Sun in these months 2–4.30*
(2) *Free*
(3) *Refreshments*
(4) *Staffordshire County Museum (same times); House, summer season only (same times)*
(5) *National Trust*

Ness

Merseyside

22. Ness Gardens (University of Liverpool Botanic Gardens)

The gardens were founded in 1898 by A. K. Bulley, the first of the great 20th-cent patrons of plant collecting. He launched George Forrest on his career as a plant collector with a trip to China in 1904, and later financed Frank Kingdon Ward and F. E. Cooper in 1913 and 1914 on expeditions to Bhutan and Asia Minor. In 1948, the estate was presented to the University of Liverpool by Bulley's daughter, Miss A. L. Bulley; since then it has been redesigned by the present director, Mr J. K. Hulme.

The garden, covering in all 45 acres (20 ha), lies on south-facing slopes of the Wirral peninsula, overlooking the Dee estuary. Shelter is provided from the north-westerly gales by plantings of Austrian pine, *Pinus nigra*; Lodgepole pine, *P. contorta*; and holm oak, *Quercus ilex*. The rose walk, with modern and old-fashioned roses, leads to a long view flanked to the west by more roses, arranged to show their development especially since the introduction from China of ancestral varieties between 1795 and 1805. To the east are serpentine borders of rhododendrons which reach their peak in late April and early May when *R. augustinii*, *R. davidsonianum* and *R. yunnanense* are covered in blue, pink and white flowers.

A woodland garden has fine specimens of the tree-like *Rhododendron arboreum* and *R. fictolacteum* as well as camellias and

southern hemisphere species such as *Desfontainea spinosa*, *Embothrium coccineum* and *Lomatia ferruginea*. The ground orchid *Pleione bulbocodioides* grows and flowers well in peat walls.

In the shrub garden, a superb specimen of *Pieris formosa* var. *forrestii* was grown from Forrest's original seed. The heather garden is famous; every important cultivar of the European species is represented. There is an azalea collection, herbaceous borders, a water garden and a rock garden in which early flowering bulbs are followed by primulas, including the highly desirable species *P. Nutans* and *P. vialii*, and saxifrages and pulsatilla species; and they in turn in autumn by crocuses, colchicum species and *Cyclamen hederaefolium*. The rock garden is overlooked by the sheltered main terrace with tender shrubs such as *Correa speciosa* and *Grevillea rosmarinifolia*.

The Ledsham Herb Garden was laid out in 1974 on a site originally levelled for tennis courts. There is a range of glasshouses, but only one is regularly open to the public.

(1) *Daily (except 25 Dec) 9–Sunset*
(2) *Free. Parking charge*
(5) *University of Liverpool*

Northwich

Cheshire

23. Arley Hall Gardens

In 1975 this 8 acre (3·6 ha) garden gained a Premier Award in the British Tourist Authority's Landscape Heritage competition. Although there has been a house, and presumably a garden, on the site since the mid-15th cent, most of the present-day garden was created by Rowland and Mary Egerton-Warburton between 1830 and 1860, within a framework of old brick walls and yew hedges. Probably the most unusual feature of the garden is an avenue of clipped ilex, *Quercus ilex*. At the end of this, steps lead to plantings of the shrub rose 'Erfurt', philadelphus varieties, *Kalmia latifolia*, *Eucryphia × intermedia* and species rhododendrons and azaleas. Splendid twin herbaceous borders are believed to be among the earliest planted in England, in c 1846. The flag garden, made in 1900, has beds of floribunda roses and lavender separated by stone paths, with *Lonicera tragophylla*, *Akebia quinata* and *Hydrangea petiolaris* growing on the curved wall. Rhododendrons and azaleas surround a pond with *Osmunda regalis*, *Peltiphyllum peltatum*, lysichitum and primula species growing at the edge of the water. More recent additions to the garden include the shrub rose beds, the herb garden and the Rough, an area that is being developed as a semi-wild garden with plants that like shelter, such as pieris, enkianthus, stewartias, embothriums, rhododendrons and azaleas. The walled garden, which was a market garden between 1946 and 1960, is now laid out with lawns and stone ornaments, and flowering shrubs and herbaceous borders frame the walls. A large glasshouse in the kitchen garden contains fig trees probably planted in c 1850. Visit from late May to mid-August.

(1) *Easter–mid-Oct: Tue–Sun and Public Holidays 2–6.30. Last admission 6*
(2) *Charge*
(3) *Tea*
(4) *Shop (same times); House can be visited by organized parties by appointment*
(5) *Viscount and Viscountess Ashbrook*

Shrewsbury
Salop
24. Quarry Park

The park stretches along the side of the river; at its centre is the Dingle, created from derelict quarry workings by Percy Thrower who was Park Superintendent in Shrewsbury from 1946 until his retirement in 1973. It has a formal lay-out with lawns, a tiny lake, a summer house, seasonal bedding (with fuchsias a special feature) flowering shrubs and several varieties of flowering cherry.

(1) *Daily Sunrise–Sunset*
(2) *Free*
(4) *Percy Thrower Garden Centre (Daily 9–6)*
(5) *Shrewsbury and Atcham Borough Council*

Southport
Merseyside
25. Botanic Gardens

The gardens, landscaped by John Shaw of Manchester, were founded by the Churchtown and Southport Botanic Garden and Museum Company in 1875 and were bought by Southport Corporation in 1936 after the company failed. The area of the garden proper is 4·2 acres (1·7 ha) and includes lawns with trees, a lake, herbaceous borders, flowerbeds with spring and summer bedding, and a fernery which was first opened in 1876.

(1) *Main garden. Daily 8–Sunset. Fernery. Easter–Sep: Daily 10–4*
(2) *Free*
(3) *Café*
(4) *Museum (Tue–Sat and Public Holidays 10–5 or 6); Sun 2–5*
(5) *Metropolitan Borough of Sefton, Parks Dept*

Stapeley, nr Nantwich
Cheshire
26. Stapeley Water Gardens

The gardens, 5 acres (2 ha) of which are open to the public, were designed in 1970 by R. G. A. Crotten and N. S. Davies. They include a small lake with beautiful Koi carp

and landscaped pools with over 60 varieties of water-lily, as well as other display pools, waterside plantings and a fish house. Visit in June and July.

(1) *Summer: Mon–Fri 9–12.30, 1.30–6; Sat and Sun 10–12.30, 1.30–7; Winter: Mon–Fri 9–12.30, 1.30–5; Sat and Sun 10–12.30, 1.30–5*
(2) *Free*
(3) *Café*
(4) *Garden shops*
(5) *Stapeley Water Gardens Ltd*

Trentham
Staffordshire
27. Trentham Gardens

The 700 acre (290 ha) grounds were originally laid out by 'Capability' Brown, who made the mile-long (1·6 km) lake. In 1834, the 2nd Duke of Sutherland commissioned Charles Barry to redesign the house and gardens, and he and W. A. Nesfield laid out large, elaborate Italian gardens between the house and the lake which, it is now claimed, form the largest formal bedding display in Europe. Besides this there are rock gardens, a peat garden, many shrubs and bulbs and some good specimen trees, such as *Sequoia sempervirens*; *Pinus strobus*; *P. ponderosa*; *Taxodium distichum*, the swamp cypress; and the umbrella pine, *Sciadopitys verticillata*.

(1) *Daily (except 25 Dec) Sunrise–Sunset*
(2) *Charge*
(3) *Restaurant*
(4) *Tree and shrub nursery; garden centre; miniature railway; swimming pool*
(5) *Trentham Gardens Ltd*

Weston-under-Lizard, nr Shifnal
Salop
28. Weston Park

The house was built in 1671 on the site of a medieval manor house. The grounds cover approx 60 acres (27 ha), including a formal woodland garden, and were laid out c 1762 by 'Capability' Brown, who was commissioned by Sir Henry Bridgeman, later 1st Lord Bradford, when he succeeded to the estate. The Temple of Diana, designed at about the same time by James Paine, is considered to be one of the most beautiful pieces of Georgian garden architecture still standing.

The path through the woods to the temple passes through clumps of rhododendrons and azaleas, and north of it lies the temple pool, spanned at the far end by Paine's Roman bridge. Around the house, the gardens are laid out in a series of three terraces running the length of the house, with fine herbaceous borders. In the middle of the large central lawn on the lower terrace stands a vast oriental plane, *Platanus orientalis*, approx 70 ft (21·3 m) high and 23 ft (6·9 m) in girth, believed to be the largest in England and to have been planted around the time that the house was built. There are extensive glasshouses and a kitchen garden. Visit in May and June.

(1) *Easter weekend: 11–7.30; Apr: Sat and Sun 11–7.30; May–Jul and 1st three weeks of Sep: Tue–Thu, Sat, Sun and Public Holidays 11–7.30; Aug: Daily 11–7.30. Last admission 5.30*
(2) *Charge*
(3) *Café and restaurant*
(4) *House; garden centre; nature trail; aquarium (days as grounds 2–6. Last admission 5.30)*
(5) *Earl of Bradford*

Willoughbridge, nr Market Drayton

Salop

29. Dorothy Clive Memorial Garden

The garden was founded in 1939 by the late Col H. Clive and now covers about 12 acres (4.9 ha). The original garden was made from overgrown woodland in an old gravel quarry; in 1961–2 a sloping field below the house was planted with Exbury azaleas, and further landscaping and planting was done after 1967. The garden contains good collections of rhododendron, both species and hybrid, azaleas, camellias and shrub roses. There are many specimen trees, including magnolias, Japanese cherries, *Styrax obassia* and *Stewartia sinensis*; there is a water garden and a large scree planted with alpines. In spring, there is a fine display of bulbs and the garden is colourful from then until late autumn.

(1) *Mar–Nov: Daily 11.30–7.30 or Sunset*
(2) *Free; collecting box*
(5) *Willoughbridge Garden Trust*

Wolverhampton, Codsall Wood

Staffordshire

30. Chillington Hall

The present house was built in 1724 by the architect Francis Smith of Warwick, with additions by John Soane in 1786. The park was landscaped by 'Capability' Brown, who incorporated an existing oak avenue, 1 mile (1·6 km) in length, and created a 75 acre (34 ha) lake, with ancillary buildings by James Paine. The garden was designed by Inigo Trigg. Some of the work was not carried out, but rose beds remain, some in a pattern of rectangular beds and some circular, with a sundial in the centre. The garden is being improved by the present owner: a herbaceous border specified by Trigg is being restored and the woodland is being planted with rhododendrons.

(1) *Early May–mid-Sep: Thu 2.30–5.30; Aug: Sun also. Other days by appointment*
(2) *Charge*
(4) *House (same times)*
(5) *P. Giffard, Esq*

Wolverhampton, Fordhouses

Staffordshire

31. Moseley Old Hall

The Elizabethan manor house, with secret hiding places, was a refuge of Charles II after the Battle of Worcester. The garden is quite small, and has been reconstructed in the style of a 17th-cent garden with a box parterre. There is also a small herb garden, an arbour, herbaceous borders and old roses; wherever possible, only plants known to have been grown in England before 1700 have been used.

(1) *Mar–Oct: Wed, Thu, Sat, Sun, Bank Holiday Mon and following Tue 2–5.30 or Sunset. Nov: Wed and Sun 2–4.30 or Sunset. No dogs*
(2) *Charge*
(3) *Tea*
(4) *House (same times)*
(5) *National Trust*

Yealand Conyers, nr Carnforth

Lancashire

32. Leighton Hall

The house has a Gothic façade of white limestone, super-imposed on the original house in 1800. The present garden dates from the early 19th cent and consists mainly of lawns backed by a wall covered with climbing roses, a long herbaceous border and a shrubbery walk, characteristic of gardens of that period. On the rose lawn near the pond is a sundial dated 1647, a relic of an earlier garden. There are fine views to the Lakeland hills.

(1) *May–Sep: Tue–Fri and Sun 2–5*
(2) *Charge*
(3) *Café*
(4) *House (May–Sep: Sun and Wed 2–5); displays of free-flying eagles and falcons (all open days 3–4, weather permitting)*
(5) *R. G. Reynolds, Esq*

ENGLAND

3. NORTH, SOUTH AND WEST YORKSHIRE, HUMBERSIDE

Richmond ● 25

9

3

16 ● Helmsley 11

19

8 ● Malton

Ripon

33
30

34

26

2

Harrogate

31

6

5
● Bridlington

15 12

36 ● York

37

24

21 14

4 1

32

20 ● Leeds

Halifax

22 23

Hull ● 18

13

10

17 ● Huddersfield

Wakefield

35

Grimsby

7

27 ● Sheffield

28 29

Kilometres 0 10 20 30

Miles 0 10 20

ENGLAND

Aberford, nr Leeds
West Yorkshire

1. Lotherton Hall

The gardens were created by Mrs Laura Gascoigne who came to live at Lotherton in the late 1890s. The garden comprises some 10 acres (4·5 ha), set in a park of 150 acres (61 ha). There are walled gardens and a rock garden dating from 1912. A bird garden is under construction.

(1) *Daily 10.30–6.15 or Sunset in Winter; also May–Sep open till 8.30 on Thu*
(2) *Charge*
(3) *Café (Summer)*
(4) *Lotherton Hall Museum of Decorative Art (same times)*
(5) *Leeds City Council*

Appletreewick, nr Skipton
North Yorkshire

2. Parcevall Hall Gardens

The estate was bought in 1927 by Sir William Milner. He restored and enlarged the house and, on the south-facing slope below it, made the terrace garden, which took three years to construct. Several semi-hardy plants grow here, including *Eucryphia glutinosa, E. × nymansensis, Crinodendron hookeranum, Cytisus battandieri* and *Solanum crispum*. The terrace has a pond with pink and white water-lilies, and at the foot of the wall supporting the bottom terrace is the camellia walk; among the varieties represented are the *williamsii* hybrids 'Donation' and 'Mary Christian'. Beyond the terrace garden lies Tarn Ghyll Wood, which is lime free and is planted with many rhododendrons, including *R. rex, R. discolor, R. thomsonii* and the August-flowering *R. auriculatum*, as well as other trees and shrubs, such as hydrangeas and cornus and two species of bamboo.

To the left of the drive is the daffodil bank, with thousands of naturalized bulbs, including the dwarf hybrid 'W. P. Milner', and several handsome conifers such as the deodar and the Serbian spruce, *Picea omorika*. The orchard is also underplanted with daffodils. Near the chapel, a stream runs between beds of candelabra primulas, then vanishes underground, reappearing in the terrace garden. Also in the chapel garden is a fine specimen of the paperbark maple, *Acer griseum*, and in the nearby courtyard are groups of agapanthus 'Headbourne Hybrids' and *Nerine bowdenii*. The rose garden, surrounded by a hedge of *Chaemaecyparis lawsoniana*, has newer varieties of rose in the centre beds and old-fashioned shrub roses round the sides. North of the house is the rock garden with beyond it the silver wood which contains a number of interesting trees, including

Magnolia sieboldii and *Ilex × altaclarensis* 'Camelliifolia', another plant raised here. Along the stream are drifts of primulas and in spring the wood is carpeted with snowdrops, daffodils and bluebells.

(1) *Easter–Sep: Daily 10–6*
(2) *Charge*
(4) *Plants for sale*
(5) *Walsingham College Yorkshire Properties*

Bedale
North Yorkshire

3. Thorp Perrow

The 60 acre (27 ha) grounds include a lake, a wild garden and an arboretum which was planted by Sir Leonard Ropner in *c* 1930 and is now reaching maturity. Approx 2,500 species of tree and shrub are represented; several are among the tallest and best specimens known in this country.

(1) *Easter–mid-Oct: Sat and Sun 2–6*
(2) *Charge*
(5) *Sir John Ropner, Bt*

Bramham, nr Wetherby
West Yorkshire

4. Bramham Park

The gardens, which extend to 66 acres (27 ha), were laid out by Robert Benson, 1st Lord Bingley, in the early 18th cent with broad walks, vistas, avenues and ornamental water features in the style of the French garden architect André Le Nôtre. The lay-out has scarcely been altered since then and when replanting has been necessary it was done in the original style, with the result that it is probably the finest example left in Britain of this type of garden. In a gale in 1962 over 400 trees were uprooted, but the beech avenues and hedges have been replanted. The walls of the original parterre now enclose a rose garden; the water gardens include a T-shaped canal, ponds and cascades and ornamental temples. In spring there is a fine display of daffodils, followed by rhododendrons in the Black Fen area. The woodlands to the south of the house cover some 400 acres (161 ha); these were laid out as pleasure grounds with rides devoted to a single species and are now productive woodland.

(1) *Good Friday–end Sep: Sun, Tue, Wed and Thu 11–6*
(2) *Charge*
(3) *Café*
(4) *House (same days 1.15–5.30)*
(5) *George Lane Fox, Esq*

Bridlington
Humberside

5. Sewerby Hall, Park and Zoo

The grounds around the hall cover approx 50 acres (20 ha) and were largely laid out in the mid-19th cent, with formal walks, terraces and statuary although many of the trees must be approx 200 years old. The formal part of the garden contains many trees and shrubs including monkey puzzles, *Araucaria araucana* and Adam's needle, *Yucca gloriosa*; in the woodland many bulbs and herbaceous plants are naturalized, such as aconites, anemones and cyclamen. Probably the most notable feature is the walled Old English Garden with a central goldfish pond with water-lilies, box-edged flowerbeds and paved paths, and one section laid out as a rose garden with climbing, rambling, Hybrid Tea, floribunda and species roses. *Pittosporum tenuifolium* from New Zealand, not usually considered hardy in the North, grows well in a sheltered, south-facing walk. A glasshouse has a fine display of potted plants.

(1) *Daily 9–Sunset*
(2) *Charge (Spring Bank Holiday–September)*
(3) *Restaurant and café (Easter–Spring Bank Holiday: Sat and Sun; Spring Bank Holiday–Sep: Daily 10–Sunset)*
(4) *House, with art gallery, museum and Amy Johnson Trophy room (Easter–Sep: Sun–Fri 10–12.30, 1.30–6; Sat 1.30–6); Zoo (same times as grounds)*
(5) *North Wolds Borough Council*

Burton Agnes, nr Great Driffield
Humberside
6. Burton Agnes Hall

The house, one of the least altered of Elizabethan country houses, was built between 1598 and 1610. The gardens immediately around it are formal, with sweeping lawns, clipped evergreens and lily-ponds surrounded by decorative urns. A woodland garden was laid out in 1970 by Messrs Notcutts of Suffolk.

(1) *Easter Sun and Mon 1.45–5; May–mid-Oct: Mon–Fri 1.45–5; Sun 1.45–6*
(2) *Charge*
(3) *Tea*
(4) *House (same times)*
(5) *Burton Agnes Hall Preservation Trust*

Cleethorpes
Humberside
7. Haverstoe Park

The 15 acre (6 ha) park is laid out with lawns, trees and flowerbeds and contains the nurseries which supply flowers for the whole of the borough council area. An interesting feature is the garden for the blind, opened by Her Majesty the Queen on her Jubilee visit to Cleethorpes in 1977. It has raised beds, approx 3 ft (91 cm) high, with a number of seats in the area; all the flowers are scented and the names are in braille as well as ordinary print.

(1) *Daily Sunrise–Sunset*

(2) *Free*
(5) *Cleethorpes Borough Council*

Coneysthorpe
North Yorkshire
8. Castle Howard

The house was designed by Sir John Vanbrugh and built between 1699 and 1726 for Charles Howard, 3rd Earl of Carlisle. Elaborate gardens around the house were designed by George London and Henry Wise; the original parterre was removed but another, simpler one, was laid out by the garden designer W. A. Nesfield in 1850. The landscaped grounds, probably planned by the Earl himself, have two splendid Classical buildings at focal points, Vanbrugh's Temple of the Four Winds and the Mausoleum by Nicholas Hawksmoor. In the valley there is a lake and a winding river spanned by a stone bridge. The grounds are planted with many trees and shrubs, including over 1,000 varieties of rhododendron.

(1) *Good Friday–early Oct: Daily 10.30–5*
(2) *Charge*
(3) *Restaurant*
(4) *House (Good Friday–early Oct: Daily 1–5; Public Holidays 11–5)*
(5) *George Howard, Esq*

Constable Burton, nr Leyburn
North Yorkshire
9. Constable Burton Hall

The beautiful 18th-cent house built by John Carr is surrounded by a large, mainly informal garden with woodland walks. There are herbaceous borders, many roses and flowering shrubs, a fine display of daffodils in spring, a small lake and a rock garden with a good collection of alpines, some rare. There is always something of interest to see throughout spring and summer.

(1) *Apr–Sep: Daily Sunrise–Sunset*
(2) *Charge for NGS*
(5) *Charles Wyvill, Esq*

Dewsbury, Temple Road
West Yorkshire
10. Crow Nest Park

The 52 acre (24 ha) park lies approx 1 mile (1·6 km) from the town centre and is laid out with a lake, trees, shrubs, flowerbeds and a conservatory containing tropical and temperate plants.

(1) *Daily Sunrise–Sunset*
(2) *Free*
(3) *Café (Apr–Oct)*
(4) *Crow Nest Mansion (same times)*
(5) *Kirklees Metropolitan Council*

Ebberston, nr Scarborough

North Yorkshire

11. Ebberston Hall

The house was built by Colen Campbell, an early protégé of Lord Burlington, who was deputy-surveyor general to William Benson, an architect who was interested in hydrostatics and certainly influenced, even if he did not actually design, the water gardens at Ebberston. The lay-out has also been attributed to Stephen Switzer who did much work in the north of England and to Charles Bridgeman who designed the gardens at nearby Scanston.

Today only about half of the original features of the water gardens remain and these are in a ruinous condition. They are, however, worth visiting as a splendid example of their period, and the original lay-out can be reconstructed from contemporary pictures and Campbell's account in *Vitruvius Britannicus*.

(1) Easter–mid-Sep: Sat and Sun 2–6
(2) Charge
(4) House
(5) West de Wend-Fenton, Esq

Follifoot, nr Harrogate

North Yorkshire

12. Rudding Park

The landscape of the park was inspired by Humphry Repton, but the most interesting part of the garden was created after World War II by the late Capt Sir Everard Radcliffe and James Russell. Much of it is a woodland garden, with clearings and glades and large plantings of rhododendrons and azaleas and drifts of candelabra primulas. There is also a beautiful walled rose garden.

(1) Easter–early Sep: Sat, Sun and Public Holidays 11–5
(2) Charge
(3) Tea
(5) Rudding Park Gardens

Halifax

West Yorkshire

13. People's Park

The 12½ acre (5 ha) park was founded by the local industrialist Francis Crossley in 1856, designed by Sir Joseph Paxton who built the Crystal Palace and was opened to the public in 1857. Basically, it remains a formal, Victorian garden, with well-planned walks and vistas, fountains and lakes, trim lawns and flowerbeds set out with spring and summer bedding, and five Italian marble statues.

(1) Daily
(2) Free
(5) Metropolitan Borough of Calderdale

Harewood, nr Leeds

West Yorkshire

14. Harewood House

The park was landscaped in 1772 by 'Capability' Brown, who enlarged the lake made about twenty years earlier by damming the stream and surrounded it with plantations. The garden as such was designed and created by Sir Charles Barry in the 1840s. There are extensive lawns; rhododendrons in flower from March to July; a herbaceous border 120 yds (110 m) long, at its best in July and early August; and about 2,000 roses as well as fine shrubs and specimen timber trees.

(1) Early Apr–late Oct: Daily 11–6
(2) Charge
(3) Café
(4) House and Bird Garden (same times and some days in Winter)
(5) Earl of Harewood

Harrogate

North Yorkshire

15. Harlow Car Gardens

The Northern Horticultural Society was formed in Manchester in 1946 and Harlow Car Gardens were founded as a 'Northern Wisley' in 1948 with the aim of helping gardeners contend with the more difficult growing conditions of the North of England. The site is in an exposed situation on a cold, heavy clay soil at an altitude of 500 ft (152 m) and covers about 60 acres (24 ha).

To the east of the broad walk leading from the main entrance lie a heath garden, a rose garden and a sandstone rock garden with a scree bed in which alpines from high altitudes flourish. A stream at the end of the walk divides the formal garden from peat terraces planted with dwarf rhododendrons, gentians, primulas and meconopsis. Beyond lies an area of woodland sheltering a large collection of rhododendrons, including particularly fine specimens of *R. calophytum*, *R. fulvum*, *R. wightii* and *R. × loderi*, as well as other trees and shrubs such as eucryphias, camellias, magnolias, maples, species of *Halesia carolina*, the 'snowdrop tree', and the rarely seen *Trochodendron aralioides*.

A limestone rock garden sited so that it can enjoy the maximum amount of sun is planted with alpine plants demanding keen drainage and an open position. To the far west of the broad walk lie borders of old-fashioned roses, a trials area, a fruit plot and an allotment-sized vegetable garden as well as a summer garden and a border devoted to winter-flowering plants such as the sweet-smelling *Viburnum × bodnantense* and *Mahonia japonica*. South-east of the entrance lies the Barbara Clough Garden, a small, enclosed garden (named in honour of a benefactor of the society), that receives maximum winter sunshine while shrubs, thought to be too tender for the North, flourish in the protection of a high wall.

Helmsley

North Yorkshire

16. Duncombe Park

The house was built for Thomas Duncombe in the early 18th cent on the edge of a plateau with the land falling away to the north and west. A long grass terrace runs along the edge of the escarpment, with two 18th-cent temples and a large statue of Father Time as ornaments. To the east of the house there is a formal garden with a green parterre and winding paths leading to the 'secret garden'.

(1) May–Aug: Wed 10–4
(2) Charge
(5) Trustees of Duncombe Park

Huddersfield

West Yorkshire

17. Greenhead Park

The park, formerly part of the estate of Sir John Ramsden, a local landowner, was bought by the Council in 1882 for £30,000, raised by public subscription. It covers 38 acres (15 ha) and is laid out with lawns, trees, shrubs and flowerbeds; a conservatory contains tropical and temperate plants.

(1) Daily Sunrise–Sunset
(2) Free
(3) Café (Apr–Oct)
(5) Kirklees Metropolitan Council

Hull, Thwaite St, Cottingham

Humberside

18. University of Hull Botanic Garden

The botanical garden was established in 1948 by Professor R. D'O. Good and has been enlarged at various times since then. Near the entrance gate is an interesting example of a graft hybrid, + Laburnocytisus adamii, which bears flowers of both its parents, Cytisus purpureus and Laburnum anagyroides. There are a number of groups of roses of various types, such as modern shrub roses, hybrid perpetuals (the ancestors of the modern Hybrid Tea roses), roses derived from R. rugosa and hybrids derived from R. cinensis.

There is an extensive glasshouse complex, part of which is open to the public. The tropical house contains plants from various countries with the emphasis on species of economic importance, although there are also ornamentals such as the bird of paradise flower, Strelitzia reginae, and the climber, Allamanda cathartica. There are two temperate houses, a fern house and two cool houses, one of which is used mainly for a collection of conifers that are not quite hardy enough to survive outside. A corridor linking these glasshouses is also planted with a number of collections, including species of citrus, hibiscus, a range of scented pelargoniums and cacti.

The rear part of the garden is planted with beds of shrubs arranged in their natural orders, and a small rock garden and scree contain mainly bulbous species.

(1) Apr–Sep: Thu 1–4.30
(2) Free
(5) University of Hull

Kirby Misperton, nr Malton

North Yorkshire

19. Flamingo Land Zoo

The 350 acre (140 ha) zoo park was founded in 1961; many of the grottoes and ornamental walks were constructed by Chinese labour imported by Alderman Twentyman, who owned the estate between 1903 and 1928. The grounds include many mature trees, including willows and flowering cherries; several ponds with water-lilies and bog plants round the edges; rose gardens; and many flowerbeds containing fuchsias, begonias and other bedding plants. Thousands of daffodil and tulip bulbs are planted each year. The Tropical House, where the collection of reptiles is kept, contains many exotic plants.

(1) Easter–Sep: Daily 10–6.30
(2) Charge
(3) Café; bar; snack bar; kiosks
(4) Zoo, with over 1,000 animals, birds and reptiles (same times); jungle cruise; fairground; haunted castle; model railway centre; miniature railway; children's farm (open 11.30 or noon)
(5) Flamingo Land Ltd

Leeds, Otley Road

West Yorkshire

20. Golden Acre Park

The park, 76·2 acres (30·5 ha) in extent, was acquired by the Council in 1946 and is being developed as a botanical garden by the Leisure Services Committee. Already, collections of acer, betula, malus, prunus, sorbus and other ornamental trees and shrubs have been established. The existing British flora in the park is being preserved and it is intended to add other British natives not indigenous to the district. There is something of interest to see at all seasons.

(1) Daily Sunrise-Sunset
(2) Free
(5) Leeds City Council, Leisure Services Dept

ENGLAND

Leeds, Headingley
21. The Hollies Park

This beautiful park with streams and ravines, was given to the city by George W. Brown. It contains lawns, herbaceous borders and rock gardens, and woodland underplanted with a comprehensive collection of rhododendrons, both species and hybrid, as well as other shrubs.

(1) Daily Sunrise–Sunset
(2) Free
(5) Leeds City Council, Leisure Services Dept

Leeds
22. Roundhay Park

The site of the present park, 616 acres (247 ha) in extent, was the subject of a charter granted by the Earl of Lincoln in the reign of Henry II giving rights of timber and pasturage to the monks of Kirkstall at 'Rundehaia'. The estate was purchased in 1804 by a London banker, Thomas Nicholson, and he landscaped the grounds, the most notable features being two lakes completed in 1815—the Waterloo Lake, covering 32 acres (13 ha) and the Upper Lake, of 6 acres (2·4 ha). The park also includes pleasure gardens, canal gardens and rose gardens with an adjoining range of glasshouses.

(1) Daily Sunrise–Sunset
(2) Free
(5) Leeds City Council, Leisure Services Dept

Leeds
23. Temple Newsam

The Tudor and Jacobean house, birthplace of Lord Darnley the husband of Mary Queen of Scots, stands in a 900 acre (360 ha) park, the largest in the city, originally landscaped by 'Capability' Brown. It was bought by the Council from Lord Halifax in 1922 at a cost of £35,000. The landscape is now being reconstructed in order to improve the various vistas, and many trees are being replanted. The grounds include a number of ornamental ponds, splendid rhododendrons and azaleas and a large rose garden.

(1) Daily Sunrise–Sunset
(2) Free
(3) Old Courthouse Restaurant
(4) House (Daily, except 25–26 Dec, 10.30–6.15 or Sunset; May–Sep open till 8.30 on Wed)
(5) Leeds City Council, Leisure Services Dept

Pocklington
Humberside
24. Burnby Hall Gardens

The gardens were founded by Major P. M. Stewart, who bought the property in 1904. He constructed two lakes: the Upper Water, now 15 acres (0·7 ha) in extent, and the smaller Lower Water. In 1935 brick-walled soil beds were built on the floor of the lakes and planted with water-lilies; the gardens now have one of the largest collections in Europe, with about 5,000 plants of more than 50 species and varieties, flowering from late May to October, although the main display is from late June until mid-September.

(1) Apr–Sep: Mon–Fri 10–7; Sat and Sun 2–7
(2) Charge
(3) Café (Jun–mid-Sep: Daily 2–5; Easter–May and late Sep: Sat and Sun 2–5
(4) Museum, with sporting trophies and curios collected by Major Stewart (same times as café)
(5) Stewart's Burnby Hall Gardens and Museum Trust

Richmond
North Yorkshire
25. St Nicholas

The garden, of great horticultural interest, was designed and planted by Robert James early in the 1900s. It includes topiary work, a rock garden and many shrubs including species rhododendrons and old-fashioned roses. Visit from April to August.

(1) Daily 10–7
(2) Charge for NGS
(5) Lady Serena James

Ripley
North Yorkshire
26. Ripley Castle

The estate has belonged to the Ingilby family since c 1350; the gatehouse leading into the courtyard was built about 100 years later. The oldest part of the house, most of which was rebuilt in 1780, is the tower, dating from 1550. The grounds were laid out by 'Capability' Brown. The soil which was dug out when he created the lake was used to make the terrace from which steps give on to a path leading to the Pleasure Grounds with flowering shrubs, a garden temple and many fine trees. Another path leads to the walled flower garden. Originally, glasshouses stretched down the length of one of the walls to the Garden House at the west end, but half of these were pulled down after World War I and replaced by a paved garden. The Palm House in the north centre of the wall still remains.

(1) Easter weekend and May–Sep: Sat, Sun and Public Holidays 10–12, 2–6

(2) Charge
(3) Refreshments (Sun and Public Holidays)
(4) House and Priest's Hole (May–Sep: Sun and Public Holidays same times. Parties on other days by arrangement)
(5) Sir Thomas Ingilby, Bt

Sheffield

South Yorkshire
27. Botanical Gardens

The gardens, which cover an area of 19 acres (7·6 ha) were founded in 1833 and designed by the first curator, Robert Marnock. They were given to the Town Trust in 1898 and have been administered by Sheffield Corporation since 1951. The ground slopes to the south-west and, although the highest point is about 450 feet (137 m) above sea level, the micro-climate is favourable, with the result that species generally considered rather tender, such as *Embothrium coccineum*, *Desfontainea spinosa* and *Cytisus battandieri*, can be grown. In all, it is estimated that 4,000–5,000 species are grown in the gardens.

Among the many features of interest are a demonstration garden, which includes collections of fuchsias and carnations; a peat garden with dwarf rhododendrons, cassiopes, ledums, primulas and meconopsis; a rock garden; a heather garden; a Victorian garden with intricate bedding displays; a formal garden; a sorbus lawn; a 'silver and gold' bed; a 'forms' bed for plants of distinctive shape and a woodland garden with rhododendrons, azaleas, *Eucalyptus gunnii* and the hardy palm *Trachycarpus fortunei*. An old bear pit now houses a collection of winter-flowering plants. The Paxton Pavilion complex, built under the chairmanship of Sir Joseph Paxton, houses an aviary, an aquarium and a half-hardy house.

(1) Daily 7.30–Sunset. Demonstration garden. 10–4 (Winter) or 6 (Summer)
(2) Free
(4) Aquarium and aviary (10–half an hour before garden closing, latest 8)
(5) City of Sheffield, Recreation Dept

Sheffield

28. Whinfell Quarry Gardens

The gardens were presented to the city in 1968 by James Neill Holdings Ltd as a memorial to Sir Frederick Neill who lived at Whinfell for 31 years. It was made from a disused quarry at the turn of the century and, because of its sheltered site, many plants normally of doubtful hardiness in the North grow and flourish. It is at its most colourful from April to June, but there is something of interest to see – flower, fruit or foliage – all the year round.

(1) Daily Sunrise–Sunset
(2) Free
(5) City of Sheffield

Sheffield
29. Whirlow Brook Park

Most of this park was presented to the city in 1946. The grounds of the house were landscaped in the late 1920s and the most notable feature is a large rock garden constructed in millstone grit that blends in with existing contours to give a natural effect. It is planted with conifers, Japanese maples and dwarf shrubs as well as alpines; a pond at the foot has water-lilies and marginal plants.

(1) Daily Sunrise–Sunset
(2) Free
(3) Restaurant
(5) City of Sheffield

Skelton, nr Ripon

North Yorkshire
30. Newby Hall

The gardens, which extend to over 25 acres (11 ha), have long herbaceous borders sloping down to the River Ure. Leading from this main axis, a number of smaller gardens were designed by the late Major Compton between 1923 and his death in 1977, with the aim of displaying colour at all seasons of the year. There are sunken gardens for old roses and spring flowers, pergolas, autumn gardens as well as many unusual trees and shrubs including magnolias, camellias, rhododendrons, azaleas and embothriums. The rock gardens are earlier than the rest of the plan, and were designed by Miss Ellen Willmott in 1915. The beautiful statuary is another interesting feature. Late summer is usually the best time to visit.

(1) Good Friday–1 Oct: Daily 11–6
(2) Charge
(3) Refreshments
(4) House (Easter, Public Holidays, Apr and May: Sun 2–6; Jun and Sep: Tue–Thu and Sun 2–6; Jul and Aug: Tue–Sun 2–6); gift shop; miniature railway rides (same times)
(5) R. E. J. Compton, Esq

Sledmere

Humberside
31. Sledmere House

The present house was built in 1751 on the site of an older one and enlarged in 1787 by Sir Christopher Sykes, who also commissioned 'Capability' Brown to lay out the 2,000 acre (800 ha) park. Lawns still sweep up to the house according to his design. An addition to the house, built in 1912, was demolished in 1945 and an Italian garden was laid out on the site. A circular pool with a fountain is set in paving; there are rose beds and 18th-cent copies of Greek and Roman statuary.

(1) *Easter Sun and Mon, Sun until mid-May and mid-May–1 Oct: Tue–Thu, Sat, Sun and Public Holidays 1.30–5.30. Last admission 5*
(2) *Charge*
(3) *Café*
(4) *House (same times)*
(5) *Sir Tatton Sykes, Bt*

Sproatley, nr Hull

Humberside

32. Burton Constable Hall

The Elizabethan house, built in 1570, is set in 200 acres (80 ha) of parkland landscaped by 'Capability' Brown. It includes 25 acres (11 ha) of lakes. An elegant orangery has now been converted into an aviary.

(1) *Easter Sat–Spring Bank Holiday: Sat and Sun noon–6; Spring Bank Holiday–last Sun in Sep: Tue–Thu, Sat, Sun and Public Holidays noon–6*
(2) *Charge*
(3) *Café*
(4) *House and model railway (open days 1–6)*
(5) *J. R. Chichester-Constable, Esq*

Studley Roger, nr Ripon

North Yorkshire

33. Studley Royal

The garden, set in a valley, was made by John Aislabie between 1720 and 1742. In the bottom of the valley is a formal water garden, a series of pools and canals made from the River Skell, which flows through it. Three ponds, the central one circular and the two flanking ones crescent shaped, are known as the Moon Ponds and are overlooked by a white Doric temple.

(1) *Mar, Apr and Oct: Mon–Sat 9.30–5.30; Sun 2–5.30; May–Sep: Mon–Sat 9.30–7; Sun 2–7; Nov–Feb: Mon–Sat 9.30–4; Sun 2–4. Closed on 24–26 Dec and 1 Jan*
(2) *Charge*
(5) *Department of the Environment*

Sutton-on-the-Forest

North Yorkshire

34. Sutton Park

The early Georgian house, built in 1730, is surrounded by a park designed by 'Capability' Brown. The gardens were created by the late Major E. C. R. and Mrs Sheffield after they bought the house in 1963. Two wide terraces were already there; part of the park, including a large cedar tree, was incorporated into the garden and a beech hedge was planted to mark the new boundary. The

top terrace is paved with old flagstones, interplanted with gold and silver thyme; flowerbeds, with six standard wistarias, are planted in a pink, grey and mauve colour scheme. The second terrace has a formal lay-out, with rectangular beds of Hybrid Tea roses and two mixed borders containing shrubs and herbaceous perennials with yellow, blue and white flowers. On the lawn below the terrace is a formal lily-pond with island beds on either side. Climbing roses are interspersed with old trees. Beyond the formal area lies a semi-wild garden with many flowering shrubs and daffodils in spring.

(1) *Good Friday, then Tue–Thu, Sun and Public Holidays until 1 Oct: 2–6*
(2) *Charge*
(3) *Café (2–5.30)*
(4) *House*
(5) *Mrs N. M. D. Sheffield*

Wakefield

West Yorkshire

35. Nostell Priory

The house, built on the site of an old priory 6 miles (9·6 km) south-east of Wakefield, dates from 1731 with a wing designed by Robert Adam added in 1766. It overlooks a lake and beyond is a garden with winding walks through shrubberies, some fine trees and a Gothic garden house.

(1) *Apr and Oct: Wed, Sat and Sun 2–6; May–Sep: Daily (except Fri) 2–6; Public Holidays (Sun, Mon and Tue) 11–6. No dogs*
(2) *Charge*
(3) *Tea*
(4) *House and motor cycle and aircraft museums (same times)*
(5) *National Trust*

York

North Yorkshire

36. University of York

The new university was built on land adjoining Heslington Hall, an Elizabethan mansion with an 18th-cent topiary garden of clipped yews. The feature of the new grounds is a 14 acre (6 ha) river-like lake, around which the new buildings have been arranged. Thousands of trees have been planted and the new garden is linked with the old by a canal pool with fountains and a sculpture by Henry Moore.

(1) *Daily Sunrise–Sunset*
(2) *Free*
(5) *University of York*

York

37. Yorkshire Museum

The Museum Gardens were founded in 1822 by the Yorkshire Philosophical Society. Interesting specimen trees, including a large monkey puzzle, *Araucaria araucana*, grow in grounds which also contain a Roman tower, the remains of the 11th- and 13th-cent St Mary's Abbey and the ruins of St Leonard's Hospital

(*1*) *Mon–Sat 8–Sunset; Sun 10–Sunset*
(*2*) *Charge*
(*4*) *Museum (Mon–Sat 10–5; Sun 1–5)*
(*5*) *North Yorkshire County Council*

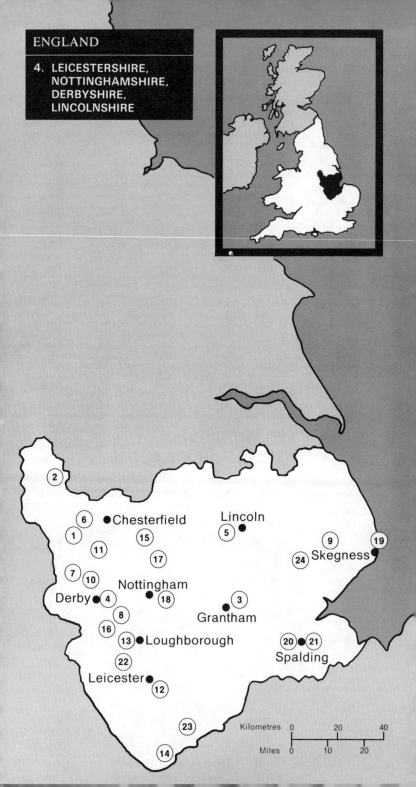

ENGLAND

4. LEICESTERSHIRE,
NOTTINGHAMSHIRE,
DERBYSHIRE,
LINCOLNSHIRE

②

⑥ ● Chesterfield   Lincoln
①   ⑤
    ⑪   ⑮
              ⑰   ⑨   ⑲
⑦ ⑩   ㉔ Skegness
Derby ● ④ Nottingham
        ⑧   ⑱   ③
    ⑯   Grantham
      ⑬ ● Loughborough   ⑳ ● ㉑
    ㉒   Spalding
Leicester ●
        ⑫
              ㉓   Kilometres 0   20   40
        ⑭   Miles 0   10   20

Bakewell

Derbyshire

1. Haddon Hall

Parts of the house, set high above the River Wye, date from the 12th cent. The gardens, mainly on the south side of the house, were constructed in the early 17th cent and take the form of a series of walled terraces leading down towards the river. By the beginning of this cent it was very much overgrown and was restored by the 9th Duke of Rutland. The Fountain Terrace has a rectangular pool with a fountain, but the dominant feature of the garden is the abundance of roses, with formal beds on the terraces and climbers on the house and terrace walls. Visit in late June and early July.

(1) *Good Friday–Sep: Tue–Sat and Public Holiday Mon 11–6; Public Holiday Sun 2–6*
(2) *Charge*
(3) *Café*
(4) *House (same times)*
(5) *Duke of Rutland*

Bamford

Derbyshire

2. High Peak Garden Centre

The 7¼ acre (3·4 ha) nursery includes an exhibition garden with over 8,000 roses, tree and shrub borders, a rock garden, a heather garden and a variety of hedges for demonstration purposes. In summer, there are rose shows every weekend.

(1) *Daily 10–Sunset*
(2) *Free; collecting boxes for NGS and GSO*
(3) *Café*
(4) *Nursery, bird garden and trout stream*
(5) *Clifford Proctor Nurseries Ltd*

Belton, nr Grantham

Lincolnshire

3. Belton House

The 17th-cent house is attributed to Sir Christopher Wren. No particular landscape artist is associated with the gardens; they are the work of various members of the Brownlow family who have lived at Belton since 1689. There are 600 acres (240 ha) of parkland. To the west of the house is a 'wilderness', bounded by the River Withen, with several cascades and sheltering Gothic 'ruins'. North of the house is a formal, sunken Victorian garden with clipped box hedges, statuary and fountain. The graceful orangery was designed by Wyatville in 1819; it is planted with camellias and the ironwork pillars support Virginia creepers. There is a Norman church in the grounds.

(1) *Good Friday–1st Sun in Oct: Sun–Fri noon–5.30*
(2) *Charge*
(3) *Restaurant/café*

(4) *House (same times); garden centre; children's play area designed as a North American timber fort.*
(5) *Lord Brownlow*

Derby

4. Derby Arboretum

The arboretum is of historical interest in that it was probably the first municipally owned public park in Britain. It was designed by the horticultural writer J. C. Loudon in 1840 for Joseph Strutt, who donated it to the city in the same year. The site has ridges and low hillocks, probably artificially made, and trees planted to no very clear plan.

(1) *Daily during daylight hours*
(2) *Free*
(4) *Bowling green*
(5) *Derby City Council*

Doddington, nr Lincoln

Lincolnshire

5. Doddington Hall

The house and the two walled gardens were completed in 1600 and the present appearance of the walled gardens dates from 1900. They are in the traditional manner, with box parterres, gravel and grass and flowerbeds, surrounded by borders of scented old-fashioned roses. The wild garden in the surrounding 5 acres (2 ha) was begun by C. F. C. Jarvis in 1930 and planted with rhododendrons, shrub roses and a number of unusual shrubs. These have been supplemented by subsequent owners. The wild garden is at its best in May; the walled garden in June and early July.

(1) *May and Jun: Wed 2–6; Jul and Aug: Wed and Sun 2–6; Sep: Wed 2–6; also Easter, 1 May, Spring and Summer Bank Holiday Mon 2–6*
(2) *Charge*
(3) *Café*
(4) *House (same times)*
(5) *Antony Jarvis, Esq*

Edensor, nr Bakewell

Derbyshire

6. Chatsworth

The present garden is mainly the creation of the 6th Duke of Devonshire, the gardener and architect Sir Joseph Paxton and the architect Sir Jeffry Wyatville, but there are traces of earlier gardens. Queen Mary's Bower, although it was reconstructed in the early 19th cent, is a relic of the garden of the Elizabethan house; and Flora's Temple, the glasshouse in the rose garden, the sea horse fountain on the south front, the cascade and the canal pond remain from the formal garden laid out in the 17th cent by George

London and Henry Wise for the 1st Duke, who built the main block of the present house. The grounds were later landscaped by 'Capability' Brown and, by the 1760s, the formal gardens had almost disappeared.

Paxton's Great Conservatory and the Lily House, a forerunner of the Crystal Palace, were demolished soon after 1918 and only low walls remain. The south part of the enclosure is planted with lupins, flowering in May and June; the central part has Michaelmas daisies and dahlias, and a maze of yew was planted in 1961. A new glasshouse with three sections at different temperature levels was designed by G. A. H. Pearce and completed in 1970.

Planting began in the arboretum and pinetum in 1835 and expeditions were sent to India and Nepal and North and South America to collect seed to grow there. To the north of the pinetum is the grotto, made in the late 18th cent., and to the east, a path through the ravine leads to the azalea dell. The rose garden is kept up to date with new plantings. Paxton's range of glasshouses nearby, which he called his 'Conservative Wall', contains camellias and other cool-house plants, including two large specimens of *C. reticulata* planted by Paxton in *c* 1850. In spring there is a mass of daffodils and other bulbs, followed by the azaleas and rhododendrons planted throughout the garden. The herbaceous borders near the orangery give colour for the rest of the summer and in autumn the many trees make a fine display.

(1) *Late Mar–early Oct: Tue–Fri 11.30–4.30; Sat and Sun 1.30–5.30; Public Holiday Sun 12.30–5.30; Public Holiday Mon 11.30–5.30*
(2) *Charge*
(3) *Café*
(4) *House (as garden but closes half an hour earlier); farmyard (Mon–Fri 10.30–4.30; Sat and Sun 1.30–5.30; Public Holiday Mon and Tue 10.30–5.30)*
(5) *Trustees of the Chatsworth Settlement*

Ednaston, nr Derby

Derbyshire

7. Ednaston Manor

The house was built for the Player family between 1913 and 1919 to the design of Sir Edwin Lutyens. The 9 acre (4 ha) garden is mainly formal and contains a wide range of interesting trees, including many sorbus and maples, rhododendrons, azaleas, roses and other flowering shrubs.

(1) *Wed and Thu 1–4.30; also early Apr–late Sep: Sun 2–6*
(2) *Charge*
(3) *Tea (Sun)*
(5) *S. D. Player, Esq*

Elvaston

Derbyshire

8. Elvaston Castle Country Park

The grounds were laid out in 1830 by William Barron, after the 3rd Earl of Harrington had invited 'Capability' Brown to design the landscape. He refused the commission because 'there is such a want of capability in it'. He did, however, give the Earl six cedars of Lebanon, which are still to be seen. Barron made a succession of gardens bounded by hedges and a series of short avenues with specimen trees at each end, and constructed the lake and rockwork to the north of the castle. He initiated topiary work with yews and much of this still remains as do many of the trees he planted, now grown to full maturity. There are collections of varieties of yew and holly.

A new rhododendron dell has been planted at the west end of the lake and more rhododendrons, acers and other trees and shrubs have been planted elsewhere in the grounds. Half of the old kitchen garden is used as a nursery and the other half has been developed into an Old English garden with herbaceous borders, a rose garden and a herb garden. The area in front of the castle has recently been replanted as a parterre in keeping with the original design.

Also in the grounds are a grotto and a curious building known as the Moorish Temple.

(1) *Daily*
(2) *Free*
(3) *Refreshments (Easter–Oct)*
(4) *House, countryside museum; trail centre; shop (Easter–Oct)*
(5) *Derbyshire County Council*

Harrington, nr Spilsby

Lincolnshire

9. Harrington Hall

The house is a Caroline manor house of mellow red brick on a medieval stone base. The high walled terrace also dates from this period but the rest of the garden, which covers 5 acres (2 ha), is 18th cent. in design with walls enclosing lawns, roses, herbaceous borders and broom borders. The terrace is the 'High Hall Garden' of Tennyson's Maud, who lived at Harrington Hall with her guardian.

(1) *Easter–Oct: Wed and Thu noon–8; also some Sun for charities*
(2) *Free; Charge on charity days and with house*
(4) *House (Tue 2–5); Garden centre (open as garden)*
(5) *Lady Maitland*

Kedleston, nr Derby

Derbyshire

10. Kedleston Hall

The property has belonged to the Curzon

family since c 1100; the present house was built, starting in 1759, for Sir Nathaniel Curzon, 1st Baron Scarsdale, largely to the design of Robert Adam, although the south front is by James Paine, at that time the more famous of the two architects. In the grounds, the orangery, the boathouse, a summer house and a graceful three-arched bridge crossing Cutler Brook were also designed by Adam. The 500 acre (202 ha) park contains a lake, a Canada goose sanctuary and many fine trees; nearer the house is a formal area with lawns, roses and flowering shrubs. Visit in early summer.

(1) Easter Sun and Mon; thereafter last Sun in Apr–last Sun in Sep: Sun and Public Holidays 12.30–6
(2) Charge
(3) Tea
(4) House; gift shop (days as above 2–6)
(5) Viscount Scarsdale

Lea, nr Matlock

Derbyshire

11. Lea Rhododendron Gardens

The gardens are large and contain a wide variety of species and hybrid rhododendrons, some rare, in an attractive hillside and woodland setting.

(1) Easter–mid Jun: Daily 10–8
(2) Charge
(3) Tea
(5) Mrs Tye and Miss Colyer

Leicester, Stoughton Drive South

Leicestershire

12. University of Leicester Botanic Garden

The present garden, about 16 acres (6·5 ha) in extent, was developed from the grounds of four houses built between 1902 and 1928, purchased by the university as halls of residence between 1947 and 1964.

In the entrance forecourt and on the terrace of the first house, Beaumont Hall, are a number of tender shrubs including *Abutilon vitifolium* and *Azara serrata* from Chile, *Penstemon isophyllus* from Mexico and several sun-loving Mediterranean shrubs. Along the east of the building, a series of shaded beds is devoted mainly to plants that flower in winter and early spring, with some later-flowering species such as azaleas, peonies and *Eucryphia x nymansensis* 'Nymansay'. Other interesting plants in the grounds include the unusual Chilean conifer *Podocarpus andinus* and the graft hybrid + *Laburnocytisus adamii*. There are two rock gardens, one built in c 1930 from waterworn Westmorland limestone, dominated by a large bristle-cone pine, *Pinus aristata*; the other constructed in c 1905 from massive carboniferous sandstone from Derbyshire, modelled on the stone gardens perfected 500 years ago by Buddhist priests

in Kyoto. A fine collection of Japanese maples reinforces the Japanese theme. Beyond Beaumont Hall lies the Formal Garden, with a long canal-pool planted with water-lilies; a sunken garden copied from a Victorian design; a fern bed; a rose garden; herbaceous borders and several plant houses including a succulent house.

Southmeade House also has tender plants on its terrace including the evergreen *Clematis armandii* and an Australian bottlebrush tree, *Callistemon citrinus*. A scree bed is mainly devoted to small plants of known wild origin and the systematic beds have representatives of twenty hardy plant families. The main glasshouse, a dwarf conifer bed and heather beds lie in the area adjoining Hastings House, and there are also some fine specimen trees including a wellingtonia, *Sequoiadendron giganteum*, and a set of the three main species of cedar: the Atlas cedar from North Africa, the cedar of Lebanon and the deodar, from Afghanistan. These are underplanted with hardy hybrid rhododendrons. The main heather garden lies on a gentle slope in the garden of The Knoll, the fourth house, and its old conservatory has been turned into an alpine house. A series of rose beds traces the history of garden roses.

(1) Mon–Fri 10–5 or Sunset. No dogs
(2) Free
(5) University of Leicester

Loughborough

Leicestershire

13. Whatton Gardens

The gardens were partly designed by Edward Dawson in the early 19th cent and were further developed towards the end of the century by the 1st Lord Crawshaw. There are many fine specimen trees, including cedars, oaks of various species, maples and wellingtonias (*Sequoiadendron giganteum*). In April thousands of daffodils planted on the lawns and under the trees make a spectacular display, and a fine herbaceous border against a south-facing wall is colourful from June onwards with the delphiniums at their best in July.

There are two rose gardens and a wild garden with winding paths, one of which is in the form of a canyon built up of rocks brought by horse and cart from Derbyshire in the late 19th cent. The Chinese Garden is a striking feature, many of the garden ornaments having been brought from China. Nearby are rhododendrons, at their best in May, and a Dutch garden with a circular azalea bed and a stone summer house.

(1) Apr–Aug: Sun and Bank Holidays 2–7
(2) Charge
(3) Tea
(4) Garden Centre (weekdays during working hours)
(5) Lord Crawshaw

Lutterworth

Leicestershire

14. Stanford Hall

The house was built in 1690. The garden is mostly laid out with lawns and shrubs, and there is a walled rose garden, at its best in early July. The River Avon runs through the park.

(1) *Easter–Sep: Thur, Sat and Sun 2–6; Easter, Spring and late Summer Bank Holiday Mon and following Tue noon–6. Other times by appointment*
(2) *Charge*
(3) *Café*
(4) *House and Motor Cycle and Car Museum (same times); craft centre (weekends)*
(5) *Lord and Lady Braye*

Mansfield

Derbyshire

15. Hardwick Hall

The house was built in 1591–7 for Bess of Hardwick, probably by the architect Robert Smythson. A 17th-cent drawing shows the courtyard planted with four grass plots and this was restored after World War I, with the addition of herbaceous borders running round the walls. Another border planted with old-fashioned roses separates the forecourt from the main garden which lies to the south of the house and is mainly the creation of Lady Laura Egerton, who spent summers at Hardwick from her marriage in 1865 until she died in 1907.

Two wide alleys, one with a beech hedge and the other with hornbeam, meet at a central *rond-point*, thus dividing the garden into quarters. One of these is a lawn with magnolias and a large beech; one has been planted as a herb garden and nuttery and the other two are orchards. Two small gazebos, one in the south-east corner of the garden and the other north-east of the house, were probably part of the original garden plan.

(1) *Apr–Oct; Daily noon–5.30*
(2) *Charge*
(3) *Lunch (May–Sep); tea*
(4) *House (Apr–Oct: Wed, Thu, Sat, Sun and Public Holiday Mon 1–5.30 or Sunset)*
(5) *National Trust*

Melbourne, nr Derby

Derbyshire

16. Melbourne Hall

The gardens, which cover approx 16 acres (6·5 ha), were laid out by Thomas Coke, Vice-Chamberlain to Queen Anne and George I from 1711 until he died in 1727. The actual design was executed in 1704

by George London and Henry Wise and this has remained almost unchanged until the present day. It is one of the finest examples left of the typically formal, late 17th- and early 18th-cent garden, similar to that of Versailles, since most of those in Britain were destroyed in the 'landscape revolution' of the mid-18th cent. An avenue extends from the east front of the house symmetrically flanked by lawns (and originally also by parterres), crossed at right angles by other paths. At the farthest end is a sheet of water with, beyond it, the famous wrought-iron pergola known as The Birdcage designed by the celebrated ironsmith, Robert Bakewell, in the early 18th cent and restored in 1956.

At the junction of the paths are clearings that contain fountains or statues including cast lead figures and vases by John Van Nost, who also worked at Chatsworth (cf). One of the most striking features in the garden is the Yew Tunnel whose age is unknown – it was already old in 1726 when the framework was decayed and had to be taken down.

(1) *Easter Sat–Tue, early Apr–late May and late Sep–early Oct: Sun 2–6; late May–mid-Sep: Wed, Thu, Sat, Sun 2–6; Public Holidays 11–6*
(2) *Charge*
(3) *Restaurant*
(4) *House; gift shop; garden produce (same times)*
(5) *Marquess of Lothian*

Newstead, nr Linby

Nottinghamshire

17. Newstead Abbey

The abbey was founded in 1170, reputedly by Henry II, as an Augustinian priory. It has many associations with the poet Byron who inherited the property in 1798. The gardens which cover 25 acres (11 ha) include a series of lakes and running streams. Parts of the gardens are formal with terraces and vistas and are probably relatively unchanged since Byron's time. The wall along the north side is supported by 14th-cent buttresses and makes a splendid background for a long herbaceous border.

The Spanish garden, a small formal garden in front of the south-east wing of the abbey, dates from early in this century; a Spanish well-head forms the centrepiece of a pattern of flowerbeds edged with clipped box. Nearby is a monument to Byron's dog, Boatswain. A rose garden with a collection of old and historical shrub roses was laid out in an old walled garden in 1965; another walled garden is planted with irises.

A Japanese garden was constructed early this century under the direction of Miss Webb, daughter of the owner of the abbey, who employed a Japanese landscape architect and imported many of the plants and ornaments from Japan. In the garden as a whole are many fine trees and shrubs, including rhododendrons.

(1) Daily 10–Sunset
(2) Charge
(3) Tea
(4) Abbey (Good Friday–Sep: Mon–Sat 2–6, guided tours every hour; Sun and Public Holidays 2–6.30, no tours)
(5) Nottingham City Council

(4) Bird museum in house (Mon–Fri 10–½ hour after Sunset; Sat and Sun by request to park keeper); aviary
(5) South Holland District Council

Radcliffe-on-Trent

Nottinghamshire

18. Holme Pierrepont Hall

The castellated brick manor house was built in c 1500 around a courtyard, which was laid out in the 1880s with elaborate box parterres, roses and a yellow herbaceous border. A large shrub garden outside the house was planted in 1973.

(1) Apr–May and Aug–Sep: Sun, Public Holidays and Easter Tue 2–6; Jun–Jul: Sun and Thu 2–6. Parties at other times by appointment
(2) Charge
(3) Buffet lunches for parties by appointment
(4) House (same times)
(5) Mr and Mrs Robin Brackenbury

Skegness

Lincolnshire

19. Foreshore Gardens

The gardens, which extend for over a mile (1·6 km) and cover approx 34 acres (15 ha), are laid out on land reclaimed from the sea. They are set out with herbaceous borders, shrubs and bedding plants (approx 65,000 are put in each year) and include a rock garden and formal and informal areas.

(1) Daily
(2) Free
(3) Café
(4) Boating lake; bowling green
(5) East Lindsey District Council

Spalding

Lincolnshire

20. Ayscoughfee Hall

The house was built in 1420 and was bought by the Council to commemorate Queen Victoria's Diamond Jubilee. The 5 acre (2·3 ha) grounds contain ancient yew trees: in 1509 some were said to be nearly 400 years old. The gardens are laid out with lawns, a formal lake, shrubberies, herbaceous borders and seasonal bedding; 35,000 tulip bulbs are planted each year. There is also a rock garden, a rose garden, a screened garden for the blind with scented plants and a conservatory.

(1) Mon–Sat 8–½ hour after Sunset; Sun 10–½ hour after Sunset
(2) Charge
(3) Café

Spalding

21. Springfields

This show garden for the British bulb industry was designed by the landscape architect Carl van Empelen and opened in 1966. It was originally intended as a spring-flowering garden, with a display of over one million tulips, daffodils, etc, but the season is now extended to October with the display of 10,000 roses – mostly new varieties supplied by the British Association of Rose Breeders – dahlias and bedding plants. There are 25 acres (11 ha) of woodland walks, lawns, formal gardens and a lake. More than 3,000 different varieties of bulbs are represented, including over 400 varieties of tulips in Collectors' Corner.

(1) 7 Apr–1 Oct: Daily 10–6. No dogs
(2) Charge
(3) Restaurant
(4) Garden shop
(5) Springfields Horticultural Society Ltd

Ulverscroft, Priory Lane

Leicestershire

22. Rockyfield Garden

The 6¼ acre (2·5 ha) garden has been developed since 1968 in an informal design; woodland walks run between rhododendrons and a variety of trees and shrubs, many unusual. A heather garden is well set off by outcrops of natural rock. In spring, there is a fine display of naturalized daffodils.

(1) Wed–Mon (except 25–26 Dec) 9–Sunset
(2) Collecting box
(4) Nursery
(5) Mr and Mrs P. B. Heslop

West Langton, nr Market Harborough

Leicestershire

23. Langton Hall

The house is a picturesque 19th-cent remodelling of a building of the late 17th and 18th cents. The garden is formal, in the French style, with lawns, yew hedges, clipped holly bushes and old and rare trees. The Revd William Hanbury of Church Langton, a friend of the composer Handel, was a keen horticulturist and helped to obtain many of the uncommon trees and shrubs. The original ha-ha remains and there are a number of 18th-cent statues. In spring the daffodils make a fine display.

(1) *Good Friday–early Nov: Sat, Sun and Public Holidays 2–6*
(2) *Charge*
(3) *Tea*
(4) *House (same times)*
(5) *Mrs Louis D. Cullings*

Woodhall Spa

Lincolnshire

24. Jubilee Park

This is a small park, approx 2 acres (1 ha) in extent, with a formal lay-out and the emphasis on roses, both in beds and on pergolas. More colour is provided by spring and summer bedding. Nearby are pine-woods planted with large areas of rhododendrons, once part of the same estate and also open to the public without charge.

(1) *Daily*
(2) *Free*
(3) *Café*
(4) *Putting, tennis, bowling*
(5) *East Lindsey District Council*

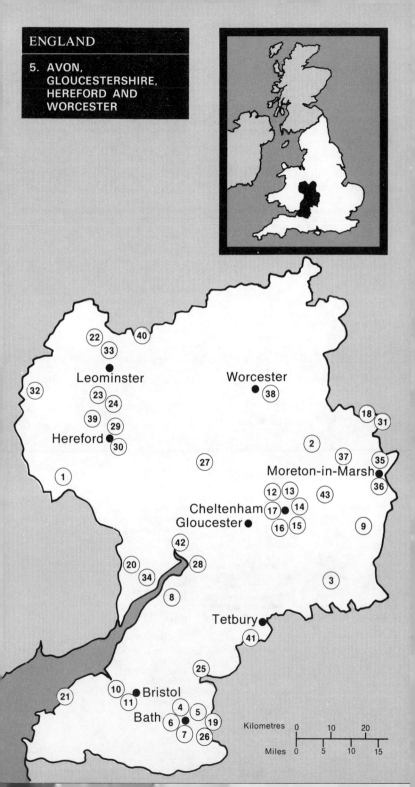

22
33
40
Leominster
Worcester
32
23
24
38
39
29
18
31
Hereford
30
2
1
27
37
35
Moreton-in-Marsh
36
12 13
43
Cheltenham
17 14
Gloucester
16 15
9
42
3
20
28
34
8
Tetbury
41
25
21
10
Bristol
11
4
Bath
5
6
19
7 26

Kilometres 0   10   20

Miles 0   5   10   15

ENGLAND

Abbey Dore, nr Hereford

Hereford and Worcester

1. Abbey Dore Court

The walled and river garden covers approx 2 acres (0·9 ha). Ferns are a speciality and the fern walk is of particular interest. There is also a young orchard.

(1) Daily 10.30–6.30
(2) Charge
(3) Café
(5) Mrs C. L. Ward

Ashton-under-Hill

Hereford and Worcester

2. Bredon Springs

The garden, approx 1½ acres (0·6 ha) in extent, has been developed since 1948 by the present owner from two cottage gardens. The lay-out is a natural one, with no specific design. There is a large collection of herbaceous plants and hardy and near-hardy shrubs, many of which come from the southern hemisphere.

(1) Apr–Oct: Sat, Sun, Wed and Public Holidays 10–Sunset
(2) Collecting box for NGS
(4) Plants for sale
(5) Ronald Sidwell, Esq

Barnsley, nr Cirencester

Gloucestershire

3. Barnsley House

The Cotswold stone house was built in 1697 and the garden wall and Gothic summer house date from 1770. A Classical 'temple' of the same date has been brought recently from Fairford Park.

The garden has been redesigned since 1960 by Rosemary Verey and is a mixture of the formal and informal. A stone path planted with helianthemums and bordered with Irish yews leads to the front door and mixed borders are colourful throughout the summer. A laburnum walk is in bloom in early June; there is a parterre with lawns and four shaped borders and a Tudor Knot garden made to a 16th-cent design. A modern stone fountain was carved by Simon Verity. The vegetable garden is now being laid out as a decorative as well as a productive potager.

(1) Wed 10–6; May–Jul: 1st Sun of month 2–7. Other times by appointment
(2) Charge (Apr–Oct); free (Nov–Mar)
(4) Plants for sale
(5) Mr and Mrs David Verey

Bath

Avon

4. Bath Botanic Gardens

Covering an area of approx 7 acres (3 ha), the gardens were formed in 1887 to accommodate a collection of over 2,000 plants from the garden of C.E. Broome, FLS, which were presented to the City by his widow. The parks superintendent, John Milburn, designed the gardens with the help of J. W. Morris, FLS.

The original collection consisted mainly of hardy herbaceous plants and flowering shrubs; other gifts of plants have been made at various times and the gardens are now believed to contain one of the finest collections of plants growing on limestone in Britain. There are handsome specimens of *Cornus controversa* and *C. nuttallii* and of the Indian bean-tree, *Catalpa bignonioides*, both in its typical form and in the golden-leaved form. There is a large specimen of *Poncirus trifoliata*, a spiny species related to citrus that is not often seen, and a fine plant of the rather tender *Azara microphylla*. A very large (115 ft; 35 m) *Sequoiadendron giganteum* provides shelter for *Paulownia tomentosa* – at 45 ft (13·7 m) itself taller than usual for this large-leaved species. There are some good magnolias and 40 different varieties of cherry. There are herbaceous borders, a rock garden and a heather garden planted mainly with varieties of the lime-tolerant *Erica carnea*.

(1) Mon–Sat 8–Sunset; Sun and Public Holidays 10–Sunset
(2) Free
(5) Bath City Council

Bath

5. Henrietta Park

7 acre (3 ha) park within easy reach of the city centre, laid out to celebrate Queen Victoria's Diamond Jubilee in 1897. There are fine trees and shrubberies, but perhaps the most interesting feature is the Garden for the Blind which was made in 1953 from the King George V Memorial Garden. It is planted with sweet-scented flowers and shrubs which are all labelled in braille.

(1) Mon–Sat 8–Sunset; Sun and Public Holidays 10–Sunset
(2) Free
(5) Bath City Council

Bath

6. Prior Park College

The house, built in c 1735 by John Wood the Elder, is now a public school. The 18th-cent landscape is noted for its covered Palladian bridge, similar to those at Stowe and Wilton House (cf) built in c 1756, which spans the nearer of two lakes and acts as a focal point in the landscape composition.

(1) Daily 11–4
(2) Charge
(4) College (May–Jul and Sep: Tue, Wed 2–6; Aug: Mon–Thu 2–6)
(5) Christian Brothers

Bath

7. Royal Victoria Park

The park, which covers 57 acres (26 ha), was first planned in 1829 with the aim of providing an arboretum comparable to that just started at Derby (cf), with as many species of shrubs and trees as possible, all clearly labelled. In 1830 the main carriage drives were laid out and in 1831 over 25,000 evergreens, forest trees and shrubs were planted and an ornamental pond was made. 7 acres (3 ha) of the park form the Bath Botanic Gardens (cf).

(1) Mon–Sat 8–Sunset; Sun and Public Holidays 10–Sunset
(2) Free
(3) Café
(5) Bath City Council

Berkeley

Gloucestershire

8. Berkeley Castle

The keep, the oldest part of the castle, dates from the mid-12th cent. The gardens cover approx 8 acres (3·5 ha), including a woodland glade and a medieval terraced garden with many attractive shrubs and climbers growing against the walls. A rectangular swimming pool is now used as a lily-pond.

(1) Easter–Apr and Sep: Tue–Sun 2–5; May–Aug: Tue–Sat 11–5; Sun 2–5; Oct: Sun 2–4.30; Public Holidays 11–5
(2) Charge
(3) Café
(4) Castle (same times)
(5) R. J. G. Berkeley, Esq

Bourton-on-the-Water

Gloucestershire

9. Birdland Zoo Gardens

The Cotswold stone house and its 3½ acre (1·6 ha) grounds were bought in 1957 by the present owner who restored the overgrown gardens and established the zoo. The garden has lawns, mature trees, pools, flowering shrubs and herbaceous borders. The tropical houses are filled with many exotic plants as well as humming birds and other tropical birds. The garden is at its best in spring, although summer is probably the best time to see the birds.

(1) Mar–Nov: 10–6 (or Sunset); Dec–Feb: 10.30–4 or Sunset
(2) Charge
(3) Kiosk
(4) Birds (same times); shop (Mar–Nov: 10–5.30); Art Gallery (Mar–Nov: Tue–Sun 11–5; Dec–Feb: Tue–Sun 2–4.30)
(5) L. W. Hill (Bourton) Ltd

Bristol, Clifton

Avon

10. Bristol Zoological Gardens

The zoo was opened in 1836 and the gardens, extending to 12 acres (4·8 ha), were laid out by Mr Forrest of Acton. There are lawns and many fine trees, flowering shrubs, herbaceous borders, spring and summer bedding displays, a rock garden, a dahlia border and a fuchsia border.

(1) Mon–Sat 9–5 or later in Summer; Sun 10–5 or later in Summer
(2) Charge
(3) Restaurant and café
(4) Zoo (same times)
(5) Bristol, Clifton and West of England Zoological Society

Bristol, North Road

11. University of Bristol Botanic Garden

The garden, established in 1882 by Adolf Leipner, the university's first Professor of Botany, has occupied its present site since 1960. It covers 5¾ acres (2·6 ha) and contains over 4,000 species. Rare plants, including local varieties, are conserved in the appropriate type of habitat, and geographical and ecological collections have been established. Visit in July to October.

(1) Mon–Fri (except Public Holidays and the following day) 9–5
(2) Charge
(4) Educational courses on natural history, gardening and conservation (details from Curator or Garden Staff)
(5) University of Bristol

Cheltenham

Gloucestershire

12. Hatherley Park

The park has an informal lay-out, with trees, shrubs, a lake, a lily-pond and a well-kept rock garden.

(1) Daily Sunrise–Sunset
(2) Free
(4) Aviary
(5) Cheltenham Borough Council

Cheltenham

13. Hesters Way Park

This large park, of informal design, contains over 300 different varieties of trees and shrubs. There are lawns, shrubberies, herbaceous borders, a rose garden and a waterfall.

(1) Daily Sunrise–Sunset
(2) Charge
(5) Cheltenham Borough Council

Cheltenham
14. Pittville Park

This 34 acre (13.7 ha) park is situated on the north side of the town and contains the Pump Room, a fine Regency building. In general, it has an informal lay-out, with many mature specimen trees, shrubberies, rock gardens and a large herbaceous border. There is also an extensive display of seasonal bedding, giving colour from April until autumn, and an ornamental lake with a collection of waterfowl.

(1) *Daily Sunrise–Sunset*
(2) *Free*
(3) *Café*
(4) *Aviaries; pets' corner; children's playground*
(5) *Cheltenham Borough Council*

Cheltenham
15. Promenade and Imperial Gardens

These gardens contain the major part of the town's spring and summer bedding schemes. The Promenade has an avenue of horse chestnuts planted in 1818 and is flanked by spacious gardens. The Imperial Gardens contain a walled garden with seasonal bedding displays.

(1) *Daily Sunrise–Sunset*
(2) *Free*
(4) *Tea garden and beer tent (Summer)*
(5) *Cheltenham Borough Council*

Cheltenham
16. Sandford Park

The 14 acre (6 ha) park near the centre of the town contains seasonal bedding displays, herbaceous borders and rose beds. A variety of trees and shrubs provide colour throughout the year from flowers, fruit and foliage. Near the College Road entrance there is a large stone fountain set among formal flowerbeds; near the Bath Road entrance is a goldfish and water-lily pool with small fountains; at the High Street entrance there is an Italian garden with seasonal bedding. Paths along the river make a pleasant walk, past artificial waterfalls and a duck pond.

(1) *Daily Sunrise–Sunset*
(2) *Free*
(4) *Children's play area*
(5) *Cheltenham Borough Council*

Cheltenham
17. Winston Churchill Memorial Garden

This garden, made from a disused burial ground, received a special commendation award in a competition run by the British Tourist Authority during European Architectural Heritage Year, 1975. It has lawns, trees, shrubs, rose beds and a pergola, as well as seasonal bedding displays.

(1) *Daily Sunrise–Sunset*
(2) *Free*
(5) *Cheltenham Borough Council*

Chipping Campden
Gloucestershire
18. Kiftsgate Court Gardens

The garden was created by the late Mrs J. R. Muir in 1918 and carried on by her daughter, the present owner. It has been planned for colour effect and also includes many rare plants, including tree peonies, hydrangeas and abutilons. There is an outstanding collection of shrub and species roses, including a specimen of *Rosa filipes* 'Kiftsgate', which is believed to be the largest rose in England. Both house and garden are splendidly sited, with fine views.

(1) *Easter Sun–Sep: Wed, Thu, Sun and Public Holidays 2–6*
(2) *Charge*
(3) *Refreshments*
(4) *Plants propagated from the garden for sale*
(5) *Mrs D. H. Binny*

Claverton, nr Bath
Avon
19. Claverton Manor

Claverton Manor, the American Museum in Britain, holds the only comprehensive collection of Americana in Europe. The grounds include 5 acres (2 ha) of lawn, herbaceous borders and specimen trees, but the most interesting features are probably the replicas of George Washington's garden at Mount Vernon, his house on the Potomac River in Virginia and a Colonial herb garden. Herbs brought from England and obtained from the Indians were used by the early settlers for cooking, medicine and making perfumes and dyes. Here, they are planted in formal beds set in a paved area, and other dye plants grow near the entrance to the Folk Art Gallery. George Washington's garden is surrounded by a white picket fence and contains a replica of the octagonal summerhouse at Mount Vernon. The flowers are in formal beds of varying shape, surrounded by clipped box and set in gravel. The plantings on and below the terrace were designed by Lanning Roper.

(1) *End Mar–last Sun of Oct: Tue–Sun 2–5; Public Holidays and preceding Sun 11–5*
(2) *Charge*
(3) *Tea and refreshments; lunch by previous arrangement*
(4) *Museum (same times)*
(5) *Trustees of the American Museum in Britain*

Clearwell, nr Coleford

Gloucestershire

20. Clearwell Castle

The castle, built in *c* 1729, is believed to be the oldest Neo-Gothic castle in Britain. It was bought in 1954 in a derelict condition and has been restored by the present owners. The 8 acre (3·5 ha) gardens are formal, on five different levels; work on them is still in progress. A bird garden has been made.

(1) Easter weekend–mid-May: Sun and Public Holidays 11–6; Mid-May–Sep: Tue–Fri 2–6; Sun and Public Holidays 11–6. Other times by arrangement
(2) Charge
(3) Tea
(4) Castle (same times)
(5) B. Yeates, Esq

Clevedon, nr Weston-super-Mare

Avon

21. Clevedon Court

The 14th-cent manor house has a 13th-cent hall and a 12th-cent tower. The garden terraces date from the 18th cent; there is a gazebo and a garden temple and a good selection of shrubs and herbaceous plants, many rare, including *Buddleia colvilei*, *B. auriculata*, *Photinia serrulata* and *Rosa brunonii*.

(1) Apr–Sep: Wed, Thu, Sun and Public Holidays 2.30–5.30. Last admission 5. No dogs
(2) Charge
(3) Café
(4) House (same times)
(5) National Trust

Croft, nr Leominster

Hereford and Worcester

22. Croft Castle

The grounds, which include an Iron-Age fort, Croft Ambrey, are noted for their trees. The Spanish chestnut avenue, thought to be about 350 years old, stretches for half a mile (800 m); a new lime avenue has recently been planted to replace one that had previously existed. Other fine trees include a Monterey pine, an incense cedar, a deodar and a large oriental plane that stands beyond the secret garden lying to the west of the castle.

The Fish Pool Valley, with its chain of ponds, was landscaped in the late 18th cent in the irregular 'Gothic' style which developed as a reaction against the calm, naturalistic style of 'Capability' Brown.

(1) 1st Wed in Apr–Sep: Wed, Thu, Sat, Sun and Public Holidays 2.15–6; Oct: Sat and Sun 2.15–6
(2) Charge
(4) House (same times)
(5) National Trust

Dinmore, nr Hereford

Hereford and Worcester

23. Dinmore Manor

The most interesting feature of the garden is the rock garden, with a good selection of alpine plants. The property includes the 12th–14th cent Chapel of the Knights Hospitaller and Cloisters.

(1) Daily (except 25 and 26 Dec) 10–6
(2) Charge (NGS)
(4) Chapel, Cloisters and Music Room (same times)
(5) G. H. Murray, Esq

Dinmore Hill, nr Hereford

24. Queen's Wood

The area, once part of a nearby estate, but derelict since timber was felled in World War I, was taken over by the Herefordshire County Council in 1935 and designated as a public open space as part of the County Memorial Scheme to celebrate the Silver Jubilee of George V. It was tidied up and many trees were planted; the most interesting feature is the arboretum, planted with many rare and exotic trees, a catalogue of which is available from the Jubilee Café.

(1) Daily Sunrise–Sunset
(2) Collecting box
(3) Café
(5) Hereford and Worcester County Council

Dodington, nr Chipping Sodbury

Avon

25. Dodington House

The house was designed by James Wyatt, and beside it he built a curved conservatory. This is unusual in having a high gallery at the back for viewing the plants. The park was designed by 'Capability' Brown in 1764 for a previous Elizabethan house on the same site, and has two lakes, cascades and an ice-house. There are small, formal gardens.

(1) Easter Sat–last Sun in Sep: Daily 11–5.30
(2) Charge
(3) Restaurant and café
(4) House and Carriage Museum (same times)
(5) Major S. F. B. Codrington

Dyrham, nr Bath

Avon

26. Dyrham Park

The house, built for William Blathwayt in 1692–1702, is surrounded by 263 acres

(106 ha) of parkland and garden. Originally a formal garden in the Dutch style was laid out, on the advice of George London, but all that now remains is the Neptune fountain, dry for almost 200 years, and the long terrace above the church. The park and garden were remodelled in c 1800 by Humphry Repton and a few trees still remain from his planting, including cedars, chestnuts, beech and two fine planes. The garden proper now lies on the west of the house and has some good specimen trees, including ilex, *Quercus ilex*, and serpentine paths. The orangery, designed by Talman and built in the early 18th cent, is one of the earliest examples of a monumentally treated glasshouse.

(1) *Garden. Apr, May and Oct: Daily (except Thu and Fri) 2–6; Jun, Jul, Aug and Sep: Daily (except Fri) 2–6. Last admissions 5.30. No dogs*
(2) *Charge*
(3) *Tea May–Sep*
(4) *House (same times)*
(5) *National Trust*

Eastnor, nr Ledbury

Hereford and Worcester

27. Eastnor Castle

The castle was built in the early 19th cent in medieval style by Sir Robert Smirke for the 1st Earl Somers. He did some planting, but most of it was carried out between 1840 and 1880 by the 2nd and 3rd Earls. The most notable feature is the pinetum, with some very fine conifers including *Abies bracteata* and *A. grandis*, but there is also a selection of broad-leaved trees including a specimen of the American beech, *Fagus grandifolia*, one of the few in this country.

(1) *Easter Mon, Spring Bank Holiday Sun and Mon and Late Summer Bank Holiday 2.15–6; late May–Sep: Sun 2.15–6. Other times by appointment for parties*
(2) *Charge*
(3) *Refreshments*
(4) *Castle (same times)*
(5) *Hon Mrs Hervey-Bathurst*

Frampton-on-Severn

Gloucestershire

28. Frampton Court

The house, built in the style of Vanbrugh, was completed in 1733. The Dutch-style water garden was made in 1760 and a 'Strawberry Hill' Gothic orangery built in the same year is reflected in the water of the long ornamental canal. Few examples of this type of garden remain.

(1) *Daily by appointment*
(2) *Charge*
(3) *Tea*

36

(4) *House (by appointment)*
(5) *Mrs Peter Clifford*

Hereford

Hereford and Worcester

29. Blackfriars Rose Garden

The garden is designed with formal beds of roses. In the centre stands one of the few surviving examples of a Preaching Cross dating from c 1300, a beautiful and interesting survivor from the Decorated period.

(1) *Daily Sunrise–Sunset*
(2) *Free*
(5) *City of Hereford*

Hereford

30. Castle Green

The park, originally the bailey of the castle, is set out with lawns, mature trees and seasonal bedding. In the centre of the green stands a 60 ft (18·3 m) high column erected in 1809 to commemorate Nelson's naval victories.

(1) *Daily Sunrise–Sunset*
(2) *Free*
(4) *Bowling green*
(5) *City of Hereford*

Hidcote Bartrim, nr Chipping Campden

Gloucestershire

31. Hidcote Manor Garden

When Hidcote was acquired in 1905 by Major Lawrence Johnston, the grounds consisted of fields with one cedar tree and two groups of beeches. Although the garden covers 10 acres (4·5 ha), it resembles a series of cottage gardens, divided by yew hedges. The forecourt is planted with hydrangeas, magnolias, Hypericum 'Hidcote', hoherias and the climbers, *Solanum crispum* and *Schizophragma hydrangeoides*. From here, one can walk through the garden yard to a large oval lawn. The long walk runs at right angles to this and at the end of it is the area known as the Wilderness, or 'Westonbirt', planted with trees and shrubs including many, like acers and sorbus, that give a good display of autumn colour, as well as spring-flowering trees.

Many of the separate gardens lie to the left of the long walk, including Mrs Winthrop's Garden with beds of yellow and blue flowers and foliage plants surrounded by beech, hornbeam and lime hedges; the Winter Border; the Stream Garden and the Bathing Pool Garden. The Old Garden is dominated by an ancient cedar of Lebanon, underplanted with shade-loving species such as the Welsh poppy, *Meconopsis cambrica*, and *Cyclamen hederaefolium*, and has borders mainly devoted to flowers in particular colour schemes; one of the borders is almost lime free, and some rhododendrons are

grown there. The White Garden is surrounded by yew and box hedges; the Red
Borders have red and orange flowers and
plants with copper foliage, and are at their
best from July until October. At Hidcote
there are a great number of rare and
interesting plants.

(1) *Apr (or Easter Sat if earlier)–Oct:
    Wed, Thu and Sat–Mon 11–8 or
    Sunset. Last admission 1 hr before
    closing. No dogs*
(2) *Charge*
(3) *Tea*
(5) *National Trust*

Kington
Hereford and Worcester
32. Hergest Croft

Laid out and planted by William H. Banks
in 1896, the gardens were gradually extended over the next thirty years and now
cover approx 50 acres (20 ha). Although
there is a rock garden and a bog garden, it is
mainly a garden of trees and shrubs from all
temperate areas of the world, many rare, including azaleas; *Sciadopitys verticillata*, the
umbrella pine; *Picea brewerana*; *Parrotia
persica*; *Koelreuteria paniculata*, the golden
rain tree; and a specimen of *Abies grandis*
planted in 1900 and now over 130 ft (40 m)
tall.

Park Wood, about half a mile from the
main garden, has a fine collection of rhododendrons, both species and hybrid, including *R. eximium*, *R. falconeri* and *R.
'Shilsonii'* as well as other interesting trees
such as *Abies bracteata* and eucryphias.
Visit in May and June

(1) *Late Apr–late Aug: Daily 11–7*
(2) *Charge*
(3) *Tea (Sun and Public Holidays in May
    and Jun)*
(4) *Plants for sale*
(5) *W. L. Banks, Esq*

Leominster
Hereford and Worcester
33. Berrington Hall

The 18th-cent house is set in a 455 acre
(183 ha) park laid out by 'Capability'
Brown in 1780. The present garden was
designed by Dobies of Chester in 1900 and
consists of lawns, trees, shrubs, herbaceous
borders and a small woodland area; it is
now in the process of modification. Some
interesting climbing plants grow on a south-
facing wall.

(1) *1st Wed in Apr (or Easter Sat if
    earlier)–Sep: Wed, Thu, Sat, Sun and
    Public Holidays 2–6; Oct: Sat and Sun
    2–6*
(2) *Charge*
(4) *House (same times)*
(5) *National Trust*

Lydney
Gloucestershire
34. Lydney Park

The garden surrounding the house is formal:
a terrace, with fine views to the Cotswolds
and the Mendips, is planted along its length
with *Chamaecyparis lawsoniana* 'Kilmacur-
ragh'. Two round, raised pools have plantings of hostas and other foliage plants round
the edge and the house walls support
wisteria and *Cotoneaster horizontalis*.

Below the house is a wooded valley
garden covering approx 8 acres (3·6 ha).
Although the soil is limestone, it is a dolo-
mitic limestone containing magnesium as
well as calcium, and rhododendrons and
azaleas flourish here. There are large plantings of hardy hybrid rhododendrons, such
as 'Cynthia', 'Purple Splendour' and 'Mrs
G. W. Leak' as well as hybrids such as
'Fortune' and 'Lady Chamberlain' and
many species, including *R. sinogrande*, *R.
falconeri*, *R. macabeanum* and *R. cinna-
barinum*. Other interesting trees and shrubs
include *Crinodendron hookeranum* and
species of magnolia, enkianthus and styrax.

(1) *Mar–late Oct: Wed 2–6; Also last Sun
    in Apr, each Sun in May and 1st Sun in
    Jun 2–6. Apr–Jun: Mon–Fri parties of
    20 or more by appointment*
(2) *Charge (GSO)*
(3) *Refreshments*
(4) *Deer park; Roman Temple site and
    museum (same times)*
(5) *Viscount Bledisloe*

Moreton-in-Marsh
Gloucestershire
35. Batsford Park Arboretum

Batsford Park, with an area of 50 acres
(20 ha), is the largest privately owned
arboretum in the United Kindom. It was
founded and planted in *c* 1880 by Lord
Redesdale, who spent some time in Japan
and developed a great interest in botanical
species while there and in Asia Minor. The
elevation (almost 800 ft, 244 m, above sea
level at the highest point) and the limy
nature of the soil limit the plants that can be
grown, but there is still a very wide range to
be seen. There are notable collections of
bamboos, maples and sorbus, and almost 40
species, sub-species and hybrids belonging
to the magnolia family.

The largest tree in the arboretum is a
specimen of the grand fir, *Abies grandis*,
almost 130 ft (40 m) high, and other fine
trees include *Davidia involucrata*; the
Macedonian oak (the largest specimen
known in England); *Cryptomeria japonica*
and *Abies nobilis*. The grounds include a
stream with a series of pools and a lake
with an island on which grows a weeping
form of *Picea omorika*, the Serbian spruce.

Mementoes brought from Japan by Lord Redesdale includes bronze statues of Buddha and deer.

(1) Apr–Oct: Daily 10–5
(2) Charge
(3) Kiosk
(4) Garden shop and garden centre
(5) Batsford Estate Company

Moreton-in-Marsh

36. Sezincote

The garden was originally designed in the early 19th cent by Humphry Repton and Thomas Daniell. The house shows considerable Indian influence in its design and in fact provided inspiration for the Royal Pavilion, Brighton. The garden, also, has an Indian flavour with its many ornaments and an oriental water-garden with cascades and a grotto containing a figure of the goddess Souriya. There are luxuriant plantings of bamboo, gunneras, primulas and other species, and many specimen trees of unusual size.

(1) Easter–Oct: Fri and Public Holidays 2–6
(2) Charge
(5) Mr and Mrs D. Peake

Snowshill, nr Broadway

Gloucestershire

37. Snowshill Manor

The house is a typical Cotswold stone manor house, built in c 1500, with a façade added in the early 18th cent; the gardens were laid out between 1919 and 1923 by the owner, Charles Wade, on the site of an old farmyard. There are terraces and ponds with rainbow trout and goldfish, and various buildings have been incorporated so that the impression is of a series of cottage-style gardens with a wide range of planting, mostly of old-fashioned flowers.

(1) 1 Apr or Easter Sat if earlier–30 Apr and Oct: Sat, Sun and Public Holidays 11–1, 2–6; May–Sep: Wed–Sun and Public Holidays 11–1, 2–6 or Sunset. No dogs
(2) Charge
(4) House (same times)
(5) National Trust

Spetchley, nr Worcester

Hereford and Worcester

38. Spetchley Park

The house was built between 1811 and 1818 by the local architect John Yasker. The gardens cover over 30 acres (14 ha) and were mainly designed by the mother of the present owner and her sister, the horticulturist Ellen Willmott. There are sweeping lawns and fine herbaceous borders; many

interesting trees and shrubs including a cedar of Lebanon mentioned by John Evelyn in his diary in c 1690; a rose lawn and a series of enclosed gardens with low yew or box hedges. The walled Melon Garden contains a number of uncommon and semi-hardy plants, such as Rosa × hardii, Penstemon cordifolius and a double-flowered pomegranate. House and garden are set in a 140 acre (56 ha) deer park with herds of red and fallow deer.

(1) Late Mar–end Oct: Mon–Fri 11–5; Sun 2–6; Public Holidays 11–6. No dogs
(2) Charge
(3) Café (Sundays)
(4) Garden centre (same times); wildfowl
(5) R. J. Berkeley, Esq

Swainshill, nr Hereford

Hereford and Worcester

39. The Weir

The garden, with fine views over the River Wye to the Welsh and Gwent hills, is laid out on a steep bank below the 18th cent house (not open to the public) with winding paths between trees and shrubs. There is a rock and water garden and a riverside walk that is at its best in spring, although also of interest in summer and autumn.

(1) Apr–mid-May: Sun–Fri (closed Good Friday) 2–6; mid-May–end Oct: Wed and Public Holidays 2–6
(2) Charge
(5) National Trust

Tenbury Wells

Hereford and Worcester

40. Burford House

The present house, a good example of early Georgian provincial architecture, dates from 1726. The 4 acre (1·8 ha) gardens were completely redesigned by John Treasure in 1954 and all that now remains of the old garden, which was mostly a wilderness, is the lawn on the north side of the house with the old moat and a few specimen trees and the lawn on the south side, although that has been largely re-shaped. The gardens, which were first opened to the public in 1959, are flanked on one side by the River Teme and contain a large number of interesting plants from many parts of the world and, notably, over 120 species and varieties of clematis, mainly grown informally among shrubs. John Treasure has tried to show how plant associations can be attractive in form and colour throughout the year.

(1) Five days over Easter and early Apr–early Oct: Daily 2–5
(2) Charge
(3) Refreshments
(4) Treasures of Tenbury Clematis Nursery (Nov–Mar: Mon–Fri 9–1, 2–5; Sat 9–1, 2–4, except Dec–Feb when it is 9–11; Apr–Oct: Mon–Fri as before; Sat

Tetbury

Gloucestershire

41. Westonbirt Arboretum

The arboretum was started in 1829 by
Robert Holford, who planted shelter belts
and designed the lay-out of wide, sweeping
rides. His son, Sir George Holford, who
continued the development of the grounds
until his death in 1926, was responsible for
the rhododendron collection and the plantings for autumn colour. He was succeeded
by Lord Morley who continued planting,
and in 1956 the arboretum with developed
parts of the nearby Silk Wood was acquired by the Forestry Commission. It now
covers approx 250 acres (100 ha) and the
setting on gentle slopes throws into focus
the skilful juxtaposition of trees to provide
an attractive range of form and colour.

The collection of trees and shrubs, one of
the finest in the world, is of interest throughout the year, with outstanding displays of
flower in spring and of leaf colour in autumn
from plants such as maples, *Euonymus
alatus*, *Parrotia persica*, and *Fothergilla*
spp. Even in winter, there is a show of
colour from the bark of trees and shrubs
such as *Cornus alba* 'Sibirica', various
species of birch, the paper-bark maple, *Acer
griseum*, and the snakebark maples such as
A. capillipes and *A. davidii*.

(1) Daily 10–Sunset
(2) Charge for car park
(3) Café
(5) Forestry Commission

Westbury-on-Severn

Gloucestershire

42. Westbury Court Garden

The gardens are of great interest in that they
have one of the few remaining 17th-cent
formal lay-outs in Britain and illustrate the
Dutch influence, with the strong horticultural emphasis, prevalent at that time; the
few other 17th-cent survivors, such as
Bramham (cf), Melbourne (cf) and Wrest
(cf), are slightly later and French in style,
with a more architectural design. The
garden was sadly neglected for 200 years
until the site was accepted by the National
Trust in 1967. Since then a considerable
restoration programme has ensued.

The central feature of the original lay-out
was a canal 450 ft (137 m) long and 22 ft
(7 m) wide, started in 1696. A long wall
parallel to the canal on the west side was
built at the same time; the T-canal was
constructed later, probably in the 1720s. In
1699, 1,000 yews and 1,000 hollies were
planted and clipped into alternate pyramids
and balls; these have since been replanted.
The summer house at the south end of the
canal was built by Maynard Colchester I in

ENGLAND

1702–3; the upper room is now used for a
display of 17th-cent botanical illustrations
and parterre designs.

Beside the T-canal is a parterre with beds
edged with dwarf box and planted with sage,
perennial candytuft, *Iberis sempervirens*,
and *Festuca glauca*, with bedding plants in
season, such as snapdragons and French
marigolds. It is surrounded by a formal
arrangement of small trees and clipped
evergreens. A small walled garden next to
the gazebo has been planted with almost
100 species of plant grown in England
before 1700, including *Daphne mezereum*,
pomegranate, *Cistus albidus* and *Yucca
gloriosa*, and many herbs. A selection of
apples, plums and pears, all in cultivation
before 1700, is grown on the west wall.
Three new *clairvoyées* have been made in
this wall, each flanked by a bay tree, *Laurus
nobilis*, with a bush of southernwood below.
In front of the fruit trees are plantings of
bulbs grown in the 17th cent. There is also a
rose garden with approx 40 different
varieties of old roses.

(1) May–Sep: Wed–Sun   and   Public
    Holidays 11–6; Apr and Oct: Sat and
    Sun 11–6. No dogs
(2) Charge
(5) National Trust

Winchcombe, nr Cheltenham

Gloucestershire

43. Sudeley Castle

The castle is of great historic interest, dating
in part from the 9th cent. The present
gardens were laid out when the castle was
restored in the mid-19th cent. There are
beautiful walled gardens around a 15th-cent
chapel and a fine double-planted yew hedge.
The Queen's Garden is a replanting of the
original Tudor herb garden under the
windows of what were the private apartments of Katherine Parr.

(1) Mar–Oct: Daily 11–5.30
(2) Charge
(3) Café
(4) Castle (Mar–Oct: Daily noon–5.30)
(5) Mrs Mark Dent-Brocklehurst

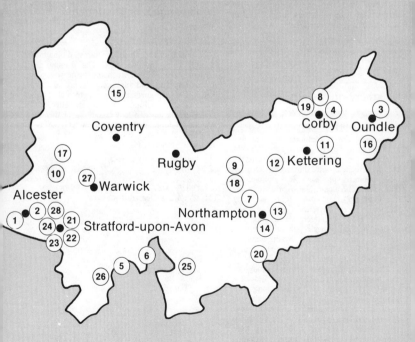

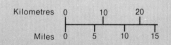

Alcester

Warwickshire

1. Pleck Gardens

In 1945, the design and lay-out of these gardens, 3¾ acres (1·5 ha) in extent was begun by the present owner in what had been a field. There are ponds, herbaceous borders, heathers, a formal rose garden, rhododendrons and azaleas and many interesting trees and shrubs, including *Acer griseum*, *A. laxifolium*, *A. palmatum* 'Senkaki', *Desfontainia spinosa*, *Drimys winteri*, *Daphniphyllum macropodum*, *Telopea truncata*, *Pseudopanax crassifolius*, *Arbutus andrachne* and a number of hydrangeas and camellias. The garden is divided into sections planted to commemorate an event: there is the Thanksgiving Garden; Peace Garden; Festival Garden (Festival of Britain, 1951); Coronation Glade and Orchard, and the Moon Garden, made with tufa stone and a gargoyle, marking the first moon landing. In spring the rhododendrons and azaleas are in bloom; in July the roses; and in August the bedding and herbaceous plants are at their best.

(1) *Apr–Sep: Daily 10–Sunset*
(2) *Charge*
(4) *Garden shop (same times)*
(5) *Miss E. C. Chapman*

Alcester

2. Ragley Hall

The park was designed by 'Capability' Brown. Near the 17th-cent house there are extensive rose gardens and in spring, naturalized daffodils make a fine display.

(1) *Gardens. Easter Mon–1 Oct: Tue–Thu, Sat, Sun and Public Holidays 1.30–5.30. Park. Same times and also Easter Mon–mid-Apr; late May–early Sep: Daily 11–7. No dogs in house, garden or adventure wood*
(2) *Charge*
(3) *Café*
(4) *House and adventure wood in park (same times)*
(5) *Marquess of Hertford*

Cotterstock, nr Oundle

Northamptonshire

3. Cotterstock Hall

The grey stone house dates from the 17th cent – it is recorded that in 1699 Mrs Elizabeth Steward was sending hampers of garden produce from Cotterstock Hall to her cousin, the poet John Dryden, in London. The grounds, approx 5 acres (2 ha) in extent, were laid out as a pleasure garden by the 3rd Viscount Melville and his successor, Lady Etheldreda Wickham, remodelled them on the lines of those at Sandringham (cf). They were again redesigned by the present owners with a

view to making them more in keeping with the 17th-cent house. There are lawns with many fine trees, including a cedar of Lebanon and an ancient mulberry; unusual shrubs and climbers, such as *Schizophragma hydrangeoides* and herbaceous borders again with some unusual plants, for example *Tanakaea radicans*.

(1) *Apr–Sep: Daily 2–5*
(2) *Charge*
(4) *House (end May–end Sep; 1st and 3rd Sun of each month; other times for pre-booked parties)*
(5) *Mr and Mrs Lewis F. Sturge*

Deene, nr Corby

Northamptonshire

4. Deene Park

Parts of the house date from the 15th and 16th cents; all that remains of the medieval house that preceded it is a portion of an archway believed to be *c* 1300. The grounds include a lake and a stone bridge and a walled garden with long mixed borders including roses and herbaceous plants, all made by the 3rd Earl of Cardigan after he inherited the property in 1703. The long border is shown on a plan of 1716. The octagonal summer house was built by the 7th Earl.

(1) *Jun and Jul: Sun and Public Holidays 2–6*
(2) *Charge*
(3) *Café*
(4) *House (same times)*
(5) *Edmund Brudenell, Esq*

Edgehill

Warwickshire

5. Upton House

The present house on the site was completed in 1695 for Sir Rushout Cullen, Bt, who probably laid out the gardens in the combe, making yew terraces on the hillsides and damming the streams to make six ponds. Now, a broad terrace runs along the south front of the house, planted with lavender, catmint and the old rose 'William Double Yellow'. The lawn appears to lead to a sloping meadow, but between them lies a wide combe containing the garden proper, still much as laid out by Sir Rushout, with a series of herbaceous borders and a walled kitchen garden laid out in formal style like a French potager with rows of vegetables and a trained fruit tree.

The shrubbery above this, between the ha-ha and the middle wall, was designed and planted with lilacs, laburnums, brooms and other flowering trees and shrubs by the architect Percy Morley Horder for the 2nd Lord Bearsted, who came to Upton in 1927. To the left of the lawn in front of the house lies a rock garden, and a path flanked by two herbaceous borders with tree peonies and geums leads to the pond, where a copse of hazels at the far end is underplanted with daffodils and primulas. A small rose garden is surrounded on three sides by yew hedges.

Another combe, at right angles to the first, originally had three ponds at the bottom. The middle one is still a pond, but the uppermost is now a bog garden with bamboos, primulas, meconopsis and ferns, and the lowest is an orchard of flowering cherries.

(1) *Apr–Sep: Mon–Thu 2–6; also some Sats and Suns 2–6*
(2) *Charge*
(4) *House (same times)*
(5) *National Trust*

Farnborough, nr Banbury

Warwickshire
6. Farnborough Hall

The house dates mainly from the 18th cent. A grass terrace walk, with views across a valley to Edge Hill, although laid out in *c* 1745–55, is in the 17th-cent tradition but less formal. It has two garden temples, one very unusual with a domed second storey, and an obelisk. It is possible that Sanderson Miller, an amateur architect who lived nearby, gave advice on the laying out of the landscape and on the design of the temples. On the valley side of the walk is a series of promontories, each fenced and hedged with a scalloped line of laurels and containing a single tree. A splendid cedar of Lebanon stands on the lawn; there is a small rose garden, a string of lakes and a collection of species of alnus which do well on the damp soil.

(1) *Apr–Sep: Wed and Sat 2–6*
(2) *Charge*
(4) *House (same times)*
(5) *National Trust*

Great Brington, nr Northampton

Northamptonshire
7. Althorp

The original Elizabethan house, built soon after 1508, was surrounded by a moat and formal garden, but these have now gone. The present gardens were designed in the 1860s by the architect William Milford Teulon and include an arboretum with many rare trees and a lake with ducks. The temple beyond the lake was bought for £3 from the grounds of Admiralty House by the 5th Lord Spencer, 1st Lord of the Admiralty.

(1) *All year: Sat and Sun 2.30–6; also Tue and Thu Apr–Jul and Sep; Aug: Daily 11–6; Public Holidays 11–6*
(2) *Charge*

(3) *Tea*
(4) *House (same times)*
(5) *Earl and Countess Spencer*

Gretton, nr Corby

Northamptonshire
8. Kirby Hall

The house, an outstanding example of a large Elizabethan stone mansion, was built in 1570 for Sir Humphrey Stafford; alterations were made by Inigo Jones in 1638–40. The gardens, which were celebrated in the 17th cent, have been laid out in accordance with the original plan. There are four large rose beds, each planted with 1,000 bushes, surrounded by yew hedges each containing four Irish yews to represent the topiary of the original garden. The roses in these beds are modern varieties, but elsewhere in the garden there are species and old-fashioned roses. The grounds cover 8 acres (3·4 ha), and besides these formal beds, there are lawns, herbaceous borders, flowering shrubs including rhododendrons and azaleas and many fine old trees, such as horse chestnuts and elms, some almost certainly as old as the house.

(1) *Mar, Apr and Oct: Mon–Sat 9.30–5.30; Sun 2–5.30; May–Sep: Mon–Sat 9.30–7; Sun 2–7; Nov–Feb: Mon–Sat 9.30–4; Sun 2–4*
(2) *Charge*
(5) *Dept of the Environment*

Guilsborough, West Haddon Road

Northamptonshire
9. Guilsborough Grange Bird and Pet Park

The house was built in the early 19th cent in a beautiful situation with fine views. The gardens include a small lake, lawns, flower-beds and a rock garden with water running through it. There is a fine tulip-tree, *Liriodendron tulipifera*, and some mature beeches.

(1) *Early Mar–late Oct: Daily 11–7*
(2) *Charge*
(3) *Refreshments*
(4) *Birds and wildlife*
(5) *Mr and Mrs S. J. Symington*

Henley-in-Arden, High Street

Warwickshire
10. Henley Bird Gardens

The gardens, approx 4 acres (1·8 ha) in extent, are attached to an Elizabethan manor house built in 1574. They have been developed since 1943 by Mrs Joan Jewsbury and rise from the back of the house in a series of lawns and steps decorated with ornamental urns. There is an interesting variety of trees, including some yews at least as old as the house, and many shrubs particularly rhododendrons, azaleas and heathers. The aviaries, with a collection of over 400 exotic birds, are in woodland at the back of the house, out of sight of the main lawns; in summer, budgerigars fly free. The grounds include a small lake with waterfowl.

(1) *Mar–Oct: Sun 10.30–Sunset*
(2) *Charge*
(4) *Aviaries; ornamental waterfowl*
(5) *Mr and Mrs C. Jewsbury*

Kettering

Northamptonshire

11. Boughton House

The house, originally a monastic property, dates from the 15th cent. It was extended, and the grounds laid out in imitation of Versailles, by Ralph, 1st Duke of Montagu, and his son John, 'the Planter', between 1680 and 1730. Avenues and lakes were created by Van der Meulen; there are many miles of lime avenues, a rose garden, a lilypond and herbaceous borders.

The garden of the Dower House, which belongs to Sir David and Lady Scott and is a plantsman's garden of particular interest, is open by appointment and occasionally for charity.

(1) *Easter Sun and Mon and Spring Bank Holiday Sun and Mon noon–6; Aug–Oct: Daily noon–6*
(2) *Charge*
(3) *Tea*
(4) *House; garden shop and children's adventure woodland play area (same times)*
(5) *Duke of Buccleuch*

Lamport, nr Northampton

Northamptonshire

12. Lamport Hall

The 3 acre (1·4 ha) garden was first laid out in 1677. It was considerably altered between 1850 and 1900, when the fine alpine garden was made. There is an Italian garden, some good specimens of Irish yews and a 17th-cent cockpit. The house dates mainly from the 17th and 18th cents.

(1) *Easter–May and Sep: Sun 2.15–5.30; Jun–Aug: Sun and Thu 2.15–5.30*
(2) *Charge*
(3) *Tea*
(4) *House (same times)*
(5) *Lamport Hall Preservation Trust Ltd*

Northampton, Wellingborough Road

13. Abington Park

The Upper Park, which was given to the town by Lady Wantage in 1895 and opened to the public two years later, contains Abington Manor, once the home of Shakespeare's last descendant, his grand-daughter

Elizabeth Barnard, who died there in 1669. On the east lawn of the house stands a white mulberry tree, grown from a cutting taken from the tree in Shakespeare's garden in New Place, Stratford-upon-Avon, planted in 1778 by the actor David Garrick. The lawns and many of the trees were set out before the garden was opened in 1897. In summer there are fine displays of carpet bedding. The Lower Park has attractive artificial lakes.

(1) *Daily*
(2) *Free*
(3) *Café*
(4) *Abington Manor Museum (Mon–Sat 10–2.30)*
(5) *Northampton Borough Council, Leisure and Recreation Dept*

Northampton, London Road

14. Delapre Abbey

Delapre Abbey and its ornamental and formal gardens cover an area of over 8 acres (3·8 ha), separated from the surrounding parkland by a ha-ha. A walled garden, surrounded by a fine 18th-cent redbrick wall, lies to the east of the abbey. Two early conservatories stand against the south-facing wall, and there are fine herbaceous borders, a topiary hedge and a collection of herbs. Beyond the walled garden is the main garden, with many vistas leading into small enclosed gardens as well as to the open parkland. There are many fine specimen trees and shrubs and a formal sunken rock garden with an ornamental stream and a pond. The nature of the planting enhances the Victorian character of the gardens. The building now contains the Northamptonshire Record Office and is also the headquarters of the Northamptonshire Record Society

(1) *Main garden. Daily 2–Sunset. Walled garden. Spring Bank Holiday–Sep: during daylight hours*
(2) *Free*
(4) *Abbey (Oct–Apr: Thu and Sat 2.30–4.30; May–Sep: Thu and Sat 2.30–6)*
(5) *Northampton Borough Council, Leisure and Recreation Dept*

Nuneaton

Warwickshire

15. Arbury Hall

The Elizabethan house was Gothicized in the 18th cent by Sir Roger Newdigate, the 5th Baronet, although an Elizabethan stable block, which was partly designed by Sir Christopher Wren, still survives. At the same time, he changed the formal Elizabethan gardens into informal landscaped gardens, according to the fashion of the times, so that they now consist of rolling lawns, serpentine paths, clumps of carefully sited trees and artificial lakes. There are large commercial gardens. Visit in early July.

(1) Easter Sun–1st Sun in Oct: Sun, Bank Holiday Mon and following Tue 2.30–6
(2) Charge
(3) Café
(4) House (same times)
(5) F. H. M. FitzRoy Newdegate, Esq

Oundle

Northamptonshire

16. Lilford Park

The house was built in 1635 and stands in 240 acres (97 ha) of parkland which includes a pinetum and an interesting rock garden built in 1900–5 and recently restored.

(1) Summer: 10–8; Winter: 10–Sunset
(2) Charge
(3) Restaurant/café
(4) Aviaries; children's farm; Museum of Rural Bygones (same times)
(5) Lilford Hall Ltd

Packwood, nr Hockley Heath

Warwickshire

17. Packwood House

The most famous feature of these gardens is the topiary of yew, probably planted between 1650 and 1670. The main part, consisting of trees of varying sizes, is supposed to represent 'The Multitude' attending the Sermon on the Mount. Beyond this, a raised walk is flanked by twelve large yews called 'The Apostles', with four others known as 'The Evangelists'. A spiral path edged with box leads to the top of the Mount, where another large specimen is known as 'The Master'.

Nearer the Tudor house is a walled garden with a brick gazebo at each corner, the oldest built in *c* 1680, another in the early 18th cent and two in modern times.

(1) Apr–Sep: Wed–Sun and Public Holidays 2–7; Oct–Easter (except 25 Dec and Good Friday): Wed, Sat, Sun and New Year Holiday 2–5
(2) Charge
(3) Restaurant/café
(4) House (same times)
(5) National Trust

Ravensthorpe

Northamptonshire

18. Coton Manor Wildlife Garden

The garden, approx 8 acres (3·6 ha) in extent, was designed in 1925 by Mr and Mrs Harold Bryant, the parents of Mrs Pasley Tyler. Terraces around the 17th-cent manor house lead to the lake that is the focus of the garden. A fine flowering cherry stands near the water, with a tulip-tree (*Liriodendron tulipifera*) beyond. There is a lovely water garden with many pools and streams, an old rose garden and three good mixed borders.

(1) Apr–Oct: Thu, Sun and Bank Holiday Mon and Tue 2–6; Jul–Aug: also Wed 2–6
(2) Charge
(3) Tea
(4) Collection of waterfowl; plants for sale
(5) Commander and Mrs H. Pasley Tyler

Rockingham, nr Corby

Northamptonshire

19. Rockingham Castle

Parts of the castle date from Norman times and there is evidence that gardens have existed on the site since the 12th cent. The present gardens originated in the 17th cent: there are 12 acres (5·5 ha) of wild and formal areas created around the fortifications, with a rose garden on the site of the old keep laid out to demonstrate where the walls and embrasures used to be. The wild garden contains over 200 species and varieties of trees and shrubs; in April and May there is a fine display of daffodils. A notable feature is a 400-year-old yew hedge shaped like elephants.

(1) Easter–1 Oct: Sun, Thu, Bank Holiday Mon and the following Tue 2–6. Other times by appointment for parties only
(2) Charge
(3) Tea (for parties, by request)
(4) House (same times)
(5) Commander Michael Watson

Stoke Bruerne, nr Towcester

Northamptonshire

20. Stoke Park

The Stoke Park pavilions were built in the Palladian style by Inigo Jones in 1630, linked by colonnades to a central block, which subsequently burned down. When the pavilions and gardens were bought by the present owner in 1954, all had been derelict since 1939. Since 1960 the gardens have been re-created by the owner and his gardener, W. H. McCaughan.

The pavilions themselves enclose a small area of lawn and flowerbeds; a long grass terrace has an ornamental *bassin* about the size of a tennis-court planted with mature *Cupressus* species. The upper part of the garden consists mainly of an old orchard, walled on three sides, with daffodils and old shrub roses growing among the fruit trees. Mixed beds of vegetables, roses, peonies and other herbaceous plants lie along the walls; on the fourth side there is a formal herb garden designed by John Codrington in the form of interlocking chessboards with alternate squares occupied by different herbs.

(1) Jun–Aug: Sat and Sun 2–6

Stratford-upon-Avon

Warwickshire

21. Anne Hathaway's Cottage

The garden of this house, where Shakespeare's wife Anne Hathaway lived before she was married, is the quintessence of an English cottage garden. It is informally laid out, with paths of broken stone dividing irregular plots planted with trees, shrubs, herbs and flowers, including everlasting pea, oxlips, primroses, crown imperials (*Fritillaria imperialis*), lavender, rosemary, peonies, hollyhocks, mulleins, globe artichokes and Judas trees (*Cercis siliquastrum*). Behind the house is an orchard with old fruit trees and many wild flowers.

(1) Nov–Mar: Mon–Sat 9–4.30; Sun 1.30–4.30; Apr–Oct: Mon–Sat 9–7 (6 on Mon–Wed and Fri in Apr, May and Oct); Sun 10–6
(2) Charge
(4) House (same times)
(5) Shakespeare Birthplace Trust

Stratford-upon-Avon

22. Hall's Croft

Shakespeare's daughter Susanna and her husband Dr John Hall lived in this fine Tudor half-timbered house. The walled garden is relatively large and, in its present form, was designed after the house was restored in 1950. A long paved path leads from a terrace at the back of the house, bordered with roses and herbaceous plants, with a sundial at the far end. The lawn has several specimen trees, including a mulberry, a medlar and an almond. A small plot is planted with medicinal herbs that would have been used by Dr Hall.

(1) Nov–Mar: Mon–Sat 9–12.45, 2–4; Apr–Oct; Mon–Sat 9–6; Sun 2–6
(2) Charge
(5) Shakespeare Birthplace Trust

Stratford-upon-Avon

23. New Place

Shakespeare spent the last five years of his retirement at New Place. The house was destroyed in 1959 and only the foundations are now left; the Great Garden occupies the estate that had belonged to the house. It has stretches of fine lawn with a specimen beech and an old mulberry believed to have been grown from a cutting planted by Shakespeare himself. A long herbaceous border with flowers such as hollyhocks, Canterbury bells, larkspur and lilies is backed by a yew hedge and divided into sections by pillars and buttresses of clipped yew. Other beds are edged with box and planted with bulbs and spring flowers such as pansies, primroses, wallflowers, snapdragons and sweet william. At the lower end of the garden is a bank planted with many herbs and flowers mentioned in the plays.

The knot garden, which occupies another part of the site at New Place, is a replica of an enclosed Elizabethan garden. It is square and slightly sunken, divided by stone paths into four beds, each with an intricate pattern made of box, santolina, thyme or other herbs, the spaces filled with bedding plants. A paved walk runs along the top of a low brick wall, bounded by an oak palisade covered with crab apple trees.

(1) Nov–Mar: Mon–Sat 9–12.45, 2–4; Apr–Oct: Mon–Sat 9–6; Sun 2–6
(2) Charge
(5) Shakespeare Birthplace Trust

Stratford-upon-Avon

24. Shakespeare's Birthplace Garden

When Shakespeare's birthplace was bought as a national memorial in 1847, the Trustees decided to lay out the plot as an association garden in memory of the poet with specimens of all the plants mentioned in his works. A long central path is flanked by wide herbaceous borders; the lawn is planted with scattered trees including mulberry, quince and medlar; there is a fig, pomegranate and grape-vine and many herbs, such as lavender, mint, savory, marjoram, rosemary, rue, hyssop, camomile, thyme and fennel.

(1) Nov–Mar: Mon–Sat 9–4.30; Sun 1.30–4.30; Apr–Oct: Mon–Sat 9–7 (6 on Mon–Wed and Fri in Apr, May and Oct); Sun 10–6
(2) Charge
(4) House (same times)
(5) Shakespeare Birthplace Trust

Sulgrave, nr Banbury

Northamptonshire

25. Sulgrave Manor

The small Elizabethan manor house was built by ancestors of George Washington and still retains many of his possessions. The garden is laid out formally in Elizabethan style.

(1) Apr–Sep: Thu–Tue 10.30–1, 2–5.30; Oct–Dec, Feb–Mar: Thu–Tue 10.30–1, 2–4
(2) Charge
(4) House (same times)
(5) Sulgrave Manor Board

Tysoe

Warwickshire

26. Compton Wynyates

The house was built at the end of the 15th cent to replace an earlier one on the same site. The estate has belonged to the Compton family, in the direct male line, since the beginning of the 13th cent. The garden dates from 1895, when it was laid out by the 5th Marquess of Northampton. A particular feature is the box and yew topiary, and there is a small formal garden in an area enclosed by the moat. The gardens are especially worth visiting in spring, when naturalized crocuses, daffodils and primroses are in flower.

(1) *Good Friday–1 Oct: Tue–Thu and Sat 2–5; Sun and Public Holidays 11–5*
(2) *Charge*
(4) *House (same times)*
(5) *Marquess of Northampton*

Warwick

27. Warwick Castle

The oldest part of the garden that remains is a pathway winding from the Watergate Tower to the summit of the Mound, made by Sir Fulke Greville at the beginning of the 17th cent. Some cedars of Lebanon date from later in the 17th cent. The general layout is attributed to 'Capability' Brown and reputed to be his first independent commission, but much of it has been obscured by later plantings. The focus of the landscape is the conservatory, erected by George Greville, the 2nd Earl, in 1774. The formal gardens, with topiary peacocks, were laid out in front of this, probably in *c.* 1900. Interesting trees, such as *Aesculus octandra*, a yellow-flowered chestnut, and flowering shrubs, particularly rhododendrons, have been planted in various parts of the grounds.

(1) *Nov–Feb: 10–4.30; Mar–Oct: 10–5.30;*
(2) *Charge*
(3) *Restaurant and café*
(4) *Castle (same times)*
(5) *Madame Tussaud's*

Wilmcote, nr Stratford-upon-Avon

Warwickshire

28. Mary Arden's House

Mary Arden's house is a half-timbered Tudor farmhouse where Shakespeare's mother lived when she was young. In front the ivy-covered boundary wall is overhung by lilac and laburnum, clipped box hedges line the path and flowerbeds, and old-fashioned roses climb over the house. Behind the house there are herbaceous borders and a lawn with a specimen oak

tree planted to commemorate the Festival of Britain in 1951.

(1) *Nov–Mar: Mon–Sat 9–12.45, 2–4; Apr–Oct: Mon–Sat 9–6; Sun 2–6*
(2) *Charge*
(4) *House and farming museum in barns (same times)*
(5) *Shakespeare Birthplace Trust*

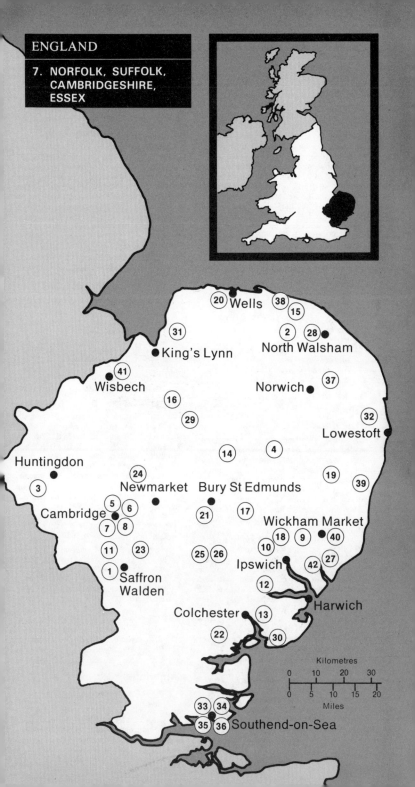

⑳ Wells
㊳ ⑮
㉛
② ㉘
King's Lynn
North Walsham
㊶
Wisbech
㊲
⑯
Norwich
㉙
㉜
Lowestoft
⑭ ④
Huntingdon
⑲ ㊴
③
㉔
Newmarket
Bury St Edmunds
⑤ ⑥
⑰
㉑
Wickham Market
Cambridge
⑦ ⑧
⑩ ⑱ ⑨ ㊵
⑪ ㉓
㉕ ㉖
㊷ ㉗
① Saffron
Walden
Ipswich
⑫
⑬
Harwich
Colchester
㉒
㉚

Kilometres
0   10   20   30

0   5   10   15   20
Miles

㉝ ㉞
㉟ ㊱ Southend-on-Sea

Audley End, nr Saffron Walden

Essex

1. Audley End

The original house was built for the Earl of Suffolk by Bernard Johnson between 1603 and 1616, but much of this was demolished on the advice of Sir John Vanbrugh and most remaining parts date from the 18th or early 19th cents. Sir John Griffin Griffin, later Lord Braybrooke, who inherited the property in 1762, did much restoration work on the house, and the gardens still remain largely as they were created in his time. In 1763, he employed 'Capability' Brown to landscape the grounds; he re-shaped the river, built a ha-ha and planted groups of trees. The garden buildings, which include two temples, a Palladian bridge, an obelisk and the rebuilt Lion Gate, were designed by Robert Adam. Much planting was done in the 19th cent, when the rose garden with its otter pit was laid out.

(1) Apr–early Oct: Tue–Sun and Public Holidays (except Good Friday) 10–6.30
(2) Charge
(3) Refreshments
(4) House (same days 10–5.30); miniature railway
(5) Dept of the Environment

Blickling, nr Aylsham

Norfolk

2. Blickling Hall

The house is Jacobean; the park is land-scaped in the manner of Humphry Repton. Three avenues of beech, horse chestnut and lime run parallel, leading in the direction of the house, crossed by another avenue of Turkey oaks. To the west of the house, a collection of magnolias is sheltered by yews; *Cyclamen hederaefolium* is naturalized in the grass. North of the house lies the mile-long artificial lake.

The parterres and formal gardens oppo-site the east front were planned by the garden designer Mrs Norah Lindsay in the early 1930s and are arranged in colour blocks, yellow and orange, and pink and blue; all surrounded by borders of roses and edged with catmint. Plants of *Yucca fila-mentosa* are scattered through the beds. On the south side is a herbaceous border, with Japanese cherries and shrub roses planted at a higher level. The orangery dates from 1781 and has a variety of plants.

The moat no longer contains water; it provides sheltered sites for many choice plants, including camellias, hydrangeas, old roses, fuchsias, myrtle and the tender South African species *Buddleia auriculata* and *Phygelius capensis*, Cape fuchsia. Through-out the park there are many fine specimen trees, such as *Parrotia persica*, *Quercus rubra* and a number of species of acer.

(1) Apr–late May and 1–14 Oct: Mon–Thu, Sat, Sun and Public Holidays 2–6; late May–Sep: same days 11–6. No dogs
(2) Charge
(4) House (same times but closed 12.30–1.30)
(5) National Trust

Buckden, 46 Church Street

Cambridgeshire

3. The Hoo

The main feature here is a herb garden divided into sections and planted in the Elizabethan manner with herbs grown with the flowers and vegetables. The Silver Jubilee Garden features silver and grey-leaved plants around a mulberry tree; the Cosmetic and Colour Garden has plants used for cosmetic purposes and for dyes; the Physic Garden has medicinal herbs and the Holy Garden contains plants of religious significance. There is also a culinary garden and an ornamental and fragrant garden.

(1) Early May–late Sep: Tue and Fri 10–4
(2) Free
(4) Herbs for sale
(5) Mrs Elizabeth Peplow

Bressingham, nr Diss

Norfolk

4. Bressingham Gardens and Live Steam Museum

The gardens covering an area of approx 6 acres (2·5 ha) were developed between 1950 and 1960 by Alan Bloom, VMH. They are laid out informally with mature trees and island beds of herbaceous perennials. It was here that the use of island beds rather than the traditional long, narrow herbaceous border, was pioneered. Many uncommon varieties were obtained by exchange with botanic and other gardens throughout the world and now the gardens contain over 5,000 species and varieties of hardy peren-nials, alpines, heathers and conifers.

(1) Early–late May and mid–late Sep: Sun and Public Holidays 1.30–6; late May–Jul and early–mid Sep: Sun and Public Holidays 1.30–6; Thu 1.30–5.30; Aug: Sun and Public Holidays 1.30–6; Wed and Thu 1.30–5.30
(2) Charge
(3) Café
(4) Steam museum and railway (Bressingham Steam Engine Trust)
(5) Blooms Nurseries Ltd

Cambridge

5. Christ's College Fellows' Garden

The garden was leased from Jesus College in 1507 and purchased in September 1554. In 1609 300 black mulberry trees, *Morus nigra*, were bought for 18*s*; it is believed that the so-called Milton's mulberry tree is the last survivor of these. The bathing pool and the summer house both date from the 18th cent. Parts of the boundary walls are medieval. The present lay-out probably dates from the late 18th and early 19th cents. There are herbaceous borders and summer bedding, wall shrubs and climbers, an apiary, and some fine trees including three cypresses, *Cupressus sempervirens*, grown from seed brought from Shelley's cenotaph in Rome.

All the courts in the college have good wall shrubs; The Master's Lodge has a fine wistaria. The Library Court contains plants mentioned in Milton's poem *Lycidas*; New Court has a hanging garden planted in 1971 and the First Court has window boxes, colourful from June to October.

(*1*) *Most weekdays (except during certain holiday periods) 10.30–12.30, 2–4*
(*2*) *Free*
(*5*) *Master, Fellows and Scholars of Christ's College*

Cambridge
6. Clare College

The River Cam, spanned by the 17th-cent Clare Bridge, runs through the college grounds. The gardens were probably first laid out in the 17th cent, possibly as a kitchen garden. In its present form, the Fellows' Garden was designed in 1946–7 by the head gardener of the time, Walter Barlow, and many different types of garden are accommodated within its 2 acres (0·9 ha). There are wide lawns and a formal water garden enclosed by tall yew hedges, a blue and yellow garden, a red border, a white border and a scented garden dominated by a silver-leaved lime, *Tilia petiolaris*. Other interesting plants include a fine swamp cypress, *Taxodium distichum*; on the river-bank, a handkerchief tree, *Davidia involucrata*, and Asiatic primulas and meconopsis in the shade of a shrubbery beyond the yew hedges. In the design of the garden much importance was attached to providing views and vistas.

As well as the Fellows' Garden, the grounds include the Scholars' Garden (17th-cent), the Master's Garden and the gardens of the Memorial Court (1924), and Thirkill Court (1956). All were rehabilitated between 1946 and 1970.

(*1*) *Mon–Fri 2–5*
(*2*) *Free*
(*4*) *Clare College (Daily during hours of daylight)*
(*5*) *Clare College (Garden Committee)*

Cambridge
7. Magdalene College

The Fellows' Garden, approx 3 acres (1·4 ha) in extent, lies beyond the oldest college buildings and borders the River Cam. A

garden has existed here since the north and south ranges of the First Court were completed by John of Wisbech, Abbot of Crowland Abbey, in *c* 1500.

The garden is secluded, being surrounded by high walls and tall trees, and has an essentially informal lay-out with a croquet lawn and a tennis court, and fine specimen trees of plane, horse chestnut and walnut. There are beds of standard roses and a fine display of crocuses in March.

(*1*) *Daily 1–6.30*
(*2*) *Free*
(*4*) *College Courts and buildings (Daily Sunrise–Sunset); Pepys Library (Michaelmas and Lent Terms: Daily 2.30–3.30; Easter Term and mid-Jul–Aug: Daily 11.30–12.30, 2.30–3.30. Closed in September)*
(*5*) *Master and Fellows of Magdalene College*

Cambridge
8. University Botanic Garden

Planting started on the present 40 acre (16 ha) site in 1846, but work did not begin on the eastern half until 1951. The garden includes systematic collections of trees and herbaceous plants and special collections of several genera, including tulipa species and European saxifrages. There are limestone and sandstone rock gardens planted geographically, a water garden, a winter garden and a wide range of glasshouses, including an alpine house, one for carnivorous plants, a cool fern house, a tropical fern house and a stove house.

(*1*) *Garden. Summer: Mon–Sat 8–7.30; Winter: Mon–Sat (except 25 and 26 Dec) 8–Sunset. Glasshouses. Summer: Mon–Sat 2–5; Winter: Mon–Sat 2–Sunset*
(*2*) *Free*
(*5*) *University of Cambridge*

Charsfield, nr Wickham Market
Suffolk
9. 1 Park Lane

This ¼ acre (0·1 ha) garden around an end-of-terrace council house is a splendid example of what can be done with a small piece of ground. Every vertical wall is covered with climbing plants and every year Mrs Peggy Cole raises approx 3,000 bedding plants. A steep embankment sloping to the road in front of the house is planted with African marigolds and geraniums, with a row of 'Evelyn Fison' roses along the top. There is a pond with a miniature bridge; about 130 varieties of fuchsia, dahlias, sweet peas, honeysuckle, and about 100 varieties of roses – it has been estimated that there are 700 or 800 types of tree, shrub and flower represented. As well as all

49

this, the garden includes a glasshouse with a display of exotics, a highly productive vegetable garden and demonstrations of home wine-making and dried flowers.

(1) *Early Jul–late Sep: Daily 2.30–6.30*
(2) *Charge, for various charities*
(5) *Mr and Mrs Cole*

Claydon, nr Ipswich

Suffolk

10. Lime Kiln

The garden was founded and designed by Countess Sophie Benckendorff in 1920, and has been converted into a rosarium since 1956 by the present owner. It is unique in this country: old and rare varieties are grown, and it is hoped that many will eventually again become commercially available. In spite of the chalk soil, over 500 varieties are represented. An early 19th-cent lime kiln in a fine state of preservation stands in the grounds.

(1) *Jun–13 Jul: Daily 2–6*
(2) *Voluntary donations*
(5) *Humphrey Brooke, Esq*

Duxford, nr Cambridge

Cambridgeshire

11. Duxford Mill

The house, converted from the old watermill and miller's house, is reputedly where Charles Kingsley wrote *The Water Babies*, and earlier it was much visited by Oliver Cromwell. The 5 acre (2 ha) garden was designed and made by the present owners and is landscaped to include vistas of the Mill Pond, Regency Temple and sculpture by Wiles. Lawns, with borders of modern roses and clumps of silver birch, run beside the River Cam.

(1) *1st two Sun in Jul and last Sun in Aug 2–7. Other times by appointment*
(2) *Charge*
(3) *Tea*
(4) *Collection of waterfowl*
(5) *Mr and Mrs Robert Lea*

East Bergholt, nr Colchester

Essex

12. Stour

Stour was the home of the late Randolph Churchill from 1953 to 1968, when it was purchased by the present owners who relandscaped the 9 acre (4 ha) garden. There are magnificent views of the Stour valley from the terraced lawns, a pleached lime walk, and a comprehensive collection of trees, shrubs, heathers and dwarf conifers as well as many unusual plants.

(1) *Good Friday–autumn: Daily 10–5*
(2) *Charge*

(3) *Tea*
(4) *Gift shop in stable block; nursery garden with containerized plants (same times)*
(5) *Mr and Mrs C. H. Gill and Mrs J. H. Gill*

Elmstead Market, nr Colchester

Essex

13. White Barn House

The garden was designed and made by the present owner, starting in 1960 with an overgrown site of approx 4 acres (1·8 ha). From this has been made an informal garden, with plants arranged in groups and provided as far as possible with the sort of growing conditions for which nature has fitted them. There are basically three types of garden: the Mediterranean garden, situated near the house on a warm gravel slope, with plants that can withstand prolonged drought and poor soil; the woodland garden, occupying an area where the soil is better and less liable to dry out; and the bog garden, which surrounds five large ponds made by damming a spring-fed ditch.

Much use is made of mulching to conserve moisture and control weeds. There are a number of unusual plants, and as much attention is paid to foliage effect as to flower colour. The result is a garden that is interesting all the year round.

(1) *Mon–Sat (except Public Holidays) 9–1, 1.30–5 (4 in winter)*
(2) *Collecting box*
(4) *Nursery garden (same times)*
(5) *Mrs Beth Chatto*

Euston, nr Thetford

Norfolk

14. Euston Hall

The lay-out of the garden and pleasure grounds, 72 acres (29 ha) in all, including the lake, dates partly from the 17th-cent. John Evelyn, William Kent and 'Capability' Brown all had a part in the design. There are herbaceous borders, shrub borders and a garden temple by Kent. Visit in June and July.

(1) *May–Sep: Thu 2.30–5.30*
(2) *Charge*
(3) *Tea*
(4) *House (same times)*
(5) *Duke of Grafton*

Felbrigg, nr Cromer

Norfolk

15. Felbrigg Hall

The handsome 17th-cent house is surrounded by a park with many fine trees, including sweet chestnuts planted by William Windham I some time after he inherited the property in 1665. West of the house is a large lawn, overlooked by the early 18th-cent orangery which contains a collection of camellias, some very large. A path running north-east from the house across the park leads to the walled garden, which the National Trust has restored to the style current in the 17th and 18th cents, where fruit, cutting flowers, herbs and vegetables are grown in formal beds set among box-edged paths. There are some large herbaceous borders and an 18th-cent dovecot.

(1) *Apr–mid-Oct: Tue–Thu, Sat, Sun and Public Holidays 2–6*
(2) *Charge*
(3) *Tea*
(4) *House (same times)*
(5) *National Trust*

Fincham

Norfolk

16. Talbot Manor

The garden, now covering approx 30 acres (12 ha) was founded in 1947 by the present owner. There is probably the largest private collection in Britain of hardy plants – trees, shrubs and herbaceous perennials – suitable for calcareous soil. The 16 glasshouses contain an extensive range, again probably the largest in the country, of tropical and tender plants, including collections of begonias and orchids. Over 20,000 taxa are represented in the garden.

(1) *Jun: Sun 2–8; Jul: 1st Sun 2–8*
(2) *Charge*
(5) *L. Maurice Mason, Esq*

Haughley, nr Stowmarket

Suffolk

17. Haughley Park

The original garden, with its walls, dates from 1620. An oak tree by the main lawn has a girth of 30 ft (9 m) and is estimated to be 600–1,000 years old; Queen Mary is said to have sat under it on her flight from London in 1553. *Magnolia soulangiana* in the centre of the lawn planted only in the late 1930s has a spread of 35 ft (10·6 m) and is in bloom in late April and early May.

The garden has been developed and re-planted since 1958 by F. G. Barcock of Drinkstone, Suffolk. It covers 6 acres (2·7 ha) and is divided into seven sections. It contains many flowering shrubs, including rhododendrons and viburnums, and a large pond with water-lilies and bog plants round the edges. The park, which contains many fine trees, covers 100 acres (40·4 ha) and adjoining this is 50 acres (20·2 ha) of mature woodland with large oaks, chestnuts, beech, hornbeam, rhododendrons, bluebells and lily-of-the-valley. From July to September the hydrangeas are in bloom.

(1) *May–Sep: Tue 3–6*
(2) *Charge*
(4) *House (same times)*
(5) *A. J. Williams, Esq*

Helmingham, nr Ipswich

Suffolk

18. Helmingham Hall

The house and garden date from *c* 1500, and the lay-out of the latter has remained unaltered. It covers approx 4 acres (1·8 ha) and is enclosed by a moat and a brick wall built in 1745. The outstanding feature is the cruciform herbaceous borders that surround areas planted with fruit and vegetables and still retain an Elizabethan flavour. Beyond lies a 400 acre (162 ha) deer park.

(1) *Easter Sun, Spring Bank Holiday Sun and each Sun thereafter–Oct: 2–6.30*
(2) *Charge*
(3) *Tea*
(4) *Safari rides in park; farm and garden produce*
(5) *Lord Tollemache*

Heveningham, Halesworth

Suffolk

19. Heveningham Hall

The mansion was built in Palladian style by Sir Robert Taylor in 1780; the orangery was built by James Wyatt, who also designed the interior of the house. The 500 acre (202 ha) park with its lake and much of the 13 acre (6 ha) gardens were designed by 'Capability' Brown; an invoice for the serpentine ('crinkle-crankle') wall surrounding the kitchen garden survives, dated 1796. Now, herbaceous borders run along the wall and the walled garden also contains roses and a double border of *Sternbergia lutea*. To the south of the house is a Victorian garden, laid out in 1877. The grounds include some fine flowering trees, including *Eucryphia* × *nymansensis*, *Laburnum* × *watereri* 'Vossii' and *Magnolia liliiflora* 'Nigra'.

(1) *Apr–mid-Oct: Wed, Thu, Sat, Sun and Public Holidays 2–6; May–Sep: also Tue. Last admission 5.30*
(2) *Charge*
(3) *Tea*
(4) *House (same times)*
(5) *Dept of the Environment administered by the National Trust*

Holkham

Norfolk

20. Holkham Hall

The Palladian house was built in 1734 by William Kent, who also designed some of the garden buildings. The grounds were landscaped in the early 18th cent, with a lake and a clump of trees; 'Capability' Brown made some alterations in 1762–4 and Humphry Repton worked here later on. In the 19th cent the architect Sir Charles

Barry designed formal terraces around the house, with geometric beds and a round pool.

(1) *Spring and late summer Public Holidays: 11.30–5; June and Sep: Thu 11.30–5; Jul–Aug: Thu and Mon 11.30–5*
(2) *Charge*
(3) *Café*
(4) *House and Holkham Pottery (same times)*
(5) *Earl of Leicester*

Horringer, nr Bury St Edmunds

Suffolk

21. Ickworth

Although the estate had belonged to the Hervey family since the mid-15th cent, building did not begin on the present house until 1795 and it was not occupied until 1829. The garden was laid out by the 1st Marquess of Bristol in the 1820s and is an early example of the return to fashion of semi-formal gardening in the Italian style, after the long vogue for naturalistic landscapes. Groves of evergreens come close to the house on the south side and a central path from the Rotunda leads up steps flanked by two mulberries to a raised, curving terrace walk which divides the garden from the park. The plantations on either side of this include yews and ilex as well as magnolias, *Phillyrea latifolia* 'Spinosa' and the golden rain tree, *Koelreuteria paniculata*. North of the house lies a pleasure ground with many large trees. The conservatory, part of the west wing, contains fuchsias, scented-leaf geraniums, *Fatsia japonica* and × *Fatshedera lizei*.

(1) *Garden. Apr–mid-Oct: Tue–Thu, Sat, Sun and Public Holidays 2–6. Park. Daily*
(2) *Garden: Charge; Park: Free*
(3) *Café*
(4) *House (same times)*
(5) *National Trust*

Layer Marney, nr Colchester

Essex

22. Layer Marney Tower

The house, with its spectacular gatehouse towers, dates from the early 16th cent. The 5 acre (2 ha) gardens were laid out in the early 20th cent by the owner, Walter de Zoëte, with lawns, yew hedges, a pond, formal rose beds and climbers such as wistaria. A loquat tree, *Eriobotrya japonica*, was planted by a later owner in the 1920s.

(1) *Apr–Sep: Thu and Sun and, in Jul and Aug, Tue 2–6; Public Holidays 11–6*
(2) *Charge*
(3) *Café*

(4) *House and tower (same times)*
(5) *Gerald Charrington, Esq*

Linton, nr Cambridge

Cambridgeshire

23. Linton Zoological Gardens

The zoological gardens occupy 10½ acres (4·2 ha) of landscaped grounds. Most of the trees and shrubs were planted in 1971, but additions are being made all the time. There are handsome specimens of the cider gum, *Eucalyptus gunnii*, and the Chusan palm, *Trachycarpus fortunei*. Colour is given by a fine collection of roses that is increased annually, by flowering shrubs and by summer bedding schemes. Most of the aviaries and enclosures are planted with creepers, trees and shrubs.

(1) *Daily (except 25 Dec) 10–7 or Sunset; last admission 45 mins before closing*
(2) *Charge*
(3) *Café*
(4) *Zoo; Pot plants for sale*
(5) *Len Simmons, Esq*

Lode, nr Cambridge

Cambridgeshire

24. Anglesey Abbey

The present house is mainly Jacobean and was bought in 1926 by Huttleston Broughton, later 1st Lord Fairhaven, and his brother, Major the Hon Henry Broughton. The 100 acre (40·4 ha) gardens, which have been described as 'among the most imaginative and successful combinations of formal landscape gardening that this century has produced', are the former's creation. East of the entrance drive lie the dahlia garden and the herbaceous garden, made in a wide semi-circle framed by large beech hedges, whose plants include *Crambe cordifolia*, *Aruncus sylvester*, peonies, lupins, salvias and delphiniums. Beyond this, a path winds through natural woodland to a wide lawn with the sunken quarry pool to the left. A brick wall, forming the north-east boundary of the garden, offers shelter to a number of shrubs including *Carpenteria californica*, *Piptanthus nepalensis* and the Beauty Bush, *Kolkwitzia amabilis*. Another path leads on to the Emperor's Walk, a broad green walk over ¼ mile (402 m) long with twelve busts of Roman emperors set against dark spruce and silver-leafed *Elaeagnus ebbingei*. The arboretum lies beside this, with many fine specimen trees such as a Japanese hop hornbeam, *Ostrya japonica*; Algerian oak, *Quercus mirbeckii*; Indian bean-tree, *Catalpa bignonioides*; and magnolias.

On the west side of the entrance, the South Glade curves to the west, culminating in the Daffodil Walk. The Great Avenue, over ½ mile (805 m) long, has eight rows of alternating planes and chestnuts, planted in 1937 to commemorate the coronation of George VI and Queen Elizabeth, while the

Temple Lawn commemorates the coronation of the present Queen in 1953. Island beds, planted with carefully composed colour schemes, alternately screen and frame the Temple. From this, a path leads past a small lawn with a statue of Narcissus beside a pool, on to the Hyacinth Garden, where 4,000 blue and white hyacinths, renewed every third year, are planted in geometric flowerbeds.

(1) *Easter Sat–mid-Oct: Daily 2–6. No dogs*
(2) *Charge*
(4) *House (Easter Sat–mid-Oct: Tue–Thu, Sat, Sun and Public Holidays 2–6; last admission 5)*
(5) *National Trust*

Long Melford

Suffolk

25. Kentwell Hall

The Elizabethan manor house is surrounded by a 15 acre (6 ha) garden, most recently laid out between 1929 and 1938 by Sir Connop Guthrie. It was subsequently sadly neglected but is being restored and replanted by the present owners. There are lawns, including a yew lawn, several moats and a fish pond, trees and shrubs, a sunken garden, a Victorian vinery and a large dovecot. A walled garden dating from the 17th cent contains espalier fruit trees, geometrically shaped flowerbeds and a yew walk, which is being recreated. In spring there is an attractive display of massed bulbs.

(1) *Easter–Sep: Wed, Thu and Sun 2–6; 15 Jul–15 Sep: Fri and Sat also*
(2) *Charge*
(3) *Tea*
(4) *House; crafts and gift shop (same times)*
(5) *J. Patrick Phillips, Esq*

Long Melford

26. Melford Hall

The 16th-cent brick manor house has a garden mainly composed of lawns and trees including an ancient mulberry. There are also rose beds, a fountain garden and a long herbaceous border in front of a wall covered with ornamental vines. An interesting feature is the octagonal pavilion dating, like the house, from the Tudor period.

(1) *Apr–late Sep: Wed, Thu, Sun and Public Holidays 2–6*
(2) *Charge*
(4) *House (same times)*
(5) *National Trust*

Lower Ufford

Suffolk

27. The Mill House

The 3½ acre (1·6 ha) garden is set on the

banks of the River Deben and contains an 18th-cent watermill in a good state of repair. It is basically a herb-growers' garden, set in the framework of a pleasure garden with ponds and mature trees. Herbs from the National Collection are grown here on trial.

(1) *May–Oct: 1st and 3rd Sun of each month 2–6*
(2) *Charge (GSO)*
(4) *Mill (same times)*
(5) *Mrs G. Le M. Croll*

North Walsham

Norfolk

28. E. B. Le Grice (Roses) Ltd

The nurseries cover 45 acres (18 ha) and many well-known varieties, such as 'Allgold' and 'News', originated here. Unusual colours are a speciality. The rose fields are a fine sight in summer. A display garden is being laid out with trees and shrubs as well as roses.

(1) *Mon–Sat 9–5; Sun 2–4*
(2) *Free*
(4) *Garden centre (same times)*
(5) *J. R. Le Grice, Esq*

Oxborough

Norfolk

29. Oxburgh Hall

The house was built by Edmund Bedingfeld in 1482, and there were some Victorian additions. Although it now belongs to the National Trust, it is still occupied by descendants of the original builder. The Gatehouse is a spectacular structure, almost unaltered since it was built, and from it a good view of the garden can be obtained.

A parterre was laid out in the French style in 1850; it is edged with box, cotton lavender, *Santolina chaemaecyparissus*, and 'Jackman's Blue' rue, *Ruta graveolens*, filled in with French marigolds and ageratum. Recently some permanent plantings have been made to reduce the labour of bedding out. Beyond this, and separated from it by a yew hedge, is a herbaceous border edged with catmint; behind this is a walled kitchen garden part of which has been grassed and planted as a formal mulberry orchard with black and white mulberries, quinces and medlars. Climbing roses and clematis grow against the walls. On the south side of the hall is a sheltered garden with crinums, fuchsias and a good specimen of *Magnolia grandiflora*.

(1) *Apr–mid-Oct: Tue–Thu, Sat, Sun and Public Holidays 2–6*
(2) *Charge*
(4) *House and gatehouse (same times)*
(5) *National Trust*

St Osyth, nr Clacton-on-Sea

Essex

30. St Osyth's Priory

The priory dates from the 16th cent and the gatehouse from the 15th. There is a formal rose garden surrounded by yew hedges and a topiary garden entered through a wistaria-covered pergola as well as lawns and some fine trees including some very old mulberries. The grounds also contain a 13th-cent chapel.

(1) May–Sep: Daily 10–5
(2) Charge
(5) Somerset de Chair, Esq

Sandringham

Norfolk

31. Sandringham House and Grounds

The house, built in the second half of the 18th cent, was bought by Queen Victoria in 1862 for the Prince of Wales, later Edward VII. A handsome pair of wrought iron gates, known as the Norwich Gates, at the north entrance to the grounds, were given in the following year to the Prince and Princess of Wales as a wedding present by the County of Norfolk and City of Norwich. From here, a path leads past banks of hydrangeas to the flower garden with formal beds filled with seasonal bedding and a massive pergola made of oak beams and brick columns, 70 yards (64 m) long and 15 feet (4·57 m) high. A range of teak glasshouses nearby was built by the Prince of Wales from the winnings of his racehorse Persimmon. The north garden was designed for George VI by the landscape architect Geoffrey Jellicoe; long, narrow flowerbeds are surrounded by box hedges and divided by grass and gravel paths. At the far end, an avenue of pleached limes leads to a bronze statue of the Buddhist divinity Kuvera, brought from China and presented to the Prince of Wales in 1869.

A path from the west terrace of the house leads to a rockery above the shore of the Upper Lake, planted with dwarf conifers, where waterside plantings include the giant *Gunnera manicata* as well as astilbes, ferns and other plants. The grounds include many fine specimen trees, such as *Davidia involucrata* var. *vilmoriniana*, *Cercidiphyllum japonicum*, magnolias and many rhododendrons, including the July-flowering tree-like hybrid *Polar Bear*, azaleas and camellias, often underplanted with polyanthus. In spring, daffodils naturalized among the trees give a fine display.

(1) Mid–late Apr and early–late Sep: Tue,
    Wed and Thu 10.30–5; May, Jun,
    early–mid-Jul and early–late Aug: Sun
    11.30–5; Mon, Tue, Wed and Thu
    10.30–5. Not open when HM The
    Queen or any member of the Royal
    Family is in residence
(2) Charge
(3) Café
(4) House (same times in Apr, May, Jun
    and Sep; closed for a longer period in
    late Jun and early Aug)
(5) HM The Queen

Somerleyton, nr Lowestoft

Suffolk

32. Somerleyton Hall

The Hall is an early Victorian house built round a Tudor-Jacobean shell. The gardens cover over 12 acres (4·8 ha) and were known for their evergreens as far back as the mid-17th cent. Now there are sweeping lawns, yew and box hedges, azaleas, rhododendrons and some fine trees, including eucalyptus; an incense cedar, *Calocedrus decurrens*; a Monterey pine, *Pinus radiata*; a tulip-tree, *Liriodendron tulipifera*; and a dawn-redwood, *Metasequoia glyptostroboides*. An avenue of 250-year-old lime trees marks the site of the original drive.

All that remains of the once-famous Winter Garden, which was designed as a miniature Crystal Palace by Sir Joseph Paxton, and was demolished in 1914–15, is a loggia surrounding the sunken garden that now occupies the site and contains much interesting statuary. A notable feature of the garden is the maze, designed by W. A. Nesfield and planted in 1846, with clipped yew hedges and a pagoda in the centre.

Also on the Somerleyton estate, approx 3 miles (4·8 km) away from the house, is Fritton Lake, worth a visit in itself. The 2 mile (3.2 km) long lake is set among trees, with an old-fashioned garden with lawns and fine herbaceous borders along one shore.

(1) Easter Sun–Sep: Sun, Thu and Public
    Holidays 2–6; Jul–Aug: Tue and Wed.
(2) Charge
(3) Refreshments
(4) House; miniature railway; aviary; children's farm; gift shop (same times)
(5) Lord Somerleyton

Southend-on-Sea

Essex

33. Chalkwell Park

The 26 acre (10·5 ha) site was purchased by the local authority in 1903 and contains an extensive rose garden and fine displays of seasonal bedding. Visit in spring and summer.

(1) Daily 7.30–Sunset
(2) Free
(5) Southend-on-Sea Borough Council

Southend-on-Sea

34. Churchill Gardens

The site was bought by the Council in 1965 and opened the following year by the Lord Lieutenant of Essex in memory of Sir Winston Churchill. The principal features are a waterfall and stream with a wide range of waterside plants. The steep banks are covered with daffodils which give a fine display in spring.

(1) Daily Sunrise–Sunset
(2) Free
(5) Southend-on-Sea Borough Council

Southend-on-Sea

35. Priory Park

The 44 acre (17·6 ha) site was acquired by the local authority between 1918 and 1931. There are many fine trees; an enclosed old world garden; a knot garden; and good displays of seasonal bedding.

(1) Daily 7.30–Sunset
(2) Free
(3) Café
(4) Prittlewell Priory Museum (Mon–Sat 10–1, 2–5.30; also Apr–Sep: Sun 2–5.30)
(5) Southend-on-Sea Borough Council

Southend-on-Sea

36. Southend Cliffs

Part of the park was purchased by the Council in 1883 and since then it has been added to until now there are 22 acres (10 ha) stretching for almost a mile (1·6 km) west of the pier. This is laid out with a variety of walks and flower gardens, colourful throughout spring and summer.

(1) Daily Sunrise–Sunset
(2) Free
(5) Southend-on-Sea Borough Council

South Walsham

Norfolk

37. Woodland Garden

The gardens, which cover approx 174 acres (70 ha), were laid out over a period of almost 30 years by the late Lord Fairhaven, who bought South Walsham Hall in 1947. He made a water garden with dykes leading to the Inner Broad and planted the woodland with shade-loving plants, including camellias, enkianthus, pieris, primulas, trilliums, lilies, and many rhododendrons, some collected in the Himalayas by Kingdon Ward. The gardens were first opened to the public in 1975.

(1) 2nd Sun in Apr–last Sun in Sep: Thu, Sat, Sun and Public Holidays 2–6
(2) Charge
(4) Bird sanctuary (by permission of warden)
(5) Fairhaven Garden Trust

Upper Sheringham

Norfolk

38. Sheringham Hall

The extensive park was landscaped in *c* 1812 by Humphry Repton, who also built the house. It has a mile-long (1·6 km) drive through spectacular rhododendron woods planted in the 19th cent.

(1) Park and rhododendron woods. May–Jun: Weekdays 10–6. Private gardens. Four or five Sun during Summer
(2) Charge
(5) T. Upcher, Esq

Westleton, nr Saxmundham

Suffolk

39. Fisk's Clematis Nursery

The nursery has displays of many types of clematis, both species and hybrid, growing on walls, pergolas and fences. An unusual feature is a flowerbed 15 ft (4·8 m) in diameter planted with several varieties of clematis pegged down to form permanent ground cover. There are also eight tunnel houses made of polythene used for bringing on young plants that visitors can walk through to compare varieties. Visit from July to the end of September.

(1) Spring and Autumn: Mon–Sat 9–5; Summer: Mon–Sat 9–5; Sun 10–5
(2) Free
(5) Fisk's Clematis Nursery

Wickham Market

Suffolk

40. Glemham Hall

The red-brick house is Elizabethan, although considerably altered between 1712 and 1722. In the garden there are extensive lawns, an avenue of Irish yews, a lily-pond and a vegetable garden. The walled garden is planted largely with roses, but also with herbaceous borders, and there are plum and cherry trees set against the walls.

(1) Easter Mon–late Sep: Sun, Wed and Public Holidays 2–5.30
(2) Charge
(3) Tea
(4) House (same times). Garden produce for sale
(5) Lady Blanche Cobbold

Wisbech

Cambridgeshire

41. Peckover House

The house was built in 1722, but the garden is basically Victorian and one of the best preserved examples of the period. The Wilderness Walk around the east lawn passes through evergreens such as laurels, spotted laurels (*Aucuba japonica*), hollies, box and yew, underplanted with ferns. On the west side are beds of evergreens and flowering shrubs. The path continues past a 19th-cent rustic Doric temple and a small rose garden with lavender-edged beds and on to the orangery, which contains some old orange trees and other flowering plants in pots. East of this is a new formal border designed to provide colour throughout the year. The orangery is linked to a second summer house by double borders edged with pinks, divided by hedges and iron cones covered with roses and clematis into sections, each planted in a different colour scheme. There are topiary peacocks and a pond surrounded by hydrangeas and peonies. The formal kitchen garden now contains a nursery border with cutting flowers, mixed borders, fruit trees, including quince and mulberry, and two glasshouses, one with a collection of tender ferns. In the grounds are some fine specimen trees including *Ginkgo biloba*, *Liriodendron tulipifera* and *Fagus sylvatica* 'Heterophylla'.

(*1*) *Apr–mid-Oct: Tue–Thu, Sat, Sun and Public Holidays 2–6. Rest of year by previous arrangement with custodian.*

(*2*) *Charge*
(*3*) *Refreshments*
(*4*) *House (same times)*
(*5*) *National Trust*

Woodbridge

Suffolk

42. Letheringham Water Mill

The watermill was mentioned in the Domesday Book. The mill house is partly Tudor and looks out on to lawns and herbaceous borders. The garden has been developed by the present owner and his wife since 1960. A stream garden is a mass of daffodils in spring, and there is colour in the garden as a whole all the year round.

(*1*) *Apr and May: Sun and Public Holidays 12.30–6; Jun, Jul and Sep: Sun and Wed 12.30–6; Aug: Sun, Wed, Thu and Public Holidays 12.30–6*
(*2*) *Charge for NGS*
(*3*) *Tea*
(*4*) *The Mill and a shop with plants and pottery. Peafowl, pheasants and ornamental ducks*
(*5*) *F. D. Ley, Esq*

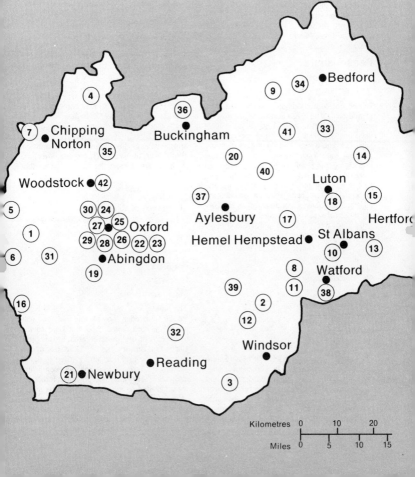

④

34 ●Bedford

9

36

7 ●Chipping Norton

Buckingham

41

33

35

20

14

Woodstock ●42

40

Luton

5

37

18

15

30 24

Aylesbury

17

Hertfor

1

27 25 Oxford

Hemel Hempstead ●

St Albans ●

29 28 26 22 23

10

13

6

31

8

● Abingdon

39

Watford

19

11

38

16

2

12

32

Windsor

● Reading

21 ●Newbury

3

Kilometres 0   10   20

Miles 0   5   10   15

ENGLAND

Bampton

Oxfordshire

1. Bampton Manor

The garden is divided into a number of sections, each with its own colour scheme. A large pond, with red and white water-lilies, is surrounded with waterside plants such as irises, marsh marigolds (*Caltha palustris*), *Rheum palmatum* and rodgersias. A circular garden surrounded by a yew hedge is planted with white-flowered plants such as the silver-leafed pear, *Pyrus salicifolia*, and the white clematis 'Marie Boisselot' trained over a wire frame. Twin herbaceous borders are set out mostly in pale colours, white, pink, blue and lemon yellow, and beyond these is a group of old shrub roses. The rose garden proper is unusual in the use of silver and grey-leaved plants, such as varieties of thyme, the lavender cotton, *Santolina chamaecyparissus*, and *Senecio greyi*, as ground cover.

(*1*) *Wed, Fri and Sun 2–5*
(*2*) *Free except when open for NGS*
(*4*) *Plants for sale*
(*5*) *Countess Münster*

Beaconsfield

Buckinghamshire

2. Bekonscot Model Village

Bekonscot Model Village was created from a muddy field in 1929 and there are now 75 miniature buildings. 200 tons of stone were used for the rockery alone and the 'countryside' is planted with 8,000 conifers of many species and varieties providing a most interesting range of forms and colours. In spite of being mostly dwarf forms, they tend to become too large after some years and have to be replaced: about a quarter are changed annually. Ground-cover plants and dwarf shrubs simulate scaled-down flowerbeds and trees and the garden is full of colour throughout the season.

(*1*) *Summer: Daily 10–6; Winter: Daily (except Christmas holiday) 10–4*
(*2*) *Charge*
(*4*) *Model railway (Easter–Oct)*
(*5*) *Bekonscot Ltd*

Bracknell

Berkshire

3. South Hill Park Arts Centre

The large Georgian house is set in a 15 acre (6 ha) natural park with two lakes and ornamental wildfowl. An Italian garden was laid out in the late 19th cent; patterned beds edged with box are filled with seasonal bedding. Elsewhere in the garden are many flowering shrubs; banks of azaleas make a fine display in May.

(*1*) *Mon–Fri 9 am–11 pm; Sat 10 am–11 pm; Sun noon–11*
(*2*) *Free*
(*3*) *Refreshments*
(*4*) *Open air sculpture exhibition; continuous programme of art events; nature trail*
(*5*) *Bracknell Development Council*

Broughton, nr Banbury

Oxfordshire

4. Broughton Castle

The moated Elizabethan mansion has a 14th-cent core. The grounds have lawns and herbaceous and mixed borders and include a walled garden laid out by Gertrude Jekyll. Visit from June to August.

(*1*) *Apr–Sep: Wed, Bank Holiday Sun and Mon 2–5; Jun–Aug: Sun also 2–5*
(*2*) *Charge*
(*3*) *Tea*
(*4*) *Castle (same times)*
(*5*) *Lord Saye and Sele*

Burford

Oxfordshire

5. Cotswold Wildlife Park

The estate was originally owned by Mr Fox, inventor of the collapsible umbrella (1806). In 1970 the wildlife park was created, covering 150 acres (60 ha), a mixture of natural park with many shrubs and landscaped gardens with lawns, seasonal bedding displays and trees. The tropical house, once the conservatory, was converted to its present lay-out in 1972. It now has plants such as hibiscus, dracaena, rubber plants, palms and bananas; and creepers, including bougainvillea, abutilons and plumbago, climb over the walls. Humming birds and sunbirds are among the many species that fly free here.

(*1*) *Daily (except 25 Dec) 10–6 or Sunset*
(*2*) *Charge*
(*3*) *Restaurant and bar*
(*4*) *Narrow-gauge railway; garden centre (same times)*
(*5*) *John Heyworth, Esq*

Buscot

Oxfordshire

6. Buscot Park

The house was built in the late 1770s by Edward Loveden Townsend; the park was probably landscaped, and the lake to the north-east of the house created, at this time. Early this century the 1st Lord Faringdon called in the architect and garden designer Harold Peto to create a link between house and lake. He made a formal, Italianate water garden, using a series of steps and a long, straight allée, with ornamental features such as marble seats, statuary and a balustraded bridge, and a rill confined by flagstone banks, sometimes falling in miniature cascades and sometimes forming basins and fountains.

(1) *Apr–Sep: Wed–Fri, 2nd and 4th Sat of every month and following Sun 2–6. No dogs*
(2) *Charge*
(4) *House (same times)*
(5) *National Trust*

Chastleton, nr Moreton-in-Marsh

Oxfordshire

7. Chastleton House

The house dates from 1603; the topiary garden was designed *c* 1700 and the lay-out has been little altered.

(1) *Mon–Fri 10.30–1, 2–5.30; Sat 2–5.30; Sun 2–5*
(2) *Charge*
(3) *Tea (Summer)*
(4) *House (same times)*
(5) *Mrs A. Clutton-Brock*

Chenies, nr Rickmansworth

Buckinghamshire

8. Manor House

The grounds around the early Tudor house are divided into a series of 'little gardens', a reconstruction of the Tudor flower and topiary gardens. There is a charming sunken garden, similar to the one at Hampton Court (cf), a topiary and herb garden and a long alley. The gardens are traversed by ancient escape passages. Visit in summer and autumn.

(1) *Wed and Thu 2–6; last Sun in Jun and 1st two in Jul 2–6. Parties at other times by arrangement*
(2) *Charge*
(4) *House (same times)*
(5) *Mr and Mrs Macleod Matthews*

Chicheley, nr Newport Pagnell

Buckinghamshire

9. Chicheley Hall

The house was built in 1719–23 by Francis Smith of Warwick and Sir John Chester, but at least part of the garden, including the three-sided canal on the south side of the house, was laid out in 1700 by Sir John Chester to the design of George London. With his partner Henry Wise, London planned the gardens at Hampton Court (cf). The grounds cover approx 25 acres (10 ha) of lake, woodland and formal and walled gardens. In June there is a fine display of roses.

(1) *Easter–Sep: Sat and Sun and Public Holidays 2.30–6*
(2) *Charge*
(3) *Refreshments*
(4) *House (same times; also late May–Sep: Wed and Thu 2.30–6)*
(5) *Hon Nicholas Beatty*

ENGLAND

Chiswell Green, nr St Albans

Hertfordshire

10. Royal National Rose Society's Garden

The 12 acre (4.9 ha) gardens were opened in 1960 and include a trial ground for new roses as well as a display garden, mainly designed by the late Harry Clacy, an architect, who was a vice-president of the Society. There are approx 30,000 roses of all types, used both formally and informally, including a section for old, historic roses. Visit from the beginning of July to mid-September.

(1) *Mid-Jun–mid-Sep: Mon–Sat 9–5; Sun 2–6. Members only mid-Sep–mid-Jun: Mon–Fri 9–5*
(2) *Charge (free to members of RNRS)*
(3) *Café*
(5) *Royal National Rose Society*

Chorleywood, Solesbridge Lane

Hertfordshire

11. Highlands Water Garden Nurseries

The nursery was founded in 1920 and was the first to specialize in water gardens. It covers over 15 acres (6 ha) and has the largest selection of aquatic and marginal plants in the country, with approx 150 varieties for sale.

(1) *Daily 10–5*
(2) *Free*
(5) *J. Kindler, Esq*

Cliveden, nr Maidenhead

Buckinghamshire

12. Cliveden

The formal gardens, which are still the basis of the present design, were laid out by Charles Bridgeman for the Earl of Orkney, probably in the 1720s. The present house was built in 1850–1 by Sir Charles Barry, replacing the original house by William Winde which was destroyed by fire. The arcaded terrace that still stands on the south side of the house was built by Winde some time after 1666. In 1852–3, Sir Charles Barry remodelled the parterre on the south side and there are now interlocking wedge-shaped beds, bordered with yew and planted with rosemary and lavender. Near the parterre, on the edge of chalk cliffs above the River Thames, stands the Octagon Temple, designed by Giacomo Leoni in the late 1730s and, below it, the path leads to Yew Tree Walk, whose trees were probably planted by the Earl of Orkney in the early 18th cent. North of the Octagon Temple, a path leads to a sheltered 'secret garden', originally conceived as an Italian garden but

59

converted into a cemetery and war memorial garden after World War I.

The Long Garden on the north side of the grounds was created by the 1st Lord Astor about the turn of the century. A long walk, bordered with box hedges and topiary, leads to a central circle with four 18th-cent stone figures. To the south of the main drive is a plantation of holm oaks, *Quercus ilex*, believed to have been planted by Frederick, Prince of Wales, in *c* 1747. The Water Garden, planted with magnolias, azaleas, bamboos and Japanese maples, was designed by Lord Astor in the 1890s. The Rhododendron Valley, to the east of the house, was first planted with rhododendrons in the 1850s, although many were added by the 1st and 2nd Lord Astors.

(1) *Wed–Sun, Good Friday and Public Holidays 11–6.30*
(2) *Charge*
(3) *Refreshments*
(4) *House (Apr–Oct: Sat and Sun 2.30–5.30)*
(5) *National Trust*

Hatfield

Hertfordshire

13. Hatfield House

The gardens were planned and planted by John Tradescant, gardener to James I and Robert Cecil, 1st Earl of Salisbury, who built the house between 1607 and 1611. They were extensively altered in the 18th cent, when they were landscaped, and then were partially returned to formality in the 19th and early 20th cents; much planning and planting is still being done.

Formal terraces link the house with the remaining wing of the Old Palace (where Elizabeth I was imprisoned as a child), with parterres containing permanent plantings of roses, shrubs or herbaceous perennials. On the east side lies a maze. A wilderness garden has good trees and rhododendrons and azaleas, and there is a newly planted scented and herb garden.

(1) *Easter–early Oct. Park: Daily 10.30–8; West Gardens: Tue–Sat noon–5; Sun 2–5.30; Mon 2–5; East Gardens (including maze): Mon 2–5*
(2) *Charge*
(3) *Restaurant and café*
(4) *House (Tue–Sat noon–5; Sun 2–5.30)*
(5) *Marquess of Salisbury*

Hitchin

Hertfordshire

14. Rose Garden

The present nursery has been devoted to specialist rose growing since 1936 and covers approx 60 acres (24 ha). Established plants make a good display, particularly in July, and the work of the hybridizing department is of interest in May and June.

(1) *Mon–Sat 9–5.30; Sun 11–5; some evenings in Jul. In Jan and Feb hours may be restricted in severe weather*
(2) *Free*
(4) *Nursery (same times); camping exhibition (Mar–Oct)*
(5) *R. Harkness and Co Ltd*

Knebworth

Hertfordshire

15. Knebworth House

The late 15th-cent mansion house has Gothic-style exterior decoration carried out by Sir Edward Bulwer-Lytton in 1843. The garden includes lawns, pleached lime avenues, roses and herbaceous borders.

(1) *Good Friday–Sep: Tue–Sun and Public Holidays 11.30–5.30; Oct: Sun 11.30–5.30*
(2) *Charge*
(3) *Licensed restaurant*
(4) *House (same times); deer park; narrow gauge railway (11–6)*
(5) *Hon David Lytton Cobbold*

Lambourn

Oxfordshire

16. Ashdown House

The house was built in the latter part of the 17th cent for the 1st Earl of Craven, possibly by the architect William Winde. In 1956 the property, in a near derelict state, was given to the National Trust by Cornelia, Countess of Craven. Apart from some tall Irish yews, little was left of the Victorian parterre to the south of the house and it now has been replaced by a new, simpler parterre with S-scrolls of box and gravel.

(1) *Apr: Wed 2–6; May–Sep: Wed and 1st and 3rd Sat of each month 2–6*
(2) *Charge*
(4) *House (same times)*
(5) *National Trust*

Little Gaddesden, nr Berkhamsted

Hertfordshire

17. Ashridge

The garden is based on plans drawn up in 1813 by Humphry Repton, who envisaged a series of small gardens. These were planted between 1814 and 1820 and since then many other features have been added. The rosarie is still basically as Repton planned it, with a wheel-spoke design planted now with modern floribunda and Hybrid Tea roses, shaded by a group of holm oaks, *Quercus ilex*. The Holy Well, at the centre of the Monks' Garden, is also close to Repton's design. The grotto, suggested by Repton, was built in 1851. The formal terrace, with clipped yews and seasonal bedding plants, is

Victorian in style and the Italian garden seems to date from the turn of the century. The conservatory, thought to have been built immediately after World War I, has its outside walls covered with *Campsis radicans* and *Vitis aconitifolia*.

Modern additions to the garden include the Lazell-Block garden, made from Westmorland water-worn limestone and planted with winter-flowering heathers, and the rose garden, made in the place of an ornamental herb garden. The Liquidambar Walk is a striking feature in autumn, when the leaves turn brilliant red.

(1) Apr–Oct: Sat, Sun and Public Holidays 2–6
(2) Charge
(4) House (4 days at Easter, 4 days over the Spring Bank Holiday weekend and 5 days at the end of Jul and early Aug 2–6)
(5) Governors of Ashridge Management College

Luton

Bedfordshire
18. Luton Hoo

The exterior of the house was begun by Robert Adam in 1767. The park was laid out by 'Capability' Brown in 1764–70, while the gardens proper were set out early this century by Romayne Walker, with lawns, herbaceous borders and a rose garden. A rock garden was created in the 1900s when it is at its best in May.

(1) Good Fri, Easter Sat and Mon 11–6; Easter Sun 2–6; late Apr–1 Oct: Mon, Wed, Thu, Sat 11–6; Sun 2–6
(2) Charge
(3) Restaurant
(4) House (same times)
(5) Wernher family

Milton, nr Abingdon

Oxfordshire
19. Milton Manor House

The original house was built in 1664, reputedly to a design by Inigo Jones; Georgian wings were later added and the garden was laid out. There are pleasure grounds with fine trees and a walled garden with a pond, shrubs and trees, a vegetable garden, cordon apple trees and a large greenhouse with peaches and nectarines. June and July are probably the best months to visit.

(1) Easter–early Oct: Sat and Sun 2–6
(2) Charge
(3) Refreshments
(4) House (same times)
(5) Surg Capt and Mrs E. J. Mockler

Mursley

Buckinghamshire
20. Stearthill

The 3 acre (1·4 ha) garden was created by Col Close-Smith and his wife. It is a typical English garden with lawns, herbaceous borders and shrubs, but the emphasis is on roses of which there is a large collection including species, old-fashioned and modern shrub roses, floribundas, Hybrid Teas and climbers. There is also an interesting semi-tropical glasshouse with a pool and seats among staged plants.

(1) Apr–Sep: Sun 2–6. Coaches weekdays, by appointment only
(2) Charge
(3) Tea
(4) Plants for sale
(5) Mrs R. S. G. Close-Smith

Newbury

Berkshire
21. Elcot Park Hotel

The original house was built in 1678, although additions have been made over the years. The 16 acre (7 ha) park which surrounds it was originally planned and laid out by Sir William Paxton in 1848, and in its heyday it was one of the showpieces of the county. A great variety of trees and shrubs, many uncommon, have been planted in the past 100 years. In spring, there is a fine display of daffodils and tree blossom, followed later on by rhododendrons.

(1) Daily during daylight hours
(2) Free (charge on two Sundays for NGS)
(3) Restaurant
(5) H. P. Sterne, Esq

Nuneham Courtenay

Oxfordshire
22. Nuneham Courtenay Arboretum

The arboretum started as an 8 acre (3.2 ha) pinetum designed by William Sawrey Gilpin as an addition to the landscape garden at Nuneham House. It now covers 50 acres (20 ha) and is an extension of the University of Oxford Botanic Garden (cf). Many of the old conifers, such as sequoias and cedars, still exist, and there has been much new planting of shrubs such as rhododendrons and camellias and heathers, as well as of trees.

(1) Apr–Oct: Mon–Sat 8.30–5
(2) Free
(5) University of Oxford

Nuneham Courtenay

23. Rose Nurseries

Mattock's Nursery was founded in 1875 by John Mattock at Headington, near Oxford; his great-grandsons now carry on the business, which was moved to its present site in 1960. From June to October over 70,000 roses are in flower in the rose fields and the garden; a notable feature is the 2 acre (0·9 ha) area planted with old garden roses, many of great historical interest. Several outstanding roses have been bred here, including 'Centurian', a fine red rose commemorating Mattock's hundred years of rose growing.

(1) *Mon–Sat 9–6 or Sunset; Sun 10–6 or Sunset*
(2) *Free*
(4) *Information centre (same times but closed 1–2); garden shop*
(5) *John Mattock Ltd*

Oxford

24. Balliol College

The college was founded in 1263 and the garden has been continuously cultivated, though re-modelled, since then. The Master's and Fellows' Gardens are not open to the public, but the quadrangles are; a wide variety of shrubs are trained up the walls of the buildings. In February and March, spring bulbs make a fine show and in May, and July to October, bedding plants take over the display.

(1) *Daily 10.30–5 (except 10 days at Christmas, 10 days at Easter and 3 weeks in Aug and early Sep)*
(2) *Free*
(5) *Master and Scholars of Balliol College*

Oxford

25. New College

The college was founded in 1379 and the garden, too, has a long history. A print dating from the 1670s shows a formal garden with a Mound in the centre, as was often a feature of Tudor gardens, with paths bordered with low hedges, probably box or yew, leading to a summer house on a higher level. Records state that the Mound was started in 1529–30 when 500 wagon loads of rubbish were used for its foundation. An early 19th-cent print shows the Mound in a state of collapse but the remains of it still exist with a number of trees growing on it including an ilex, *Quercus ilex*; a Lucombe oak, *Q. × hispanica*; a Manna ash, *Fraxinus ornus* and a golden yew. Recently more trees and shrubs have been planted on it.

Over the centuries the garden has changed but some old trees remain, such as a group of horse chestnuts and a tulip-tree, *Liriodendron tulipifera*. The rose on the west side of the Cloisters is the same rose from which Florence Nightingale was given a spray when she visited the college and the wistaria on the east face of the north range of the Garden Quad is thought to have been planted *c* 1830. Many evergreens were planted in the 19th cent while a mulberry in the sunken lawn was planted between the two world wars.

Recent plantings include a fastigiate hornbeam; a tree of heaven, *Ailanthus altissima*; a dawn redwood, *Metasequoia glyptostroboides*; a maidenhair tree, *Ginkgo biloba* and a handkerchief tree, *Davidia involucrata*. The garden contains the finest remaining section of the old city wall. Visit in March–April and July–August.

(1) *University terms: Daily 2–5; Vacations: Daily 11–5*
(2) *Free*
(3) *Tea (Jul and Aug)*
(4) *College Hall and Chapel (same times)*
(5) *Warden and Fellows of New College*

Oxford

26. Queen's College

Most of the grounds have been in the possession of the college since its foundation in 1341. They consist of a series of small gardens, not all of which are open to the public, separated by old stone walls and containing some rare shrubs. Visit in April and May.

(1) *University terms: Mon–Sat 2–5; Sun 10–5; Vacations: Daily 10–5*
(2) *Free*
(4) *Chapel, Hall and quadrangle (same times)*
(5) *Master, Fellows and Scholars of Queen's College*

Oxford

27. St John's College

The grounds were laid out in the style of 'Capability' Brown in 1776–7 and the general pattern remains the same, although a large rock garden was added between 1893 and 1900, and flower borders were planted around the lawn in the present century, with particularly fine displays of irises, peonies, shrub roses and azaleas. Visit from April to June.

(1) *Mon–Sat 1–5; Sun 9–1. Closed on Public Holidays*
(2) *Free*
(4) *College Hall and quadrangle (same times)*
(5) *Master, Fellows and Scholars of St John's College*

Oxford

28. Trinity College

The college was founded in 1554 by Sir

Thomas Pope on the site of the monastic Durham College, and the buildings date from the 14th to the 20th cents. The gardens are composed mainly of lawns and herbaceous borders, with some fine trees.

(1) *Daily (except 24–26 Dec, Easter weekend and mid-Aug–mid-Sep) 2–Sunset*
(2) *Free*
(4) *College and Chapel (same times)*
(5) *Master, Fellows and Scholars of Trinity College*

Oxford, Rose Lane

29. University Botanic Garden

This is the oldest botanical garden in the country, founded in 1621 by Henry Danvers, Earl of Danby, on the site of the old Jewish cemetery. The main gateway was designed by Inigo Jones. Besides the botanical specimens, there are collections of old roses, variegated plants and tropical and sub-tropical plants, including ones of economic importance. Just outside the gate facing the High Street is a memorial rose garden designed by Dame Sylvia Crowe after World War II.

(1) *Garden. Mar–Oct: Mon–Sat 8.30–5; Sun 10–noon, 2–6; Oct–Mar: Mon–Sat 9–4.30; Sun 10–noon, 2–4.30. Glasshouses. Daily 2–4*
(2) *Free*
(5) *University of Oxford*

Oxford

30. Worcester College

The grounds of Worcester College were landscaped between 1817 and 1821 according to the well-established principles of providing variety, surprise, flowing lines and a lake. There are some fine specimen trees, including Indian bean-tree, *Catalpa bignonioides*; tulip-tree, *Liriodendron tulipifera*; maidenhair tree, *Ginkgo biloba*; tree of heaven, *Ailanthus altissima* and weeping ash, *Fraxinus excelsior* 'Pendula'.

(1) *University terms: 2–Sunset; Vacations: 9–noon, 2–Sunset*
(2) *Free*
(5) *Master, Fellows and Scholars of Worcester College*

Pusey, nr Faringdon

Oxfordshire

31. Pusey House

The present house, believed to have been designed by John Wood of Bath, was built in 1748. The garden, originally landscaped in the style of 'Capability' Brown, was altered in the mid-19th cent by Philip Pusey, possibly on the advice of J. C. Loudon, the garden writer and designer. The stream was later enlarged into a lake, although the Chinese bridge dates from the mid-18th cent.

The house changed hands in 1935 and the garden was redesigned in 1937 by Geoffrey Jellicoe, who added a wide stone terrace on the south side of the house and introduced many more flowering shrubs and plants. One of the features of the garden is a herbaceous border over 150 yds (137 m) long, with blue the predominating colour. Another area is planted largely with old-fashioned roses. Beyond the Chinese bridge is the water garden, planted with primulas, yellow loosestrife *Lysimachia punctata* and hostas. There are many interesting trees, including several species of maple such as *Acer capillipes*, *A. drummondii* and *A. griseum*. Maples are noted for their autumnal colours, and this is further provided by *Cercidiphyllum japonicum* and *Liquidambar styraciflua*. Lady Emily's Garden is a walled area planted largely with roses and silver-leaved plants.

(1) *25 March–1 Jul: Wed, Thu, Sun and Public Holidays 2–6; 4 Jul–19 Oct: Tue–Thu, Sat, Sun and Public Holidays 2–6*
(2) *Charge*
(3) *Tea*
(5) *Pusey Garden Trust*

Rotherfield Greys, nr Henley-on-Thames

Oxfordshire

32. Greys Court

The Jacobean manor house has a complex of outbuildings, some Tudor, including the Bachelors' Hall (now called the Dower House), the Old Stables and the Well House with a donkey wheel. In a small courtyard between the stables and the Bachelors' Hall is a medieval archway leading into a rose garden, planted mainly with old-fashioned roses, which in turn leads to a circular walled garden containing some very old wistarias, and beyond that, fruit and vegetables and flower borders. East of the Bachelors' Hall is a very fine tulip-tree and a weeping ash. A garden of Japanese cherries and a Swiss 18th-cent fountain are enclosed by the walls of the old tithe barn, while the tower garden is planted with white flowers and shrubs and has a lily-pond. Beyond the kitchen garden is a nut avenue underplanted with daffodils and over the ha-ha there are irises and shrubs. In front of the house there are banks of cistus, rosemary and lavender.

The grounds contain some very old trees, including a larch to the north-west of the house that is thought to be one of the oldest in the country.

(1) *Apr–Sep: Mon–Sat 2.15–6*
(2) *Charge*
(3) *Tea (Sat and Public Holidays and at other times for booked parties)*

(4) House (dates as garden: Mon, Wed and Fri 2.15–6)
(5) National Trust

Silsoe

Bedfordshire

33. Wrest Park

About 9 acres (4 ha) of the garden were laid out early in the 18th cent in the French style with a long canal pool sited between groups of trees and leading to the domed Archer pavilion. The woodland has intersecting paths with statues and other garden ornaments strategically placed. 'Capability' Brown worked here later in the 18th cent and, untypically, left the formal area intact; he surrounded it with a winding, artificial river. In the 19th cent an Italian-style garden was made, linking the French garden with a new house. It has formal terraces, parterres, statues and clipped evergreens.

(1) May–Sep: Sat, Sun and Public Holidays 10–7
(2) Collecting box for GSO
(3) Refreshments
(5) National Institute for Agricultural Engineering

Stagsden

Bedfordshire

34. Stagsden Bird Gardens

The gardens, 8 acres (3·2 ha) in extent, have a large collection of shrub and species roses as well as modern varieties, mainly located in the East Garden, but also planted throughout the grounds. Visit in June and early July.

(1) Daily 11–7 or Sunset
(2) Charge
(3) Kiosk; tea (Summer)
(4) Rare pheasants; old breeds of poultry; collection of waterfowl
(5) Mr and Mrs R. E. Rayment

Steeple Aston

Oxfordshire

35. Rousham House

This is one of the classic landscape gardens of England, the most complete surviving example of the work of William Kent. He began work here in the 1730s and the garden is designed as a series of scenes, each leading to a new vista, with cascades, a stone-lined stream, a valley enclosed by woods and a wide avenue with a statue of Hercules at one end and a temple at the other.

(1) Daily 10–6
(2) Charge
(4) House (Apr–Sep: Wed and Sun 2–6; parties by arrangement)
(5) C. Cottrell-Dormer, Esq

Stowe

Buckinghamshire

36. Stowe Gardens

This is one of the most important landscape gardens in England and most of the great names of 17th- and 18th-cent design are associated with the house or garden. Although small formal gardens already existed here, it was in c 1715 that the important work began when Sir Richard Temple, later Viscount Cobham, engaged Charles Bridgeman to design the gardens. He built ha-has to open the garden to the surrounding countryside and made a parterre and a central walk to an octagonal lake.

In c 1730 William Kent, the 'inventor' of landscape gardening, came to work at Stowe. He altered Bridgeman's straight lines and changed the octagonal lake to an informal shape, and developed the eastern area of the park creating the parts known as the Elysian Fields and the Grecian Valley. He and others, including Sir John Vanbrugh, designed the many garden buildings and temples. One of the best known is the Temple of British Worthies, containing busts of heroes, poets and philosophers. 'Capability' Brown came to work at Stowe as head gardener in 1741 and his influence can also be seen.

(1) Mid-Jul–early-Sep: Daily 10–6; also some days during Easter school holidays
(2) Charge
(5) Governors of Stowe School

Waddesdon, nr Aylesbury

Buckinghamshire

37. Waddesdon Manor

The house was designed in the style of a French château for Baron Ferdinand de Rothschild by the French architect Gabriel-Hippolyte Destailleur in 1874–89; the gardens were laid out by the French landscape gardener Lainé. Around the house are formal terraces, one planned around a large, elaborate aviary. Flowerbeds are filled with seasonal bedding, and there is much use of statuary and fountains. The park contains some fine specimen trees.

(1) Late Mar–late Oct: Wed–Sat 2–6; Sun 11.30–6; Public Holidays 11–6
(2) Charge
(4) House (late Mar–late Oct: Wed–Sun 2–6)
(5) National Trust

Watford, Nascot Wood Road

Hertfordshire

38. Cheslyn Gardens

There are approx 4 acres (1·6 ha) of grounds, which comprise a large area of woodland garden with many fine trees, including acers and cedars, and rhododen-

drons and azaleas. Elsewhere there are
lawns with bedding displays and herbaceous borders and a pond.

(1) May–Sep: Daily (except Tue and Thu)
    10–5; Oct–Apr: Daily (except Tue and
    Thu) 10–4
(2) Free
(4) Aviary (same times)
(5) Watford Borough Council

West Wycombe
Buckinghamshire
39. West Wycombe Park

The original house was built between 1710
and 1715, but it was considerably extended
by Sir Francis Dashwood, later Lord
Despencer, between 1735 and 1781. He was
largely responsible for the lay-out of the
park in a semi-formal style, with a mixture
of straight avenues and winding paths, the
great lake and cascade and serpentine
streams. The garden temples were built at
the same period. Thomas Cook, a pupil of
'Capability' Brown, worked here after 1770
and probably gave the landscape a more
'natural' appearance; Humphry Repton was
employed in c 1794–5, but seems to have
effected few changes beyond thinning the
trees and demolishing some of the buildings.
The architect Nicholas Revett worked at
West Wycombe and was responsible for
some of the garden buildings, including the
Music Temple on the island in the lake.

(1) Easter and Spring Bank Holiday Sun
    and Mon 2.15–6; Jun: Mon–Fri
    2.15–6; Jul and Aug: Sun–Fri 2.15–6
(2) Charge
(4) House (Jun: Mon–Fri 2.15–6; Jul and
    Aug: Sun–Fri 2.15–6)
(5) National Trust

Wing
Buckinghamshire
40. Ascott

The present house dates mainly from the
latter half of the 19th cent. The 30 acre (12
ha) gardens were laid out later in the same
century by Leopold de Rothschild, with the
advice of Sir Harry Veitch of the Chelsea
nursery firm of James Veitch & Son, and
combine formal and informal styles. Below
the house lies a series of grass terraces with,
at one end, a topiary sundial made from
clipped box. The central feature of the
terrace is an ornamental pool with a large
bronze fountain group by the American
sculptor Julian Story, who was also responsible for a marble fountain in a formal
flower garden west of the terrace. There are
two rock gardens, one made from tufa; a
lily-pond with several varieties of water-lily,
and numerous fine specimen trees, many
selected for their autumn colour.

(1) Apr–Sep: Wed, Sat and Public
    Holidays 2–6; Jul and Aug: Sun also
(2) Charge

ENGLAND

(4) House (same times)
(5) National Trust

Woburn, nr Bletchley
Bedfordshire
41. Woburn Abbey

The abbey was founded in 1145 by the
Cistercian Order but most of the present
house was built in 1750–60. The 3,000 acre
(1200 ha) deer park was designed by
Humphry Repton in 1802, with rolling turf,
clumps of trees and lakes. The gardens
proper surrounding the house cover 40
acres (16 ha) and include lawns and many
specimen trees, a rock garden and an
octagonal 'Chinese dairy', designed by
Henry Holland, set beside a pool. A curving
glasshouse designed by Sir Jeffry Wyatville
in c 1818 is now used as a camellia house.

(1) Late Mar–Aug: Mon–Sat 10.30–5;
    Sun 10–5; Sep–late Oct: Mon–Sat 11–
    4.30; Sun 11–5; late Mar–late Oct:
    Daily 11–3.30
(2) Charge
(3) Restaurant; bar
(4) Wild Animal Kingdom (Daily from 10);
    Garden centre, pottery (same times as
    grounds); Antique centre (Daily from
    10); House (late Mar–Aug: Mon–Sat
    11.30–5.45; Sun 11.30–6.15; Sep–late
    Oct: Mon–Sat 11.30–5.15; Sun 11.30–
    5.45; late Oct–late Mar: Daily 1–4.30;
    last admission 45 mins before closing)
(5) Marquess of Tavistock and the
    Trustees of the Bedford Estates

Woodstock
Oxfordshire
42. Blenheim Palace

The gardens were originally laid out for the
1st Duke of Marlborough by Queen Anne's
gardener, Henry Wise. A military garden, as
it was then called, there were terraces and
parterres, outlined in dwarf box, leading to a
'formal wilderness'. Sir John Vanbrugh, the
architect of the palace, constructed a canal
and built the elaborate stone bridge. In the
1760s 'Capability' Brown was called in and
he swept away the formal garden in accordance with the new fashion for landscape
gardening. He widened the canal into a
serpentine lake and constructed a cascade at
the western end. He left the elm avenues and
Wise's kitchen garden with its massive
walls.

In the early years of the 20th cent the 9th
Duke of Marlborough decided to restore
formal plantings near the palace and employed the French landscape architect
Achille Duchêne. He made the Italian
garden, a parterre with scrolls of clipped
box, and later, in the 1920s, he made the
water parterre, reminiscent of the one at
Versailles and now one of the most striking
features of the garden.

ENGLAND

(1) *Late Mar–Oct: Daily 11.30–5*
(2) *Charge*
(3) *Refreshments*
(4) *House (same times); Park; Garden centre (9–5)*
(5) *Duke of Marlborough*

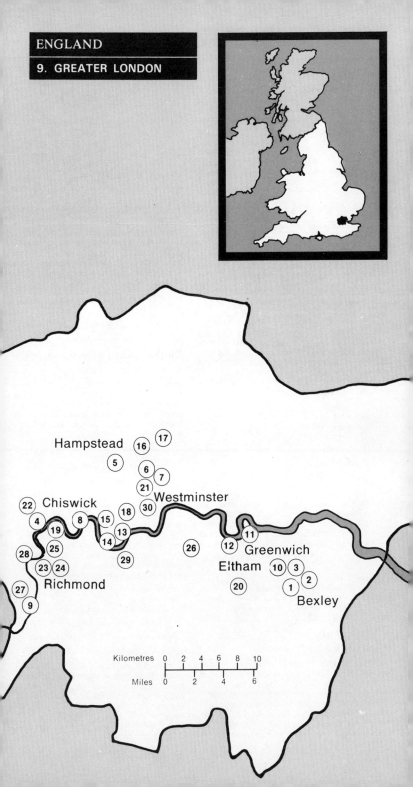

Hampstead

Chiswick

Westminster

Richmond

Greenwich

Eltham

Bexley

Kilometres 0 2 4 6 8 10

Miles 0 2 4 6

ENGLAND

Bexley, Bourne Road

1. Hall Place

The house is partly medieval and partly Georgian. The grounds include a notable display of topiary, with a set depicting the Queen's Beasts, an enclosed flower garden, rose garden, water garden, rock garden, heather garden and herb garden with a wide range of medicinal and culinary herbs with labels in braille. A conservatory contains floral displays and a collection of exotic plants.

(1) Garden. Mon–Fri 7.30–Sunset: Sat and Sun 9–Sunset; closed 25 Dec. Conservatory. Daily 10.30–12.30, 1.30–4.30
(2) Free
(4) House (Mon–Sat 10–Sunset)
(5) London Borough of Bexley, Parks, Recreation and Cemeteries Dept

Bexley

2. Lesnes Abbey Wood

This was originally the site of a 12th-cent abbey destroyed during the Dissolution of the Monasteries. Its main item of interest is the magnificent display of 20 acres (8 ha) of wild daffodil, in late March and April, although it is also worth a visit in autumn for the autumn colours.

(1) Daily
(2) Free
(3) Refreshments
(5) Greater London Council

Bexleyheath

3. Danson Park

The grounds, which include a 20 acre (8 ha) boating lake, were landscaped by 'Capability' Brown in c 1760. Notable features include a rhododendron and heather garden, a heather walk, a rock and water garden and an old-fashioned garden.

(1) Mon–Fri 7.30–Sunset; Sat and Sun 9–Sunset
(2) Free
(4) Boating; angling; putting; bowls; tennis
(5) London Borough of Bexley, Parks, Recreation and Cemeteries Dept

Brentford

4. Syon Park

The 60 acre (24 ha) grounds were designed by 'Capability' Brown in c 1770; the Great Conservatory, with its large glazed dome, was designed by Charles Fowler and built in c 1820. The grounds include many fine specimen trees, including species of oak and maple, several good examples of the swamp cypress, *Taxodium distichum*, and species

of zelkova. In the 1960s, part of Syon Park was set aside as a permanent gardening exhibition; a 6 acre (2·2 ha) rose garden is planted with more than 12,000 roses of over 300 varieties and herbaceous perennials are displayed in island beds.

(1) Apr–Sep: Daily 10–6; Oct–Mar: Daily 10–5 or Sunset
(2) Charge
(3) Café and restaurant
(4) Aviary, insectarium and aquarium in Great Conservatory (same times); Garden centre (Daily 10–5.15); World of Motoring Exhibition (Daily 10–5)
(5) Duke of Northumberland

Camden

5. Kilburn Grange Park

The 8 acre (3·6 ha) park was once part of the Grange estate and was opened to the public in 1913. It includes an old English garden surrounded by flowering shrubs and reached through an arbour covered in roses, clematis and wistaria.

(1) Daily 7.30–Sunset
(2) Free
(3) Kiosk
(5) London Borough of Camden

Camden, Gray's Inn Road, WC1

6. St Andrew's Gardens

This 2 acre (0·9 ha) garden, on the site of an 18th- and 19th-cent burial ground, was opened to the public in 1885. There are lawns, rosebeds and good displays of bedding plants and an old weeping ash, *Fraxinus excelsior* 'Pendula'.

(1) 7.30–Sunset
(2) Free
(5) London Borough of Camden

Camden

7. St George's Gardens

Opened to the public in the 1880s, this is on the site of an early 18th-cent burial ground, and some old stone memorials remain. Paths wind among lawns, trees, shrubs and bedding plants, and there is a rock garden and a scented garden for the blind.

(1) 7.30–Sunset
(2) Free
(5) London Borough of Camden

Chiswick

8. Chiswick House

The grounds, 66 acres (26·5 ha) of a large estate dating from at least the beginning of the 17th cent, were laid out in more or less their present form in the 1730s and were the first in England in the new Italianate, picturesque style. Lord Burlington, and William Kent, who designed the Palladian villa, collaborated also on the lay-out of the gardens; Charles Bridgeman was also involved. There are formal vistas, a temple, summer houses, Classical statuary and obelisks and a serpentine strip of water. Later additions include a bridge by James Wyatt; a 19th-cent conservatory by Joseph Paxton, designer of the Crystal Palace; and there are displays of seasonal bedding. The grounds have been neglected, but some restoration work is taking place.

(1) *Daily Sunrise–Sunset*
(2) *Free*
(3) *Kiosk (Summer)*
(4) *House (May–Sep: Daily 9.30–1, 2–7; Oct: Daily 9.30–1, 2–5.30; Nov–Feb: Wed–Sun 9.30–1, 2–4; Mar: Wed–Sun 9.30–1, 2–5.30)*
(5) *London Borough of Hounslow (House: Dept of the Environment)*

East Molesey

9. Hampton Court Palace

Although Cardinal Wolsey made a garden here in the early 16th cent, the gardens as they are today date mainly from the late 17th cent, when they were laid out by the nurserymen George London and Henry Wise in the formal French style, with parterres, radiating avenues of trees, a canal pool, and clipped trees and shrubs. The maze was planted in Queen Anne's time. The famous Great Vine near the end of the formal Privy Garden, planted in 1769, is thought to be the oldest vine in the country. The orangery was designed by Sir Christopher Wren; the wilderness is planted with daffodils, primulas and lilies. More recent additions include the knot garden, laid out in 1924 as an example of the type of garden fashionable in the late 16th cent, the reconstructed herb garden, and a large rose garden in the old tilt-yard.

(1) *Dec–Feb: 7.30–Sunset; Mar–Nov: 7–Sunset*
(2) *Free*
(3) *Restaurant*
(4) *State Apartments, Great Hall and Lower Orangery (Mar–Apr and Oct: Mon–Sat 9.30–5; Sun 2–5; May–Sep: Mon–Sat 9.30–6; Sun 11–6; Nov–Feb: Mon–Sat 9.30–4; Sun 2–4; closed 24–26 Dec, 1 Jan and Good Friday. Charge); Great kitchen and cellars, banqueting house and Tudor tennis court, Vine (Apr–Sep times as above. Free); Maze (May–Sep: Mon–Sat 10–6; Oct and Mar–Apr 10–5; Sun as above but opening at 11); Upper Orangery (Apr–Sep: as State Apartments but closed Mon)*
(5) *Dept of the Environment*

Eltham

10. Avery Hill Winter Garden

The winter garden was built in c 1890 by Col J. T. North, then owner of the Avery Hill estate, as a place to exercise during

'inclement weather'. It is 100 ft (30·5 m) square and 90 ft (27·4 m) high, with a total length of glass of 750 ft (228·6 m); the roof is supported by iron pillars. The estate was bought by the London County Council in 1902.

There are three temperature-controlled glasshouses containing trees, shrubs, herbaceous plants and ferns from all over the world. A notable feature is a Chinese palm, at least 100 years old, presented by the Royal Botanic Gardens, Kew (cf) when the garden was reopened to the public in 1962 after war damage, which stands under the centre of the glass dome in the temperate house. The adjoining cool house contains plants such as camellias, oleanders and acacias set around an ornamental pool with fountains. The tropical house includes bananas, coconut palms and pineapples.

The park at Avery Hill also has 19 acres (7·6 ha) of plant nurseries where most of the plants used in the GLC parks are grown, and part of this is open to the public.

(1) *Mon–Fri 1–4; Sat and Sun 11–4 (except 25 Dec and the 1st Sun of each month)*
(2) *Free*
(5) *Greater London Council*

Greenwich

11. Castlewood, with Jackwood and Oxleas

These properties together make up almost 300 acres (121 ha) of woodland and include the 18th-cent Severndroog 'Castle' with steep terracing and a beautiful rose garden; also the fine terraced garden with mellow brick walls and a fountain at Jackwood, set among woodland with oak, silver birch and hornbeam.

(1) *Daily*
(2) *Free*
(3) *Café*
(4) *Putting green*
(5) *Greater London Council*

Greenwich

12. Greenwich Park

Greenwich Park was the first of the Royal Parks to be enclosed: the licence was granted in 1433 by Henry VI to his uncle, Humphrey, Duke of Gloucester. The Queen's House, designed by Inigo Jones, now forms part of the National Maritime Museum, and the Old Royal Observatory has a collection of astronomical instruments. The park is set out with tree-lined avenues, woodland dells, a lake, a rose garden and a flower garden, with herbaceous borders and a dahlia border, at its most colourful in late August, and bedding plants. The park has many fine specimen trees, including magnolias and catalpas.

(1) Traffic. Daily 7—Sunset. Pedestrians. Daily 6—Sunset
(2) Free
(3) Tea
(4) National Maritime Museum; Old Royal Observatory (Mon—Fri 10—5; Sat 10—6; Sun 2.30—6)
(5) Dept of the Environment, Royal Parks Divison

Hammersmith

13. Fulham Palace Grounds and Botanic Garden

About 11 acres (5 ha) of the grounds of Fulham Palace, former residence of the Bishops of London, are open to the public and consist mainly of sweeping lawns and fine mature trees, including cedar of Lebanon, *Cedrus libani*, black walnut, *Juglans nigra*, and recent plantings of species of acer and magnolia. Part of the former kitchen garden has been developed as an educational Botanic Garden. Plant families of use to man, such as *Gramineae* (grasses), *Rosaceae* (roses), *Umbelliferae* (parsley) and *Cruciferae* (cabbage) are well represented. There is also a newly established woodland garden and collections of heathers and bulbous plants.

(1) Palace Grounds. Daily 7.30—Sunset. Botanic Garden. Apr—Oct (same times)
(2) Free
(5) London Borough of Hammersmith

Hammersmith

14. Memorial Gardens, Bishop's Park

Bishop's Park, over 30 acres (12 ha) in extent, has a long stretch of riverside walk, bordered with London planes. The Memorial Gardens, occupying a section of the park, have recently been laid out as a garden for the blind. The design is informal with an emphasis on aromatic shrubs such as rosemary and lavender, and on plants with textured leaves, such as hostas, to provide contrasting surfaces to touch.

(1) Daily Sunrise—Sunset
(2) Free
(5) London Borough of Hammersmith

Hammersmith

15. Ravenscourt Park

The park covers over 30 acres (12 ha); the most interesting feature is the scented garden for the blind which is set in an old walled garden and has a formal lay-out, with a central fish-pool surrounded by herbs, old roses and scented shrubs. Many have grey-green foliage and the flowers are all in pastel colours – white, pink, pale blue and pale yellow, for the benefit of those with partial sight.

(1) Daily Sunrise—Sunset
(2) Free
(5) London Borough of Hammersmith

Hampstead

16. Fenton House

The 1¼ acre (0·7 ha) garden is large for a town house. Most of its lies behind the 17th-cent house, enclosed within high brick walls with fine wrought-iron gates by Jean Tijou. The terrace walks are probably relics of the original 17th-cent design when they would have overlooked a sunken parterre. Visit in summer.

(1) 2 Jan—Mar and Nov: Sat and Sun 2—5; Apr: Wed—Sat and Public Holidays 11—5; Sun 2—5 or Sunset; closed Good Friday
(2) Free
(4) House (same times)
(5) National Trust

Highgate

17. Waterlow Park

The 27 acre (12 ha) park was given to the public by Sir Sydney Waterlow in 1889. It is set on an undulating hillside and contains rock gardens, a scented garden for the blind, shrubberies, herbaceous borders and an unusual three-level lake. The fine specimen trees include copper beech; silver lime; golden catalpa, *Catalpa bignonioides* var. *aurea*; tulip-tree, *Liriodendron tulipifera*; maidenhair tree, *Ginkgo biloba*; and hand-kerchief tree, *Davidia involucrata*. Within the grounds is Lauderdale House, where Charles II and Nell Gwyn are said to have stayed; near the house is a sundial that is level with the top of St Paul's Cathedral.

(1) Daily 7.30—Sunset
(2) Free
(5) London Borough of Camden

Kensington

18. Kensington Gardens

The gardens are approx 230 acres (93 ha) in extent. The Flower Walk, with ornamental trees, herbaceous perennials and bedding plants, has been planned so that there is colour from early spring to autumn. The Broad Walk is flanked by limes and Norway maples and off it, beside Kensington Palace, lies the Sunken Garden, formal in design with a rectangular pond and flowerbeds, and surrounded by pleached limes.

(1) Daily 5 am—Sunset
(2) Free
(3) Restaurant
(4) Kensington Palace (Mar—Sep: Mon—Sat 10—6; Sun 2—6; Oct and Feb: Mon—Sat 10—5; Sun 2—5; Nov—Jan: Mon—Sat 10—4; Sun 2—4)

(5) *Dept of the Environment, Royal Parks Division*

Kew

19. The Royal Botanic Gardens

The gardens were started in *c* 1759 by Augusta, Dowager Princess of Wales, and became famous during the reign of George III when Sir Joseph Banks was the unofficial Director and William Aiton the Head Gardener. In 1841 the gardens were taken over by the State; the first Director was Sir William Hooker who increased their size from their original 9 acres (3·6 ha) to over 200 (80 ha) and started the Herbarium, Library and the Department of Economic Botany and Museums.

Part of the gardens were landscaped by 'Capability' Brown – he made the long lake and the dell now used for rhododendrons. In the mid-19th cent this was planted up as a Himalayan rhododendron valley, but now many of the plants are garden hybrids. Although the peak season for the rhododendrons is May, some flowers can be seen from January to August. There is also a collection of rhododendron species, underplanted with primulas, meconopsis and hostas. There are collections of many other groups of plants, including oaks, elms, poplars, limes, birches, lilacs and conifers. 'Individual' gardens include the azalea garden, heath garden, rock garden and scree beds, rose garden, bamboo garden and the Queen's Garden. The last is a replica of a 17th-cent garden, formal in design, with pleached alleys, parterres, a fountain and a gazebo. Only plants known to have been grown in gardens in the 17th cent are planted here.

A notable feature of Kew is the glasshouses, dominated by the huge palm house designed by Decimus Burton and built in 1844–8. Other houses include the tropical water-lily house, the temperate house, the succulent house, orchid houses, alpine house, Australian house, tropical and temperate fern houses and filmy fern house. The orangery was built in 1761 to the design of Sir William Chambers and now contains the bookstall as well as a collection of citrus and ferns.

(1) *Daily (except 25 Dec and 1 Jan) 10–4 or 8, according to season. Glasshouses open at 11*
(2) *Charge*
(3) *Refreshments*
(4) *Bookstall*
(5) *Ministry of Agriculture, Fisheries and Food*

Lewisham

20. Horniman Gardens

The 11 acres (5 ha) of gardens, opened in 1895, surround the Horniman Museum which houses a fine archaeological collection. There are lawns, a rose garden, a wide variety of trees and shrubs and a rock garden.

(1) *Daily*
(2) *Free*
(3) *Café*
(4) *Museum*
(5) *Greater London Council*

Marylebone

21. Regent's Park

Regent's Park began as Marylebone Park, enclosed as a hunting park by Henry VIII. Remodelling started in 1812, and it was opened to the public under its new name in 1835. The flower gardens along the Broad Walk are kept colourful with bedding plants, but the most interesting part of the park from the horticultural point of view is Queen Mary's Garden, within the area known as the Inner Circle. This is one of the finest rose gardens in the world, with large beds, generally with considerable blocks of one variety. It was begun in 1932 and new varieties are constantly being added. As well as the roses, there are herbaceous borders and a lake with an island in it built up as a rock garden.

(1) *Daily 5 am–Sunset (gates to Outer Circle 7–midnight)*
(2) *Free*
(3) *Restaurant*
(4) *Dept of the Environment, Royal Parks Division*

Osterley

22. Osterley Park

The original Elizabethan house was greatly altered by the architect Robert Adam between 1760 and 1780; the Tudor stable block still remains. It is set in grounds of 140 acres (56 ha) that consist mainly of lawns and specimen trees, including some fine cedars believed to have been planted in 1764, and three lakes formed by damming a stream. A semi-circular garden house built by Robert Adam *c* 1780 faces another garden temple believed to date from 1720.

(1) *Daily 10–8 or Sunset*
(2) *Free*
(3) *Refreshments (Summer)*
(4) *House (Apr–Sep: Tue–Sun and Public Holidays 2–6; Oct–Mar: Tue–Sun noon–4; closed on Good Friday, 24–26 Dec and 1 Jan. Charge)*
(5) *National Trust and Victoria and Albert Museum, London*

Petersham

23. Ham House

The garden surrounding the Jacobean house has one of the few remaining 17th-cent layouts, with a terrace, parterres and a wil-

71

derness. This has recently been restored and must now once again resemble what the diarist John Evelyn saw and described when he visited Ham House in 1678.

(1) *Apr–Sep: Tue–Sun and Public Holidays 2–6; Oct–Mar: same days noon–4; closed on Good Friday, 24–26 Dec and 1 Jan. No dogs*
(2) *Free*
(4) *House (same times); shop*
(5) *National Trust and Victoria and Albert Museum, London*

Richmond
24. Isabella Plantation, Richmond Park

The Isabella Plantation is a 42 acre (18 ha) woodland garden set in the middle of the 2,500 acre (1000 ha) Royal Richmond Park. Rhododendrons, azaleas, magnolias, camellias and other woodland subjects grow under a canopy of oaks. The stream and three ponds have waterside plantings of primulas and meconopsis. The garden serves also as a bird sanctuary.

(1) *Summer: 7–Sunset; Winter: 7.30– Sunset*
(2) *Free*
(4) *Richmond Park*
(5) *Dept of the Environment, Royal Parks Division*

Richmond
25. Terrace Gardens

The Terrace Gardens were opened in May 1887, having been formed from the grounds of three large private estates. In 1977 a Silver Jubilee plaque was unveiled describing what can be seen. The gardens are laid out with lawns, trees and flowering shrubs.

(1) *Daily*
(2) *Free*
(5) *London Borough of Richmond*

Southwark
26. Dulwich Park

This 72 acre (29 ha) park is noted for its fine display of rhododendrons and azaleas in spring, and there is also a rock garden, silver birches and other fine trees and a sculpture by Barbara Hepworth.

(1) *Daily*
(2) *Free*
(3) *Café*
(4) *Putting; boating; aviary*
(5) *Greater London Council*

Teddington
27. Bushy Park

Bushy Park covers more than 1,000 acres (402 ha) and was laid out soon after 1514, when Cardinal Wolsey took over Hampton Court Palace (cf). The famous chestnut avenue was laid out by Sir Christopher Wren. The Waterhouse Plantations are woodland gardens, themselves 100 acres (40 ha) in extent, with a watercourse and the Longford River, made by Charles I, running through them. Planting was started in 1949 by J. W. Fisher using many rhododendrons, species and hybrids, camellias and azaleas. There are many other interesting trees, and shade and moisture-loving herbaceous plants such as *Meconopsis betonicifolia*, primulas, hostas and rodgersias. Visit from April to June.

(1) *Daily*
(2) *Free*
(3) *Tea*
(5) *Dept of the Environment, Royal Parks Division*

Twickenham
28. York House

The 17th-cent mansion is now the offices of Richmond Borough Council. The garden in front of the house is colourful with seasonal bedding; behind it is a sunken lawn, flower-beds, herbaceous borders, shrubberies, a water garden and some fine specimen trees. A notable feature is the large group of Italian marble statuary of maidens disporting themselves in a fountain. A bridge leads from the main garden over a road to a terrace overlooking the Thames.

(1) *Daily*
(2) *Free*
(5) *London Borough of Richmond*

Wandsworth
29. Battersea Park

Probably the most striking thing about this park is the fine specimen trees, including *Catalpa bignonioides* and *Paulownia tomentosa* set out on wide lawns. There are also flowering shrubs and flowerbeds giving a fine show throughout the summer.

(1) *Daily*
(2) *Free*
(3) *Café*
(4) *Fishing; boating; bowling*
(5) *Greater London Council*

Westminster
30. St James's Park

This is the oldest of London's Royal Parks, 'acquired' by Henry VIII in 1532. Charles II laid it out after the style of Versailles, converting the various swamps and ponds into a canal pond, making lawns and planting trees, and then opened it to the public. It was redesigned by John Nash, the Regency architect, who converted the formal French lay-out into a more-or-less natural English one which remains basically unchanged to this day. The park has some fine weeping willows and splendid displays of seasonal bedding. The waterfowl are of particular interest.

(1) Daily 5 am–midnight
(2) Free
(3) Café
(5) Dept of the Environment, Royal Parks Division

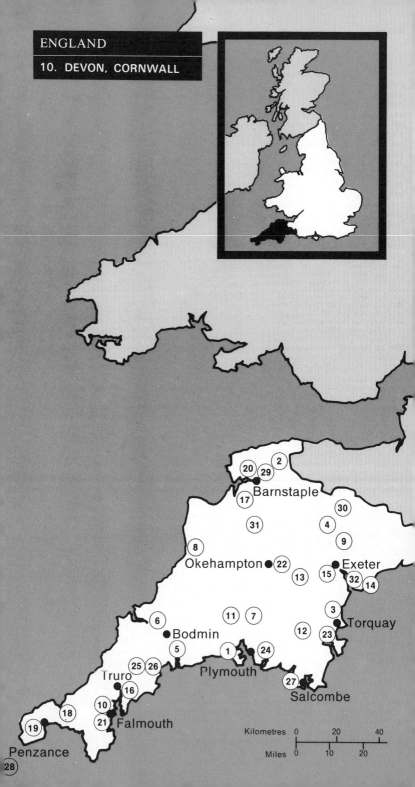

Barnstaple

Okehampton

Exeter

Torquay

Bodmin

Plymouth

Truro

Salcombe

Falmouth

Penzance

Kilometres 0   20   40

Miles 0   10   20

Antony, nr Torpoint

Cornwall

1. Antony House

The present house was built in 1721. A gravel walk leads from it, beside a great yew hedge, to a huge temple bell, brought from Burma after the Burma Wars by Sir Reginald Pole-Carew, flanked by granite lanterns from Japan. In front of the hedge is a large topiary arbour, cut from yew. From near the bell, a yew alley takes the visitor back to the terrace where a flight of steps leads to the lawn north of the house and to radiating avenues of trees, each made of one species, such as horse chestnut, oak and lime. Notable trees include the cork oak, *Quercus suber*, and a particularly large specimen of the maidenhair tree, *Ginkgo biloba*.

(1) *Early Apr–Oct: Tue–Thu and Public Holidays 2–6*
(2) *Charge*
(4) *House (same times)*
(5) *National Trust*

Arlington, nr Barnstaple

Devon

2. Arlington Court

The present house was built for Col Chichester by the architect Thomas Lee in *c* 1820. The park contains mainly woodland and ponds, but near the church is a formal Victorian flower garden on three levels and a conservatory.

(1) *Apr–Oct: Daily 11–6. Last admission 5.30; Nov–Mar: Daily during daylight hours*
(2) *Charge*
(3) *Tea*
(4) *House; horse-drawn vehicles in the stable (Easter–Oct: Daily 11–6)*
(5) *National Trust*

Babbacombe, nr Torquay

Devon

3. Babbacombe Model Village

The model village was created, on a scale of 1 in to 1 ft, by T. F. Dobbins in 1963, on a 4 acre (1·8 ha) site in a combe running down to the sea. About 800 varieties of trees and shrubs are planted, including good selections of hebe, viburnum, hydrangea, potentilla and euonymus, and larger trees like *Embothrium coccineum* var. *lanceolata* and *Eucalyptus gunnii*, as well as a notable collection of dwarf conifers. More colour is provided by bedding plants such as begonias. Many tons of local limestone were used in the making of the village but the rocks in the waterfalls are of Westmorland limestone.

(1) *Easter–Oct: Daily 9 am–10 pm, illuminations from Sunset; Nov–Easter: Daily 9–5*
(2) *Charge*

(3) *Kiosk*
(5) *T. F. Dobbins, Esq*

Bickleigh, nr Tiverton

Devon

4. Bickleigh Castle

The history of the house extends over almost nine centuries, but the gardens were designed and laid out by the late Col Jasper Henson in the 1930s. Part of the medieval moat, in front of the 14th-cent gatehouse, has been converted into a water garden with pink and white water-lilies and irises. A picturesque bridge leads across the moat and into the courtyard. The 11th-cent chapel stands in its own small courtyard, surrounded by rose-covered cob and stone walls. Behind the gatehouse is a huge mound which must once have been part of the fortifications and is now covered with rhododendrons, at their most colourful in May and early June. A steep zig-zag path leads to the top, whence there are magnificent views over the castle complex and the Exe valley. The garden also includes rose beds and many uncommon shrubs and trees, including several ginkgos.

(1) *Apr–Sep: Wed and Public Holidays 2–5; Jul–Aug: also Tue, Thu, Fri*
(2) *Charge*
(3) *Café*
(4) *Castle (same times)*
(5) *Mr and Mrs O. N. Boxall*

Bodmin

Cornwall

5. Lanhydrock

The 17th-cent house was extended in *c* 1857 for the 1st Baron Robartes by the architect Gilbert Scott (later Sir Gilbert) who also laid out formal gardens. This house was gutted by fire in 1881, and rebuilt by the 2nd Baron. The gatehouse, with its columns and arches, is mid-17th cent. The formal gardens, originally very elaborate, have been simplified and now consist mainly of rose beds set in lawns, flanked by clipped Irish yews, *Taxus baccata* 'Fastigiata'. On the walls of the house are some good specimens of *Magnolia grandiflora*. A gate in the wall on the north side of the formal garden opens onto a path that leads to the shrub garden, mainly planted since 1931. It includes several species of magnolia, many rhododendrons, both species and hybrid, the mountain laurel *Kalmia latifolia* and hydrangeas, which give colour later in the year. The Holy Well is on the site of what was called Well Park on a 1694 map, and has bamboos and New Zealand Flax, *Phormium tenax*, growing around it. From here, one path leads uphill and another runs along the west edge of the garden, past a border with rhododendrons, azaleas, mag-

75

nolias, flowering cherries, crab apples and hydrangeas, to a little formal garden with a circle of beds filled with summer-flowering plants. To the right of the tennis court stand two copper beeches, one planted by Gladstone and the other by Lord Rosebery.

Outside the gatehouse, a path leads to the Great Wood, mainly beech underplanted with rhododendrons and azaleas and with a splendid display of bluebells in spring.

(1) *Apr–Oct: Daily 11–6; last admission 5.30; Nov–Mar: Daily during daylight hours*
(2) *Charge*
(3) *Restaurant*
(4) *House (times as for Summer season of grounds)*
(5) *National Trust*

Bodmin

6. Pencarrow House

The house dates from c 1770. The formal Italian gardens in front of the house and the large granite rockery were designed by the Victorian politician Sir William Molesworth in c 1835. The gardens contain notable collections of rare specimen conifers, rhododendrons and camellias, many of which, together with hydrangeas, flank the mile long (1·6 km) drive which was laid out in 1842. In all, there are about 35 acres (14 ha) of woodland gardens, including a lake and an ancient British encampment.

(1) *Easter Sat–Sep: Daily during daylight hours*
(2) *Charge*
(3) *Café*
(4) *House (Easter Sat–Sep: Tue–Thur and Sat 1.45–5.30; last admission 5; Public Holidays 11–5.30)*
(5) *Molesworth-St Aubyn family*

Buckland Monachorum

Devon

7. Garden House

The garden has been made by the present owners since 1948 on neglected terraces below the house with high retaining walls, believed to have been made several hundred years ago for growing vines. The whole area, including new borders and lawns outside the walled garden, covers approx 2½ acres (1·1 ha) and contains a wide range of shrubs and trees – flowering cherries, magnolias, rhododendrons, azaleas and camellias, as well as herbaceous perennials. The upper levels of the site are acid, while the lower are alkaline, which adds greatly to the variety and interest of the plants which can be grown. Great attention has been paid to the grouping of plants with regard both to colour and form.

(1) *Early Apr–early Sep: Wed 3–7 or by appointment*

(2) *Charge (NGS)*
(5) *Mr and Mrs L. S. Fortescue*

Bude

Cornwall

8. Ebbingford Manor

The house dates from the 12th cent and the basic shape of the walled garden has remained the same for many hundreds of years. It is a typical walled Cornish manor house garden which seems to have happened naturally rather than to have been consciously designed. A fine specimen of the trumpet vine, *Campsis radicans*, growing on the right-hand wing of the house, a fig tree and two bay trees in the entrance drive all testify to the mildness of the climate, if wind shelter can be provided. What happens when it is not, is demonstrated by a large western red cedar, *Thuja plicata*, overshadowing the courtyard, which has developed the shape of a bush rather than a tree by the effect of the wind blowing over the ridge of the roof. Visit in July and August.

(1) *Spring Bank Holiday Mon–Jun: Tue–Thu 2–5.30; Jul–Sep: Tue–Thu and Sun 2–5.30*
(2) *Charge*
(3) *Refreshments*
(4) *House (same times)*
(5) *B. Dudley Stamp, Esq*

Budlake, nr Exeter

Devon

9. Killerton

The garden was laid out after the Napoleonic wars by Sir Thomas Acland with the assistance of the nurseryman Robert Veitch, and since then has been added to by every generation of the Acland family. Many of the trees and shrubs have been grown from seed brought back by plant-hunting expeditions. Near the house is a terrace with dwarf flowering shrubs and other plants, mostly evergreen, such as bergenias, yuccas and lavender; in front of this is a herbaceous border designed to give colour from July on. Beyond are sweeping lawns with some fine specimen trees, such as *Nothofagus obliqua*. The rock garden was probably made in the second half of the 19th cent from a hard rock quarried on the spot. The rest of the 15 acre (7 ha) garden is largely woodland, with a very good selection of rhododendrons, including some interesting species and hybrids such as *R. auriculatum* and the tender *R.* 'Fragrantissimum'. There are many magnolias, including a fine *M. campbellii*, and a number of trees and shrubs from the southern hemisphere, such as *Eucalyptus coccifera* from Tasmania, and *Desfontainea spinosa* and *Embothrium coccineum* from Chile.

(1) *Daily during daylight hours*
(2) *Charge*

(3) *Restaurant*
(4) *House (Apr–Oct: Daily 11–6; last admission 5.30)*
(5) *National Trust*

Budock, nr Falmouth

Cornwall

10. Penjerrick

Although this famous rhododendron garden which has one of the most beautiful of all hybrids named after it is now sadly overgrown, there is still much for the enthusiast to see. As well as rhododendrons, there are some fine Californian redwoods, magnolias, camellias, tree ferns and other tender plants. Visit in April–May.

(1) *Apr–Oct: Tue–Sun 10–5. No dogs*
(2) *Charge*
(5) *Mrs J. M. E. Fox*

Calstock

Cornwall

11. Cotehele

The house is medieval in origin, with many unusual shrubs and climbers growing on the walls. The garden is on a number of different levels and is divided by walls and hedges into a number of sections. In the upper garden, a golden ash, *Fraxinus excelsior* 'Aurea', and a tulip-tree, *Liriodendron tulipifera*, grow near a pond and there is a good specimen of the unusual conifer *Podocarpus salignus*. On the north side of the house there are terraces and flowerbeds and two large magnolias, *M. soulangiana* and *M. soulangiana* 'Rustica Rubra'. The ground slopes to a valley, with a pond and a stream whose edges are planted with primulas, irises, ferns and *Gunnera manicata*. Nearby stands an old beehive-shaped dovecot and there are plantings of Japanese maples, palms, bamboos, enkianthus and other shrubs. In spring the slopes near the house have a splendid display of daffodils.

(1) *Apr–Oct: Daily 11–6 or Sunset; last admission 5.30; Nov–Mar: Daily during daylight hours*
(2) *Charge*
(3) *Café*
(4) *House (same times)*
(5) *National Trust*

Dartington, nr Totnes

Devon

12. Dartington Hall

Modern landscape garden based around a 14th-cent courtyard. The main designers involved were the American Beatrix Farrand and, later, Percy Cane. An old tiltyard is integrated into the scheme with steps and terraces. There is a variety of trees and shrubs and a statue of a reclining figure by Henry Moore.

(1) *Daily 9–1, 2–5*
(2) *Charge*
(4) *Garden centre (same times); cider press; textile mills; farm trials*
(5) *Dartington Hall Trust*

Drewsteignton

Devon

13. Castle Drogo

The castle and terraced garden were built for Julian Drewe, a wealthy businessman, by the architect Sir Edwin Lutyens on a granite outcrop overlooking the entrance to the steep gorge of the River Teign. The foundation stone was laid in 1911, but the castle was not completed until 1930. The garden is invisible from the castle, lying north of the entrance drive. A path leads from the terrace to a rectangular lawn, surrounded by flowerbeds raised on retaining walls, hedged in by yew. At each corner, weeping elms (*Ulmus glabra* 'Camperdownii') have been trained to form a square 'tent'. The path continues up through banks of azaleas to a large, circular lawn surrounded by high yew hedges. To the west of the terrace is a rhododendron garden.

(1) *Apr–Oct: Daily 11–6 (last admission 5.30)*
(2) *Charge*
(3) *Restaurant*
(4) *House (same times)*
(5) *National Trust*

East Budleigh

Devon

14. Bicton Gardens

The Italian Gardens at Bicton were laid out in the mid-18th cent from plans said to have been made by Le Notre, though they were probably made for another garden. They are bounded by the temple and its conservatories (from where the best view is obtained) at one end, by a bank of trees beyond the ornamental canal at the other and by brick walls on the remaining sides. The many interesting trees and shrubs include three deodars; a variegated *Arbor vitae* (*Thujopsis dolabrata* var. *variegata*); *Magnolia campbellii* with its magnificent pink flowers in early spring; the less spectacular *M. tripetala*; *Eucryphia nymansensis* and *E. cordifolia*; *Desfontainea spinosa*, a Chilean shrub with holly-like leaves and red and yellow tubular flowers; and the tea plant, *Camellia sinensis*.

The American garden lies beside the Italian garden – the original intention was that it should contain trees and shrubs from the American continent, although it now contains some plants of different origin. There is the Mexican pine, *Pinus montezumae*; the madrona, *Arbutus* andrachne; *Nyssa sylvatica*, which turns fiery red in autumn, and *Styrax japonica*, as well as rhododendrons, azaleas and other shrubs. To the west of the Italian garden is the pinetum, laid out in 1840, which now contains fine specimens of many species uncommon in Britain. The lower pinetum houses conifers collected in China by E. H. Wilson at the beginning of this century.

Bicton has five glasshouses: the tropical house which, as well as decorative species, has a collection of both botanical and economic interest; the temperate house; the cactus house; the cool house and the palm house. All plants are labelled. Guide books available in French and German.

(1) *Easter–Oct: Daily 10–6*
(2) *Charge*
(3) *Restaurant*
(4) *James Countryside Museum; Narrow-gauge railway (same times)*
(5) *Clinton Devon Estates*

Exeter

Devon

15. Estate of the University of Exeter

An amalgamation of several Victorian estates with a large collection of trees and shrubs from all temperate and warm temperate areas of the world.

One of the most interesting features is the 18 acre (8 ha) arboretum centred on Reed Hall and laid out in the 1860s by the firm of Veitch, who were among the leading horticulturists of the time. The evergreen and slightly tender *Cornus capitata*; *Crinodendron hookeranum*; *Eucryphia glutinosa*; *E. × nymansensis*; *Catalpa bignonioides*, the Indian bean-tree; *Embothrium coccineum* and *Nothofagus antarctica*, the southern beech, are among the interesting plants grown there, but probably the best representation is of the coniferales, with over 150 species from many genera including picea, abies, pseudotsuga, cephalotaxus, pinus, cupressus, sciadopitys and sequoiadendron. Also in the grounds are a rock garden and a pond.

The other estates are also rich in botanical interest. A number of Japanese cherries, *Prunus serrulata*, were given to the then University College of the South-West by the Japanese Government in 1937, and make a fine display in spring. An interesting collection of tender shrubs is planted against the south-facing walls of Northcote House, including the Chilean jasmine, *Mandevilla suaveolens*; *Azara petiolaris*, also from Chile; the lobster claw, *Clianthus puniceus* from New Zealand; and *Carpenteria californica* from California. More unusual plants grow in the botanic garden which was laid out in the 1960s, and there are four parallel ranges of glasshouses.

The halls of residence have their own gardens; that of Thomas Hall includes a stream and a bog garden with groups of *Gunnera chilensis* with leaves 6 ft (1·8 m) in diameter. There is something of interest at all times but parking may be a problem in term time.

(1) *Daily*
(2) *Free*
(5) *University of Exeter*

Feock, nr Truro

Cornwall

16. Trelissick Garden

Much of the park planting, including some of the older exotics, was done by the Gilbert family who owned the property between 1844 and 1913, but the garden lay-out is due largely to Mr and Mrs Copeland, who inherited the estate in 1937 and in 1955 presented the house, with 376 acres (151 ha) of surrounding parkland and woods, to the National Trust.

The first part a vistor comes to is a walled garden with two enclosures, one with several fig trees and the other with an assortment of trees, shrubs and climbers including *Cestrum newellii*, *Grevillea rosmarinifolia*, *G. sulphurea*, and *Trachelospermum jasminoides*. The main garden is noted for the display of camellias, magnolias, rhododendrons and azaleas, and there is a collection of over 100 kinds of hydrangea, both species and hybrid.

The situation near the sea and the shelter of woodland allows many tender plants to be grown, including many from the southern hemisphere, such as *Gevuina avellana*, *Crinodendron hookeranum* and *Podocarpus andinus* from Chile; *Nothofagus fusca*, *Leptospermum scoparium* and *Hoheria glabrata* from New Zealand and *Eucalyptus subcrenulata* from Tasmania.

(1) *Mar–Oct: Mon–Sat 11–6; Sun 2–6 or Sunset. No dogs.*
(2) *Charge*
(4) *Garden shop with plants for sale*
(5) *National Trust*

Instow

Devon

17. Tapeley Park

The Italian garden was created at the beginning of this century by Lady Rosamund Christie to the architectural design of John Becher (also responsible for the present exterior of the William and Mary house). There are terraces, statues, sundials and summer houses, an ilex hedge tunnel and a fishpond; a long flight of steps leads towards the old walled kitchen garden, with glasshouses erected in the 1920s, and a shell house of 18th-cent origin. The garden contains a wide variety of plants, many rare, including a collection of lilies presented by Jan de Graaff; plants of dracaena and trachycarpus give it a sub-tropical atmosphere. There are magnificent views across the bowling green to the Taw and Torridge estuary and the sea beyond. The wild garden and lily pond were made to commemorate the last of the Clevelands (owners of Tapeley 1702–1854), who was killed in the Crimea in 1854. The estate subsequently passed through the female line to the Christie family of Glyndebourne, who own it still. An interesting feature is a brick, igloo-like ice-house near the dogs' gravestones. About 10 acres (4·5 ha) are open to the public. Visit in late spring, the end of June and early August.

(1) Easter–Oct: Tue–Sun and Public Holidays 10–6
(2) Charge
(3) Tea
(4) Conducted tours of 12–25 people over part of the house; putting green
(5) Miss R. A. H. Christie

Lelant, nr St Ives

Cornwall

18. Lelant Model Village

The water gardens are set in the grounds of the model village, which was first opened to the public in 1972. There are fountains and waterfalls powered by electric pumps, as well as lily-ponds and a natural stream. The stonework is of local materials, and the gardens have been planted with over 100 different species and varieties of shrubs and herbaceous plants, many too delicate to grow in the open in most parts of Britain.

(1) Easter–early Nov: Daily 10–5; high season 10–10
(2) Charge
(3) Kiosk
(4) Model village; museum; art gallery; exhibitions; playground (same times)
(5) Mr L. C. and Mrs D. C. Caswell

Madron, nr Penzance

Cornwall

19. Trengwainton Garden

There has been a house here at least since the 16th cent. In 1814 the estate was bought by Sir Rose Price who started planting trees, made a new drive (now the Long Walk) and built a series of walled gardens at the foot of the drive with raised, terraced beds. The house was bought in 1867 by T. S. Bolitho; in 1925 it came to his great-nephew, Lt-Col E. W. W. Bolitho, and he and his head gardener Mr Creek virtually created the present gardens, with advice from owners of other great Cornish gardens. He subscribed to Kingdon Ward's 1927–8 expedition to Assam and Upper Burma and the rhododendron collection at Trengwainton is founded on seeds collected on this expedition, although the oldest specimen in the garden is probably a *Rhododendron falconeri* planted in the 1880s. Sir Rose Price's plantations and walled gardens were used to give them shelter. More tender

rhododendrons grow and flourish out of doors at Trengwainton than in any other garden on the mainland of Britain.

There are many other interesting plants to be seen, including the tree fern *Dicksonia antarctica*; *Magnolia × veitchii*, *M. mollicomata*, *M. delavayi*, *M. sprengeri*, *M. campbellii* and several other species; *Leptospermum scoparium* from New Zealand; *Azara serrata* and *Lomatia ferruginea* from Chile; *Schima argentea* from Szechwan; and several species of acacia, eucryphia and embothrium. In c 1950 a stream garden was made, planted with primulas and other moisture-loving plants.

(1) Mar–Oct: Wed–Sat and Public Holiday Mon 11–6
(2) Charge
(5) National Trust

Marwood, nr Barnstaple

Devon

20. Marwood Hill

The garden, which has a total area of 10 acres (4·5 ha), has been made since 1960 by the present owner from a field on a valley slope. A stream at the bottom has been dammed to form two lakes with waterside plantings. There is a large collection of camellias, both outside and under glass, and many rhododendrons, a rock garden and a heather garden. Daffodils make a fine display in spring. The garden is continually being added to: recently a new area was planted to form an arboretum.

(1) Feb–Oct: 9–Sunset
(2) Charge
(4) Plants for sale (same times)
(5) Dr J. A. Smart

Mawnan Smith, nr Falmouth

Cornwall

21. Glendurgan Garden

The garden at Glendurgan was first planted in the 1820s and 1830s by Alfred Fox, who built the present house after the original thatched cottage burnt down. He planted the laurel maze in 1833. Successive generations of the family continued with the planting until the property was given to the National Trust in 1962.

Much of the garden is set in a wooded valley, and there are many uncommon and tender plants. There is a good selection of rhododendrons, including *R. sidereum*, *R. griersonianum*, *R. auriculatum*, *R. crassum*, *R.* 'Penjerrick' and 'Lady Alice Fitzwilliam'. A specimen of *Araucaria bidwillii* from Queensland, a relative of the monkey puzzle, is said to be the only specimen growing naturally in England. The many magnolias include the large-leaved *M. delavayi*, and there are tree ferns, *Dicksonia antarctica*, as well as a good collection of native ferns, and some tall eucryphias. Near the house is a formal garden, the many shrubs gaining protection from the walls, including *Acacia dealbata* and *A. longifolia* from Australia; *Feijoa sellowiana* from Brazil and *Hoheria sexstylosa* and the climber *Clianthus puniceus* from New Zealand.

(1) *Mar–Oct: Mon, Wed, Fri (except Good Friday) 10.30–4.30*
(2) *Charge*
(5) *National Trust*

Okehampton

Devon
22. Wood Country Hotel

The garden was designed at the turn of the century by the garden architect T. H. Mawson to complement the Elizabethan-style house built at the same time for the Lethbridge family. The garden covers approx 20 acres (8 ha), all landscaped, and includes 12 acres (5 ha) of parkland and formal and informal areas. There is a lake with rare ferns planted around it, and massed plantings of rhododendrons and azaleas. Visit in May and June.

(1) *Mar–Sep: Daily noon–5*
(2) *Charge*
(3) *Café*
(5) *J. C. Canning, Esq*

Paignton

Devon
23. Paignton Zoological and Botanical Garden

The only combined zoological and botanical gardens in Britain, extending to 75 acres (30 ha). There is a good collection of trees and shrubs, many rare or too tender to grow in the open in most parts of the country, underplanted with unusual bulbs, ferns and herbaceous plants arranged largely by family. Some of the aviaries, cages, houses and paddocks are planted with interesting specimens. A sub-tropical house, heated only by the sun, is divided into two compartments, planted geographically. Birds fly freely inside the house.

The tropical house is arranged so as to display a number of habitat groups including a tropical forest, succulents and a tropical pond, as well as a collection of tropical crop plants and a series of plant family groups.

(1) *Daily (except 25 Dec) 10–7 or Sunset. No dogs*
(2) *Charge*
(3) *Restaurant and bar*
(4) *Jungle Express miniature railway (same times)*
(5) *Herbert Whitley Trust*

Plympton

Devon
24. Saltram

The house was built in the Tudor period with classical façades added in the 18th cent; the park was landscaped in *c* 1769 in the manner of 'Capability' Brown. The garden lies mainly to the west of the house and has lawns backed by fine trees and many flowering shrubs including rhododendrons, azaleas, camellias, magnolias, eucryphias, *Crinodendron hookeranum* and hydrangeas. *Cyclamen hederaefolium* has become naturalized under a clump of lime trees and under the limes lining the long avenue. A herbaceous border near the chapel was planted in the early 1970s.

The orangery was built in 1773–5, when orange trees were imported from Italy. Orange trees are still grown here, and every year on Oak Apple Day, 29 May (commemorating the Restoration of King Charles II), they are moved to the orange grove, a sheltered area behind the chapel, where they are arranged around a central fountain pool. Traditionally, they are moved indoors again on Tavistock Goose Fair day, the second Wednesday in October. In the wood behind the orangery is a small 18th-cent classical temple, known as Fanny's Bower.

(1) *Apr–Oct: Daily 11–6 or Sunset (last admission 5.30); Nov–Mar or Easter: Daily during daylight hours. No dogs*
(2) *Charge*
(3) *Restaurant*
(4) *House (same times); shop*
(5) *National Trust*

Probus, nr Truro

Cornwall
25. County Demonstration Garden and Arboretum

The purpose of the centre, which was started in 1970, is to illustrate in the form of permanent demonstrations and planting displays a wide range of garden practices, plant use and the results of modern research. It is also hoped to emphasize the association between plants and medicine, history and geography.

Among the features demonstrated are patio gardens, using a variety of materials, container gardens, wall plantings, a labour-saving garden, rose cultivation and propagation, herbs, a historical garden, shrubs and herbs for shade, fruit and vegetable gardens. There are collections of hydrangeas, heathers, pinks and carnations, lilies, hardy annuals, hardy fuchsias, bamboos, ornamental grasses, and plants of exotic appearance such as *Phormium tenax*, New Zealand flax, and *Cordyline australis*, the cabbage palm. There are trials of eucalyptus and dwarf conifers and an arboretum.

(1) *Oct–Apr: Thu 2–5; May–Sep: Mon–Wed and Fri 2–5; Thu 2–8; Sun 2–6*

(2) *Charge*
(5) *Cornwall Education Committee*

Probus, nr Truro

26. Trewithen

The 20 acre (8 ha) garden was originally laid out to set off the 18th-cent house and was further developed by G. H. Johnstone in 1908. It is basically a woodland garden, with an internationally famous collection of magnolias, camellias and rhododendrons and, besides these, there are embothriums, azaras and tree ferns.

(*1*) *Mar–Sep: Mon–Sat 2–4.30*
(*2*) *Charge*
(*3*) *Café*
(*4*) *House and garden shop (same times)*
(*5*) *Mr and Mrs A. M. J. Galsworthy*

Salcombe

Devon

27. Sharpitor

The first house on the site overlooking the sea and estuary was built in the 1890s; in 1901 the owner, Edric Hopkins, bought additional land and started to lay out the garden, terracing the steepest parts and planting many trees and shrubs. One of these early plantings is a fine *Magnolia campbellii* that is covered with large pink flowers in March. The garden was further extended in 1913 to approx 6 acres (2·7 ha) and the present house was built. In 1937 Sharpitor was left to the National Trust.

Frost is rare in the Salcombe area and because of this many tender plants can be grown. There is a collection of palms, mostly the Chusan palm, *Trachycarpus fortunei*, which flowers and sets seed freely, but also the only European native palm, *Chamaerops humilis*, and many southern hemisphere plants such as *Callistemon* spp. from Australia; *Drimys winteri* and *Hoheria* spp. from New Zealand and *Crinodendron hookeranum* and *Cunninghamia lanceolata* from Chile. Other interesting plants include a large free-standing *Magnolia grandiflora*; *Metasequoia glyptostroboides*, the dawn redwood; *Musa basjoo*, the Japanese banana; and the prickly *Colletia cruciata*. Much use is made of ground-cover plants between the shrubs, such as periwinkle, bergenias and geraniums.

(*1*) *Daily*
(*2*) *Charge*
(*4*) *Museum (Apr–Oct: Daily 11–1, 2–6)*
(*5*) *National Trust*

Scilly Isles

Cornwall

28. Tresco Abbey

The garden was founded in 1834 by Augustus Smith, the first Lord Proprietor of the Isles of Scilly. Despite the fierce, salty Atlantic winds, many tender and exotic plants flourish in the mild climate, forming a collection of outstanding botanical interest. A small formal garden surrounds the ruins of a 10th-cent Benedictine priory and throughout the grounds long paths are flanked by sub-tropical plants which grow as they would in their natural environment. Plants from the southern hemisphere are well represented, including the magnificent red-flowered *Metrosideros tomentosa* and *M. robusta*, and species of grevillea, eucalyptus, callistemon and hakea, from New Zealand and Australia, *Leucadendron argenteum*, the silver-tree, proteas and *Erica canaliculata* from South Africa and *Myrtus luma* from Chile.

(*1*) *Mon–Sat (except 25 Dec) 10–4*
(*2*) *Charge*
(*3*) *Refreshments*
(*4*) *Abbey (Apr–1 Oct: Mon–Fri 11–4); collection of figureheads and other items salvaged from wrecks*
(*5*) *R. A. Dorrien Smith, Esq*

Shirwell, nr Barnstaple

Devon

29. Youlston Park

This is mainly a woodland garden, including a small lake. Restoration is still in progress after years of neglect. There is a walled vegetable garden. Visit in June.

(*1*) *May–Sep: Tue–Sun 10–1, 2–5*
(*2*) *Charge*
(*3*) *Tea*
(*4*) *House (same times)*
(*5*) *J. J. C. Clarke, Esq*

Tiverton

Devon

30. Knightshayes Court

The house was built in the 1860s by the architect William Burges for John Heathcoat-Amory, but although many of the specimen trees and the yew hedges date from that period, the garden as it is now has mostly been made since the end of World War I. It now covers 25 acres (11 ha) and its sheltered site on south-facing rising ground enables a wide range of plants to be grown. There is a notable collection of rhododendrons growing in woodland, including a good representation of large-leaved species such as *R. falconeri*, *R. macabeanum*, *R. sinogrande*, *R. mollyanum* and *R. rex* as well as other interesting trees and shrubs such as drimys, camellias, elaeagnus and olearia, and an unusual variety of herbaceous plants such as trilliums and erythroniums. Dwarf rhododendrons are grown in raised beds made from peat blocks. There is also a fine selection of magnolias, including *M. campbellii*, *M. delavayi*, *M. dawsoniana*, *M.*

kobus, M. mollicomata, M. salicifolia and *M. sprengeri*. A pool garden with statues set against hedges and an adjoining paved formal garden were completed in 1959; a scree bed lies beneath the terrace wall. Another pool was enlarged in 1972 as a setting for a willow garden.

(*1*) *Apr–Oct: Daily 12.30–6*
(*2*) *Charge*
(*3*) *Refreshments*
(*4*) *House (Daily 1.30–6)*
(*5*) *National Trust and Knightshayes Garden Trust*

Torrington

Devon

31. Rosemoor Garden Charitable Trust

The garden, extending to approx 5 acres (2 ha), is situated in a wooded valley, sheltered from east winds. It was started in 1959 by the present owners and contains many rare plants. The genus that is most widely represented is rhododendron, both as a species and a hybrid; a collection of dwarf species grow on peat terraces or raised beds. There are also many species of cistus, a collection of old-fashioned and species roses, raised alpine beds and a scree. An arboretum was planted in 1975 and 1976.

(*1*) *Apr–Oct: Daily Sunrise–Sunset*
(*2*) *Charge*
(*3*) *Tea for groups by arrangement*
(*4*) *Plants for sale*
(*5*) *Col J. E. and Lady Anne Palmer*

Woodbury, nr Exeter

Devon

32. The Warren

The 12 acre (5 ha) woodland garden is set in a sheltered valley and contains many fine trees, including Californian redwoods, *Sequoiadendron giganteum*, and many flowering shrubs, particularly rhododendrons and azaleas, many introduced from the Himalayas in 1908 by Mr Bowden-Smith. There is a lake, a water-lily pond and a bog garden containing a number of plants including primulas and rare ferns.

(*1*) *Mid-May–mid-July: Sun and Wed 2–7. Other days by appointment for parties. No dogs.*
(*2*) *Charge (NGS)*
(*5*) *Mrs Anita G. A. Jones*

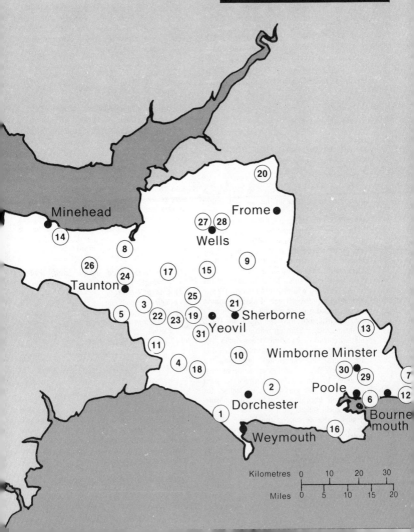

ENGLAND

11. DORSET, SOMERSET

Minehead

Frome

Wells

Taunton

Sherborne

Yeovil

Wimborne Minster

Poole

Dorchester

Bournemouth

Weymouth

Kilometres 0   10   20   30

Miles 0   5   10   15   20

ENGLAND

Abbotsbury

Dorset

1. Abbotsbury Sub-tropical Gardens

The gardens, approx 17 acres (6·8 ha) in extent, were originally part of the grounds of Abbotsbury Abbey and were probably first planted in the latter half of the 18th cent. Since 1969 much restoration work has been done by the late Lord Galway and Lady Galway (now Lady Teresa Agnew). The original garden is walled and semi-formal; the rest is a natural wild garden on several levels, in woodland with a lake. There are almost 1,000 rhododendrons, including many Chinese and Himalayan species grown from seed in the 19th cent, and also from seed sent by E. H. Wilson in the early 20th cent. The many other exotic trees and shrubs include magnolias, camellias, *Crinodendron hookeranum*, *Acacia dealbata*, *A. baileyana*, *Cornus* spp., *Myrtus* spp., *Hoheria* spp., *Pittosporum* spp. and approx 12 species of eucalyptus. Peacocks wander around the garden.

(1) Mid-March–Sep: Mon–Sat 10–5; Sun 2–5
(2) Charge
(4) Plants for sale
(5) Strangways Estate

Athelhampton, nr Dorchester

Dorset

2. Athelhampton

The house is essentially medieval. A *Magnolia grandiflora* on the wall is thought to be approx 200 years old. The gardens contain both formal and informal areas.

The formal gardens lie mainly to the south-east of the house – 40,000 tons of Ham stone were used in the building of the terraces. The corona, in the Elizabethan manner with clipped yews and a fountain, is at the centre of this. To the north is the Private Garden, which leads into the White Garden with the River Piddle running through it and a white marble group bought from the International Exhibition of 1862. The new Cloister Garden with an octagonal pool surrounded by lime trees links the White Garden with the Kitchen Garden with several fine magnolias, including the large-leaved *M. delavayi*, growing against the walls. Inside, the walls support trained fruit trees. A new glasshouse on the south-facing wall contains a collection of sub-tropical and tropical plants.

East of the corona is the Lion's Mouth with a cascade and pool; this garden was altered in 1977 to provide a habitat for rock plants. Tudor archways lead to the Lime Walk, where flowering shrubs are backed by a double row of pleached limes. To the south, the corona leads into the largest formal garden with the Great Terrace and a sunken lawn with a fishpond. A canal was constructed in 1969–70.

(1) Wed before Easter–1st Sun in Oct: Wed, Thu, Sun, Public Holidays and Tue in Aug 2–6
(2) Charge
(3) Tea
(4) House (same times)
(5) R. G. Cooke, Esq

Barrington, nr Ilminster

Somerset

3. Barrington Court

The house is Tudor, built in *c* 1520, linked to what was originally a stable block dating from 1670. The gardens were planned – by post – by Gertrude Jekyll in the 1920s, when she was over 80. Around the Tudor house there are mainly lawns, with aquatic plants in the moat, but around the 'newer' part there are a number of separate sections, including a formal iris garden with box-edged beds, herbaceous borders, flower-beds, an orchard with rose borders round the edges and a walled garden with a lily-pool in the centre.

(1) Easter–Sep: Wed 10.15–12.15, 2–6; Oct–Easter: Wed 10.15–12.15. Also some days for charity. No dogs
(2) Charge
(4) House (same times)
(5) National Trust

Beaminster

Dorset

4. Parnham House

The 16th-cent house is surrounded by a 14 acre (6 ha) garden, largely redesigned early in this century. Formal terraces, with 50 clipped yews, are bisected by spring-fed cascades, while north of the house lie an Italian garden, the glade and the wilderness. A riverside walk runs alongside the River Brit.

(1) Apr–Oct: Wed, Sun and Public Holidays 10–5, or by arrangement
(2) Charge (in aid of NGS and GSO)
(3) Refreshments
(4) House; John Makepeace furniture workshop in former stables (same times)
(5) John Makepeace, Esq

Blagdon Hill, nr Taunton

Somerset

5. Widcombe Bird Gardens

Widcombe House, built in the early 19th cent, stands in 36 acres (16 ha) of grounds, of which approx 20 acres (8 ha) were converted into a bird sanctuary in 1970. The lake and lower informal gardens, including the arboretum, were created in the 19th and early 20th cents and contain many unusual trees and shrubs, including rhododendrons and azaleas, camellias, cedars, eucalyptus, maples and viburnums. Visit in May and June.

(1) Mar–Oct: Daily 10.30–7 (last admission 6); Nov–Feb: Sun 10.30–7
(2) Charge
(3) Restaurant (10.30–6)
(5) Leslie Strong, Esq

Bournemouth

Dorset

6. Compton Acres

Compton Acres comprises ten individual gardens: the Roman garden; herbaceous borders; Italian garden; palm court and wishing well; rock and water gardens; woodland and sub-tropical glen; English garden; heather garden; garden of memory; Japanese garden. The idea was conceived by Thomas William Simpson, who bought the house after World War I, but never lived in it. Thousands of tons of soil and stone were brought in and also a collection of marble, bronze and lead statuary.

There are many uncommon trees and shrubs some of which, like *Rhododendron spinulosum*, *Azara microphylla*, *Leptospermum scoparium* and *L. humifusum*, are too tender to be grown in the open in most parts of the country. Other interesting species include *Embothrium coccineum* 'Longifolium', *Desfontainea spinosa*, *Crinodendron hookeranum*, *Rhododendron augustinii*, *R. thomsonii* and the rhododendron with the largest leaves of all, *R. sinogrande*.

(1) Apr–Oct: Daily 10.30–6.30
(2) Charge
(3) Refreshments
(4) Plant stall (Daily)
(5) Mr and Mrs J. R. Brady

Bransgore

Dorset

7. MacPennys

MacPennys nursery covers 12 acres (5 ha). 3 acres (1·4 ha) of this consists of a woodland garden on undulating ground, planted with fine trees and shrubs including acers, camellias, embothriums, eucryphias and rhododendrons. Visit in spring and late autumn.

(1) Mon–Sat 8–noon, 2–5
(2) Collection box
(4) Nursery garden (same times)
(5) D. B. and Tim Lowndes, Esqs

Cannington, nr Bridgwater

Somerset

8. Cannington College

The Somerset College of Agriculture and Horticulture, founded in 1921 by Somerset County Council, has ornamental and educational gardens on two adjoining sites. The walled gardens of the 12th-cent priory, 3

acres (1·4 ha) in extent, are divided into several sections. The Winter Garden contains established specimen shrubs and small trees, such as *Carpenteria californica*, *Garrya* spp. and *Chimonanthus praecox*, underplanted with ground-cover plants. The Tennis Garden has acid borders for plants such as rhododendrons, camellias and eucryphias which cannot be grown in the alkaline soil of the rest of the garden, and also contains shrub roses and a number of marginally hardy plants, including a collection of salvia species, *Solanum crispum*, *Leptospermum scoparium* 'Nichollsii', *Sophora tetraptera* and *Azara lanceolata*. On the south wall is a collection of about forty species and cultivars of ceanothus. In the Bee Garden a small apiary is surrounded by interesting plants, many from Australia and New Zealand, and has a fern garden in a shady corner. The Bishop's Garden is planted with plants of Biblical significance, such as the Judas tree and figs. A new range of glasshouses has recently been completed.

The gardens around the new college buildings date from 1963. A collection of eucalyptus contains approx fifty species, and tender plants against a wall, including *Cestrum fasciculatum*, *Mimulus aurantiacus* and *Callistemon citrinum*. The Sub-tropical Garden contains architectural plants like phormium, cordyline, beschorneria and opuntia, while the Shade Quadrangle features plants of the aralia family such as ivies, *Fatsia japonica* and *Pseudopanax arboreus* as well as some tender species of buddleia. Other features of interest include a rose garden, a vista garden and a rock wall.

(1) College Open Day (Sat nearest 21 May) 2–6; other days for NGS and GSO; Mon–Fri 9–5 by previous arrangement with Head of Horticulture Dept, S. H. Brookfield
(2) Free
(4) Horticulture shop (Mon, Tue, Thu and Fri 10–noon, 2–4)
(5) Somerset County Council

Castle Cary

Somerset

9. Hadspen House

The 8 acre (3·2 ha) garden, laid out in the early years of this century on the 18th-cent foundation, is of considerable horticultural interest with new plantings of shrubs, many tender, shrub roses and hostas. There is a particular emphasis on trees and shrubs with bark and foliage interest, and on Australasian plants.

(1) All year round: Thu 10–5; Apr–Oct: Sun also 2–5. No dogs
(2) Charge
(4) Nursery
(5) Mr and Mrs David Hobhouse

85

Cerne Abbas,

Dorset

10. Minterne

The arboretum was formed and landscaped in 1765. There is a fine collection of trees, including magnolias, and the rhododendrons are of particular interest as they have been introduced from all the major Himalayan expeditions by E. H. Wilson, George Forrest, Kingdon Ward, Rock and Professor Hu.

(1) Easter Mon and Spring Public Holiday 2–7; Apr–Jun: Sun 2–7. Parties by appointment on weekdays
(2) Charge
(5) Lord Digby

Chard

Somerset

11. Forde Abbey

The house was originally a Cistercian monastery and part of it dates from the 13th cent. The garden was started by the Gwyn family in the 18th cent, when the lawns and drives were laid out and the ponds dug. Many conifers were planted during the 19th cent, and at the turn of the century it was a typical Victorian garden dominated by laurel shrubberies. In the 20th cent the garden has been altered by two generations of the Roper family and there is now a large rock garden, a bog garden with Asiatic primulas, gunneras, royal ferns, skunk cabbage, and several ponds including a canal pond. At the foot of the stone steps leading to the rock garden is a yew hedge covered with the vivid scarlet climber *Tropaeolum speciosum*. The long border, at its best in July, is planned so that there are sections of contrasting colours – blue, yellow and red. There are many interesting and uncommon trees and shrubs both in the garden and in the arboretum, including a 100-year-old *Pinus radiata*, eucryphias, *Magnolia sargentiana robusta*, *Azara serrata*, *Nandina domestica*, *Carpenteria californica* and *Feijoa sellowiana*.

(1) Easter Sun 2–6; May–Sep: Wed, Sun and Public Holidays 2–6
(2) Charge
(3) Refreshments
(4) House (same times); Garden centre (Mon–Fri 9–5)
(5) M. Roper, Esq

Christchurch

Dorset

12. Red House Museum, Art Gallery and Gardens

The house was built in *c* 1764 as a parish workhouse, but in 1886, when a new work-

house was built, it was sold and the yard was partially converted into a garden. In 1951 this was redesigned as the museum garden by the curator, J. H. Lavender. There is a walled herb garden and a carp pool, while the larger south garden includes formal lawns, a peony terrace, a woodland walk and a collection of old garden roses, best seen in May and June.

The plants grown are particularly suited to light soils and include fine specimens of hornbeam, weeping ash, twisted willow and the maidenhair tree, *Ginkgo biloba*. Among the herbaceous plants there is an emphasis on those with good foliage, such as hostas and euphorbias.

(1) Tue–Sat 10–5; Sun 2–5; closed on 25 Dec
(2) Charge
(4) Museum and Art Gallery (same times)
(5) Hampshire County Museum Service

Cranborne

Dorset

13. Manor House

The garden of approx 11 acres (4 ha) was originally laid out in 1609–11 by John Tradescant, gardener to Robert Cecil and James I. Although the garden has been much altered since then, particularly just before and after the last war, the framework as designed by him is still there – courtyard, yew allée, bowling green and mount. There is a walled herb garden, a knot garden planted with Elizabethan flowers, a white garden in the North Court, a water garden, orchards and a wild garden with spring bulbs.

(1) Mar–Oct: 1st Sat and Sun of each month and Public Holidays; Sat 9–6; Sun 2–5. For other times tel Cranborne 248.
(2) Charge
(4) Garden centre (Mon–Sat 10–6; Sun 2–6)
(5) Marquess of Salisbury

Dunster

Somerset

14. Dunster Castle

Most of the castle, whose origins date from the 13th cent, was remodelled by the architect Anthony Salvin in 1868–72. He added the towers, turrets and battlements that give the building a spectacular appearance as it rises from the wooded slopes of the Tor. Although the site is exposed, the area is mild and the slopes and terraces around the castle offer good habitats for semi-hardy and sun-loving plants, such as *Acacia dealbata*, *Cordyline australis*, yuccas, *Beschorneria yuccoides* and *Correa spinosa*. Perhaps the most famous feature of the garden is a huge lemon tree that stands against part of the façade, receiving only slight protection in winter; the same tree is mentioned in records of 1830.

(1) Mid-Apr–Sep: Daily (except Fri and
    Sat) 11–5; Oct: Tue, Wed and Sun 2–4
(2) Charge
(4) Castle (same times); shop; deer park
(5) National Trust

Ilchester

Somerset

15. Lytes Cary

The garden gate leads to a paved walk with stone balls set between buttresses of the yew hedge. A raised walk to the east looks over an orchard with intersecting avenues planted with different kinds of fruit tree, and black walnuts in the angles. The border along the south front of the house, parts of which date from the 13th cent, is planted with species known to have been in cultivation in the 16th cent. From the east front, a stone path leads between lawns and clipped yews.

(1) Mar–Oct: Wed and Sat 2–6. Last admission 5.30. No dogs
(2) Charge
(4) House (same times)
(5) National Trust

Kimmeridge, nr Wareham

Dorset

16. Smedmore House

The first record of gardens at Smedmore dates back to *c* 1620, when Sir William Clavell, according to a local chronicle, 'built a little newe house at Smedmore and beautified it with pleasant gardens'. The present lay-out dates from 1958, when Sir William Clavell's descendants returned to the house. There are large herbaceous borders, fuchsias, hydrangeas and other shrubs and a mulberry tree.

(1) Jun, Jul and Aug: Wed 2.15–5.30; Sep: 1st two Wed 2.15–5.30
(2) Charge
(5) Major and Mrs John Mansel

Langport

Somerset

17. Kelways Nurseries

The nursery was established in 1851 and contains the largest collections of peonies and irises to be found in Europe, as well as many other herbaceous and bulbous plants. June is the most colourful month.

(1) Daily during working hours
(2) Charge
(5) Kelways Nurseries

Mapperton, nr Beaminster

Dorset

18. Mapperton

10 acres (4 ha) of terraced hillside garden are planted with trees and shrubs, banks of

daffodils and formal borders. There is an orangery in classical style, 18th-cent stone fishponds, a summer house and a modern Italianate formal garden. Visit in April to June.

(1) Mar–Sep: Mon–Fri 2–6
(2) Charge
(3) Tea
(4) House (by appointment for organized parties)
(5) Victor Montagu, Esq

Montacute

Somerset

19. Montacute House

Although the raised walk running along the boundaries of the garden to the north of the 16th-cent house could be a relic of the Elizabethan garden, the lay-out of the present garden, with its green parterres and yew hedges, dates mainly from the mid-19th cent. Below the raised walk is a border with old shrub roses planned by V. Sackville-West. She also planted the flower borders in the forecourt. A long yew walk to the south of the house leads to an arcaded garden house and beyond this a semi-circular garden has a stone pool and beds of *Yucca recurvifolia*. The grounds contain some fine trees, including cedars of Lebanon; golden yews, *Taxus baccata*, 'Aurea', and an exceptionally tall *Cupressus macrocarpa*.

(1) Apr–Oct: Daily (except Tue) 12.30–6 or Sunset. Other times by written appointment with the administrator
(2) Charge
(3) Café (Easter–Sep)
(4) House (same times)
(5) National Trust

Norton St Philip, Trowbridge Road

Somerset

20. Oldfield Nurseries

The land was planted as vineyards up to 1720, when the vines were destroyed by a virus and damsons were planted, probably to make gin. The garden as it is now has been designed and planted by the present owner since 1965, with the aim of developing an old-fashioned nursery garden, as distinct from a modern garden centre. Lime-tolerant trees and shrubs, including conifers and dwarf conifers, climbers, herbaceous plants, alpines and herbs are all grown; propagating material is collected from the mature plants.

(1) Mon–Sat 8–1, 2–5.30
(2) Free
(4) Nursery garden
(5) Gerald A. Thompson, Esq

Sherborne

Dorset

21. Sherborne Castle

The castle was built by Sir Walter Raleigh in 1594 and has been in continuous occupation by the Digby family since 1617. The gardens, with lawns, wooded valleys and open views, were redesigned by 'Capability' Brown when the original Elizabethan gardens were submerged under a 50 acre (20 ha) lake. The castle and its grounds sit in a natural amphitheatre of 250 acres (101 ha). Ruins of a 12th-cent castle can be seen across the lake. Visit in spring.

(1) *Easter Sat–Sep: Thu, Sat, Sun and Public Holidays 2–6*
(2) *Charge*
(3) *Café*
(4) *Castle (same times)*
(5) *S. K. Wingfield Digby, Esq*

South Petherton

Somerset

22. East Lambrook Manor

The 15th-cent house was bought by Walter and Margery Fish in a derelict condition in 1937, with an acre of overgrown garden. The garden was redesigned in the style of an old English cottage garden, with the aim of providing colour and interest at all times of the year. Exotic and unusual herbaceous perennials, trees, shrubs and climbers flourish beside more typical cottage garden plants. An interesting feature is the use of herbs as garden subjects.

Margery Fish made the garden famous in her book *We Made a Garden*, and there came to be so much demand for the plants she used that she started a commercial nursery. She died in 1969, and the house and garden are carried on by her nephew, the present owner.

(1) *Daily 9–5*
(2) *Charge*
(4) *House (Mar–Oct: Thu 2–5); Nursery garden (same times as garden)*
(5) *Henry Boyd-Carpenter, Esq*

Stoke-sub-Hamdon

Somerset

23. Little Norton Mill

The property was bought by the present owners in 1962; the 1½ acre (0·7 ha) garden was designed and planted to accommodate stock plants for the nursery which covers approx 3 acres (1·2 ha). It has terraces with lawns and rock plants, an ornamental pool, flowering shrubs, conifers, heathers and ground-cover plants.

(1) *Mon–Sat 9–5.30; Sun 2–5.30*
(2) *Free*

(4) *Nursery*
(5) *Mr and Mrs J. W. J. McClintock*

Taunton

Somerset

24. Hestercombe House

The landscape and combes behind the house were planned by Coplestone Warre Bamfylde, a landscape gardener who inherited the house in 1759. The gardens proper were designed and laid out by Sir Edwin Lutyens and Gertrude Jekyll between 1904 and 1910 and are probably the finest example of their collaboration. The orangery on the east side of the house was also designed by Lutyens. As tastes changed, the garden was altered, but recently its historic importance has been recognized and in 1970 restoration began, using the original plans. In 1975 the restoration scheme received a Heritage Year Award in connection with European Architectural Heritage Year. The split level terraces, the stonework and waterways are of particular interest.

The house is now the Headquarters and Administrative Centre of Somerset Fire Brigade.

(1) *May–Sep: Thu noon–5; last Suns of May, Jun, Jul: 2–6*
(2) *Collection box*
(5) *Somerset County Council*

Tintinhull

Somerset

25. Tintinhull House

The house is mainly early 17th cent, with the west front added in *c* 1720. Just before the end of the 19th cent it was bought by the botanist Dr S. J. M. Price who laid out the series of formal gardens that lead from the west front of the house. In 1935 the property was bought by Capt and Mrs F. E. Reiss, who made further changes to the garden. A tennis court to the north of the house was made into a formal garden with a loggia, rectangular pool and borders backed by yew hedges. Mrs Reiss set out all the borders with a clever choice of plants, using contrasting foliage shapes and harmonizing colours. Most of the borders are mixed, with flowering shrubs and trees growing among herbaceous and bulbous plants, including lilies. Like Hidcote in Gloucestershire (cf), it is a formal garden with informal planting.

(1) *Apr–Sep: Wed, Thu, Sat and Public Holidays 2–6. No dogs*
(2) *Charge*
(4) *House (same times)*
(5) *National Trust*

Tolland, nr Taunton

Somerset

26. Gaulden Manor

The history of the manor house goes back to the 12th cent. The garden is being remade by the present owners and will become a plantsman's garden. A bog garden contains many varieties of plant, especially primulas; there is a herb garden and a rose garden; a 'secret garden' is being laid out. Visit at the end of May and in June.

(1) Apr–Sep: Wed, Thu, Sat and Public Holidays 2–6. No dogs
(2) Charge
(3) Tea
(4) House (same times)
(5) Mr and Mrs James Le Gendre Starkie

Wells

Somerset
27. Bishop's Palace

The palace, of which the oldest part dates from the 13th cent, is set in spacious lawns with mature specimen trees, some being unusual examples to find in the British Isles. A moat is fed by streams diverted from the wells. The Jubilee Arboretum was established in 1977 and, although it is not yet open to the public, will be an interesting feature in later years when the trees and shrubs are fully established.

(1) Easter–Sep: Thu and Sun 2–6; Aug: Daily 2–6
(2) Charge
(3) Tea (Aug)
(4) The old Bishop's Palace (Easter–Sep: Sun 2–6; Aug: Daily 2–6)
(5) Church Commissioners for England

Wells

28. Milton Lodge

The 7 acre (2·8 ha) arboretum was originally an extension to the gardens of The Cedars, now part of Wells Cathedral School. A stretch of mown grass in the centre is surrounded by plantings of trees and shrubs on steep banks. It has been planted by successive generations of the Tudway family and extensively altered by the present owner, who has extended the range of planting with trees and shrubs such as maples, sorbus, species of birch, *Davidia involucrata*, *Paulownia fargesii*, flowering cherries, crab apples, hawthorns, lilacs, cornus and hydrangeas. There are many fine specimens of native forest trees, and native plants, such as ferns, violets and primroses, are used as ground cover along with alchemillas, geraniums, *Symphytum grandiflorum* and daffodils. Visit in May, June and mid-October. The gardens at Milton Lodge are open under the NGS on two Sundays each summer, and at other times by appointment.

(1) Easter–Oct: Sat and Sun 2–7
(2) Free; voluntary contributions for benefit of Wells Cathedral Appeal
(5) D. C. Tudway Quilter, Esq

Wimborne Minster

Dorset
29. Merley Bird Gardens

The bird gardens, situated in what was once the walled garden of Merley House, built c 1850, were created in 1968 by Mr and Mrs J. Hudson and opened to the public the following year. Large outdoor aviaries are set in 3 acres (1·2 ha) of lawns, trees, herbaceous borders and seasonal bedding.

(1) Daily 10.30–6.30 or Sunset
(2) Charge
(3) Café
(4) The birds; children's pet corner
(5) Compton Acre Gardens Ltd

Wimborne Minster

30. Wimborne Minster Model Town

The model town is a miniature replica, 1 : 10 scale, of Wimborne Minster. The gardens of the houses are also beautifully reproduced in miniature, with pocket-sized lawns and dwarf trees, shrubs and flowers, forming an interesting example of an extreme case of 'planting to scale'.

(1) Summer: Daily 9–9; Winter: Daily 9–5
(2) Charge
(5) T. E. Salter, Esq (Director)

Yeovil

Somerset
31. Brympton d'Evercy

The west front of the house is of Tudor design, while the south front was built in the late 17th cent. Most of the garden was laid out by the late Mrs Clive in the early 20th cent and it has been restored in recent years by Mrs Clive-Ponsonby-Fane. The forecourt is planted in a yellow and white colour scheme; there are shrubs, pot pourri beds, a pond and a commercial vineyard.

(1) Easter weekend and May–late Sep: Sat–Wed noon–6
(2) Charge (NGS)
(3) Tea
(4) House and agricultural museum (same times); cider and wine for sale
(5) Charles E. B. Clive-Ponsonby-Fane, Esq

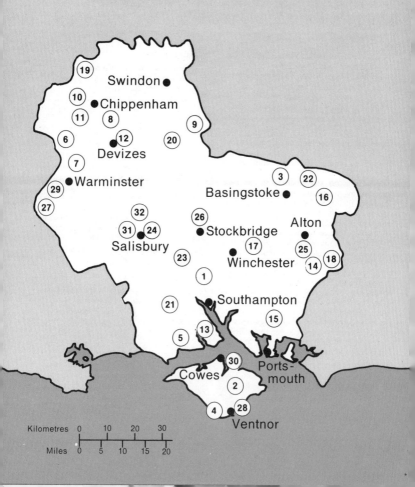

⑲
Swindon ●

⑩ ● Chippenham
⑪ ⑧
⑥ ⑫ ⑨
⑦ Devizes ⑳

⑳ Warminster
㉙ ③ ㉒
㉗ Basingstoke ● ⑯

㉜ ㉖ Alton ●
㉛ ㉔ Stockbridge ● ㉕
Salisbury ⑰ ⑭ ⑱
㉓ Winchester

①
㉑ Southampton ●
⑤ ⑬ ⑮

㉚ Ports-
Cowes ② mouth

④ ㉘
Ventnor

Kilometres 0   10   20   30
Miles   0   5   10   15   20

Ampfield, nr Romsey

Hampshire

1. The Hillier Arboretum

The arboretum, now over 100 acres (40·5 ha) in extent, contains the largest collection in the world of trees and shrubs hardy in temperate regions; it is estimated that over 15,000 species and varieties are represented. It was founded in 1953 by Harold Hillier, CBE, owner of the famous nursery firm. As well as the tree and shrub collection, there are scree beds for alpines and dwarf bulbs; a bog garden; a pond; and the Centenary Border, two pairs of beds constructed in 1964 to celebrate the firm's centenary, running diagonally for approx 800 ft (244 m) across the original 10 acre (4 ha) arboretum, and planted alternately with Hybrid Tea and floribunda roses and herbaceous perennials.

In spring, the main display of colour comes from camellias and daffodils, followed by flowering cherries, magnolias and many of the comprehensive collection of rhododendrons. After them come the deciduous azaleas and in summer roses and herbaceous perennials take over. The autumn colour is spectacular and even in winter a number of plants are in flower. In October 1977 Harold Hillier gave the arboretum to the Hampshire County Council.

(1) Mon–Fri (except Public Holidays) 9– 4.30
(2) Charge
(5) Hampshire County Council

Arreton

Isle of Wight

2. Arreton Manor

Although the main feature of interest here is the early 17th-cent manor house, the 4½ acre (2 ha) grounds, which twenty years ago were derelict, have been greatly improved: new gardens have been laid out and much planting done. A wild flower garden is under construction. A specimen of *Cupressus sempervirens* was planted by Queen Victoria in 1897 and a pine tree by Queen Mary.

(1) Easter–1st week of Nov: Mon–Sat 10– 6; Sun 2–6
(2) Charge
(3) Café and restaurant
(4) House (same times)
(5) Count Slade de Pomeroy

Basingstoke

Hampshire

3. The Vyne

The house dates from the 16th cent; the park is little altered since it was landscaped in 1755–6 by John Chute, who enlarged the lake north of the house. A red-brick pavilion in the garden was probably designed by

John Webb, a pupil and nephew of Inigo Jones. There are sweeping lawns, a very fine herbaceous border and some good trees, including white willows (*Salix alba*) and *Phillyrea latifolia*.

(1) Apr–Oct: Tue, Wed, Thu, Sat and Sun 2–6 (5.30 in Oct); Public Holidays 11–1, 2–6. Parties on other days by arrangement with the administrator
(2) Charge
(3) Tea
(4) House (same times)
(5) National Trust

Blackgang, nr Ventnor

Isle of Wight

4. Blackgang Chine

Situated on a clifftop on the southern point of the Isle of Wight, 400 ft (122 m) above sea level, the gardens were created in 1843 by Alexander Dabell, whose great-grandson is the present owner. They have been expanded by successive generations into the present-day leisure park.

Because of the exposed situation, privets, escallonias, olearia, elaeagnus and griselinia have been planted as windbreaks. The water gardens were constructed in 1961–2, with pools, waterfalls and fountains and over 120 species of evergreen and flowering shrub. There is a maze, a gnome's garden and a model village, including a scale model of Osborne House, Queen Victoria's residence on the Isle of Wight. June–September the gardens are floodlit in the evenings.

(1) Late Mar–May and Oct: Daily 10–5; Jun–Sep: Daily 10–10
(2) Charge
(3) Cafés
(4) Museum; model dinosaurs (same times)
(5) F. R. Dabell, Esq

Boldre

Hampshire

5. Spinners

The present owner and his wife bought a derelict stable block in 1958, converted it into a house and started to create the 2 acre (0·9 ha) garden in 1960. This was done without outside help and the garden is still maintained by the owner and his wife. The garden is mostly woodland and contains a wide range of plants, many rare and unusual, and it includes rhododendrons, azaleas, camellias and magnolias underplanted with primulas, meconopsis and other shade-loving and ground-cover plants. Visit in May and June.

(1) Last week of Apr–mid-Jul: Tue–Sun 2– 7. Other times by appointment
(2) Charge
(4) Plants for sale
(5) P. G. G. Chappell, Esq

Bradford-on-Avon

Wiltshire

6. The Hall

The house, which is not open to the public, dates from 1600. The garden is extensive, with lawns, terraces, trees and herbaceous borders.

(1) Daily 9–5
(2) Collecting box
(5) Alex Moulton, CBE

Brokerswood, nr Westbury

Wiltshire

7. Woodland Park

This piece of natural woodland, one of the last in the area of a primeval forest, contains a very wide range of trees native to this country. There are cherries, crabs, aspens, sweet chestnuts and a large specimen of the uncommon wild service tree, *Sorbus torminalis*.

(1) Daily 10.30–Sunset
(2) Charge
(3) Café
(4) The Phillips Countryside Museum (same times)
(5) A. G. Phillips, Esq

Calne

Wiltshire

8. Bowood

The park, laid out to plans of 'Capability' Brown in the 1760s, is one of the finest examples of landscape gardening, the lake set against a backdrop of fields and beech woods, with the Wiltshire downs beyond.

The Lake Walk includes a Doric temple, hermit's cave and a cascade in the Rococo style designed by Charles Hamilton in 1785. The pleasure grounds have a magnificent display of spring flowers and in summer there are roses on the terraces in front of the house. The arboretum has a collection of 200 different kinds of trees and shrubs. The 60 acres (24 ha) of rhododendrons, which are separate from the rest of the garden, are dominated by the mausoleum designed by Robert Adam in 1761.

(1) Gardens and Grounds. Good Friday–Sep: Daily 2–6. Rhododendron Walks. Mid-May–mid-Jun: Daily 2–6. No dogs
(2) Charges
(3) Tea
(4) Picture Gallery and Chapel (same times as Gardens and Grounds)
(5) Earl of Shelburne

Chilton Foliat, nr Hungerford

Wiltshire

9. Littlecote House

A Tudor house set in approx 8 acres (3·2 ha) of walled garden including a trout stream and ponds. There are broad lawns, fine specimen trees, shrubs, roses, herbaceous borders and bedding plants. Visit in July.

(1) Easter–Sep: Sat, Sun and Public Holidays 2–6; by appointment for organized parties
(2) Charge
(3) Tea
(4) House (same times)
(5) D. S. Wills, Esq

Chippenham

Wiltshire

10. Sheldon Manor

The house dates from the 13th cent and the first mention of a garden is in 1287. It is approx 5 acres (2 ha) in extent and was considerably refurbished in 1935 and 1953. There is a formal garden around the house, many roses, a water garden and some very old yew trees. In recent years a number of interesting trees and shrubs have been planted.

(1) Easter–Oct: Sun, Thu and Public Holidays 2–6. Other times by arrangement
(2) Charge
(3) Tea
(4) House (same times)
(5) Major Martin Gibbs

Corsham

Wiltshire

11. Corsham Court

The grounds of the Elizabethan manor house were originally designed by 'Capability' Brown in 1760. He made the lake, built an ornamental bath house and planted many trees, including an oriental plane, *Platanus orientalis*, which now has a perimeter of 200 yds (183 m), with branches that have layered themselves where they touch the ground. In 1799 Humphry Repton enlarged the lake and planted a great avenue of elms. Other notable trees include large specimens of the maidenhair tree, *Ginkgo biloba*, and black walnut and a copper beech. Behind the bath house is a flower garden, with rose beds and herbaceous borders.

(1) Mid-Jul–mid-Sep: Tue–Sun and Public Holidays 11–12.30, 2–4.30; mid-Sep–mid-Jul: Sun, Wed, Thu 11–12.30, 2–4.30
(2) Charge
(4) House (same times)
(5) Lord Methuen

Devizes, Hillworth Road

Wiltshire

12. The Pygmy Pinetum

The pinetum, which covers approx $3\frac{1}{2}$ acres (1·4 ha) was founded in 1958 by the present owner with the intention of establishing a standard reference collection of dwarf and slow-growing conifers. It is now the largest collection in existence with about 1,200 species and cultivars growing in a landscaped setting. The excellent conifer library may be visited only by *bona fide* researchers, at the owner's discretion.

(*1*) *Mon–Fri 8–5; Sat 8–noon. Other times by appointment*
(*2*) *Free*
(*4*) *Wansdyke Nursery (same times)*
(*5*) *H. J. Welch, Esq*

Exbury

Hampshire

13. Exbury Gardens

In the 1920s, the late Lionel de Rothschild started breeding rhododendrons at Exbury and many famous hybrids have been raised there, including 'Hawk', 'Lady Bessborough', 'Lady Chamberlain' and 'Lionel's Triumph', as well as the strain of Exbury deciduous azaleas which, perhaps more than any other type, combines beauty of flower with perfume. There is also a fine collection of species rhododendrons, such as *R. sinogrande*, *R. falconeri*, *R. concatens* and *R. wardii*.

The garden is largely woodland, interplanted with the rhododendrons and azaleas, and with a fine display of daffodils in spring. As well as the rhododendrons, there are many other interesting shrubs and trees, including *Magnolia* × *veitchii*; the spectacular pink-flowered *M. campbellii*; the Hungarian oak *Quercus frainetto*; *Q. canariensis*; and some interesting conifers such as the South American *Fitzroya cupressoides* and the California nutmeg *Torreya californica*.

(*1*) *Early Apr–mid-Jun: Daily 2–6.30*
(*2*) *Charge*
(*5*) *E. L. de Rothschild, Esq*

Greatham, nr Liss

Hampshire

14. Greatham Mill

The gardens, approx $1\frac{1}{2}$ acres (0·7 ha) in extent, lie on two sides of the 17th-cent mill house, and are bounded by the River Rother. It is a plantsman's garden, full of uncommon plants, and has been designed and planted over the past 25 years by the present owner and her gardeners.

(*1*) *May–Oct: Sun 2–7*
(*2*) *Charge*
(*4*) *Small nursery garden (same times)*
(*5*) *Mrs Frances Pumphrey*

Hambledon

Hampshire

15. The Vineyard

The vineyard was planted in 1951; it covers 5 acres (2 ha) and produces an average of 15,000 bottles a year of white wine. The soil is chalky, as in Champagne, and the same types of vine are used. There are pleasant views over Broadhalfpenny Down, the cradle of cricket. Around the house there is a pleasant small, mainly formal, garden.

(*1*) *Late Jul–early Oct: Sun 2.30–5.30 or by appointment*
(*2*) *Charge*
(*3*) *Café*
(*4*) *Winery*
(*5*) *Maj.-Gen Sir Guy Salisbury-Jones*

Hartley Wintney

Hampshire

16. West Green House

The early 18th-cent house is surrounded by a 4 acre (1·8 ha) garden, with terraced lawns and a wide range of shrubs, roses, herbaceous perennials and herbs, as well as a wild garden with pools and water-lilies. The walled kitchen garden contains old fruit trees.

(*1*) *Apr–Sep: Wed, Thu and Sun 2–6, also two Sats for NGS. No dogs*
(*2*) *Charge*
(*4*) *House (3 rooms only) (Wed 2–6 by previous appointment with Secretary – 7 days notice)*
(*5*) *National Trust*

Itchen Abbas, nr Winchester

Hampshire

17. Avington Park

The 17th-cent red-brick house is set in a wooded park. The River Itchen, spanned by an iron bridge, flows through the grounds. There are extensive lawns and many fine trees, an orangery and conservatories. Avington Church stands in the grounds.

(*1*) *May–Sep: Sat, Sun and Public Holidays 2.30–5.30*
(*2*) *Charge*
(*3*) *Tea (Sun and Public Holidays)*
(*4*) *House (same times)*
(*5*) *J. B. Hickson, Esq*

Liphook

Hampshire

18. Bohunt Manor

The garden was redesigned in 1952 and unusual plants have been added each year. There are lakeside and woodland walks, a bog garden, flowering shrubs, bulbs and outstanding herbaceous borders.

(1) Apr–Sep: Mon–Sat (except Public Holidays) 11–5
(2) Charge
(3) Tea
(4) Waterfowl, cranes and ornamental pheasants
(5) World Wildlife Fund

Luckington

Wiltshire

19. Luckington Court

The house was mainly built in the Queen Anne period but parts of it are much older. The well-designed garden, largely formal, has a good collection of flowering cherries as well as other interesting trees and flowering shrubs.

(1) Wed 11–6
(2) Charge
(4) House (by appointment)
(5) Hon Mrs Trevor Horn

Milton Lilbourne, nr Pewsey

Wiltshire

20. Manor House

The house, which dates from the late 17th or early 18th cent, has a 3 acre (1·2 ha) garden that was redesigned by Robert Stent in 1947, with lawns, roses, herbaceous borders and shrubs, including rhododendrons and azaleas.

(1) May–Oct: Wed 2–6
(2) Collecting box
(4) Antique shop in house (same times)
(5) Mrs R. Gentle

Minstead, nr Lyndhurst

Hampshire

21. Furzey Gardens

Furzey house was built on open pastureland by Boulton and Paul in 1922 for three brothers Dalrymple, of whom Hugh Dalrymple was chiefly responsible for the design of the 8 acre (3·2 ha) garden. Soil was imported by horse and cart to bury the forest clay.

The garden consists mainly of lawns with large island beds and grassy walks forming glades and includes one of the most comprehensive collections of heathers in the country, with some very large tree heaths. There are many azaleas and rhododendrons and a profusion of spring bulbs and bluebells, and many unusual trees and shrubs, quite a number from South America, including a specimen of Eucryphia × nymansensis over 50 ft (15 m) high, E. cordifolia, E. glutinosa and Embothrium coccineum. Nyssa sylvatica and Parrotia persica provide

brilliant autumn foliage. The garden is of considerable botanical interest and is beautiful at all times of year, although probably it is most colourful in spring.

(1) Daily 10–7 or Sunset
(2) Charge (proportion to NGS); Dec: Free
(4) Will Selwood Art and Craft Gallery (same times)
(5) H. J. Cole, Esq

Riseley, nr Reading

Hampshire

22. Stratfield Saye House

The main part of the house was built in c 1630; it was bought by the 1st Duke of Wellington with the money voted to him by Parliament after his victory at Waterloo in 1815. The gardens became run down, but a comprehensive programme of restoration has been undertaken.

On the east side of the house, between it and the river Loddon which runs through the grounds, lies the 6 acre (2·3 ha) main lawn, laid down in 1973. The Pleasure Grounds on either side of the house have an interesting collection of trees, some planted by the 1st Lord Rivers in the 18th cent, others by the 1st Duke of Wellington, and a considerable number by the 8th Duke since his succession to the property in 1972. A fine group of wellingtonias (Sequoiadendron giganteum) was planted in 1857 by the 2nd Duchess: the tree was introduced to this country in 1853, the year after the 1st Duke's death, and was named after him.

The American Garden was created in the early 19th cent, using mainly trees and shrubs from North America; it was largely replanted in 1973 and is at its best in early summer. A recently planted rose garden lies between the Ice House Paddock (which contains the grave of the Duke's battlecharger Copenhagen) and the walled garden. The latter covers about 3 acres (1·2 ha) and has recently been redesigned.

(1) Sun before Easter–last Sun in Sep: Sat–Thu 11–6. Last admission 5.30
(2) Charge
(3) Refreshments
(4) House (same times); Wellington Country Park (Daily, except 25 Dec 10–Sunset)
(5) Duke of Wellington

Romsey

Hampshire

23. Mottisfont Abbey

A 12th-cent abbey church survives behind 18th-cent elevations. The park contains some fine trees, including walnuts, Spanish chustnuts, cedars of Lebanon, a giant London plane, Platanus × hispanica, believed to have the largest girth of any specimen in Britain, and an oak thought to be 800 years old. A Neo-Gothic summer house dates from the 18th cent, but the present garden is largely the creation of Mr and Mrs Gilbert Russell, who bought the property in 1934. The lawn north of the house and the pleached lime walk along its western border were designed by the landscape architect Geoffrey Jellicoe in 1936–7. The limes are underplanted with the spring-flowering bulb *Chionodoxa luciliae*. The retaining wall of the terrace, which is decorated with lead vases, has various species of hydrangea, fuchsia and yucca growing against it.

There are many summer-flowering shrubs, such as varieties of *Hibiscus syriacus*, ceanothus and potentillas; Russell Page advised on the planting.

South of the house is a small parterre on the site of the old cloister garth, laid out by Norah Lindsay in 1938, edged with box and lavender and filled with seasonal bedding. The walled garden behind the stables was laid out by the National Trust's garden adviser, Graham Thomas, and planted in 1972–3 with his collection of historic roses. Cross paths, bordered with dwarf box, meet at a fountain and pool flanked by Irish yews. One of the central walks has herbaceous borders backed by rambling roses trained on poles.

(1) *Apr–Sep: Tue–Sat 2.30–6*
(2) *Charge*
(4) *House: Whistler room and cellarium (Apr–Sep: Wed and Sat 2.30–6)*
(5) *National Trust*

Salisbury, The Close

Wiltshire

24. North Canonry

There has been a domestic garden on the 2 acre (0·8 ha) site since the 13th cent. The design of the present garden of the 17th-cent house is reputedly by Gertrude Jekyll. The most striking feature is a double herbaceous border, at its best in summer, that leads to the banks of the Hampshire Avon.

(1) *Apr–Sep: Daily noon–6*
(2) *Charge*
(5) *Mrs Y. M. Cory*

Selborne

Hampshire

25. The Wakes

The Wakes was the home from 1729 to 1793 of the Revd Gilbert White, the naturalist and author of *The Natural History of Selborne*; he and his brother Henry landscaped the garden between 1758 and 1761. The grounds are surrounded by a ha-ha, built up with flint stones. An arched pergola of laburnum leads to the water garden with a lily pool and topiary hedges and the rose garden which is planted with 18th-cent varieties – gallicas, damasks, albas, provence and moss. In the herb garden are species such as southernwood, winter savory, soapwort, sweet cecily, hore-

ENGLAND

hound and salad burnet. A brick path laid by Gilbert White himself leads to a reconstruction of his bird-watching hide. The garden also contains some fine specimen trees, including *Ailanthus altissima*, the tree of heaven; *Ginkgo biloba*, the maidenhair tree, and *Liriodendron tulipifera*, the tulip-tree.

(1) *Mar–Oct: Tue–Sun and Public Holidays noon–5.30. Last admission 5*
(2) *Charge*
(4) *Gilbert White Museum and Oates Memorial Library and Museum (same times)*
(5) *Oates Memorial Trust*

Stockbridge

Hampshire

26. Longstock Park Gardens

These gardens were started early in this century and were developed by the founder of the John Lewis Partnership and successive chairmen. In all there are 170 acres (68 ha) of gardens, but only about 7 acres (3 ha) of woodland and water garden are open to the public. The water garden, with its extensive collection of bog and aquatic plants, is said by many to be the best in Europe. As well as this, there is a pinetum, a rose garden, herbaceous borders including summer bulbs, a herb garden and a grey garden.

(1) *Apr–Sep: 3rd Sun of each month 2–5*
(2) *Charge*
(4) *Plants for sale*
(5) *Leckford Estate Ltd*

Stourton, nr Mere

Wiltshire

27 Stourhead House

The grounds at Stourhead form one of the greatest surviving examples of the 18th-cent English landscape garden. The house was built by Colen Campbell in the early 18th cent for Henry Hoare I. His son, Henry Hoare II, started to create the Stourhead landscape in *c* 1744, advised by Henry Flitcroft, an exponent of the Palladian style of architecture. The grotto and the Temple of Flora were built around the site of existing springs; the lake and Pantheon were created in *c* 1754. Over the next few years, more temples were built and in 1785, Henry Hoare died leaving the property to his grandson Richard Colt Hoare, who had a greater knowledge of plants than his predecessor and in 1791–2 began a comprehensive planting programme around the lakeside, using mainly broad-leaved species including many varieties of oak, elm, willow, phillyrea, holly, crataegus and aesculus. He planted the first rhododendrons, *R. ponticum*, in 1791; two plants of *R. arboreum* were bought in 1834.

Many conifers were planted in the mid-19th cent, and in the first half of the 20th cent many rhododendrons and azaleas were introduced, as well as other flowering trees and shrubs. Although this planting has to a certain extent reduced the stylistic effect of the original scheme, the pictorial effect still remains.

(1) *Daily 11–7 or Sunset. Last admission half an hour before closing*
(2) *Charge*
(3) *Refreshments*
(4) *House (Apr, Sep and Oct: Mon, Wed, Sat and Sun 2–6 or Sunset; May–Aug: Daily except Fri, 2–6)*
(5) *National Trust*

Ventnor
Isle of Wight
28. Ventnor Botanic Gardens

The garden was planned and constructed in 1969 by the present curator, R. Dore, in close consultation with H. G. Hillier of Winchester. It covers an area of approx 22 acres (8·8 ha) and contains over 10,000 plants of over 3,500 species. As it has a climate similar to that of the Mediterranean seaboard, trees (including palms), shrubs, herbaceous plants and succulents from all parts of the world's temperate zones grow and flourish here.

(1) *Summer: Sunrise–midnight; Winter: Sunrise–Sunset*
(2) *Free*
(3) *Restaurant (in season) 10 am–11 pm*
(4) *Smuggling Museum (Good Friday–Spring Bank Holiday and Sep: 10–5; Jun–Aug 10–5, 7–9)*
(5) *South Wight Borough Council*

Warminster
Wiltshire
29. Longleat House

The park at Longleat was landscaped by 'Capability' Brown, who made the lakes from the small stream or 'leat' from which the house takes its name. There are many fine trees, including deodars, *Cedrus deodora*; wellingtonias, *Sequoiadendron giganteum*, and redwoods, *Sequoia sempervirens*. The formal gardens were laid out in 1952 by the present owner in conjunction with the landscape architect Russell Page. In addition, there is a splendid azalea and rhododendron drive, a rose garden and an orangery with citrus trees that successfully bear fruit. Visit in late May and early June.

(1) *Easter–Sep: Daily 10–6; Oct–Easter (except 25 Dec): Daily 10–4*
(2) *Charge*
(3) *Restaurant and Café*

(4) *House (same times); Safari park (Daily 10–6 or Sunset); Kitchen shop, garden shop and boat rides (Easter–Sep: Daily 10–6)*
(5) *Marquess of Bath*

Whippingham, nr East Cowes
Isle of Wight
30. Barton Manor

The property was originally a 13th-cent monastery, mentioned in the Domesday Book, but the present house is mainly 16th-cent. It was bought by Queen Victoria in 1854, and the house was restored and the gardens laid out by Prince Albert. They have recently been extended and now cover 20 acres (8 ha), including mature specimen trees, flowering shrubs, a plantation of cork oaks, herbaceous borders, a water garden, a lake and the progeny of 225,000 daffodils that were planted in 1922. A 5 acre (2 ha) commercial vineyard was added in 1976.

(1) *Easter Sun and Mon, thereafter each Sun till late May 2–6; 30 May–mid-Sep: Thu, Fri, Sun and Public Holidays 2–6*
(2) *Charge*
(5) *A. H. Goddard, Esq*

Wilton, nr Salisbury
Wiltshire
31. Wilton House

The present house was built in *c* 1650 to a design by Inigo Jones to replace the earlier Tudor house that was almost completely destroyed by fire in 1647. The landscaped grounds include 20 acres (8 ha) of lawn with giant cedars of Lebanon, the oldest of which were planted in 1630 and were among the first cedars brought from the Lebanon. The River Nadder runs to the south of the house and is spanned by a Palladian Bridge built in 1737 by Henry, 9th Earl of Pembroke.

(1) *Easter–early Oct: Tue–Sat and Public Holidays 11–6; Sun 2–6. No dogs*
(2) *Charge*
(3) *Café and licensed restaurant*
(4) *House (same times); Garden centre*
(5) *Earl of Pembroke*

Woodford, nr Salisbury
Wiltshire
32. Heale House

Charles II hid in this 17th-cent manor house after his defeat at the Battle of Worcester. The River Avon runs through the garden which is laid out with lawns, herbaceous and mixed borders and roses. There is an authentic Japanese tea house surrounded by an attractive water garden and a wild garden.

(1) Mid-Apr–late Sep: Tue and Public Holidays 2–6. Other times by special arrangement for parties
(2) Charge
(3) Tea
(4) Garden produce and plants for sale
(5) Major and Mrs David Rasch

(29) ● Staines
(30)

(7)

Woking ● (21)

(27)

(13) (12)

(25) Guildford ● Dorking

(19)

● Godalming ● Crawley ●

(9) (4)

(10) (1) (23)

(14) (18) (15)

● Haslemere (6)

(17) Cuckfield ● (16)

(22) Haywards Heath

(20)

Midhurst ● ● Pulborough

(24) (2)

(5)

(28) (26)

(8)

● Chichester (11) ●

(3) ● Worthing

Bognor Regis

| Kilometres | 0 | 10 | 20 |
| Miles | 0 | 5 | 10 | 15 |

Ardingly, nr Haywards Heath

West Sussex

1. Wakehurst Place

Bequeathed to the National Trust in 1963, Wakehurst Place has been leased for the use of the Royal Botanic Gardens, Kew (cf) since 1965. The higher rainfall, relative freedom from frost and the rich soil provide a wide range of growing conditions. The gardens contain a fine collection of temperate trees and shrubs established 1903–6 by Lord Wakehurst (Gerald Loder), since enlarged from the Kew collections. Among the multitude of interesting plants are a selection of Australasian and South American shrubs in the heath garden and a notable collection of rhododendrons, including large-leaved species such as *R. sinogrande* and other fine foliage species such as *R. bureavii* and 'Sir Charles Lemon'. There is a magnificent specimen of the pink-flowered *Magnolia campbellii* which, at over 60 ft (18 m) high, is probably the largest in the British Isles.

Attractive use has been made of the garden's natural features – valley, lake and outcrops of rock – and there is much to see from the flowering of the *Magnolia campbellii* in early spring to the brilliance of the autumn leaves.

(1) Nov–Jan: Daily (except 25 Dec and 1 Jan) 10–4; Feb and Oct: Daily 10–5; Mar: Daily 10–6; Apr–Sep: Daily 10–7
(2) Charge
(3) Restaurant
(5) Royal Botanic Gardens, Kew

Ashington, Billingshurst Lane

West Sussex

2. Ashington Botanical Collection

This is the largest nursery in the country specializing in cacti, succulents, xerophytes and *Bromeliaceae*, and the reference collection is one of the most comprehensive in Europe. It is housed in two glasshouses and the plants are displayed in a natural setting in raised beds. Some other exotic plants, including bulbs, are also represented.

(1) Daily (except 25–26 Dec) 10.30–5
(2) Charge
(4) Nursery (Daily 9–5)
(5) Holly Gate Nurseries Ltd

Bognor Regis

West Sussex

3. Hotham Park

Near the gates of the park are lawns, with a bandstand, and seasonal bedding. Beyond this is an area of woodland with a rock garden and a pool.

(1) 7.30–½ hour before Sunset
(2) Free
(5) Arun District Council

Coldharbour, nr Dorking

Surrey

4. Leith Hill Rhododendron Wood

The wood was formerly part of the estate of Leith Hill Place, once the home of the composer Ralph Vaughan Williams. There are rhododendrons and azaleas and it is very colourful in April and May when these and the bluebells are out. Although the plants are not labelled, there are some interesting rhododendron species, including *R. edgeworthii, R. fargesii* and a very large specimen of *R. falconeri*.

(1) Daily
(2) Collecting boxes
(5) National Trust

Cootham, nr Pulborough

West Sussex

5. Parham Park

The grounds consist of a pleasure garden bordering a lake, with a beech grove planted by Sir Cecil Bysshopp in the 18th cent, and a walled garden, in all approx 7 acres (3 ha) in extent. The walled garden contains an orchard, herbaceous borders, lawns and glasshouses and collections of clematis and roses.

(1) Easter Sun–1st Sun in Oct: Sun, Wed, Thu and Public Holidays 1–6
(2) Charge
(3) Tea
(4) House (same days 2–5.30)
(5) Mr and Mrs P. A. Tritton

Cuckfield

West Sussex

6. Cuckfield Park

The Elizabethan manor house is surrounded by a large garden containing sweeping lawns, many fine trees, two lakes and flowering shrubs, including a good display of rhododendrons.

(1) Easter Sun–early Oct: Wed, Sun and Public Holidays 2.15–5.30
(2) Charge
(3) Tea
(4) House (same times)
(5) M. J. Holt, Esq

Esher

Surrey

7. Claremont Landscape Garden

Claremont, one of the earliest examples in England of the 'natural' landscape garden, was described in 1725 as 'the noblest of any in Europe'. Sir John Vanbrugh, Charles Bridgeman, William Kent and 'Capability' Brown all worked here.

ENGLAND

The estate was split up in the 1920s: the house became a school and the landscape garden, in a derelict condition and overgrown by laurel and rhododendrons, was acquired by the National Trust in 1949. Because of lack of money, restoration work on the garden did not start until 1975, when a grant from the Slater Foundation made it possible.

Much of the undergrowth has now been cleared and the outline of Charles Bridgeman's great turf amphitheatre, constructed in the 1720s on a steep slope by the lake, has reappeared. It is the only surviving one of its kind in Britain. The grotto and the pavilion on an island in the lake have now been restored, as has the Camellia Terrace, where plants that are 150 years old still grow and flower. The grounds include some fine old trees, such as a specimen of the Chinese conifer, *Cunninghamia lanceolata*.

(*1*) *Oct–Feb: Mon–Fri 8–4.15; Sat and Sun 9–4.15 Mar: Mon–Fri 8–5.30; Sat and Sun 9–5.30; Apr: Mon–Fri 8–7; Sat and Sun 9–7; May–Jul: Mon–Fri 8–8; Sat and Sun 9–8; Aug: Mon–Fri 8–7.30; Sat and Sun: 9–7.30; Sept: Mon–Fri 8–6.30; Sat and Sun 9–6.30. Public Holidays as Sat and Sun.*
(*2*) *Free*
(*5*) *National Trust*

Fishbourne

West Sussex

8. Roman Palace and Museum

When part of the palace was excavated in 1961–8, it was found that the original layout of the garden, dating from *c* AD 75, was visible because of the contrast between the dark soil in the beds and the yellow clay of the site itself. It seemed to be a formal garden, and this has been reconstructed, with lawns, hedges, paths and espalier trees.

(*1*) *Mar, Oct and Nov: Daily 10–4; Apr: Daily 10–5; May, Jun and Sep: Daily 10–6; Jul and Aug: Daily 10–7*
(*2*) *Charge*
(*3*) *Café*
(*4*) *Museum (same times)*
(*5*) *Sussex Archaeological Trust*

Godalming

Surrey

9. Hydon Nurseries Ltd

The nursery was founded by Arthur George in 1956 and is now one of the foremost rhododendron nurseries in the country with a wide range of species, many rare, as well as hybrids and deciduous and evergreen azaleas. Plants that associate well with rhododendrons, such as camellias, eucryphias and pieris, are also grown. Many specimens are grown in a 2 acre (0·9 ha) woodland garden. Visit in spring.

(*1*) *May–Sep: Mon–Fri 8.30–5*
(*2*) *Free*
(*4*) *Nursery, with containerized plants always available (Mar–May and Sep–Nov: Mon–Sat 8–5; Jun–Aug and Dec–Feb: Mon–Fri 8–5; Sat 8–1)*
(*5*) *A. F. George, Esq*

Godalming

10. Winkworth Arboretum

The arboretum is over 100 acres (40 ha) in extent and includes two lakes. The first plantings were made in 1938 by Dr Wilfred Fox and were mainly of trees and shrubs on steep slopes overlooking one of the lakes. There are collections of acers, magnolias, sorbus, ilex, quercus and rhododendrons. The autumn display in October and November is still an outstanding feature, and in spring there is a fine show of azaleas and bluebells.

(*1*) *Daily Sunrise–Sunset*
(*2*) *Charge*
(*3*) *Tea*
(*5*) *National Trust*

Goring-by-Sea, nr Worthing

West Sussex

11. Highdown

This famous garden was made by Col (later Sir) Frederick Stern on a chalk down and in an old chalk quarry, starting in 1909. In spite of the unpromising site, it was found that many plants would grow here, provided that the ground was broken up at planting; virtually no soil was brought in. The garden has an informal design, with lawns, ponds and trees underplanted with bulbs and corms, many of which have become naturalized, including daffodils, the beautiful blue *Anemone blanda* and many species of crocus, cyclamen and snowdrop. There are herbaceous borders with plants such as peonies, irises and lilies, and many fine specimen trees, including a fine *Arbutus* × *andrachnoides*; *Cornus capitata*; *Acer griseum* and *Magnolia* × *highdownensis*. Visit from April to June.

(*1*) *Oct–Mar: Mon–Fri 10–4.30; Apr (or Easter if earlier)–Sep: Mon–Fri 10–4.30; Sat and Sun 10–8*
(*2*) *Charge*
(*5*) *Worthing Corporation*

Great Bookham, nr Dorking

Surrey

12. Polesden Lacey

The original house on the site was built in 1632 and was bought by the playwright Richard Brinsley Sheridan in 1797. He lived there until his death in 1816. In 1818 the house was sold to Joseph Bonsor who demolished it and built the present house in 1821–3, designed by Thomas Cubitt. All that remains of any early garden is the long terraced walk, begun in 1761 and extended by Sheridan. The rest of the garden was laid out early in this century in Edwardian style with lawns and fine trees, including some large specimens of *Parrotia persica* underplanted with spring bulbs. The formal part is planted as a series of gardens – a lavender garden, an iris garden, peony borders and a large rose garden with the main walk passing under arches covered with rambling roses. On the east side of the garden is a collection of conifers including *Podocarpus andinus, Cephalotaxus harringtonia drupacea* and the Spanish fir, *Abies Pinsapo*.

(1) Daily 11–Sunset
(2) Charge
(3) Refreshments
(4) House (Mar and Nov: Sat and Sun 2–5 or Sunset; Apr–Oct: Tue–Thu, Sat, Sun and Public Holidays (closed following Tue) 2–6. Last admission ½ hour before closing)
(5) National Trust

Guildford

Surrey

13. Guildford Castle

The 12th-cent castle, now a ruin, is set on a steep mound thickly planted with daffodils. At the foot, the area once occupied by the moat is laid out in a formal style with grass and geometrically shaped beds with seasonal bedding, at its most colourful in May. A small pool with a fountain is set in paving stones.

(1) Daily 7.30–Sunset
(2) Free
(3) Café
(4) Castle keep (Apr–Sep: 11–6)
(5) Guildford Borough Council

Hambledon, nr Godalming

Surrey

14. Feathercombe

The house was built in 1910 for Eric Parker, editor of *The Field*. The grounds cover 15 acres (6 ha) and include a steeply sloping lawn flanked by rhododendrons, azaleas and tree heaths leading through herbaceous borders to a topiary garden. The Glade is planted with species of sorbus underplanted with daffodils, bluebells and lupins. There is a heath garden, many flowering shrubs, a rock garden and a pool. Visit in May and June.

(1) Mar–Oct: Sun and Public Holidays 2–6
(2) Charge
(4) Garden centre (Mon–Fri 9–5; Sun 2–6)
(5) Miss M-R. Parker and Mrs E. A. Wieler

Handcross

West Sussex

15. Nymans

The garden at Nymans, which covers approx 30 acres (12 ha), was begun in 1889 by Ludwig Messel.

The path from the entrance leads through new plantings to the pinetum, which was planted in the 1890s and has many fine, mature trees, including a specimen of *Cryptomeria japonica* 'Spiralis', thought to be the second largest in Britain. The trees are interplanted with eucryphias and many rhododendrons collected in China and the Himalayas by George Forrest and Kingdon Ward, as well as hydrangeas and azaleas sent from the Arnold Arboretum in the USA. A temple designed by the architect Alfred Messel is framed by large-leaved rhododendrons: *R. macabeanum, R. magnificum* and *R. sinogrande*.

The Victorian Laurel Walk leads from the pinetum to the Sunk Garden, where a Byzantine urn is set among bedding plants, surrounded by camellias. Recently, summer flowering shrubs have been planted including *Genista virgata, G. aetnensis* and deutzia, philadelphus and ceanothus species. South of this lies the Heather Garden, with clumps of cistus, lavender and alpines as well as heathers. There are dwarf rhododendrons such as *R. pemakoense* and *R. forrestii* as well as other shrubs including enkianthus, *Callistemon citrinus, Hakea acicularis* and *Pieris formosa* var. *forrestii* 'Wakehurst'.

Beside the road there is a pergola and from there lawns sweep up to the house. The picturesque ruins of the house destroyed by fire provide shelter for a number of tender plants. Before the west front of the house there are massed banks of azaleas, and behind them specimens of *Rhododendron arboreum* with huge trunks more than a century old.

The Wall Garden, originally an orchard, was the first part of the garden that was made by Ludwig Messel. Herbaceous borders run from side to side and there are flowering shrubs, a spring bulb border and some fine specimen trees, including species of magnolia, nothofagus, davidia, cornus, *Umbellularia californica, Staphylea colchica* 'Coulombieri' and many rhododendrons. Here also are the original trees of *Eucryphia glutinosa* and *E. cordifolia* which were crossed in the early years of the century by Ludwig Messel to produce the now-famous *Eucryphia × nymansensis*.

A path leads to an area of woodland underplanted with rhododendrons and also *Crinodendron hookeranum* and *Cardiocrinum giganteum*. Further on, there are more plantings of rhododendrons, azaleas and lilacs and two fine hybrids that originated at Nymans, *Magnolia* 'Leonard

101

Messel' and *Camellia* 'Leonard Messel'. These plants were named after Ludwig Messel's son, Lt-Col L. C. R. Messel, who greatly enlarged the garden and the collection in the period between the two wars.

In the Top Garden are glasshouses, more flowering trees and shrubs and the rose garden, with a good collection of old shrub roses and climbing roses on arches and pillars.

Across the road lie the rhododendron wood and the wild garden, where many of the rhododendron species are grown as well as a collection of berberis and a number of plants from Tasmania such as *Drimys lanceolata*, *Nothofagus cunninghamii* and *Lomatia tinctoria*.

Under the terms of Col Messel's bequest the gardens are managed by his daughter, the Countess of Rosse.

(*1*) *Apr–Oct: Tue–Thu and Sat 2–7; Sun and Public Holidays 11–7 or Sunset. Last admission 1 hour before closing*
(*2*) *Charge*
(*3*) *Tea*
(*4*) *Plants for sale*
(*5*) *National Trust*

Haywards Heath

West Sussex

16. Borde Hill

The property, made up of over 300 acres (120 ha) of garden, woodland and park, was bought in 1893 by Col Stephenson Clarke (grandfather of the present owner) who helped to finance many expeditions of plant collectors to the Himalayas, South America and Tasmania. The garden is famous for its collection of rhododendron species from seed sent by all the famous collectors – Hooker, Wilson, Farrer, Forrest, Rock, Ludlow and Sherriff, Professor Hu and in particular Kingdon Ward, but there are also hybrid rhododendrons and azaleas and a wealth of other trees and shrubs, many rare. These include magnolias, camellias, *Stewartia malacodendron*, *Emmenopteris henryi*, *Umbellularia californica*, maples and some fine conifers. A collection of nerines in the glasshouses is one of the finest in the country. Visit in spring and early summer.

(*1*) *Late Mar–late Aug: Wed, Sat, Sun and Public Holidays 10–6*
(*2*) *Charge*
(*3*) *Tea*
(*5*) *Borde Hill Garden Ltd*

Hollycombe, nr Liphook

West Sussex

17. Hollycombe House

The gardens were designed at the turn of the century by J. C. Hawkshaw, then owner of the property. The woodland garden and arboretum contain many unusual trees, including the Californian nutmeg, *Torreya californica*; the cork oak, *Quercus suber*; *Trochodendron aralioides* and *Disanthus cercidifolius*. Colour is provided by camellias, large banks of rhododendrons and an azalea walk. An ice-pit, which before the days of refrigerators was used for storing ice throughout the summer, is an interesting feature of the grounds.

(*1*) *Easter Sun–mid-Oct: Sun and Public Holidays noon–6*
(*2*) *Charge*
(*3*) *Tea*
(*4*) *Collection of working steam engines, including steam fairground and railways with spectacular views over the Downs; souvenir shop (Sun and Public Holidays 2–6)*
(*5*) *J. M. Baldock, Esq*

Lower Beeding

West Sussex

18. Leonardslee

The garden was created by Sir Edmund Loder, Bt (grandfather of the present owner), who started planting the woodland in 1887, although some of the larger conifers were already there. The house lies 300 ft (91.4 m) above sea level and the gardens, which are 82 acres (33 ha) in extent, slope down to a stream and a chain of lakes: these are hammer ponds made over 300 years ago by excavations for iron ore. Running water provided power and the trees provided fuel. There are fine views over the valley to the South Downs.

This is one of the finest woodland gardens in Britain, particularly noted for its rhododendrons, both species and hybrids, including the beautiful scented *R.* × *loderi*, which was raised there. There is a splendid collection of camellias, some in cold glasshouses for protection. There is also a temperate glasshouse, kept above 40°F (4°C), that contains plants too tender to be grown outside, such as *Myrtus luma*, *Acacia baileyana* and bougainvilleas. Near the house is the rock garden, planted with Kurume azaleas and other low-growing rhododendrons as well as dwarf conifers and other shrubs. All the named forms of *R.* × *loderi* and massed azaleas are planted in the Coronation Garden, which was laid out in the early 1950s. The many interesting trees include *Magnolia macrophylla*, *Nothofagus procera*, *Betula utilis*, *Quercus alnifolia* and a number of specimen conifers.

(*1*) *End of Apr–early Jun: Wed, Thu, Sat, Sun and Public Holidays 10–6; Oct: some Sats and Suns*
(*2*) *Charge*
(*3*) *Tea*
(*5*) *Sir Giles Loder, Bt*

New Chapel, nr Lingfield

Surrey

19. London Temple

Parts of the manor house date back to Elizabethan times; there has been a garden on the site since then, but it was modernized when the Temple was built. The River Eden runs through the grounds. The gardens, 12–15 acres (5.5–7 ha) in extent, surrounding the Temple are colourful from spring onwards, with massed bulbs followed in June by the rhododendrons in the 100-year-old Rhododendron Walk. Later, the display is provided by roses and the herbaceous border, 95 yards (87 m) long. A reflecting pool mirrors the Temple in the water.

(1) *Daily 10–Sunset*
(2) *Free*
(4) *Visitors' centre (same times)*
(5) *Church of Jesus Christ and the Latter-day Saints*

Petworth

West Sussex

20. Petworth House

The house dates mainly from the late 17th cent and the park, created in the 18th-cent, is one of the finest achievements of 'Capability' Brown, painted frequently by Turner. Brown was first consulted by the 2nd Earl of Egremont in 1751 and over the next few years he dammed the stream to make a serpentine lake, planted many trees and swept away the existing formal gardens. In the Pleasure Grounds, north of the house, he retained the outline of the Elizabethan rectangle, modified later by George London: he added serpentine gravel paths, two temples and made many new plantings. Between 1870 and 1914, a good selection of rhododendrons was planted, including *R. campylocarpum, R. concatens* and *R. bureavii*, and a number of exotic trees such as *Davidia involucrata, Cornus florida, C. kousa* and *C. nuttallii*.

(1) *Pleasure Grounds. Apr–end Oct: Tue–Thu, Sat and Public Holiday Mon (closed following Tue) 2–6. Park. Daily*
(2) *Charge*
(4) *House (same times)*
(5) *National Trust*

Ripley

Surrey

21. Wisley Garden

The Wisley estate was given to the Royal Horticultural Society in 1904. At that time approx 6 acres (2·4 ha) were under cultivation – mainly the wild garden – while now almost 200 acres (81 ha) are incorporated in the garden. Wisley has a number of functions: to maintain a garden with as full a range as possible of ornamental plants; to

advise Fellows of the RHS on horticultural problems; to carry out trials of new varieties of flowers, fruit and vegetables; to carry out research work and to train young gardeners.

There is always something of interest to see at Wisley. In late March and early April the Alpine Meadow is outstanding, with naturalized specimens of the hoop-petticoat daffodil, *Narcissus bulbocodium*; these are followed by species and varieties of 'Angel's Tears', *Narcissus triandrus*, and the dog's-tooth violet, *Erythronium dens-canis*. Above the Alpine Meadow is the rock garden with winding paths and bridges across small streams where there is always something in flower. The heather garden, in the area known as Seven Acres, has curved beds planned so as to give colour from either flower or foliage all the year round while dwarf conifers ensure that there is not too much uniformity in shape. Most of the shade-loving plants are grown on Battleston Hill; there are many species and varieties of rhododendron, camellia and magnolia and, in May, evergreen and deciduous azaleas provide a spectacular display. In summer and late summer, the long herbaceous borders are full of interest.

The new glasshouses were opened in 1970; the dominating feature is the display house which covers an area of 10,000 square feet (929 sq m) and is divided into three sections – warm, with a minimum temperature of 60°F (15·6°C), intermediate (temperate), with a minimum temperature of 50°F (10°C), and cool, with a minimum temperature of 40°F (4·4°C). Other houses are for cacti and succulents, orchids and epiphytes.

(1) *Feb–Oct: Daily 10–7 or Sunset; Nov–Jan: Daily 10–4.30 (except 25 Dec)*
(2) *Charge, except for Fellows of the RHS*
(3) *Restaurant (Mar–Oct; 10.30–5.30); café*
(4) *Information centre and shop; plant sales centre (same times)*
(5) *Royal Horticultural Society*

Roundhurst

Surrey

22. Farall Demonstration Gardens

The garden was designed and planted in 1947 by the present owner with the aim of demonstrating how shrub beds can give continuous colour from May to October and, when planted densely (the close boskage system), reduce maintenance to a minimum. The colour is provided mainly by camellias, evergreen azaleas and rhododendrons in early spring; by deciduous azaleas and hardy hybrid rhododendrons in late spring; by roses, philadelphus, genistas, heaths and hydrangeas in mid-summer and by genistas, heaths and hydrangeas in late summer. There are many fine specimens of

103

flowering trees including embothriums, cornels, hoherias, styrax and eucryphias. All plants are labelled. The total area is 6 acres (2·4 ha) including a water garden and 3 acres (1·2 ha) of wild garden where rhododendrons and magnolias grow in woodland.

(1) *Mon–Sat 9–1, 2–5*
(2) *Charge*
(4) *Garden centre (same times)*
(5) *M. Haworth-Booth, Esq*

Sharpthorne

West Sussex

23. Tanyard

The medieval tannery, with half-timbered additions dating from the 16th and 17th cents, is set in a walled garden laid out informally with lawns, flowering shrubs and herbaceous borders. It is atttractive throughout spring and summer.

(1) *May–Sep: Mon and Wed 2–5*
(2) *Charge*
(4) *House, with remains of tanning pits (same times)*
(5) *M. R. Lewinsohn, Esq*

South Harting, nr Petersfield

West Sussex

24. Uppark

The gardens, approx 5 acres (2 ha) in extent, were originally laid out by the Earl of Tankerville in 1690, when the house was built. They were redesigned in 1810 by Humphry Repton and now consist mainly of lawns, with flowering shrubs and many mature trees, including deodars, tulip-trees (*Liriodendron tulipifera*), *Picea smithiana*, *Abies cephalonica* and *Pittosporum tenuifolium*.

(1) *Apr–Sep: Wed, Thu, Sun and Public Holidays 2–6*
(2) *Charge*
(4) *House (same times)*
(5) *National Trust*

Tilford, Reeds Road

Surrey

25. Old Kiln Agricultural Museum

The grounds around the museum cover approx 10 acres (4 ha), part of which forms an arboretum consisting of natural woodland planted approx twenty years ago with native and exotic trees: an incense cedar, *Libocedrus decurrens*, *Sequoia sempervirens*, *Cedrus deodora* and various species of larch. The rest of the grounds are planted with a variety of ornamental trees, such as flowering cherries and Japanese maples, and near the buildings is a bank planted with dwarf rhododendrons and daffodils and other bulbs, as well as plantings of shrubs including *Garrya elliptica*, and species of elaeagnus and euonymus.

(1) *Apr–Sep: Wed, Sat, Sun and Public Holidays noon–6*
(2) *Charge*
(4) *Wheelwright's shop; forge; dairy hand-tools and waggons (same times)*
(5) *Henry Jackson, Esq*

Washington

West Sussex

26. Goatcher's Nurseries

The nursery was founded in 1845 and now some 40 acres (16 ha) are under cultivation growing roses, perennials, fruit trees, etc, but specializing in ornamental trees, shrubs and conifers. Although there is no demonstration garden as such, many visitors come in summer to see the colourful mixed borders and the mature specimens of fine trees such as *Ginkgo biloba*, *Styrax japonica* and *Fagus heterophylla*.

(1) *Mon–Fri 8–5; Sat 8–noon*
(2) *Free*
(5) *A. Goatcher & Son*

West Clandon, nr Guildford

Surrey

27. Clandon Park

The house was built in c 1733 by the Venetian architect Giacomo Leoni for the 2nd Baron Onslow; the park, designed by 'Capability' Brown, is not open to the public, but from the entrance drive there is a pleasant view of a narrow lake with red-stemmed cornus on the far side and a garden temple on the other. On the walls of the house are some large specimens of *Clematis armandii*; elsewhere in the garden much of the planting is recent, although there are some large old cypresses and a big wellingtonia, *Sequoiadendron giganteum*. At the back of the house are formal, rectangular beds, some planted with hornbeams. Island beds set in the lawn, which has clumps of cowslips, are planted mainly with ground-cover plants such as bergenias and geraniums, with some taller shrubs such as *Mahonia japonica* and *Phlomis fruticosa*. Drifts of daffodils make a good display in spring. There is an early Maori meeting-house in the garden.

(1) *Apr–mid-Oct: Tue–Thu, Sat, Sun and Public Holidays 2–6 (last admission 5.30). Closed Tue after Bank Holiday Mon*
(2) *Charge*
(3) *Restaurant*
(4) *House (same times)*
(5) *National Trust*

West Dean, nr Chichester

West Sussex

28. West Dean Gardens

The original manor house was built towards the end of the 16th cent and there have been gardens here at least since then. The contemporary gardens are largely informal and, although many of the trees are very old, much of the planting has been done by the James family who bought the estate in 1893. The specimen trees include two trees of heaven, *Ailanthus vilmoriniana*, believed to be the tallest in southeast England; a group of foxglove-trees, *Paulownia tomentosa*; corkscrew hazels, *Corylus avellana 'Contorta'*; tulip-trees, *Liriodendron tulipifera*; *Nothofagus obliqua*; *Zelkova serrata*; and the Californian nutmeg, *Torreya californica* as well as some fine conifers. A pergola leads from a sunken garden dominated by three Japanese maples, *Acer palmatum*, to a gazebo with a floor made from knapped flint and horses' molars. There is a spring garden with many bamboos.

(*1*) *Apr–Sep: Sun–Fri and Sat of Bank Holiday weekends 2–6*
(*2*) *Charge*
(*3*) *Tea*
(*4*) *Garden shop (same times)*
(*5*) *Edward James Foundation*

Windsor Great Park

Surrey

29. Savill Garden

The Savill Garden, 35 acres (14 ha) in extent, occupies a small area of Windsor Great Park. It was created by Sir Eric Savill, then Deputy Ranger, and was started in 1932 although planting was not completed until the early 1950s. Many of the plants in the garden were raised from seed sent home by collectors, and others have been presented by people from all over the world.

The Savill Garden combines to a remarkable degree beauty of design with interesting and rare plants. There is a good collection of rhododendrons and azaleas, both species and hybrid, including a number of large-leaved species such as *R. rex*, *R. sinogrande*, *R. mollyanum* and *R. basilicum*, and many magnolias, including the March-flowering species *M. sargentiana 'Robusta'* and *M. dawsoniana*. Tender rhododendrons grow in the Temperate House, where the temperature does not fall below 40°F; March and April are good months to see these. Notable trees and shrubs include many acers, nothofagus, camellias, stewartias, flowering cherries and hydrangeas.

The woodland areas provide ideal conditions for meconopsis and primulas; more primulas are found in the Peat Garden, which also has a collection of hardy terrestrial orchids. The various ponds provide suitable habitats for many waterside and

bog plants such as *Lysichitum* spp., the skunk cabbages, the giant rhubarb, *Gunnera manicata*, and irises. The alpine meadow is covered with *Narcissus bulbocodium*, *N. cyclamineus* and other wild daffodils in March and early April.

Alpine plants proper are grown in seven raised beds with a range of soils varying from acid to alkaline alongside a south-facing wall covered with climbers, some only semi-hardy, such as *Clematis armandii*, *Campsis radicans*, *C. grandiflora* and *Azara serrata*. In the more formal part of the garden there are lawns and herbaceous borders and a wide range of roses, old-fashioned and shrub roses as well as Hybrid Teas and floribundas.

(*1*) *Mar–Oct: Daily 10–6*
(*2*) *Charge*
(*3*) *Licensed restaurant and café*
(*4*) *Plant shop*
(*5*) *Crown Estate Commissioners*

Windsor Great Park

30. Valley Gardens

This area was developed as a woodland garden by Sir Eric Savill, starting in 1947. It can be divided into three main areas: the Valley Garden, the Heather Garden and the Rhododendron Species Collection; and two smaller areas: the Pinetum and the Hydrangea Garden.

The collection of rhododendrons is world famous. It was originally formed by the late J. B. Stevenson at Tower Court, Ascot, between 1900 and 1950. After his death in 1951, it was acquired by the Crown Estate Commissioners and eventually transferred to its present site, a task that took four years to complete. It occupies an area of 50 acres (20 ha) and is planted in series grouped according to the current classification; each specimen is labelled with name and collector's number. They are in flower from January and February, when the rosy-purple flowers of *R. dauricum* and *R. mucronulatum* appear, until July when the scented, tree-like *R. auriculatum* flowers and August when *R. serotinum* flowers, the latest of all. As well as rhododendrons, there are many other interesting trees, such as magnolias, nothofagus, maples and birches.

In the Valley Garden, one of the most striking features is the Punchbowl, planted with evergreen azaleas that are a blaze of colour in May. The Azalea Valley is planted with both evergreen and deciduous varieties, the latter carrying the season well into June. Many cultivars of *Camellia japonica* and *C. × williamsii* are grown; they are at their best in March and April. Other trees and shrubs include magnolias, flowering cherries, maples, hamamelis, enkianthus and amelanchier. The Heather Garden was made in 1954 from an old gravel pit and different species and cultivars provide colour for every month of the year. Dwarf conifers, dwarf rhododendrons, brooms and potentillas are among the other plants represented there.

The Hydrangea Garden was planted in 1963–4 so as to provide a varied display from July to October. There are cultivars of *Hydrangea macrophylla*, both the hortensia type and lace-caps, as well as species such as *H. aspera*. The Pinetum has been planted since 1935. There is a good representative collection of conifers, including some plants of the dawn redwood, *Metasequoia glyptostroboides*, grown from the original introduction of seed in 1947. In spring, the floor of the Pinetum is covered with a mass of *Narcissus bulbocodium* var. *citrinus* and *N. pseudonarcissus*.

(*1*) *Daily Sunrise–Sunset*
(*2*) *Free: a car-park adjoining the gardens, for which a fee is charged, is available Apr–Jun, Mon–Fri and daily in autumn*
(*5*) *Crown Estate Commissioners*

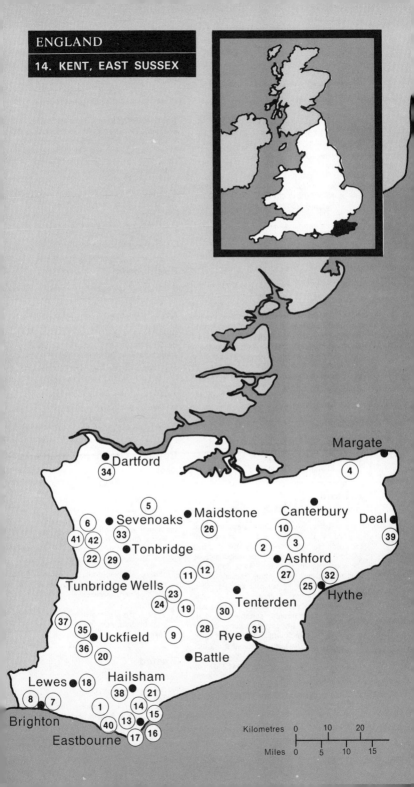

ENGLAND

14. KENT, EAST SUSSEX

ENGLAND

Alfriston

East Sussex

1. Drusillas

The 2 acre (0·9 ha) garden was founded by Douglas Ann. Lawns, with a pond and specimen trees and a formal lay-out of roses, adjoin a courtyard and a 16th-cent cottage

(1) *Easter–Oct: Daily 11–6*
(2) *Free*
(3) *Restaurant and tea kiosk*
(4) *Zoo Park; English wine centre; railway; garden centre; gift shop; bakery; pottery; collection of tropical moths and butterflies* (*same times*)
(5) *M. D. and C. A. Ann*

Ashford

Kent

2. Godinton Park

The present house dates mainly from Stuart times. The park and gardens were first laid out in the 18th cent but the gardens, 12 acres (4·8 ha) in extent, were altered to a formal design by the architect Sir Reginald Blomfield in the late 19th cent. He enclosed the whole area with a large yew hedge and it now includes formal paths, topiary, statues, lily ponds, an Italian garden, herbaceous borders and a box-hedge garden. A wild garden is colourful in spring with daffodils and other bulbs.

(1) *Easter Sat, Sun and Mon 2–5; Jun–Sep: Sun and Public Holidays 2–5 or by appointment*
(2) *Charge*
(4) *House* (*same times*)
(5) *A. Wyndham Green, Esq*

Ashford

3. Withersdane Hall Gardens

The gardens were mainly designed and planted in 1948–55, using the grounds of the old Hall and especially the kitchen garden, although some of the trees, such as the mulberry on the main lawn, date from Victorian times. The main garden covers approx 4½ acres (2 ha) and consists of a series of enclosed gardens divided by yew hedges with collections of trees, shrubs and herbaceous perennials suitable for calcareous soil. A number of half-hardy shrubs grow well, including trumpet vines (*Campsis radicans*), an olive and a double-flowered pomegranate. The rose garden contains a collection of the newer varieties of delphinium presented by the National Delphinium Society as well as roses; the sundial garden has a collection of silver, gold and purple foliage plants. A small peat garden has recently been constructed for plants that like an acid soil.

The conservatory, reached from Olantigh

Road and Occupation Road, has three compartments. The cool house contains cacti and other succulents, orchids (at their best in February and March) and plants from South Africa and Australia. The hot house is planted with representatives from a number of tropical families and demonstrates some of the components of a tropical forest. There are collections of begonias and *Bromeliaceae* and insectivorous plants. The economic house contains a collection of hot house orchids arranged according to present ideas of classification and evolution and a simulation of a peasant garden with representative tropical crops and weeds.

(1) *Some Sun for charity; other times by appointment with the Estates Bursar, Wye College, Ashford, Kent.*
(2) *Charge*
(4) *College Agricultural Museum at adjacent village of Brock*
(5) *Wye College* (*University of London*)

Birchington

Kent

4. Powell-Cotton Museum

Quex Park mansion, now a museum, is set among lawns and fine trees. In the formal part of the garden there is a small rose garden, shrubs and herbaceous borders, a sunken garden and an ornamental pond.

(1) *Easter–Sep: Sun, Wed, Thu 2.30–6; mid-July–early Sep: Tue–Fri and Sun 2.30–6*
(2) *Charge*
(4) *Museum* (*same times, also Thu throughout the year*)
(5) *C. Powell-Cotton, Esq.*

Borough Green, nr Sevenoaks

Kent

5. Great Comp Garden

The 7 acre (3 ha) garden has been skilfully designed and constructed by the present owners since 1957, with lawns, paths and a plantsman's collection of trees, shrubs, heathers and herbaceous plants; much use has been made of interesting ground-cover plants. The colours in autumn are notable.

(1) *Early May–mid-Oct: Wed, Sun and Public Holidays 11–6; parties on other days by arrangement*
(2) *Charge*
(3) *Tea (3.30–5); morning coffee for parties by arrangement*
(5) *Mr and Mrs R. Cameron*

Brasted

Kent

6. Emmetts Garden

The 'Old Garden' between the house and drive was made from a field and laid out in 1893–5 by Frederic Lubbock. The Shrub Garden was set out in 1900–8 using plants bought from Coombe Hill Nurseries, Kingston-upon-Thames, when the nursery was sold up. The next owner, C. W. Boise, extended the plantings of rhododendrons and azaleas.

The garden as a whole totals 4 acres (1·6 ha) and contains a fine collection of trees and shrubs, many rare, including several species of cornus, such as *C. kousa*, *C. controversa* and *C. macrophylla*, and many rhododendrons including large-leaved species such as *R. hodgsonii* and the elegant *R. calophytum*.

(1) *Apr and Jul–Oct: Sun and Wed 2–6; May–Jun: Sun, Tue–Thu 2–6. Last admission 5.30*
(2) *Charge*
(5) *National Trust*

Brighton
East Sussex
7. Preston Park and Rock Garden

The park, which was bought with the manor house by the town in 1883, covers an area of approx 63 acres (25 ha) and includes an enclosed garden and a garden for the blind as well as various recreational areas. It contains part of the town's floral bedding displays, a dahlia border and an annual border and the summer International Gardens of Greeting Competition. The rock garden was made on a railway bank in 1935.

(1) *Daily (rock garden closed on 25 Dec)*
(2) *Free*
(3) *Kiosks*
(4) *Preston Manor; bowling greens; cricket ground; croquet lawn*
(5) *Borough of Brighton, Parks and Gardens Dept*

Brighton
8. Withdean Park

Planting started on the 38 acre (15 ha) site in 1960 to plans prepared by the Director of the Brighton Parks and Gardens Dept. The park contains the largest collection of syringas in the country, with some 350 species and cultivars. There are also large collections of floribunda and shrub roses, viburnum, cotoneaster, hebe and berberis. It is at its best in May.

(1) *Daily*
(2) *Free*
(5) *Borough of Brighton, Parks and Gardens Dept*

Burwash
East Sussex
9. Bateman's

The house was built in 1634. Its most famous owner was Rudyard Kipling, who lived here from 1902 until his death in 1936. The lawns are surrounded by thick yew

hedges, and a pair of Irish Yews, planted in 1902, stand inside the entrance gate. In front of the house a drive leads to the walled garden and the kitchen garden, past a herb garden planted with culinary and medicinal herbs. A wrought-iron gate with the initials R. K. leads to the pleached pear walk with clematis growing over the trees. On the flagged south terrace, a trumpet vine, *Campsis grandiflora,* climbs round the drawing-room windows. The formal gardens behind the house were designed by Mr and Mrs Kipling, although the two rows of lime trees were already there. A gate leads into a wild garden with flowering shrubs and trees, underplanted with bulbs. A stream has *Lysichitum americanum* and *Gunnera manicata* growing beside the water.

(1) *Mar–May and Oct: Daily (except Fri, but open Good Friday pm) 2–6; Jun–Sep: Mon–Thu 11–6; Sat and Sun 2–6*
(2) *Charge*
(3) *Café*
(4) *House and water-mill (same times)*
(5) *National Trust*

Chilham
Kent
10. Chilham Castle

Although the keep of the original 12th-cent castle survives, the present castle is Jacobean, built by Sir Dudley Digges. A large old holm oak (*Quercus ilex*) is supposed to have been planted in 1616 to mark the completion of the house. The long avenue of chestnuts may also have been there at that time, and there are many other interesting old trees, including three fine black mulberries, reputed to be over 500 years old, a large black walnut and a tulip-tree, *Liriodendron tulipifera*. There are records of formal gardens laid out in 1637 by John Tradescant, but the grounds as they are today are mostly the work of 'Capability' Brown. They include a lake, a rose garden and a water garden, and are beautiful at any time of year.

(1) *Week before Easter–mid-Oct: Tue–Thu, Sat, Sun and Public Holidays noon–7*
(2) *Charge*
(3) *Tea*
(4) *Battle of Britain Museum and garden shop (same times)*
(5) *Viscount Massereene and Ferrard*

Cranbrook
Kent
11. Angley Park

There has been a garden at Angley since the 16th cent and some trees still survive from that time. The garden as it is now is basically a 12 acre (4·8 ha) 18th-cent pleasure garden which was improved extensively in Victorian times when the lake was made and many trees and shrubs, including rhododendrons walks, were planted. More recently, more rhododendrons and azaleas and specimen trees and shrubs have been added. One striking old tree is an oriental plane, *Platanus orientalis*, five branches of which were layered in 1890, as it was thought then that the tree was about to die. The layered branches are now mature trees, giving the impression of one enormous plant. Peacocks, ornamental pheasants and waterfowl run free and no dogs are allowed.

(*1*) *Apr–Jul: Daily 11–7; Oct: Daily 11–6*
(*2*) *Charge*
(*5*) *D. R. Snell, Esq*

Cranbrook
12. Sissinghurst Castle

The Tudor and Elizabethan mansion was bought in a neglected state in 1930 by the politician and writer, Sir Harold Nicolson, and his wife, V. Sackville-West. The garden was derelict, with some high Tudor brick walls remaining and two stretches of water. The design was based on a combination of axial walks, usually with terminal features such as statues or an archway, with small geometrical gardens opening off them; as V. Sackville-West said, 'There should be the strictest formality of design, with the maximum of informality in planting.'

Among the sectional gardens are ones with a seasonal basis: the spring garden, at its best from March to mid-May; an early summer garden, May to July; a late summer garden, July to August, and an autumn garden, September to October. Other areas have predominant colour schemes, such as the White Garden, by the Priest's House. The Cottage Garden is planted mainly in orange and yellow; the north side of the front courtyard is dark blue and purple.

The rose garden contains mainly old-fashioned roses, but other plants have a home there, too, including paulownia species, *Caryopteris × clandonensis*, *Clerodendrum foetidum* and *Acanthus spinosus*. There is a nuttery and beyond this lies the herb garden where even the path and a garden seat are covered with aromatic plants; just outside it, on the edge of the moat, is a small lawn made of thyme. The moat walk runs between the herb garden and the orchard which is filled with old apple trees supporting climbing roses and underplanted with daffodils. The Tower Lawn, on the site of the courtyard of the Elizabethan house, is planted with magnolias on its south side. A small sunken garden has been made from an old cellar and is planted with meconopsis and alstroemerias.

(*1*) *Apr–mid-Oct: Mon–Fri noon–6.30; Sat, Sun and Public Holidays 10–6.30. No dogs*

(*2*) *Charge*
(*3*) *Refreshments*
(*4*) *Part of the Castle (same times)*
(*5*) *National Trust*

Eastbourne
East Sussex
13. Carpet Gardens

These 2 acre (0·9 ha) gardens, situated along the sea front adjacent to the pier, form the principal floral feature of the town. It is known that the area was set out as lawns after the sea defences were constructed in 1870 and photographs exist showing gardens laid out in 1904. The design is formal, with spring and summer bedding; the summer carpet beds are in a Victorian geometric design relying mainly on dwarf foliage plants. Visit in April, May, August and September.

(*1*) *Daily Sunrise–Sunset*
(*2*) *Free*
(*3*) *Kiosks*
(*5*) *Eastbourne Borough Council*

Eastbourne
14. Gildredge Park and Manor Gardens

The park was purchased by the Council in 1908, while the adjoining Manor Gardens and House were bought in 1923 with a legacy from Alderman J. C. Towner. The whole area covers approx 16 acres (7 ha) and the gardens are colourful throughout the year with rock gardens and herbaceous borders.

(*1*) *Daily Sunrise–Sunset*
(*2*) *Free*
(*4*) *Towner Art Gallery in Manor House; small aviary*
(*5*) *Eastbourne Borough Council*

Eastbourne
15. Hampden Park

The 82 acres (33 ha) of land were bought by the Council in 1898 and laid out as a park at a total cost of £10,000; it was opened to the public in 1902. A lake with ornamental wildfowl is surrounded by mixed woodland, and seasonal interest throughout the year is provided by flowering shrubs and bedding plants.

(*1*) *Daily Sunrise–Sunset*
(*2*) *Free*
(*3*) *Refreshments*
(*5*) *Eastbourne Borough Council*

Eastbourne
16. Holywell Italian Gardens and Parades

The whole area covers 12 acres (4·8 ha). The Italian gardens, laid out in a formal style with bedding plants, were formerly a chalk quarry and were developed in 1904–5 and extended in 1921–2. The Parades include areas of carpet bedding, the Wish Tower and the Western Lawns; the Wish Tower is one of the martello towers built in the early 19th cent when an invasion by Napoleon's troops seemed likely. The Western Lawns, a large expanse to the west of the Tower, were very popular in Victorian and Edwardian times.

(1) *Daily Sunrise–Sunset*
(2) *Free*
(3) *Refreshments*
(4) *The Wish Tower; museum of military defences against Napoleon*
(5) *Eastbourne Borough Council*

Eastbourne

17. Motcombe Gardens

The old garden, approx 2 acres (0·9 ha) in extent, was given to Eastbourne in 1908 by the Duke of Devonshire. It includes a circular stone dovecot, thought to be medieval in date, and a pond that is said to be the source of the Bourne stream from which Eastbourne takes its name. Colour is provided throughout the year by flowering shrubs and bedding plants.

(1) *Daily Sunrise–Sunset*
(2) *Free*
(5) *Eastbourne Borough Council*

Glynde, nr Lewes

East Sussex

18. Glynde Place

The beautiful Elizabethan manor house, built of Sussex flint and Caen stone, encloses a courtyard with smooth lawns on each side of a central path and roses and other climbers covering the walls. The balustraded forecourt is raised on a terrace with varied plantings against the walls. The house is screened from the road by an avenue of beech trees and a high bank thickly planted with many different kinds of spring-flowering bulbs.

(1) *Easter Sat, Sun and Mon 2.15–5.30; May–early Oct: Wed, Thu and Public Holidays 2.15–5.30*
(2) *Charge*
(3) *Refreshments*
(4) *House (same times)*
(5) *Viscount Hampden*

Goudhurst

Kent

19. Bedgebury National Pinetum

The pinetum was started in 1925 to replace the Kew Gardens collection and avoid atmospheric pollution. It now covers 100 acres (40 ha) of undulating ground with two streams and a lake, and it contains the most comprehensive collection of conifers in

ENGLAND

Europe, with over 200 species and a greater number of varieties and cultivars. There are very large specimens of *Abies grandis* and *Araucaria araucana*, planted before the pinetum was founded. Not only conifers are represented: there is an avenue of *Liquidambar styraciflua*, which provides brilliant colour in autumn, as well as maples, rhododendrons and azaleas. The Chilean beech, *Nothofagus obliqua*, seeds itself freely and has become well established.

(1) *Daily 10–8 or Sunset*
(2) *Charge*
(3) *Refreshments (weekends)*
(5) *Forestry Commission*

Halland, nr Lewes

East Sussex

20. Bentley Wildfowl Collection

The collection, one of the largest in private hands in the country, was founded in 1962 by Gerald Askew, who also designed the 23 acres (10 ha) of fox-proofed enclosures and gardens. There is an avenue of sweetly scented balsam poplars and many unusual trees and shrubs, including quite a number of shrub roses such as 'Penelope' and 'Frau Dagmar Hastrup', and drifts of daffodils in spring.

(1) *Easter–1 Oct: Daily (except Good Friday) 10.30–6*
(2) *Charge*
(3) *Tea*
(4) *Ornamental wildfowl*
(5) *Mrs Gerald Askew*

Herstmonceux

East Sussex

21. Herstmonceux Castle

The garden was founded by Sir Paul Latham, Bt, in 1933 and was designed by Capt Danials of Wood & Ingrams. It covers 62 acres (25 ha), with lawns and an avenue of sweet chestnut trees estimated to be 500–600 years old. There are three large herbaceous borders and 3 acres (1·2 ha) of spring bulbs.

(1) *Easter–1 Oct: Mon–Fri 2–5.30; Sat, Sun and Public Holidays 10.30–5.30*
(2) *Charge*
(3) *Refreshments (Jun–Sep)*
(4) *Royal Greenwich Observatory exhibition and souvenir shop (same times)*
(5) *Royal Greenwich Observatory*

Hever, nr Edenbridge

Kent

22. Hever Castle

The gardens were created in 1903–7 by William Waldorf Astor, later 1st Viscount Astor, and consist mainly of extensive pleasure grounds with flowering trees and shrubs and large herbaceous borders. The 4 acre (1·6 ha) Italian garden has Roman and Renaissance sculptures, rock gardens, grottoes, cascades and fountains, and a large loggia with a colonnaded piazza overlooking the 35 acre (14 ha) lake. The castle, part of which dates from the 13th cent, where Anne Boleyn was born, is surrounded by an inner and outer moat, and between these are lawns, topiary hedges, including a set of chessmen, cut from yew, a maze and paved gardens planted by J. Cheal and Sons of Crawley.

(1) *Easter–Sep: Tue, Wed, Fri, Sun and Public Holidays 1–7*
(2) *Charge*
(3) *Café*
(4) *Castle (same days 1.30–7; 1.30–6 on Tue and Wed when extra rooms are shown); Garden shop*
(5) *Lord Astor of Hever*

Lamberhurst

Kent

23. The Owl House

This 16th-cent half-timbered cottage is surrounded by a relatively new garden, 13 acres (5·2 ha) in extent. Near the house, it is designed in the traditional cottage-garden style with herbaceous borders and clipped box hedges. Further afield there are ponds, a woodland garden with rhododendrons and azaleas and a profusion of roses, both as bushes, trained on pergolas or tripods, and also growing in the woods.

(1) *Mon, Wed–Fri and Public Holiday weekends: 11–6; Sun 3–6*
(2) *Charge*
(5) *Maureen, Marchioness of Dufferin and Ava*

Lamberhurst

24. Scotney Castle

The 14th-cent castle is now a picturesque ruin; a new house has built in 1837 by Anthony Salvin for Edward Hussey. William Sawrey Gilpin, the artist and landscape gardener, advised on the laying out of the grounds in a pictorial and romantic style, and over the next hundred years the landscape matured with little alteration. When the writer, the late Christopher Hussey, inherited the property in 1952, he extended the planting to provide more variety with the result that the garden is now beautiful at all seasons of the year, with magnolias and daffodils followed by hybrid rhododendrons and azaleas and, in summer, a great variety of roses. Later in summer, herbaceous perennials take over the display and in autumn there is a splendid display of coloured foliage. Around the castle are roses and there are also formal

beds of herbs and geraniums. Stone for the new house was quarried just below the site, and this became a rock garden.

(1) *Apr and Oct: Wed–Sun and Public Holidays 2–5; May–Sep: same days 2–6. Last admission half an hour before closing. No dogs*
(2) *Charge*
(4) *Shop*
(5) *National Trust*

Lympne, nr Hythe

Kent

25. Port Lympne Wildlife Sanctuary and Gardens

The mansion was built early this century by the architect Sir Herbert Baker for Sir Philip Sassoon. It was bought in 1973, in a neglected condition, by John Aspinall, who is restoring the house and gardens to their original high standard. The gardens were largely designed and planted by Sir Philip Sassoon and Philip Tilden: Russell Page is advising on their restoration.

The most striking feature is the elaborate terracing with a long York stone stairway. The four western terraces are planted with dahlias and roses; the eastern terraces are grassed and will be planted with Mediterranean fruit trees such as pomegranates, loquats and citrus. A herbaceous border was treated with 200 tons of elephant dung before planting. A striped garden, a chequer-board garden and clock garden have all been recently replanted.

(1) *Daily (except 25 Dec) 10–6 or Sunset*
(2) *Charge*
(3) *Café*
(4) *Wildlife Sanctuary and house (same times)*
(5) *John Aspinall, Esq*

Maidstone

Kent

26. Leeds Castle

The stone castle, romantically set in the middle of a lake, dates from Norman times and was the royal palace for eight of England's medieval queens. No trace remains of any early garden. The park was landscaped by 'Capability' Brown and the 6 acre (2·4 ha) woodland garden, with its streams and ponds, was created by the late Lady Baillie between 1930 and 1970. The beautiful blue *Anemone blanda* is naturalized among the trees and these and daffodils give a fine display from April to mid-May.

(1) *Late Mar–late Oct: Tue–Thu, Sun and Public Holidays (except Good Friday) 1–5. No dogs*
(2) *Charge*
(3) *Refreshments*
(4) *Castle; aviary; shop (same times); 9-hole golf course (open daily)*
(5) *Leeds Castle Foundation*

Mersham, nr Ashford

Kent

27. Swanton Mill

The 3 acre (1·2 ha) garden was designed by the owner on a site around the watermill, the restoration of which won the 1975 European Architectural Heritage award. The garden has lawns, trees, herbaceous borders and roses, the main feature being a water garden with bog plants around the edge of the stream.

(1) Apr–Oct: Sat and Sun 3–6 or by appointment
(2) Charge
(3) Refreshments
(4) Working watermill with flour for sale (same times)
(5) Mrs Gay Christiansen

Northiam

East Sussex

28. Great Dixter

The house, built in c 1450, is one of the finest examples of a large, timber-framed house. It was bought in 1911 by Nathaniel Lloyd and restored by the architect Sir Edwin Lutyens, who added to it a 16th-cent hall house. The gardens, once a farmyard, were also designed by Lutyens, largely in an informal manner. The different sections include a topiary garden, a rose garden, a small orchard underplanted with bulbs and large mixed borders where shrubs, herbaceous perennials and annuals all blend felicitously. A sunken garden with a central lily-pool was designed by Mr Lloyd in 1923. Christopher Lloyd, the horticultural writer, now looks after the garden and is responsible for its great variety of unusual and interesting plants.

(1) Easter–mid-Oct: Tue–Sun and Public Holidays 2–5
(2) Charge (sometimes for NGS)
(4) House (same times); Nursery garden (Mon–Fri 9–5; Sat 9–1)
(5) Quentin Lloyd, Esq

Penshurst

Kent

29. Penshurst Place

Parts of the house, where Sir Philip Sidney was born, date from the mid-14th cent, but most of the garden was designed in the mid-19th cent in a formal style, echoing that of the 17th cent, with terraces and a parterre. Some of the beds are filled with solid box, clipped level, and they surround a central pool with a fountain.

(1) Easter Sat–late May: Sat, Sun, Tue–Fri and Public Holidays 1–6; late May–1 Oct: same days 11.30–6
(2) Charge
(3) Refreshments

(4) House; toy museum (same times, except Easter–late May 2–6)
(5) Viscount de L'Isle

Rolvenden

Kent

30. Great Maytham Hall

The present house, on the site of an older building and incorporating part of it, was built in 1909–10 to a design by Sir Edwin Lutyens. To the front is a terrace with a variety of plants grown against the wall and below this lies a walled garden with iron gates, older than the house, planted with lawns and roses, which is the original 'Secret Garden' of the book by Frances Hodgson Burnett, who lived for some time in the house. Beyond the walled garden is another stretch of lawn, and a fish pool with water-lilies.

(1) May–Aug: Wed and Thu 2–4
(2) Charge
(5) Mutual Households Association Ltd

Rye

East Sussex

31. Lamb House

The early 18th-cent house was the home of the writer Henry James from 1898 until his death in 1916. The walled garden, approx 1 acre (0·45 ha) in extent, was largely laid out for Henry James by his friend, the landscape painter Alfred Parsons. It contains roses, clematis and a variety of flowering shrubs, herbaceous perennials and fruit trees – apples, pears, plums and figs. A walnut tree at the south-west corner of the lawn was planted by the writer himself.

(1) Early Apr–Oct: Wed and Sat 2–6. Last admission 5.30
(2) Charge
(4) House (same times)
(5) National Trust

Saltwood, nr Hythe

Kent

32. Saltwood Castle

The medieval castle, with dungeons and crypt dating from the 13th cent, was the subject of a quarrel between Henry II and Thomas a Becket. There are fine sea views from the grounds which are laid out with lawns, herbaceous borders and trees. Roses and other climbing plants cover the walls.

(1) Late May–Jul: Sun and Public Holidays 2–5.30; Aug: Tue–Fri, Sun and Public Holidays, 2–5.30
(2) Charge
(3) Tea
(4) Castle (same times)
(5) The Hon Alan Clark MP

(4) House (by appointment)
(5) Mrs Vera Thomas

Sevenoaks

Kent

33. Riverhill House

The house was bought by John Rogers in 1840 with the intention of creating a garden from the fine natural site, south-facing, sheltered and lime free. The situation is ideal for growing rhododendrons, azaleas and magnolias as well as other shrubs and roses. Every generation has added to the garden, with the result that introductions from a great succession of plant hunters are represented, from Joseph Hooker and Robert Fortune in the mid-19th cent to Ludlow and Sherriff in the mid-20th cent. There are huge clumps of *Rhododendron arboreum* and good specimens of *R. sinogrande, Magnolia campbellii* and *M. soulangiana*. In all there are about 9 acres (4 ha) of woodland, including many mature specimen trees such as *Cedrus deodara* and *Araucaria araucana*, the monkey puzzle.

(1) Mid-Apr–mid-Jul: Sat and Sun noon–6
(2) Charge
(5) Major and Mrs David Rogers

Sutton-at-Hone, nr Farningham

Kent

34. St John's Jerusalem

Although the house, which was once a church of the Knights Hospitallers, was built in 1199, the garden, which covers approx 5 acres (2 ha) within the old moat, was first planted 130 years after the Dissolution of the Monasteries (1540) when the church was converted into a private house. Since then, the garden has been replanned about every 100 years, according to the current fashion. Now flowering shrubs have been planted to take the place of time-consuming seasonal bedding. A notable feature is the number of butterflies attracted by the flowering shrubs, such as buddleia. Visit during high summer.

(1) Apr–Oct: Wed 2–6
(2) Free
(5) National Trust

Uckfield

East Sussex

35. Beeches Farm

The 16th-cent farmhouse is surrounded by an attractive small garden designed and developed by the present owner since 1946. There are lawns, roses, herbaceous borders, yew trees, shrubs and a sunken garden; there is something of interest to see from spring until early autumn.

(1) Daily 10–5
(2) Charge

Uckfield

36. Horsted Place

The Victorian Gothic mansion is on a site giving fine views over the Downs and towards Chanctonbury Ring. The gardens, redesigned and landscaped by Geoffrey Jellicoe in the 1960s, are an attractive mixture of the formal and informal, with pleached limes, rose-covered arches, a laburnum tunnel and woodland glades. Many varieties of rose are grown, some in painted iron 'baskets', following the plans of Humphry Repton for Brighton Pavilion. Throughout the garden there is an emphasis on scented and aromatic plants; a myrtle bush was grown from a sprig from Queen Victoria's wedding bouquet.

(1) Apr–Sep: Wed, Thu, Sun and Public Holidays 2–6
(2) Charge
(4) Farm and garden produce for sale
(5) Lord and Lady Rupert Nevill

Uckfield

37. Sheffield Park Garden

Although the park was landscaped by 'Capability' Brown in c 1775 for the 1st Lord Sheffield and further developed for the 3rd Earl approx 100 years later, much of the plantings as they are today were made by Arthur G. Soames between 1909, when he bought the property, and his death in 1934. The grounds cover approx 100 acres (40 ha), including five lakes and a cascade, and contain one of the finest collections of trees in the British Isles. There are many conifers and a particular emphasis on trees and shrubs that give good autumn colour, such as maples, *Fothergilla monticola, Sorbus* spp., and *Nyssa sylvatica*. In spring, a fine display of flowering trees and shrubs includes *Amelanchier* spp., *Cornus florida*, flowering cherries and thousands of rhododendrons and azaleas, as well as a mass of colour from naturalized daffodils and, later in the season, bluebells. A number of southern hemisphere species are represented, including *Eucalyptus gunnii*, one specimen of which is over 90 ft (27·4 m) tall; *Eucryphia glutinosa*; *Nothofagus obliqua* and the Chilean fire bush, *Embothrium coccineum*.

(1) Apr–Sep: Tue–Sat 11–7; Sun 2–7; Public Holidays 11–7; Oct–mid-Nov: Tue–Sat 11–5 or Sunset; Sun 2–5; Public Holidays 11–7. Last admission 1 hour before closing time
(2) Charge
(3) Refreshments in Oak Hall (not NT) adjoining garden (tel. Danehill 338); season may differ from garden
(5) National Trust

Upper Dicker, nr Hailsham

East Sussex

38. Michelham Priory

The 13th-and 16th-cent priory is surrounded by a large moat that encloses 7 acres (3·2 ha) of garden with lawns, a wide variety of trees and shrubs, water gardens, rose borders and herbaceous borders. 10,000 daffodils give a splendid display in spring.

(1) *Easter–mid-Oct: Daily 11–5.30*
(2) *Charge*
(3) *Licensed restaurant and buffet*
(4) *Priory (Easter–mid-Oct: 11–1, 2–5.30); restored working water-mill (same times)*
(5) *Sussex Archaeological Society*

Walmer

Kent

39. Walmer Castle

The Tudor castle, built in 1538–40, is now the official residence of the Lord Warden of the Cinque Ports. The garden was originally laid out by the traveller Lady Hester Stanhope, a niece of William Pitt. It has a formal lay-out with clipped hedges and fine herbaceous borders. Summer is the best time to visit.

(1) *Apr: Tue–Sun and Bank Holiday Mon 9.30–5.30; May–Sep: same days 9.30–7*
(2) *Charge*
(4) *Castle (Apr–Sep: same times but closed from 1–2; Mar and Oct: Tue–Sat 9.30–1, 2–5.30; Sun 2–5.30; Nov–Feb Tue–Sat 9.30–1, 2–4; Sun 2–4. Closed when the Lord Warden is in residence)*
(5) *Dept of the Environment*

West Dean, nr Seaford

East Sussex

40. Charleston Manor

The manor is a mixture of Norman, Tudor and early Georgian architecture, with a famous Romanesque window. The tithe barn, one of the largest in the country, dates from the 15th cent, and the circular dovecot is even earlier. There are lawns, herbaceous borders, yew hedges and a large collection of old-fashioned roses, climbing and shrub, at their best in June and July. The lower orchard has clematis and roses climbing over the old apple trees; anemones, narcissi and *Fritillaria meleagris* flower in spring and *Cyclamen hederaefolium* gives a fine display of pink and white in autumn. There is a walled kitchen garden.

(1) *Apr–Oct: Daily (weather permitting) 11–6*
(2) *Charge*
(4) *Festival exhibitions of paintings, ceramics, etc in Jun and Jul; House (Wed 2.15–6 by appointment)*
(5) *Lady Birley*

Westerham

Kent

41. Chartwell

The main feature of the garden is the stream that runs down the slope to the lakes. Sir Winston Churchill divided the two bottom lakes by a dam and created the island; he himself built the wall that surrounds what was until recently the kitchen garden, between 1925 and 1932. The Golden Rose Walk was a gift from their family to Sir Winston and Lady Churchill on their golden wedding anniversary. Lanning Roper has advised the National Trust on the planting and planning of the grounds and gardens.

(1) *Apr–Jun and Sep–mid-Oct: Tue–Thu 2–6 or Sunset; Sat, Sun and Public Holidays 11–6 or Sunset; Jul and Aug: Tue 2–6 or Sunset; Wed, Thu, Sat and Public Holidays 11–6 or Sunset. Closed Tue after Public Holiday*
(2) *Charge*
(4) *House (Mar–Nov same times)*
(5) *National Trust*

Westerham

42. Squerryes Court

The house dates from 1681; the gardens were laid out and terraced at about the same time. This formal area features roses and herbaceous borders; the rest of the garden has woodland walks, a lake and many fine trees and flowering shrubs including rhododendrons and azaleas. There is a particularly fine display of spring-flowering bulbs.

(1) *Mar–Oct: Wed, Sat, Sun and Public Holiays 2–6. Last admission 5.30*
(2) *Charge*
(4) *House; Regimental Museum of Kent and Sharpshooters' Yeomanry (same times)*
(5) *John St A. Warde, Esq*

SCOTLAND

NORTHERN SCOTLAND

Kilometres
0
20
40
60
0
10
20
30
Miles
10
Dornoch
18
Ullapool
Nairn
14
Inverness
Huntly
11
21
12
Aberdeen
2
3
1
Ballater
Banchory
7
Montrose
Dundee
Perth
16
8
Crieff
15
19
St Andrews
5
4
9
Dunblane
17
6
13
20
Stirling
Kirkcaldy

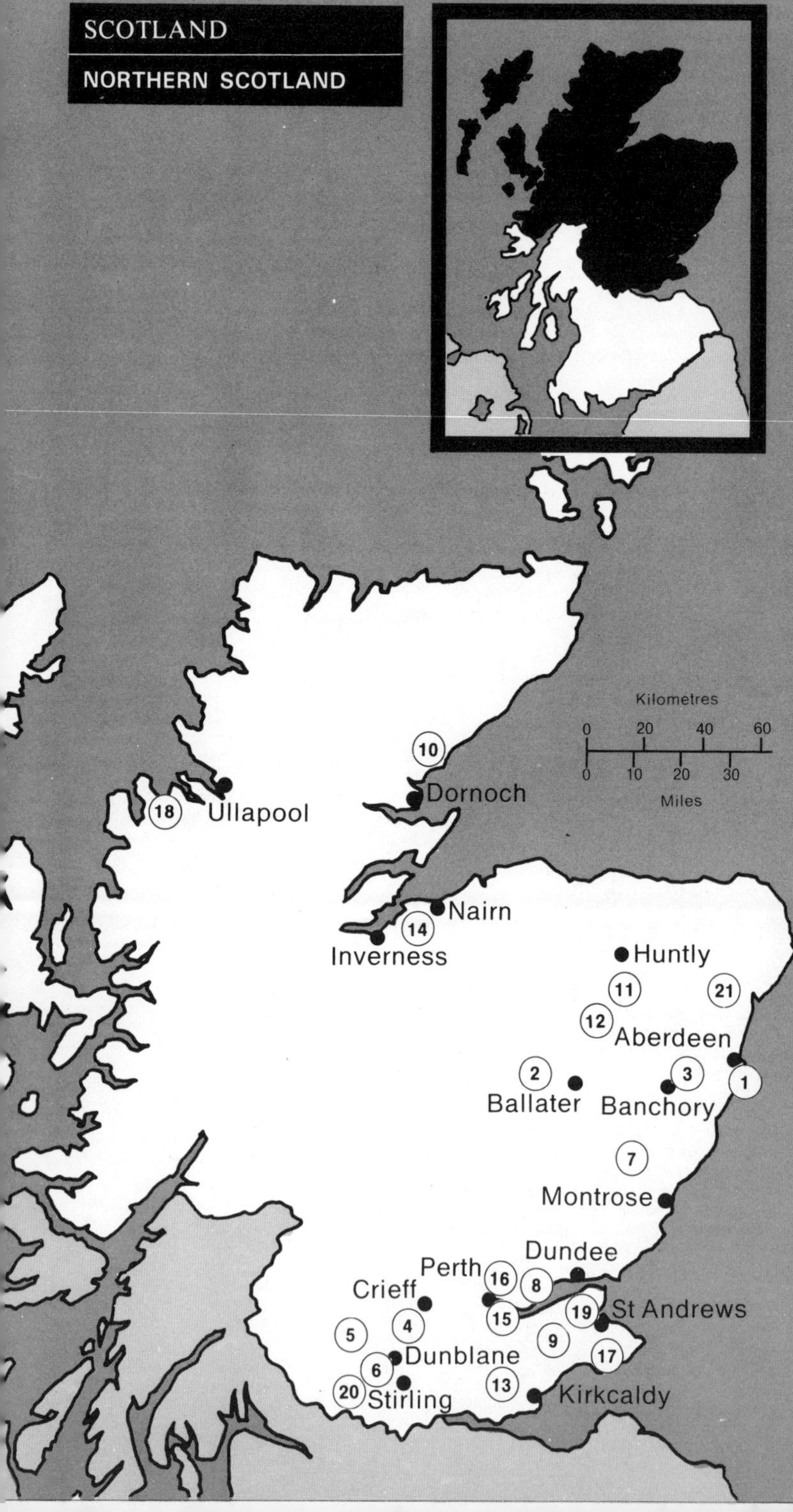

Aberdeen, St Machar Drive

Grampian

1. Cruickshank Botanical Gardens

The gardens, lying to one side of the Ballater–Huntly road, were founded through the generosity of Miss A. H. Cruickshank in 1898 under the direction of Professor J. W. H. Traill on the present site covering 6 acres (2·4 ha) near King's College in Old Aberdeen. Although little survives of the original design (by George Nicholson of Kew in 1899), the purpose of furthering 'university interests and the public good' remains unchanged and close association with the university's Department of Botany is maintained. Large rock and water gardens and the sunken heather garden hold extensive collections of shrubs, herbaceous and alpine plants of botanical and horticultural interest: succulents kept under glass may be seen by arrangement with the head gardener. Visit from May to June and August to September.

(1) *Mon–Fri 8.30–4.45; May–Sep: Sat and Sun 2–6*
(2) *Charge*
(5) *Cruickshank Trust and University of Aberdeen*

Ballater

Grampian

2. Balmoral Castle

Since Prince Albert bought Balmoral Castle and laid out the gardens in 1855, successive sovereigns have cared for the estate and made various improvements. The approach to the castle is lined by mature trees, many dating from the 19th cent. As well as gardens in the immediate vicinity of the castle – rose gardens to the west and the Tower Garden on the east front – there are spacious lawns and a walk along the bank of the River Dee. A fountain garden devised by Queen Mary in the early 1920s has recently been extended to incorporate a large kitchen garden.

(1) *May–Jul: Daily (except Sun) 10–5*
(2) *Charge*
(5) *HM the Queen*

Banchory

Grampian

3. Crathes Castle

The castle, dating from the 16th cent, stands in grounds covering approx 6 acres (2·4 ha) almost completely enclosed by a high stone wall and divided into several gardens by hedges or borders. Although the present lay-out has been established in the 20th cent, yew hedges dating from 1702 suggest the earlier existence of a formal garden. Each section of the garden develops a particular theme; the focus may be a colour, a season, or the provision of year-round interest. There is an outstanding collection of hardy shrubs and herbaceous plants and recent developments include the creation of a 'golden garden' and a 'red garden'. The walls are covered with climbers, and the avenues to east and west feature a number of interesting trees. Visit in June, July or August.

(1) *Daily 9.30–Sunset*
(2) *Charge*
(3) *Restaurant (May–Sep)*
(4) *Castle (Oct: Wed 11–1, 2–6; Sat and Sun 2–6; May–Sep: Mon–Sat 11–6; Sun 2–6. Last admission 5.30); nature trails*
(5) *National Trust for Scotland*

Crieff

Tayside

4. Drummond Castle

The great parterre of approx 13 acres (5·2 ha) is in the form of a St Andrew's cross, at the centre of which is a multi-faceted sundial, dated 1630. Laid out in the 19th cent, it is composed of widely spaced topiary, flowerbeds of elaborate form and statuary. A copper beech was planted by Queen Victoria in 1842 and this may be the date of the completion of the parterre.

A stone stairway descends the side of the valley forming a dramatic link between the castle, altered by John Mylne (by whom the sundial was probably also made) in 1629–30 and remodelled by G. T. Ewing in 1878, and the formal garden. On the opposite side of the valley is woodland with a ride on the axis of the stairway and the sundial.

(1) *Apr–Oct: Wed and Sat 2–6*
(2) *Charge*
(5) *Grimsthorpe and Drummond Castle Trust Ltd*

Doune, nr Dunblane

Central

5. Doune Park Gardens

The gardens, created in the early 19th cent by the 10th Earl of Moray, were rehabilitated between 1969 and 1972. They cover 60 acres (24·2 ha). A particular feature is the walled garden divided into four distinct areas that are separated by a double herbaceous border and a double annual border backed by a pergola of climbing roses. There is a formal rose garden, a 'house' garden with fruit, vegetables and flowers for cutting, a spring garden and an autumn garden. The pinetum, planted in the 1860s, has an interesting collection of exotic conifers, including some exceptionally tall trees – a wellingtonia, a Douglas fir and a Lawson's cypress.

In the area around the Gardener's Cottage, a 19th-cent ornamental building, there are species rhododendrons and azaleas, at

117

their best in May and June. There are woodland walks with bluebells in spring and autumn colour in September and October. The banks of the Buchany Burn have daffodils and shrubs beneath the trees. These include *Fagus sylvatica 'Cristata'* and *Fraxinus excelsior 'Glomerata'*.

(1) *Apr–Oct: Daily 10–6*
(2) *Charge*
(3) *Restaurant*
(4) *Doune Motor Museum (same times); Doune Castle (Apr–Oct: Daily, except Thu in Apr and Oct, 10–6); Garden Centre*
(5) *Earl of Moray*

Dunblane

Central

6. Keir Garden

The extensive garden surrounding Keir House remains much as it was laid out by Sir William Stirling Maxwell in the 1860s. Special features, approached by woodland paths, include a yew-tree house, the tree planted in *c* 1850, a water garden with a pond which was cleared and replanted in the 1960s, an arboretum of rare conifers, herbaceous borders and flowering shrubs, notably rhododendrons and azaleas. The woodland contains many rare and interesting trees.

(1) *Tue, Wed, Thu 2–6 or by appointment with the Head Gardener*
(2) *Charge (SGS)*
(5) *Lt-Col William Stirling*

Edzell, nr Brechin

Tayside

7. Edzell Castle

The original walled garden was created by Sir David Lindsay in 1604 and restored after it was taken over by HM Office of Works in 1932. The three red sandstone walls are divided into 43 panels, niches for flowers alternating with heraldic and symbolic sculptures that are unique in Scotland. Above the panels are nesting holes for birds.

No trace remained of the original parterres and these have been re-created with low box hedges.

(1) *Apr–Sep: Mon–Sat 9.30–7; Sun 2–7; Oct–Mar: Mon–Sat 9.30–4; Sun 2–4. Closed 25 and 26 Dec and 1 and 2 Jan*
(2) *Charge*
(3) *Dept of the Environment*

Errol

Tayside

8. Megginch Castle

The ancient physic garden grew up round the castle of 1460 and as the castle was al-

tered or added to, so too was the garden. A 16th-cent rose garden with box hedges and a paved walk was added to the original walled garden and in the 18th-cent the walled garden was expanded. In the early 19th cent the formal flower garden was laid out to the west of the building within the framework of four clumps of ancient yews, which were, according to legend, the hedge of a monastery garden. There are a number of interesting plants in the garden brought from the botanic garden at Macao in the 1790s.

(1) *Mar–Aug: Wed 2–6*
(2) *Charge*
(5) *Capt and the Hon Mrs Drummond of Megginch*

Falkland

Fife

9. Falkland Palace

In 1947, the present Hereditary Constable, Captain and Keeper of the Palace re-created the lay-out shown in 17th-cent records after the alteration and replanting of the garden in 1628.

The design of the garden, which is relatively small, imparts a satisfying impression of space; views of the palace building from the grass walk around the garden are framed between flower borders and the hill slopes beyond. The garden holds a varied selection of herbaceous plants, notably irises and lupins, flowering shrubs, climbing roses and a fine specimen of the rose 'Frühlingsgold'. It is attractive from the opening of the cherry blossom in spring to the turning of the maples in autumn. The gardens contain the original royal tennis court of 1539.

(1) *Mid-Apr–end Oct: Mon–Sat 10–6; Sun 2–6*
(2) *Charge (Scots Guards and members of Scots Guards Association free)*
(4) *Palace and Visitor Centre (same times)*
(5) *National Trust for Scotland*

Golspie, nr Dornoch

Highland

10. Dunrobin Castle

The 15th-cent castle was rebuilt by Sir Charles Barry between 1835 and 1850 and it was probably he who laid out the imposing parterres, one circular and two rectangular, which lie between the castle and the sea. There are fine trees, a collection of azaleas, floribunda roses in the parterres, fuchsias and mixed borders. The castle was again restored, by Sir Robert Lorimer, after a fire in 1915.

(1) *May–last Fri in Sep: Mon–Fri 11–6; Sun 1–6*
(2) *Charge*
(3) *Tea*
(4) *Castle (same times)*
(5) *Countess of Sutherland*

Kennethmont, nr Huntley

Grampian

11. Leith Hall

The garden at Leith Hall, home of the head of the Leith family since 1650, was the work of Charles Leith-Hay, who inherited the estate in 1900, and of his wife, Henrietta. Though small, it was created to blend peacefully with its natural and historical background; a winding herbaceous bed leads the eye southward to trees and distant hills. Attractive features include a walled garden with the Chinese 'moon gate', and a rock garden in which celmisias flower freely. Visit in August. There is a pond walk with an observation hide. Practicable for wheelchairs.

(1) *May–Sep: Daily 10–Sunset*
(2) *Charge*
(4) *House (May–Sep: Mon–Sat 11–1, 2–6; Sun 2–6. Last tour starts 45 min before closing time); woodland walk; picnic area*
(5) *National Trust for Scotland*

Kildrummy, nr Alford

Grampian

12. Kildrummy Castle Garden

The ruins of a medieval castle, ancient seat of the Earls of Mar, stand above the gardens, which are of considerable botanical interest. In the quarry, from which the stone for the castle was hewn, there is an alpine garden begun early this century by Col James Ogston. It was he who employed Japanese landscape gardeners to construct a water garden in c 1904 on the banks of the burn which runs beneath his replica of the 14th-cent Auld Brig o' Blairgowny. The south-facing garden, sheltered by a band of silver fir, larch and tsuga established in the 19th cent, contains good collections of bulbs, ground-cover plants, conifers, species and hybrid rhododendrons and shrubs from many parts of the world.

(1) *Apr–Oct: Daily 9–5*
(2) *Charge*
(4) *Castle ruins (Dept of the Environment, open at all reasonable times)*
(5) *Kildrummy Castle Gardens Trust*

Kinross

Tayside

13. Kinross House

The 17th-cent house built by Sir William Bruce is approached by an avenue of trees and fronted by a broad expanse of lawn. Formal gardens centred on a pool and fountain behind the house remain as they were re-created early this century by Sir Basil Montgomery, who laid out the rose garden and herbaceous borders, divided by yew trees and hedges.

(1) *May–Sep: Daily 2–7*
(2) *Charge*

SCOTLAND

(4) *House (by appointment)*
(5) *Sir David Montgomery, Bt*

Nairn

Grampian

14. Cawdor Castle

Cawdor Castle, fortress home of the Thanes of Cawdor since the early 14th cent, is set in peaceful grounds, with sweeping lawns punctuated by hedges and trees. The present garden was laid out by Sir Hugh Campbell and his wife, Lady Henrietta, who married in 1662. There is a fine vegetable garden, a woodland garden by the burn created in 1959, apple trees supporting clematis and climbing roses and the drive flanked by cherries. Visit in June and August.

(1) *Late May–mid-Sep: Daily 10–5.30*
(2) *Charge*
(3) *Restaurant and snack bar*
(4) *Castle (same times)*
(5) *Earl of Cawdor*

Perth, 116 Dundee Road

Tayside

15. Branklyn

Starting with a very small garden when they built Branklyn House in 1922, John and Dorothy Renton extended it in stages to the present area of 2 acres (0·8 ha) and worked on its development until their deaths in the 1960s. The sloping garden, overlooking Perth, is noted for the perfection of its design as a setting for the rich collection of plants, which includes small rhododendrons, meconopsis, over eighty varieties of primula and many such rarities as *Paraquilegia anemonoides*. The scree gardens form an interesting feature. To see the greatest profusion of colour, visit in late May or early June, although there is much of interest throughout the summer and autumn.

(1) *Mar–Oct: Daily 10–Sunset*
(2) *Charge*
(5) *National Trust for Scotland*

Perth

16. Scone Palace

Scone has one of the finest collections of rare conifers in the country, started in 1848. There is a woodland garden with rhododendrons and azaleas, the walks winding through the old Friars' Den and Monks' Playgreen of the former Abbey of Scone. The Douglas firs are named after the botanist and traveller David Douglas, who was born and worked as under-gardener on the estate. He sent the seed to the Earl of Mansfield and this was planted in 1834.

(1) *May–Sep: Mon–Sat 10–6; Sun 2–6. Last admission 5.30*

119

(2) Charge
(3) Café
(4) Palace (same times)
(5) Earl of Mansfield

(1) Daily Sunrise–Sunset.
(2) Charge
(3) Restaurant (mid-Apr–Sept)
(4) Trout fishing; Visitor centre (mid-Apr–mid-Oct: Mon–Sat 10–6.30; Sun 1–6.30 or Sunset)
(5) National Trust for Scotland

Pittenweem

Fife

17. Kellie Castle

Kellie Castle, mainly dating from the 16th and 17th cents and virtually abandoned in the 19th cent was restored by Prof James Lorimer, whose family rented the property from the 1870s before buying it in 1948. The castle is enclosed on the north and east sides in a Victorian walled garden, sheltered by trees, containing herbaceous plants, shrub roses and rose arches and joined and divided by box-edged paths. Visit in July.

(1) Mid-Apr–Sep: Daily 10–Sunset
(2) Charge
(4) Castle (mid-Apr–Sep: Daily, except Mon and Tue, 2–6)
(5) National Trust for Scotland

Poolewe

Highland

18. Inverewe

A magnificent natural garden flourishing on a once-barren headland on the shore of Loch Ewe, behind a thick belt of sheltering trees planted by Osgood Mackenzie, owner of the estate from 1862, who described his development of the garden in the book *A Hundred Years in the Highlands*. His work was continued by his daughter, Mrs Mairi Sawyer, until the year before her death in 1953; the garden was then cared for (1954–60) by Dr J. M. Cowan on behalf of the National Trust for Scotland.

Noted for its profusion of tender, exotic plants, thriving in the warm, humid climate of the Gulf Stream, the garden offers something of interest all the year round: rhododendrons first come into flower very early in the year, reaching the height of their display from mid-April to mid-May and followed by azaleas; a fine specimen of *Magnolia campbellii* blooms in March and April: rock plants flowering throughout the summer are at their best in May and June, as are meconopsis and primulas; an early herbaceous border in the walled garden and long beds of roses edged with dianthus make a striking display in June, followed by herbaceous beds below the house and a collection of *Cardiocrinum giganteum*; hydrangeas which flower in August sometimes continue until November; autumn flowers include kniphofia, agapanthus, watsonia, eucryphia and numerous heathers, while maples and other trees provide a brilliant variety of colour in November, with the scarlet berries of viburnum and cotoneaster. Practicable for wheelchairs.

St Andrews

Fife

19. University Botanic Garden

A teaching garden attached to the university's Department of Botany, covering 20 acres (8 ha) in two areas of the town, contains a variety of interesting botanical specimens. The original garden was founded in 1889 by Dr John Wilson and recently developed. The main garden is approached from the Canongate; a smaller annexe, known as Dyers Brae, from Queen's Terrace. A large glasshouse section is partly open to the public. The garden contains something of interest all the year round but is seen at its best from May to July.

(1) Mon–Fri (except Local Holidays) 10–4
(2) Free
(5) University of St Andrews

Stirling

Central

20. Gargunnock House

Mansion house dating from the 16th–18th cents surrounded by a small shrub and flower garden and large policies. It has been created over a period of two centuries and the woodland garden is now in course of further development. There is a fine display of daffodils in April and May, and many flowering shrubs and trees in spring. The garden is also worth visiting in October for the autumn colours.

(1) Mid-Apr–end Jun and mid-Sep–end Oct: Wed 1–5
(2) Collecting box
(5) Miss V. H. C. Stirling of Gargunnock

Udny, nr Oldmeldrum

Grampian

21. Pitmedden

Restoration of the Great Garden laid out by Sir Alexander Seton in the 17th cent was begun in 1955, after the presentation of Pitmedden to the National Trust for Scotland by Major James Keith in 1952. The four rectangular parterres are planted out each May with annuals raised at Pitmedden, the intricate patterns defined by box hedges. The design of the north-west parterre incorporates the Seton arms and family mottoes, while the other patterns are based on a 17th-cent garden at one time at the Palace of Holyroodhouse, Edinburgh. There are two herbaceous borders around the formal garden. Reconstructed fountains and garden ornaments include fragments of the original stonework. Twin pavilions stand to north and south of the garden. Practicable for wheelchairs.

(1) Daily 9.30–Sunset
(2) Charge
(3) Morning coffee and tea (Jun–Sep)
(5) National Trust for Scotland

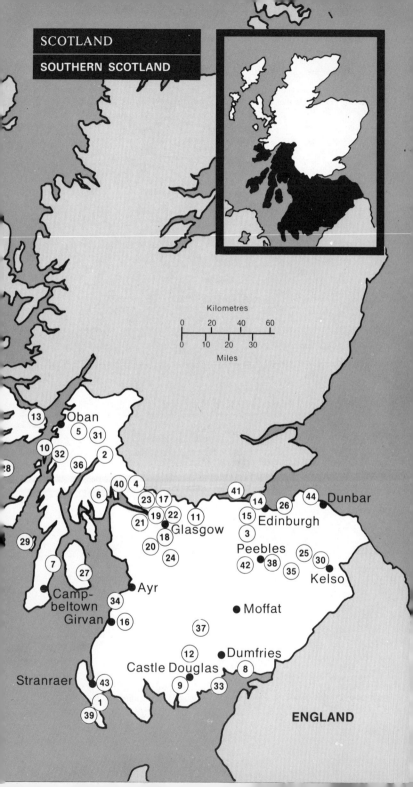

SCOTLAND

SOUTHERN SCOTLAND

Ardwell, nr Stranraer

Dumfries and Galloway

1. Ardwell House

A personal garden planted by the family of the present owners, Ardwell contains tree rhododendrons and a number of hybrids. Spring flowers include daffodils and many shrubs. There are also dahlias, roses, a crazy paving, at its best in mid-summer, and a number of fine trees.

(1) *Mar–Oct: Mon–Fri 10–6*
(2) *Contribution box*
(5) *Mr and Mrs H. J. Brewis*

Ardkinglas, nr Arrochar

Strathclyde

2. Strone

The garden, which covers approx 12 acres (4·8 ha), contains a pinetum, established in 1860, and many species and hybrid rhododendrons planted since 1930 by the present owner. The collection of trees and shrubs also includes camellias, magnolias and a number of exotics, as well as the tallest giant fir, *Abies grandis*, in Britain.

(1) *Easter–Sep: Daily Sunrise–Sunset*
(2) *Charge*
(5) *Lord Glenkinglas*

Balerno, nr Edinburgh

Lothian

3. Malleny Garden

Malleny House dates from the 17th cent. The grounds in which it stands have been developed with the intention of providing a personal garden which has something attractive to offer all the year round by Commander and Mrs Gore-Brown Henderson, who bought the estate in 1960. It was presented to the National Trust for Scotland in 1968. While its essential shape remains unchanged, the garden has been extensively replanted since 1961. There is a good collection of shrub roses. Visit in July and August. Practicable for wheelchairs.

(1) *May–Sep: Daily 10–Sunset*
(2) *Charge*
(5) *National Trust for Scotland*

Balloch, nr Dumbarton

Strathclyde

4. Cameron Loch Lomond
Wildlife and Leisure Park

Beside Loch Lomond, gardens and a woodland walk covering an area of 25 acres (10 ha). They were laid out by the landscape gardener Lanning Roper and form a series of separate gardens: the Rhododendron and Azalea Garden, the Flower Garden and the Water and Primula Garden. The house, home of the 18th-cent author Tobias Smollett and of the Smolletts of Bonhill, was rebuilt in 1865 after a fire.

(1) *Easter–Oct: Daily 10–6*
(2) *Charge*
(3) *Restaurant*
(4) *Wildlife Park (same times); House (Easter–Oct: Daily 10.30–6)*
(5) *Mr and Mrs Patrick Telfer Smollett*

Barguillean, nr Taynuilt

Strathclyde

5. Angus's Garden

A garden designed and built by Mr and Mrs Neil Macdonald in memory of their son who died in 1956. The 6 acre (2·4 ha) woodland area has been planted with a predominance of hybrid rhododendrons, deciduous and evergreen azaleas which blend into the Highland setting. The loch has now been designated a bird sanctuary. The garden was created entirely without professional help and has been open to the public since 1976.

(1) *Mar–Oct: Daily 9–7*
(2) *Charge*
(5) *Mr and Mrs Neil Macdonald*

Benmore, nr Dunoon

Strathclyde

6. Younger Botanic Garden

A wooded garden of 100 acres (40 ha), set on the Benmore Estate, which was presented to the nation in 1928. The garden's earliest trees, Scots pines extending from Benmore House to the Golden Gates, were planted in 1820, and an avenue of wellingtonia, *Sequoiadendron giganteum*, with the surrounding forest, about 50 years later. A fine collection of trees and shrubs introduced by Mr H. G. Younger forms the basis of the present garden, together with rhododendrons planted since Benmore came under the control of Edinburgh's Royal Botanic Garden (cf) in the 1930s. Suggested walks pass a stream and pond, surrounded by azaleas, maples and water-loving flowers, and a formal garden of conifers selected for variety in shape and foliage. The Younger Memorial Walk is flanked by fine trees and shrubs, many planted by the owner in 1916. Rhododendrons throughout the garden are arranged in their natural groups, flowering from January to September, with the greatest profusion from late April to early June. There are views over the garden to Beinn Ruadh or along the River Echaigh to the Holy Loch and the distant Ayrshire hills.

(1) *Apr–Sep: Daily 10–6*
(2) *Charge*
(3) *Tea (Apr–Sep: Daily except Sat)*
(5) *Dept of Agriculture and Fisheries for Scotland*

Carradale, nr Campbeltown

Strathclyde

7. Carradale House

The walled garden, approx 2 acres (0·8 ha) in size, probably dates from 1780, when Carradale House was rebuilt for the then owners, the Buchanans. There is also a wild garden with an iris pond. Recently redesigned for easier maintenance, the garden contains over 100 varieties of rhododendrons and azaleas which, with other flowering shrubs, make a good display until June; huge clumps of *R. barbatum* and *R.* 'Shilsonii' are at their best in early April.

(1) Apr–Sep: Daily 10–5
(2) Charge
(4) House (by appointment); plants for sale in spring, vegetables in summer
(5) Lady Mitchison

Carrutherstown, nr Annan

Dumfries and Galloway

8. Kinmount Gardens

The house was built by Sir Robert Smirke in 1815 for the Marquess of Queensberry, and there are 20th-cent alterations. There is a natural rock garden and woodland walks, with recommended routes taking half an hour, an hour and two hours. The rhododendrons and azaleas are the most notable features of the gardens.

(1) Easter–Oct: Daily 10–5
(2) Charge
(3) Kiosk
(5) Hoddom and Kinmount Estates

Castle Douglas

Dumfries and Galloway

9. Threave Garden

The Victorian mansion now houses the School of Practical Gardening run by the National Trust for Scotland. The original walled garden, the work of Major Alan Gordon, who presented the estate to the Trust in 1948, has glasshouses. Around it, a terraced peat garden, a rock garden grown on a natural outcrop, a vegetable garden, woodland and water gardens, winter borders and a nursery have evolved from the activities of the School, in an effort to create settings in which all important groups of ornamental plants may grow as well as soil and climate allow.

The pond and herbaceous beds are in front of the house; to the north-east the rose garden contains a large selection of shrub roses, old fashioned and modern, which flower from July to September. The formal Longwood Steps are flanked with Hybrid Tea, floribunda and climbing roses. Beyond the heather garden there is a collection of

dwarf conifers. A road past the arboretum and orchard leads to natural woodland carpeted in spring and early summer with daffodils and woodland flowers. Ornamental cherries and crab apples, underplanted with daffodils and at their best in April and May, lead to a newly cultivated bog garden. Practicable for wheelchairs.

(1) Main garden. Daily 9–Sunset. Walled garden and glasshouses. Daily 9–5
(2) Charge
(4) Visitor centre (mid-Apr–Oct); Threave Wildfowl Refuge (Nov–Mar: Daily, except Mon, by arrangement with the Warden, Kelton Mill, Castle Douglas. Tel. Bridge of Dee 242)
(5) National Trust for Scotland

Clachan Bridge, Isle of Seil

Strathclyde

10. An Cala

The garden of An Cala was created in the 1930s by Col and Mrs Arthur Murray. It lies in a spectacular setting, with a background of conifers and shrubs planted on the rock face that shelters it to the north and east, and overlooking the Isles of the Inner Hebrides. A natural outcrop forms the basis of the rock garden, and the burn feeds a water garden at the foot of a waterfall. Cherries, azaleas and a threefold terrace of roses provide outstanding displays. Visit from mid-April to June

(1) Apr–Sep: Thu 2–6
(2) Charge (SGS)
(5) Mrs H. I. Blakeney

Clarkston, Airdrie, nr Glasgow

Strathclyde

11. Greenbank

A garden of 2·5 acres (1 ha) and 13 acres (5·2 ha) of policies established as a Gardening Advice Centre intended to help, in particular, the owners of small gardens. Before its formation as such, this was already an established garden and contains a good collection of plants, particularly shrub roses. Information about courses obtainable from Greenbank or from the headquarters of the National Trust for Scotland, 5 Charlotte Square, Edinburgh (Telephone 031-226-5922).

(1) Garden. Daily 10–5. Advice Centre. Mon–Fri 10–5, also Apr–Oct: Sat and Sun 2.30–5
(2) Charge
(5) National Trust for Scotland

Corsock, nr Crocketford

Dumfries and Galloway

12. Corsock House

A woodland walk, the circuit comprising approx 1 mile (1·6 km), known for its collection of species rhododendrons, many of them raised from seed collected on Himalayan expeditions in the 1930s. In the late spring and autumn the water garden with its maples, *Cercidiphyllum japonicum* and enkianthus is worth particular notice.

(1) *May: Sun 2.30–6.30*
(2) *Charge*
(5) *Mrs F. L. Ingall*

Craignure, Isle of Mull

Strathclyde

13. Torosay Castle

The mid-Victorian castle, designed by David Bryce, is set in 11 acres (4·4 ha) of formal and wild gardens. Three Italianate terraces and a statue walk were laid out by Sir Robert Lorimer at the turn of the century. Near the water garden there is a plantation of Australian gum trees, one of the most northerly in the world. Eucryphias flower in late summer. Visit from May to August. Torosay is reached by ferry from Oban to Craignure or from Loch Aline to Fishnish.

(1) *Daily*
(2) *Contribution box*
(4) *Castle (Daily 11–5); small-gauge steam railway*
(5) *Torosay Estate Trustees*

Edinburgh, Inverleith Row

14. Royal Botanic Garden

Founded as a physic garden at Holyrood in 1670, the Royal Botanic Garden was transferred to the present site in 1820. Trees and shrubs throughout the garden provide interest and beauty at all times of year and include a collection of plants with coloured bark which are at their most spectacular in the winter and early spring. Peonies, meconopsis and primulas are among the notable collections of herbaceous plants, and a long herbaceous bed provides a fine display against the background of a tall beech hedge. The Heather Garden holds all but the most tender specimens in the heather collection, some of which are in flower throughout the year. The present Rock Garden, constructed between 1908 and 1914, was adapted in 1938 and again in the late 1960s; it contains brooms and genistas as well as ranges of conifers and dwarf rhododendrons, and mountain plants from many parts of the world. Bulbs and tuberous plants in the woodland garden are protected by conifers and evergreens, chiefly rhododendrons. Dwarf rhododendrons and other *Ericaceae* are also a feature of the Peat Garden, interplanted with a wealth of small herbaceous plants, such as primulas and terrestrial orchids. The Plant Houses, opened in 1967, contain plants adapted to many climatic environments, including succulents, water plants, ferns and orchids, and an Exhibition Hall (opened 1970) houses changing displays of information on many aspects of plant biology: Sound

SCOTLAND

Guide Tours are available. The Demonstration Garden gives a systematic view of plant families and the relationships between them.

(1) *Garden. Summer: Mon–Sat 9–1 hour before Sunset; Sun 11–1 hour before Sunset. Winter: Mon–Sat 9–Sunset; Sun 11–Sunset. Plant Houses and Exhibition Hall. Mon–Sat 10–Sunset (latest 5); Sun 11–Sunset (latest 5). Closed 1 Jan*
(2) *Free*
(3) *Tea (Apr–Oct)*
(4) *Scottish National Gallery of Modern Art (Summer: Mon–Sat 10–6; Sun 2–6; Winter: Mon–Sat 10–1 hour before Sunset: Sun 2–1 hour before Sunset)*
(5) *Dept of Agriculture and Fisheries for Scotland*

Edinburgh, 43 Gogarbank

15. Suntrap

Suntrap House and the surrounding gardens were presented to the National Trust for Scotland in 1966 by the late G. Boyd Anderson. The Gardening Advice Centre, the first of its kind in Scotland, was opened in 1968 to give advice and practical instruction to amateur gardeners. The grounds contain a wide range of attractive and interesting plants. Practicable for wheelchairs.

(1) *Gardens. Daily. Advice Centre. Mon–Fri 9–5, also Mar–Oct: Sat and Sun 2.30–5*
(2) *Charge*
(4) *Plants for sale*
(5) *National Trust for Scotland*

Girvan

Strathclyde

16. Bargany

Situated in the Valley of the Girvan Water, the woodland garden at Bargany was begun by the late Col Sir North Dalrymple Hamilton in 1910. The lily-pond, which is at the centre of the garden, is surrounded by azaleas and rhododendrons and to the west is a rock garden with shrubs and some heath plants. To the east is the old bowling green, the beech hedge now mature trees. The fine trees on the estate include wellingtonias. *Abies alba*, *Abies grandis*, *Abies nobilis* and a ginkgo. The flowering shrubs are at their best in May and June and earlier there are snowdrops, daffodils and wild hyacinth. In October there is a good display of autumn colour.

(1) *Feb–Oct: Daily 10–7*
(2) *Contribution box*
(5) *Capt N. E. F. Dalrymple Hamilton*

Glasgow, 730 Great Western Road

17. Glasgow Botanic Gardens

The gardens were founded by Thomas Hopkirk in 1817 and have occupied their present site since 1842. They cover 42 acres (17 ha) on the banks of the River Kelvin and include natural woodland and parkland. There are small rock and scree gardens and the Chronological Border shows the date of introduction of some common plants into British gardens. This is next to a series of genetic beds demonstrating the Mendelian laws of inheritance. The Systematic Garden represents the main families of annuals and herbaceous plants that are hardy in Scotland and there is a herb garden laid out in 1957 with plants used in medicine, cooking and the production of natural dyes. The Kibble Palace, one of the largest glasshouses in Britain, was transferred from Coulport, Loch Long, and was opened at the gardens in 1873; it was converted into a winter garden in the 1880s and now houses a fine collection of tree ferns and other plants not normally hardy in Scotland, grouped according to geographical origin. In the main range of glasshouses, the conservatory contains a colourful display throughout the year, and there are specialist collections of orchids, begonias and economic plants. A new arboretum was opened in 1977.

(1) *Gardens. Daily 7–Sunset. Kibble Palace. Daily 10–4.45. Main range of glasshouses. Mon–Sat 1–4.45; Sun noon–4.45. Kibble Palace and glasshouses close at 4.15 in winter*
(2) *Free*
(5) *Corporation of Glasgow, Parks and Botanic Gardens Dept*

Glasgow, 100 St Andrew's Drive

18. Haggs Castle Museum

Haggs Castle, which was built in 1585, is now a museum about history designed for children. The garden surrounding the building is an extension of this, recreating some popular features of gardens in the 16th and 17th cents. There is a knot garden, a herb and vegetable plot, a raised border, a cottage garden and a dovecot. A particularly good explanatory leaflet has been produced.

(1) *Mon–Sat 10–5.15; Sun 2–5*
(2) *Free*
(5) *City of Glasgow District Council, Parks Dept*

Glasgow, Kelvingrove

19. Kelvingrove Park

Richly wooded parkland covering 85 acres (34 ha) on the banks of the River Kelvin, purchased in 1852 and laid out by Sir Joseph Paxton; the granite steps near Park Gardens were built in 1854. As well as a fine border of roses and mixed shrubs, there are many other floral features, a number of unusual trees, including weeping varieties of ash, elm and birch, and an ornamental pond.

(1) *Daily*
(2) *Free*
(5) *City of Glasgow District Council, Parks Dept*

Glasgow, 97 Haggs Road and 2060 Pollokshaw Road

20. Pollok Park

The gardens of Pollok House were created over many years by Sir John Stirling Maxwell, who died in 1956. The gardens contain a valuable collection of trees and shrubs, including rhododendrons, azaleas, Japanese maples, magnolias, prunus and a specimen of *Davidia involucrata*, the handkerchief tree. Near the house are a display rose garden laid out in 1972, another, formal, rose garden and terraced lawns. The surrounding woodland contains a variety of trees in a natural setting. The park covers 361 acres (144·4 ha). Visit in spring for the daffodils and during May and June for rhododendrons and woodland bluebells.

(1) *Mon–Sat 10–5; Sun 2–5*
(2) *Free*
(4) *Pollok House (same times); nature trails*
(5) *City of Glasgow District Council, Parks Dept*

Glasgow, Victoria Road

21. Queen's Park

The park, now covering 148 acres (59·2 ha), was laid out by Sir Joseph Paxton and features a granite stairway leading to an extensive terrace which gives fine views of the Campsie Hills and Ben Lomond. Well-maintained lawns are surrounded with flowering plants in the summer months, and the walled garden, laid out in 18th-cent Dutch style, contains roses and herbaceous beds. As well as sub-tropical and economic plants, the glasshouses have a display of house plants with instructions on their care.

(1) *Park. Daily 7–Sunset. Glasshouses. Mon–Fri 11–4.15; Sat and Sun 11–6*
(2) *Free*
(5) *City of Glasgow District Council, Parks Dept*

Glasgow, Crookston Road

22. Ross Hall Park

The estate, named after the Ross family, once owners of Hawkhead Castle, was landscaped at the beginning of this century and adapted and extended in 1908. A variety of plant life flourishes among artificial lakes and rockeries with waterfalls and grottoes. There are fine heather and rock gardens; meadows and woodland lead down to the River Cart.

(1) *Apr–Sep: Daily 1–8; Oct–Mar: Daily 1–4*
(2) *Free*
(4) *Nature trails; children's playgrounds; putting green*
(5) *City of Glasgow District Council, Parks Dept*

Glasgow, Thornliebank, Rouken Glen Road

23. Rouken Glen Park

A park originally owned by the Montgomeries of Eglinton Castle and covering 156 acres (62·4 ha) approx 6 miles (9·6 km) from the city centre. Tree-shaded walks pass displays of rhododendrons in summer and fine shows of autumn colour. At the head of the glen the Auldhouse Burn rushes down a cascade. The boating pond, opened in 1924, has picturesque islands of trees and shrubs. The roses, rock plants and herbaceous beds in the walled garden are of interest to gardeners, and there is a rare collection of alpines.

(1) *Park. Daily 7–Sunset. Alpine House. Mid-Feb–mid-Oct: Daily 1.30–4*
(2) *Free*
(3) *Tea (Apr–Sep)*
(4) *Nature trail*
(5) *City of Glasgow District Council, Parks Dept*

Glasgow, Victoria Park Drive

24. Victoria Park

The park covering 58 acres (23.2 ha) was acquired by the Burgh of Partick in 1886, a year before the discovery of the fossilized stumps of a grove of trees which flourished 330 million years ago, now a feature of the garden. A large formal garden is protected from north and east by an artificial bank planted with hollies and cherries. Seen from the highest point of the bank, the flower garden is bright with polyanthus, wallflowers, myosotis and tulips in spring, and a great variety of plants in summer. There is a wide range of trees and shrubs throughout the park and the arboretum in the north-east corner contains about 35 labelled species. The rock garden adjoining the Fossil Grove has been reconstructed in recent years and now contains many shrubs and annuals as well as alpine plants; at its foot, there is a goldfish pond with a good display of waterlilies. Shelter has been provided for other

water plants growing round a small pond devoted to ducks and other fowl.

(1) *Park. Daily 7–Sunset. Fossil Grove. Mon–Sat 8–Sunset; Sun 10–Sunset*
(2) *Free*
(5) *City of Glasgow District Council, Parks Dept*

Gordon, nr Kelso

Borders

25. Mellerstain

Mellerstain, built by William Adam and completed by his son Robert, stands in richly wooded parkland. Fine lawns sweep from formal Italian gardens on terraces below the house to a lake stocked with waterfowl. In the gardens designed by Reginald Blomfield in 1910 there is a unique collection of old-fashioned and modern roses.

(1) *May–Sep: Daily (except Sat) 1.30–5.30. Last admission 5*
(2) *Charge*
(3) *Tea*
(4) *House (same times)*
(5) *Lord Binning*

Inveresk, nr Musselburgh

Lothian

26. Inveresk Lodge

Garden of a 17th-cent house in Inveresk, restored in 1959, displaying a range of plants suitable for a small garden. There is a border of old-fashioned and shrub roses as well as a selection of climbing roses, and an area devoted to peat beds.

(1) *Mon, Wed, Fri 10–4.30; Sun (when house is occupied) 2–5*
(2) *Charge*
(5) *National Trust for Scotland*

Isle of Arran

Strathclyde

27. Brodick Castle

Brodick Castle, home of the Dukes of Hamilton from 1503 to 1895, is famed for the beauty of its gardens, set against a background of the Arran Hills with the sea below. The woodland garden was laid out in the 1920s by the Duchess of Montrose, with the help of her son-in-law, Major J. P. T. Boscawen. Their shrub collection includes introductions from South America and the Far East brought in at a time of great botanical exploration. An outstanding collection of rhododendrons are in flower from January to August. Trees and shrubs from Australia and New Zealand also do well here. A large walled garden contains fine herbaceous borders, and lawns slope down to a pond garden.

127

(1) *Daily 10–5*
(2) *Charge*
(3) *Tea*
(4) *Castle (mid–end Apr: Mon, Wed and Sat 1–5; May–Sep: Mon–Sat 1–5, Sun 2–5*
(5) *National Trust for Scotland*

Isle of Colonsay
Strathclyde
28. Kiloran

An island garden noted for its rhododendrons, particularly big-leaved varieties, which seed freely. There are also magnolias, a path flanked with scarlet embothriums and a number of plants which are tender in most parts of Britain. Visit in spring.

(1) *Daily Sunrise–Sunset*
(2) *Charge*
(5) *Lord Strathcona*

Isle of Gigha
Strathclyde
29. Achamore House

The garden surrounding Achamore House was created by Sir James Horlick after his acquisition of the island in 1944, and his valuable plant collection was presented to the National Trust for Scotland in 1962.

Established behind thick belts of shelter which were added to existing trees, the garden covers 50 acres (20 ha) and has interesting collections of shrubs, notably rhododendrons and azaleas, sorbus, pine trees, waterside irises and spring bulbs, in a series of small 'gardens within a garden', many of which feature specimens of particular botanical interest. Plants from many parts of the world flourish in the island's temperate climate. Visit from March to June, taking the ferry from Tayinloan.

(1) *Apr–Sep: Daily 10–Sunset*
(2) *Charge*
(5) *D. W. N. Landale, Esq, and National Trust for Scotland*

Kelso
Borders
30. Floors Castle

The gardens lying to the west of the house were laid out in the mid-18th cent and the garden buildings were built by the architect James Playfair, who was employed at Floors in c 1840. In the walled gardens, where flowers, vegetables and fruit for the house are grown, there are fine herbaceous borders. Floors is well known for its carnations and several varieties were propagated here.

(1) *Early May–late Sep: Sun–Thu 12.30–4.30*

(2) *Charge*
(3) *Tea*
(4) *Castle (same days 1.30–4.45); Garden centre*
(5) *Duke of Roxburghe*

Kilchrenan, nr Taynuilt
Strathclyde
31. Ardanaiseig

The walled garden and many of the trees in the grounds date back to c 1830, when the house was built by Col Campbell. The main planting of rhododendrons and other flowering shrubs in the woodland garden, begun in the late 19th cent, was later carried out by Sir Thomas Ainsworth. The gardens are noted for fine displays of spring bulbs, flowering shrubs and autumn colour. There are magnificent views across Loch Awe. Visit in May, June or October.

(1) *Apr–Oct: Daily 10–6*
(2) *Charge (SGS)*
(5) *Mr and Mrs J. M. Brown*

Kilmelford, nr Oban
Strathclyde
32. Arduaine Gardens

Planting of the gardens, which extend to some 22 acres (8·8 ha) was begun in c 1910 by Arthur Campbell with the help of Osgood Mackenzie, creator of the garden at Inverewe (qv under Poolewe). Together, they made a fine collection of trees and shrubs, including tender species of rhododendrons and azaleas. After some years of neglect since World War II, the gardens have been restored. Visit in April, May or June.

(1) *Apr–Oct: Daily (except Thu and Fri) 9–8*
(2) *Charge*
(5) *Edmund Wright, Esq, and Harry Wright, Esq*

Kirkbean, nr Dumfries
Dumfries and Galloway
33. Arbigland Gardens

The grounds of Arbigland House are situated by a sandy beach at the tip of a peninsula on the Solway Firth. The gardens have evolved from a lay-out devised in the 18th cent by William Craik, the great Scottish land improver. To the north of an avenue, the Broad Walk, there are formal, woodland and water gardens. The climate is sufficiently mild for the growing of tender shrubs and flowers normally associated with southern or foreign gardens. Rhododendrons, azaleas and camellias are at their best in May and early June.

(1) *May–Sep: Tue, Thu, Sun 2–6*
(2) *Charge*
(3) *Tea*
(5) *Capt J. B. Blackett*

Maybole, nr Ayr

Strathclyde

34. Culzean Country Park

The castle, built by Robert Adam around an ancient tower, dates mainly from 1772–92. At that time the terraced gardens laid out during the reign of Charles II were embellished with parapets and pavilions. Developments in the 1960s included the introduction of many new shrubs and flowering trees, a large herbaceous bed in the centre of the walled garden and a collection of crab-apple trees, as well as the restoration of the 18th-cent pleasure garden. The formal Fountain Court extends over 7 acres (2·8 ha) in front of the castle; beyond it is the Camellia House. The castle grounds became Scotland's first Country Park in 1969. Practicable for wheelchairs.

(1) Daily
(2) Charge
(3) Restaurant (Apr–Sep: Daily 10–6; Oct: Daily 10–4)
(4) Castle (mid-April–Sep: Daily 10–6; Oct: Daily 10–4). Country Park (Daily). Information and Exhibition Centre (mid-Apr–Sep: Daily 10–6; Oct: Daily 10–4); Ranger Naturalist service.
(5) Managed by the National Trust for Scotland with Strathclyde Regional Council; the District Councils of Kyle and Carrick; Kilmarnock and Loudoun; Cunninghame; Cumnock and Doon Valley

Melrose

Borders

35. Priorwood Gardens

Adjacent to Melrose Abbey, a special garden displaying flowers for drying.

(1) Mid-Apr–mid-Oct: Mon–Sat 10–6; Sun 1.30–5.30; mid-Oct–24 Dec: Mon 2–5.30; Tue–Sat 10–5.30
(2) Free
(5) National Trust for Scotland

Minard, nr Inverary

Strathclyde

36. Crarae Woodland Garden

The garden established early this century on the steep slopes of a highland glen by Lady Campbell, aunt of the explorer and plant collector Reginald Farrer, was extended and developed by Sir George Campbell from 1925 until his death in 1967. Now covering an area of approx 40 acres (16 ha), the garden contains trees and shrubs from all temperate areas of the world, including both species and hybrid rhododendrons, a collection of decorative deciduous trees which provide a spectacular autumn colour, eucryphia, embothrium, nothofagus, the southern beech, and approx 25 different species of eucalyptus. Visit at the end of

SCOTLAND

May and early June or the last two weeks of September.

(1) Mar–Sep: Daily 8–7
(2) Charge
(4) Plants for sale
(5) Sir Ilay Campbell, Bt

Moniaive

Dumfries and Galloway

37. Maxwelton House

The gardens surrounding Maxwelton House, originally a stronghold of the Earls of Glencairn and birthplace of Annie Laurie, are thought to date from the 17th cent. Set among mature trees, with views of distant hills, they are designed to form an attractive background to the ancient building. Since restoration of the house, beginning in 1969, a fine collection of unusual shrubs and bulbs has been introduced. Visit throughout the summer from early May.

(1) May–Sep: Wed and Thu 2.30–5
(2) Charge
(4) House and museum of agricultural and early domestic life (same times)
(5) Maxwelton House Trustees

Peebles

Borders

38. Kailzie Gardens

These gardens in the Tweed Valley were first laid out at the end of the 18th cent, and the walled garden was made in the 1850s and redesigned by the owner after World War II. It now has climbing roses and island beds of shrub roses and hardy shrubs. The wild garden is at its best in spring, with snowdrops and then later daffodils and bluebells; in May there are azaleas. The larches, planted in 1725, may be the oldest in Scotland. The burnside walk is known as 'The Major's Walk'. There are glasshouses, which include a conservatory and fruit houses.

(1) Easter–Oct: Daily 10–6.30
(2) Charge
(3) Tea
(5) Mrs M. A. Richard

Port Logan, nr Stranraer

Dumfries and Galloway

39. Logan Botanic Garden

The garden, founded by the McDoualls of Logan, an ancient Galloway family, is now an important annexe of the Royal Botanic Garden, Edinburgh, and covers 3½ acres (1·4 ha). The mild climate encourages the growth of a notable collection of tender plants from the warm temperate areas of the southern hemisphere. There is an avenue of Cordyline australis. The garden is of interest throughout the summer and autumn.

(1) *Apr–Sep: Daily 10–5*
(2) *Charge*
(3) *Café*
(5) *Dept of Agriculture and Fisheries for Scotland*

Rhu, nr Helensburgh

Strathclyde

40. Glenarn

Most of the garden, now some 8 acres (3·2 ha) in extent, has been laid out since 1924. As well as the species rhododendrons, some dating from the 1840s and many others grown from seed introduced by the great plant collectors, there are some fine magnolias, a good collection of Chilean shrubs, and displays of primulas, meconopsis and lilies. Visit from April to June.

(1) *Mar–Aug: Daily Sunrise–Sunset*
(2) *Charge*
(5) *J. F. A. Gibson, Esq*

South Queensferry, nr Edinburgh

Lothian

41. Hopetoun House

Hopetoun House, home of the Marquess of Linlithgow, is set in 100 acres (40 ha) of parkland on the shores of the Forth. The grounds, first laid out in 1699, were re-designed with spacious lawns and avenues of trees to provide a magnificent setting for the house when it was enlarged by William Adam in the 1750s. To the south of the house is the famous Lime Walk and a walled garden; deer parks to the north and south hold herds of red and fallow deer. Visit in spring for the daffodils, late May for the rhododendrons, or later in the summer for the roses in the walled garden.

(1) *Daily 11–5.30*
(2) *Charge*
(3) *Café*
(4) *House and Museum (Daily, except Thu and Fri, 1.30–5.30, last admission 5.15); Nature trail*
(5) *Hopetoun House Preservation Trust*

Stobo, nr Peebles

Borders

42. Dawyck House Gardens

As it is today the garden was planted and planned by Col. F. R. S. Balfour. The terraces and stonework around the house date from 1820, but the present house was built in 1930 by William Burn, with later additions. There is a walled garden, best seen in summer; but Dawyck is principally known for its fine trees. A larch, *Larix decidua*, is believed to have been planted by the Swedish botanist Linnaeus in 1725; and of particular interest are the Dawyck beeches, *Fagus sylvatica* 'Dawyck', and the *Picea brewerana*. Species and hybrid rhododendrons flourish in the sheltered 'glen'.

(1) *Easter–Sep: Daily noon–5*
(2) *Charge (SGS)*
(5) *Lt-Col and Mrs A. N. Balfour*

Stranraer

Dumfries and Galloway

43. Castle Kennedy

The gardens around the Old Castle Kennedy on the neck of land between the Loch of Inch and Loch Crindl, were laid out in the early 18th cent by soldiers under the command of the 2nd Earl of Stair. After years of neglect, the grounds were restored and developed in the 19th cent. Additions were made to the original design of avenues radiating from a circular lily-pond, and flower gardens were laid out beside Loch-inch Castle, which was built in 1867. The gardens are notable for the collection of rhododendrons, azaleas, camellias, the scarlet embothrium and magnolias, which are seen to their best effect from mid-May to early June. Some specimens of *Rhododendron arboreum* were planted 100 years ago from seed brought back from the Himalayas by Sir Joseph Hooker. The walled kitchen garden contains a double herbaceous border which is at its best in August and September.

(1) *Apr–Sep: Daily (except Sat) 10–5*
(2) *Charge*
(3) *Kiosk*
(4) *Shop and garden centre (same times)*
(5) *Earl and Countess of Stair*

Tyninghame, nr Dunbar

Lothian

44. Tyninghame House

The most ancient part of the policies to be seen by the visitor is the triple avenue of beeches and the extensive woodland planted by the 6th Earl of Haddington between 1681 and 1735 and greatly added to throughout the centuries. Recent plantings include a collection of eucalyptus species.

Surrounding the house, which was extended and partially remodelled by the architect Sir William Burn in 1828, is a formal parterre, terraces and borders which today contain roses, shrubs and herbaceous plants. These were also designed originally by Burn. There is a walled garden and grass walks with statues and yew hedges, and apple tree espalier tunnels. Within the garden walls the path leads to a small knot garden with weeping mulberry trees.

(1) *May–Sep: Mon–Fri 1.30–4.30*
(2) *Charge*
(5) *Earl of Haddington*

WALES

Llandudno
Rhyl
(17) (2) (26) (22)
Bangor (14)
(18)
Wrexham (28)
Porthmadog
(21)
(1)
Welshpool (27)
(12)
Aberystwyth

Brecon
(11)
Abergavenny (19)
(24) (20)
Haverfordwest
(13)
Swansea
(3) (25)
(15) Cardiff
(4) (16) (5) (6)
(23) (10) (7)
(9) (8)

Kilometres 0   20   40
Miles 0   10   20

WALES

Arthog
Gwynedd
1. Ty'n-y-coed
The gardens, set on the lower slopes of Cader Idris, were founded in c 1870. They are made up of approx 3 acres (1·2 ha) of woodland surrounding a light triple waterfall, fountains and a lawn. There is a fine selection of trees and shrubs, including the second largest *Magnolia soulangiana* in Wales, rhododendrons, azaleas, flowering cherries, and Chusan palms, *Trachycarpus fortunei*. Visit in May and June.

(*1*) *May–Oct: Mon–Sat 10.30–5.30; Sun 1–5.30*
(*2*) *Charge*
(*3*) *Refreshments*
(*5*) *Dowager Viscountess Chetwynd*

Bangor
Gwynedd
2. Penrhyn Castle
The neo-Norman castle was rebuilt in 1830 for the 1st Lord Penrhyn by the architect Thomas Hopper around an earlier neo-Gothic house. The garden is divided by two terraces into three main areas. The upper area is laid out with a loggia, a parterre and three lily-ponds; a number of unusual plants grow on the walls. The middle area is dominated by an old specimen of *Pinus nigra maritima* and is planted with flowering trees and shrubs such as viburnums and witch hazel, *Hamamelis mollis* to provide flowers in winter; camellias, azaleas and magnolias for spring; cornus, honeysuckles, embothrium and hydrangeas for summer, followed by eucryphias in late summer. The lowest part is a wild garden with a small stream, planted with Japanese maples, bamboo, berberis and the giant *Gunnera manicata*. The slope above the drive to the Grand Lodge is planted with fuchsias, rhododendron and buddleias, and there are also some fine trees including redwoods, *Sequoia sempervirens*, wellingtonias, *Sequoiadendron giganteum*, and Douglas fir, *Pseudotsuga menziesii*.

(*1*) *Apr–May and Oct: Daily 2–5; Jun–Sep: Daily 11–5; Bank Holiday weekends 11–5*
(*2*) *Charge*
(*3*) *Refreshments*
(*4*) *Castle; locomotive museum; doll museum (same times)*
(*5*) *National Trust*

Blackpill, nr Swansea
West Glamorgan
3. Clyne Castle
The Clyne estate belonged to the Phillips family from 1790 and was acquired by Admiral Sir Vyvyan Heneage Vyvyan in 1859. His collection of rhododendrons, azaleas and other exotic trees and shrubs, as well as herbaceous plants such as primulas, is probably the finest in South Wales. In 1955 Clyne Castle was bought by Swansea University College as a Hall of Residence and the City Council acquired the grounds as a public park. Visit from mid-April to mid-June.

(*1*) *Mon–Fri 8–Sunset; Sat and Sun 10–Sunset*
(*2*) *Free*
(*5*) *Swansea City Council*

Bridgend
Mid-Glamorgan
4. Merthyr Mawr
The present house was built in 1809 by the architect Henry Wood for Sir John Nicholl, MP. The gardens were originally laid out by him and have been expanded by later generations. There are lawns and terraces; the top terrace has rockeries and sink gardens while the lower terrace has a red and silver border. Tender plants are grown in a bed on the south side of the house. There are many flowering trees and shrubs, including 14 magnolias; a formal rose garden in the form of a Maltese cross and a herb garden, planted in 1976. Chapel Wood contains many shrubs and specimen trees and the 'secret garden', originally made last century; it was replanted and the vista cleared in the late 1960s. Within the grounds are several swallow-holes which are part of a cave system, a 14th-cent chapel and the remains of an Iron Age fort.

(*1*) *Mid-May–Aug: Wed afternoons (other times by appointment)*
(*2*) *Charge*
(*5*) *Mrs McLaggan*

Cardiff
South Glamorgan
5. Bute Park
The whole area, covering over 350 acres (140 ha), contains Cardiff Castle and its grounds, including Sophia Gardens, and the areas known as Pontcanna and Llandaff Fields. Throughout the park there are many fine trees and shrubs; a path winds among specimens such as *Paulownia tomentosa*, *Ginkgo biloba* and species of magnolia, maple, birch, crataegus, eucalyptus, and flowering crab apples. Behind the nursery, beside the River Taff, a collection of trees and shrubs is known as the Camellia Section, where, besides camellias, are specimens of strawberry tree, *Arbutus unedo*; paperbark maple, *Acer griseum*; Turkish hazel, *Corylus colurna*; Golden Ontario poplar, *Populus × candicans* 'Aurora'; the Japanese bitter orange, *Poncirus trifoliata*, and a small collection of

rhododendrons. In spring, thousands of wild daffodils, *Narcissus pseudo-narcissus*, give a brilliant display. Elsewhere in the park, there are good displays of seasonal bedding.

(1) Daily 8.30—Sunset
(2) Free
(4) National Recreation Centre: Equitation Centre
(5) Cardiff City Council

Cardiff
6. Parc Cefn-Onn

The 200 acre (80 ha) park, situated on the northern outskirts of Cardiff, about 5 miles (8 km) from the city centre, includes wooded hillsides with fine views and a dingle planted with rhododendrons, azaleas and exotic trees. Most of the planting was done before and after World War I by T. M. Jenkins, the late head gardener who was in charge for over 30 years under both private ownership and the Council, who bought the area in 1944.

The park is divided into two separate sections; the south part was not planted until after its acquisition by the Council and is basically a woodland garden, with streams and a water-lily pool. Large oaks and conifers provide shelter for shrubs such as rhododendrons and *Pieris formosa* var. *forrestii*. The Upper Park, the site of the original garden, also has a stream and a pool. There are many fine specimen trees such as blue cedar, *Cedrus atlantica glauca*; Brewer's weeping spruce, *Picea brewerana*, and *Embothrium coccineum*, as well as clumps of rhododendrons and camellias, bamboos and Kurume azaleas. Along the waterside are plantings of ferns, astilbes and the American skunk cabbage, *Lysichitum americanum*. A rock garden contains heathers and other plants that like an acid soil.

(1) Daily 8.30—Sunset
(2) Free
(3) Refreshments (Summer)
(5) Cardiff City Council

Cardiff
7. Roath Park

This park, first opened to the public in 1894, covers over 100 acres (40 ha), and includes a landscaped 30 acre (12 ha) lake and a large conservatory, opened in 1975. The park can best be viewed by following the Nant Fawr Walk which is 3 miles (4·8 km) long. It starts in the Waterloo Gardens (qv) and leads through Roath Mill Gardens and Roath Brook Gardens to Roath Pleasure Gardens, with lawns, a fine collection of trees and shrubs, a floribunda rose garden and flowerbeds with seasonal bedding. In spring there is a good show of crocuses.

Roath Park Botanic Garden is famous for its rose garden with over 50 beds of Hybrid Teas and many shrub roses and climbers; the Royal National Rose Society sends for display purposes new roses that

have recieved Trial Awards. National dahlia trials are also held here and a chrysanthemum house, with hundreds of plants of many different varieties, is open to the public in November. There is also a fine collection of trees and shrubs from all over the world, two herbaceous borders, a bog garden, a rock garden and an acer lawn. In spring the grass slope leading to the rock garden is covered with daffodils and crocuses; in autumn there is a good display of coloured foliage, and in winter colour is provided by berries and the stems and trunks of trees and shrubs such as cornus, willows and birches. Most of the plants in the garden are labelled.

The path leads on beyond the lake, where there is a wild garden.

(1) Daily 8.30—Sunset
(2) Free
(3) Lakeside café (summer)
(4) Boating; fishing
(5) Cardiff City Council

Cardiff
8. Rumney Hill Gardens

The notable feature of this 9 acre (4 ha) park is the rock garden with a wide collection of alpine plants, mostly labelled.

(1) Daily 8.30—Sunset
(2) Free
(5) Cardiff City Council

Cardiff
9. Tremorfa Park

The 30 acre (12 ha) park, once part of Pengam Airfield, formerly Cardiff's airport, is noted for its large heather garden which contains a wide range of species and varieties.

(1) Daily Sunrise—Sunset
(2) Free
(5) Cardiff City Council

Cardiff
10. Waterloo Gardens

This 3 acre (1·4 ha) garden, first opened in 1910, is particularly attractive in spring and summer. Japanese flowering cherries are followed by rhododendrons, roses and herbaceous perennials and there is always a colourful display of seasonal bedding.

(1) Daily 8.30—Sunset
(2) Free
(5) Cardiff City Council

Crickhowell
Powys
11. Gliffaes Country House Hotel

The hotel is reached by a quarter-mile (0·4

km) drive flanked by rhododendrons, at their best in May and June. The grounds cover 27 acres (11 ha) and contain many rare trees and shrubs and terraced lawns.

(1) Daily Mar–Dec
(2) Free
(3) Tea
(5) Mr and Mrs S. G. Brabner and Mr and Mrs N. S. Brabner

Eglwysfach, nr Machynlleth

Dyfed

12. Ynyshir Hall

The hotel garden was started in the 1920s and the designer is unknown. There are lawns and many fine specimen trees, including magnolias, rhododendrons, camellias, hydrangeas and other shrubs such as *Clerodendrum trichotomum*. Visit in spring and autumn.

(1) Mid-Mar–mid-Oct: Daily 2–5
(2) Collecting box for National Trust
(5) Mrs Penny Roberts

Haverfordwest

Dyfed

13. Picton Castle

The castle, built in 1190, is one of the most ancient in Britain and is still occupied by descendants of the original founder. The most interesting part of the garden has been developed over the past 25 years by Lady Marion Philipps, making use of existing woodland and streams. Shelter from the salt winds has been provided, and now shrubs and trees are in flower in every month of the year – rhododendrons, camellias, magnolias, cherries, crabs, embothriums, liquidambar, leptospermum, callistemon species, eucryphias and escallonias, as well as herbaceous and bulbous plants including agapanthus and crinum and arum lilies.

(1) Late Mar–Sep: Daily 10.30–12.30, 1.30–5.30
(2) Charge
(4) Graham Sutherland Art Gallery (same times)
(5) Hon Hanning and Lady Marion Philipps

Hawarden, nr Deeside

Clwyd

14. Hawarden Castle

The garden was founded by Sir John Glynne in 1730–40 and changes have been made at various later dates. There are some fine rhododendrons and azaleas, a rock garden, a bog garden and a picturesque view of the 13th-cent castle. Wild flowers are encouraged to grow. Visit in April and May.

(1) Easter–Sept: Sat, Sun and Public Holidays 2–5.30
(2) Charge
(4) Garden centre
(5) Sir William Gladstone

Llandaff, nr Cardiff

South Glamorgan

15. Llandaff Court

The 8 acre (3·2 ha) park, entered through an avenue of horse chestnuts, is made up of lawns, many interesting trees and shrubs, including two fine cedars of Lebanon, roses, fuchsias and wall shrubs.

(1) Daily Sunrise–Sunset
(2) Free
(5) Cardiff City Council

Llandaff

16. Old Bishop's Palace

The public gardens on the site of the courtyard of the former Bishop's Palace were laid out in 1972 and have received Civic Trust and Wales in Bloom awards. The palace, parts of which may date from the 13th cent, is now a ruin although some parts, such as the gatehouse and turrets, have been restored. The central part of the garden is lawn, with apple trees and fig trees. A foliage shrub border lies in front of a Victorian garden wall on the foundations of an older wall; at right angles to that is an aromatic shrub border. At the north end of the garden is a paved area and a herb border. Plants have been selected for their suitability to the monument as a whole.

(1) Daily 8.30–Sunset
(2) Free
(4) Palace ruins
(5) Cardiff City Council

Llanfairpwll, Isle of Anglesey

Gwynedd

17. Plas Newydd

The house dates from the early 16th cent, with 18th-cent additions. Humphry Repton laid out the park and gardens producing one of his famous Red Books for Plas Newydd in 1799, although many of the trees are much older than this. There has been much replanting since the war; this includes a very large hedge of *Viburnum plicatum* 'Lanarth', some fine specimens of *Embothrium coccineum lanceolatum* and many rhododendrons. A formal Italianate rose garden has a group of Mediterranean cypresses as a focal point. The garden is at its most colourful in May and June, although shrubs such as potentillas and hydrangeas and roses continue the display until late summer.

(1) Mid-Apr–end Oct: Daily (except Sat, but open Bank Holiday Sat) 12.30–5.30
(2) Charge

Llanrug, nr Caernarvon

Gwynedd

18. Bryn Bras Castle

The castle was built in Romanesque style in 1830, around a pre-1750 structure. The garden is one of the largest private gardens in Wales to be open to the public, and although situated in the north-west foothills of Snowdon, with fine views to the mountains, it is sheltered from the south-westerly gales. The woodland garden, with rhododendrons and azaleas, walks, pools, waterfalls and walled kitchen garden, were all laid out between 1839 and 1850 and the basic design has remained largely unchanged since then. In the 1920s the kitchen garden was converted into a knot garden, which has been restored by the present owners after a period of neglect; in 1970 hundreds of rose bushes were planted in its geometric beds.

(1) Spring Bank Holiday–mid-Jul and Sep: Sun–Fri 1–5; mid-Jul–Aug: Sun–Fri 10.30–5
(2) Charge
(3) Tea
(4) Part of castle (same times)
(5) Mrs M. Gray-Parry and R. D. Gray-Williams

Llanvihangel, nr Abergavenny

Gwent

19. Llanvihangel Court

The house, which dates from 1550, is approached by stone steps leading up between grass terraces and old stone walls. The garden covers approx 2 acres (0·8 ha) and consists mainly of lawns, shrubs and trees. Behind the house is a fine avenue of Spanish chestnut trees, brought originally as seedlings from Spain.

(1) Jun: some Sun 2.30–6; Jul and Aug: Sun and Bank Holiday Mon 2.30–6
(2) Charge
(3) Tea
(5) Col and Mrs Somerset Hopkinson

Lydart, nr Monmouth

Gwent

20. The Yew Tree

The 3 acre (1·2 ha) garden is set on a hillside and is divided by shelter belts of trees and shrubs into a series of small compartments. Terraces of sloping lawns are divided by low dry-stone walls planted with alyssum, aubrieta, mossy saxifrages and helianthemums, while the beds at the top of the walls are planted with low-growing shrubs, including several varieties of hebe. In the lowest bed, there are Japanese hybrid tree peonies and hy-drangeas. The yew trees that give the house its name are thought to be over 300 years old; one is covered with the scarlet *Tropaeolum speciosum* and *Aconitum volubile* and the other with *Clematis macropetala* and *Eccremocarpus scaber*.

At the foot of the garden is a stream whose banks are planted with many waterside and bog plants, including meconopsis and primulas; behind the water garden is an area devoted to rare local flowers such as various orchids, *Lilium martagon* and *Helleborus foetidus*. Rhododendrons are a speciality, both dwarfs and taller species such as *R. oreotrephes* and 'Lady Chamberlain'. A collection of dwarf conifers is top-dressed with seashells.

At the rear of the house, many tender plants are grown, such as *Ozothamnus rosmarinifolius*, *Callistemon* spp. and *Phygelius aequalis*.

(1) Apr–Oct: Sun and Bank Holiday Mon 2–7 or by appointment
(2) Charge
(5) Lt-Col A. F. Collett

Portmeirion

Gwynedd

21. Gwyllt Gardens

The village of Portmeirion is the creation of the architect Sir Clough Williams-Ellis. The whole peninsula, an area of approx 175 acres (70 ha), forms the gardens. The original landscaping was 18th cent, but there has been much replanting, particularly by the botanical experts Mr Westmacott and Sir William Fothergill Cook. There are outstanding rhododendrons and azaleas as well as many other trees and shrubs including embothriums, eucalyptus, ginkgo, camellias and hydrangeas.

(1) Easter–Oct: Daily 9.30–5.30
(2) Charge
(3) Café and restaurant
(4) Portmeirion Village
(5) Trustees of the Portmeirion Foundation

Rhuddlan

Clwyd

22. Bodrhyddan

The 17th-cent manor house is surrounded by parkland and a woodland garden. A formal garden was designed by Nesfield in the mid-19th cent for the grandfather of the present owner.

(1) Jun–Sep: Tue and Thu 2.30–5.30
(2) Charge
(3) Tea
(4) House (same times)
(5) Col Lord Langford

WALES

St Nicholas, nr Cardiff

South Glamorgan

23. Dyffryn Gardens

The gardens, 73 acres (29.2 ha) in extent, were founded by Reginald Cory in 1900–14, but most of the planting dates from 1920–34. There are extensive lawns, water-lily pools and fountains, an arboretum with an interesting collection of trees, shrub borders, herbaceous borders, seasonal bedding, a collection of dwarf conifers and a rose garden with over 2,000 roses. A number of individual garden designs are each enclosed by fine yew hedges.

Plant houses contain a wide range of tropical, temperate and cool-house plants, including several of economic importance such as coffee, cocoa, ginger and citrus. There are collections of orchids and cacti and display houses with flowering pot plants.

(1) *Easter Sat–mid-May and Sep: Daily 1–6; Oct: Sat and Sun 1–6; plant houses close at 5; mid-May–Aug: Daily 10–7, plant houses close at 6*
(2) *Charge*
(3) *Café*
(5) *Mid Glamorgan and South Glamorgan County Councils*

Scolton, nr Haverfordwest

Dyfed

24. Scolton Manor Country Park Museum

The present house, which replaces a previous Tudor one, was designed by the local architects William and James Owen and completed in 1840. The grounds cover approx 40 acres (16 ha) and consist mainly of woodland, with many species and varieties of trees and shrubs from different parts of the world. In spring, rhododendrons and azaleas are in bloom.

(1) *Times of opening from Dyfed Town Council: 0437 3708*
(2) *Free*
(3) *Restaurant*
(4) *Museum*
(5) *Dyfed County Council*

Swansea

West Glamorgan

25. Educational Gardens, Singleton Park

The Educational Gardens in Singleton Park occupy a part of what was, before the acquisition of the park by the City Council, part of the kitchen garden attached to Singleton Abbey. They were laid out in 1923 and contain many rare trees and shrubs, including sub-tropical species; collections of herbaceous plants and bulbs; and a range of glasshouses with one of the best collections in Wales of tropical and cool-house plants, including plants of economic importance and orchids.

(1) *Winter: Daily 9–1, 2.15–4; Summer: Daily 9–1, 2.15–7*
(2) *Free*
(3) *Kiosk*
(5) *Swansea City Council*

Tal-y-Cafn, Colwyn Bay

Gwynedd

26. Bodnant Garden

The 90 acre (36 ha) grounds, with beautiful views to Snowdon, were first laid out in c 1875. In 1900 the 2nd Lord Aberconway started planting on a grand scale: below the house he designed and constructed five terraces in the Italian style. Two large cedars were already there; these were incorporated and, between them, he made a formal lily-pool. The lowest terrace has a canal pool with at one end an open air stage and, at the other, the elegant Pin Mill, an 18th-cent building, originally an old pin factory, saved from demolition in Gloucestershire and re-erected here. One of the features of the garden is the collection of rhododendrons, both species, grown from seed collected on botanical expeditions, and hybrids, many grown at Bodnant. Most of these are planted in a sheltered valley that has been made into a beautiful woodland garden. There are many other choice plants, such as eucryphias, embothriums, magnolias and camellias, and also collections of daphnes and conifers, a large rock garden with many evergreen azaleas and a laburnum walk.

(1) *Mid-Mar–Oct: Mon–Sat 10–5; Sun 1–5. No dogs or prams*
(2) *Charge*
(3) *Refreshments*
(5) *National Trust*

Welshpool

Powys

27. Powys Castle

The castle stands on a rocky slope; the garden terraces are reputed to have been designed by the architect William Winde, who visited the castle in 1697, and are the only formal gardens of that date still existing in their original form. Four terraces, two with balustrades decorated with urns and figures, nearly 200 yards (185 m) long, stretch across the east front of the castle. The top terrace is planted with clipped yews and many interesting shrubs; creepers grow against the retaining walls. An orangery is built into one of the terraces and above it is a loggia with arches. Besides this, there is a woodland garden underplanted with rhododendrons and a pinetum with some fine trees.

(1) *Easter Sat–end Sep: Daily (except Mon and Tue) 2–6; Public Holidays 11.30–6. Also Wed and Sun mornings from 11.30 in Jul and Aug*
(2) *Charge*
(3) *Refreshments*
(4) *Castle (Easter Sat–early Sep: same times but not mornings in Jul and Aug)*
(5) *National Trust*

Wrexham

Clwyd

28. Erddig

The house dates from 1680, with 18th-cent additions. The gardens have been restored to their 18th-cent formal Dutch style, with walks, a canal pond and a double avenue of pleached limes (*Tilia × euchlora*) that follows the line of walls demolished in the late 18th cent. The walled garden was replanted in 1975–7, using 18th- and 19th-cent cultivars of fruit; the walls also support clematis, *Hydrangea petiolaris* and roses; the borders at the foot of the walls contain a collection of rare old varieties of narcissus as well as summer-flowering plants. A parterre with stalagmite fountains is a Victorian addition.

(1) *Apr–Oct: Tue–Sun and Bank Holiday Mon noon–5.30*
(2) *Charge*
(4) *House (same times. Last admission 4.30)*
(5) *National Trust*

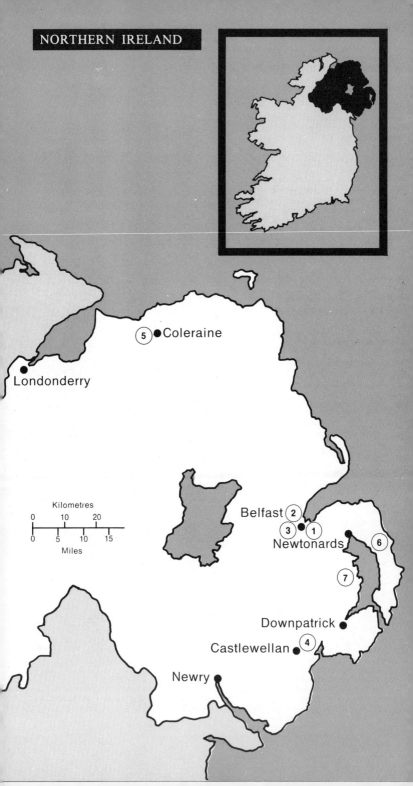

NORTHERN IRELAND

⑤ ●Coleraine

●Londonderry

Kilometres
0   10   20
0   5   10   15
Miles

Belfast ②
③ ● ①
Newtonards   ⑥

⑦

Downpatrick ●

Castlewellan ● ④

Newry ●

Belfast, Stranmillis Road

1. Botanic Gardens

The gardens were founded in 1829 under the auspices of the Belfast Botanic and Horticultural Society and became a public park, the oldest in the city, in 1895.

The glasshouses are of particular interest, the Palm House, of 1840, being one of the last examples of 19th-cent conservatories of curvilinear design of cast-iron construction. It was designed by Charles Lanyon and is currently undergoing major refurbishing. The Tropical Ravine, a unique piece of horticultural Victoriana of 1886, was constructed by Richard Turner of Dublin, who was also responsible for the construction of the Great Palm House at Kew (qv). It comprises a ravine within the glasshouse surrounded on three sides by a raised walk with narrow, winding paths along the bottom of the ravine which lead to a small pool and waterfall.

In the open area the most interesting horticultural feature is a rose garden. There is also a neolithic tomb – the Ballintaggart Court cairn – which was moved from Co Armagh.

(1) *Daily 8–Sunset*
(2) *Free*
(4) *Ulster Museum*
(5) *City of Belfast Parks Dept*

Belfast

2. Musgrave Park

The site of the 52 acre (21 ha) park was presented to the Belfast Corporation in 1920 by Henry Musgrave. A traditional municipal park, the horticultural features have recently been extended with a model ornamental garden. It is used as a training centre by the Parks Department and comprises shrubs, heathers, herbaceous borders, a bog garden and seasonal bedding plants.

(1) *Daily 8–Sunset*
(2) *Free*
(5) *City of Belfast Parks Dept*

Belfast

3. Sir Thomas and Lady Dixon Park

The estate of 134 acres (54 ha), bounded on one side by the River Lagan, was given to the Belfast Corporation in 1959 by Lady Edith Stewart Dixon. There is a small formal walled garden, lawns and parkland with fine, mature trees. Since 1965 part of the park has been laid out as the City of Belfast International Rose Trial ground, now containing over 20,000 roses. Each trial is judged over a two-year period. The trial beds and large display beds are interspersed with shrub planting and trees for ornament and shelter. Each year the Belfast Parks Department organizes a Belfast Rose

Week in July and most of the events are centred in the park.

(1) *Daily 8–Sunset*
(2) *Free*
(5) *City of Belfast Parks Dept*

Castlewellan

Co Down

4. Castlewellan National Arboretum

Part of what is now the Castlewellan Forest Park, the arboretum was originally planted by the 5th Earl Annesley in the 1870s. Covering an area of 80 acres (32 ha), it contains a comprehensive collection of conifers and many rare hardwood trees and shrubs. It is recognized as one of the most interesting arboreta in the British Isles. There is a walled garden (the Annesley Garden), with herbaceous borders and glasshouses, a rhododendron wood, an autumn wood, a spring garden, a winter garden and in the park at some distance from the arboretum a collection of chamaecyparis.

(1) *Daily*
(2) *Parking charge*
(5) *Dept of Agriculture, Forest Service*

Coleraine

Co Londonderry

5. Guy L. Wilson Daffodil Garden

Situated in the grounds of the New University of Ulster, the garden was begun in 1971 in memory of Guy L. Wilson. It was opened to the public in 1974.

New bulb plantings are made every year and the aim is to display a comprehensive collection of the cultivars of Guy L. Wilson, a noted daffodil hybridist, and of J. Lionel Richardson, a daffodil breeder from Waterford. A botanic garden is under construction which will contain a collection of trees, shrubs and herbs arranged according to their geographical origin. It will include a section devoted to British plant ecology and an important collection of rare and endangered species.

(1) *Daily during daylight hours*
(2) *Free*
(4) *University refectory*
(5) *New University of Ulster*

Greyabbey

Co Down

6. Mount Stewart

Edith, 7th Marchioness of Londonderry, started to create the gardens at Mount Stewart in 1921. Situated beside Strangford Lough, the extremely soft climate and

139

shelter of woodlands permit many exotic species to flourish here in a setting that blends the formal with the informal.

In the south front is the Italian Garden, a long terrace giving on to a sunken lawn with twin parterres surrounded by walls set with unusual stone ornaments made to Lady Londonderry's design and alluding to the Ark Club, a London club of the 1930s. The Spanish Garden has a sunken pool and a garden house roofed with Spanish tiles.

The west front looks on to a sunken garden surrounded by a raised walk overhung by climbers and planted with beds of azaleas. *Rosa gigantea*, ceanothus, solanums and delphiniums grow well here. Beyond is a paved garden in the form of a shamrock in which a topiary harp stands over the Red Hand of Ulster set in flowers in the paved area.

At the east end of the house lies the Mairi Garden, with a summer house and dovecot, where the nursery rhyme 'Mairi, Mairi, Quite Contrary' can be traced with the 'silver bells and cockle shells and pretty maids all in a row'.

Avenues, many of them lined with rhododendrons, lead from the house to many parts of the estate and a path from the entrance front takes the visitor to the lake. Near the lake is the private burial ground, *Tir Nan Og* (Land of the Ever Young).

The garden, with its interesting collection of plants from all over the world, was transferred to the National Trust in 1955.

(1) *Apr–Sep: Daily (except Fri, but open on Good Friday) 2–6*
(2) *Charge*
(3) *Tea (Apr–Aug: Daily; Sept: Weekends)*
(4) *House (same times)*
(5) *National Trust*

Saintfield

Co Down

7. Rowallane

The garden was created in this century by Hugh Armytage Moore, a distinguished plantsman. Originally a wasteland of rock, the 200 acre (81 ha) Rowallane is today famous for the arrangement and the rarity of its collection of trees, shrubs, plants and bulbs. Of particular note are the rhododendrons and azaleas. *Chaenomeles* 'Rowallane', *Hypericum* 'Rowallane', *Primula* 'Rowallane Rose' and *Viburnum plicatum var. tomentosum* 'Rowallane' are all named after the garden.

There is a walled garden and also a spring garden, situated in rocky pastures intercepted by dry stone walls, where uncommon shrubs and trees blend with the landscape. The garden is at its best between mid-May and mid-June.

(1) *Mon–Fri 9–6; Sat and Sun 2–6; also May and Jun on fine evenings 7–9*

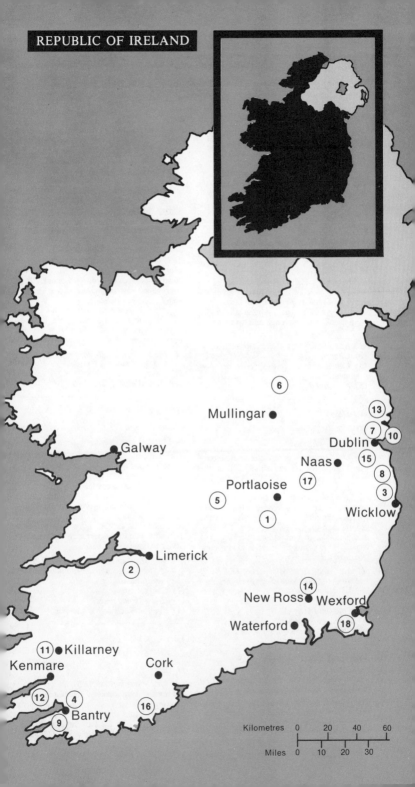

REPUBLIC OF IRELAND

Mullingar ●

⑥

⑬

⑦ ⑩

Dublin

Galway ●

Naas ●

⑮

⑧

Portlaoise

⑰

⑤

●

③

①

Wicklow

Limerick

●

②

New Ross ⑭

● Wexford

Waterford ●

⑱

⑪ ● Killarney

Kenmare

Cork ●

⑯

⑫

④

⑨ Bantry

Kilometres 0   20   40   60

Miles 0   10   20   30

REPUBLIC OF IRELAND

Abbeyleix

Co Laois

1. Abbey Leix

The house was built by the architect Sir William Chambers in 1773 and the terraces to the west date from the early 19th cent. They were made by Emma, wife of the 3rd Viscount de Vesci, and modelled on the Woronzow palace in the Crimea, the home of her mother's family. Parkland stretches down to the River Nore and beside it is the Wilderness. On the far side of the river is woodland which is of particular interest because in it survive oaks (*Quercus pedunculata*) that are the last remaining trees of the primaeval forest of Ireland. Abbey Leix is also notable because it was one of the first estates in Ireland to undertake commercial sylviculture. Known as Parkhill, the woodland has a carpet of bluebells in spring.

The King's Garden is on the site of the original Cistercian abbey and here lies the tomb of Malachy O'More, the last king of Leix. There is a large lily-pond surrounded by azaleas, a lime avenue and, to the north of the house, a pinetum.

(1) Easter Sat–Sep: Daily 2.30–6.30
(2) Charge
(3) Lunch and morning coffee by arrangement; Tea
(5) Viscount de Vesci

Adare

Co Limerick

2. Adare Manor

The Box Garden with four geometrical box-edged parterres on the south side of the house was laid out in the 19th cent by the architect P. C. Hardwick, who also worked on the house. Beside the formal garden is a bowling green and a rose border, beyond which steps lead down to the river. In the grounds are tulip-trees, a cedar of Lebanon that is 200–250 years old and the largest in Ireland, and a ginkgo; there is also a cork tree, now rare in Ireland.

(1) Apr and Oct: Mon–Fri 10.30–4.30; Sun 2–4.30; May–Sep: Mon–Fri 10–5.30; Sun 2–5.30
(2) Charge
(3) Café (mid-May–Sep)
(4) House (same times)
(5) Earl of Dunraven and Mount Earl

Ashford

Co Wicklow

3. Mount Usher

The original garden, surrounding a corn mill that was on the site of the present house, was founded by Edward Walpole and dates from *c* 1860. Early in the 1880s George and Edward Walpole, the founder's sons, fell under the influence of William Robinson, author of *The English Flower Garden* (1883), and, following his advice, they started to plant trees and shrubs so that they appeared to grow naturally and freely. Gradually acquiring more land and with the expert help of Sir Frederick Moore, director of the National Botanic Gardens at Glasnevin, Dublin (qv), they created a romantic garden of great horticultural interest. They obtained seeds from New Zealand, Australia, South America, Japan and China, and North Africa, as well as from Europe. The exotic grows side by side with indigenous species.

Extending today to 20 acres (8 ha), the garden has a natural axis in the River Vartry. Bridges and weirs break up views of the water from various different points. A feature of the garden is the great variety of moisture-loving and waterside plants that grow on the banks and also beside the pond. One of the glories of the garden is the Montezuma pine, and there are fine eucalyptus trees, hybrid rhododendrons, eucryphias and magnolias and a remarkable *Libocedrus chilensis*.

Although strictly a plantsman's garden, the atmosphere of the place should appeal to the general visitor. Visit in May, September or October.

(1) Mon–Sat 10–5.30; also May–Sep: Sun 2–5.30. Closed at Christmas
(2) Charge
(5) R. B. Walpole, Esq

Bantry

Co Cork

4. Bantry House

The Italianate terraces, situated on steeply rising ground above Bantry Bay, were laid out by the 2nd Earl of Bantry in *c* 1840. A staircase of 100 steps leads to a viewpoint behind and high above the Georgian house. There are rhododendrons, camellias and azaleas, and palm trees stand straight and tall among the shrubs. In front of the house are balustraded grass terraces with statuary, urns and flower-filled basins.

(1) Mid-Mar–mid-Oct: Mon–Fri 10–1, 2–6; Sun 2.30–6. Parties at other times by appointment
(2) Charge
(4) House (same times)
(5) Egerton Shelswell-White, Esq

Birr

Co Offaly

5. Birr Castle

Birr Castle was built in 1620, incorporating the remains of a medieval structure, and the planting of the grounds which cover approx 100 acres (40.5 ha) began in the late 18th cent. The park in front of the castle slopes down towards a lake and the River Camcor.

The River Walk takes the visitor along the river, on the far side of the lake, and into the arboretum, leading finally to the formal Walled Gardens in the north-west corner. The box hedges, at 34 feet (10 m) in height, are reputedly the tallest in the world and date from the 18th cent, as also do the terraces; but the French-style lay-out, with hornbeam alleys, box parterres, garden ornaments, yew hedges and borders of irises and peonies, dates from 1935. Here also are lawns with ancient trees and glasshouses, and rugosa and other shrub roses.

On the south-west of the castle are the terraces, with a herbaceous border on the site of the old moat and against the wall *Magnolia delavayi*. Beside the path are tubs of lilies and agapanthus. The Low Walk leads to the River Garden, where there are fine trees, notably *Magnolia Charles Raffill*. Here there are beds of moisture-loving plants. On the opposite bank of the river is *Magnolia dawsoniana* set against the dark background of *Cupressus macrocarpa lutea*, and a collection of viburnums and other flowering shrubs on the slopes. Further to the west is the Lagoon Garden, planted with trees that are notable for their blossom in spring and for their colour in autumn.

At the boat house the High Walk leads back towards the castle. This has shrub borders and in spring there is a fine display of blue-eyed Mary, *Omphalodes cappadocica*, and lungwort. In the park there is a lilac walk, collections of *Rosaceae* and the Giant Telescope, constructed in 1845 and for 70 years the largest in the world. A museum has recently been installed at the base of the tube.

The 5th Earl of Rosse and his son, the present Earl, were among the sponsors of Chinese and Himalayan expeditions, in return for which they received seeds of species collected there in the wild. In 1977 it was stated in the report *Heritage at Risk* that the gardens at Birr are 'scientifically the country's most important collection of trees and shrubs outside the National Botanic Gardens in Dublin' (qv).

(1) *Winter: Daily 9–1, 2–5.30; Summer: Daily 9–1, 2–6*
(2) *Charge*
(4) *Plants for sale*
(5) *Earl and Countess of Rosse*

Castlepollard
Co Westmeath
6. Tullynally

Set in rolling 18th-cent parkland above Lough Derravaragh, the battlemented castle acquired its present appearance in 1840. The gardens cover approx 30 acres (12 ha) and were laid out in the 18th and early 19th cents.

The Pleasure Ground has winding paths leading past fine specimen trees and shrubs. Stone steps lead down through a beech grove to the River Sham (an artificial lake)

and the Forest Walk. The central gravel walk leads to the walled flower garden, planted originally in 1740, and thence to the large kitchen garden, where the central avenue of Irish yews survives. Here there is an unusual hedge of mixed mahonia, box, yew and holly. Another path from the Pleasure Ground leads to the early 19th-cent grotto.

(1) *Jun–Sep: Sun and Public Holidays 2.30–6*
(2) *Charge*
(3) *Tea*
(4) *House (same times)*
(5) *Thomas Pakenham, Esq*

Dublin, Glasnevin
7. National Botanic Gardens

The gardens were founded by direction of the Irish Parliament, the acquisition of 27 acres (10·5 ha) of land outside Dublin by the Dublin Society taking place in 1795. The site now extends to 48 acres (19·4 ha).

The original lay-out was altered by Ninian Niven, designer of Phoenix Park, Dublin, in the 1830s and modifications to his plan were made by later curators. The arrangement of plants is botanic rather than geographical and the River Tolka, which forms the boundary of the gardens on one side, is incorporated in the lay-out. A feature of the gardens is the range of curvilinear glasshouses, erected in 1843, comprising the Green House and Stove House. The palm house range, built in 1884, comprises the Palm, Orchid and Camellia Houses.

The specimen of *Cedrus atlantica pendula* is said to be one of the finest weeping cedars in cultivation and there is a good herbaceous border.

(1) *Gardens. Summer: Mon–Sat 9–6; Sundays 11–6; Winter: Mon–Sat 10–4.30; Sun 11–4.30. Glasshouses. Summer: Mon–Sat 9–12.45, 2.15–5.45; Sun 2–5.45; Winter: Mon–Sat 10–12.45, 2.15–4.15; Sun 2–4.15*
(2) *Free*
(4) *National Herbarium (by appointment)*
(5) *Dept of Agriculture and Fisheries*

Enniskerry
Co Wicklow
8. Powerscourt

The great formal garden was conceived by the 6th Viscount Powerscourt in *c* 1840 and carried out by his son with the architect Daniel Robertson between 1843 and 1875. Fountains, statuary and ornamental stonework, a perron (or platform) of black and white stones and flower-filled parterres are the principal elements of the curving terraces that descend to the circular Triton Lake, guarded by winged horses – the

143

heraldic supporters of the Wingfield coat of arms.

The wrought-iron gates on the west of the main axis came from Bamberg Cathedral, Bavaria, and much of the statuary was collected by the 6th Viscount on his travels in Europe. In the area of the Green Pond are fine eucalyptus trees, planted in 1897, and nearby is a remarkable *Cupressus macrocarpa*, planted in 1898. The Japanese Garden, of which a striking feature is *Trachycarpus fortunei*, was made in 1908 by the 8th Viscount and his wife on reclaimed bogland.

The Italian formality of the terraced gardens contrasts with unconfined views of the parkland and surrounding country, with the distant Sugar Loaf Mountain. Throughout the estate there are fine trees, including one of the best collections of mature conifers in Western Europe, and there is an avenue of monkey puzzles, a collection of southern hemisphere beeches and exceptionally good specimens of *Drimys winteri* and *Eucalyptus globulus*.

4 miles (6·4 km) from the house, which was extensively damaged in 1974, is a 400 ft (122 m) waterfall.

(1) *Garden. Easter–Oct: Daily 10.30–5.30. Waterfall. Daily 10.30–8*
(2) *Charge*
(3) *Café*
(5) *Powerscourt Estate Trust*

Garinish Island

Co Cork

9. Garinish Island

In 1910 Annan Bryce, a Belfast merchant, commissioned the landscape architect Harold Peto to design a house and garden on the 37 acre (15 ha) island (also known as Ilnacullin) in Bantry Bay. The gardens were conceived as the setting for an Italianate mansion that was never built.

First a shelter of trees was planted, in soil brought from the mainland, enabling the shrubs in the woodland garden – which runs the length of the island from east to west – to withstand the winds. Most of the tender plants were established after Roland Bryce inherited the property in 1939. In 1953 it was bequeathed to the nation.

The focus of the garden is a rectangular paved area with a lily-pond surrounded by bonsai and a pavilion at one end. There is a walled garden with herbaceous border , a Grecian temple, a martello tower built in 1815 and terraces, steps and ornamental stonework that add a note of formality to the wild garden.

Among the interesting plants and trees are olearias, abutilons, many uncommon rhododendrons, *Dacrydium cupressinum* and, from Australia, a Manuka tea tree.

The island is reached by a 15-minute journey by boat from Glengariff Quay.

(1) *Mar–Oct: Mon–Sat 10–5.30; Public Holidays 10–6; Sun and Church Holidays 1–6*
(2) *Charge*
(5) *Commissioners of Public Works*

Howth

Co Dublin

10. Howth Castle

The most notable feature at Howth is the rhododendron gardens, situated approx half a mile (0·8 km) from the castle, next to the Deer Park Hotel and golf courses. Planting began in *c* 1850, when holes in the cliff face were filled with earth and peat. There are today specimens of approx 400 species, 100 crosses and 500 hybrids. Including duplicates and un-named rhododendrons there are in all approx 2,000 in the 30 acres (12 ha).

(1) *Daily (except 25 Dec) 8–Sunset*
(2) *Charge (Easter–July)*
(5) *Capt C. S. Gaisford-St Lawrence*

Killarney

Co Kerry

11. Muckross House

Adjoining Muckross House, built in 1843, is a woodland garden with magnificent views of the mountains and Lough Leane. The original planting was done in the 1770s by the owner, Edward Herbert, in the grounds of a Franciscan friary and church that were sacked by order of Cromwell. Today the lawns are punctuated with clumps of mature hybrid rhododendrons. There is a stream garden with waterside plants and a rock garden created on a natural outcrop of fissured limestone and planted with an extensive collection of dwarf and slow-growing conifers, prostrate shrubs and climbers and alpine perennials. Among the fine trees are several kinds of eucalyptus, *Dicksonia antarctica* and *Nothofagus cunninghamii*.

In 1932 the entire estate of 11,000 acres (4,452 ha) was presented to the nation by William Bowers Bourn and Arthur Vincent to be used as a national park, the largest in Ireland.

To the south of the gardens an arboretum is being developed that will be complementary to the J. F. Kennedy Park at New Ross (qv) but with the emphasis on less hardy trees that would not flourish in harsher conditions.

(1) *Easter–Jun and Sep–Oct: Daily 10–7; Jul and Aug: Daily 9–9; other times: Daily (except Mon) 11–5*
(2) *Free*
(3) *Café*
(4) *Kerry Folk Life Centre (same times)*
(5) *National Parks and Monuments Branch of the Office of Public Works*

Lauragh, nr Kenmare
Co Kerry
12. Derreen

The garden, situated on a small peninsula in Kilmackillogue Harbour, was begun by the 5th Marquis of Lansdowne in 1870. While Viceroy of India, he collected specimens of rhododendrons and also profited from the many expeditions that set out at this period collecting plants for the gardens at Kew (qv).

A notable feature of Derreen is the grove of New Zealand tree ferns, *Dicksonia antarctica*, which flourish in the mild climate. *Cryptomeria japonica elegans*, which leans across the Rock Garden Walk, is said to be the largest tree of its kind in the British Isles. It was planted in *c* 1870 and the tallest of its four great arms measures 60 ft (18 m). Visit in April, May and June to see the rhododendrons and azaleas for which the garden is famous.

(*1*) *Apr–Sep: Tue, Thu, Sun and Public Holidays 2–6*
(*2*) *Charge*
(*3*) *Tea*
(*4*) *Plants for sale*
(*5*) *Hon David Bigham*

Malahide
Co Dublin
13. Malahide Castle

The 268 acre Malahide Demesne was acquired by Dublin County Council in 1977 and is now open as a public park.

The gardens of Malahide cover approx 20 acres (8 ha) and were largely created by Lord Milo Talbot de Malahide between 1950 and 1973. The core of the gardens is an 18th-cent walled garden. Shrubberies link this to the castle and shrub-bordered lawns to east and west of the castle, and trees and shrubs have been planted along the Dublin Drive.

Genera well represented here are olearia, euphorbia, eryngium and ceanothus. Of particular note is *Buddleia auriculata* growing against the wall of the East Lawn, the scented flowers appearing in October, and in the border is a 15 ft (3·5 m) specimen of *Cytisus battandieri*. In the south-west corner is a heather garden. Elsewhere there is a pond with water-lilies, peat beds, a border of Hybrid Tea roses and glasshouses.

Many of the plants, of which there are altogether more than 5,000 species and varieties, were collected by the former owner on his travels and are rarely seen in cultivation in Europe.

(*1*) *Park. Apr and Sep: Daily 10–7; May–Aug: Daily 10–9; Oct–Mar: Daily 10–5. Gardens. For groups by appointment*
(*2*) *Charge*
(*4*) *Castle (Mon–Fri 10–5; Sun 2–5)*
(*5*) *Dublin County Council*

New Ross
Co Wexford
14. John F. Kennedy Park

The park, which covers 480 acres (194 ha) and is situated 6 miles (10 km) south of New Ross, was founded jointly by the Irish Government and Irish-American interests in memory of the President of the United States. The intention is to form a comprehensive collection of trees and shrubs that can be grown outdoors in Ireland. 240 acres (96 ha) is devoted to specimen trees, and there is to be 90 acres (36 ha) of forest plots, each planted with a particular species. The park was opened to the public in 1968.

(*1*) *Apr and Sep: Daily 10–6.30; May–Aug: Daily 10–8; Oct–Mar: Daily 10–5*
(*2*) *Parking charge*
(*3*) *Café*
(*5*) *Forest and Wildlife Service, Dept of Fisheries*

Rathfarnham, Grange Road
Co Dublin
15. Marlay Park

Surrounding Marlay House is a landscaped garden with lawns, shrub borders and fine trees, including rare species of conifers such as *Sciadopitys verticillata*. The Dargle River flows through the woodland beyond, widening into two ponds and with a number of water courses with waterfalls. The whole estate, which was acquired by Dublin County Council from the Love family in 1972, extends to 214 acres (86 ha).

(*1*) *Apr and Sep: Daily 10–7; May–Aug: Daily 10–9; Oct–Mar: Daily 10–5*
(*2*) *Free*
(*5*) *Dublin County Council*

Timoleague
Co Cork
16. Castle Gardens

On the edge of the village with a magnificent view across the river to the ruins of the 13th-cent Franciscan friary are the house and gardens. There are shrubs, fine trees including cypresses, poplars and Irish yews and the ruins of a 14th-cent Norman castle. The gardens include picnic sites and a children's playground.

(*1*) *Jun–Sep: Mon–Sat 11–6*
(*2*) *Charge*
(*5*) *Mr and Mrs N. R. E. Travers*

Tully, nr Kildare

Co Kildare

17. Japanese Gardens

Devised by Col William Hall-Walker (later Lord Wavertree), the Japanese Gardens were created under the direction of the Japanese gardener Tassa Eida between 1906 and 1910. A tea house was brought from Japan, as were some of the plants and a collection of bonsai, which includes some of the finest and oldest in Europe.

The lay-out is symbolic of the life of man and the Pilgrim Soul enters the garden through the Gate of Oblivion and journeys towards Life's end at the Gateway to Eternity. The pathways of the garden symbolize the pathways of Life and the difficulties man has to face.

(1) *Easter–Oct: Mon–Sat 10.30–1, 2–5; Sun 2–5.30. Groups advised to book in advance*
(2) *Charge*
(4) *Irish National Stud and Irish Horse Museum (same times)*
(5) *Irish National Stud*

Wexford

18. Johnstown Castle

The appearance of the Gothic Revival castle and its grounds as seen today is due to John Knox Grogan, his son Hamilton Knox Grogan-Morgan and the architect Daniel Robertson. The signposted route through the grounds, which are noted for their fine, mature trees, leads from the castle, first to the Heather Bed. The walled gardens were originally created in 1844–51 and planted with a teaching collection of fruit trees, shrubs and plants in 1946–59. The lower garden has a herbaceous border and borders for bedding plants that are changed twice a year. The hothouses, specializing in house plants, are of interest at all times of the year. The upper garden is primarily devoted to tree propagation. To the south of the castle are three lakes and Rathlannon Castle, a derelict tower house.

(1) *Daily 9–5*
(2) *Free*
(5) *Am Zoras Taluntais (Agricultural Institute)*

Augrés Manor, Trinity

Jersey

1. Jersey Wildlife Preservation Trust

The Trust was founded by the zoologist Gerald Durrell in 1959; the park and gardens have been designed in order to incorporate many old and rare trees, with new plantings planned to create a suitable micro-climate for the animals displayed. Wherever possible, the trees and shrubs surrounding the enclosures are species originating from the same continent as the animals.

(1) *Daily 10–6*
(2) *Charge*
(3) *Refreshments (Summer)*
(5) *Jersey Wildlife Preservation Trust*

Gorey

Jersey

2. La Colline

The early 19th-cent house, which had been empty for three years before it was bought in 1957 by Capt Lort-Phillips, is surrounded by terraced gardens covering 2 acres (0·9 ha) with magnificent sea views. The garden includes a new lawn and borders designed by the garden architect, John Brookes; Japanese- and Chinese-style gardens; species roses growing in a quarry setting, and a collection of Australian and New Zealand shrubs grown from seed donated by the Melbourne Botanical Gardens. Magnolias grow well despite the salt winds, likewise camellias, many of which were collected in Japan.

(1) *Mid Mar–Oct: Mon, Thu, Sat 2.30–6. Other times by appointment*
(2) *Charge*
(5) *Channel Islands Garden Conservation Trust Ltd*

St Helier

Jersey

3. Fort Regent

This Napoleonic fortress has been converted into a leisure centre. The gardens include a rose garden and water gardens and there are magnificent views from the rampart walks.

(1) *Summer: Daily 10–10; Winter: 10–Sunset*
(2) *Charge*
(3) *Café*
(5) *States of Jersey*

St Mary's

Jersey

4. The Fantastic Tropical Gardens

The 4 acre (1·8 ha) gardens were founded in 1958 by the present owners with the purpose of growing plants used as sources

for drugs, fibres, dyes, spices, flavourings and cosmetics in, as nearly as possible, their natural habitat. No artificial sprays or fertilizers are used and no digging is done. The uses of the plants are explained on plaques, as are the ancient beliefs and customs of India, China, Japan, Islam and pre-Columbian America. There are shrines and temples for a number of faiths.

(1) *Early May–early Oct; Tue–Sun 10–6*
(2) *Charge*
(3) *Kiosk*
(5) *Mr and Mrs H. W. Bexon*

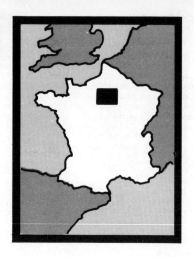

Chantilly ●
①

④

Meaux ●
⑨

⑳

⑲

㉒   ㉑
Versailles ●㉓
⑰ ⑫ ⑭
⑩
⑥ ⑪ ⑮ ⑬ ⑯

③

⑧
⑱ ● Rambouillet

● Chartres

②

⑦

⑤ ●
Fontainebleau

Kilometres 0   5   10   15   20
Miles 0   5   10   15

Chantilly

Oise

1. Château de Chantilly

The garden was founded by the Montmorency family in the 16th cent and was remodelled in the 17th cent by André Le Nôtre and La Quintinie. It was enlarged in the 18th and 19th cents. It consists of parterres surrounded by canals, ornamental ponds and cascades, statues and a grand canal and there is also an English garden, a hamlet and Sylvia's House.

(*1*) *Daily (except Tue) 10.30–5 or 6*
(*2*) *Free*
(*4*) *Château de Chantilly; Condé Museum; Library*
(*5*) *Institut de France*

Courances

Seine-et-Oise

2. Château de Courances

The château was built in 1622 for Claude Gallard, son of one of Louis XIII's officials. He was also responsible for the original gardens which, after falling into dereliction after the Revolution, were restored by a new owner, the Marquis de Ganay, in the 1870s. The design has often been attributed to Le Nôtre, but there is no proof of this. It is a composition of great dignity and calm. Rows of fine trees and carpets of mown grass, contrasted with mirror-like *pièces d'eau* are the principal elements. The fountains, for which Courances was once famous, are no more, but it is water still that animates and beautifies this famous garden.

The approach to the château is flanked by twin *tapis verts*, which are matched by rectangular pools separating their smooth turf from outer rows of magnificent planes planted in 1782. Passing to the left of the château the gravel driveway skirts the moat which is filled by a spring that falls from the gaping head of a sandstone dolphin and meets the axis of transverse *allées* lined with statues. To the right is a *pièce d'eau*, half-moonshaped and known as the *Fer à Cheval* (Horseshoe) and over which a marble nymph, by Poirier and once in the garden at Marly, presides by a flowing spring.

In the centre below the château is a parterre of box and gravel making patterns of sinuous arabesques, and beyond this is the *Grand Miroir*, a great rectangle of water (656 ft (200 m) long), lying like a sheet of glass in a tree-fringed frame of shaven lawn.

To the left an *allée* leads past the end of the Grand Canal, which lies parallel to the axis of the château, to a ten-sided pool. On the other side of the Grand Canal is a long glade where the water drops gently from one level to another in a series of shallow cascades and which is guarded at either end by sentinel pairs of wolves and dozing lions.

Nearer the château is a Japanese garden laid out by the Marquise de Ganay, an informally planted area with moss-covered rockwork, ferns, weeping willows and Japanese maples, which colour richly in autumn. It adjoins the *foulerie*, now a summer house, but where in the 18th cent grapes were prepared for wine-making.

(*1*) *Apr–Nov: Sat, Sun and Public Holidays 2–6*
(*2*) *Charge*
(*5*) *Marquis de Ganay*

Dampierre

Seine-et-Oise

3. Château de Dampierre

The first château (1180–1351) is attributed to the architect Jean Duval. Another built after this was partly burnt down and a new château was built in c 1660 by Mansard and the gardens laid out by André Le Nôtre.

Wrought-iron gates lead into the *cour d'honneur* in front of the château, flanked by buildings with open arches. On one side of the château is a lake; on the other a bridge crosses a canal which surrounds an island parterre of lawn with paths and a central fountain.

The château itself is surrounded by canals. Steps lead down to the formal garden which is on a lower level with paths surrounding a large parterre of lawn bordered with small circular flowerbeds. An inner path surrounds the floral design of the parterre's centre. Beyond the parterre is an ornamental pond with two urns of flowers at either end of a small balustrade.

(*1*) *Apr–mid-Oct: Daily (except Tue) 2–6*
(*2*) *Charge*
(*5*) *Duc de Luynes*

Ermenonville

Oise

4. Château d'Ermenonville

The Château d'Ermenonville was built in 1776 for the Marquis de Girardin. It is surrounded by an attractive landscaped park, designed largely under the direction of the Marquis, which contains various buildings including the Temple of Philosophy and the tomb of Jean-Jacques Rousseau, thought to have been designed by Hubert Robert who died while staying with the Marquis de Girardin in 1778.

(*1*) *Daily Sunrise–Sunset*
(*2*) *Free*
(*5*) *Touring Club of France*

Fontainebleau

Seine-et-Marne

5. Château de Fontainebleau

The château, inhabited and altered by a succession of French sovereigns, bears witness to the Renaissance, 17th- and 18th-cent styles in architecture. The gardens originated under François I and were altered under Louis XIV and Napoleon I.

In front of the château are four lawn parterres with topiary and flowerbeds. To one side of the château is a large lake bordered with avenues. Behind the château is the *grand parterre* designed by André Le Nôtre. This consists of four lawn parterres with topiary and flowerbeds situated around a central square pond. On one side is a further oval-shaped pond surrounded by a crescent of trees and on another side the Grand Canal designed under Henri IV. Further gardens are the English Garden and the Jardin de Diane, both designed under Napoleon I.

(1) *Winter: Daily 9–5.30; Summer: Daily 9–8*
(2) *Free*
(4) *Château (Daily, except Mon, 10–12.30, 2–5 or 6); Forest of Fontainebleau*
(5) *French State*

L'Hay des Roses, rue Albert Watel

Marne

6. Regional Park and Rose Garden

The park and the magnificent rose garden are situated on a hill overlooking the valley of the Bièvre. They were created in 1899 by Jules Gravereaux to a design by the landscape architect Edouard André. In 1968 they were given to the *département* of the Marne Valley. The park covers 40 acres (16 ha), the rose garden almost 5 acres (2 ha).

The rose garden has 2,800 varieties of roses. The collections include wild roses, China roses, polyantha roses, rose varieties grown by the Empress Josephine at the Château de la Malmaison, a collection illustrating the history and development of roses, the Theatre of the Rose as well as new varieties. The Rose Museum displays works of art inspired by the rose. Visit in June or during the first fortnight of July.

(1) *Jun–Sep: Daily 10–6. (Night-flowering plants: Fri and Sat until 11)*
(2) *Charge*
(4) *Rose Museum (same times)*
(5) *Préfecture of the Marne Valley*

Maincy

Seine-et-Marne

7. Château de Vaux-le-Vicomte

The celebrated gardens at Vaux were the first commission of André Le Nôtre. They were designed for Nicolas Fouquet, superintendent of finance under Louis XIV, and

completed in 1661. Here a quite new approach to garden design was put into effect for the first time: symmetry on a grand scale, whose form is at once apparent, but whose detail is only gradually revealed through changes in level and the subjugation of the surrounding landscape to the demands of the grand design.

From the terrace of the château a vast and intricately patterned carpet rolls away into the middle distance, contained on either side by banks of trees. The parterre in the foreground, of box and rosy powdered brick, introduces a vividly polychromatic theme which strengthens the analogy with an oriental carpet. Beyond is a canal, invisible from the terrace, which separates the parterre from twin lawns, scalloped pools with fountains in the centre of each and the perspective emphasized by pyramids and cones of clipped yew and sculpture on pedestals. Beyond again lies a larger canal hidden behind a blind arcade of rusticated stone; this is the famous *théâtre d'eau*. There are more statues and fountains (operated on the second and last Sunday of each month, 3–6) and two stalactite-hung caves, in which statues symbolic of rivers recline holding gushing urns. From here the eye is led by a tree-lined vista to the skyline and the silhouette of an immense statue of the Farnese Hercules leaning on his club.

The château was begun in 1656 to the designs of Le Vau and the interior decorated by Le Brun.

(1) *Apr–Oct: Mon–Sat 10–noon, 2–6; Sun and Public Holidays 10–6*
(2) *Charge*
(3) *Café*
(4) *Château (same times)*
(5) *M Patrice de Voguë*

Maintenon

Eure-et-Loir

8. Château de Maintenon

The park and gardens were created in the mid-17th cent for Louis XIV and Madame de Maintenon by André Le Nôtre. The château dates back to the Middle Ages. The aqueduct was built by the Marquis de Vauban and La Hire for Louis XIV to carry water from the River Eure to Versailles but it was not completed.

(1) *Mid-Oct–Mar: Sat, Sun and Public Holidays 2–5.30; Apr–mid-Oct: Mon–Sat (except Tue) 2–6.30; Sun and Public Holidays 11–noon, 2–6.30*
(2) *Charge*
(5) *Mme Raindre*

Meaux

Seine-et-Marne

9. Jardin Bossuet

The bishop's palace, now a museum, is surrounded by beautiful 18th-cent formal gardens.

(1) Daily 9–noon, 1.30–6
(2) Free
(4) Palace museum (Summer: 2.30–6.30;
Winter: 2.30–4.30
(5) Town of Meaux

Paris, Bois de Boulogne
10. Bagatelle

In the summer of 1777 the young Comte d'Artois, in order to please his sister-in-law, Marie Antoinette, offered to build her a palace in two months. The queen, delighted, wagered 100,000 livres none the less that such a thing was not possible. The outcome was the enchanting *pavillon* of Bagatelle, completed at vast expense in 64 days. The architect was Alexandre Bélanger, and the designer of the English landscape garden in which it was set was a Scot, Thomas Blaikie. Of his work a group of artificial ruins, a lake, some rockwork and many fine trees survive today. Though the grounds were parcelled out to various leaseholders in 1797 and the *pavillon* itself became a celebrated restaurant, the estate was in due course repurchased by Napoleon, the *pavillon* refurnished and the gardens restored. At the Restoration the Comte d'Artois regained possession.

In 1835 Bagatelle was bought by the immensely rich Marquess of Hertford, who enlarged the house, extended the park, swept away the grottoes, bridges and Chinese tea houses provided by Blaikie for the Comte d'Artois and embellished the garden with sculpture from Vaux-le-Vicomte and Versailles and the exotic oriental *Kiosque de l'Impératrice*, named for the Empress Eugénie. On the death of Lord Hertford in 1870 Bagatelle passed to his natural son, Sir Richard Wallace, who removed the famous contents to London for safety during the Commune and built the adjacent Trianon to the designs of Léon de Sauges. In 1904, some years after the death of Wallace, Bagatelle was sold to the City of Paris. Thereafter 62 acres (24 ha) of garden were gradually developed according to an imaginative grand design inspired by Kew Gardens and prepared by the noted gardener J. C. N. Forestier.

Most famous of the modern gardens is the Rose Garden, laid out on the site of Lord Hertford's *manège* in 1906 by Quentin Bauchart. It contains about 20,000 plants of 2,650 varieties of rose and here the International Show for New Roses is held annually. New types of rose are constantly being grown, studied and disseminated throughout the world. In one of Thomas Blaikie's lakes is a collection of lotus, water-lilies and other aquatic plants. In April and May there are fine displays of narcissi and tulips, succeeded in June and July by rhododendrons, magnolias and irises.

(1) Summer: Daily 8.30–8; Winter: Daily 9–5
(2) Charge

(3) Restaurant and café
(4) Château (or pavillon) by appointment
(5) City of Paris

Paris, 3 avenue Porte d'Auteuil
11. Fleuriste Municipal

The nursery raises well over a million plants a year for use in the Paris parks and it provides one of the world's greatest floral displays. The garden covers 32 acres (13 ha), comprising an arboretum and a collection of 140 varieties of camellia. The 94 glasshouses contain exceptional collections of exotic and tropical plants including collections of palms, rock-garden plants, house plants, orchids, cacti and succulents and *Bromeliaceae*. Visit in April for the azaleas and in October and November for the chrysanthemums.

(1) Apr–Sep: Daily 10–6; Oct–Mar 10–5
(2) Free
(5) Paris Parks Dept

Paris, quai du 4 Septembre
12. Jardins Albert Kahn

The gardens were founded by Albert Kahn, the banker, when between 1895–1900 he purchased three large properties. The designers were Réverol and Duchesne. They created a rose garden with an orchard, a French garden, an English garden, *la forêt bleue* and a Vosges forest or mountain garden with rocks brought from the Vosges region of Gérardmer.

The trees in the Japanese garden were brought over from Japan; two bridges cross a stream which winds through it and there are five buildings and 300 bonsai trees. In 1930 the property was put up for auction and in 1936 the *département* of the Seine bought the gardens which today cover approx 12 acres (5 ha).

(1) Mid-Mar–mid-Oct: Sun–Fri 2–6; Sat and Public Holidays 2–7
(2) Free
(5) Paris Parks Dept

Paris, 57 rue Cuvier
13. Jardin des Plantes

This was founded in 1635 as the king's medicinal garden by Guy de la Brosse, physician to Louis XIII. It has been called the Jardin des Plantes since 1718. Many famous names are associated with this garden, including Tournefort, Jussieu, Dufay, Buffon, Daubenton and Lamarck.

There is a garden 656 yds (600 m) long in the French style and a maze on an artificial hill, covering approx 5 acres (2 ha), laid out in *c* 1640 with some old trees including a Cretan maple (1702), yews and thujas (1735) and a cedar of Lebanon almost 66 ft

(20 m) high and with a trunk approx 13 ft (4 m) in circumference.

The School of Botany was remodelled in 1954 and has a large collection of European and exotic plants including collections of economic and medicinal plants arranged systematically. It also boasts the oldest tree in Paris: a locust-tree (false acacia) which is over 300 years old. The alpine garden was created in 1931 and has over 2,000 varieties arranged geographically from all over the world: the Alps, Pyrenees, the Caucasus, the Rockies, Greenland and the Himalayas. Xerophilous plants of the lower Alps of the Mediterranean area grow on south-facing terraces and sub-alpine plants grow on the slopes opposite these. There is also an area for plants arranged ecologically.

A variety of collections are housed in glasshouses, arranged geographically or according to botanical specification. There are glasshouses for collections of tree ferns such as *Angiopteris erecta* and for *Aroideae*, and a unique collection of *Bromeliaceae* and a collection of palms, almost 2,000 varieties of cacti and succulents, a collection of tropical economic plants and a large collection of orchids, including cultivars. Near the glasshouse is the aquarium containing the giant waterlily, *Victoria regia*, and *Eurale ferox* of the same family. Small glass aquariums contain collections of aquatic plants including *Ouvirandra fenestralis*.

The garden also contains a menagerie with reptiles, monkeys, deer, elephants and an aviary. Galleries contain exhibitions of mineralogy and paleontology.

(1) *Daily 9–5*
(2) *Free*
(4) *Menagerie (Daily, except Tue); Maze and Exhibition Galleries (Daily, except Tue, 1.30–5)*
(5) *Musée Nationale d'Histoire Naturelle*

Paris, place de la Concorde
14. Jardin des Tuileries

The garden of the Louvre and of the Tuileries covers approx 74 acres (30 ha). The main design is by André Le Nôtre although the garden has been altered over the years. There are many flower parterres and also avenues of trees and two ornamental ponds. There is marble statuary of the 18th cent and 20th-cent statuary by Aristide Maillol. The main avenue is on the axis of the place de la Concorde and the Arc de Triomphe.

(1) *Early–mid-Mar: Daily 6 am–8 pm; mid–end Mar: Daily 6 am–9 pm; Apr–May: Daily 6 am–10 pm, Jun–Aug: Daily 6 am–10.45 pm; early–mid-Sep: Daily 6 am–10 pm; mid–end–Sep: Daily 6 am–10 pm; mid-end–Sep: pm; Nov–Feb: Daily 6.30 am–8 pm*
(2) *Free*
(3) *Kiosk*

(4) *Musée du Jeu de Paume and Musée de l'Orangerie (Daily, except Tue, 10–5)*
(5) *Ministère de la Culture et de l'Environnement*

Paris, 77 rue de Varenne
15. Musée Rodin

The garden surrounds the Rococo mansion built in 1728–31 by Jean Aubert to designs by Jacques Gabriel. The Maréchal de Biron, who owned the mansion after 1753, laid out the park in the landscape style with pavilions, trellis arbours, kitchen and flower gardens, and opened it to the public. Later both mansion and gardens underwent changes. The museum was opened in 1919.

On the northern side of the museum are lawns on either side of the forecourt with statues by Rodin: The Thinker (1880), Balzac (1891–7), The Burghers of Calais (first casting in Calais 1895) and The Gates of Hell (1880–1917, cast 1937) framed by figures of Adam and Eve. On the southern side of the museum are flower parterres. On the eastern side of the central parterre are The Caryatid Carrying a Stone (1881) and The Caryatid with Urn (1888) and at the far end of the parterres is a sloping lawn with Rodin's Call to Arms (1879). The garden contains several varieties of shrub rose.

(1) *Oct–Mar: Daily (except Tue) 10–5; Apr–Sep: Daily (except Tue) 10–6*
(2) *Charge*
(3) *Refreshments (Jun–Sep)*
(4) *Museum (same times)*
(5) *Musée Rodin*

Paris, route de la Pyramide
16. Parc Floral

The park was created in 1969 for the International Flower Shows of that year by the landscape architect Daniel Collin. Situated in the Bois de Vincennes, it covers 69 acres (28 ha) and includes a valley of flowers, the *jardin sculpté*, aquatic gardens, a pinewood, an alpine garden and rockeries, a rose garden and a dahlia garden. Visit in May and June for the tulips, irises, peonies, azaleas, rhododendrons, roses and lilies, and in September and October for the dahlias. Glasshouses contain a variety of displays according to season.

(1) *Daily 9.30–6*
(2) *Charge*
(3) *Refreshments*
(5) *Paris Parks Dept*

Paris, St-Cloud
17. St-Cloud

The château beside the River Seine was built in the 17th cent by Monsieur, brother of Louis XIV, and it was later enlarged by Marie Antoinette. In the 19th cent it was a favourite residence of Napoleon I, Charles X, Louis Philippe and Napoleon III. The château, together with most of the buildings in the park, was burnt down in 1870 at the time of the fall of the Second Empire. Only the guardroom, stables and Pavillon de Valois were restored, and the Pavillon de Breteuil was the only building to escape the fire. The 1,112 acre (445 ha) park, designed by André Le Nôtre, retains some of the former magnificence of the estate.

The site of the *cour d'honneur* and of the château are marked by lawns with flowerbeds and yew trees. To the west and south is the 17th-cent *jardin privé*. The parterre on the western side was once bordered by an orangery and, at the far end of this, is an ornamental pond surrounded on three sides by 24 fountains. Beyond, a *tapis vert* leads to a round pond, La Grande Gerbe, from which seven avenues lead in different directions into the park. On the southern side is the horseshoe pond (*Bassin du Fer à Cheval*), from which an avenue leads to the Rond-point de la Balustrade with a fine view over Paris.

Situated below the château terrace and along the bank of the River Seine is the Jardin Bas. This contains the famous waterfall, created in 1677 by P. Le Pautre and J. Hardouin Mansart and restored in the 18th cent, when new statuary was added. It is 295 ft (90 m) long. Here also in the centre of a lawn is a fountain which can reach 138 ft (42 m). South of these an avenue leads to the Pavillon de Breteuil (not open to the public), the Sèvres Porcelain Manufactory rebuilt under Napoleon III and the Sèvres Porcelain Museum. On the northern side of the site of the château is the 19th-cent Jardin du Trocadéro in the English style.

The original design by Le Nôtre is evident in the park, although more trees have been planted since, at the end of the 18th cent and beginning of the 19th cent.

(1) *Mar–Apr: Daily 7–9; May–Aug: Daily 7–10; Sep–Oct: Daily 7–9; Nov–Feb: Daily 7–8. Cascade and fountain. May–Sep: 2nd and 4th Sun of each month 4–5*
(2) *Parking charge*
(3) *Café*
(4) *Guardroom Museum (Sat, Sun and Wed 2–6); Sèvres Porcelain Museum: (Daily, except Tue, 9.30–noon, 1.30–5.15)*
(5) *French State*

Rambouillet
Seine-et-Oise
18. Château de Rambouillet

The formal garden was laid out during the reign of Louis XIV. There are canals, parterres with flowerbeds and topiary, a dairy built as a Greek temple designed by Savage and in the English garden a shell-covered pavilion decorated by the Duke of Penthièvre in 1778. Both buildings were erected by Louis XVI for Marie Antoinette. The château is the presidential summer residence.

FRANCE

(1) *Apr–Sep: Daily (except Tue and when the President is in residence) 10–noon, 2–6; Oct–Mar: Daily (except Tue and when the President is in residence) 10–noon, 2–4*
(2) *Charge*
(4) *Château (same times)*
(5) *French State*

Rosny
Seine-et-Oise
19. Château de Rosny

The 17th-cent château was built for Maximilien de Béthune, Duke of Sully and Minister to Henri IV. The Duchesse de Berry lived here between 1820 and 1830 and the painter Corot stayed here in the 1840s and painted the château and gardens on a number of occasions. The park and gardens are in the formal French manner and run along the banks of the River Seine.

(1) *Mar–Oct: Daily (except Tue and Wed unless Public Holidays) 2–6; Nov–Feb: Sat, Sun, Mon and Public Holidays 1.30–5*
(2) *Charge*
(5) *Dr Herz*

Rueil-Malmaison
Seine-et-Oise
20. Château de la Malmaison and Château de Bois-Préau

The park of the Château de la Malmaison was well known in the 18th cent as a park in the English style with a rose garden, glasshouses and many exotic plants. However, these features no longer exist and plans for restoration have been drawn up. The partly restored park of Bois-Préau is only partially open to the public.

(1) *Oct–Mar: Daily (except Tue and some Public Holidays) 10–noon, 1.30–4.30; Apr–Sep: Daily (except Tue and some Public Holidays) 1.30–5.30*
(2) *Park of Malmaison: Charge; Park of Bois-Préau: Free*
(4) *Napoleonic Museum in the Château; National Museum of Château Bois-Préau (same times)*
(5) *French State*

Sceaux
Île de France
21. Château de Sceaux (Musée de l'Île-de-France)

The magnificent 450 acre (180 ha) park was designed by Le Nôtre for Colbert and it was restored after World War II. The original château designed by Claude Perrault for Colbert was destroyed in 1798 and the present château was built by the Duke of

Trévise in the 19th cent. The orangery, built by Jules Hardouin Mansart in c 1684, was restored in 1974 and is used for exhibitions and concerts. There are two pavilions: the 18th-cent Hanover Pavilion, designed by Chevotet for Richelieu, and the Aurora Pavilion, built by Mansart with a cupola by Lebrun. The park contains lawn parterres with flowerbeds, topiary and hedges, a large dahlia collection, a grand canal over 1½ miles (2·5 km) long, an octagonal pond and waterfalls. A long avenue leads to the château.

(1) *Daily Sunrise–Sunset*
(2) *Free*
(4) *Museum (Mon and Fri 2–6; Wed, Thu, Sat and Sun 10–noon, 2–7 or 5 in Winter)*
(5) *Département des Hauts-de-Seine*

Thiverval-Grignon

Seine-et-Oise

22. Botanical Garden and Arboretum

Founded in 1875 by Prof Mussat and Mouillefert, the garden and aboretum cover almost 4 acres (1·5 ha). The special features of the botanical garden are a collection of ornamental perennials and an ecological garden with plants of calcareous soils.

(1) *Daily 9–6*
(2) *Free*
(5) *Ministry of Agriculture*

Versailles

Seine-et-Oise

23. Château de Versailles and Petit Trianon

No garden has achieved greater renown, nor spawned more imitations, than the great Baroque lay-out at Versailles. Since the end of the 17th cent it has been the wonder and the envy of the civilized world.

Louis XIII came often to hunt in the woods around the village of Versailles and there, in the first decade of the 17th cent, he built a small château as a hunting lodge. The appearance of the gardens is not recorded, but they were probably the work of Jacques Boyceau. They were later extended, and in 1613 the château itself was enlarged.

In 1643 the four-year-old Louis XIV succeeded to the throne. During his childhood Versailles was neglected, but in 1660 he began to develop both the château and the gardens. More land was acquired and the services of Le Nôtre enlisted to contrive under the king's direction the grand design that survives today. The essence of Le Nôtre's plan lies in the complete subordination of nature to the demands of a plan conceived as an extension of the archi-

tecture of the château. This was a temple to the glory of the Sun King, and the gardens, with their clipped trees, geometrical *pièces d'eau*, radiating avenues, carefully manicured parterres and great works of sculpture by Tubi, Le Hongre, Coysevox and Regnaudin are designed to demonstrate the divine right of the monarch to supremacy in his kingdom.

Before the château lies an immense artificial plateau with parterres of flowers and water. In the centre the *parterre d'eau* – twin rectangles of water – mirrors the façade of the château. At each corner are statues symbolizing the rivers of France. To right and left are parterres of clipped box, grass, marble urns and bedding plants. Still further to the right is the orangery, completed in 1683 to a design of Mansard. Here in winter the citrus trees, palms, olives, oleander (*Nerium oleander*), pomegranates (*Punica granatum*), medlars and carobs are stored, which in summer are brought out in their tubs to stand in formal array around the pool. The orangery has no artificial heat, but the windows are double glazed and the doors are by tradition sealed with hay against the draughts of an alien climate.

Passing down the central axis that separates the twin pools of the *parterre d'eau*, the terrace is reached. Below is the Fountain of Latona and, beyond, the gravelled axis passes once more between parterres before abruptly narrowing to form the famous *tapis vert*. This is flanked by towering forest trees, in front of which alternating vases and human figures in white marble face each other like troops lining a ceremonial route. The sudden narrowing of perspective draws the eye on into the middle distance, where it pauses to take in the vast circular pool, the Bassin d'Apollon.

In 1715 Louis XIV died and the gardens were for some years again neglected. In 1722 the Court returned to Versailles and the interest of Louis XV in botany led to the establishment at Trianon of a botanical garden under the direction of Claude Richard and Bernard de Jussieu. The king spent much time in this new garden and a small house was built overlooking it, soon to be known as the Petit Trianon. This exquisite little building owes its design to the collaboration of Madame de Pompadour, the architect Gabriel and the king himself.

Marie Antoinette, to whom Louis XVI gave the Petit Trianon, swept away most of Richard's botanical garden and replaced it by a landscape in the newly fashionable English/Chinoiserie style under the direction of the Comte de Caraman. It was given a mountain, a grotto, graves and a small, apparently natural lake, overlooked by a belvedere designed by Mique, who was also responsible for the nearby Temple of Love.

In 1783 Mique was again called upon, this time to construct the famous hamlet at one end of the lake, where the queen and her friends indulged in games of pastoral make-believe. Here and there rare trees survive from the era of Louis XIV. Near the lake are specimens of sweet gum, swamp cypress (*Taxodium distichum*) and the tulip-tree (*Liriodendron tulipifera*); near the Petit Trianon specimens of the pagoda tree (*Sophora japonica*), pencil cedar (*Juniperus virginiana*), Crimean pine (*Pinus pallasiana*) and Turkey oak (*Quercus cerris*). Other trees include the European hop-hornbeam (*Ostrya carpinifolia*), zelkova, cedar of Lebanon and the large-leafed cucumber tree (*Magnolia macrophylla*).

On the whole the gardens of Versailles suffered during the Revolution from nothing more serious than another period of neglect. Napoleon had them put in order, but he had no affection for Versailles, nor did Louis XVIII or Charles X ever live in the château. It was Louis Philippe who turned it into a museum to the glory of France and ensured thereby the preservation of the gardens in the state in which they have come down to us today.

The aboretum of Chèvreloup lies to the north-east of the château, between the Trianons and the village of Rocquencourt.

(*1*) *Daily (except Mon) 9.45–5.30*
(*2*) *Charge*
(*3*) *Café*
(*4*) *Château (Daily, except Mon, 9.45–5.30); Chapel, State Apartments and Galerie des Glaces (Tue–Sat 10.30–3; Sun and Public Holidays 10.30–1.30); Musée de l'Histoire de France and Galerie des Batailles (Daily, except Mon, 2–5); Other rooms (Guided tours by arrangement Daily, except Mon); Grand Trianon (Daily, except Mon, 10–5); Petit Trianon (Daily, except Mon, 2–5)*
(*5*) *French State*

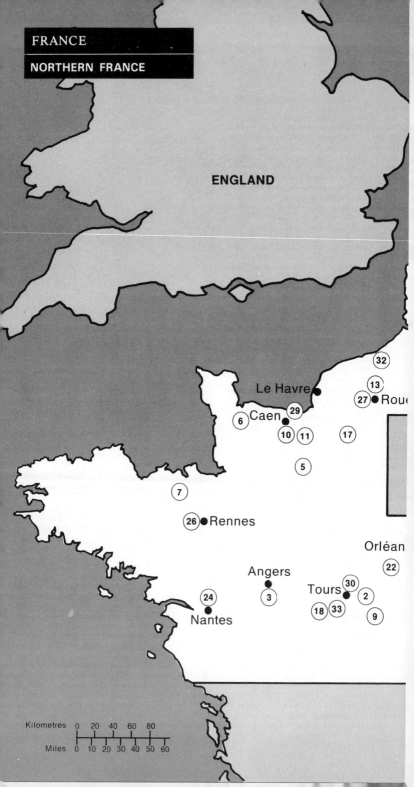

FRANCE

NORTHERN FRANCE

ENGLAND

(32)

Le Havre (13)
(29) (27) Rou
(6) Caen
(10) (11) (17)

(5)

(7)

(26) Rennes

Orléan

(22)

Angers (30)
(3) Tours (2)
(24) (18) (33) (9)
Nantes

Kilometres 0 20 40 60 80
Miles 0 10 20 30 40 50 60

Abbeville, 131 route de Paris

Somme

1. Château de Bagatelle

The garden was created during the transitional period when the English style of gardening was taking over from the formal French style. It has since been restored several times. A formal parterre serves as the garden extension of the château and a landscaped park lies beyond. An avenue of limes arranged in a horseshoe ring and dating from the 18th cent forms one side of the garden.

(1) *Jul–Aug: Daily (except Tue) 10–12.30, 2–7*
(2) *Charge*
(4) *Château*
(5) *Mme de Wailly*

Amboise

Indre-et-Loire

2. Château d'Amboise

The palace was built in the 15th and 16th cents and overlooks the River Loire. It is surrounded by a garden with attractive flowerbeds and trees that are many centuries old.

(1) *Daily 9–noon, 2–7 or 5 in winter*
(2) *Charge*
(4) *Château; chapel (same times)*
(5) *Fondation Saint-Louis*

Angers, promenade du Bout du Monde

Maine-et-Loire

3. Château d'Angers

The garden was created when the Renaissance palace was restored in 1950–60. It is a formal garden with floral parterres designed in geometrical patterns and with topiary and hedges. There is a small terraced garden on the château ramparts.

(1) *Summer: Daily (except 1 May) 9.30–noon, 2–5.45; Winter: Daily 10–noon, 2–5*
(2) *Charge*
(3) *Tea (Jul, Aug and Sep)*
(4) *Château (same times)*
(5) *French State*

Apremont-sur-Allier

Cher

4. Parc Floral

The park was founded in 1970 and opened to the public in 1977. It covers 9 acres (3·6 ha) and contains trees, shrubs, perennial plants and aquatic plants. There are ponds with waterbirds and a waterfall.

(1) *Late Mar–mid-Nov: Daily 10–noon, 2–7*
(2) *Charge*
(3) *Refreshments*
(4) *Musée des Calèches (horsedrawn carriages) (same times)*
(5) *Duchesse de Brissac*

Argentan

Orne

5. Château de Sassy

The château was built in 1760 and has gardens descending from the château on three levels. At the lowest level canals surround a formal garden of scroll parterres with topiary. At the far end of this is a small summer house from which the visitor looks back up to the château.

(1) *Easter–1 Nov: Sat and Sun 3–6; Jul and Aug: Daily 3–6*
(2) *Free*
(4) *Château, chapel and library (same times)*
(5) *Duc d'Audiffret Pasquier*

Balleroy, nr Bayeux

Calvados

6. Château de Balleroy

The 17th-cent Château de Balleroy, designed by Mansart, is situated on a hillside overlooking the River Dromme. In front of the château is a formal garden with parterres of clipped box and clipped trees in tubs, and a terrace flanked by twin pavilions.

(1) *Easter–Oct: Sun, Tue, Thu, Sat and Public Holidays 2–6*
(2) *Charge*
(5) *Marquise de Balleroy*

Becherel

Côte-du-Nord

7. Château de Caradeuc

A park has surrounded the château since it was built in 1723. In the 19th cent it was partly remodelled in the English style but, starting in 1898, it was extended and restored to the classical style by Edouard André. There is a formal parterre divided into four sections and containing flowerbeds planted alternately with red and yellow roses and bordered with clipped yew. There is a *tapis vert* bordered by English oaks and clipped hedges, statues, monuments, ornamental ponds and avenues. From the northern terrace of the château there is a magnificent view over the upper valley of the River Rance.

(1) *Daily during daylight hours*
(2) *Charge*
(5) *Marquis de Kernier*

Besançon, place Maréchal Leclerc

Doubs

8. Town and University Botanical Garden

A botanical garden in Besançon was first created in c 1580, followed by eight successive gardens, and the present garden was created in 1956–61. The open area, covering 4 acres (1·6 ha), contains flowerbeds with plants arranged according to a botanical system, a large rockery, an artificial peat bog, an artificial river and ponds with aquatic plants, a medicinal garden and an arboretum with 225 varieties of trees. Glasshouses contain tropical and sub-tropical plants with many unusual varieties such as the giant water-lily, *Victoria regia*. There are collections of succulents and cacti, over 50 varieties of begonia and also economic plants.

(1) *Mon–Fri 8.30–11, 2–4.30; Sat 8.30–11*
(2) *Free*
(5) *Town of Besançon and Besançon University*

Bléré

Indre-et-Loire

9. Château de Chenonceaux

The château was built on a bridge crossing the River Cher, in 1513. The first garden was founded in c 1547 by Diane de Poitiers, to whom Henri II made a gift of Chenonceaux. In c 1560 a second garden was founded by Catherine de Médicis. The well-maintained park and gardens, together covering approx 800 acres (324 ha), were designed by Bernard Palissy.

An avenue of plane trees leads to the château. On one side is the garden of Diane de Poitiers, with clipped trees and hedges, flowers and ornamental fruit and vegetables. On the other side is the formal garden of Catherine de Médicis, with parterres, topiary and hedges and flowerbeds. Visit between April and mid-June and between July and September.

(1) *Mid-Mar–Sep: Daily 9–7; Oct: Daily 9–6; Nov: Daily 9–5; Dec–Jan: Daily 9–noon, 2–4; Feb–mid-Mar: Daily 9–5*
(2) *Charge*
(3) *Restaurant and café (Feb–Nov)*
(4) *Château; Musée des Cires (Wax museum)*
(5) *Société Civile Chenonceaux-Rentilly*

Caen, 5 place Blot

Calvados

10. University and Town Botanical Garden

The first botanic collection in Caen was created in 1689 and a botanical garden containing 3,500 varieties was founded in

1736 at its present location. In the 19th cent this garden was enlarged and an orangery and a botanical institute were added; the garden was modernized in the 1950s.

It contains collections of alpine plants, economic plants, medicinal plants, horticultural plants and the wild flowers of Normandy. Among the rare trees are dawn redwood, a dove-tree and various cedars. The orangery and glasshouses contain tropical plants: vanilla, coffee-shrubs, aquatic plants such as the South American water-lily *Victoria cruziana*, as well as grasses, cacti and a collection of freshwater exotic fish.

(1) *Garden: Daily 8–7. Glasshouses: Wed and Sun*
(2) *Free*
(5) *Town of Caen and Caen University*

Canon

Calvados

11. Château de Canon

The 17th-cent château is in the Italian style. The garden was created in c 1730 in the French style and was remodelled in 1770–83 by the lawyer, Elie de Beaumont, friend of Voltaire and Horace Walpole. In front of the château is an ornamental pond supplied with water from canals which are in turn supplied by springs in the garden. Four avenues cross the grounds at right angles: there is one of beeches and another of 200-year-old limes leading to the Temple de la Pleureuse. The grounds, with trees and hillocks, contain other small temples, many statues and waterfalls. The main feature of the garden is the 13 walled gardens, or *chartreuses*, connected by arches and planted with spring flowers. Visit in the spring, August and September.

(1) *In groups by appointment. Apply to Château de Canon, 14270 Mézidon-Canon, Calvados*
(2) *Free*
(4) *Château (same times)*
(5) *Mme Delom de Mézerac*

Chalon-sur-Saône

Saône-et-Loire

12. Parc Nouelle

The park has a deer park of 12 acres (5 ha) created in 1972, a lake of 51 acres (20·4 ha) with protected birds, a large aviary and, separated by fencing and a stone gateway, a botanical garden. The park contains many old trees and shrubs; the botanical garden contains plants of the temperate zones; the lake has aquatic plants and on the side opposite the botanical garden are trees, shrubs and lawns.

(1) *Park. Daily Sunrise–Sunset. Botanical Garden. Daily 8–noon, 2–7*

(2) *Free*
(5) *Town of Châlon-sur-Saône*

Clères

Seine-Maritime

13. Château de Clères

The park was founded as a private collection of birds and animals and gardens designed by Avray Tipping were added later, in 1860. The park contains a variety of trees, shrubs, perennial plants, colourful flowerbeds, alpine plants and cacti. The 11th-cent château was rebuilt in the 13th and 15th cents.

(1) *Summer: Daily 9–6 or 7; Winter: Daily 9–noon, 1.30–5*
(2) *Charge*
(4) *Château*
(5) *M J. Delacour, M P. Ciarpaglini (Administrators)*

Col de Saverne, nr Strasbourg

Bas-Rhin

14. Botanical Garden

The alpine garden is situated at 984 ft (300 m) and covers approx 6 acres (2·5 ha). It was founded in 1930 and was restored after World War II by the Association of the Friends of the Col de Saverne and the Faculty of Sciences at Strasbourg. The garden contains ravines and escarpments especially suited to the alpine collections of saxifrage and crassula. The plants are arranged in ecological order.

A path leads under a high rock bearing ferns and rue to an area planted with alpine anemones, gentians, primulas and aconites from the Alps and Pyrenees. Beyond this is a humid ditch planted with bamboos and giant umbellifers followed by a small spring garden of tulips, narcissi and irises. The arid rockeries include collections of wild pinks and potentillas while the humid rockeries contain tree and mountain ferns with the tiny *Helxine soleirolii* from Corsica and the purple-flowered *Ramonda myconi*. In the north-eastern corner of the garden is an arboretum with several hundred varieties of trees and shrubs including rare varieties from China, the Himalayas and North America.

(1) *May–Sep*
(2) *Free*
(5) *Association of the Friends of the Col de Saverne and the Faculty of Sciences at Strasbourg*

Col de la Schlucht, nr Gérardmer

Vosges

15. Alpine Garden Haut-Chitelet

The garden is situated at 4029 ft (1228 m), the highest altitude of any garden in France, and covers 25 acres (10 ha). An alpine garden near the present site was created in 1900 but fell into ruin during World War I and was never restored. The present garden was founded at the source of the Vologne, a tributary of the Moselle, in 1966 and opened to the public in 1969. It contains 2,914 varieties of alpine plants arranged geographically and ecologically in groups. Of particular interest are the collections of flora from the Vosges area and mountain turf-moor. There are also fine collections of alpine plants from North America, China, Japan, the Himalayas, the Caucasus, the Carpathians, the Alps, the Jura and the Massif Central, including some rare varieties.

(1) *Jun–mid-Oct: Daily 8–6; Sep–Oct: Daily 8–5.30. Guided tours by previous arrangement: Jardin d'Altitude du Haut-Chitelet, Col de la Schlucht, 88400 Gérardmer. Tel: 16 (29) 631146*
(2) *Free*
(5) *City and University of Nancy*

Dijon, 1 avenue Albert I

Côte-d'Or

16. Botanical Gardens of L'Arquebuse

The botanical garden was founded in 1771 by B. Legouz de Gerland and was transferred to its present location in 1833. It consists of two parts: the School of Botany and a small arboretum. The School of Botany consists of four large squares with 66 flowerbeds enclosed by boxwood. These contain approx 3,500 varieties of plants: Burgundian plants, French plants and exotic plants. West of these is the arboretum which was renovated in 1960 and contains interesting species of oaks, planes, sequoias, nettle-trees and a Chinese cedar (*Cedrela sinensis* or 'Bastard Cedar'), which is said to be the oldest in France. To the north of the arboretum are collections of medicinal and economic plants. A rose garden is being created.

(1) *Summer: Daily 6 am–10 pm; Winter: Daily 7–5*
(2) *Free*
(4) *Museum of Natural History (Wed–Sun 2–5)*
(5) *Town of Dijon*

Harcourt

Eure

17. Château d'Harcourt

The château was built in the 11th–14th cents and has undergone restoration since

1958. The arboretum of 12 acres (5 ha) was founded by L. G. Delamarre, who planted many varieties of pine. On his death he bequeathed the property to the French Academy of Agriculture.

The park contains specimens of Douglas fir (*Pseudotsuga menziesii*), Incense cedar (*Libocedrus decurrens*), sequoias and giant sequoia (*Sequoiadendron giganteum*), Western red cedar (*Thuja plicata*), Japanese red cedar (*Cryptomeria japonica*) and coast redwood (*Sequoia sempervirens*). A forest adjoins the arboretum.

(1) *Jun–mid-Sep: Daily 2–6; mid-Sep–Nov and Feb–May: Sun and Public Holidays 2–6*
(2) *Charge*
(5) *French Academy of Agriculture*

Langeais

Indre-et-Loire

18. Château de Langeais

This Loire valley château was built in *c* 1465–7. The garden, which was laid out in the 19th or early 20th cent, consists of geometrically laid out parterres, including a floral crown and fleur-de-lys. In the park is one of the oldest stone keeps in France.

(1) *Summer: Daily (except Mon) 9–12, 2–6.30; Winter: Daily (except Mon) 9–noon, 2–4.30*
(2) *Charge*
(4) *Château*
(5) *Institut de France*

Les Laumes

Côte-d'Or

19. Château de Bussy-Rabutin

The gardens were created by André Le Nôtre for Count Roger de Rabutin. The estate covers 84 acres (34 ha) and is situated on a hillside. At the entrance is an ancient lime tree. On the south side of the château, which is surrounded by a moat, are woods and a long avenue of old limes. On the north side is the French Garden. This has parterres, a small canal leading to a pond – beyond which is a terrace and then a cascade – and a larger canal, springs and statuary.

(1) *Early May–Sep: Daily (except Tue) 9–11, 2–5; Oct–Apr: Daily (except Tue) 10–11, 2–4*
(2) *Charge*
(3) *Café*
(4) *Château (same times)*
(5) *French State*

Lille

Nord

20. Jardin des Plantes

The first botanical garden in Lille was founded at the end of the 16th cent, another in 1750 and several gardens followed. The

FRANCE

present garden was founded in 1940 by M. J. Marquis and covers 27 acres (11 ha).

The open area contains trees and shrubs arranged both in ecological and in systematic groupings, beds of plants arranged in family groupings, collections of economic and medicinal plants and of annuals and biennials and also a research area. The alpine garden in the western part of the garden contains a variety of alpine plants and a waterfall, and a pool is to be added for aquatic plants. Near this are a Japanese garden, an iris garden, a peony garden and a heather garden. The rose garden is terraced with supporting walls, stairs, basins, a pergola and a T-shaped pool. It contains both modern and old varieties of rose.

Exotic plants are cultivated in glasshouses and are displayed in the large glass display house which was built in 1966. This consists of three hexagonal structures, each side measuring 13 ft (3·9 m), on an understructure of reinforced concrete. Banana, coffee, tea, cotton, eucalyptus, palms, cacti and succulents, orchids, *Bromeliaceae*, hibiscus and bougainvillea are among the plants growing here. The orangery is used for the winter storage of seeds. There is a children's playground and, planned for the future, are a leisure terrace on a lawn decorated with Mediterranean plants, a garden for the blind, a reading garden and a small open-air theatre.

(1) *Summer: Daily 8–noon, 2–9; Winter: Daily 8–noon, 2–5*
(2) *Free*
(5) *Town of Lille*

Lunéville

Meurthe-et-Moselle

21. Château de Lunéville

The château was designed in 1703 by the architect Germain Boffrand for Duke Leopold of Lorraine and it is in the neo-classical style. The park, created by Yves des Hours between 1711 and 1718, is an example of the transition from the formal 17th-cent French style to the English landscaped style. The gardens were extended in 1724 and to them were added statues or groups of statuary by the sculptors Renard, Guibal and Jacob Sigisbert Adam.

When Stanislas Leszczyński made Lunéville his principal residence, he not only did a considerable amount of work on the interior of the château but also on the gardens. He instructed the architect Héré, who was succeeded by Miqué, to build a number of pavilions. Several of these are in the Oriental style and the most important of them is the pavilion of Chanteheux, which is in effect the Petit Trianon of Lunéville.

The formal gardens have flowerbeds and topiary surrounding a large pool and, beyond, there is a park in the English landscaped style.

(1) *Apr–Sep: Daily 9–noon, 2–6; Oct–Mar: Daily 9–noon, 2–4*
(2) *Charge*
(4) *Château (same times)*
(5) *French State*

Ménars

Loir-et-Cher

22. Château de Ménars

The château, situated by the Loire, was bought in 1760 by Mme de Pompadour and in 1764 inherited by her brother, the Marquis de Marigny, under whose direction Jacques Germain Soufflot designed the vestibule, the rotunda, the grotto and the orangery. The park and garden were also laid out for him.

A gate leads into the château forecourt which has in its centre a large lawn and which is bordered by trees. Behind the château are lawn parterres edged with flowerbeds within dwarf clipped hedges, gravel paths and urns. Beyond these extends a vast park which contains an alley of old trees and the Temple of Love designed by Soufflot.

(1) *Palm Sunday–last Sun of Oct: Sat, Sun and Public Holidays*
(2) *Charge*
(4) *Château (8.30–11.30, 2–6)*
(5) *Compagnie de Saint-Gobain*

Nancy

Meurthe-et-Moselle

23. Parc de la Pépinière

A royal park was created in 1757 for Louis XV and in the mid-19th cent this became municipal property and was opened as a public park. The English garden was founded in 1877; the rose garden was begun in 1927, although it has since been enlarged; and there is also a fountain and formal pond. The park contains floral mosaics, a floral clock, a variety of shrubs and trees, including a large-leafed lime, a tulip-tree 115 ft (35 m) high and a Japanese red cedar 66 ft (20 m) high.

(1) *Summer: Daily 5–midnight; Winter: Daily 6 am–9 pm*
(2) *Free*
(5) *Town of Nancy*

Nantes, rue Stanislas Baudry

Loire-Atlantique

24. Botanical Garden

The garden was created as it is today in *c* 1850 by Dr Ecorchard and consists of a botanical garden and an arboretum, together covering 17 acres (7 ha). There are magnificent collections of magnolias and of camellias (visit between March and April),

and also of roses. The glasshouses contain exotic plants: orchids, cacti, palms and *Bromeliaceae*. There are over 1,700 plants in the botanical garden as well as seasonal displays of tulips and dahlias.

(1) *Summer: Daily 8.30–8.30; Winter: Daily 8.30–5.30*
(2) *Free*
(5) *Town of Nantes*

Orléans

Loiret

25. Floral Park

The 1,013 acre (410 ha) property of La Source, situated a short distance south of Orléans, was acquired by the city of Orléans and the Département du Loiret in 1959 for the purpose of founding a university and satellite town. At the same time permission was obtained to lay out almost 87 acres (35 ha) of the land as a park. This area contains the Château de la Source and the source of the River Loiret. It was designed by Albert Poyet. Part of it was opened in 1964, the remainder in 1967.

The administration buildings are set to the left of the entrance to the park, on a terrace. In front of these a floral mosaic is planted in summer to represent a stylized rose. On either side of the entrance are ponds and flowerbeds. An avenue to the right of the buildings leads to a magnificent iris garden containing 25,000 rhizomes and one of the four rose gardens, which together contain 200,000 roses.

An avenue of mature trees leads to the source of the River Loiret which is surrounded by cotoneaster, hypericum and flower parterres. On the right river bank are flamingoes, swans and ducks, an aviary with pigeons, pheasants, doves and peacocks.

Surrounding a cottage is a typical Tours landscape with a regional rose garden. The Japanese Garden contains a lotus pond. The *miroir*, the lake fed by the Loiret in front of the château, is separated from the château by a mosaic scroll design of clipped box and red sand. On the opposite side of the lake is another of the rose gardens with pergolas and behind it Atlas cedars, cedars of Lebanon and a Breton mill. (The mill then operates on Public Holidays). Another rose garden contains displays of Belgian polyantha roses and Alsatian rambling roses on pergolas, and nearby is a landscaped garden. At the far end of the park a bridge over the Loiret leads to a memorial erected to the botanist Raymond Chenault and to a variety of flora from his property at Clos Fleuri.

On returning to the spring, a hilly path leads to the large restaurant-display house containing collections of tropical plants. A broad avenue bordered by various floral displays leads back to the flowerbeds at the entrance and small paths lead off amongst the shrubs and grounds. The park also contains a rock garden and from spring until late autumn the park is filled with a wide variety of flowers.

(1) Daily Sunrise–Sunset
(2) Free
(3) Restaurant
(4) Miniature railway
(5) Town of Orléans and Département du Loiret

Rennes, place Ste Malaine

Îlle-et-Vilaine

26. Jardin du Thabor

The garden was first documented as the bishop's palace garden in 1610 and it was gradually enlarged thereafter. Large glasshouses were built in the 19th cent. The garden covers 25 acres (10 ha). There are avenues of old trees including oaks, one of which, the so-called 'Oak of Ste Malaine', is several centuries old. There is a French Garden with magnificent mosaic flowerbeds, a botanical garden with 3,000 indigenous and exotic plant varieties arranged in concentric flowerbeds bordered with box, a small Italian parterre with topiary, large collections of roses, dahlias, perennials and bulbous plants and a rock garden with rhododendrons, azaleas and camellias nearby. Part of the garden is a landscaped park of lawns and avenues with a grotto and aviary and with deer. Giant sequoia, cedar, fir, pine, cypress, lime, maple, beech, birch, poplar, oak and magnolia all grow here. Visit the garden in April for the camellias, rhododendrons and tulips, in July and August for the French Garden and the roses and at the end of October for the chrysanthemums.

(1) Winter: Daily 7.30–6; Summer: Daily 7–9.30
(2) Free
(3) Refreshments
(5) Town of Rennes

Rouen, 114 avenue des Martyrs de la Résistance

Seine-Maritime

27. Park and Botanical Garden

The botanical garden was laid out in 1832 when the town acquired what was formerly a private park, founded in 1691 by Louis de Carel. There are lawns, flowerbeds, rockeries, a rose garden, iris gardens, aquatic plants, displays of rhododendrons, azaleas and camellias and a variety of medicinal plants and glasshouses that contain collections of orchids, *Bromeliaceae* and *Araceae*. In summer may be seen the giant water-lily, *Victoria regia*, the leaves of which measure up to 3 ft (1 m) in diameter.

There is a late 17th-cent pavilion, erected by Louis de Carel, at the entrance to the park with an 18th-cent wrought-iron gateway; and in the park itself a large and typical 19th-cent metal-framed glasshouse

FRANCE

and a reconstructed cider-press. The park covers *c* 25 acres (10 ha).

(1) Park. Summer: Daily 8–8; Winter: Daily 8–5.30. Glasshouses. Daily 10–11.30, 2–5
(2) Free
(5) Town of Rouen

Strasbourg-Cedex, 28 rue Goethe

Bas-Rhin

28. Botanical Garden of the University Louis Pasteur

A botanical garden was inaugurated in 1619 but the present university garden was founded in 1880–2 around an abandoned gravel pit. It was remodelled in 1965–7. It is divided into three sections: the scientific collection, the distribution of plants according to their ecology and the systematic collection. Of particular interest are the rockeries, the collection of medicinal plants, the pond with aquatic plants and the arboretum which includes zelkova, ginkgo (*Ginkgo biloba*), Japanese nutmeg (*Torreya nucifera*), Kentucky coffee tree (*Gymnocladus dioicus*) and Caucasian wing-nut (*Pterocarya caucasica*). There are also hothouses and temperate glasshouses. The garden covers almost 9 acres (3·5 ha).

(1) Summer: Mon–Sat 7–noon, 2–6; Sun 7–noon; Winter: Mon–Sat 8–noon, 2–4; Sun 8–noon
(2) Free
(5) University Louis Pasteur

Thaon

Calvados

29. Château de Fontaine-Henry

The park was created at the beginning of the 19th cent in the English style by the Marquis de Carbonnel et Canisy. It surrounds the magnificent château which was built in the 15th and 16th cents. The park contains interesting trees and many springs. There is also a 13th-cent chapel in the park, and there is a pleasant view over the valley of La Mue.

(1) Summer: Daily (except Tue and Fri) 2.30–6.30; Winter: Sun and Public Holidays 2–6
(2) Charge
(4) Château (same times)
(5) Comte Jacques d'Oilliamson

Tours, 33 boulevard Tonellé

Indre-et-Loire

30. Botanical Garden of Tours

The garden of 12 acres (5 ha) was founded in 1843 by the chemist Jean Margueron and is in two parts: the landscaped park and the

School of Botany. The former, with lawns, flowers, ponds and a river with aquatic plants, contains over 300 varieties of trees: ginkgo (*Ginkgo biloba*), cypress (*Taxodium sempervirens*), tulip-tree (*Liriodendron tulipifera*), Caucasian wing-nut (*Pterocarya caucasica*) and cucumber-tree (*Magnolia acuminata*). There are also deer, an aviary and waterbirds. The School of Botany, covering 2½ acres (1 ha), contains approx 2,000 varieties of plants grouped according to their taxonomy. The two glasshouses contain tropical plants, a large pool contains aquatic plants and the orangery, erected in 1843 by Louis-René Madelin, shelters deer.

(*1*) Daily 8–7, 8 or 9
(*2*) Free
(*5*) City of Tours and Laboratory of Plant Biology, Faculty of Pharmacy

Valençay

Indre

31. Château de Valençay

The Renaissance château, built in the 16th and 17th cents, has a formal garden of geometrically designed lawns with ponds, ornamental urns and topiary. The Jardin de la Duchesse has a parterre with flowerbeds.

(*1*) Palm Sunday–Oct: Daily 9–11.30, 2–6.30; Winter: Sun and Public Holidays 10–11.30, 2–Sunset
(*2*) Charge
(*4*) Château
(*5*) M J. G. Morel

Varengeville-sur-Mer, route de l'Eglise

Seine-Maritime

32. Parc Floral Des Moutiers

The house was built by Sir Edwin Lutyens in 1898 for Guillaume Mallet and the garden was designed by Lutyens and Miss Jekyll. It is situated in a small valley and covers 25 acres (10 ha). The main quadrangle with four cypresses, white flagstones and brickwork echoes the Japanese and Tudor styles of the house. Near this is a series of enclosed gardens: a floral parterre, a quadrangle, a pergola, a rose garden and then a path bordered by Portuguese laurel and yews which leads to a Japanese tea house. There are roses, clematis, jasmine and narcissi. Paths lead to clearings where shrubs are arranged together for effects of colour or for their scent. There are magnificent rhododendrons, azaleas and magnolias and a variety of well-established trees: oaks, sweet gums, eucryphia and swamp cypress.

(*1*) Easter–1 Nov: Daily 10–12.30, 2–Sunset
(*2*) Charge
(*5*) Mallet family.

Villandry, nr Tours

Indre-et-Loire

33. Château de Villandry

The gardens, as reconstructed early in this century by the late Dr Carvallo, are a unique example of an early 17th-cent garden plan and are thus of the greatest importance. They comprise 12 acres (4·8 ha) of intricately patterned squares and rectangles, terraced out of the hillside and confined by rows of pleached lime, trellis, and changes in level. The château, rebuilt in 1532 by Jean Lebreton, a minister of François I, is moated and beyond the moat to the west the gardens extend at an oblique angle. Though obliterated in the 19th cent, enough of the structural detail survived in the way of paths and terrace walls to make the restoration possible.

The garden is on four levels, and from this fact much of its charm and interest derives. Of the uppermost two, carved out of the hillside, the second connects with the upper floor of the château and provides a gallery along two sides, from which the pleasure garden and the *potager* can be surveyed from above. The former is predominantly green, an elaborate and crisply drawn series of interlocking patterns in broad bands of box; fountains and box 'finials' give vertical emphasis here and there. The *potager*, by contrast, is multicoloured. Nine squares, outlined in dwarf box and each with a different pattern within the square, are planted in blocks of vegetables according to variety, with a resulting chequer-board of contrasting foliage. The squares are enclosed by trellis, rising at the angles to form rose-covered arbours.

The inspiration for the garden derives from the decorative concepts of the designer and architect, Jacques du Cerceau, in particular that for the gardens at Fontainebleau (qv). The result is a garden of remarkable charm and unparalleled documentary interest. Nowhere else is it possible to see an example of a garden that antedates the influence of Boyceau and Le Nôtre. Though much larger than any medieval garden would ever have been, it belongs nonetheless to the tradition of the *Hortus inclusus*, an enclosed space oblivious of nature outside.

Dr Carvallo died in 1936. His son has maintained the garden since then and has added a great apple orchard on the hillside to the south. Nearly 2,000 apple trees are planted in 46 intersecting lines in the manner shown in the engravings of du Cerceau.

(*1*) Mid-Mar–mid-Nov: Daily 8–Sunset; mid-Nov–mid-Mar: Daily 9–Sunset
(*2*) Charge
(*3*) Refreshments
(*4*) Château (Apr–Nov: Daily 9–6)
(*5*) M Robert Carvallo

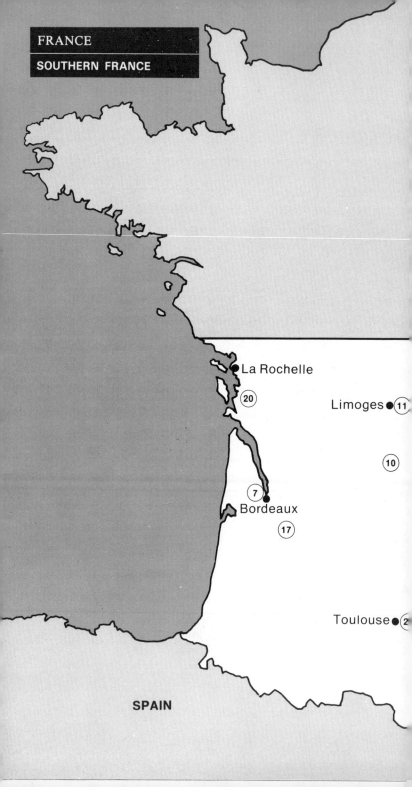

FRANCE
SOUTHERN FRANCE

La Rochelle
(20)

Limoges ●(11)

(10)

(7)
Bordeaux
(17)

Toulouse ●(2)

SPAIN

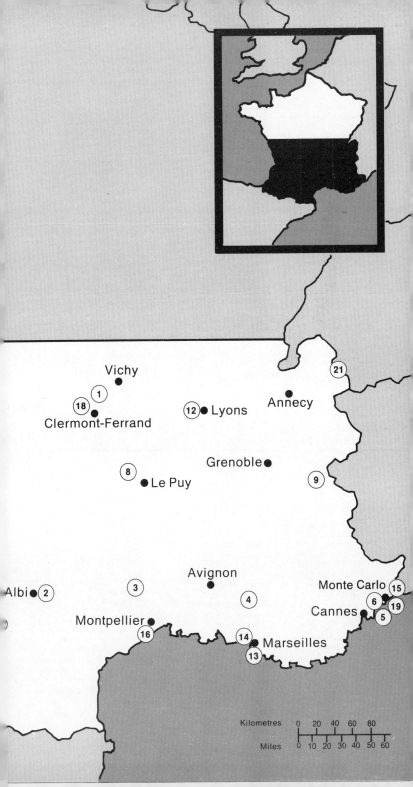

FRANCE

Aigueperse
Puy-de-Dôme
1. Château d'Effiat

The garden was designed by André Le Nôtre and laid out in 1626–40; the château was built in 1627. The garden is in the 17th-cent style with terraces, canals, ponds, topiary, a grotto and mature oaks and sweet chestnuts.

(1) June–Sep: Daily 9–noon, 2–7; Oct and Palm Sun–May: Sat, Sun and Public Holidays 9–noon, 2–7
(2) Charge
(4) Château (same times)
(5) M Guy de Moroges

Albi
Tarn
2. Palais de la Berbie

The small garden was once the courtyard of the episcopal palace and was laid out in the 18th cent with flowerbeds and scroll-patterned parterres. The garden and palace overlook the River Tarn and the town of Albi.

(1) Daily 9–noon, 2–6
(2) Free
(4) Musée Toulouse-Lautrec (same times)
(5) City of Albi

Anduze
Gard
3. Bambuseraie de Prafrance

This bamboo garden was created in 1855 by Eugéne Mazel and Paoletti and was restored after 1902. It covers 99 acres (40 ha). The collection is unique to Europe with over 30 varieties, including giant varieties such as *Phyllostachys pubescens* that grow to a height of 31 ft (9·5 m) and a circumference of 24 in (60 cm). There is a 437 ft (133 m) long avenue of bamboos. Prafrance also has some rare trees: an avenue of giant sequoias (*Sequoiadendron giganteum*), coast redwood (*Sequoia sempervirens*), Chusan palm (*Chamaerops excelsa*), Lawson cypress (*Chamaecyparis Lawsoniana*), red cedars and male and female ginkgos. In the flower-beds are mimosa, magnolia, azaleas, camellias and rhododendrons. There are also ponds with water-lilies and Egyptian lotus.

(1) Daily 9–noon, 2–7
(2) Charge
(5) M Yves Crouzet

Ansouis
Vaucluse
4. Château d'Ansouis

The château was first mentioned in 960 and its architecture ranges from the 10th to the 17th cents. The gardens, designed by Péresque, are composed of a formal garden, terraces and copses. The formal garden consists of ornate arabesques of clipped box leading to a long pool, cascade and a pentagonal pond.

(1) Daily (except Mon) 2–7
(4) Château (same times)
(5) Comte de Sabran

Antibes, chemin Raymond
Alpes-Maritimes
5. Botanical Garden of Villa Thuret

The garden covers approx 12 acres (5 ha) and was founded in 1856 by Gustave Adolphe Thuret, a botanist and algae expert. There are over 1,000 varieties of trees and shrubs. Among the ancient trees are species of eucalyptus, acacia and melaleuca, and there are collections of cypress, podocarpus and giant palms. There are also many sub-tropical and Mediterranean plants. Visit in May–June and September–October.

(1) Daily (except Sat, Sun and Public Holidays) 8–6
(2) Free
(5) INRA Station of Botany and Pathology, and National Institute for Agronomic Research

Beaulieu-sur-Mer
Alpes-Maritimes
6. Le Léonina Botanical Garden

The garden covers 5 acres (2 ha) and was founded in 1937 by Arpad Plesch who over the years has made various improvements. The entrance gate is flanked by two white stone lions. The garden contains over 3,500 plant varieties including many ornamental plants, although the owner's main interest is in plants with a practical purpose. There are collections of nutritional plants (edible beans, seeds, roots, stems, herbs and spices), medicinal plants, oil-yielding plants and sugar-manufacturing plants. It represents one of the most comprehensive collections of economic plants in the world.

The garden also contains a large number of trees, including almost 300 varieties of fruit trees: citrus fruits, bananas, anona, diospyros and eugenia. It also contains shrubs, climbing plants, formal ponds and display houses. A very fine botanical and horticultural library adjoins the garden.

(1) By arrangement
(2) Charge
(4) Library
(5) M Arpad Plesch

Bordeaux, place Bardineau

Gironde

7. Botanical Garden

The present botanical garden was founded in 1859 by Durieu de Maisonneuve. It contains 1,500 plant varieties, mostly indigenous varieties but also exotic plants from China, Japan and North America. It is situated in a large public park with fine trees.

(1) Daily
(2) Free
(5) Town of Bordeaux

Chavaniac-La Fayette

Haute-Loire

8. Château de Chavaniac-La Fayette

The château, situated in a magnificent park on a mountainside, was built at the beginning of the 14th cent by the Suat family and rebuilt in 1701 after a fire. It was the birthplace of General La Fayette. In 1790–91 it was restored by the architect Laurent Vaudoyer and further restoration took place in the present century. On one side is a large sloping lawn with flowerbeds. There is a formal rose garden and, beyond, a wooded area with streams and cascades.

(1) Easter–Oct: Mon, Thu, Sat, Sun and Public Holidays 10–noon, 2–6
(2) Charge
(4) Château (same times)
(5) Musée La Fayette

Col du Lautaret, nr Briançon

Hautes-Alpes

9. Alpine Garden du Lautaret

This alpine garden was founded in 1894 by the Touring Club of France and the University of Grenoble. It was restored after World War II. The garden, but not the laboratory, is open to the public. The garden, covering 5 acres (2 ha), is in a remarkable geographical position at 6,000 ft (1,829 m) and is rich in flora. It contains approx 3,500 species of alpine plants from all over the world, including rare species. Visit in July.

(1) Late Jun–mid-Sep: Daily 8–6
(2) Free
(5) University of Grenoble

Hautefort

Dordogne

10. Château de Hautefort

The 17th-cent château has a park of 99 acres (40 ha) and terraced gardens with fine flower parterres set in lawns, as well as an iris garden planted by the French Iris Society. The château was restored after a fire in 1968.

(1) Palm Sunday–1 Nov: Daily (except Tue) 9–noon, 2–7
(2) Charge
(4) Château and chapel (same times)
(5) Baronne de Bastard

Limoges

Haute-Vienne

11. Cathedral and Botanical Gardens

The gardens are situated behind the Cathedral and the Bishop's Palace (now the Municipal Museum containing a collection of Limoges enamel, modern art, egyptology, etc). The cathedral garden, founded in the late 18th cent, covers 10 acres (4 ha) and was remodelled as a formal garden in 1975. It consists of terraced lawns and parterres wtih clipped yew and decorative shrubs. The botanical garden, founded in 1959, consists of parallel beds bordered with clipped box and containing approx 1,250 varieties of annual, biennial and perennial indigenous and exotic plants as well as a collection of conifers with some rare varieties.

(1) Daily 8–Sunset
(2) Free
(4) Cathedral and Municipal Museum (Oct–May: Daily, except Tue, 10–noon, 2–5; Jun–Sep 10–noon, 2–6)
(5) Town of Limoges

Lyons, boulevard des Belges, boulevard de Stalingrad

Rhône

12. Parc de la Tête d'Or

The park was designed in the English style by the brothers Bühler in collaboration with the chief municipal engineer Bonnet between 1856 and 1862. It covers 260 acres (105 ha) and is situated beside the River Rhône.

There are several entrances to the park but near the Winston Churchill Bridge is the main entrance with the Monument des Enfants du Rhône, erected in 1887. A magnificent wrought-iron gate leads through to lawns, avenues of mature trees and the lake with its islands and swans. The avenue to the right leads past the villas along the boulevard des Belges. Facing is an avenue which skirts part of the southern side of the lake, leading into the centre of the park and thence to the zoological and botanical gardens and aviary which are situated in the south-east corner of the park. Just after passing the lake the avenue branches: to the right it leads to a children's garden and a deer park beyond which are glasshouses and the Mexican garden of the botanical garden; to the left it crosses a bridge and leads past a new pavilion restaurant on to bowls and mini-golf. The avenue to the left of the main entrance skirts the northern side of the lake past the Petite Suisse, a grove of conifers including magnificent cedars of Lebanon and sequoias. In this part of the park is the statue, Dancer with Castanets, by J. Bernard. An underground passage leads to the Île des Cygnes. Another smaller island, Île des Tamaris, has ducks and other waterbirds.

The rose garden which is 12 acres (5 ha) in area, is situated near the Palais des Congrès. It was first planted in 1964 and contains 350 varieties of roses, 63,000 roses in all. There is also a variety of other flowers and shrubs, including rhododendrons and azaleas. The garden is laid out with avenues, paths, pools, a pergola 49 yds (45 m) long, a small stream with a rustic bridge and a statue of a woman by Tajana. Beyond the rose garden is the northern entrance to the park, a miniature railway and a bicycle track on the lake's largest island.

The park, consisting of areas of wood and lawn with flowers or flowerbeds, has many statues and trees which include magnolias, Judas trees, black walnut, varnish trees, ginkgos, tulip-trees, beeches, copper beeches, maples and planes. Some of the trees are over 100 years old.

(1) Summer: Daily 6 am–11 pm; Winter: Daily 6 am–8 pm
(2) Free
(3) Restaurant
(5) Town of Lyons

Marseilles, avenue Clôt Bey, avenue Borély

Bouches-du-Rhône

13. Borély Parc and Botanical Garden

The park was created in the 18th cent by the Borély family and was acquired by the city in c 1860. It was restored after being badly damaged during World War II. There are grounds in the French style, consisting of parterres and ponds, and grounds in the landscaped style with lawns, shrubs and trees including large planes, ginkgos and tulip-trees. There is also a large rose garden. The botanical garden, which adjoins the park, was created in 1880 under Dr Heckel and enlarged in 1913. It is currently being redesigned. It covers 2½ acres (1 ha) and contains approx 1,500 exotic and indigenous plant varieties.

(1) Park. Daily 8–6. Botanical Garden. Daily (except Sat, Sun and Public Holidays) 8–6
(2) Free
(4) Museum Borély
(5) City of Marseilles

Marseilles, chemin de la Palud, le Merlan

14. Parc de Font Obscure

The park, which has been open to the public since 1976, consists of three formerly private properties. It comprises an English garden, wooded hills and a lake.

(1) Daily 8–6
(2) Free
(5) City of Marseilles

Menton-Garavan, avenue Saint-Jacques

Alpes Maritimes

15. Val Rahmeh Botanical Garden

The garden covers approx 2½ acres (1 ha). It was created in 1905 by Lord Radcliffe, who also built a villa at this time, and it has been successively enlarged and improved. It was acquired by the State in 1966. The garden contains approx 500 varieties of herbaceous plants, all clearly labelled. Narrow paths lead through the garden, arrows marking a suggested route.

At the entrance a short avenue bordered on one side by the palm Phoenix canariensis leads to the villa, the walls of which are covered with vines and climbing plants: jasmine, plumbago, Tonkin's vine and the rare Passiflora quadrangularis. On the south side of the villa a terrace overlooks the gardens. Beyond the lawns are a supporting wall and a pergola with climbers such as Thunbergia grandiflora, clematis and passiflora. A sunken garden, which contains a variety of interesting shrubs and trees – avocado (Persea americana), Cape gooseberry (Actinidia chinensis) and the soap-bark tree of Chile (Quillaia saponaria) – leads from here. Nearby is a pond containing Egyptian papyrus (Cyperus papyrus) and beyond this a further pool with water-lilies and lotus (Nelumbo nucifera).

An area is reserved for economic plants such as citrus trees, avocados, bananas and sugar cane. On the northern side of the villa a path leads up a small hill amongst olive trees and rare shrubs such as Bauhinia grandiflora, Caesalpinia sepiaria and Solandra hartwegii as well as mimosa and buddleia. In this area are cyclamen, gladioli, poinsettia and dahlias. The garden also has jacaranda trees, bamboos, olive trees, bougainvilleas, rambler roses, orange and grapefruit trees, a pepper tree from South America (Schinus molle), the Lion's ear (Leonitis leonurus), hibiscus and castor-oil plant (Ricinus communis). The visit ends along an avenue bordered by camellias, a huge Datura arborea as well as D. sanguinea and D. versicolor.

(1) Oct–Apr: Daily (except Tue) 10–noon, 2–4; May–Sep: Daily (except Tue) 10–noon, 3–7

(2) *Free*
(5) *French State*

FRANCE

Montpellier, 163 rue Auguste Broussonnet

Hérault

16. Botanical Garden of Montpellier

This is the oldest university garden in France, founded in 1593 by Henri IV and first laid out in 1598 by Pierre Richer de Belleval. The School of Botany was created by Aimé Chicoyneau. The garden was enlarged at the beginning of the 19th cent by the addition of an orangery, glasshouses, canals, ponds and extra grounds. Today it covers 15 acres (6 ha). There are specimens of ginkgo (*Ginkgo biloba*), holm oak (*Quercus ilex*), nettle tree (*Celtis occidentalis*), Judas tree (*Cercis siliquastrum*), wistaria and palms. The glasshouses contain interesting collections of succulents, orchids and of medicinal plants. There is also an English garden, a fine alpine collection and a lotus pond.

(1) *Summer: Daily (except Sat afternoons and Sun) 8–noon, 2–6; Winter: Daily 8–noon, 2–5.30*
(2) *Free*
(5) *University of Montpellier*

Preignac

Gironde

17. Château de Mâle

The late 17th-cent château has gardens in the Italian style arranged in terraces and containing 17th-cent Italian statuary and fountains. There is an open-air theatre in the Italian style with a rock and pebble nymphaea and alcoves containing statues of characters from the Italian Commedia dell'Arte. The château has an important vineyard and produces three excellent wines: Château de Mâle, Château de Cardaillon and Chevalier de Mâle. Visit in the spring or in September.

(1) *Easter–mid-Oct: Daily (except Wed) 3–7 or by arrangement*
(2) *Charge*
(4) *Château (same times)*
(5) *Comte de Bournazel*

Romagnat nr Clermont-Ferrand

Puy-de-Dôme

18. Château d'Opmes

The fortress of Opmes was rebuilt as a residential château in 1613 and the formal gardens were laid out at the same time. They are in two terraces with a Renaissance fountain in one and a pond and fountain in the other.

(1) *Daily (except Wed) 9–noon, 2–6.30*
(2) *Charge*

(4) *Château (in groups by arrangement)*
(5) *M Victor Basse*

Saint-Jean-Cap-Ferrat

Alpes Maritimes

19. Les Cèdres Botanical Garden

The garden covers approx 37 acres (15 ha) and commands magnificent views. It is situated in the centre of the Cap Ferrat peninsula at 164 ft (50 m). In the 19th cent the property belonged to the Pollonais family and at that time only part of the villa existed. At the end of the century it was acquired by King Leopold II of Belgium, who enlarged the villa and after whose death in 1909 it was divided into lots. The present garden area was bought by an Englishman and in 1924 by the father-in-law of the present owner who introduced many exotic plants and designed the tropical garden. The present owner and her late husband have continued to enrich the garden's collections and it now contains approx 5,000 varieties of plants.

The garden nearest the villa is formal with terraces, pathways, ponds and a long canal bordered by cypresses and flower borders. An artificial lake surrounded by a variety of shrubs contains a collection of tropical water-lilies including the rare Amazonian *Victoria cruciana* and *Euryale ferox*, lotus (*nelumbo*) and Egyptian lotus (*Nymphaea lotus*) while a special pool contains insectivorous plants and more aquatic plants. This is one of the few European botanical gardens in which species of lotus and water-lily thrive in the open. The garden further away from the villa is laid out in the English style but contains tropical and sub-tropical trees, shrubs and ferns. There are avenues bordered with palms with epiphytic plants on the trunks or with bromeliads and orchids.

The tropical garden contains tree ferns such as *Alsophila excelsa*, *Cibotium regale* and *Cyathea medullaris*, 30 varieties of bamboo including *Dendrocalamus giganteus* from Indo-China, *Phyllostachys sulphurea*, from Japan, and many trees including palms, umbrella pines, olives and avocados.

The orange garden contains approx 40 varieties of citrus trees including orange, lemon, grapefruit and kumquat trees.

The garden also contains, both outside and in glasshouses, several thousand varieties of cacti and succulents. There are almost 400 varieties of *Mesembryanthemaceae* and possibly the world's most complete collection of *Crassulaceae* and of *Euphorbiaceae*, including the rare South African *Euphorbia obesa*.

(1) *By arrangement with the Secretary*
(5) *Mme Marnier-Lapostolle*

FRANCE

Saint-Porchaire, La Roche-Courbon

Charente-Maritime

20. Château La Roche-Courbon

The extensive formal gardens were magnificently reconstructed in 1925–30 from a painting by the Dutch artist Hackaert depicting the gardens as they were in the 17th cent. The northern part of the gardens has been restored on what formerly was marshy land. An avenue leads to the 15th-cent château which is approached through an ilex forest, the ilex being a very rare tree in France.

On the other side of the château, facing the terrace, are the formal gardens. These consist of parterres, some with clipped yew trees and ornamental urns, and a knot garden. Facing these is a large ornamental pool designed by the architect Duprat, bordered with lawns and fed by several canals with a waterfall constructed over a series of stone terraces facing the château.

(1) Daily 8–Sunset
(2) Charge
(4) Château; Museum of Prehistory; prehistoric caves
(5) Society of the Estate of La Roche-Courbon

Samöens

Haute-Savoie

21. Botanical and Alpine Garden La Jaÿsinia

The garden is situated at 2,296–2,559 ft (700–780 m) in the town centre. It is a landscaped garden of over 8 acres (3·5 ha) on a south-facing chalk slope with gullies, waterfalls, small ponds and bogs. It was founded in 1905 by Madame Cognacq-Jaÿ and in 1906 given by her to the town of Samöens. It was designed by the Genevan architect Allemand. The garden was restored after 1935, when a laboratory for biology and alpine ecology was founded.

A steep winding path leads up into the alpine garden. There is a world-wide collection of alpine plants arranged geographically, a variety of shrubs and of flowers. At the highest point in the park is a terrace. Areas of the garden are reserved for sun-loving plants, including wild irises, and African plants such as kniphofia, plants of the north and east Mediterranean including acanthus, wulfenia, pinks and peonies, plants of the Sierras and Pyrenees including *Genista hispanica* and the rare *Lithospermum oleifolium*, a pond with aquatic saxifrage (*Saxifraga aquatica*), Chinese and Japanese plants. The garden contains an arboretum with red oak (*Quercus rubra*), incense cedar (*Libocedrus decurrens*), honey-locust (*Gleditsia triacanthos*), thujas,

yellow buck-eye (*Aesculus flava*) and dawn redwood (*Metasequoia glyptostroboides*). Near the laboratory is a research garden. Visit between mid-May and mid-July for the flowers and between mid-September and mid-October for the autumn colours and fruit.

(1) Daily 8–noon, 1.30–7 (Sunset in winter)
(2) Free
(5) Town of Samöens and Fondation Cognacq-Jaÿ (Paris)

Toulouse

Pyrénées

22. University Botanical Garden

The botanical garden was founded in 1969 and covers approx 2½ acres (1 ha). It forms a small part of the Jardin des Plantes, a public park founded by Picot de Lapeyrouse and Ferrière which was presented to the city by Napoleon in 1806. It contains an interesting collection of old trees including a fine group of *Pinus strobus*. The botanical garden contains medicinal plants, about 500 varieties of herbaceous plants and areas for research.

(1) Daily by appointment
(5) University and City of Toulouse

MONACO

Monte Carlo

Exotic Garden

The garden was founded on a steep, rocky slope by Prince Albert I in 1913 and was remodelled and opened to the public in 1933. It contains large collections of succulents, cacti, mesembryanthemum, crassula, amaryllis as well as aloes, agaves and euphorbias. Visit in winter and spring for the flowering of mesembryanthemum and aloes but the garden has specimens of interest throughout the year.

(1) Jun–Sep: Daily 9–7; Oct–May: Daily 9–noon, 2–6
(2) Charge
(4) Observatory Grotto; Museum of Prehistoric Anthropology (same times)
(5) M Marcel Kroenlein (Director)

BELGIUM

Annevoie
Namur

1. Château d'Annevoie

The late 18th-cent château and gardens were designed by Charles-Alexis de Montpellier between 1758 and 1776 and have been little changed except for the recent addition of a rose garden and several pieces of sculpture. The original canalizations carrying water from four springs in the woods still supply the fountains and cascades for which the gardens are famous. Here elements of French and Italian formal gardening are combined with the English style of landscape gardening.

The gardens are entered from the west side of the courtyard of the château. There is a flower garden, with parterres bordered by low hedges, and beyond a circular basin with a central fountain the eye is led towards a statue of Minerva, by Detombay. A winding path leads to a sculpture of a boar, a copy of the Florentine model. To this side there is also a canal, extending the view from a window of the château and terminating in a cascade, a lily pond, pools with figures of children spitting water and riding dolphins and a grotto sheltering a sculpture of Neptune.

In front of the château is a lake and a *buffet d'eau* and two parallel rows of four small spouts of water on the rising ground. Beyond is a group of Neptune and Amphitrite and an alley of fine trees on the far side of the supply canal extends to a statue of Minerva.

On the east side is the curving French cascade and closer to the château the less formal English cascade. A pool overhung by trees and with banks covered by red, yellow and white tulips in spring has a fountain from which water fans out in the shape of a peacock's tail, and there are further flower-filled parterres.

(1) Apr–Oct: Daily 9–7
(2) Charge
(3) Restaurant and café
(4) Château (Easter–Jun: Sat, Sun and Public Holidays 9.30–1, 2–6; Jul–Aug: Daily 9.30–1, 2–6) Garden Centre (Daily, except Feb, 9–7)
(5) M. and Mme de Montpellier d'Annevoie

Antwerp, Koningen Astridplein 24

2. Botanical Gardens of Antwerp Zoo

The Winter Gardens were opened by Leopold II in 1897 and contain a rich and varied collection of tropical and exotic plants. Palms are well represented with several types of phoenix palm and remarkable examples of the *Corypha australis*, *Livistona altissima* and *Washingtonia*

gracilis. There are important collections of orchids and *Bromeliaceae*.

Each year some 2,000 flowering plants are bedded out in the Zoological Gardens. In spring there are crocuses, primroses, hyacinths and tulips; in summer, geraniums, petunias, begonias, heliotropes and dahlias, as well as the palms, ferns and exotic plants that winter in the hothouses; in autumn, asters and chrysanthemums. The arboretum is also worthy of note, with good examples of honey-locusts, araucarias, a *Ginkgo biloba* and a 125-year-old paulownia.

(1) Daily 8.30–Sunset
(2) Charge
(3) Café-restaurant
(4) Zoo (same times); Natural History Museum (same times); Library (Mon–Fri 9–Noon, 2–6); Planetarium (opens Wed 2 pm); Concert halls
(5) Antwerp Zoological Society

Antwerp, Rubenstraat 9–11

3. House of Rubens

The garden of the house in the centre of Antwerp that belonged to Rubens provides a good example of an urban garden. Rubens settled in Antwerp in 1615 and made this house his permanent home until his death in 1640.

The City of Antwerp acquired the property in 1937 and the original garden has now been re-created by reference to Rubens's own paintings – in particular the portrait in Munich of his wife, Helen Fourment, with the artist's eldest son Nicolas which shows the garden in detail – and the engravings of Jacobus of Harrewijn executed between 1684 and 1692.

Linking the painter's house with his studio is a Baroque portico, through which the garden is first glimpsed. It is a garden of great simplicity divided into four rectangular parterres edged with low yew hedges, each with narrow borders of flowers to add a touch of colour. By the first parterre to the left is a great yew tree. The central axis terminates with a pavilion at the end of the garden housing a fine statue of Hercules, attributed to the sculptor Lucas Faid'herbe. Nearby there are two rectangular grass parterres. Towards the right is a fountain, close to the original pergola, which has been restored. In the corner is the gardener's cottage, overgrown with honeysuckle, also identifiable from the painting.

(1) Daily (except Mon) 10–5
(2) Free
(5) City of Antwerp

Antwerp, Middelheimlaan 61

4. Middelheim Park and Open-air Sculpture Museum

Part of the 459 acre (184 ha) area of park and woodland forming the Nightingale Park, acquired in 1910 by the City of Antwerp.

Among the fine trees are a swamp cypress (*Taxodium distichum*), several araucarias and catalpas, and a cedar, tulip-tree and two copper beeches of impressive growth. Lily-of-the-valley and willow-herb grow beneath the trees and in spring there is a fine display of rhododendrons and azaleas. The Mosberg, as the name suggests, is an area of moss-covered banks.

Since 1950 there has been a biennial international sculpture exhibition in the Nightingale Park, lasting from the beginning of June to the end of September, and in the Middelheim Park there is also a permanent exhibition of approx 200 pieces of sculpture from the late 19th cent onwards. The Louis XVI house, built by the architect Barnabé Guimard, in the middle of the estate from which this part of the Nightingale Park was created, is now a restaurant. The orangery is an exhibition hall.

(1) *Daily Nov–mid-Feb: 10–5; mid-Feb–mid-Mar: 10–6; mid-Mar–mid-Apr: 10–7; mid-Apr–May: 10–8; Jun and Jul: 10–9; Aug: 10–8; Sep: 10–7; Oct: 10–6*
(2) *Free (except during Biennial Exhibition)*
(3) *Restaurant (closed in Feb and on Wed)*
(5) *City of Antwerp, Parks Dept*

Antwerp, Leopoldstraat 24
5. Public Botanical Gardens

Until the beginning of the 19th cent the gardens were the property of St Elizabeth's Hospital and medicinal plants were grown here. The gardens were enlarged later and now contain a collection of rare plants.

(1) *Gardens. Daily 8–6. Glasshouses. Sat and Sun 10–1*
(2) *Free*
(5) *City of Antwerp, Parks Dept*

Attre
Hainaut
6. Château d'Attre

The present château was built in 1752 by François-Philippe de Gomegnies. It is approached through an entrance flanked by rose-coloured marble columns and to the other side lies an interesting landscaped garden with a 15th-cent dovecot, ruined tower, village pillory, bath house and 19th-cent Swiss chalet. The principal feature is a rock tower, *le Rocher*, erected as a hunting lodge and observatory in honour of the Archduchess Marie-Christine, eldest daughter of the Empress Maria Theresa of Austria, and her husband, the Duke of Saxe-Teschen, governors-general of the Low Countries. The summit is reached by winding paths and at the foot is a small lake and a grotto hung with stalactites.

Among the fine trees are catalpas, copper beeches, tulip-trees, a paulownia, chestnut and oak, several of which date from the time

BELGIUM

of Napoleon, to whom Count du Val de Beaulieu, son-in-law of François-Philippe de Gomegnies, was a page.

(1) *Mid-Mar–Oct: Sat, Sun and Public Holidays 10–noon, 2–6; Jul and Aug: Daily (except Wed) same hours*
(2) *Charge*
(4) *Château (same times)*
(5) *M and Mme Anatole de Meester de Heyndonck*

Les Awiers
Liège
7. Château d'Aigremont

The present château, which was built in 1716 in the traditional Liège style, occupies a fine position overlooking the Meuse. Only the framework of the original garden survives. The courtyard has two rocky recesses with fountains dedicated to Neptune and Amphitrite. A wrought-iron gate leads to a walled garden on two levels: the first has a fountain and ornamental pool at the centre; the second is composed of four parterres.

(1) *2 Apr–1 Nov: Daily (except Tue) 10–noon, 2–6*
(2) *Charge*
(5) *Royal Society for Belgian Historical Buildings*

Belœil
Hainaut
8. Château de Belœil

The imposing château was rebuilt by Sanson after a fire in 1900. Before, it was reached by a 2½ mile (4 km) avenue. It looks out over a large rectangular *pièce d'eau* with a statue of Neptune at the far end. French formal gardens, begun in the second half of the 17th cent and attaining their present form by 1760, lie parallel to the water on either of the long sides. These are composed of parterres, ornamental pools and fountains, bosquets and alleys of trees and shrubs. There are 6 miles (9 km) of hornbeam hedge at Belœil and 6,000 pink and red roses. Of particular interest is the open-air theatre (*le boulingrain*), an 18th-cent bathing pool and a revolving bridge. Until 1925 ice was taken from the ice pond to an ice-house situated beyond the kitchen garden.

The deer park, Island of Flora, on which there is a summer house, obelisk, Temple of Morpheus designed by F.-J. Bélanger and romantic ruin were created as an English garden in the late 18th cent. They are not open to the public. On the east side is the kitchen garden with the pavilion known as the Temple of Pomona at the centre and to the south, facing east, the orangery.

(1) *Daily 9–Sunset*

(2) *Charge*
(3) *Restaurant and café*
(4) *Château (Apr or Easter–1 Oct: Daily 10–noon, 2–5*
(5) *S.A. Prince Antoine de Ligne*

Brussels, avenues Emile Duray and Emile Demot

9. Abbaye de la Cambre

Cistercian convent founded in 1196 with the help of Henri I, Duke of Brabant, by Gisela, a Benedictine nun. It was built on the edge of the Forêt de Soignes by the source of the River Maelbeek. The convent was named Camera Beatae Mariae after the Virgin Mary's room at Nazareth.

In 1796 the convent was dissolved and after passing through several hands its restoration was taken on by the Ligue des Amis de la Cambre in 1921. The 14th-cent church was re-opened in 1927 and between 1930 and 1932 the main formal gardens, of which only a part of the 18th-cent terracing and *cour d'honneur* remained intact, were reconstructed by the landscape gardener, Jules Buyssens, after an engraving by Sandérus. The work was carried out by the City of Brussels and the Borough of Ixelles.

From the pond which marks the source of the Maelbeek a good view can be had of the terraced gardens with their lawns, stairs and ramps, clipped hedges and trees. The buildings are now occupied by the Institut Cartographique Militaire and by the Ecole Supérieure d'Architecture et des Arts Visnels.

(1) *Daily*
(2) *Free*
(5) *City of Brussels and Borough of Ixelles*

Brussels, avenue du Parc Poyal

10. Laeken Royal Conservatories

The Royal Conservatories are open to the public for a brief few days each year, when the passages of geraniums and tropical plants are displayed.

(1) *Mid-May. See local press or write to the Maître des Ceremonies de la Cour, Palais Royal de Bruxelles, for times*
(2) *Free*
(5) *Belgian Royal Family*

Brussels

11. Parc de Bruxelles

Laid out between 1774 and 1787 by Barnabé Guimard, architect of many of the houses bordering the park, and planted by Charles Zinner, it is on the site of an earlier royal garden. The park has belonged to the City of Brussels since 1817. Following the model of Versailles (qv), avenues converge from three points on a large circular basin

and a *rond point* of espaliered limes; a smaller basin is situated in the central avenue. Of the many fine sculptures, some were originally at Tervuren (qv).

(1) *Nov–Apr: Daily 7–9; May–Oct: 6–11*
(2) *Free*
(3) *Café*
(5) *City of Brussels*

Gaasbeek

Brabant

12. Château de Gaasbeek

Between 1887 and 1898 the château (originally a fortified building dating from 1240) and gardens were restored by the Marquise Arconati-Visconti with the help of the architect Charle-Albert, following the ideas of Viollet-le-Duc. Of the Renaissance garden created by the Counts of Renesse de Warfusée only the enclosed garden remains and this is not open to the public. The interior courtyard of the château is in the manner of an Italian Renaissance garden with flowerbeds bounded by box hedges and a fountain at the centre. To this side of the château lies the *étang de Ste-Gertrude* and in the woods is the chapel of Ste-Gertrude. In the centre of the lawn extending towards the entrance of the château is a fine two-tiered marble fountain in the Baroque style and at the edge of the park is an *arc de triomphe* erected by a member of the Arconati-Visconti family in 1803 in honour of Napoleon. The property has belonged to the Belgian State since 1921.

(1) *Apr, May, Jun, Sep and Oct: Tue, Wed, Thu, Sat, Sun and Public Holidays 10–6; Jul and Aug: Daily (except Fri) 10–6*
(2) *Charge*
(4) *Château (same times)*
(5) *Belgian State (Park: Administration des Eaux et Forêts)*

Ghent, K. L. Ledeganckstraat 35

East Flanders

13. Botanical Collection of the State University

Originally situated in the grounds of the Abbaye de Baudeloo, the collection was transferred in 1903 to the Citadelpark. The gardens are particularly well known for their orchids, *Asclepiadaceae* and succulents, best seen in June, July and August.

(1) *Sun and Public Holidays 9–noon; Wed and Thu 2–5*
(2) *Free*
(5) *State University*

Hanzinelle

Namur

14. Château de Hanzinelle

18th-cent château and garden set in the valley of the Ry Massart. Of the original symmetrical garden in the French style a few traces remain, such as a magnificent hornbeam arbour and clipped yews. It was refashioned in *c* 1885 by Mme Emile Pirmez with the help of the landscape-gardener Fuchs. Together they created the present English romantic garden with its 5 acre (2 ha) lake lying in front of the château, its rockery and lawn planted with fine trees. There is also an orangery, an ice-house and a small enclosed garden completely surrounded by a high yew hedge.

(1) Jul–Aug: Sat, Sun and Public Holidays 10–6
(2) Charge
(5) Baron and Baronne Jacques Fallon

Jehay-Bodegnée

Liège

15. Château de Jehay

The château is surrounded by water on three sides, a courtyard and stable block occupying the fourth side. The chapel is on a separate island. The château is mainly 16th cent, with a fine chequerboard façade. A bridge leads to the gardens, remodelled by the present owner. These are laid out with strict symmetry. A central pathway stretches towards an araucaria, its lower branches pruned to allow an unimpeded view. The pathway is bordered by a small wall and a stepped waterfall. Two parterres studded with pairs of conical shaped trees and other single trees of similar shape lie to either side. A path cuts transversely across the centre of the garden and disappears into a tunnel reached by narrow steps. At the top of the waterfall is a sculpture by the present owner, composed of two nymphs and known as 'The Source', The waterfall was inspired by that of the Villa d'Este (qv). There are openings at intervals in the far hedges to the right and left of the main pathway providing views of the country beyond.

The ground to one side of the château was cleared in 1974 and planted with trees. The Count has also restored an old avenue of lime trees at the end of the driveway which leads to a green lawn with a round central pond where he has placed another of his sculptures. Beyond this is a menhir (ancient standing stone) dating from 1500 BC.

(1) Mid-May–Aug: Sat, Sun and Public Holidays 2–6
(2) Charge
(4) Archaeological Museum, collections of silver, porcelain, etc (same times)
(5) Comte Guy van den Steen de Jehay

Kortrijk

West Flanders

16. West Flanders Rosarium

Garden of the Kasteel 't Hooghe comprising a collection of roses for the purpose of

instruction, tracing the history of their cultivation; a demonstration garden with a hundred or so varieties that are available commercially; and a collection of new varieties which each year are judged by an international jury and the Rose d'Or awarded to the winner. The Rosarium is best visited from the end of June to the middle of August.

(1) Daily Sunrise–Sunset
(2) Free
(5) N. V. Kasteel 't Hooghe

Liège, Domaine du Sart-Tilman

17. Botanical Gardens of Liège University

The university botanical collections owe their foundation, in 1816, to the king, Guillaume I. In 1836 they were moved to a site in Liège where, in 1944, the glasshouses were damaged by a bomb. In 1961 the decision was taken to move them again to a position close to the new university buildings in the Domaine du Sart-Tilman, which is a conservation area. In it is included part of the original park of the Château de Colonster. Work began in 1968 and continues still.

The grounds extend to 78 acres (32 ha), comprising areas of natural landscape with streams and woodland and systematic collections, collections of ornamental, aquatic and marsh plants and plants that are useful to man, a rock garden and a heath garden, as well as glasshouses. There are fine views over the valleys of the Meuse and the Ourthe.

(1) Gardens. Daily Sunrise–Sunset; Glasshouses. summer weekends and by request
(2) Free
(3) Café (weekdays)
(5) University of Liège

Loppem

West Flanders

18. Château de Loppem

19th-cent château with a maze (one of the few surviving mazes in the country) and park dating from 1859. The estate consists of 99 acres (40 ha) of park and farmland; there are two grottoes and some fine oak trees. The maze is 98 yds (90m) long and over 32 yds (30m) wide.

(1) Daily Sunrise–Sunset
(2) Charge
(4) Château (Apr–Nov: Daily, except Fri, 10–noon, 2–6)
(5) Fonds van Caloen e.s.b.l. (Park: Locality of Loppem)

BELGIUM

Malines

Antwerp

19. Vrijbroekpark

An area of great natural beauty which in the Middle Ages was Common Land, covering 100 acres (40·5 ha), planted after 1918 by the Town of Malines. It was bought in 1928 by the Province of Antwerp who laid it out as a public park. There is a fine 4 acre (2 ha) rose garden planted with 10,000 roses of 120 different species and many rare trees.

(1) *Summer: Daily 6 am–Sunset; Winter: Daily 7 am–Sunset*
(2) *Free*
(3) *Cafés*
(5) *Province of Antwerp*

Meise

Brabant

20. Domaine de Bouchout and National Botanical Garden of Belgium

The château of Bouchout, remodelled in the 1830s in neo-Gothic style, is set at the edge of a small lake and surrounded by lawns, paths and woodland. In 1879 it was bought by King Leopold II for his sister Charlotte, Empress of Mexico, after Tervuren (qv) had been destroyed, and she lived there until her death in 1927. The neighbouring property of Meise was acquired in 1882. In 1938 the Belgian State took over the main park and adjoining meadows, totalling 227 acres (93 ha), to preserve an area of parkland 6 miles (10 km) from the centre of Brussels and to create a new botanical garden.

On the south side of the park is the *Palais des Plantes*, a glasshouse complex constructed between 1947 and 1958. Of the 13 large glasshouses open to the public, ten are organized by geographical groups; two are reserved for economic plants – producing edible fruits, natural fibres, etc. – and the last is known as the Victoria hothouse. There the water is kept at a constant temperature of 30°C for the tropical water-lilies, notably the *Victoria amazonica* and the *Victoria cruziana*, whose leaves may span 6½ ft (2 m) and support the weight of a child. Rare orchids and carnivorous plants grow in hanging baskets.

The 22 smaller glasshouses are open only to specialists; the orangery in the park is a cafeteria and restaurant.

(1) *Park. Daily 9–Sunset; Glasshouses. Mon–Thu 2–5; Easter–Oct: Sun and Public Holidays 2–6*
(2) *Park: Free, Glasshouses: Charge*
(3) *Café and restaurant*
(5) *Belgian State, Ministry of Agriculture*

Morlanwelz, Chaussée de Mariemont 90

Hainaut

21. Mariemont Park

The history of the park dates back to 1546, when the first palace was built by Mary of Austria, sister of Charles V. The 16th-cent garden, and the 17th-cent garden inspired by Aranjuez (qv) that replaced it, have disappeared. (In 1668 the property passed to Louis XIV and Mariemont is depicted in *Les Maisons Royales*, the famous Gobelins tapestries woven under the direction of Lebrun.)

In 1766 Charles de Lorraine rebuilt the palace and laid out gardens in the formal manner of Schönbrunn (qv) in Austria. Part of the beech avenue from Mariemont to Morlanwelz has survived and the orangery and kitchen garden, together with the winter garden dating from the 19th cent, are now run as a school of horticulture. During the French Revolution the palace was burnt down and the property abandoned. In 1830 Nicolas Warocqué created an English landscape garden around a new palace: this was destroyed by fire in 1960.

The garden is noted for its rose garden and the many fine trees: a magnificent cedar, beeches, and chestnuts dating from the time of Charles de Lorraine, oaks and several species of lime, at their best in June and July. In early May there is a fine display of rhododendrons and azaleas. The Museum exhibits the collections of works of art bequeathed to the nation in 1917, at the same date as the park, by Raoul Warocqué.

(1) *Daily 9–4, 5 or 6*
(2) *Free*
(4) *Museum (Daily, except Mon, 10–12.30, 1.30–6)*
(5) *Belgian State*

Le Rœulx

Hainaut

22. Château du Rœulx

The château of rose-coloured brick was built in c 1740 and is set in front of a large semi-circular lawn bordered by trees. Beyond the stableyard to the south-west of the château is the rose garden. Inspired by the famous rose gardens of Pachy, now disappeared, the landscape designer, René Pechère, in 1961 converted the original kitchen garden into an octagonal rose garden, framed by two rows of limes and enclosed by walls. There are five ornamental ponds surrounded by beds. Each rose is labelled and in July over 100,000 roses are in bloom.

The orangery has been converted into a small exhibition hall. The park has fine trees and two lakes, one of which has an island with a thatched Swiss chalet on the site of a chapel where St Feuillen took refuge in c 655.

(1) 8 Apr–Sep: Daily (except Tue) 10–noon, 1.30–6

(2) Charge

(4) Château (same times)

(5) S.A.S. Prince de Cröy-Rœulx (Park: Province de Hainaut)

Tervuren

Brabant

23. Tervuren Park

From *c* 1200, when the first château was built in the centre of the St Hubert Lake by Henri I, Duke of Brabant, Tervuren was the summer residence of the dukes, sovereigns and governors of this part of present-day Belgium. Charles de Lorraine, who died there in 1780, had laid out by the architect J. A. Anneesens a *rond point* in the park, from which radiate eight avenues, and the stables in the shape of a horseshoe. The park was then neglected until it was restored by King Leopold II. He gave the château, rebuilt between 1817 and 1822, and part of the park to his sister Charlotte, Empress of Mexico, and the rest of the park was opened to the public. In 1879 the château was destroyed by fire. For the Brussels Exhibition of 1897 the great avenue of 1868 was widened and extended to the Cinquantenaire, thus linking Tervuren with the capital; fruit and vegetable gardens were laid out; and a formal garden, with an ornamental pond crowning a series of terraces dropping down to a lake, was designed by the landscape architect, Lainé.

In 1910 the Musée Royal de l'Afrique Centrale was inaugurated and two of the existing lakes were merged to form the Lake of Vossem.

The estate covers an area of 556 acres (225 ha) and the woodland borders the Forêt de Soignes.

(1) Daily

(2) Free

(4) Musée Royal de l'Afrique Centrale (Daily 9–5.30)

(5) Belgian State, Administration des Eaux et Forêts and Service du Plan Vert

Waulsort

Namur

24. Château de Freyr

The château, dating from the 16th, 17th and 18th cents, has terraced gardens that extend along the banks of the Meuse. They were designed in the manner of the *grand siècle* by Guillaume and Philippe de Beaufort-Spontin in 1759, retaining the framework of the earlier Renaissance gardens.

The designers were extremely strict in their observance of the spirit of Descartes and a module regulates all the proportions, the axes and perspectives. As at Vaux le Vicomte (qv), France, designed by Le Nôtre, there are no flowers. The round pond and fountain lie on the central axis, flanked

by parterres and basins parallel to the river. On a crossing axis an oval pond is supplied by a cascade, and beyond and above this there is a Louis XVI domed pavilion with stucco decoration by the Moretti. The best view of the gardens and river may be had from here.

Lime trees, topiary and bosquets are features of the garden, the last surviving French garden in Belgium, and Freyr is famous for its 33 orange trees. These were bought from Stanislas Leszczyński, king of Poland and father-in-law of Louis XV, and by the standards of the Low Countries they are of an exceptional age.

(1) Jul–Aug: Sat, Sun and Public Holidays 2–6.30

(2) Charge

(5) Baronne Francis Bonaert

Zottegem

East Flanders

25. Château de Leeuwergem

Perfect example of a Louis XV château and garden, famous for its open-air theatre which seats 1,200. The stage, auditorium and box seats are of clipped hornbeam. The garden is a blend of the classic French and the English romantic styles. The château is set on a rectangular island with symmetrical parterres and with the water of the 5 acre (2 ha) *pièce d'eau* stretching out before it. The far end is guarded by two sphinxes and great copper beeches. The gardens continue beyond this to a pool. To the east an obelisk is set among the trees. A winding path through woodland leads to a smaller lake with an islet on which there is a tomb.

On the north-east side of the château is a kitchen garden and pavilion.

(1) Mid-May–Sep: Sun 10–5

(2) Charge

(5) Baron and Baronne Guy della Faille D'Huysse

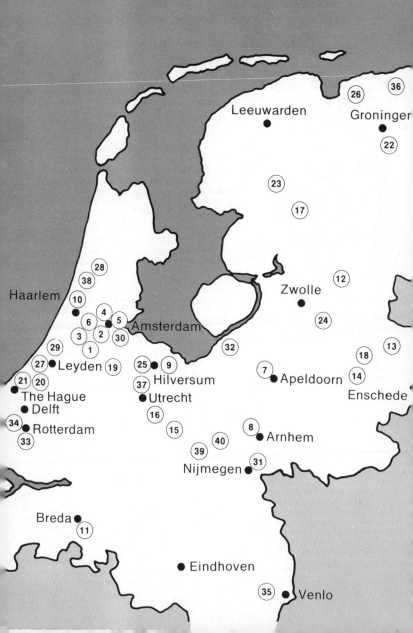

HOLLAND

Kilometres 0 10 20 30
Miles 0 10 20

Leeuwarden

Groninger

㉖

㊱

㉒

㉓

⑰

Haarlem

㉘

㊳

⑩

④

⑤

⑥

③ ② ⑫

Amsterdam

① ㉚

Zwolle

㉙

㉔

㉗ Leyden ⑲

㉝

㉜

The Hague

Delft

⑯

⑮

Rotterdam

㉞

㉝

Breda

⑪

Eindhoven

Venlo

㉟

Utrecht

㊲

Hilversum

㉕ ⑨

⑦

Apeldoorn

⑬

⑱

⑭

Enschede

⑧ Arnhem

㊵

㊴

Nijmegen ㉛

Amstelveen

North Holland

1. Jacques P. Thijsse Park

A wild garden laid out in 1939–40 by the Municipal Public Gardens Department of Amstelveen. There are marsh and woodland plants and water gardens.

(*1*) *Daily*
(*2*) *Free*
(*5*) *Amstelveen Council*

Amsterdam

2. Amstelpark

When the 1972 Floriade, the horticultural exhibition, came to an end, a park was created that is now one of the most interesting and beautiful parks in Amsterdam. It covers approx 95 acres (38 ha) and has acquired many animals from the Amsterdam Zoo.

Especially worthy of note are the Rhododendron Valley with an invisible sprinkling system, the Iris Garden with a collection of Japanese *Iris kaempferi*, the Rose Garden with 160 species, the Dahlia Garden, laid out in landscape style, the Belgian garden and the Conifer Garden. There are glasshouses and pavilions and, beyond the lake at Amstelrust, a nature reserve where, in accordance with the theories of L. D. Le Roy, nature is allowed to take her natural course. There is also an area devoted to plants in danger of extinction.

(*1*) *Daily 6.30 am–Sunset*
(*2*) *Free*
(*3*) *Restaurant*
(*5*) *Amsterdam Council*

Amsterdam

3. Het Amsterdamse Bos

Woodland and parkland on the southern side of the city laid out since 1934. The area covers 2,350 acres (952 ha) and lies 13 ft (4m) below sea level. It offers facilities for a number of recreations and there is a woodland museum (Bosmuseum).

(*1*) *Daily*
(*2*) *Free*
(*3*) *Café*
(*4*) *Bosmuseum (Easter–mid-Oct: Daily 10–4; mid-Oct–Easter: Daily, except Thu, 25 and 26 Dec and 1 Jan, 10–4)*
(*5*) *Amsterdam Council*

Amsterdam

4. Artsenijhof

Three gardens with medicinal herbs assembled according to the ailments for which they offer a cure. It was laid out at the time of the Floriade in 1972.

One of the gardens is planted with herbs for complaints of the stomach, liver, heart and lungs, another for the common cold and constipation, while in the third are remedies

for toothache and throat infections. All the plants are labelled and name the disease for which they offer a remedy.

(*1*) *Summer: Daily Sunrise–Sunset*
(*2*) *Free*
(*5*) *Amsterdam Council*

Amsterdam, Plantage Middenlaan 2

5. Botanical Garden of Amsterdam University

The botanical garden dates from 1618, when it comprised rectangular beds in which medicinal herbs were cultivated. In *c* 1870 these rectangular beds were abandoned and the garden was radically altered. Glasshouses were added and the garden was laid out in the manner of a landscape garden. The orangery dates from this period.

The plant collection comprises all the more advanced plant families together with sporophytes such as ferns. Apart from the tropical collection, there is a large collection of sub-tropical plants which includes palm trees, tree-ferns, a comprehensive collection of plants from the Cape and from Australia and a large number of plants in cultivation.

(*1*) *Mon–Fri 10–12.30, 1.30–4; Sat, Sun and Public Holidays 1–4*
(*2*) *Charge*
(*5*) *University of Amsterdam*

Amsterdam—Buitenveldert, van der Boechorststraat 8

6. Botanical Garden of the Free University

Founded in 1954, the botanical garden was moved to its present site in 1967. It contains a wild garden, a systematic garden, glasshouses, including one for succulents, a fern house and tropical houses. On the dyke along the Kalfjeslaan there is an arboretum.

From the middle of May to the middle of October a large collection of tropical and sub-tropical plants is on display outside.

(*1*) *Mon–Fri 8–4.30*
(*2*) *Free*
(*5*) *Free University of Amsterdam*

Apeldoorn

Gelderland

7. Het Loo

The Stadtholder William III, King of England from 1689 to 1702, bought this estate in 1684 and built a palatial hunting lodge, designed by the architect Daniel Marot. This today is known as the Palace of Het Loo. At the same time he gave orders that a

French garden should be laid out. William's physician-in-ordinary, Walter Harris, was a keen and observant botanist and he left a detailed and accurate description of these gardens on which the model for restoration has been based. This will take place in the near future.

The site, at the edge of the Veluwe heath and with numerous streams, was ideal for this type of garden with its pools, lakes and fountains. From engravings by Gerard Valck and others it is possible to gain a clear picture of the size of this garden. People from all over Europe came to see this 'wonder of the world'.

With the arrival of the French and the proclamation of the Batavian Republic these spendid gardens fell into decay and were ultimately destroyed. Then, in 1807, Louis Bonaparte gave instructions for the design of a landscape garden in the English style. King William I and his successors did a great deal to improve the 1,625 acres (650 ha) of park, planting a large number of trees, many of which still survive. The west part has maintained its natural character and there is a look-out post from which wild boar and deer can be observed. The east part around the palace has beautiful water gardens with three lakes and fine trees, including some indigenous species. Behind the Royal Stables stands the oldest Douglas fir wood in the Netherlands, planted in the mid-19th cent. Noteworthy, too, are the tulip-trees, mammoth trees, swamp cypresses and some enormous specimens of the European larch.

The Orange Museum in the palace and the Royal Stables, containing a permanent exhibition of coaches, vintage cars and horse-drawn sleighs, are well worth a visit.

(1) Park. Daily 9 at Pijnboomlaan entrance or 10 at Amersfoortseweg–Sunset (6 latest). Arboretum, glasshouses and orangery: by appointment
(2) Charge (including museum and stables)
(3) Tea
(4) Museum (Daily 10–5). Stables (Apr–Oct: Daily 10–5)
(5) Dutch State

Arnhem

Gelderland

8. Herb Garden of the Netherlands Open-air Museum

The botanical garden, dating from 1927, contains a monastery garden which is a replica of the oldest known herb garden in Europe, that of the monastery of St Gallen in Switzerland (an abbey founded in the Middle Ages by monks from Scotland and Ireland). Other features are culinary and medicinal herbs and plants which produce dyes; also herbs that play a role in folklore.

The park has original buildings from all over the Netherlands, re-erected here in an attempt to show the daily life of the Dutch in previous centuries. There is a paper mill, village school, brewery and farmhouse kitchens.

(1) Apr–Oct: Mon–Sat 9–5; Sun 10–5; Jun–Aug closes 5.30
(2) Charge
(3) Restaurant
(5) Ministry of Cultural Affairs, Recreation and Social Welfare

Baarn

Utrecht

9. Cantonspark

Cantonspark was originally laid out as a private garden. It was bequeathed to the State University of Utrecht and transformed into a botanical garden with lawns, exotic trees, herbaceous borders and a border with succulents.

The winter garden building is one of the tallest glasshouses in the Netherlands. There are plants from the Cape which are placed outside in tubs in summer, an interesting collection of orchids, carnivorous plants, *Bromeliaceae* and other tropical plants.

(1) Mon–Fri 9–noon, 2–4.30
(2) Free
(5) State University of Utrecht

Bloemendaal

North Holland

10. Thijsse's Hof

Laid out as a wild garden, this specializes in the flora of Kennemerland – plants of the dunes, woods and marshland. An aviary is included in the 10 acres (4 ha) of garden.

(1) Apr–Oct: Tue–Fri 9–noon, 1.30–5; Sat 9–5; Sun 9–1; Nov–Mar: Tue–Fri 9–noon, 1.30–4; Sat 9–4. Closed 25 and 26 Dec, 1 Jan, 30 Apr and in bad weather
(2) Free
(3) Café
(5) Thijsse's Hof Institute at Bloemendaal

Breda, Catharinastraat

North Brabant

11. Kruidentuin Begijnhof

The charm of the herb garden lies in the 16th-cent atmosphere of this typically Dutch beguinage (beguines were members of a religious lay sisterhood not bound by vows). In 1969 the Town Council had the herb garden laid out following the historical evidence and planted with medicinal and culinary herbs and herbs for warding off the evil influence of witches. There is also a bleachery. A herb shop can be found round the corner.

(1) Daily 8–6
(2) Free
(5) Breda Council

Dedemsvaart

Overijssel

12. Tuinen van Mien Ruys

The principal feature of the garden, named after the Dutch landscape architect, Miss Ruys, is a display of various types of small garden: a garden with ornamental grasses and a millstone filled with water; a 100 ft (30 m) herbaceous border; a wild garden with a pond and a globe from which water trickles down on to boulders and a large collection of shade-loving plants.

There is a water garden, a bog garden, and a rock garden, an old-fashioned herb garden with a well and a small town garden containing tall ornamental grasses and a variety of shrubs, perennials and conifers. It covers an area of 5 acres (2 ha).

(1) *May–Oct: Mon–Sat 10–5*
(2) *Charge*
(5) *Tuinen van Mien Ruys Foundation*

Delden

Overijssel

13. Kasteel Twickel

The rectangular ornamental garden with yew topiary was laid out by Hugo Poortman. The park as it now stands was laid out in the 19th cent by J. D. Zocher and E. C. A. Petzold, and Daniel Marot played an earlier part in its design. From the end of May to the beginning of June there is a display of rhododendrons and azaleas.

(1) *Wed and Sat conducted tours by appointment: 1.30, 2.45 and 4*
(2) *Charge*
(5) *Twickel Institute*

Diepenheim

Overijssel

14. Kasteel Warmelo

The lay-out of the gardens is geometrical, with canals, clipped hedges and 18th-cent statuary. There is a garden with a pond and rosebeds and a 'green room', a garden of fuchsias enclosed by green hedges with a well in the centre. Beyond the canals is the pinetum.

From the middle of May to the end of June there is a fine display of rhododendrons and azaleas.

(1) *Mid-May–mid-Sep: Tue and Thu 1.30– 4.30; first Sun of the month, Ascension Day and Whit Mon noon–5*
(2) *Charge*
(5) *Dr Arenarius*

Doorn

Utrecht

15. Von Gimborn Arboretum

This private collection, covering approx 65 acres (26 ha), was laid out in the 1920s by Mr von Gimborn in a landscape style. As

well as the many deciduous trees, shrubs and an interesting heather garden, it contains a number of conifers, some of which measure as much as 131 ft (40m).

(1) *Mon–Fri 9–4.30*
(2) *Free*
(5) *State University of Utrecht*

Driebergen-Rijsenburg

Utrecht

16. Heather Garden

A heather garden lying among Scots pines and woodland plants laid out in 1955. There are approx 400 cultivars and species of the calluna and erica genera.

(1) *Daily*
(2) *Free*
(3) *Driebergen Council*

Frederiksoord, Majoor van Swietenlaan 15

Drenthe

17. Gerard Adriaan van Swieten Horticultural College

Numbered arrows indicate a route through the most interesting parts of the garden. In the rose garden, which was laid out at the end of the 19th cent, there are espaliered pear trees. There is also an instruction and demonstration border of herbaceous plants, a sorbus collection and a rose collection. In spring the chaenomeles are spectacular. To the right of the main path there is a demonstration garden of clipped hedges.

(1) *Whitsun–Sep: Mon–Fri 9–noon, 2–5; Sun 2–5*
(2) *Charge*
(5) *Benevolent Society at Frederiksoord*

Goor

Overijssel

18. Kasteel Weldam

The formal garden of Weldam Castle was laid out in 1886 by the landscape gardener Hugo Poortman, evidently influenced by his master, the Frenchman Edouard André. The principal features of the garden are clipped hedges, a maze and a pleached beech walk; a swamp cypress and a fir tree are both 150 years old.

(1) *Mon–Fri 10–noon, 1–4.30*
(2) *Charge*
(5) *Countess Solms-Bentinck*

Haarzuilens

Utrecht

19. Kasteel de Haar

The formal garden and landscape park were

designed by Henri Copijn in *c* 1895, at the same time as the castle was rebuilt in a neo-Gothic style. There is a rose garden, a forecourt with flowering plants and a canal in the manner of Le Nôtre.

(1) *Jan–mid-Aug and mid-Oct–Dec: Daily 9–6*
(2) *Charge*
(4) *Castle (mid-Feb–Jul and Oct–mid-Nov: Mon–Sat 9–noon, 1.30–5; Sun 1.30–5; Aug and Sep: Tue and Wed 10–noon*
(5) *T. F. E. H. Baron van Zuylen van Nyevelt de Haar*

The Hague
20. Park Clingendael

The original formal garden is known only from engravings. In the 19th cent the estate was altered first by the landscape gardener J. D. Zocher and later by E. C. A. Petzold. They created a landscape park with magnificent vistas and tall deciduous trees planted in groups.

Notable features are a small Dutch garden with low clipped box hedges and red gravel paths at the foot of a flight of steps and a rose garden with modern as well as old-fashioned roses. There is a Japanese garden, the only one in the Netherlands, with a tea house and a small red lacquered bridge, Buddhist lanterns, moss ground cover and, in spring, the spectacular beauty of the Japanese azaleas. There is also a small wood with radiating paths and a large collection of rhododendrons, a paddock and a children's tiled playground with an old serpentine wall (formerly a protected place for espaliered fruit trees).

(1) *Japanese Garden. Mid-May–mid-Jun: Daily 8.30–8. Main Garden. Daily*
(2) *Free*
(3) *Café*
(5) *The Hague Council*

The Hague
21. Rosarium Westbroekpark

The park contains seven rose gardens, planted with modern floribunda, Hybrid Tea, climbing and miniature roses, all labelled with their names and that of the grower.

The annual international rose festival held here is a great occasion: a permanent committee of inspection awards points for growth performance, flower abundance, fragrance and colour, resistance to weather conditions and disease. This is one of the few gardens in Holland where the public is allowed to walk on the grass.

(1) *Mid-Apr–mid-Oct: Daily 8–8*
(2) *Free*
(3) *Restaurant*
(5) *The Hague Council*

Haren, Kerklaan 30
Groningen
22. Hortus de Wolf

The history of this collection dates back to 1642, when the apothecary Henricus Munting founded his herb garden. The original lay-out of a wild garden with the maximum variety of growing conditions has been retained: there is grassland, dry rock and dry slope, calcareous and acid soil, ponds and heathland with small marsh pools. There is also a large tropical glasshouse which is divided into five climatic sections: monsoon, savannah, desert, sub-tropical and tropical.

(1) *Mon–Fri 1.30–4.45; Sat 9–4.45; Sun 2–4.45*
(2) *Charge*
(3) *Café*
(5) *State University of Groningen*

Heerenveen
Friesland
23. President Kennedy Landscape Garden

This is an experimental area laid out according to the theories of L. G. Le Roy. It covers 3,281 ft (1 km) by 65 ft (20m) in the middle of a dual carriage-way that runs through one of the suburbs of Heerenveen. It was started in 1966 on the south side with strips of land planted with trees, heather and marsh plants. There are alternating low-lying and elevated parts made with dry walls, heaps of rubble and sleepers. Using various kinds of soil (peat, sand, loam and lime), different plant environments have been created. Indigenous as well as exotic species have been planted, both mixed and side by side. The pruned and dead parts of the plants are not removed and no artificial fertilizer or insecticides are used.

(1) *Daily*
(2) *Free*
(5) *Heerenveen Council*

Heino
Overijssel
24. Kasteel van het Nijenhuis

19th-cent landscape garden with a beech hedge clipped in the shape of a tunnel; also 18th-cent statuary. There are canals and a moat, and a number of 17th-cent outbuildings. The castle houses the famous Hannema-de-Stueurs Collection of works of art.

(1) *Tue, Wed, Thu 1–5*
(2) *Free*
(4) *House (Summer: Daily 10–5; Winter: Daily 10–3)*
(5) *Province of Overijssel*

Hilversum, r.d. Lindelaan 25

North Holland

25. Pinetum Blijdenstein

Founded in 1928, this is a small, well-kept pinetum with mature conifers. There are two small glasshouses for non-hardy conifers. The collection comprises approx 225 species and 200 varieties.

(2) Mon–Fri (except Public Holidays) 10– 12.30, 1.30–4
(2) Charge
(5) Botanical Garden of the University of Amsterdam

Leens

Groningen

26. Verhildersum Bulb Garden and Park

A lime avenue leads to Verhildersumborg, a moated castle built in the 14th cent and transformed into a manor house in the 17th and 18th cents. It lies opposite the old-Carolingian Leemsterterp and is surrounded by an interesting landscape of 'house mounds' *(terpen)*. An old canal encircles the house and the formal garden in front of it. Apart from a herb collection, there is a display of typical Groningen borgenflora, mainly bulbous and tuberous plants that flower in the Spring.

The house has been a museum since 1953 and, among other items on display, there is a permanent exhibition on the history of the tidal flats and the land.

(1) Easter–1 Nov: Daily (except Mon) 11–6
(2) Free
(3) Tea, coffee, sandwiches on request
(4) House (same times)
(5) Leens Council

Leyden, Rapenburg 73

South Holland

27. Botanic Garden of the State University

Founded on 13 April 1587, the Leyden Botanic Garden is one of the oldest in Europe. Planting was begun when the famous botanist Carolus Clusius was appointed professor at the university. More than a thousand different species and varieties of plants were cultivated. Fortunately there is in existence a plan and a planting list of the garden which provide detailed information about the plant collection and design of the garden from 1594 to 1609, the year in which Clusius died. This made it possible in 1932 to reconstruct the garden not far from its original site.

Since Clusius's day the garden has been enlarged at various times. The most radical extension was effected in 1818. The glasshouses, built between 1850 and 1890, were later replaced by a large group of modern hothouses, and in most of the garden formal

planting was substituted for the landscape design. The laburnum planted by Clusius in 1601 survives and there is also a tulip-tree of *c* 1715 and a copper beech of *c* 1820. The orangery was built between 1740 and 1744.

Dr Philip Franz Balthazar von Siebold, who practised medicine in Japan between 1823 and 1829, presented the garden with various plants native to that country, some of which he was the first to import into Europe: a Japanese quince and an *Akebia quinata*; also a *Juglans ailantifolia*.

In the systematic garden, the plants are arranged according to families. In it stands a bust of the Swedish botanist Linnaeus, who spent some time at Leyden in 1735.

Among the noteworthy trees in the garden are the fern-leaf beech (1818), the Caucasian wing-nut (1818), the weeping beech (*c* 1840), and the Japanese pagoda-tree (*c* 1850). The greater part of the plant collection is to be found in the glasshouses: plants attracting much attention are the *Victoria regia* which flowers every summer in the Victoria House, surrounded by a large number of tropical plants, and the orchids. Tall plants, such as the banana, are to be found in Hothouses 2 and 3.

(1) Garden. Apr–Sep: Mon–Sat 9–5; Sun 10–4; Oct–Mar: Mon–Sat 9–noon, 1.30–4. Glasshouses. Apr–Sep: Mon–Fri 9–12.30, 1.30–4.30.; Oct–Mar: Mon–Fri 9–noon, 1.30–4
(2) Charge
(5) State University of Leyden

Limmen, Dusseldorpweg 81

North Holland

28. Bulb Garden

Specialized collection of bulbs assembled by P. Boschman that are no longer available commercially – tulips, hyacinths and daffodils. The collection is of historical and scientific interest.

(1) Apr, May and early Jun: Mon–Sat 9–5
(2) Free
(5) Netherlands Society for Furthering the Scientific Propagation of Ornamental Plants

---

Lisse, Stationsweg 166A

South Holland

29. Keukenhof

In spring the Dutch bulb-growers arrange a magnificent display of more than six million narcissi, tulips, crocuses and hyacinths in the 70 acre (28 ha) park and in the glasshouses and roofed-in area. There are fine trees and shrubs, water gardens and a heather garden and, at one end of the park, a windmill from Groningen; also a collection of sculpture. Exhibitions and demonstrations of flower arranging are held in the Queen Juliana Pavilion.

The garden is laid out on what was originally the hunting grounds of Jacqueline of Hainaut. The estate passed into the hands of the Van Lynden family and it was from the Van Lyndens that the Dutch bulbgrowers first leased the property in 1949.

(1) *23 Mar–21 May: Daily 8–8*
(2) *Charge*
(3) *Restaurant and coffee shop*
(4) *Flower shop*
(5) *Keukenhof Institute*

Muiden

North Holland

30. Kruidhof van het Muiderslot

In the days of P. C. Hooft, the famous 17th-cent Dutch poet and governor of Muiderslot, the herb garden was indispensable to life at the castle. It produced medicinal herbs, dyes for wool and cotton, culinary herbs, fruit and flowers. The plants and layout of the garden are based on documentation from the 17th cent so that the 1955 reconstruction is historically accurate. An attempt has been made to adhere, as far as possible, to the bulbs, and the apple and pear varieties of that period, which makes an interesting study. The herb garden contains some 400 species.

Also in 1955 the plum trees to the west of the castle and the elms on the ramparts were replanted following the original design.

(1) *Tue–Sat 9–5; Sun 1–5*
(2) *Free*
(3) *Café*
(4) *Castle (Mon–Sat 9–5 pm; Sun 1–5)*
(5) *Ministry of Cultural Affairs, Recreation and Social Welfare*

Nijmegen

Gelderland

31. Botanical Garden of the University of Nijmegen

Laid out in 1959, the principal part of the garden is planted according to the theories of the late Dr J. P. Thysse, the plants grouped in the manner in which they grow naturally in the area. There is an oak and beech wood, an oak and hornbeam wood and an ash and elm wood. The alpinum is laid out according to the geographical origins of the plants, and there is a sunken road with ferns and mosses and areas of heath and bog land.

(1) *Summer: Daily 9–8; Winter: Daily 9–6*
(2) *Free*
(5) *University of Nijmegen*

Putten, Garderenseweg 93

Gelderland

32. Schovenhorst Arboretum and Pinetum

Over a century ago an area of approx 200 acres (81 ha) of heathland was bought at public auction by J. H. Schober, a barrister from Utrecht, in order to grow new varieties of conifers. This was the start of what is now an impressive collection, comprising among other things, the Large and the Small Pinetum and the Arboretum, where trees have been planted according to their country of origin under the botanical geographical system of Engler and Prantl. The total property now covers an area of approx 815 acres (330 ha)

(1) *Mon–Sat 9–5*
(2) *Charge*
(5) *Institute of the Estate of Schovenhorst*

Rotterdam, Honingerdijk 64

33. Arboretum Trompenburg

The Arboretum Trompenburg lies sheltered by the dyke which through the ages has been Rotterdam's main line of defence agains the floods of the tidal river Maas.

Outstanding species of trees from Europe, Africa, Asia and America, crowned by a collection of stout cedars, have been brought together here. A well-balanced layout accentuates the natural effect both of specimens and groups. About 2,000 varieties of trees and shrubs, collected by five generations of the Van Hoey Smith family, are to be found in the Trompenburg catalogue. It covers an area of approx 13 acres (5 ha) and is divided into five main parts.

The central part, dating from 1820, is laid out in the English landscape style. The cedar collection, planted later, is the pride of Trompenburg. The oldest trees in the Arboretum originate from plantings in 1820, 1870 and 1900; the younger trees from 1928 onwards and new species and varieties are still being added. It is especially worth visiting from April to June for the rhododendrons.

(1) *Mon–Sat 9–5*
(2) *Tickets from the Tourist Information Office, Stadhuisplein 19, Rotterdam; or by writing to Mr J. R. P. van Hoey Smith, Groene Wetering 46, Rotterdam*
(5) *Arboretum Trompenburg Foundation*

Rotterdam

34. Kralingse Bos Wild Garden

In 1911 the Municipal Council of Rotterdam decided to lay out a large park around the lake, the Kralingse Plas. The level of this land was first raised by pumping mud from the Waal and Merwe ports and, after 1945, this was again raised with rubble from the bombed city and finally earthed over. The wild garden, laid out in 1971 and covering an area of about 7 acres (2·8 ha), is situated on a secluded stretch of land on the north shore of the Kralingse Plas. There are roughly 350 species of plants, the seeds of which are harvested and exchanged with other gardens of this kind.

(1) Daily Sunrise–Sunset
(2) Free
(5) Rotterdam Council

Steyl, Maashock 26
Limburg
35. Botanical Garden Jochum-Hof

The garden lies on the east bank of the River Maas. It has a magnificent collection of plants, some extremely rare, some less so, from all parts of the world, collected by missionaries from Steyl and planted by Father Jochum.

There is a glasshouse with tropical and sub-tropical plants and a newly designed herb garden and a heather garden. The wild garden concentrates on plants indigenous to North Limburg. There is also an information centre where fossils from the clay pits of Tegelen are exhibited.

(1) May–Sep: Daily (except Carnival Season) 10–6; Oct–Apr: Daily (except 25 Dec and 1 Jan) 2–5
(2) Charge
(5) Institute Botanical Garden Jochum-Hof

Uithuizen
Groningen
36. Menkemaborg

The ornamental garden comprises a maze, topiary, roses and rose walks, statuary and a tea house. In the orchard are apple and pear trees and a pleached pear alley, and the herb garden contains culinary as well as medicinal herbs. The manor house, now a museum, lies in the centre of these gardens. Beyond the canals is grassland with fishponds and a dovecot.

The gardens were restored in 1924, when use was made of the original scheme dating from the first half of the 18th cent.

(1) Daily 9–6
(2) Charge
(3) Café
(4) Museum (same times)
(5) Menkemaborg Museum

Utrecht, De Uithof, Heidelberglaan 2
37. Fort Hoofddijk

In 1965 Fort Hoofddijk was made into a rock garden, mainly for alpine plants. The stone, the plants and the seeds came from all over the world. There is a large sys-

HOLLAND

tematic garden with woodland and herbaceous plants.

(1) Mon–Fri 9–4.30
(2) Free
(5) State University of Utrecht

Velsen-Haarlem
North Holland
38. Beeckestijn

In 1953 Beeckestijn was restored to its 18th-cent appearance. The reconstruction of the garden was based on the 1772 design of the garden designer J. G. Michaël. At the back of the house is a Baroque garden with a hollow (dry, which is unusual in Holland) and a pond at the intersection of a number of avenues. There is also a herb garden with many of the plants grown in an 18th-cent herb garden and a flower garden with a rose pergola and three serpentine walls. The far end of the park to the rear of the house is landscaped, the earliest example of landscaping in Zuid-Kennemerland.

(1) Daily
(2) Free
(3) Café
(4) Museum (Jun–Sep; Tue–Sat 10–noon, 2–5; Sun 2–5; Oct–May: Daily, except Mon, 2–5)
(5) Velsen Council

Wageningen, Gen. Foulkesweg 94
Gelderland
39. Arboretum Belmonte

In 1951 the replanting of the arboretum, comprising approx 40 acres (16 ha), which had been badly damaged during World War II, was taken on by the Agricultural College of Wageningen for purposes of instruction and research. Ornamental trees and shrubs are grown here which are of great value to those who plant trees.

Of particular interest are the maples, apple trees, prunus, oaks, philadelphus, rhododendrons, hamamelis, sorbus, thorns, elms and birches. Visit in April and May, September and October.

(1) Daily 8–Sunset
(2) Free
(5) Wageningen Agricultural College

Wageningen, Gen. Foulkesweg 37
40. Arboretum de Dreyen

This is a botanical garden of an earlier date than the Belmonte (qv above) laid out around the Laboratory for Plant Taxonomy and Geography. It contains a collection of ornamental shrubs and hardy perennials as well as a number of conifers. Special mention should be made of the rose garden with wild roses, moss roses, and old cultivars.

(1) Daily 8–Sunset
(2) Free
(5) Wageningen Agricultural College

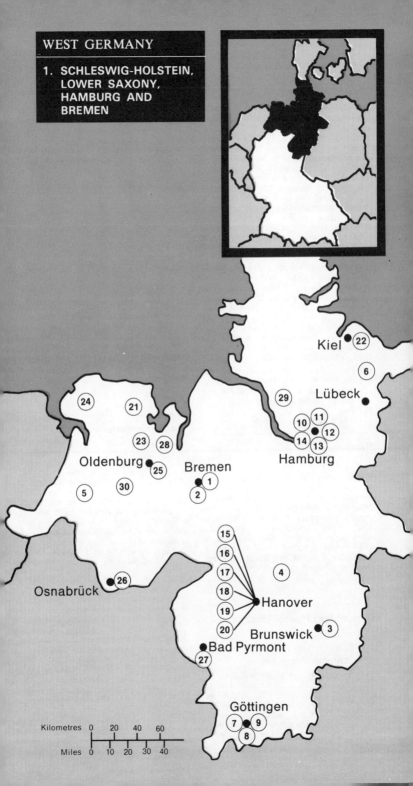

WEST GERMANY

1. SCHLESWIG-HOLSTEIN,
LOWER SAXONY,
HAMBURG AND
BREMEN

Kiel ●22

6

29   Lübeck ●

24   21   10 11
              ●12
23 28   14 13
Oldenburg ●   Hamburg
        25
       Bremen
5   30   ●1
            2

        15
        16
        17   4
        18   ● Hanover
        19
        20   Brunswick
Osnabrück ●26   ● 3
        Bad Pyrmont
        ●27

        Göttingen
        7 ●9
        8

Kilometres 0   20   40   60

Miles 0   10   20   30   40

Bremen, Marcusallee 60

1. Botanical Garden and Rhododendron Park

The Rhododendron Park was established in 1936–38, when the German Rhododendron Society was founded. The Society retains a close connection with the park, which has as a result become internationally famous. It is now part of the Botanical Garden, which was created in 1949–51. This covers an area of 86 acres (35 ha) and contains 8,000 varieties of plants divided into sections. The largest of these is the geographical section containing plants from Africa, America, Asia, Australia and the Mediterranean region. There is a heather garden, a display house for *Ericaceae*, an azalea museum, a display house for the fuchsia collection, one for tropical rhododendrons and a glasshouse for tropical and sub-tropical rhododendrons from Central Asia, the Himalayas, Burma, Tibet, China, Formosa and southern Japan. In all there is a collection of approx 1,600 different varieties and species of rhododendrons and the fuchsia collection comprises approx 350 varieties and species. Visit in June to see the rhododendrons at their best.

(*1*) *Park. Daily 7.30–Sunset. Botanical Garden. Apr–Sep: Daily 7.30–Sunset. Rhododendron House. Mon–Fri and Sun 10–4; Sat noon–4*
(*2*) *Free*
(*3*) *Snack Bar*

Bremen

2. Bürgerpark

Together with the city woods, the grounds cover 499 acres (202 ha). The park was planned in 1866 by Frederick William Benque and created on what had been marshy cattle pasture. It was extended in 1907 by the creation of the city woods. There is a variety of indigenous trees, a yellow-wood, a locust tree, a tulip-tree, a Caucasian wing-nut and North American sweet-gums as well as rhododendrons.

(*1*) *Daily*
(*2*) *Free*

Brunswick, Humboldtstrasse 1

Lower Saxony

3. Botanical Garden of the Technical University

Founded in 1840, the garden is situated by the River Oker. It covers almost 4 acres (1·6 ha) and is chiefly a garden for botanical research, best visited during the summer. There are marsh and aquatic plants, trees, which include many conifers, and a variety of shrubs. The alpine garden contains plants from alpine and sub-alpine mountains, the Prairies and the Steppes, but the area is too polluted for high-alpine plants.

The garden has areas for medicinal plants and for systematic grouping, and there is also a pergola and a fern gully. The glasshouses include one for succulents, one for plants from the tropical rain forests, one for tropical and some sub-tropical plants, an orchid house and a cultivation house which also has some unusual plants such as *Welwitschia mirabilis* from South-West Africa and the rootless fern *Psilotum triquetum*.

(*1*) *Garden. Mon–Fri 8–5; Sat and Sun 8–noon. Glasshouses. Tue–Thu 1–4*
(*2*) *Free*

Celle, Wehlstrasse

Lower Saxony

4. Französischer Garten

A park was laid out in the 16th cent and after 1670 remodelled in the formal French style by Henri Perronet, who also built the orangery, which since 1927 has housed the Regional Institute of Apiculture. There is a lake and an avenue of 250 lime trees in four rows which was created by René Dahuron, Perronet's successor, and renewed and extended in 1951–3. The southern part of the park was remodelled in the English style after 1820.

(*1*) *Daily*
(*2*) *Free*

Clemenswerth

Lower Saxony

5. Clemenswerth

A typical 18th-cent park located north-east of Meppen. The hunting lodge was built in 1737–47 by the Westphalian master-builder Johann Conrad Schlaun. The park covers 42 acres (17 ha) and has eight avenues radiating out from the lodge. It was probably designed by Dominique Girard. There is an avenue of lime trees 850 yds (800 m) long and a yew hedge over 250 yds (230 m) long, 6–9 ft (2–3 m) wide and over 200 years old.

(*1*) *Daily*
(*2*) *Free*

Eutin

Schleswig-Holstein

6. Schlosspark

The park is on one side of the Grosser Eutiner Lake, covering 36 acres (15 ha), and was laid out in the Baroque manner in *c* 1700. It was remodelled by Daniel Rastedt at the end of the 18th cent in the English landscape style. It surrounds the *schloss* and contains indigenous trees as well as Indian bean-trees and other exotic trees, a double lime avenue and various monuments, one of which is a memorial to Carl Maria von Weber, the composer. There is an open-air stage.

(1) Daily
(2) Free
(3) Café
(4) Schloss (Mid-May–Sep: Daily, except Mon, guided tours at 11, 3, 4)

Göttingen, Büsgenweg 2

Lower Saxony

7. Forestry Botanical Garden and Arboretum of Göttingen University

This was founded in 1971–2 and is not yet completed. It covers 74 acres (30 ha) and specializes in trees of the northern temperate zone. Visit in the spring and autumn.

(1) Mon–Sat 7–6
(2) Free

Göttingen, Grisebachstrasse 1a

8. New Botanical Garden of Göttingen University

This was founded in 1967 and is still under construction. Its special features are the flora of Central Europe and woodland flora of the world's temperate zones. There is a special section for economic plants from the tropics.

(1) Daily until 4
(2) Free

Göttingen, Untere Karspüle 1

9. Old Botanical Garden of Göttingen University

The park was founded in 1736 and today covers 12 acres (5 ha). It contains a comprehensive collection of alpine plants. The glasshouses contain orchids, *Bromeliaceae*, ferns, succulents and a fine collection of insectivorous plants. The alpine plants are at their best from April to July. The giant tropical water-lily, *Victoria regia*, may be seen flowering from July to October.

(1) Summer: Mon–Sat 7–6; Winter: Mon–Sat 8–4; Sun and Public Holidays 8–noon
(2) Garden: Free; Glasshouses: Charge

Hamburg

10. Ausstellungspark 'Planten un Blomen' and Old Botanical Garden

Hamburg's most popular park has three times been the site of the International Horticultural Exhibition. It was created by Karl Plomin in 1934–5 for the Federal

Horticultural Show in 1936 and remodelled in 1953 and 1963. Since 1973 it has included the city's old botanical garden. The park consists of ornamental gardens and of larger recreational areas. There is a rose garden, a rich assortment of shrubs, a magnificent iris collection – in particular *Iris kaempferi* – herb gardens and a warm pool with tropical aquatic plants, also a large landscaped lake.

The botanical garden, founded in 1821, includes an alpine garden, a palm house, a cactus collection and a glasshouse for the giant water-lily *Victoria regia*, as well as orchids and a fine specimen of *Lapageria rosea*.

(1) Daily 8 am–11.30 pm
(2) Charge
(3) Revolving restaurant in television tower

Hamburg, Flottbek

11. Botanical Garden of Hamburg University

The garden, covering 58 acres (23·8 ha), was founded in 1971 and opens to the public in 1979. It contains approx 20,000 varieties of plants from all regions of the world. Glasshouses contain tropical and sub-tropical plants. There will also be a systematic section, plants arranged by geographical grouping, an alpinum, collections of rhododendrons, roses, irises, lilies, perennial plants, conifers, medicinal plants, economic plants, protected plants and other specialized collections. It is one of West Germany's most modern and instructive botanical gardens.

(1) Daily 7–Sunset
(2) Free

Hamburg

12. Elbchaussee

The Elbchaussee, a 5 mile (8 km) avenue, is bordered by about 15 parks, such as Donners Park (with fine trees); a rose garden of 10 acres (4 ha); Schröders Elbpark, a landscaped park; the Hindenburgpark, the Reemtsmapark and the Wesselhoeftpark, with ponds and old trees; and the Hirschpark of 111 acres (45 ha), with ancient oaks, avenues and rhododendrons. Many of the parks were originally private estates and some are of considerable horticultural interest. Jenisch-Park (qv) is one of the most attractive.

(1) Daily
(2) Free

Hamburg, Elbchausee in Klein-flottbek

13. Jenisch-Park

A park was created in the English style in 1797 and the present Jenisch-Park, situated by the River Elbe, was its central part. It is a spacious, natural park of 108 acres (45 ha) with attractive individual and grouped oaks, beeches and other trees. A row of exotic trees includes one of North Germany's largest and finest specimens of *Ginkgo biloba*. The Jenisch house in the north-west part of the park was built in 1829–32 to a design by K. F. Schinkel and has been a museum since 1927. Near the Jenisch house stands the Ernst Barlach Museum built in 1961–2 by Werner Kallmorgen. The glasshouses in the park may also be visited.

(1) Tue–Sun 10–5
(2) Charge
(4) Jenisch house museum (same times); Ernst Barlach Museum (Tue–Fri 11–1, 3–5; Sat and Sun 11–5)

Hamburg

14. Stadtpark

Hamburg's largest park covers 452 acres (183 ha). It was founded by Alfred Lichtwark and Fritz Schumacher in 1910–14. It contains a large lake, a rose garden, a rock garden and a heather garden. There is also an open-air theatre, sports facilities and a 197 ft (60 m) viewing tower and planetarium.

(1) Daily
(2) Charge
(3) Restaurant

Hanover, Herrenhäuser Strasse

Lower Saxony

15. Berggarten

This began as a kitchen garden, the first glasshouse being erected in 1666, and after *c* 1750 it developed into a botanical garden. For over 100 years mulberries were grown here to supply the Royal Silk Manufactory at Hamelin until this was closed by Napoleon. In 1851 the giant water-lily, *Victoria regia*, flowered in the glasshouse, the first time in Europe; in 1862 the first flamingo flower, *Anthurium scherzerianum*, was introduced; and in 1891 the first Usambara violet, *Saintpaulia ionantha*. In 1903 the Berggarten had the most comprehensive collection of orchids in Europe and it still is a notable collection.

Today, modern glasshouses contain cacti, succulents, and tropical plants. The garden also contains a library pavilion by Laves, built in 1816–19, a mausoleum by Laves, built in 1842–7 and containing the sarco-

phagi of German electors and dukes, and of George I of England and his parents. The show borders of perennials are worth visiting at all seasons.

(1) Garden: Daily 7–Sunset; Glasshouses: Daily 8–Sunset
(2) Free

Hanover

16. Georgengarten and Herrenhäuser Allee

This once consisted of private gardens but by 1859 the entire area had become royal property. It is in the style of an English landscaped park, with expansive lawns and lakes. The buildings include the Wallmoden château (built in 1780–96 for the Count of Wallmoden, son of George II, who began to unite the gardens), which now houses the Wilhelm Busch Museum. In the garden is a temple to the philosopher G. W. Leibnitz with a bust by Iren Hewetson. The Herrenhäuser Allee of 1,300 lime trees, replanted in 1972–4, leads from the gallery of the Grosser Garten through the Georgengarten to the centre of Hanover.

(1) Daily
(2) Free
(3) Kiosk
(4) Wilhelm Busch Museum (Summer: Daily 10–6; Winter: Daily 10–5)

Hanover, Kirchröder Strasse

17. Hermann-Löns-Park

Created in 1946–8 in the style of an English park and gardens with the Anna Lake as its central point, it covers an area of approx 988 acres (400 ha). There are old timber windmills which in earlier times stood in the square where the opera house now stands.

(1) Daily
(2) Free
(3) Restaurant

Hanover

18. Herrenhausen Grosser Garten

Herrenhausen, which became the summer residence of the dukes of Hanover in 1665, was destroyed in World War II, but the Grosser Garten, the immense Baroque layout constructed between 1666 and 1714 which was its setting, was reconstructed in 1945. It is aligned on the axis of the site of the principal façade of the palace and owes something to Le Nôtre and something to Dutch gardens of the 17th cent.

The garden is enclosed on three sides by a continuous canal and the furthest half is taken up by a great parterre centring on a circular basin and the highest garden fountain in the world, throwing a jet to a height of 220 ft (67 m). Nearer the site of the palace are a series of small enclosed gardens, each with a different theme, and also the Sylvan Theatre (1689–93) with hornbeam hedges and gilded statuary, a maze, a cascade of rocaille work, a grotto and a large orangery with fine old plants in tubs. Statuary, topiary (of hornbeam, in particular) and coloured gravels and sand are recurring elements. The Gallery, an independent wing of the palace which survived the war, has frescoes by the Venetian Tommaso Giusti.

(1) Daily 8–Sunset
(2) Free
(3) Restaurant
(4) Herrenhausen Museum (Summer: Daily 10–6; Winter: Daily 10–4)

Hanover
19. Stadtpark at the Stadthalle

Created before 1951 for the first Federal German Garden Show after World War II, this is noted for its fountain garden.

(1) Daily 8–Sunset
(2) Free
(3) Café

Hanover
20. Welfengarten

This was laid out in 1720 as a Baroque garden and in 1779 changed into a landscaped park. In 1843–4 Laves built his first iron spanned bridges here, of which one has survived. The Welfenschloss now houses the Technical University and also the Central Technical Library of the German Federal Republic.

(1) Daily
(2) Free

Jever
Lower Saxony
21. Schlosspark

The park, situated in the centre of the town, covers 7½ acres (3 ha) and surrounds the castle which was constructed in 1505. The park in the English style dates from 1820–30. Among its trees are a sweet-gum with a trunk diameter of 16 in (40 cm) and a huge larch. Thousands of winter aconites herald the spring.

(1) Daily
(2) Free

Kiel
Schleswig-Holstein
22. Botanical Garden of Kiel University

This was founded as the university *hortus medicus* in 1669 by Duke Christian-Albrecht. It was moved several times before the move in 1872 by the famous botanist Adolf Engler. It is shortly moving again to

the city's new university complex. Kiel has one of Europe's best collections of succulents, including the only European examples of varieties of South African succulents, and a large alpinum.

(1) Garden. Mon–Fri 9–4; Sat and Sun 9–1. Glasshouses. Tue and Fri 2–4, also Apr–mid-Oct: Sun 9–noon
(2) Free

Linswege, nr Westerstede
Lower Saxony
23. Rhododendronpark Hobbie

The estate, which has belonged to the Hobbie family for many years, was laid out by Dietrich C. Hobbie as a rhododendron park in 1929. It contains thousands of species and hybrids, including some new cultivations such as hybrids of *R. Williamsianum* and of *R. repens*, for example the famous hybrid 'Scarlet Wonder' (Essex Scarlett × *repens*). The park covers 161 acres (65 ha) and also includes a water-lily pond. Visit in May and June.

(1) Daily 7–7
(2) Apr–early Jul: Charge; mid-Jul–Mar: Free

Lütetsburg, nr Nordern in Ostfriesland
Lower Saxony
24. Schlosspark

The park surrounds the castle moat and covers 62 acres (25 ha). It is a landscaped park with lakes and ponds, created by Carl Frederick Bosse in *c* 1790 replacing an earlier garden, and it contains many rare trees including one of Germany's oldest Douglas firs. There are many spring flowers and in May and June the rhododendrons and azaleas are in flower. Lütetsburg forest containing some fine silver firs (*Abies alba*) adjoins the park.

(1) Mon–Fri 8–6; Sun 10–7
(2) Free

Oldenburg
Lower Saxony
25. Schlossgarten

This classical English landscaped park covering almost 45 acres (18 ha) was created by Duke Peter Frederick Ludwig von Oldenburg with the help of Carl Frederick Bosse in 1806–13. The Association of Friends of Oldenburg Castle Park, founded in 1953, extended the park in 1956. The oldest part of the park, dating from 1603, contains some of the park's most interesting trees: twelve tulip-trees, all over 170 years old; hollies over 39 ft (12 m) high and just over 4 ft (1·30 m) in trunk circumference; a giant sequoia over a hundred years old; an old and fine specimen of ilex; large magnolias, and 300-year-old oaks, beeches and limes.

The main features of the park are the rose garden (1954) and adjoining nursery (1809). There is also a tropical glasshouse. Visit in May and June for the rhododendrons and azaleas; from June to September for the irises and roses.

(1) Daily: closes at Sunset
(2) Free
(3) Café

Osnabrück

Lower Saxony
26. Botanical Nursery Garden

The garden covers $2\frac{1}{2}$ acres (1 ha) and is the remaining part of the Schlosspark which was destroyed in World War II. It demonstrates the regional flora and also has a medicinal and herb garden.

(1) Daily 8–Sunset
(2) Free

Bad Pyrmont

Lower Saxony
27. Kurpark

Originating with an avenue of limes, planted in 1668, the park was extended at the beginning of the 18th cent by the addition of other avenues; and in 1906 it was further altered. The avenues are today of lime and chestnut.

The park is landscaped and contains rare and old trees: Serbian spruce, Oriental spruce, sumach, Indian bean-tree, Hinoki cypress and copper beeches that are from 160 to 180 years old. In 1967, the founder of the International Dendrological Society, Jacques Lombards-Middell, found a unique form of tulip-tree (*Liriodendron tulipifera*) in the park and named it *Pyrmonter Welle*.

A palm garden was created in 1904–6. This contains a variety of palms, including *Trachycarpus fortunei*, *Chaemaerops humilis*, *Rhapis excelsa*, *Howea forsteriana* and *Rhopalostylis Baueri*.

(1) Daily
(2) Charge
(3) Café

Rastede

Lower Saxony
28. Parks von Rastede

An extensive landscaped park covering 740 acres (300 ha), consisting of the Grossen Forst, the Vorpark and the Schlosspark. The Grossen Forst has many paths leading through mixed woodland; the Vorpark has lakes, pools and a variety of rhodo-

dendrons bordering the paths and banks; the Schlosspark is private. The park has very favourable conditions for the cultivation of rhododendrons. It contains many hybrids and there is a 492 ft (150 m) long rhododendron bank which is over 160 years old.

Rastede has a long history. There was a Benedictine Monastery here in 1091 but this was dissolved in 1546 during the Reformation by the Counts of Oldenburg. Later a palace was built in its place by Count Anton Günther, who established the famous Oldenburg stud farm, which may be visited. The park was created after 1667 by Carl Frederick Bosse and was continued after his death by Christian Ludwig Bosse.

(1) Daily
(2) Free
(3) Café

Uetersen

Schleswig-Holstein
29. Rosarium

The Rosarium surrounds the mill pond in the centre of the town, with many points of access, and it covers 20 acres (8 ha). Begun by the German Rose Society in 1925, it was opened in 1934 and has a collection of approx 900 varieties of roses, all labelled. Visit from June to autumn.

(1) Daily 7am–8 pm
(2) Free
(3) Café

Bad Zwischenahn

Lower Saxony
30. Kurpark

The park covers 48 acres (20 ha) and is situated on the bank of the Zwischenahner Meer in Ammerland. It was laid out in 1929 and considerably extended in 1950. The central features of the park are the lake and the Baroque garden, which is bordered on either side by landscaped grounds in the English manner. The rhododendrons do exceptionally well here on account of the climate and the soil. On the north side of the lake is the ancient 'Church Lime'. Visit in May and June.

Bad Zwischenahn is a centre for growing rhododendrons and evergreens.

(1) Daily
(2) Free

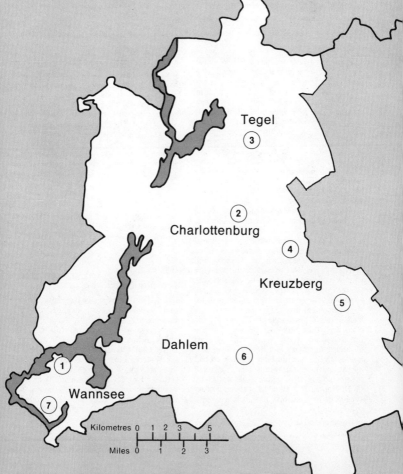

Tegel

③

②

Charlottenburg

④

Kreuzberg

⑤

Dahlem

⑥

Wannsee

①

⑦

Kilometres 0 1 2 3 5

Miles 0 1 2 3

WEST GERMANY

Berlin

1. Pfaueninsel

The Peacock Island, situated in the River Havel, is almost a mile (1,500 m) long and approx 550 yds (500 m) wide. The Prussian king, Frederick William III, commissioned Peter Joseph Lenné in 1822 to model the island as an English park in the style of the Jardin des Plantes in Paris. The island became a nature reserve in 1924. The trees include two tulip-trees, a Weymouth pine, a cedar of Lebanon, a ginkgo and a Caucasian wing-nut. There is a Swiss Cottage built by K. F. Schinkel, the ruined Jacob's Fountain, the guest-house with the façade of a Danzig nobleman's house (*Kavalierhaus*), also by Schinkel, and the ruined Gothic church or dairy-farmhouse (*Meierei*). The latter was built at the same time as the palace, in 1793.

(*1*) *Daily 8–8*
(*2*) *Charge (included in ferry ticket at Nikolskoer Weg)*
(*4*) *Schloss (Daily, except Mon, 10–5)*

Berlin

2. Schloss Charlottenburg

The summer palace was built in 1695–9 for Sophie Charlotte of Hanover, wife of King Frederick I, to designs by Johann Arnold Nering. It was altered and enlarged in 1701–12 and 1740–2. The park was created in 1697 by Siméon Godeau, a pupil of Le Nôtre, in the formal French style. In *c* 1816 it was remodelled under Frederick William III by the palace gardener Steiner and by Peter Joseph Lenné as an English landscaped park. The park covers 128½ acres (52 ha) and is bordered on its eastern side by the River Spree. Both palace and park were damaged during World War II.

The grounds directly behind the palace were restored as a Baroque garden, following old designs, including parterres with changing displays of flowers from spring to autumn, topiary and a fountain. The palace terrace has plants such as oleander and myrtle in tubs. In the park there is a lake with water-lilies and near the eastern wing of the palace is the Schinkel Pavilion, containing furniture and paintings, built by K. F. Schinkel in 1825 in the style of the Villa Reale Chiatamone in Naples. At the north end of the park near the River Spree is the Belvedere, a tea house built by Karl Gotthard Langhans in 1789–90 which now houses a porcelain museum. At the west end of the park is the Mausoleum, a small temple built in 1810 with marble statues by C. D. Rauch. It is situated at the end of an avenue of fir trees and near it is a swamp cypress that is approx 150 years old.

(*1*) *Summer: Daily 8 am–10 pm; Winter: Daily 8–7*

(*2*) *Free*
(*4*) *Schloss, State apartments (Tue, Thu–Sun 9–5; Wed 10–6); Schinkel Pavilion and Belvedere (Daily, except Mon, 9–5)*

Berlin

3. Schloss Tegel

The *schloss* of 1550 was extended in 1821–3 by K. F. Schinkel for the philologist and diplomat Wilhelm von Humboldt. The landscaped park covers 36 acres (14·7 ha). A lime avenue planted in 1792 leads to the mausoleum designed by Schinkel. Other trees include a 500-year-old oak, known as the '*Humboldteiche*', and a large Kentucky coffee-tree, *Gymnocladus dioicus*.

(*1*) *Apr–Oct: Daily*
(*2*) *Charge*
(*4*) *Humboldt Museum (Wed, Sat, Sun and Public Holidays guided tours at 2, 3, 4 and 5)*

Berlin

4. Tiergarten

Berlin's largest, oldest and most famous park, covering 413 acres (167 ha), originated as a game reserve at the beginning of the 16th cent and in *c* 1700 King Frederick I had a park created. It was further developed by Frederick the Great who had the park laid out as a French park by the architect Georg Wenzeslaus von Knobelsdorff. It was later adapted by Peter Joseph Lenné to the English style, the work being completed in 1838. Destroyed in World War II, the park was afterwards restored by the planting of over a million trees and shrubs. The park contains the *Bremer Sommerblumengarten*, a savannah-area with grasses and shrubs, a large rhododendron grove and an English garden.

(*1*) *Daily Sunrise–Sunset*
(*2*) *Free*
(*3*) *Café*
(*4*) *Zoo (Apr–Sep: Daily, except Sun and Public Holidays, 9–8; Sun and Public Holidays 8–8; Oct–May: Daily 9–Sunset); Aquarium (Daily 9–7)*

Berlin

5. Victoriapark

Created to the designs of Hermann Mächtig in 1888–94 on former vineyards, this hilly landscaped park of 39½ acres (16 ha) contains a waterfall in an artificial ravine and a medicinal plant garden. On the ravine is the 66 ft (20 m) National Monument to the Wars of Liberation set up in 1821 and designed by K. F. Schinkel. There are statues by C. D. Rauch, Tieck and Wichmann representing the principal victories. The Kreuzberg, an artificial mound, is the highest point in the centre of Berlin.

(*1*) *Daily*
(*2*) *Free*

Berlin-Dahlem, Königin-Luise-Strasse 6–8

6. Botanical Garden

In 1801 Carl Ludwig Willdenow, first professor of botany at Berlin University, founded a collection of medicinal plants which in 1815 was established as a botanical garden by Heinrich Friederich Link. Adolf Engler, who worked out a natural system for the classification of plants, laid out the systematic garden on its present site in 1897–1903.

The garden extends to 104 acres (42 ha) and contains 18,000 varieties of plants. It is recognized as one of the most important botanical collections in the world. The principal section, representing the vegetation of Germany and the mountain regions of the northern hemisphere, is laid out geographically, as a woodland garden, with a network of walks and streams. The arboretum, which lies beyond, is also highly regarded internationally. There are collections of economic and medicinal plants, marshland and aquatic plants and alpine plants. The large glasshouse complex includes the Great Tropical House (Victoria House), completed in 1968, which displays plants and trees of the Americas in the northern area and of Africa, Asia and Australia in the southern area. The collection of insectivorous plants is remarkable. The Italian garden is a formal garden with clipped yew and box. In the northern corner of the botanical garden is the Botanical Museum.

(1) *Daily (except Sun and Public Holidays) 8–Sunset (latest 8 pm); Sun and Public Holidays (except 25 Dec and 1 Jan) 9–Sunset (latest 8 pm). Guided tours on Sun at 10*
(2) *Charge*
(4) *Botanical Museum (Tue, Thu, Fri, Sat, Sun 10–5; Wed 10–7)*

Berlin-Wannsee

7. Park Kleinglienicke

The present palace was built in 1826 by K. F. Schinkel and in 1951 restored for use as a convalescent home. The park was laid out on the bank of the Havel in the 19th cent and was later extended as a public park of 287 acres (116 ha). It is one of West Germany's most important landscaped parks, planned by Peter Joseph Lenné. The park buildings include the Kasino, an Italianate villa with pergolas by Schinkel; the Kleine Neugierde and the Grosse Neugierde, summer houses built by Schinkel; and the Klosterhof, which has medieval works of art.

(1) *Daily*
(2) *Free*
(3) *Café*
(4) *Kasino, Kleine Neugierde, Gross Neugierde and Klosterhof (usually open)*

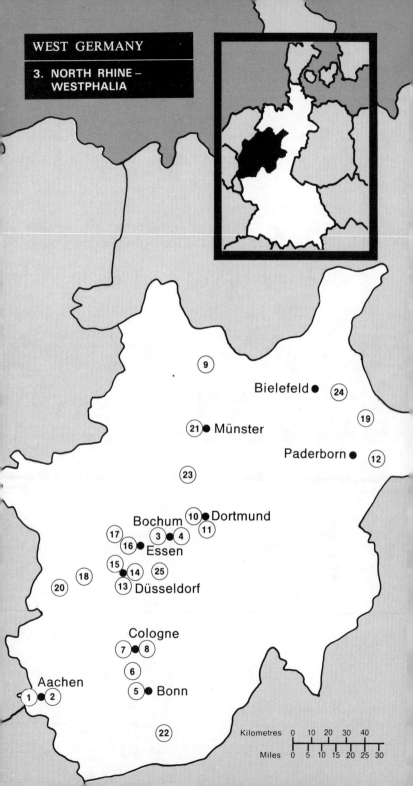

WEST GERMANY

3. NORTH RHINE – WESTPHALIA

⑨

Bielefeld ● ㉔

㉑ ● Münster

㉓

Paderborn ● ⑫

⑲

Bochum ⑩ ● Dortmund
⑰ ③ ● ④ ⑪
⑯ ●
Essen
⑮
⑭ ㉕
⑱
⑬ Düsseldorf
⑳

Cologne
⑦ ● ⑧

⑥

Aachen ⑤ ● Bonn
① ● ②

㉒

Kilometres 0 10 20 30 40

Miles 0 5 10 15 20 25 30

Bad Aachen, Alte Maastrichter Strasse 30

1. Botanical Garden of the Rhine-Westphalian School of Technology

This was founded in 1898 as an experimental garden and extended as a botanical garden after 1963. It specializes in native flora and has three display houses.

(1) Mon–Fri 8–4
(2) Free

Bad Aachen, Monheim Allee

2. Kurpark

A landscaped park with attractive old trees and colourful flowerbeds in summer. The grounds were founded in 1852 by Peter Joseph Lenné and cover 31 acres (12·5 ha). They were greatly damaged in World War II but have since been restored.

(1) Daily
(2) Free
(3) Café

Bochum, Universitätsstrasse 150

3. Botanical Garden of the Ruhr University

This was founded in 1966 and covers 42 acres (17 ha). Special features of the open area are the geo-botanical section, an alpinum, the economic plants, the biological-ecological plant groupings and a dahlia collection. The glasshouse complex includes a tropical house, succulents and cacti, plants of the Mediterranean countries and Canary Islands and insectivorous plants.

(1) Garden. Apr–Sep: Daily 9–6; Oct–Mar: Daily 9–4. Glasshouses. Apr–Sep: Daily 9–noon, 2–5; Oct–Mar: Daily 10–noon, 2–4
(2) Free

Bochum

4. Stadtpark

The town park covers 77 acres (31 ha) and is laid out as a natural park with a rose garden and a dahlia garden. The first part of the park was created in 1876 and it was enlarged in 1899 and 1903–7. There is a game park and the Bismark tower.

(1) Daily
(2) Free
(3) Café

Bonn, Poppelsdorfer Schloss

5. Botanical Institute of Bonn University

Founded in 1818, the site was previously

the garden of the Baroque Schloss Clemens-ruh, built in 1715–23, which now belongs to the university. It covers 16 acres (6·5 ha) and includes glasshouses, an arboretum with a number of old and rare trees and horticultural areas. The chestnut avenue leads to the Poppelsdorfer Schloss.

(1) Apr–Oct: Mon–Fri 8–7; Sat 8–noon; Sun 10–1; Nov–Mar: Mon–Fri 8–5
(2) Free

Brühl

6. Schloss Augustusburg and Schloss Falkenlust

The two palaces and parks are connected by an avenue. The park of the Baroque Schloss Augustusburg, by J. C. Schlaun and, after 1728, F. Cuvilliés the Elder, was created between 1728 and 1740 by Girard, a pupil of Le Nôtre, and Cuvilliés, who completed the palace, under the direction of the Elector Clemens August. The parterre was changed into an English park but restored to its original design from plans of 1750 after 1946. There are long canals, fountains and box parterres. The forest park dates back to the late 12th cent and was little altered by Girard. Schloss Falkenlust was also built by Cuvilliés in 1729–40 as a hunting lodge.

The trees include dawn redwoods (Metasequoia glyptostroboides), swamp white oaks (Quercus bicolor), katsura trees (Cercidiphyllum japonicum), sweetgums (Liquidambar), paulownias and wild cherry, all over 100 years old.

(1) Daily Sunrise–Sunset
(2) Free
(3) Café

Cologne

7. Flora-Park and Botanical Garden

The Flora-Park, opened in 1864 and designed by Peter Joseph Lenné, is the oldest part of the park. It retains the style of the English landscaped garden and now includes a heather and a fern garden. The Botanical Garden was opened in 1914 and the two were united in 1920 to cover 28 acres (11·5 ha). The Flora Park has lawns planted with plane trees, horse chestnuts and wing-nuts, some of which are over 130 years old; the largest tree is a copper beech, and there are 110-year-old hornbeams.

The Botanical Garden has many unusual trees, such as the Chinese fir; an alpine garden; an iris and lily garden; a kitchen garden; collections of poisonous and protected plants, ranunculus and saxifrage. The large tropical hothouse contains the giant bamboo and cacao, palm, fig and banana trees. The small tropical hothouse contains orchids, ferns and Bromeliaceae. There is

199

also a hothouse for succulents and a display house for the sub-tropical collection, which includes eucalyptus and orange trees.

(1) *Park and Garden. Daily 8 am–9 pm or Sunset. Glasshouse. Daily 10–6 or Sunset. Closed noon–1 Mon–Fri*
(2) *Charge*
(3) *Restaurant*

Cologne
8. Rheinpark

The park is situated on the right bank of the Rhine and covers 104 acres (42 ha). Re-planned for the Federal Garden Show of 1957, it was partially altered again for the Show in 1971. There are mature poplars, willows and acacias, an iris garden, a rose garden and a water garden, shrubs and individual gardens. A 9 mile (15 km) promenade leads from the park along the Rhine.

(1) *Daily*
(2) *Free*
(3) *Cafés*
(4) *Chairlift; miniature railway (Sun and Public Holidays)*

Dörenthe, nr Ibbenbüren
9. Botanical Garden 'Bauern Arboretum'

A small private botanical garden created in 1911 by Bernhard Loismann. It contains many unusual trees planted on the soil that was displaced for the construction of the Weser-Ems-Canal. These include the Japanese red cedar (*Cryptomeria japonica*), Chinese cow's tail pine (*Cephalotaxus fortunei*), snowbell tree (*Styrax japonica*), a rare Chinese fir (*Cunninghamia sinensis 'Glauca'*), downy tree of heaven (*Ailanthus vilmoriniana*), snake-branch spruce (*Picea abies 'Virgata'*) and a rare beech (*Fagus sylvatica 'Cristata'*).

(1) *Summer: Daily; Winter: Sat and Sun*
(2) *Charge*

Dortmund
10. Botanical Garden

The garden extends over 161 acres (65 ha). It contains a rhododendron wood with 350 varieties, an alpine garden, a primula valley, a rose garden, an arboretum with approx 5,000 species and varieties of trees, a good display of orchids, a school garden for school botanical studies and an area for the cultivation of shrubs. it was founded in 1930 and is situated in the Romberg Park.

(1) *Garden. Daily. Glasshouses. 9–Sunset*
(2) *Garden: Free; Glasshouses: Charge*
(3) *Café*

Dortmund
11. Westfalenpark

Created in 1959 for the Federal Garden Show and enlarged for the Show ten years later, it now covers 173 acres (70 ha). There are lawns, lakes, a large assortment of trees and shrubs, especially rhododendrons, flowerbeds and pergolas, cold and warm pools with indigenous and tropical plants and a rosarium with a geographical arrangement and over 3,000 varieties and species owned by the Rose Association. There is also an open-air theatre, a children's playground and a large exhibition hall for flower and art displays, fountains and a water organ. Demonstration areas for the amateur gardener and a Japanese garden are also included. A landmark in the park is the Florian Tower with a revolving restaurant and viewing platforms.

(1) *Daily 9 am–11 pm*
(2) *Charge*
(3) *Restaurant, café, kiosk*

Bad Driburg
12. Kurpark

A park in the landscaped style with huge poplars, a rose garden, rock garden, goldfish ponds and a lake. It was created in c 1782 and covers 69 acres (28 ha).

(1) *Daily*
(2) *Charge*

Düsseldorf, Benrath
13. Schloss Benrath

Both the palace and the park were created by Nicolas de Pigage for the Elector Carl Theodor and were completed in 1769. The grounds cover 158 acres (64 ha).

The woods are divided by a main aisle which strikes through the centre to the so-called 'star', where eight other aisles meet. The East Garden retains the French geometrical style in which Pigage created the park. The West Garden was remodelled in the landscaped style by Weyhe in c 1814. A notable feature of the park is the way in which pools are linked with the lake by an underground canal system.

(1) *Daily*
(2) *Free*
(4) *Schloss (Daily, except Mon and Public Holidays, 9–5)*

Düsseldorf
14. Hofgarten

The park, which covers 67 acres (27 ha), was created around the palace by Nicolas de Pigage under the patronage of Ludwig Friedrich von Goltstein after 1769 and extended in 1803 by Frederich von Weyhe, who in part altered the lay-out to a landscaped park. The four-rowed main avenue leading from the palace to a large pond with a statue and fountain remains from Pigage's design. There are several monuments and sculptures in the park and the head gardener's house is the Goethe Museum. The palace contains the North Rhine-Westphalia art collection.

(1) Daily
(2) Free

Düsseldorf, Stockum

15. Nordpark

The park was created for a horticultural show in 1937 and restored after its destruction in World War II. It is a city park with canals, fountains, pools, a rose garden, flowerbeds, lawns and sculptures. In 1974–5 a large Japanese garden was created by the landscape gardener Ishiguro. It leads into the Rheinpark.

(1) Daily
(2) Free
(3) Kiosk and restaurant

Essen

16. Grugapark and Botanical Garden

The grounds cover 197 acres (80 ha) and consist of the Botanical Garden, created in 1972, the Alten Grugapark and a leisure park, together forming one large and magnificent park. The Grugapark was originally laid out in 1929 and the most recent alterations were made in 1965 for the Federal Garden Show; the leisure park dates from 1965.

There are a variety of fine trees, a kitchen garden, dahlias and other flowers, a rhododendron valley, Mediterranean garden, rose garden, shrub garden, alpine garden, an aquarium and terrarium, and a belvedere. There are collections of conifers and climbing plants, a home garden demonstration area and display houses for tropical and sub-tropical plants, including orchids and house plants.

(1) Daily 9–Sunset
(2) Charge
(3) Restaurant
(4) Narrow-gauge railway

Gelsenkirchen

17. Schloss Berge

The moated *schloss* was built in *c* 1550 and restored in *c* 1780, and the park was created at this time. The garden, on the south-eastern side of the *schloss* and leading to the park, was created in *c* 1700. The garden was restored in 1924 and today consists of grass parterres with flower borders and clipped hedges; there are magnolias, tuliptrees and Indian bean-trees. The park was restored in 1926. Together the grounds cover 180 acres (73 ha). Nearby is the Berger Lake, a dahlia garden and a water-lily pond. *Schloss* Berge is now a hotel and restaurant.

(1) Daily
(2) Free
(3) Restaurant

Krefeld, Sandberg 1

18. Botanical Garden

This was created in 1928 and today covers 10 acres (4 ha). It includes alpine, medicinal, aquatic and marsh plants, a heather and rhododendron garden, a rose garden, a garden of flora of the Lower Rhine and an arboretum.

The garden is situated in the Schönwasserpark, a landscaped park with a small topiary garden which is open at all times.

(1) Good Friday–Oct: Daily 8–6 or 7
(2) Free

Bad Meinberg

19. Kurpark

The park, situated in the centre of the spa and covering 49 acres (20 ha), was created in 1767. A layer of carbonic acid covering the ground is responsible for the healthy growth of the plants in the park. The park consists of three parts: the Alter Kurpark which is landscaped, with two avenues of limes and chestnut trees intersecting at its centre; the Berggarten which is laid out in symmetrical terraces as a typical rock garden; and the park around the Stauteich, in which the River Werre rises. The park is adjoined by a large forest park.

(1) Daily (Old Spa Park closes Mon, Tue, Thu, Fri at 3; Wed, Sat, Sun at 2)
(2) Free

Mönchen-Gladbach

20. Bunter Garten

The park has lawns, shrubs, trees and wild flowers and also geometrically laid-out gardens with flowerbeds and fountains. There is a heather garden with birches and juniper trees, genista and a variety of grasses, and the spring flowers are a feature of the park.

(1) Daily
(2) Free

Münster

21. Botanical Garden of Münster University

Founded in 1804 on the site of kitchen and herb gardens. Of particular interest are the *Bromeliaceae*, succulents, ferns and aquatic plants. The insectivorous plants are in a small showcase on their own near the glasshouses. Adjoining the botanical garden is a park with fine trees and an exhibition of contemporary sculpture.

(1) *Summer: Daily 7.30–5; Winter: Daily 7.30–4*
(2) *Free*
(3) *Restaurant*

Bad Neuenahr

22. Kurpark

This consists of five separate parks situated along the banks of the River Ahr: Kaiser Wilhelm Park, Lenné Park, Kurgarten, Dahliengarten and Kaiserin Augusta Viktoria Park. The earliest was laid out in the mid-19th cent by Peter Joseph Lenné. The peach and almond blossoms are worth seeing in the spring and in late summer the park is famous for its dahlias. The Grosser Sprudel, a hot-water fountain, plays at midday on Sundays and Mondays at 11.30.

(1) *Daily Sunrise–Sunset*
(2) *Charge*
(3) *Café*

Nordkirchen

23. Schloss Nordkirchen

The *schloss* and park date from 1705 onwards and were created under the direction of the Prince-Bishop Friedrich Christian von Plettenburg according to designs by the architects Pictorius and Schlaun. The park is a successful imitation of the park at Versailles and, with its ornamental lakes and chestnut and lime avenues, it is the finest Westphalian park of this kind. It extends to 556 acres (225 ha).

(1) *Daily*
(2) *Free*

Bad Salzuflen

24. Kurpark

Covering 148 acres (60 ha), the park was created in *c* 1885. There is a rose garden, a water-lily pond and in spring a fine display of primulas, narcissi and tulips; also small lakes, terraces and fountains and a landscaped area with lawns and trees.

(1) *Daily 8–Sunset*
(2) *Charge*
(3) *Café*

Wuppertal

25. Botanical Garden

The garden with its glasshouses covers 5 acres (2 ha) and specializes in medicinal and aromatic plants, rhododendrons, irises and cyclamen. It is situated on a hill in the middle of the town with a good view over the valley.

(1) *Mar–Sep: Mon–Sat 7.30–7; Sun and Public Holidays 9–7; Oct–Feb: Mon–Sat 9–Sunset; Sun and Public Holidays 9–Sunset*
(2) *Free*

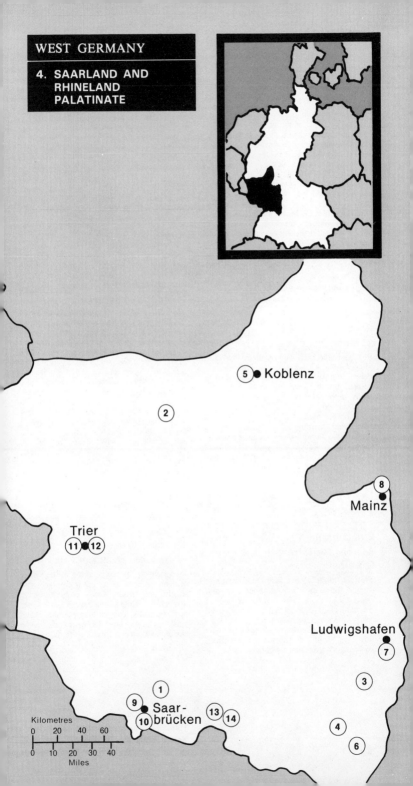

WEST GERMANY

4. SAARLAND AND
   RHINELAND
   PALATINATE

⑤● Koblenz

②

⑧● Mainz

Trier
⑪●⑫

Ludwigshafen●
⑦

③

①

⑨● Saar-
⑩ brücken   ⑬⑭

④

⑥

Kilometres
0   20   40   60
0 10 20 30 40
     Miles

WEST GERMANY

Bexbach, nr Homburg
Saarland
1. Blumengarten

This is a modern park of 15 acres (6 ha) created in 1951 for the garden and flowers exhibition with the aim of providing inspiration for the home gardener. There are shrubs and flowers, a heather garden, rose garden, rock garden, water-lily pond and a fountain. The grounds surround the 131 ft (40 m) tower, Hindenburgturm, which commands a view over the surrounding countryside. This tower houses the Grubenmuseum (Mining Museum) with a subterranean mining lay-out. Concerts take place in the park and there is a children's traffic-ground, mini-golf course and aviary.

(1) Garden. May–Oct: Daily 9–7. Tower and museum. May–Oct: Daily 10–6
(2) Charge
(3) Restaurant, café, kiosk

Bürresheim
Rhineland Palatinate
2. Barockgärtchen

Schloss Bürresheim was begun in 1157 and altered in the 17th cent. It was a private residence until 1938. The garden typifies those created by the lesser aristocracy in Germany: although only 2,390 sq yds (2,000 sq m) in extent, it is a well-kept formal garden with lawns, paths and clipped trees and shrubs, centring on a small ornamental pool. There are attractive rambling roses on the garden walls and a pergola. The *schloss* and garden are situated at the junction of two streams in a wooded valley.

(1) Daily 8–5
(2) Free
(4) Schloss (Apr–Oct: Daily 8–1, 2–6; Nov and 2 Jan–Mar: Daily 9–1, 2–5)

Bad Dürkheim
Rhineland Palatinate
3. Kurpark

This is a modern park with indigenous and foreign trees, including almonds, figs and sweet chestnuts, all of which flower early in the mild climate, blue cedars, Indian bean trees, paulownias, ginkgos and a 150-year-old nettle-tree (*Celtis occidentalis*). Of the flowering shrubs in the park, the winter-flowering varieties do particularly well.

(1) Daily
(2) Free
(3) Café

Bad Gleisweiler, nr Landau
Rhineland Palatinate
4. Sanatoriumspark

The sanatorium, built in the classical style in 1840 to plans by the landscape architect Leo von Klenze, was founded by Dr Ludwig Schneider, who chose this place on account of the mild climate. The park was created by his son in the 1870s, with the emphasis on exotic plants, and extended in 1916–19. It covers 5 acres (2 ha) and is partly in the English landscape style and partly wooded. There are hollies, cherry-laurels, Germany's largest coast redwood (*Sequoia sempervirens*), swamp cypresses, Atlas cedars, a ginkgo and bamboos. A sun temple was designed by Vauban, the French fortifications architect.

(1) Daily
(2) Free

Koblenz
Rhineland Palatinate
5. Rheinanlagen

The earliest work on public grounds along the banks of the Rhine was undertaken in 1809 by the French *préfet* of the Rhine and Mosel departement, Lezay-Marnésia, but was uncompleted when he left Koblenz. The Prussian Princess Augusta took great interest in the lay-out of the grounds and helped to finance their completion. She consulted Peter Joseph Lenné the Younger. The grounds were remodelled in 1889 and again after World War II. There are fine trees – such as the tulip-tree, the giant sequoia, the ginkgo, the Atlas cedar, the pagoda-tree, the Indian bean-tree and the dawn redwood – and flowerbeds. The promenade adjoins the palace garden (Apr–Sep: 8–8; Oct–Mar: 8–4.30).

(1) Daily
(2) Free
(3) Café and restaurant

Landau
Rhineland Palatinate
6. Goethe and Schiller Parks

Two well-kept parks, situated in the centre of the town, with lawns, paths, fine trees and shrubs and, from March onwards, good displays of tulips, heliotropes and other bedding plants. There is also a dahlia testing garden. Created after 1870 they are on the site of the town's fortifications.

(1) Daily
(2) Free

Ludwigshafen
Rhineland Palatinate
7. Ebertpark

This is a public, recreational park with land-scaped areas and flowerbeds, a lake with interesting aquatic flora and fountains. It was created for the South-West German Horticultural Exhibition in 1925. Concerts and firework displays take place here and there is a children's playground. It covers 72 acres (29 ha)

(1) Summer: Daily 6 am–10 pm; Winter: Daily 6 am–9 pm
(2) Free
(3) Café and kiosk

Mainz

Rhineland Palatinate

8. Botanical Garden of Mainz University

This garden was founded in 1946 by Wilhelm Troll together with the university's botanical institute. It covers 20 acres (8 ha). The garden has been extended and improved since its foundation and contains an arboretum, alpine garden and area for systematic groupings.

(1) Daily 7.30–5
(2) Free

Saarbrücken

Saarland

9. Deutsch-Französischer Garten

A landscaped park of 83 acres (34 ha) created for the Franco-German Garden Show of 1960. In World War II this was the site of defences against the French. The park lies on the border between France and West Germany. Its chief attraction is the mill pond with flamingos and other birds. There are a variety of shrubs and flowers and roses of French and German origin. There are fountains, a woodland theatre and also Europe's largest water organ. The park contains a chairlift, a miniature railway, a clock golf course, a music pavilion and a Gulliver's Mini-World, built in 1969.

(1) Daily 8.30–Sunset
(2) Charge

Saarbrücken

10. Schlosspark

A park surrounded the *schloss* as early as 1605 but both *schloss* and park were destroyed in 1793. The park was remodelled in 1955 and consists of several different gardens separated by stairways, retaining walls and terraces. There is a Baroque parterre and a rose garden, and the remains of Baroque buttresses and a turret of the garden pavilion of 1577. The flowerbeds and lawns of the Theatre Grounds lie on the opposite bank of the River Saar.

(1) Daily
(2) Free

WEST GERMANY

Trier

Rhineland Palatinate

11. Nell's Ländchen

The park, situated in the north of the town, is named after the prebendary of St Paulin, Nikolaus Nell, who created the park on what was formerly a swamp area in 1792–1801. Covering 25 acres (10 ha), it is in the English-Dutch style with mature oaks, beeches, elders and chestnuts, ponds, fountains and statuary. There are rhododendrons, many flowerbeds, a rosarium (1951), a pavilion and an orangery. There are amenities such as mini-golf and boating and in the first week of September a special flower exhibition with music and fireworks.

(1) Daily
(2) Free
(3) Café

Trier

12. Palastgarten

This was the garden of the 17th-cent elector's palace, now used for local government offices. Covering 30 acres (12 ha), it was laid out as a public park in 1935–50. In front of the palace is the Rococo garden created in 1762 by F. J. Puscher. Trimmed hedges with arches enclose lawns with flowers and Baroque statuary around an ornamental pond. On one side is a parterre of clipped box scrolls filled with flowers and gravel. The statuary is by Ferdinand Tietz (1759): these are copies of the originals, which may be seen in the municipal museum. The park has a number of fine trees, including planes, poplars and locust-trees.

(1) Daily
(2) Free
(4) Roman Imperial Baths (Apr–Sep: Daily 8–7; Oct–Nov and mid-Jan–Mar: 9–noon, 1–4)

Zweibrücken

Saarland

13. Fasanerie

Situated in a hilly landscape, this formerly belonged to the Polish king and father-in-law of Louis XV, Stanislas Leszczyński. He lived here from 1714–8, naming it 'Tschifflick', Turkish for country seat. A new palace was begun after 1720 for Duke Gustav Samuel Leopold and a new park laid out. Since 1767 it has been called the Fasanerie, the pheasant reserve. Today there is a magnificent forest park with long, straight paths and canals. Near the ruins of the palace is a rectangular garden with winding paths leading to a pavilion, and there is an informal rose garden. The grounds contain the ruins of a medieval palace, a pheasant reserve, a race course and a camping ground.

(*1*) *Daily*
(*2*) *Free*

Zweibrücken

14. Rosengarten

The rose garden in the centre of the town is one of Europe's largest. Covering approx 14 acres (6 ha) it has 60,000 roses of over 2,000 varieties. There is also an iris and lily garden.

The first rose show in Zweibrücken took place in 1880 and was thereafter repeated annually. The varieties of rose represented were rapidly increased and in 1914 the town opened a rosarium in grounds belonging to a former ducal estate. It was remodelled after being destroyed in World War II. The best months to visit the garden are June and August.

(*1*) *Mid-Apr–Oct: Daily 8–Sunset*
(*2*) *Charge*
(*3*) *Restaurant*

WEST GERMANY

5. HESSE

Kassel ● (16)(17)(18)

(19)● Marburg an der Lahn

(22)

(12)● Giessen   (11)● Fulda

(20)

(21)

(15)

Frankfurt ●
Wiesbaden   (13)● (14) Hanau
(23)●(24)
(5)(6)(7)(8)(9)(10)

(2)● (3)
Darmstadt

(1)

(4)

Kilometres 0   10   20   30
Miles 0   5   10   15   20

Bensheim-Auerbach, Bergstrasse

1. Staatspark Fürstenlager

A landscaped park in a sheltered valley with fine trees, notably a swamp cypress, a western red cedar that is more than 125 ft (38 m) high, a paulownia, a group of tall cedars of Lebanon and a group of tulip-trees, and West Germany's tallest giant sequoia measuring approx 174 ft (53 m). The park dates back to the mid-18th cent and was laid out by C. L. Geiger. It covers 62 acres (25 ha). There are pavilions and monuments, and fine views over the Rhine Valley and surrounding countryside. The house was the summer residence of the house of Hesse-Darmstadt under the Landgrave Ludwig X. The park has been a nature reserve since 1954.

(1) Daily
(2) Free
(3) Café

Darmstadt

2. Botanical Garden of the School of Technology

This was founded in 1814 and covers 12 acres (5 ha). It contains large collections of *Bromeliaceae*, cacti, succulents and insectivorous plants in the glasshouses. The arboretum has 2,000 varieties of trees, including 50 varieties of juniper, some of which were planted nearly a century ago. The dendrologists Purpus and Boerner worked here and helped to form the collection. There are also alpine plants, ferns and grasses. There is a lake and the River Darmbach flows through the arboretum.

(1) Summer: Daily 7.30 am–8 pm; Winter: Daily 7.30–5
(2) Free

Darmstadt

3. Prinz-Georg-Garten

The park was laid out as a pleasure garden in 1625 but the present park dates from *c* 1700. It is a garden in the French Rococo style with an open-air theatre and topiary in the formal gardens surrounding the palace (*c* 1700). Alleys provide views of pavilions in the grounds. In 1951 it was merged with the Prettlackian garden and remodelled, but it retained the formal style. It covers 10 acres (4 ha) and adjoins the Herrngarten. In the *schloss* are collections of porcelain and faience.

(1) May–Sep: Daily 7 am–8 pm; Oct–Apr: Daily 8–3.45
(2) Free
(4) Schloss (Mon–Thu 10–1, 2–5; Sat and Sun 10–1)

Eulbach

4. Schlosspark

The landscaped park with classical features was founded by Franz I Count of Erbach-Erbach in 1802 according to designs by F. L. von Sckell. The park is entered by an avenue of pleached lime trees. There are two small lawns with trees and shrubs leading to an obelisk erected by Franz I and beyond this lie further lawn areas with a variety of fine trees – yews, oaks, larches, firs and cypresses. The park was extended in 1818 by the addition of three small lakes and the aritificial ruin of the Eberhardsburg. The park also contains several commemorative statues, Roman stone fragments and an animal reserve. It covers 11 acres (4·5 ha)

(1) Daily 8–5
(2) Charge
(3) Café
(4) Museum (Mar–Oct: Daily 8.30–noon, 1.30–5)

Frankfurt am Main

5. Bethmannpark

This was once a private park but since 1941 it has been publicly owned. It contains annuals, perennials, bulbs, flowering shrubs, conifers and creepers. There are also plots to serve as examples for window-boxes and a glasshouse with indoor plants. The park is intended as a practical guide to the laying out of a garden and free advice may be obtained.

(1) Daily 7–Sunset
(2) Free

Frankfurt am Main, Siesmayerstrasse 72

6. Botanical Garden of Johann Wolfgang Goethe University

The garden covers 21 acres (8·5 ha) and adjoins the Palmengarten (qv) on one side and Grüneburgpark, a landscaped park with shrubs and exotic trees, on the other. There is an arboretum with trees from North America and East Asia, an alpine garden with flora from Central Europe, the Pyrenees, the Carpathians and the Himalayas, collections of bog, heath and dune plants, medicinal and ornamental plants, and there are also systematic, geographical and ecological groupings. Visit from April until June and in September.

(1) Mon–Sat 8–Sunset; Sun 9–1
(2) Free

Frankfurt am Main

7. Goldstein Demonstration Garden

Created in 1935–6 by the City Park Authorities as an advisory centre, this adjoins the Goldsteinpark. It is divided into demonstration areas for annual vegetables, perennial vegetables, fruit, herbs and ornamental plants.

(1) *Summer: Mon–Fri 8–4; Sat 9–noon*
(2) *Free*

Frankfurt am Main

8. Ostpark

This was Frankfurt's first public park, created by Karl Heicke in 1900–8 and covering 77 acres (31 ha). There is a large lake with moisture-loving plants growing beside it and a number of fine trees.

(1) *Daily*
(2) *Free*

Frankfurt am Main, Siesmayerstrasse

9. Palmengarten

This was founded in 1869–71, soon after the Palm Garden Society was founded in 1868. It acquired the famous plant collection of Duke Adolph von Nassau after his dethronement in 1866. The Palm House, the largest and oldest in West Germany, was built a year later. This contains a notable collection of over 1,000 varieties of cacti, succulents, *Bromeliaceae* and other tropical plants. In 1932 the Society was dissolved and the park is now under municipal control. It has been considerably extended over the years and now covers over 53 acres (22 ha) consisting of a landscaped park with lakes and lawns. There is a greenhouse complex with fourteen glasshouses, a cultivation garden, an alpine garden, a collection of evergreens and a rose garden. There is a yew tree which is 400 years old. In the open area is a large and notable collection of *Iris germanica* and hemerocallis.

The Palmengarten adjoins the Botanical garden (qv) and Grünebergpark.

(1) *Daily 8–Sunset*
(2) *Free*
(3) *Restaurant, café, kiosks*

Frankfurt am Main

10. Wallanlagen

The grounds are situated where formerly a fortified castle stood, whose ramparts were planted with trees in 1765 and converted into promenades in 1806–12 by Sebastian Rinz. A conservation order to prevent building was placed on the grounds as early as 1807. The grounds were extended and improved after World War II. They cover 55½ acres (22·5 ha) and consist of seven areas: the Untermain next to the playhouse; the Gallus with flowers and benches; the Taunus with the rampart ruins; the Bockenheimer with a lake, fountains and trees; the Eschenheimer with the only remaining tower of the castle; the Friedberger with

trees and a pond; and the Obermain with remains of the walls and moat and plane trees.

Nearby, running beside the river, is the Nizza Park created by Rinz in 1860. The climate is not as good as in Nice, in the South of France, after which the park is named, but very good by local standards. Fig, bay and lemon trees grow here. There is a cast-iron fountain with sulphurous water and a sundial (1951) designed by L. M. Loske.

(1) *Daily*
(2) *Free*

Fulda

11. Schlossgarten

Attached to the palace of the prince-abbots of Fulda, this garden is laid out with Baroque parterres and terraces. On the staircase to the orangery is a magnificent *floravase* of 1728. There is a small rose garden, fine old tub plants and, further away from the *schloss*, a small lake.

(1) *Daily*
(2) *Free*
(4) *Café*

Giessen

12. Botanical Garden of Justus-Liebig University

This is West Germany's oldest remaining botanical garden, founded in 1609 by Ludwig Jungermann. In c 1800 Frederick Luther Walther created the world's first university forestry garden and this was later combined with the botanical garden. The arboretum contains trees 150–200 years old. There is a glasshouse complex, an alpine garden, collections of plants from the steppes and prairies, medicinal, poisonous and edible plants, aquatic and marsh plants together with systematic and biological groupings. The Castle Garden contains plants that were grown in the gardens of medieval castles and monasteries.

(1) *Garden. Apr–Sep: Mon–Fri 8–5; Sat, Sun and Public Holidays 8–noon. Glasshouses. Apr–Sep: Mon–Fri 10–noon, 2–4; Sat, Sun and Public Holidays 10–noon*
(2) *Free*

Hanau

13. Schlossgarten

A landscaped park of 14 acres (5·6 ha) situated around a Baroque-style parterre laid out in 1897 and remodelled in the 1960s. The trees include swamp cypresses, magnolias, shingle oaks, copper beeches, Indian bean-trees and a paulownia. The stream running through the park widens into a pond.

(1) Daily 8–Sunset
(2) Free
(3) Café

Hanau
14. Schlosspark Philippsruhe

The park is situated by the River Main and covers 22 acres (9 ha). It was created as a formal French garden in 1696 under the direction of Max Dossmann and was later extended and an orangery added. In 1815 it was remodelled as an English landscaped park but the original avenues of lime trees were retained. The spring flowers, in particular the *Scilla sibirica* are a feature of the park. The Baroque *schloss* was begun by Julius Ludwig Rothweil in 1701–26 and the work was later taken over by Girard.

(1) Daily 8–Sunset
(2) Free

Bad Homburg
15. Schlosspark

This is a landscaped park attached to the residence of the Landgraves of Hesse-Homburg, bearing traces of the original French design of 1766. It covers 42 acres (17 ha) and has a lake, streams, rare and exotic plants and shrubs, a group of sweet chestnuts (*Castanea sativa*) and cedars of Lebanon (*Cedrus libani*) planted in 1820.

(1) Daily 7–Sunset
(2) Free
(3) Restaurant and café
(4) Schloss (Daily except Mon)

Kassel
16. Karlsaue

The park stretches into the centre of the city and covers 371 acres (150 ha). It was begun in 1568 but it was principally developed in the late 17th and early 18th cents under the Landgrave Karl of Hesse. He enlarged the park with the intention of forming a counterpart to the park of Schloss Wilhelmshöhe (qv). In *c* 1800 the Baroque garden was altered to a landscaped park. There are lawns, canals, lakes, flowerbeds and the flower island Siebenbergen, on which there are many rare flowers and trees. There is also an orangery (1705–11) and a marble boating-house, or pavilion, rebuilt after World War II.

Large-scale restoration to the park was effected for the Federal Garden Show in 1955 and work is in progress here and in Fulda, which lies opposite, on a large recreational park. Both will play a part in the 1981 Garden Show.

(1) Daily
(2) Park: Free; Siebenbergen: Charge
(3) Café
(4) Marble pavilion (Easter–mid-Oct: Sat 1–6; Sun 10–6)

Kassel
17. Schlosspark Wilhelmshöhe

This is one of Hesse's most famous parks and Europe's largest park in the mountains, extending to 740 acres (300 ha). Monks settled here as early as 1143 but the history of the park began when hunting and summer palaces were built in 1701 under the park's greatest patron, the Landgrave Karl of Hesse. The park was extended by the Landgrave Friedrich II in the second half of the 18th cent and remodelled in the English style with further fountains by his son Wilhelm, after whom the park is named. Under Karl, cascades were created by the Italian architect Giovanni Francesco Guerniero. Water cascades over 24 steps into the Neptune basin and the cascading fountain is bordered by staircases of 542 steps.

Guerniero also built the huge castle of volcanic limestone at the head of the cascades which is called the Octagone. A 98 ft (30 m) high pyramid base on the Octagone bears a copper statue of Hercules, a copy of the Farnese Hercules, made in 1713–17 by Johann Jakob Anthoni. The Wilhelmshöhe Palace was built for the Landgrave Wilhelm IX by Simon Louis du Ry and Heinrich Christoph Jussow and was completed in 1798. Schloss Löwenburg was built in 1793–8.

The park contains a Chinese village, the Mulang (1782–5); an aqueduct which is an artificial ruin (1788–92); the Devil's Bridge; the New Waterfall; a lake with the Great Fountain of 171 ft (52 m); and various garden temples and grottoes. There are 800 varieties of trees and shrubs and the Great Glasshouse of 1822 contains camellias, azaleas, palms, ferns and orchids.

In the *schloss* is a tapestry museum with important collections.

(1) Park. Daily. Glasshouses. Jan–Apr: Daily 10–5. Fountains. Wed, Sun and Public Holidays 2.30
(2) Free
(3) Café
(4) Schloss, Art Gallery and Löwenburg (Mar–Oct: Daily, except Mon, 10–5; Nov–Feb: Daily, except Mon, 10–4); Octagone (mid–end of Mar and Oct: Daily, except Mon and in snow, 10–5; Apr–Sep: Daily, except Mon, 10–6; 1 Nov–mid-Nov: Daily, except Mon and in snow, 10–4)

Kassel
18. Schlosspark Wilhelmsthal

A 5½ mile (9 km) long grass avenue connects this park with that of Wilhelmshöhe (qv). The park was formerly an estate belonging to the monastery of Helmarshausen. A Rococo *schloss* and garden were created in the Dutch style in 1743. From 1796 to 1814 this garden was remodelled as an English landscaped park. The architect was François Cuvilliés and the park was created in collaboration with Carl and Simon Louis du Ry. There are huge oaks and old lime trees in the park as well as a small lake, a belvedere, a Rococo grotto with a canal and fountains and a Rococo garden.

(1) Daily Sunrise–Sunset
(2) Free
(4) Schloss (Mar–Oct: Daily, except Mon, 10–5; Nov–Feb: Daily, except Mon, 10–4)

Marburg an der Lahn
19. Botanical Garden of Phillips University

A botanical garden existed at the time of the foundation of the university in 1527 but Marburg did not have a public botanical garden until 1786. In 1970 there was no room for extension and the garden was transferred to its present site in the east of the town. Its special features are the alpine garden, the sunken fern garden and the rhododendron collection. The glasshouses include tropical plants, succulents, economic and aquatic plants. There are also heathers, conifers and deciduous trees.

The former botanical garden is now a park.

(1) Mon–Fri 9–3.30. (Guided tours by previous arrangement on Sun and Public Holidays)
(2) Free
(3) Kiosk

Bad Nauheim
20. Kurpark

A large park laid out in the English landscape style with extensive lawns, ponds and foreign and indigenous trees. These include beeches, oaks, yews, limes, Indian bean-trees, tulip-trees, pagoda-trees and downy trees of heaven. It consists of the old park, laid out in the mid-19th cent, and the new park, laid out in c 1900.

(1) Daily
(2) Free

Bad Salzhausen
21. Kurpark

The park of 185 acres (75 ha) is situated on volcanic rock on the slope of the Vogelsberg. It contains over 350 varieties of deciduous and coniferous trees from all over the world as well as salt flora. There is an old water-mill in the grounds.

(1) Feb–Dec: Daily
(2) Charge

Weilburg
22. Schlossgarten

The *schloss* and garden are situated on the banks of the River Lahn. The grounds were laid out at the beginning of the 18th cent by Count Johann-Ernst von Nassau-Weilburg, who also had built the Baroque *schloss* around the earlier Renaissance structure. The Baroque gardens descend in three large terraces, the highest one planted with lime trees and decorated with a balustrade and ornamental vases. There is an orangery in the style of the Grand Trianon at Versailles (qv). The trees include bay and pomegranate trees. The grounds were owned from 1890 to 1935 by the Grand Duke of Luxembourg.

(1) Daily 9–Sunset
(2) Free
(3) Café (Apr–Sep)
(4) Schloss (Apr–Sep: Daily 10–6; Mar and Oct: Daily 10–5; Nov–Feb: Daily 10–4. Closed some Public Holidays)

Wiesbaden
23. Kurpark

The park was laid out in 1852 and consists of lawns with well-kept paths, a lake with a fountain and a *Nizzaplätzchen* with two Baroque basins. Rhododendrons and azaleas grow here and the planes, which were planted earlier, in 1810, are among the finest of the trees. The pump room dates from 1810. There is a bronze statue, The Flautist, which was added in 1965.

(1) Daily
(2) Charge except on Mon, Wed, and Sun mornings
(3) Restaurant and café

Wiesbaden
24. Schlosspark Biebrich

This park was the last work of F. L. von Sckell. He began landscaping the park behind the *schloss* in 1817, under the patronage of Prince Wilhelm von Nassau-Weilburg. The *schloss* was built over the years from 1698 to 1744 and is one of the loveliest of the Baroque period. The park contains an artificial hill, lake and the Moosburg (1806).

(1) Daily 6 am–Sunset
(2) Free
(3) Restaurant

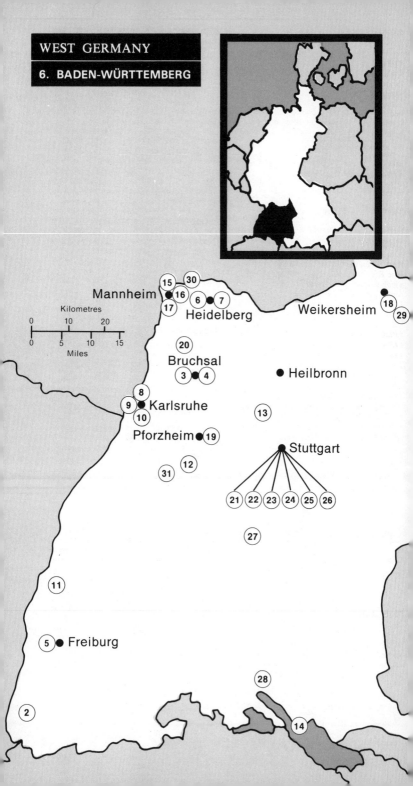

WEST GERMANY

6. BADEN-WÜRTTEMBERG

Mannheim

Heidelberg

Weikersheim

Kilometres
0   10   20
0   5   10   15
Miles

Bruchsal

Heilbronn

Karlsruhe

Pforzheim

Stuttgart

Freiburg

Baden-Baden

1. Lichtentaler Allee

The avenue, which leads past several of the spa's hotels, the pump room and art gallery, was laid out in the 17th cent as an oak avenue. It consists of many indigenous and foreign trees: beeches, oaks, tulip-trees, cedars, limes, ginkgos, maples, cypresses, Indian bean-trees, pines, giant sequoias, acacias, mulberries and magnolias. There are banks of rhododendrons and azaleas. Nearby is the Gönneranlage with pergolas and fountains flanking a rose garden, where international rose competitions are held regularly. It is situated on the opposite side of the River Oos.

(*1*) *Daily*
(*2*) *Free*

Badenweiler

2. Kurpark and Schlosspark

The Kurpark dates from 1758 and its principal creator was Ernst Krautinger, who, under the direction of the Grand Duke Friedrich I von Baden laid out the landscaped park with its small lake in 1850–71. Among the trees are Oriental planes (*Platanus orientalis*), Japanese thuja (*Thuja standishii*), Atlas cedars (*Cedrus atlantica*), giant sequoias (*Sequoiadendron giganteum*), sugar maples (*Acer saccharinum*), dawn redwoods (*Metasequoia glyptostroboides*), a huge paulownia and a magnolia that is nearly 100 years old. There are kitchen and medicinal herbs of the Mediterranean growing around the ruin of the Roman bathing-house and the park also has irises, narcissi, roses, lilies and a very varied collection of shrubs. There is a music pavilion, the castle ruins, hot springs and a new pump room.

The adjoining Schlosspark was opened to the public in 1952 after the death of the Grand Duchess Hilda von Baden and it contains an interesting variety of trees. Together the parks cover 54 acres (22 ha).

(*1*) *Daily*
(*2*) *Schlosspark: Free; Kurpark: Charge for concerts (Feb–Nov)*

Bruchsal

3. Schlosspark

The castle park, covering 17 acres (7 ha), was created in 1724 in the French style by Sickora, the court gardener, under the patronage of the Cardinal and Prince-Bishop Damian Hugo Philip von Schönborn. It is situated behind the Baroque *schloss*, which was built between 1722 and 1733, almost completely destroyed in World War II and is currently being restored. The park was remodelled in 1746 according to designs by Balthazar Neumann. It fell into decay in the mid-19th cent but has now been restored. The trees include horse chestnut, copper beech, hornbeam, black poplar, maple, sycamore, ash, weeping birch, lime, tulip-trees and Indian bean-tree, as well as shrubs such as lilac, forsythia, snowberry, privet and syringa. There are also many fine old plants in tubs.

(*1*) *Daily*
(*2*) *Free*

Bruchsal

4. Stadtgarten

A small park situated on a hill which was once a Merovingian cemetery dating from the 6th cent. It contains a reservoir and a belvedere built by the Cardinal of Schönborn in 1738. There are many foreign and indigenous trees and shrubs, such as magnolia, copper beech, hornbeam, ash, maple, sycamore, an Indian bean-tree, a cedar and a tulip-tree, syringa, lilac, jasmine, privet, Japanese quince and yuccas.

(*1*) *Daily*
(*2*) *Free*

Freiburg

5. Botanical Garden of Freiburg University

Founded in 1620 as a medicinal garden, it was established in its present location in 1912–14 and remodelled in 1960–75. The garden includes an arboretum with conifers and trees of North America and eastern Asia and glasshouses with a variety of plants including ferns.

(*1*) *Garden. Daily 10–6. Glasshouses. Tue, Thu, Sat 2–4; Sundays 10–noon, 2–4*
(*2*) *Free*

Heidelberg

6. Botanical Garden of Heidelberg University

The garden was first laid out by Smetius in 1593 as a medicinal garden and ranks as one of the oldest botanical gardens in the world. It was moved and redesigned in 1679, 1805, 1834, 1879 and 1915 and today covers 10 acres (4 ha). There is an open area and a large glasshouse complex. Among the garden's specialities are its collections of succulents, orchids, *Bromeliaceae*, ferns and tropical and subtropical plants. The head of the Botanical Garden is the world-famous expert on *Bromeliaceae* and succulents, Professor Rank.

(*1*) *Garden. Daily Sunrise–Sunset. Glasshouses. Mon–Thu, Sun and Public Holidays 9–noon, 1–4*
(*2*) *Free*

WEST GERMANY

Heidelberg
7. Schlossgarten

A terraced park which in the 17th cent was known as the *Hortus Palatinus* and was world famous. Work to replace a smaller garden was begun in 1616 for the Elector Friedrich V by the French architect Salmon de Caus, but it was not completed. The park fell into decay during the Thirty Years War and the *schloss* was destroyed by the French in 1689 and again in 1693. In 1804, Carl Friedrich von Baden created the present castle park out of the remains of the *Hortus Palatinus*. Four of the five connecting terraces remain. The bottom terrace has a collection of conifers. The *schloss*, which now contains the Deutsche Apotheken Museum, was partially ruined by lightning in 1764.

(1) Daily 7–midnight
(2) Charge during the Heidelberger Blumentage *in early Aug*
(3) Café
(4) Schloss ruins

Karlsruhe
8. Old Botanical Garden at the Schloss

This was created in part of the pleasure garden of the Margrave Karl Wilhelm von Baden-Durlach, who also founded the town. He filled the garden with varieties of tulips, exotic plants collected from all over the world, some housed in glasshouses, and many exotic trees and shrubs including sassafras, cladrastis, cedars, wellingtonias and magnolias. Here the first aloe flowered in Europe in 1748, the first tulip-tree flowered in Europe in 1774 and in 1808 the first double dahlia was cultivated. The garden covers 5 acres (2 ha).

(1) Daily 9–Sunset
(2) Garden: Free; Glasshouses: Charge
(3) Café

Karlsruhe
9. Schlossgarten

For the Federal Garden Show of 1967 the original wooded park to the north of the *schloss* was replanted with 400 trees and 9,000 rhododendrons, and the lake was enlarged; the parterres to the right and left of the *schloss* and the forecourt were redesigned to great effect. Adjoining the Old Botanical Garden (qv), it extends to 161 acres (54 ha), and the *schloss* contains the Baden Regional Museum.

To the east of the park is the Faisanerie, begun as a game park in 1714 and altered to the English style by Schweykert in 1780–90. Beyond the buildings of the Technische Universität are the New Botanical Gardens of the University.

(1) Daily Sunrise–Sunset
(2) Free
(3) Restaurant
(4) Museum (Apr–Sep: Daily, except Tue, Thu and Public Holidays, 10–5; Thu 10–5, 8 pm–10 pm; Oct–Mar: Daily, except Tue, Thu and Public Holidays, 10–4; Thu 10–4, 7 pm–9 pm)

Karlsruhe
10. Stadtgarten

This became a public park in 1967 for the Federal Garden Show. Two lakes joined by a canal give the impression of a riverbank landscape. There is a Japanese garden, created in 1920 and restored for 1967, a rose garden and a 'gondoletta'. Open-air concerts are given in the park and there is also a theatre. The zoo is at the south and east ends of the park.

(1) Daily Sunrise–Sunset
(2) Charge
(3) Café
(4) Zoo

Lahr
11. Stadtpark

The park was founded in 1860–2 and covers 18 acres (7·5 ha). It is laid out in the English style and contains old and attractive trees, flowerbeds, roses and dahlias, a lake and glasshouses with orchids, succulents and cacti.

(1) Daily Sunrise–Sunset
(2) Free
(3) Restaurant (Summer)

Bad Liebenzell
12. Kurpark

The park is situated on the bank of the River Nagold and covers 7 acres (3 ha). Its central feature is the Promenadenallee dating from the 18th cent. The park was laid out in 1900–15 and extended and remodelled in 1953–4. It contains elegant fountains. Concerts are sometimes given here, for which a fee is charged.

(1) Daily
(2) Free

Ludwigsburg
13. Schloss Ludwigsburg

The palace was built between 1704 and 1733 and is Germany's largest palace in the Baroque style. It consists of 18 buildings situated around 3 courtyards and has 452 rooms. The Ludwigsburg porcelain factory is housed in part of the palace.

The park was remodelled in 1954 under the direction of A. Schöchle to celebrate the 250th anniversary of the palace. In front of the palace on the south side is the formal Baroque garden. A path with flowerbeds leads to a round pond with fountains and on either side of the path are large lawns. Beyond the pond the path continues and on either side are formal Baroque parterres of grass with floral designs and topiary. Beside these are plain parterres with fountains and high clipped hedges and, beyond, displays of roses. Directly in front of the palace there are plantings of spring flowers and on each side dahlias.

Behind the palace on one side is a Renaissance garden and an intricate Baroque broderie with a central pond and fountain. On the other side and extending beyond the palace is a natural area of lawns and trees. 500,000 tulips flower in April and May and there are displays of roses, dahlias and other flowers throughout the spring and autumn. There are over 800 varieties of shrubs, a rhododendron glen, azaleas and an avenue of plane trees called the Brückenweg; flamingoes, a large aviary, a children's playground and the Fairy Tale Garden (Märchengarten) for children, with gondolas and groups depicting the characters and animals of German fairy tales.

In the furthermost part of this area is a lake, the Schlüsselsee, with a large fountain floodlit in the evenings and, nearby, a garden of rare plants. Beside the lake is a pavilion.

The grounds also contain the romantic ruins of Emichsburg on a rock outcrop and the Rococo Schloss Monrepos built in 1760–5 by De la Guepière. Through a deer park is the Lustschlösschen Favorite (1718–23) with a large boating lake.

(1) *Park. End Mar–mid-Oct: Daily 7.30 am–8.30 pm. Fairy Tale Garden. End Mar–mid-Oct: Daily 7.30–6*
(2) *Charge*
(3) *Café and restaurant*
(4) *Schloss (March–mid-Oct: Daily 9–noon, 1–5. Conducted tours in several languages)*

Mainau Island, Lake Constance

14. Mainau Island

The island covers 111 acres (45 ha) and is less than a mile (1·6 km) across at its greatest extent. Two-thirds of it are gardens.

There was a monastery here in the 9th cent and in 1271 the Prebend Mainau was founded. In 1491 the island passed to the Electors of Baden. The Baroque *schloss* was built in 1738–46. In 1853 the island was inherited by Grand Duke Friedrich I of Baden who laid out the gardens in 1860–80, planting trees brought back from his travels in and beyond Europe, such as orange and lemon trees, cedars and giant sequoias. In 1932 the island was inherited by Count Lennart Bernadotte who further developed the gardens. Since 1974 the island has been a foundation for the public benefit.

The island is generally reached by a long bridge on the western side. A smaller bridge

takes the visitor to the entrance to the gardens and thence through the lower gardens, reaching an animal enclosure with ponies and miniature animals, a pond with water-birds, goldfish and a fountain and then a stone statue, The Fisherwoman of Lake Constance. Above these a path bordered with 250 varities of roses leads to a grove of apple trees.

On the southern side of the island there is a garden of irises and rare lilies. In the lower gardens, in summer, flowerbeds contain 550 varieties of tulips including wild, Darwin hybrid and other varieties. Here, too, exotic trees surround flowerbeds containing over 180 varieties of dahlias. Above the dahlia display a path leads up through trees to the gardens laid out before the *schloss*. A lime tree commemorates the poet Scheffel and there is a stone memorial to Queen Victoria, daughter of Grand Duke Friedrich I of Baden. To the right of the terraces is the Tropical Garden. Here are palms, bananas, eucalyptus, Indian cane, tropical trumpets and many other sub-tropical plants. Some of these are housed in temporary glasshouses for protection during the winter which are then dismantled in the spring.

To the left is the rose garden, laid out in the Italian style with pergolas and flowerbeds around a central urn. This area has been enlarged and, in summer, over 30,000 roses flower in the garden and its extensions. The Tea rose from China, 'Maréchal-Niel', which has flowered here for over 100 years and Hybrid Teas including 'Virgo', standard and rambler roses grow in this area, and there are other plants such as hibiscus and heliotrope and also cypress trees.

Steps lead to the *schloss* terrace, from which there is a magnificent view. This has palms, orange and lemon trees and orchids – all protected during the winter – as well as exotic birds. On one side of the palace is the Baroque chapel (1739). On the western side are lawns with great cedars and flowerbeds around a fortified tower. Below these is a terrace with cypresses, palms, Mexican agaves, bougainvillea, cordyline and other sub-tropical plants. Through a Baroque wrought-iron gate the visitor may return to the lower gardens.

On the inland side an avenue of sweet chestnuts and the Spring Promenade (crocuses, hyacinths, daffodils and narcissi) lead to the Swede's Tower and to the arboretum, planted by the Grand Duke. This is a 100-year-old collection of 750 varieties and includes cedar of Lebanon, ginkgo trees, giant sequoias, Atlas cedars, deodars and Austrian pines. An avenue of dawn redwoods (*Metasequoia glyptostroboides*) has been planted.

(1) *Apr–Oct: Daily 8–7*
(2) *Charge*
(3) *Restaurants and kiosks*
(4) *Chapel*

Mannheim

15. Friedrichsplatz

Created in 1907 for the 300th anniversary of the town when there was an international art exhibition and landscape gardening show. It has ornamental fountains and geometrically laid-out flowerbeds and is surrounded by a crescent of arcaded Art Nouveau buildings. The water tower dominates the square. The fountains which play from April to October are illuminated on Saturdays and Sundays.

(1) Daily
(2) Free

Mannheim

16. Herzogenriedpark

Originating in 1928, the park was redesigned for the Federal Garden Show of 1975. There are large shrubberies, a rose garden, a wildlife enclosure, a pond for model boats and the Multihölle, a wooden lattice structure with a foil roof that is the first of its kind in the world.

(1) May–Sep: Daily 9 am–10 pm; Oct–Apr: Daily 9–9
(2) Charge

Mannheim

17. Luisenpark

Laid out between 1892 and 1903, this contains many old and rare trees, shrubs, a glasshouse for tropical and sub-tropical plants, an aviary and a 'gondoletta'. It was turned into a multi-purpose park for the 1967 Federal Garden Show, when the terrarium, aquarium and lakeside theatre were added.

(1) Park. May–Sep: Daily 9 am–10 pm; Oct–Apr: Daily 9–9; Glasshouse. May–Sep: Daily 10–6.30; Oct–Apr: Daily 10–4.30
(2) Charge
(3) Café; revolving restaurant in television tower

Bad Mergentheim

18. Schlosspark

The park attached to the 16th-cent Castle of the Teutonic Order was originally laid out in 1606. In 1791, after the schloss was renovated, it was transformed into a landscape park and extensively restored in 1950. There are ancient plane trees, a honey locust and an Indian bean-tree. It is linked by bridges with the Kurpark, where at certain hours the fountains play.

(1) Daily
(2) Free

(4) Schloss (Feb–Nov: Mon, Tue, Wed tour at 10.30; Thu and Fri tour at 3.30; Dec–Jan: Wed tour at 10.30)

Pforzheim

19. Alpine Garden

This is a small garden situated on a mountain-side in the Würmtal National Park. It was laid out in 1927–39, completely destroyed in World War II and restored in 1954–9. It contains an important world-wide collection of alpine plants, with over 5,000 varieties of mountain and rock-garden plants. There are also dwarf conifers, dwarf shrubs, rhododendrons and azaleas.

(1) Apr–Oct: Mon–Sat 8–6; Sun and Public Holidays 7–7
(2) Charge
(3) Café
(4) Plants for sale

Schwetzingen

20. Schlosspark Schwetzingen

The earliest mention of a schloss at Schwetzingen was in 1350. In 1699–1715 the Elector Johann Wilhelm had the schloss rebuilt as it stands today.

The gardens were created by Carl Theodor, the last Elector Palatine, in 1752, and laid out in the formal French style by Nicolas de Pigage and Johann Ludwig Petri. After 1778 F. L. von Sckell, Germany's first landscape gardener, created an English garden which was set apart from the French garden. The gardens were remodelled according to the original designs in 1974.

In the cour d'honneur in front of the schloss there is lilac which was brought from Asia. The gardens extend behind the schloss, on its western side. Directly behind the schloss and at a lower level are the parterres, the gardens' central feature, which form a large circle flanked by a circle of buildings. The parterres consist of grass with designs in clipped dwarf hedges and coloured gravel and of grass with flower borders. Each area has an ornamental pond, fountain or marble urn at its centre and all are grouped around a central pond with a fountain. Rows of ancient limes border the paths between the parterres: four rows from west to east and ten rows from north to south. At the point of the circle opposite the schloss is a very fine group of stags by the sculptor Peter Anton von Verschaffelt.

Following a path to the right, a pond and fountain with lead sculptures by Barthélemy Guibal are reached, and a little further on are statues in the Rococo style by Konrad Linck. Also in this wooded area of the gardens is a statue of Pan playing his pipe, sitting on a rock, by Simon Peter Lamine.

Beyond this woodland area is a lower level of garden with an orangery, behind which Rococo wrought-iron gates by Rabaliatti lead into an arboretum. To the west of both the orangery and the arboretum is the Temple of Apollo for which the statue of Apollo was designed by Verschaffelt and the area surrounding the temple by Pigage. Steps lead up to a fountain beneath the temple which is set on a small artificial hill. Nearby is a small stone grotto.

The Bath House was designed by Pigage in 1766. There are statues, including some ornamented in gold leaf, a painted ceiling and rosewood panelling. Behind the Bath House is a Rococo feature: through a pergola covered with vines is the Fountain of Birds: a ring of birds spit water into basins beneath them.

Beyond and over a canal is the English garden containing the Temple of Botany by Pigage and a romantic artificial ruin of a Roman fort covered in ivy.

Returning in a western direction the visitor crosses the Chinese Bridge over a canal and comes to a large lake surrounded by tall trees. A row of limes separates this area of the gardens from the French Garden, which lies between the lake and the parterres. This lake contains two reclining statues of water-gods which represent the Danube and the Rhine. The sculptor, Verschaffelt, died before completing statues to represent the Mosel and the Maas.

On the southern side of the lake is a further area in the English style containing the Temple of Mercury ruin and, nearby, the Turkish Garden and the Mosque by Pigage of c 1780. The Temple of Minerva was restored in 1951.

Another remarkable feature of the gardens is the richly decorated Rococo theatre, built by Pigage in 1752–62. Since 1952 plays have been performed here during the *Schwetzingen Festspiele*, which takes place each year from mid-May to mid-June.

(1) Daily 8–Sunset
(2) Charge
(3) Restaurant

Stuttgart, Hohenheim

21. Botanical and Exotic Gardens of Hohenheim University

The Botanical Garden was founded for the royal agricultural academy of Hohenheim in 1829 in what was the park of Hohenheim Palace, which now forms part of the university buildings. It was extended in 1975 to include a historical vegetation area – the natural and anthropological development of woodland vegetation in Central Europe over the past 12,000 years and the development of agriculture – and a systematic section with approx 2,000 varieties of ornamental shrubs and plants. There are also examples of rare deciduous and coniferous trees.

The Exotic Garden, which was formerly a school for the study of exotic trees, adjoins the Botanical Garden and the area planted with trees covers approx 17 acres (7 ha). It was created in 1813 as a school of forestry and in 1922 it became part of the

grounds of Hohenheim University and thus under the same administration as the Botanical Garden.

(1) Daily
(2) Free
(4) Museum in Exotic Garden (Sat 2–5; Sun 10–1, 2–5); Agricultural Museum (Wed–Sat 2–5; Sun 10–5)

Stuttgart

22. Höhenpark Killesberg

A modern landscaped park covering 123 acres (50 ha), first laid out by Professor Hermann Mattern for the Reichs Garden Exhibition of 1939. After its destruction in World War II it was remodelled for the Federal Garden Shows of 1950 and 1961. Special features of the park are the rose garden, the spring flowers and in particular the primulas, the parterre, the sunken garden, the marsh and aquatic plants of the water-lily pond and lake terraces, the tulips, gladioli, dahlias and the conifer collection.

(1) Apr–Oct: Daily
(2) Charge
(3) Café
(4) Belvedere, chair-lift, narrow-gauge railway

Stuttgart, Bad Cannstatt

23. Park Wilhelma

The park is a zoological and botanical garden with flora and fauna from all over the world. The original Wilhelma was built as a country palace and park in the Moorish style for Wilhelm I in 1837–53. It was opened as a botanical garden for the public after World War I, destroyed during World War II and remodelled in its present form, with a zoological garden, by 1953.

The park's chief features are the Moorish Garden which contains Europe's largest magnolia grove (visit in April), an orchid collection of 10,000 plants and 100-year-old azaleas and camellias (visit in March and April). There are many further plant collections in the glasshouses, including tropical water-lilies such as *Victoria regia*. The park covers 49 acres (20 ha).

(1) Summer: Daily 7–7; Winter: Daily 8–4
(2) Charge
(3) Restaurant

Stuttgart

24. Rosensteinpark

Founded by King Wilhelm I of Württemberg in 1820, the landscaped park in the English manner and Schloss Rosenstein were designed by Giovanni Salucci. The park covers 148 acres (60 ha) and contains many rare trees. It is linked to the Schlossgarten (qv) by footbridges and adjoins the Park Wilhelma (qv). Schloss Rosenstein houses the regional museum of natural history.

(1) *Daily*
(2) *Free*
(4) *Schloss (Tue–Sat 10–4; Sun 10–5)*

Stuttgart
25. Schlossgarten

The park, stretching from the New Palace and central station in the centre of the town to the River Neckar, was founded by Friedrich I of Württemberg in 1805, the year he was proclaimed king. It covers 79 acres (32 ha) and consists of an upper, middle and lower garden. The upper garden contains the rose garden and 'theatre lake', illuminated in the evening. The middle garden has a lake, fountains and the ruins of a pavilion, considered a masterpiece of the German Renaissance, which formerly stood in the town square. Both the upper and middle gardens were remodelled for the Federal Garden Show of 1961. The lower garden, which was remodelled for the Federal Garden Show of 1977 and has a magnificent avenue of old plane trees, stretches down to the River Neckar and adjoins the Rosenstein Park (qv).

(1) *Daily*
(2) *Free*
(3) *Café and restaurant*

Stuttgart
26. Villa Berg

The villa was built in 1848–53 in the Italian Renaissance style. Since 1950 it has been used by South German Radio.

The park, linked to the Schlossgarten (qv) since 1977 and situated on high ground with views over the River Neckar, was created originally in 1853. It was badly damaged in World War II and redesigned in 1966. There is now a terraced garden laid out above an underground car park which consists of concrete areas with shrub beds. This forms a modern parterre in front of the villa. Water from a fountain and basin cascades over concrete basins decorated with majolica tiles to collect in a large ornamental pool in the terraced garden, from where it is pumped back again. Among the old trees in the park are huge copper beeches, Indian bean-trees, cedars, nettle trees, paulownias and dawn redwoods.

(1) *Daily*
(2) *Free*

Tübingen
27. Botanical Garden of Tübingen University

The new botanical garden was opened in 1969 and covers 25 acres (10 ha). Its history dates back to a *hortus medicus* of 1675 which was extended in 1806. There are individual gardens for flowering shrubs, for cacti and grasses and for rock-garden plants; there is an iris and lily collection, a Japanese lake surrounded by azaleas and areas for the botanical system and plant family groupings; there is an alpine collection and a large collection of Bavarian wild flowers.

The glasshouse complex contains a large variety of tropical and sub-tropical plants. There are orchids, cacti and succulents, insectivorous plants and Louisiana and Virginia moss (*Tillandsia usneoides*). The tropicarium represents the tropical rain forest with palms, bananas, tropical marsh and aquatic plants such as Egyptian papyrus (*Cyperus papyrus*), Indian lotus-blossom (*Nelumbo nucifera*), water hyacinths (*Eichhornia crassipes*) and tropical water-lilies. There are also epiphytes and food plants such as cocoa and vanilla from tropical regions. There are botanical rarities from the high mountains of Kenya, South America and the northern tundra. The national flower of Chile, *Lapageria rosea*, flowers constantly in the sub-tropical glasshouse. A recent addition is a sempervivum collection.

(1) *Garden. Mon–Fri 7–4.45; Sat, Sun and Public Holidays 8–4.45. Glasshouses. Mon–Fri 7–11.45, 1–4.45; Sat, Sun and Public Holidays 10–11.45, 1.30–4.45. Arboretum. Mon, Wed, Thu 7–4.30; Tue and Fri 7–noon*
(2) *Free*
(3) *Café*

Uberlingen
28. Stadtgarten

A landscaped park covering 9 acres (3·5 ha) laid out in 1875–6 on the site of a vegetable garden and vineyard. Among the fine deciduous trees and conifers are Western red cedars (*Thuja plicata*), sequoias and Lawson cypresses (*Chamaecyparis lawsoniana*). A large collection of cacti is exhibited in the open in the summer. The park is particularly worth visiting in spring when the magnolias are in flower.

(1) *Daily*
(2) *Free*

Weikersheim
29. Schloss Weikersheim

One of the few formal parks in Franconia which has remained unaltered since it was founded by Count Karl Ludwig of Hohenlohe in 1709. The designer was Mathieu.

The park is situated beyond the moat of the *schloss*, built between 1580 and 1680 and containing fine interiors and a collection of works of art. The park contains numerous sculptures by Christopher and Philip Jacob Sommer, including sixteen figures on the balustrade of the moat. There is an orangery (1719), belvedere and avenues of chestnut trees.

(*1*) *Summer: Daily 7–8; Winter: Daily 9–6*
(*2*) *Charge*
(*4*) *Schloss (Apr–Oct: Mon–Sat 8–noon, 1–6; Nov–Mar: Tue–Sat 10–noon, 2–4)*

Weinheim

30. Schlosspark and Exotenwald

The gardens were laid out in *c* 1790 by F. L. von Sckell in the English landscape style. They contain the largest and oldest cedar of Lebanon in Germany, planted in *c* 1790, and 230-year-old hedges of clipped box. The *schloss* is in the Renaissance style and dates from 1537.

The Exotenwald was created by Baron von Berckheim in 1868 and is one of the most notable artificially created forests in the world. It contains sweet chestnuts, giant sequoias, Austrian pines, incense cedars, Japanese umbrella pines, tulip-trees, and mountain pines and many other exotic trees.

(*1*) *Park. Daily 8–Sunset. Forest. Apr–Sep: Daily. Guided tours through the Park and Forest on Saturdays at 4*
(*2*) *Free*
(*3*) *Café*

Wildbad

31. Kurpark

Situated beside the River Enz and covering 32 acres (13 ha), the park was founded by Duke Eberhard Ludwig von Württemberg, who planted a double-rowed hornbeam avenue in 1699. Roses, azaleas and rhododendrons surround the pump room, which was renovated in 1958.

(*1*) *Daily*
(*2*) *Free*

Kilometres

0   20   40   60

0   10   20   30   40

Miles

(11)

(21)

(12) (13)

Coburg

(20)

(3)

Aschaffenburg

Bamberg

Bayreuth

(4)

(10) (9)

(7) (8)

(32) (36)

(34)

(30)

(38) (37)

(1)

(39) Würzburg

(16)

Nuremberg

(17)

(27)

(2)

(29) Regensburg

(28)

(15) Eichstatt

(33)

(31)

(6)

Augsburg

(14) (23)

(5)

(25) (24)

(26) Munich

(35)

(19)

Garmisch-
Partenkirchen

(22)

(18)

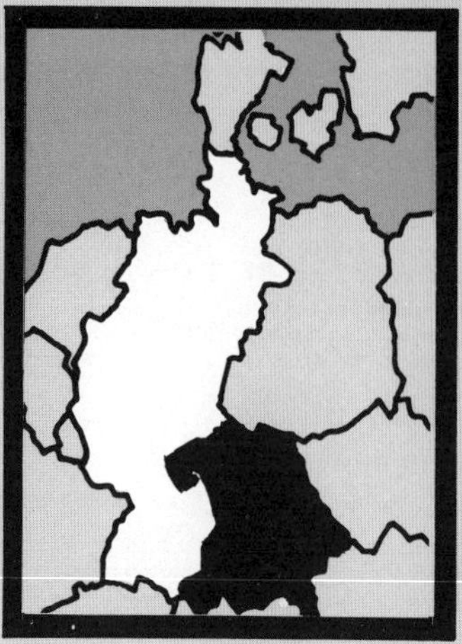

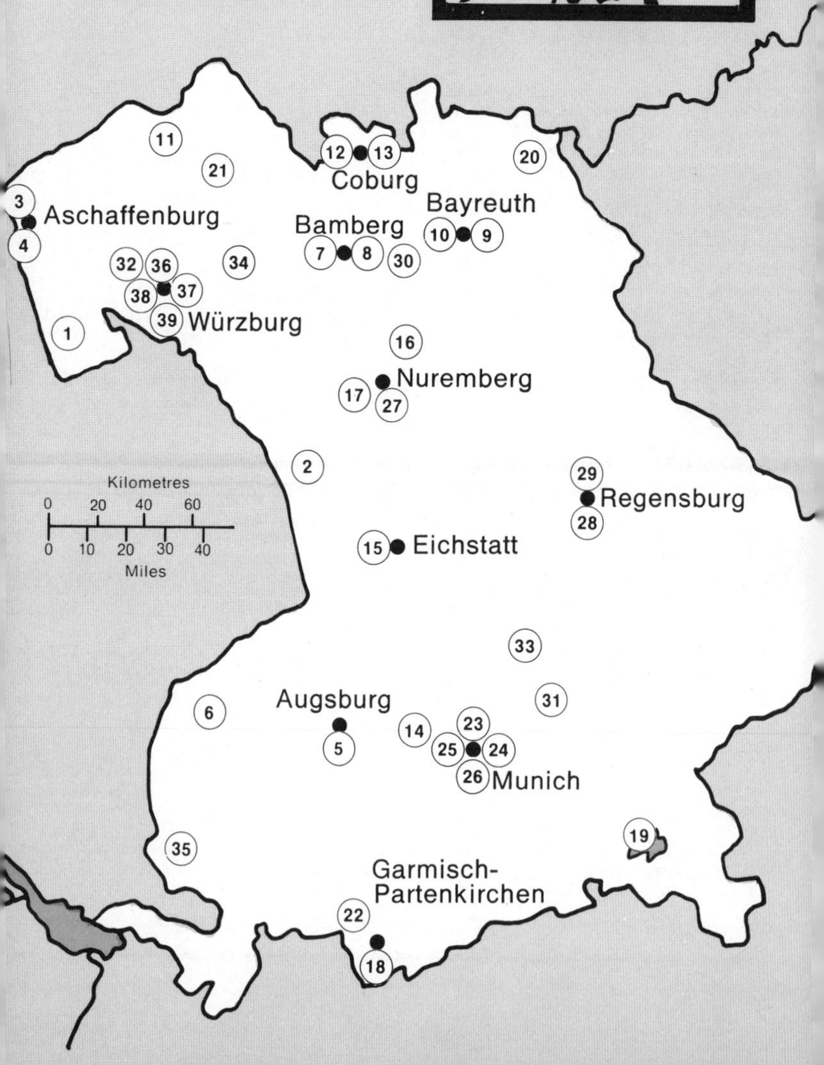

Amorbach

1. Seegarten

This was originally the garden of the Benedictine Abbey of Amorbach but after the princes of Leiningen took up residence in 1802 it was transformed into an English landscaped garden according to a design by F. L. von Sckell. The park is named after the many fishponds maintained by the monastery and displays magnificent specimens of silver maple. The café is in the former monastery mill of 1448.

(1) Daily
(2) Free
(3) Café
*(4) Abbey church (Apr–Sep: Mon–Sat 8–
    6.30; Oct–Mar: Mon–Sat 2–4.30; Sun
    and Protestant Festivals 12.30
    onwards)*

Ansbach

2. Hofgarten

The garden covers 42 acres (17 ha) and is situated near the residence of the Margrave. The original palace was burnt down in 1667 and in 1726–8 an orangery was built in its place by Karl Friedrich von Zocha. The French formal garden was altered to an English garden in *c* 1770–80, but there is a Baroque parterre in front of the orangery. A double avenue of limes was planted by the Margravine Christiane Charlotte von Ansbach in 1723 and now forms a green arcade in summer.

On alternate years the Rococo festival takes place over a weekend in July.

(1) Daily
(2) Free

Aschaffenburg

3. Park Schöntal

The park, which is situated 2 miles (3 km) to the west of the town and covers 23 acres (9·6 ha), originated as a zoological garden in the 15th cent. In 1775 it was remodelled as a park in the English landscape style. It has a lake, old trees and the ruins of the moated monastery. It is opposite the Park Schönbusch (qv below).

(1) Daily Sunrise–Sunset
(2) Free
(3) Café

Aschaffenburg

4. Schönbusch

This was Germany's first landscaped park in the English style. Formerly a game reserve, the park was founded by the Minister of State, Wilhelm von Sickingen in 1775 and further developed by the Portuguese architect Joseph Emanuel d'Herigoyen. The *schloss* was completed in 1780. After Sickingen left the Elector Carl von Erthal's service, F. L. von Sckell

became responsible for the park and it was his first great achievement. Covering 395 acres (160 ha), it contains a number of fine and unusual trees such as the copper beech, ginkgo, Indian bean-tree, tulip-tree, swamp cypress and dawn redwood. There is a maze, a belvedere, a lake and a canal with bridges, a temple – the Temple of Friendship – and pavilions. The park is situated in a loop of the River Main.

(1) Daily
(2) Free
(3) Restaurant
*(4) Schloss (Apr–Sep: Daily 8–1, 2–6;
    Oct–Mar: Daily 10–noon, 2–4)*

Augsburg, Parkstrasse 15a

5. Botanical Garden and Siebentisch Grounds

The garden was laid out in 1936–7 next to the Siebentisch grounds, a park designed by Karl von Effner, and covers nearly 4½ acres (2 ha). It consists of open grounds with summer flowers, shrubs, a variety of tulips, a rose garden, aquatic plants and trees, and of glasshouses containing tropical and sub-tropical plants which include palms, cacti, orchids, *Bromeliaceae* and the giant water-lily, *Victoria regia*. Visit in May and September.

*(1) May–Sep: Mon–Sat 9–6; Sun 9–5;
    Oct–Apr: Daily 9–5*
(2) Charge

Babenhausen

6. Schlosspark

The 5 acre (2 ha) park is attached to Schloss Rechberg with the Fugger Museum which belonged to the princes Fugger. Its present lay-out dates from 1911. There is a parterre in the French style and hornbeam alleys which are over 250 years old. The mature trees include one of Germany's oldest Weymouth pines (*Pinus strobus*) and six limes thought to be over 350 years old.

(1) Daily 10–noon
(2) Free
*(4) Fugger Museum (Mar–Oct: Tue–Sat
    10–noon, 2–5; Sun 10–noon, 1–6)*

Bamberg, Domplatz

7. Rosengarten

This small rose garden was designed in 1733 by Balthazar Neumann for the Prince-Bishop Friedrich Carl von Schönborn. Laid out on a terrace around a central pool with paths and pergolas, it contains old and new varieties of shrub and climbing roses, floribundas and Hybrid Teas. Copies of sculptures made by Ferdinand Tietz in 1760–1 adorn the garden.

(1) Daily
(2) Free

Bamberg

8. Theresien and Luisenhain

The parks are situated between two arms of the River Regnitz and cover 128¼ acres (52 ha). After 1803 they were remodelled as a park in the English style under the direction of King Maximilian I and opened to the public. There are mature trees, notably oaks, hornbeams and black poplars. One grove of oaks is 150 years old and consists of twenty varieties; another plantation of oaks dates back to 1440. A former hunting lodge has been a café since 1764 and E. T. A. Hoffmann often came here. A small part of the park was laid out as a botanical garden with ponds in 1923.

(1) Daily
(2) Free
(3) Café
(4) Karl May Museum (Mon–Fri 10–noon, 2–4; Sat and Sun 10–noon)

Bayreuth

9. Eremitage Garten

2½ miles (4 km) from the centre of Bayreuth to the east, this landscaped park surrounds two palaces.

The Altes Schloss was begun in 1715 by the Margrave Georg Wilhelm von Brandenburg-Bayreuth as a country retreat from his principal residence. Monastic cells, in which guests could make believe they were hermits, open on to the inner courtyard, and there is also a grotto. The gardens were first laid out in 1718 by Gabriel Lück. From 1736 onwards the Margravine Wilhelmina laid out part of the gardens as a landscaped park.

The semi-circular Neues Schloss, situated only a few yards west of the Altes Schloss, was built for the Margravine in 1749–53 and rebuilt in 1945. It is surrounded by formal gardens with fountains, statuary, staircases and a grotto with fountains. The grounds were remodelled in the English style after the Margravine's death. She had many artificial ruins built in the wooded park surrounding this garden such as the theatre built as a ruin in 1743 by Joseph Saint-Pierre and the hermitage cottage. The park now covers approx 116 acres (47 ha). From May to mid-October the fountains play each day at 11–11.30 and 3.30–4.

(1) Daily
(2) Free
(3) Café
(4) Altes Schloss (Apr–Sep: Daily, except Mon, 9–11.30, 1–4.30; Oct–Mar: Daily, except Mon, 10–11.30, 1–2.30)

Bayreuth

10. Hofgarten

Covering 33 acres (13·5 ha) the park is situated behind the Neues Schloss in the centre of Bayreuth. It was originally a vegetable garden, then a pleasure garden, and it was extended in 1670 by the addition of a grotto with a mineral spring, a tennis court, an orangery and two parallel avenues. In 1753 the Altes Schloss burnt down and the Neues Schloss was built here in 1753–4 for the Margrave Friedrich and his wife Wilhelmina, sister of Frederick the Great. At the same time the garden was extended and transformed into a landscaped park under her direction. This style did not replace the formal French style elsewhere in Germany until c 1790. A canal was completed in 1755 which retains the Baroque style yet resembles a natural river. This forms the central axis. After the deaths of the Margrave and his wife, the park was remodelled c 1790 as an English park. The *schloss* contains richly decorated apartments and the Bavarian art gallery.

(1) Daily
(2) Free
(3) Café
(4) Neues Schloss (Summer: Daily, except Mon, 10–noon, 1.30–5; Winter: Daily except Mon, 10–noon, 1.30–3.30)

Bad Brückenau

11. Kurpark

The grounds were first laid out in c 1747 and have since been enlarged. The old spa park, remodelled in 1890 and 1954, consists of terraced gardens and lawns with flowerbeds, shrubs and hedges, boskets and avenues. The new spa park, laid out in 1954, consists of expansive lawn areas, flowers and woods and connects the grounds with the surrounding woods and fields. The most remarkable trees are a tall tulip-tree, a ginkgo and an oak that is 1,000 years old.

(1) Daily
(2) Free except for concerts

Coburg

12. Hofgarten

Connecting the castle square in the town centre with the Veste Coburg, a 16th-cent fortress, the garden was founded in c 1860 in the English landscaped style by Duke Ernst II of Saxe-Coburg-Gotha. It contains a small rose garden, restored in 1962, and trees which date from the creation of the garden. It covers 161 acres (65 ha).

(1) Daily
(2) Free
(3) Café
(4) Veste Coburg (Apr–Oct: Daily, except Mon, 10–1; 2–4; Nov–Mar: 2–3.30)

Coburg

13. Rosengarten

This garden was laid out to the south of the town as an exhibition park for the German Rose Show in 1929 and remodelled in 1947. As well as roses, the garden contains sunken gardens, rock gardens, water-lily ponds, fountains and displays of tulips and dahlias. Glasshouses contain exotic plants. It covers 20 acres (8 ha).

(1) Daily
(2) Free

Dachau

14. Schlosspark

The park, situated behind Schloss Dachau, dates from the beginning of the 15th cent and covers 23 acres (9·5 ha). It was remodelled as a Baroque garden after 1716 and by 1791 it was laid out in the English style with lawns and rows of fruit trees. An arcade of limes planted in c 1790, cuts across the park. There is an attractive view over the surrounding countryside. The *schloss* was used by Bavarian counts, electors and kings before the building of the palaces at Nymphenburg (qv under Munich) and Schleissheim (qv).

(1) Daily Sunrise–Sunset
(2) Free

Eichstätt

15. Hofgarten

The town has a long horticultural tradition. As early as 1597 the Nuremberg apothecary Basilius Besler laid out a famous botanical garden for Prince-Bishop Johann Conrad and in 1613 the *Hortus Eystettensis* was produced in Eichstätt with copper engravings by Besler of plants in the Prince-Bishop's collection. A new Rococo-style garden was laid out for Prince-Bishop Franz Ludwig Schenk von Castell after the completion of a new Residenz in 1735. The three remaining pavilions in the garden date from 1757–81.

The garden was extended in 1786 and in the first half of the 19th cent it was transformed into a garden in the English style. It retains this form today, but the fountains and statues of the Rococo garden remain. It covers 5 acres (2 ha) and contains a ginkgo, a honey locust, a giant sequoia and an Indian bean-tree.

(1) Daily
(2) Free

Erlangen

16. Erlangen University Botanical Garden

Soon after the university was founded in 1743, plans for a botanical garden were drawn up. However, the garden was not established until the medicinal garden of

WEST GERMANY

Altdorf Academy was closed in c 1818. It contains a wide variety of plants from different soils and climates, glasshouses, an arboretum, a systematic section and a morphological-ecological section. The oldest plant, which probably came from the garden at Altdorf, is a palm fern (*Cycas circinalis*) that is almost 300 years old.

(1) Mon–Thu, Sun and Public Holidays 9.30–11.30; also Tue and Wed 1.30–4
(2) Free

Fürth

17. Stadtpark

The park, founded in 1870 and extended several times since, covers 40 acres (16 ha). There are lawns, flower gardens and many trees, including a 100-year-old mulberry tree, a Japanese pagoda-tree and swamp cypresses. An avenue of limes leads to a fountain near an open-air theatre. There are two lakes with water fowl and there are many statues. Besides a rose garden, there are herbaceous and shrub borders, a 'desert' garden, rhododendrons, an iris garden and a wall planted with mosses. The botanical nursery, founded in 1920, forms part of the park.

(1) Daily
(2) Free
(3) Café
(4) Botanical Nursery (Daily 8–3.30)

Garmisch-Partenkirchen

18. Alpine Garden 'auf dem Schachen'

This was laid out by Munich University's Professor of Botany, Dr von Goebel and opened in 1901. It is under the administration of the Munich Botanical Garden (qv). It covers 2½ acres (1 ha) and is situated at 6,070 ft (1,850 m) on Mount Schachen. It contains over 1,000 varieties of plants arranged geographically, including flora of the European Alps, North American Rockies, Carpathian Mountains, the Near East, the Pyrenees, the Balkans, the Caucasus and the mountains of Asia. There is also a bed containing the rare *Wulfenia carinthiaca*. It is one of the alpine gardens with the greatest variety of plants.

(1) Jul–Sep: Daily 8–6
(2) Free

Herrenchiemsee

19. Schloss Herrenchiemsee

In 1873 Ludwig II of Bavaria bought the island, which covers 593 acres (240 ha), and attempted to create a castle and gardens in emulation of the sumptuousness of Versailles. The work of 1878–85 was, however, never completed and the king spent only a week there before his death.

The geometrical lay-out of the gardens was designed by Ludwig II together with Karl von Effner. The terraced gardens on the western side of the *schloss* consist of parterres with statuary and basins, between which a grand staircase leads to the Latona Fountain. Beyond the large flower-filled parterres lawns lead to the Apollo Basin and a canal. The fountains play during the summer. Avenues of limes form an east–west axis to either side of the castle, and there are 69 acres (28 ha) of natural woodland.

It is reached by boat from Prien-Stock.

(1) *Apr–Sep: Daily 9–5; Oct–Mar: Daily 10–4*
(2) *Free*
(3) *Café*

Hof

20. Stadtpark Theresienstein

A landscaped park covering 136 acres (55 ha). It includes a botanical garden which contains a rosarium and a wide variety of garden plants arranged in flowerbeds. It was created in 1816–18. There is also a 52 ft (16 m) tower and an artificial ruin.

(1) *Daily*
(2) *Free*
(3) *Restaurant (Sun)*

Bad Kissingen

21. Kurpark

The Kurgarten, Rosengarten and Luitpoldpark in the town centre together cover 99 acres (40 ha). They are situated along the banks of the River Saale, connected by bridges.

(1) *Daily*
(2) *Free*

Linderhof, nr Oberammergau

22. Schloss Linderhof

This is the most individual of Ludwig II's romantic castles, built between 1870 and 1878, and is situated in a valley between two mountains. The park, which covers 94 acres (38 ha), was laid out by Karl von Effner when the *schloss* was built in 1869. It consists of the French Garden of geometrically laid-out grounds around the palace with terraces, statuary and cascades and, beyond this, the English Garden – landscaped grounds with pines, sycamores and wing-nuts merging into the Alpine landscape.

In front of the *schloss* is a parterre bordered with clipped hornbeams and containing a central basin with a group of gilded figures and a fountain. The parterre is embellished with statuary. Beyond this are further parterres. The west parterre, bordered with clipped hornbeams, is divided into four sections. It consists of lawns, flowerbeds and clipped box with a central basin and gilded statue. There is a fountain and gilded statue of Amor and dolphins, urns and pavilions. The east parterre of lawns and flowerbeds bordered with hornbeam espaliers has in its centre stone statues of Venus and Adonis, a fountain with gilded putti and cast-zinc Amor on one side as well as statuary along the sides. At one end of the parterre is a pavilion, from which steps lead up to an area containing a star-shaped flowerbed surrounded by beeches.

Opposite the *schloss*, across the main parterre, steps lead up on the sides of three terraces. There are fountains, basins, niches and statuary. Each terrace has flowerbeds and clipped box trees. The top terrace has a rotunda and marble statue of Venus. Near the lowest terrace is the 300-year-old lime from which the *schloss*'s name is derived.

Behind the *schloss* on the northern side are steep slopes and a cascade of 32 marble steps with vases and *amoretti*. At the bottom of the cascade is a basin with fountains and a Neptune group and in front of this is a fleur-de-lys parterre with two stone vases. On either side of the cascade are pergolas of limes with small pavilions and statues. At the top of the cascade is a rotunda.

The park contains King Maximilian's hunting lodge, transferred to its present site when the *schloss* was built, and St Anne's Chapel built in 1864 for the abbot of Ettal Monastery. The hermitage was destroyed in 1945. The grotto, created in 1876–7 by August Dirigl, consists of a main grotto and two side grottoes with stalagmites and stalactites in the interior. The grotto was once illuminated by means of 24 dynamo engines made by Werner von Siemens. Today it is illuminated by spotlights.

The Moorish Kiosk was bought by Ludwig at the Paris Exhibition of 1867. It is constructed of iron with relief ornament and has a cupola and four turrets. The richly decorated interior contains the Peacock Throne made for Ludwig in 1877 by Le Blanc-Granger.

The *schloss* was built on a site near King Maximilian's hunting lodge between 1869 and 1878. The architect was Georg Dollman and the interior was principally designed by Frank Seitz.

(1) *Summer: 9–12.15, 12.45–5; Winter: 9–noon, 1–4. Closed on some Public Holidays*
(2) *Charge*
(3) *Café*
(4) *Schloss (same times)*

Munich

23. Botanical Garden

The garden originally belonged to the Bavarian Academy of Sciences and was laid out by Frederick P. von Schrank. In 1914 the garden was transferred to a new site adjoining the park of Schloss Nymphenburg (qv below). It covers nearly 50 acres (20 ha).

The ornamental garden has trees and shrubs and displays flowers throughout the year. The Spring Garden, surrounded by locust, honey-locust and pagoda trees, specializes in spring flowers and shrubs. The Alpine House has two sections, one unheated and one kept continually above frost-level. There is a large section for ecological and genetic plant groupings surrounded by a pergola and a section for plants grouped according to family. The extensive arboretum contains a lake, heather garden, alpine garden, fern glen and a rhododendron collection. There are collections of protected cereal and medicinal plants and a rose garden. The large glasshouse complex includes large collections of orchids, palms, small and large cacti, succulents including African and American varieties, ferns, mosses, insectivorous plants and water-lilies.

Large coloured parrots and figures of boys in local Nymphenburg pottery ornament the architectural features of the garden: the terraces, stairways and pergolas.

(1) *Summer: Daily 9–7; Winter: Daily 9–5*
(2) *Charge*
(3) *Café*

Munich

24. Englischer Garten

One of Europe's largest parks within a city, in all extending to 902 acres (365 ha), it was created under the direction of the Elector Carl Theodor at the suggestion of his minister Count von Rumford (the American Benjamin Thompson). The architect was F. L. von Sckell and the park was laid out, as the name suggests, in the English style. It was opened to the public in 1793, although not completed until 1803.

Paths lead through the parkland. There are tall elms, copper beeches and limes. The buildings include the Monopteros – a circular temple – and the Chinese tower. The large Kleinhesseloher lake lies to the north of the park.

(1) *Daily*
(2) *Free*
(3) *Café*

Munich

25. Hofgarten

This is one of Munich's oldest parks, dating from 1597. The present design dates from 1613–17 and it was created under the direction of Maximilian I. It was opened to

the public by the Elector Carl Theodor in 1790. The central point of the square garden is the Brunnentempel (1615), a twelve-sided pavilion by Heinrich Schön the Elder. This is surrounded by a Renaissance parterre with paths and hedges. There are avenues of horse chestnuts and of limes. The park was restored after damage in World War II and covers 15 acres (6 ha).

(1) *Daily*
(2) *Free*
(3) *Café*
(4) *Residenzmuseum (Apr–Sep: Tue–Sat 9–12.30, 1.30–5; Oct–Mar: 10–12.30, 1.30–4; Sun 10–1)*

Munich

26. Schlosspark Nymphenburg

The summer residence of the Bavarian ruling family was built from 1664 onwards by A. Barelli and E. Zuccalli. The park was first laid out as an Italian garden in 1671 under the direction of Adelaide of Savoy, wife of the Elector Ferdinand Maria. In 1701 it was remodelled as a French Baroque garden with Dutch-style canals by Charles Carbonet, a pupil of Le Nôtre. From 1715 to 1730 it was extended by Dominique Girard, to become one of Germany's greatest Baroque gardens. Fountains were added and also the Würm canal with avenues of limes on either side. In 1804–23 F. L. von Sckell transformed the gardens into an English landscape park. He preserved part of the Baroque gardens by incorporating the large parterre, in a simplified form, together with the canal, into his design.

The *schloss* is approached from the eastern side. Facing it is a crescent of pavilions, and among them the Nymphenburg Porcelain Manufactory. In front of these is a canal leading to the 18th-cent *cour d'honneur*.

The 500 acre (220 ha) park stretches out from the double staircase on the western side of the *schloss*. Immediately in front lies the large parterre, consisting of lawns with borders, besides which are paths with statues of gods and vases of Sterzing marble of c 1769. On the northern side of the parterre is a greenhouse by von Sckell (1807). Beyond the parterre the Würm Canal cuts straight through the park as its central axis, leading to a cascade designed by Joseph Effner and statuary including a reclining river god and nymph (1717) by G. Volpini. On either side of the canal are the landscape grounds with the Badenburg Lake to the south side and the Pagodenburg Lake to the north. Directly on either side of the *schloss* galleries and pavilions are the Cabinet Gardens laid out in the early 18th cent with statuary and, on one side, a small cascade.

The park contains three beautiful

pavilions, the Pagodenburg, the Badenburg and the Amalienburg. The Pagodenburg (1716) was built by Joseph Effner, who also built the Badenburg (1718) containing a Delft-tiled swimming-pool. The most famous is the Rococo Amalienburg which was built by Cuvilliés in 1734 as a hunting-box for the Electress Amalia. Between the Amalienburg and the Badenburg is the Menagerie (1791), the *Dörfchen* (small village) and the *Brunnhaus* (pump-house) built in 1762 and later rebuilt. This supplied water for the fountain of the parterre and for the palace. Near the eastern end of the Badenburg Lake is a sculpture depicting Pan playing the flute and a goat by P. Lamine (1815). Between the Badenburg and the cascade is the Monopteros (1865). There is also a hermitage named the Magdalenenklause, which is an artificial ruin with a grotto, built by Effner in 1725.

(*1*) *Apr–Sep: Daily 7 am–8 pm; Oct–Mar: Daily 7–5*
(*2*) *Free*
(*3*) *Café*
(*4*) *Schloss (Apr–Sep: Daily 9–5; Oct–Mar: Daily 10–4); Carriage Museum (same times as Schloss); Amalienburg (Summer: Tue–Sun 9–5; Winter: Tue–Sun 9–4); Badenburg (Summer: Tue–Sun 10–12.30, 1.30–5); Pagodenburg (Summer: Daily 10–noon, 2–6); Magdalenenklause (Summer: Tue–Sun 10–12.30, 1.30–5)*

Nuremberg
27. Stadtpark

The landscaped park with fine mature trees, flowerbeds and fountains covers 44 acres (18 ha). The flowers include tulips, roses, dahlias and climbing plants. The park was created in 1896 and was remodelled after being destroyed in World War II.

(*1*) *Daily*
(*2*) *Free*
(*3*) *Restaurant, kiosk*

Regensburg
28. Alleen

The former city ramparts were laid out as a park in 1790 and this was restored in 1947–9. Regensburg was the first city in Germany to create grounds of this kind. The 'green belt' is 900–1,300 ft (300–400 m) wide and is planted with limes, planes, maples, sycamores, *Corylus colurna*, honey-locusts and trees of heaven. There are monuments, fountains and flowers. The avenues link the Dörnberg-Park (qv below), the Stadtpark and the Herzogpark.

(*1*) *Daily*
(*2*) *Free*

Regensburg
29. Dörnberg-Park

The park was founded by Count von Dörnberg and was laid out by Karl von Effner in 1863–7 in the English style. It was restored and partly remodelled in 1954–7. There are lawns, avenues of magnificent trees including copper beeches, a rose garden, the *schloss* and its guest house.

(*1*) *Summer: Daily 6–Sunset: Winter: Daily 7–Sunset*
(*2*) *Free*
(*3*) *Café*

Sanspareil, nr Bayreuth
30. Sanspareil

A game park was begun in 1744 under the Margrave Friedrich von Bayreuth but the Margravine Wilhelmina soon became influential in the creation of a park in the English landscape style and this was completed in 1748. It is one of the oldest surviving landscape gardens on the Continent. The park was restored in 1951 and opened to the public in 1956. It covers 32 acres (13 ha) and is situated on the northern side of the fortress Zwernitz. The park takes its name (*Felsengarten*) from the rock and stone outcrops.

After passing through the chapel courtyard on the lower level of the fortress, the visitor passes through a narrow gully (*Eiskeller*) and comes to a sunken parterre. Formerly this was laid out with box and coloured sand but it has not been maintained since the end of the 19th cent. It was surrounded by four buildings of which two remain, the partly maintained *Küchenbau* and opposite this the Schloss Hainbau, or *Morganländischer Bau*. The latter was built as a rustic hermitage in 1746–7 for the Margravine Wilhelmina by the Bavarian court architect Joseph Saint-Pierre.

The park, with its huge rocky outcrops, extends behind this building. The *Felsenrondell* is an area surrounded by mountains and rocks. Here paths lead through trees to the Mentor Grotto and the Diana Grotto. The park now becomes less rocky and more wooded. The chapel, the statuary and the pavilion that were once here no longer remain, although stairs lead up the rock on which the pavilion was built.

At the foot of this rock is the Calypso Grotto, the Vulcan Grotto or Cave and the Ruins-and-Grotto Theatre. The latter, the park's most remarkable feature, was probably built by Saint-Pierre. North of this was formerly a geometrically laid out area but this no longer exists. Beyond it, in the furthermost part of the park is another group of rocks where there were originally grottoes and a temple.

(*1*) *Apr–Sep: Daily (except Mon) 9–noon, 1.20–5*
(*2*) *Charge*
(*3*) *Café*
(*4*) *Fortress (same times)*

Schleissheim, nr Munich

31. Schloss Schleissheim

One of the few German *Schlossparks* that has retained its Baroque design to the present day, it was laid out with the building of the palace by Carbonet; the first design was by Enrico Zuccalli, c 1684. It was remodelled for the ·Elector Max Emanuel c 1720 in the Dutch style by Dominique Girard. Both F. L. von Sckell and Karl von Effner retained the original design when working on the park in the first half of the 19th cent. There is a canal as the central axis of the park with canals on either side of it and cascades. Between these lie parterre and bosket gardens linked with paths and hedges. It covers 205 acres (83 ha).

The Baroque old and new palaces were both damaged during World War II and only the Neues Schloss has been restored. At the end of the main canal opposite the Neues Schloss is the Lustheim, a hunting lodge which now contains an important collection of Meissen porcelain.

(1) *May–Aug: Daily 8–8; Sep: Daily 8–7; Oct: Daily 8–6; Nov–Apr: Daily 8–5*
(2) *Free*
(3) *Café*
(4) *Neues Schloss and Lustheim (Summer: Daily 10–12.30, 1.30–5; Winter: Daily 10–12.30, 1.30–4)*

Veitshöchheim, nr Würzburg

32. Schloss Veitshöchheim

The palace was built in 1680–2 as a summer residence for Prince-Bishop Peter Philipp von Dernbach by Heinrich Zimmer, to designs by Petrini. It was extended in 1749–53 to designs by Balthazar Neumann. The garden was first laid out in 1702–3 and extended during the first half of the 18th cent by Neumann. The founder of the garden as it is seen today was Adam Friedrich von Seinsheim in 1763–74 with the garden architect Johann Mayer.

Veitschöchheim is one of Germany's greatest gardens and its oldest surviving garden in the French manner. It has been called 'Germany's Rococo Garden' and is a perfect example of south German Rococo. Characteristic of German Baroque and Rococo gardens are the many decorative sculptures and statuary. It covers 32 acres (13 ha).

The palace terrace and balustrade, created in 1702–3 and extended in 1753, has sculptures created in 1775–7 by Johann Peter Alexander Wagner of children, putti and ornamental vases.

The parterre garden around the palace dates in its present form from 1768 and consists of twelve flowerbeds and four fountains with trees planted during the 19th cent. The two western corners have octagonal pavilions of wooden treillage. It is laid out on an enclosed terrace, and a decorated staircase on the western side leads into

another area of garden. The western and southern walls enclosing the parterre garden have statues of gods and muses by J. W. van der Auvera, L. van der Auvera and Peter Wagner. On the southern side is another decorated staircase leading down from the parterre garden.

On the western side and leading west is an avenue bordered with hedges. Behind these on either side are two oval pools. On the northern side are buildings erected in 1749 by Neumann on the site of a demolished castle which are now used by the Regional Institute for Viticulture, Fruit-growing and Horticulture. The avenue leads to a circular area decorated with statuary at the main entrance and a gate-way to the grounds. From here an avenue leads southwards to the end of the large lake.

To the east is the rectangular bosket garden, crossed from east to west by a central axis which cuts through the large lake and circle and from north to south by an avenue of limes beginning at the western end of the parterre garden and an avenue of firs beginning on the southern side of the palace. This area of bosket garden is in three parts: the large and small lakes; the hedge and shrub area; and, on the eastern side, a wooded area.

The lakes are surrounded by gardens, enclosed mainly by hornbeam hedges. The design of the large lake was probably by Petrini and the path around it has figures of gods and allegorical figures by Ferdinand Tietz who was responsible for much of the sculpture at Veitshöchheim. In the centre of the lake there are statues representing Parnassus with Pegasus and other figures. A path leads from the southern side of the large lake to the small lake laid out in 1721. It has an artificial island with willows, and there are fountains, a water-spitting bird and allegorical statues. Around the lake are huge plane trees planted c 1825.

Crossing the magnificent lime avenue near the south entrance, the second area of the bosket garden may be entered. This narrow rectangular area consists of hedge-lined gardens with pergolas, statuary and an ornamental circular area in the central part. On the south side of the circle is a wooden treillage pavilion with carvings and paintings and on the north side a corresponding pavilion decorated with sculptures. The circle is the central point of the bosket garden. It is surrounded by a ring of limes forming a high hedge. In the centre are four great plane trees. The circle has fine sculptures including allegorical, hunting and pastoral figures.

At the northern end of this area the visitor crosses the fir avenue and comes to the wooded area of the bosket garden, first reaching the open-air theatre with hedges of hornbeam. South of this is a densely wooded area with paths, two springs laid out as sunken gardens and with statuary

227

and two canopied structures in Chinese style created in 1768. South of this area is an octagonal garden and next to this is an area of trees laid out in the form of a chessboard, called the *Lindensaal*.

At the southernmost end of the fir avenue in a niche is a figure of Orpheus surrounded by various beasts. Following the path on the southern side of the garden eastwards the grotto building and belvedere may be reached. The cascade was almost entirely destroyed in World War II. The grotto building has two floors, the lower forming the grotto and the upper a pavilion and belvedere. Both are decorated. It was created by Johann Philipp Geigel and Materno Bossi in 1772–3. This area also contains a 16th-cent watchtower.

(1) *Summer: Daily 7.30 am–8 pm; Winter: Daily 8–4*
(2) *Free*
(3) *Café*
(4) *Schloss (Apr–Sep: Daily 9–5)*

Weihenstephan
33. Horticultural Garden

Created in 1948, together with the State Teaching and Research Institute for Horticulture. It covers 12 acres (5 ha) and comprises collections of ornamental and other hardy perennials and ornamental trees and shrubs, including 250 varieties of *Paeonia lactiflora* and 800 varieties of rose.

It is the centre of German shrub testing and also the headquarters of the international shrub register and an international phenological garden. The garden was created and designed by Professor Dr Richard Hansen as Director of the Institute for Shrubs, Woods and Applied Botanical Sociology.

(1) *Daily 7–6*
(2) *Free*

Wiesentheid, nr Würzburg
34. Schlossgarten

A park in the English landscape style with lawns, trees, paths and a lake. The palace of the Counts of Schönborn was built in the second half of the 16th cent and between 1708 and 1724 the gardens were remodelled in the Baroque style. The park, replacing the gardens, assumed its present appearance in the 1860s.

(1) *Daily*
(2) *Free*

Bad Wurzach, nr Memmingen
35. Schlosspark and Kurpark

The parks adjoin one another and together cover 34 acres (14 ha). The Schlosspark in the English landscape style is situated behind the Baroque building and is noted for its lime trees. It was laid out in the second half of the 18th cent. The Kurpark was developed after World War II. It is landscaped with shrubs and ornamental flowers and the River Ach flows through it. Wurzach marsh with unusual flora and fauna extends beyond the park grounds.

(1) *Daily*
(2) *Free*

Würzburg
36. Botanical Garden of Julius-Maximilian-University

The garden belongs to the university's botanical institute. The University has had a botanical garden since 1695 but the present garden was built only in 1960. It covers approx 22 acres (9 ha). The modern glasshouse complex contains approx 4,000 and the open area approx 3,500 plant varieties. The plant stock is increased by the exchange of seed with 350 botanical gardens of the world. It has many divisions but can be divided into three main groups: plants according to their geographical and sociological groups, plants for medicinal and culinary purposes and flowering plants of both cultivated and wild varieties.

(1) *Garden. Apr–Sep: Daily 8–6; Oct–Mar: Daily: 8–4. Glasshouses. Wed and Sat 2–4; Sun and Public Holidays 10–noon, 2–4*
(2) *Free*

Würzburg
37. Hofgarten

The Residenz was created in 1720–44 for Johann Phillipp Franz von Schönborn by Balthazar Neumann. The park was designed by Neumann and his son Hildebrandt and Cuvilliés the Elder. Towards the end of the 18th cent the park was adapted to the Rococo style for the Prince-Bishop Adam Friedrich von Seinsheim by Johann Prokop Mayer. After the Prince-Bishop's death, part of the park was remodelled in the English landscape style. It covers 37 acres (15 ha). The trees include yews, cypresses, magnolias, downy trees of heaven, magnificent planes, limes, elms, mulberries and an avenue of ginkgos.

(1) *Daily Sunrise–Sunset*
(2) *Free*
(3) *Café*
(4) *Residenz (Apr–Sep: Daily 9–5; Oct–Mar: Daily, except Mon and 25 Dec, 10–4)*

Würzburg
38. Marienbergpark

One of Germany's oldest fortresses, situated in a commanding position above the town overlooking the River Main. There was a parterre here in the 16th cent and the staircases, balustrades and cascading fountains were added later. The garden with eight flowerbeds of roses and a fountain was restored in 1937–8.

(1) Daily Sunrise–Sunset
(2) Free
(3) Café
(4) Fortress (Apr–Sep: Daily 9–5; Oct– Mar: Daily, except 25 Dec: 10–4. Closed some mornings in winter)

Würzburg

39. Ringpark

The park begins and ends at the River Main, forming a curve through the city centre. It covers almost 69 acres (28 ha) and was created in 1883–1900 by Jens Lindahl on the site of the city's original fortifications. It is made up of four parts and contains old and many exotic trees, lawns and a rose garden with pergolas. Some of the unusual trees and shrubs were brought back by P. F. van Siebold from his explorations in Japan. The park was restored after damage during World War II.

(1) Daily
(2) Free

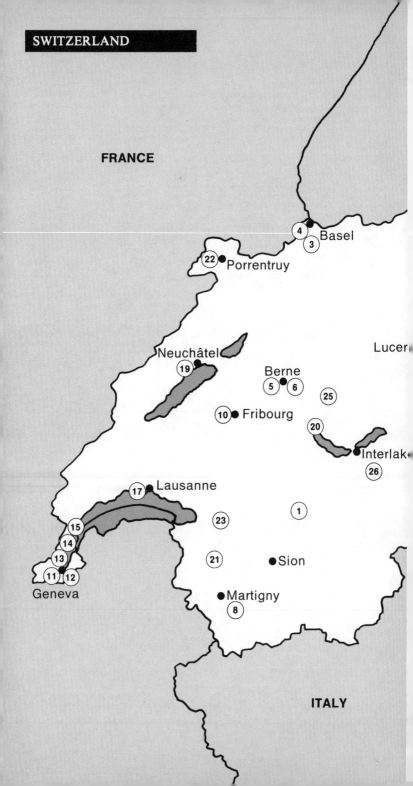

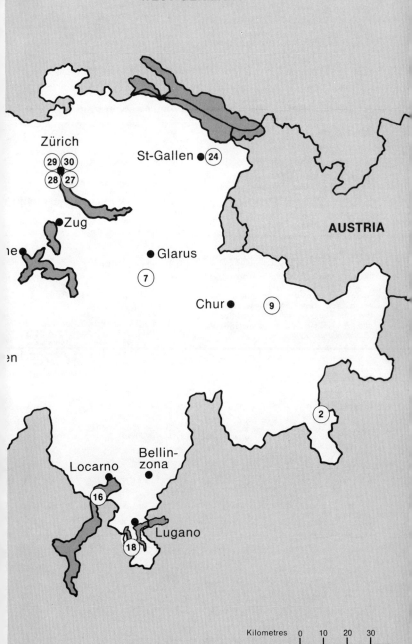

SWITZERLAND

Adelboden

Berne

1. Alpine Garden Höreli

This was laid out by the present owner, Otto Walter, in 1968 and is extended each year. It contains over 3,000 alpine plants from all areas of the world. Visit in July and August. It is thirty minutes walk from Adelboden via Schlegeli and Hoernliweg.

(1) Daily
(2) Free
(5) Herr Otto Walter

Alp Grüm

Graubünden

2. Alpine Garden Alp Grüm

Situated at 6,860 ft (2,091 m) and covering 2½ acres (1 ha), this is not so much a horticultural garden as a garden representing the region's wild flowers, with all the plants identified by labels. The flowering season is from mid-April to the end of October. The plants include some which it is surprising to find growing at such a high altitude. Typical of the Puschlav region is the fescue grass. Also on display are anemones (Pulsatilla vernalis, Pulsatilla sulphurea), clover (Trifolium alpinum) and Campanula barbata. Mare's tail (Hippuris vulgaris) and similar plants grow around the artificial pond and there are plants growing on stone-free soil and on chalky soil, such as the edelweiss (Leontopodium alpinum).

(1) Daily 9–5
(2) Free
(3) Restaurant
(5) Rhaeto Railway Administration

Basel, Brülingen

3. Botanical Garden

This covers 32 acres (13 ha) and was founded in 1968. It consists of open areas only, with agricultural buildings built in 1837–9, a summer villa and its park dating from 1810. The garden contains Europe's largest iris collection with about 1,500 varieties. There are garden 'plots' where indoor, window-box and roof-garden plants may be bought. The garden is being extended for the second Swiss horticultural exhibition in 1980.

(1) Daily
(2) Free
(5) Botanical Garden Co.

Basel, Schönbeinstrasse 6

4. Botanical Garden of Basel University

This originated as a university medicinal

garden in 1588. It was moved in 1692, 1840 and finally in 1898 to its present location. There are almost 8,000 varieties of plants from all over the world. These include camellias, strawberry trees (arbutus), photinia, rock-garden plants, and sub-tropical and tropical plants in the large glasshouse complex. The new Tropical House (1968) contains plants of the tropical rain forests such as orchids, Araceae and Bromeliaceae.

(1) Summer: Daily 7 am–8 pm; Winter: Daily 7–5
(2) Garden: Free; Tropical House: Charge
(5) University of Basel

Berne, Altenbergrain 21

5. Botanical Garden of the University

This was established in its present location, descending in terraces to the bank of the River Aare, in 1863. It covers an area of 5·5 acres (2 ha). In the open are alpine plants arranged geographically, plants of the dry vegetation area of the Valais and a Swiss farm garden. The glasshouses contain plants of the topical rain forests and of the deserts, and a collection of economic plants.

(1) Daily 8–6
(2) Free
(5) University of Berne

Berne, Aargauerstalden

6. Rose Garden

The garden was opened as a park in 1914 and, in 1917, 3,700 roses of 130·varieties were planted. Since then it has been altered from time to time. There is a pergola, a basin and fountain, an iris garden, spring flowers, azaleas and rhododendrons and a water-lily pond. From the garden there is a good view of the city.

(1) Daily
(2) Free
(3) Restaurant (Summer)
(5) City of Berne

Braunwald

Glarus

7. Alpine Rose Nursery

This was founded in 1968 by the Swiss Rose Society under Dr Woessner. The grounds consist of eight rose gardens containing 3,500 plants of 300 varieties. They are laid out on ground varying from 4,265 ft (1,300 m) to 6,234 ft (1,900 m) above sea level. Visit between mid-July and October.

(1) Daily
(2) Free
(5) Swiss Rose Society and Town of Braunwald

Champex, nr Martigny

Valais

8. Alpine Garden Florealpe

Situated at 4,500 ft (1,372 m), this large and beautiful alpine garden was founded in 1927 by Jean-Marcel Aubert and has since been extended. Of particular interest are its alpine section with a rockery, ornamental ponds and artificial moraine (debris deposited by a glacier), its nursery garden and the specialized collections of primula, sempervivum, saxifrage and other alpine plants from all over the world. Visit during June and July.

(1) Daily (except Sun and Mon) 10–noon
(2) Free
(5) Foundation Jean-Marcel Aubert

Davos-Schatzalp

Graubünden

9. Alpine Garden Schatzalp

The garden covers 8 acres (3 ha) and is situated at 6,234 ft (1,900 m) in a beautiful valley of the Guggerbach river. It was founded in 1967 by Oscar Lucius Miller. It contains about 10,000 alpine plants, representing some 1,000 varieties.

(1) Early Jun–end Sep: Daily 8–5
(2) Charge (included in funicular railway ticket)
(3) Restaurant
(5) Hotel Schatzalp, Herr Oscar L. Miller

Fribourg, rue A. Gockel 3

10. Botanical Garden of Fribourg University

This was planned in 1902 and was opened in 1937 as the university's botanical garden, covering 4 acres (1·5 ha). It was extended by the construction of additional glasshouses in 1965–6 and by a medicinal garden in 1968. It specializes in medicinal plants, alpine plants and systematic groupings.

(1) Mon–Sat 8–5; Apr–Oct: First Sun of each month 9–noon, 2–5
(2) Free
(5) University of Fribourg

Geneva, 192 route de Lausanne and 1 chemin de l'Impératrice

11. Botanical Garden and Conservatory

The first botanical garden was built in 1817–8 by A. P. de Candolle. In 1902 it was transferred to its present site and it has been enlarged since that date by extending the grounds and adding buildings such as a library and herbarium, orangery, aviary and also a deer park. Today it covers 34 acres (14 ha). Of particular interest are the rockeries with plants arranged geo-

graphically, the arboretum which includes an interesting collection of conifers such as *Metasequoia glyptostroboides*, economic plants, displays of wild and cultivated tulips, dahlias and alpine plants. Two of the glasshouses are open to the public and these contain tropical and equatorial as well as European plants.

(1) Garden. Apr–Sep: Daily 7–6.30; Nov–Feb: Daily 8–5; Mar and Oct: Daily 8–6. Glasshouses. Daily (except Fri) 9–11, 2–4.30. Conservatory. Mon–Fri 7.45–noon, 1.30–5
(2) Free
(3) Café (May–Oct)
(5) City of Geneva

Geneva

12. Jardin Anglais

Laid out in 1854 and extended in 1862 and 1870, the most notable feature of the 7 acre (3 ha) park is the floral clock. This was created in 1955. Some 6,300 plants are used for it annually.

(1) Daily
(2) Free
(5) City of Geneva

Geneva

13. Parc de la Grange

The distinguished engineer, William Favre, donated this property to the City of Geneva in 1917. Surrounding the Louis XV-style house is a garden of approx 50 acres (20 ha), the most notable feature of which is the rose garden created in 1945 by Eric Bois, director of the Service des Parcs et Promenades, and the landscape architect Armand Auberson. Altogether there are 12,000 roses of 180 varieties: it is the finest rose garden in Switzerland. Dry walls separate the plants. Close to the orangery is a nursery garden where plants for all the municipal gardens of Geneva are grown. Each June there is an international rose competition.

(1) Daily Sunrise–Sunset
(2) Free
(5) City of Geneva

Geneva

14. Parc des Eaux-Vives

Adjoining the Parc de la Grange (qv above), this was acquired for the city by public subscription in 1913. The house dates from 1750. In spring there is a fine display of rhododendrons and azaleas, presented by the Dutch people after World War II.

(1) Daily
(2) Free
(5) City of Geneva

233

SWITZERLAND

Geneva

15. Parc Villa Barton, La Perle du Lac, Parc Moynier and Parc Mon Repos

Four adjoining parks on the edge of Lake Geneva with fine trees, flowerbeds and lawns. The Villa Barton is now the Institut Universitaire des Hautes Études Internationales and there is a museum of the history of science in the Italianate villa that was formerly the property of the Bartholomy family (La Perle du Lac).

(1) Daily
(2) Free
(3) Restaurant (La Perle du Lac)
(5) City of Geneva

Island of Brissago

Ticino

16. Botanical Garden

Founded in 1890 by the Baroness of St Légéer, it has been a public park since 1950. Its geo-botanical divisions contain plants from New Zealand, Australia, California, Florida, northern Japan, northern and central China, South and Central America, the Mediterranean regions and other countries. Visit from the end of March until May, and in August and September. The island is reached by scheduled boat from Locarno and Porto Ronco.

(1) Mid-Mar–mid-Nov: Daily 9–6
(2) Charge
(3) Restaurant
(5) Canton of Ticino

Lausanne, 14 bis avenue de Cour

Vaud

17. Botanical Garden

The botanical garden was created in 1892 and remodelled in 1946. It contains a varied collection of plants, in particular medicinal and alpine plants. It covers 5 acres (2 ha).

(1) Mar–Oct: Daily 8–noon, 2–7
(2) Free
(5) Canton of Vaud

Morcote

Ticino

18. Scherrer Park

The park contains Mediterranean plants and trees and buildings and monuments of architectural interest. There is a good view over Lake Lugano.

(1) Apr–Oct: Daily 9–5. Guided tours every Tue at 10
(2) Charge

234

Neuchâtel, 11 rue Emile-Argand

19. Botanical Garden of the University

This was founded in 1954 and a cultivation glasshouse was added later. It contains an alpine garden with a rockery and an artificial peat bog, trees and shrubs, an orangery, ponds and tropical plants from all over the world. The garden specializes in natural and artificial hybrids and in the study of plants, such as sempervivum, sedum, cerastium, cytisus and genista. Visit during May and June.

(1) Mar–Oct: Daily 8–6
(2) Free
(5) Neuchâtel University Institute of Botany

Oberhofen, Lake Thun

Berne

20. Oberhofen Castle

The castle has a long history, dating back to the 12th cent. The interior was restored in 1962. The park consists of a box garden, lawns with trees, an alpine rock garden with rare conifers and a Swiss cross laid out in flowers by the lakeside. There is a children's chalet and playground.

(1) May–Oct: Daily (except Mon mornings) 9.30–noon, 2–6
(2) Charge
(4) Castle (May–Oct: Daily, except Mon mornings, 10–noon, 2–5)
(5) Bernese Historical Museum

Pont de Nant sur Bex

Vaud

21. Alpine Garden La Thomasia

The garden, established in 1890, is situated at approx 4,000 ft (1,219 m) and contains a large collection of alpine plants. Visit in June and July.

(1) May–Oct: Daily
(2) Free
(5) University of Lausanne

Porrentruy, route de Fontenais 22

Berne

22. Botanical Garden

This dates from 1750, when it belonged to the Jesuits. Since 1815 it has belonged to the Cantonal School of Porrentruy. It contains tropical plants, plants of the Jura region, rose and iris collections and a rockery. Visit from June until October.

(1) Mon–Fri 9–noon, 2–5; Sat 9–noon, 3–5; Sun 10–noon
(2) Free
(3) Café
(5) Cantonal School of Porrentruy

Rochers de Naye, nr Montreux

Vaud

23. Alpine Garden La Rambertia

At 6,700 ft (2,042 m), this is the highest alpine garden in Europe. It contains more than 1,000 varieties of alpine plants from Switzerland and other countries. It may be reached by taking the mountain railway from Montreux.

(1) Jun–Oct: Daily
(2) Free
(5) Rambertia Society

St-Gallen, Brauerstrasse 69

St-Gallen

24. Botanical Garden

The designer of the botanical garden, founded in 1945, was P. Zülli. It contains a variety of trees and shrubs, a rock garden, indigenous alpine plants, many small specialized flower gardens, an alpine house and glasshouses with approx 1,000 varieties of orchids as well as cacti and succulents, tropical economic plants and ferns. Since 1954 the garden has also been a meteorological station. Guided tours with particular themes take place at 10 and 3 on the first Sunday of each month.

(1) Daily (except Sat) 9–noon, 1.30–5
(2) Free
(5) Town of St-Gallen

Schlosswil, nr Berne

Berne

25. Schlosswil Castle

Schlosswil Castle is first documented in 1146. It was built in the 10th and 11th cents, possibly on the site of a Roman fortress, and, with the exception of the tower, was destroyed by fire in 1546. The castle was subsequently rebuilt. Today it houses local government offices. In the garden there are fine trees and shrubs, a pool and parkland.

(1) Daily
(2) Free
(3) Restaurant
(4) Castle (Mon–Fri 8–noon, 2–6)
(5) District of Konolfingen

Schynige Platte, nr Interlaken

Berne

26. Alpine Garden Schynige Platte

This was founded in 1928 and opened in 1929. There is an alpine pasture and bog and a collection of medicinal plants. It contains approx 500 varieties of flowering plants and ferns and covers 2 acres (0·8 ha). Towered over by the Jungfrau, it may be reached by mountain railway from Wilderswil, near Interlaken.

(1) Daily
(2) Charge
(5) Alpine Garden Schynige Platte Co

Zürich, Seestrasse

27. Belvoir Park

The park and mansion were created from 1826 to 1830 by Heinrich Escher-Zollikofer. Alfred Escher resided here until his death in 1882, when the city acquired the estate. The park contains rare exotic trees including a swamp cypress (*Taxodium distichum*), bitternut (*Carya amara*), giant sequoia (*Sequoiadendron giganteum*), black walnut (*Juglans nigra*), incense cedar (*Thuja gigantea*) as well as oaks and wing-nuts. The park is situated opposite the Rieter Park (qv below). Visit between May and September.

(1) Daily
(2) Free
(3) Restaurant
(5) Zürich Horticultural Authority

Zürich, Zollikerstrasse 107

28. Botanical Garden of Zürich University

The first botanical garden to be created outside Italy was at Zürich, in 1560. In 1834 Zürich University was founded and a university botanical garden was created. However, its location became unfavourable for a botanical garden on account of increased building and traffic pollution. The present botanical garden was opened to the public in May 1977. It contains a variety of flora, including Mediterranean, aquatic, alpine, medicinal and economic plants, heathland and marshland plants, rhododendrons, indigenous trees and wild flowers. There is a complex of dome-shaped display houses.

(1) Garden. Summer: Daily 7–7; Winter 7.30–6. Glasshouses. Daily 8–11.30, 1–4
(2) Free
(3) Café
(5) Canton of Zürich

Zürich, Mythenquai 88

29. City Succulent Collection

Founded in 1931, since 1950 this has been the collection and herbarium for the international organization of succulent research. The collection on display consists of approx 20,000 succulents from 28 families. There are many rare varieties, such as *Notocactus rutilans*, *Parodia rigidispine*, *Ferocactus schwarzii* and the smallest variety of cactus, *Blossfeldia liliputana*. The main flowering season is from April until June.

(1) *Mon–Sat 8–11.45, 1.30–5; Sun and Public Holidays 10–noon, 2–5*
(2) *Free*
(5) *City of Zürich*

Zürich

30. Rieter Park

The park surrounding the Wesendonck Villa, now a museum containing the collections of Baron von der Heydt, was created in 1857 by L. Zeugheer and has been a public park since it was acquired by the City in 1945. It contains rare trees such as an Oriental spruce (*Picea orientalis*), a West Himalayan spruce (*Picea morinda*), a magnificent red oak (*Quercus rubra*) and a coast redwood (*Sequoia sempervirens*). The park is situated opposite the Belvoir Park (qv above).

(1) *Daily*
(2) *Free*
(4) *Rietbergmuseum (Tue–Sun 10–5; Wed also 8 pm–10 pm)*
(5) *Zürich Horticultural Authority*

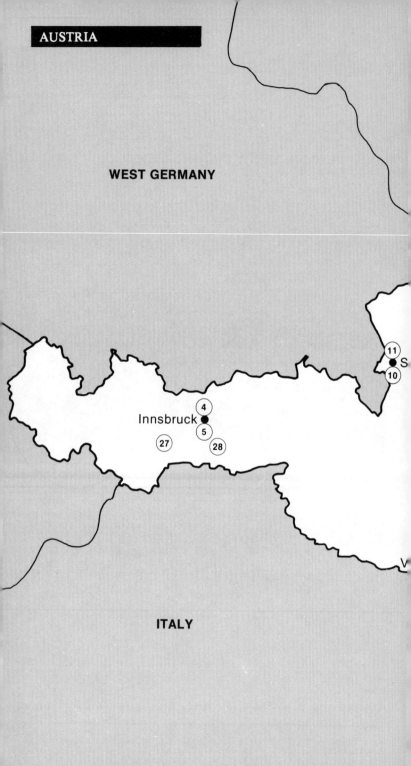

CZECHOSLOVAKIA

Linz ● ⑨

Wels ● ㉓

St Polten ● ㉛

⑫ ⑬ ⑭ ⑮ ⑯ ⑰ ⑱ ⑲ ⑳ ㉑

Vienna ●

zburg

⑧

Wiener Neustadt ●

⑥

㉚

㉖

㉔

Leoben ●

①

Graz
② ● ㉙
③

㉕

ach ●㉒ ⑦ ● Klagenfurt

YUGOSLAVIA

| Kilometres | 0 | 20 | 40 | 60 |
| Miles | 0 | 10 | 20 | 30 |

AUSTRIA

Frohnleiten

Styria

1. Franz Mayr-Meinhof Alpine Garden

The garden, situated 14 miles (23 km) north of Graz and covering 20 acres (8 ha), was founded in 1947 and opened to the public in 1950. It is a world-wide alpine collection with approx 10,000 varieties. From mid-May until mid-June the azaleas are in flower. A small zoo lies in the eastern part of the garden.

(1) Mar–Nov: Daily 8–6. Guided tours on Sun and Public Holidays at 2
(2) Charge
(5) Baron Franz Mayr-Meinhof

Graz

Styria

2. Botanical Garden of Graz University

The garden covers 5 acres (2 ha) and is affiliated to the Institute of Systematic Botany of Graz University. It was founded in 1888–9. The glasshouses were extended after World War II, and in 1977 a cactus house was added. The garden specializes in alpine plants.

(1) Apr–Oct: Mon–Fri 7–7; Sat and Sun 7–1
(2) Free
(5) Graz University

Graz

3. Schlossberg

The clock tower and the bell tower are all that remain of the original fortifications, dismantled at the time of the Napoleonic wars. Today there are terraces, shady avenues and winding paths, and beds of massed flowers. In the Bastion Flower Garden the colour scheme is changed every few weeks.

(1) Daily
(2) Free
(5) Town of Graz

Innsbruck, Botanikerstrasse 10

Tyrol

4. Botanical Garden of Innsbruck University

The garden covers 5 acres (2 ha) and specializes in alpine and Mediterranean plants. Among the 1,200 species of alpine plants are those from non-European mountain ranges.

(1) Summer: Daily 8–6
(2) Free
(5) Innsbruck University

Innsbruck, Rennweg 8

5. Hofgarten

In 1410 a kitchen garden was established here and by the end of the 16th cent trees had been planted and the garden extended. In the mid-18th cent Maria Theresa had the present palace built, and the garden was altered at this time. It was opened to the public in 1797.

Under the Bavarian King Maximilian it was remodelled as an English park in 1858. Today it covers 25 acres (10 ha) and has lakes and fine trees, an orchid house (1954) and a glasshouse for tropical plants. Concerts are given here in summer.

(1) Daily
(2) Free
(3) Café
(4) Palace (Daily 9–4; mid-Oct–mid-May closed on Sun and Public Holidays); Palace Church (May–Sep: Daily 9–5; Oct–Apr: Daily 9–noon, 2–5); Tyrolean Folk Art Museum (Mon–Sat 9–noon, 2–5; Sun and Public Holidays 9–noon)
(5) Administration of Austrian National Gardens, Innsbruck

Bad Ischl

Upper Austria

6. Kaiservilla

The villa was given as a wedding present to the Emperor Franz Josef and the Empress Elizabeth by the Archduchess Sophia. The fine landscaped park covering 60 acres (24 ha) was created by Franz Josef with the gardener Franz Rauch. In the park is the Marmorschlössel, a small marble château used by the Empress as her 'Trianon'. It houses a museum of the history of photography.

(1) End Apr–Nov: Daily 9–noon, 1–5
(2) Charge
(3) Café
(4) Villa and Marmorschlössel (same times)
(5) Markus Salvator Habsburg Lothringen

Klagenfurt, Kinkstrasse 6

Carinthia

7. Botanical Garden of Carinthia

The garden was founded in 1865 and was laid out at its present location in the ancient quarry of Klagenfurt in 1958. It contains indigenous species such as *Wulfenia carinthiaca, Waldsteinia ternata* subsp. *trifolia* and *Bulbocodium vernum*; a variety of plants of the central and southern Alps; marsh and aquatic plants; an artificially created high and low moorland with plants such as *Betula humilis*, *Betula nana*, andromeda and drosera; and insectivorous plants. The glasshouse contains tropical and sub-tropical plants.

Laxenburg

Lower Austria

8. Schloss Laxenburg

8 miles (15 km) to the south of Vienna, Laxenburg was the summer residence of the Austrian imperial house. After World War II it was taken over in part as a convalescent centre. The park covering 618 acres (250 ha) has a lake, streams and paths that wind through the woodland and open areas. It is interesting today principally for its garden buildings: a temple, the Green Pavilion, a dovecote and, in particular, the small castle in medieval style, the Franzensburg, on an island in the lake. To the south-west is a grotto, a bridge with a pointed Gothic arch and a jousting arena. These structures date mainly from the 19th cent.

(1) Daily
(2) Charge
(3) Café

Linz, Roseggerstrasse

Upper Austria

9. Botanical Garden

The garden, founded in 1950 and extended in 1961 to cover approx 10 acres (4 ha), is one of Austria's most interesting botanical gardens. There are areas for irises and flora of the Steppes and for rhododendrons and ferns. There are collections of economic plants, climbing plants, plant mutations, an area for morphological and biological groupings and a systematic section. The rock garden contains plants arranged in fourteen geographical groups and there is also a heather garden and a garden representing the history of the rose. An area with ponds has marsh and aquatic plants and the garden contains a large variety of native flora, of spring and summer flowers and of trees.

There are glasshouses for tropical plants, tropical water-lilies, cacti and succulents and orchids and a display house which also serves to protect certain plants in winter. The alpine plants are best seen from April to June, the local wild flowers from May to July and the giant water-lily, *Victoria cruziana*, which is in the tropical house, during the summer.

(1) Glasshouses. Daily 8–noon, 1–5. Open area. Oct–Mar: Daily 8–5; Apr and Sep: Daily 8–6; May–Aug: Daily 8–7
(2) Free
(5) City of Linz

AUSTRIA

Salzburg

10. Schloss Hellbrunn

Hellbrunn, situated approx 5 miles (8 km) to the south of Salzburg, was built under the direction of Marcus Sitticus von Hohenems, Prince-Archbishop of Salzburg. It was built by the Italian architect Santino Solari in the Italian High Renaissance style and completed by 1615. The gardens were remodelled by Franz Anton Danreiter in c 1730 and were extended in c 1790 with an English park. They are divided by two principal avenues. The main avenue leads to the palace and the second leads, at an angle to the first, to Hellbrunn hill, the Watzmann viewpoint, the zoo, the *Steintheater* (rock theatre) and the Monatsschlössl.

Hellbrunn is famous for its *Wasserspiele* (or *jeux d'eau*). The main feature is the Roman theatre built in 1750 on the north-west side of the palace. This has a semi-circular wall with the statue of a Roman emperor, and niches contain further statuary. Facing the theatre is an ornamental pond with a reclining statue of Neptune. In the centre is the Prince's Table made of marble with ten marble stools. This was used by the Prince-Archbishop to entertain guests, and wine was cooled in a trough of water in the table centre. A secret tap can be turned on so that water spouts from the centre of each stool, excluding the Prince's. On one side of the pond is the Orpheus Grotto with statues of Orpheus and Eurydice and there are further fountain statues and a small cascade. At the palace end of the pond is a statue of Bacchus and on one side of this the Wine Cellar (1660).

Passing through a gate into the gardens facing the palace, there is the Star Pool and behind it a semi-circular wall and a grotto, on either side of which are statues representing the Four Seasons. Five grottoes are situated beneath the palace: the Neptune Grotto, where again water can be made to flow, the Shell Grotto, the Ruins Grotto, the Mirror Grotto and the Bird Song Grotto, so-called because a water mechanism simulates bird song. A canal and a walk lead from the Star Pool southwards to the main gardens. First there are the mechanical peepshows, the figures made to move by running water: among them are a knife-grinder, Apollo and Marsyas, a miller, Perseus and Andromeda and a potter. Facing these is the Venus Grotto and Fountain. Passing more statuary, the mechanical theatre is reached, created in 1750–4 by Lorenz Rosenegger. Running water turns a wheel causing by means of further wheels and wires about half of the 256 figures, in and before a town-hall stage, to move. A water organ attempts to conceal the sound of the moving figures. Beyond this is the Crown Grotto with a fountain. Water can be turned on to form a rain arcade to the entrance. Beyond are the Perseus, Eurydice and Neptune Fountains.

The main gardens are designed around two small and two large ornamental ponds, connected by canals forming an island parterre in the centre. There are parterres with flower borders. To the north is the English Garden (1790) with a statue of the Empress Elizabeth (1900). To the south-east is Hellbrunn hill, and in this part of the grounds is Monatsschlössl, the villa built by Solari in 1615, now containing a folk museum. Here also is the *Steintheater*, an open-air theatre built in a cave caused by quarrying for the stone for the palace. The zoo was originally established in the 15th cent.

(1) *Gardens. Daily 7–Sunset; during Hellbrunn Festival in Aug: 7–noon Wasserspiele. End Mar, Apr, Sep: 9– 4.30; May–Aug: Daily 8–5.30; during Hellbrunn Festival in Aug: 8–noon; Oct: Daily 9–noon, 1–4*
(2) *Gardens: Free; Wasserspiele: Charge*
(3) *Restaurant and kiosks*
(4) *Palace and Museum (same times as Wasserspiele)*
(5) *City of Salzburg*

Salzburg

11. Schloss Mirabell

The palace was built in 1606 for Bishop Wolf Dietrich and remodelled by Johann Lukas von Hildebrandt in 1721–7. In 1818 fire destroyed all but the chapel, hall and grand staircase.

The original gardens were altered by J. B. Fischer von Erlach in *c* 1700 with Ottavio Mosto, laid out in the Baroque manner with parterres, statuary, pools and fountains and a maze. The open-air theatre was designed by Matthias Diesl in *c* 1710– 18. Although much simplified, the garden retains many of the features and the architectural framework of this formal layout.

(1) *Daily 7–Sunset*
(2) *Free*
(5) *City of Salzburg*

Vienna

12. Augarten

The park was laid out for the Imperial summer residence, Alte Favorite, in 1649. It was opened to the public in 1755 by the Emperor Josef II. The park was restored after World War II in the landscaped style with sports and recreation areas and a parterre with flowerbeds. This park occupies the site of the first Viennese porcelain factory (1717).

(1) *Daily Sunrise–Sunset*
(2) *Free*
(5) Bundesgartenverwaltung (*Federal Park Administration*)

Vienna, Prinz-Eugen-Strasse and Rennweg

13. Belvedere

The two palaces of the Belvedere were built by Johann Lukas von Hildebrandt for Prince Eugene of Savoy, conqueror of the Turks. The Lower Belvedere (1714–16) was his summer residence and the Upper Bel-vedere (1721–3) was used for entertaining.

Between the palaces are the gardens, which cover an area of 50 acres (20 ha). They were designed by Dominique Girard and created by Anton Zinner; they were completed in 1725 and opened to the public in 1776–7.

They are Baroque terraced gardens with lawn parterres, flowerbeds, topiary and ornamental pools with fountains, statuary and cascades. The garden of the Upper Belvedere comprises an alpine garden, the oldest alpine collection in Europe with 6,000 species from all over the world. It originated as a botanical garden laid out at the end of the 18th cent by Gerard van Swieten and Herman Schuurmans Steckhoven. This was replaced in 1865 and later neglected until 1926, when it was restored and enlarged. It was again restored after World War II.

Although small in area, it is a remarkably comprehensive collection, with saxifrage, sempervivum, sedum, anemones, arenaria, irises, campanulas, dianthus, gentians, dwarf alpine rhododendrons and rare plants such as *Adonis amurensis*, *Erinacea pungens*, *Rosa Watsoniana*, *Rosa persica*, *Jankaea heldreichii* and *Genista holo-petala*. The glasshouses also contain inter-esting collections.

(1) *Apr–Sep: Mon–Sat 9–6; Sun 9–7*
(2) *Free*
(4) *Lower Belvedere (Museum of Austrian Medieval Art) and Upper Belvedere (Gallery of the Nineteenth and Twen-tieth Centuries) (Mon–Sat 10–4; Sun and Public Holidays 9–1)*
(5) *Federal Park Administration*

Vienna, Rennweg 14

14. Botanical Garden of Vienna University

The garden was founded in 1754 under the patronage of Maria Theresa. There is a systematic garden, an arboretum, an econ-omic plant collection and a collection of aquatic plants. Of particular interest are the alpine plants and the large outdoor col-lection of cacti and succulents.

The garden covers 20 acres (8 ha) and is situated close to the Belvedere (qv above). The glasshouses are not open to the public.

(1) *Mid-Apr–mid-Oct: Daily 9–Sunset*
(2) *Free*
(5) *University of Vienna*

Vienna

15. Burggarten

This was laid out as the private garden of the Emperor Franz I in 1820 and has been a public park since 1919. There are flowers, mature trees, a palm house and a pond with water birds. At the entrance is a statue of Goethe and there are statues of the Emperor Franz Josef and Franz I; also the Mozart Memorial.

(1) *Daily Sunrise–Sunset*
(2) *Free*
(5) *Federal Park Administration*

Vienna

16. Donaupark

The park was created for the International Horticultural Exhibition of 1964 and covers 250 acres (101 ha). It contains miniature gardens, roses, irises, alpine plants, dahlias, heather and rhododendron gardens and unusual trees. The Tower Glasshouse has plants on a moving belt and the 830 ft (252 m) Danube Tower has a revolving restaurant near its top. This is Vienna's most popular park.

(1) *Daily*
(2) *Free*
(3) *Restaurant*
(5) *City Park Authority*

Vienna

17. The Prater

Austria's largest park is situated between two arms of the Danube and is traversed by an avenue almost 3 miles (4·5 km) long. Originally a royal hunting park, it was opened to the public by the Emperor Josef II in 1766. As well as the woods and marshland, there are areas of lawns with flowers and shrubs, and fountains and basins.

(1) *Daily*
(2) *Free*
(3) *Restaurant*
(5) *City Park Authority*

Vienna

18. Schloss Schönbrunn

Following the destruction of a hunting lodge in the Turkish invasion in 1683, the Emperor Franz I commissioned J. B. Fischer von Erlach to create a palace and park on the scale of, and in imitation of, Versailles (qv). Gardens in the formal French manner were completed with the help of Jean Trehet in *c* 1714. The Gloriette, Roman Ruins and Fountain of Neptune were added during the reign of the Empress Maria Theresa (1740–80), when Schönbrunn was the summer residence of the court, by Gerard van Swieten and Herman Schuurmans Steckhoven.

On the opposite side of the palace from the *cour d'honneur* are large parterres with colourful planting of flowers, separated by

broad gravel paths. These are bordered by stone sculptures, by Wilhelm Beyer, and tall hedges. Beyond is an ornamental pool and the Fountain of Neptune. Paths zigzag up a small grassy hill to the Gloriette, an eye-catcher built to commemorate the Battle of Kolin in 1757. This is bordered by woodland.

To the south-west of the palace is a small zoo with an aquarium and beyond this the Tyrolean Garden. The glasshouse complex of display and service houses includes the Palm House, with palms and ferns, orchids, bromeliads and insectivorous plants. The Mexican display house has night-flowering cacti and other rare plants, and there is an orangery dating from 1767 with evergreen shrubs and citrus trees. There are avenues of splendid limes in the gardens and a large pagoda-tree (*Sophora japonica*).

(1) *Gardens. Daily 6 am–Sunset. Palm House. Daily 9–5*
(2) *Free*
(3) *Restaurant and café (Apr–Oct)*
(4) *Palace May–Sep: Daily 9–noon, 1–5; Oct–Apr: Daily 9–noon, 1–4*
(5) *Federal Park Administration*

Vienna

19. Stadtpark

The park covers 17 acres (7 ha) and straddles the River Wien. It was created in 1863–7 by J. Selleny and Dr Siebeck as a public park. There are commemorative statues of Austria's famous composers.

(1) *Daily*
(2) *Free*
(3) *Café*
(5) *City Park Authority*

Vienna

20. Volksgarten

This popular park was laid out in 1819–23 by Ludwig Remy as the city's first public park and extended in 1862. It contains a rose garden, a famous fountain, the Temple of Theseus and memorials to among others the Empress Elizabeth and to the poet Grillparzer.

(1) *Daily: Sunrise–Sunset*
(2) *Free*
(3) *Café*
(5) *Federal Park Administration*

Vienna

21. Wertheimsteinpark

The park was laid out in 1830 as a private park and in 1908 was bequeathed to the city. There are ponds, streams, an alpine garden and a variety of flowers. The most famous feature of the park is the Viennese Garden for the Blind (1959). Blind visitors may find their way around the garden by the handrails, the labels are in braille and the plants, chosen for their scent, may be touched. Nearby is a singing acoustic cymbal fountain.

(*1*) *Daily*
(*2*) *Free*
(*5*) *City Park Authority*

Villach, Villacher Alpenstrasse

Carinthia

22. Alpine Garden Villacher Alpe

The garden was founded in 1966 and opened to the public in 1973. It is situated at 4,921 ft (1,500 m), at a height where alpine and sub-alpine plants flourish. The garden specializes in plants from the southern Alps.

(*1*) *Mid-Jun–end Aug: Daily 9–6*
(*2*) *Charge*
(*3*) *Café*
(*5*) *Alpengarten Villacher Alpe Company*

Wels

Upper Austria

23. Stadtpark

Founded in the 19th cent, the park has flowerbeds and fine trees. There is a palm and cactus house and a small zoo.

(*1*) *Summer: Daily 7 am–8 pm; Winter: Daily 7–7*
(*2*) *Free*

Other Alpine Gardens

Alpine Gardens, open for a season during the summer, are situated at or near the following places:

24. Bad Aussee, Styria
25. Gaal, nr Knittelfeld, Styria
26. Bad Goisern, Upper Austria
27. Kühtai, Tyrol
28. Patscherkofel, nr Innsbruck, Tyrol
29. Rannach, nr Graz, Styria
30. Reichenau an der Rax, Lower Austria
31. Schönbühel, nr Melk, Lower Austria

ITALY

NORTHERN ITALY

WE

SWITZERLAND

●Aosta

⑩

㉖ ⑯
⑮
㉞ ㉟

⑤

⑨
⑧

●Como

⑦
⑥ ㉓
② ③

④

⑲ ㉛
Milan●⑳
㉑
㉚
Pavia●㉙
㉒

Brescia●

●Turin

⑪

㉗ ●Par

㉜

●Genoa

㊷
●
Ventimiglia

Kilometres 0   20   40   60
Miles   0 10 20 30 40

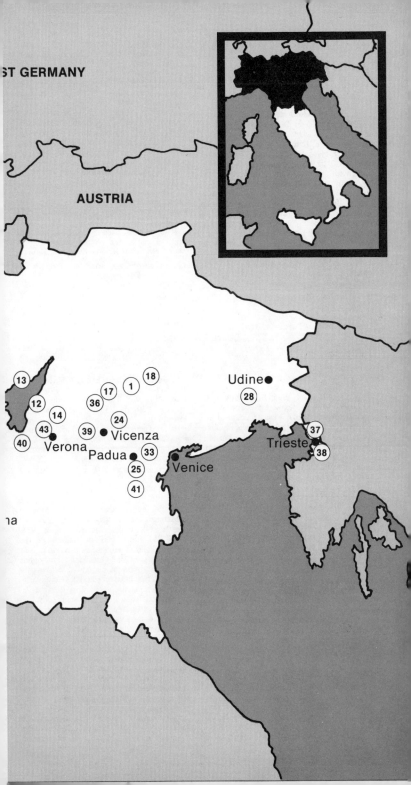

ITALY

Bassano del Grappa

Veneto

1. Parolini Gardens

The Parolini Gardens were founded by Alberto Parolini in 1805 with the intention of creating an ornamental park that would at the same time provide facilities for botanical research and study. By dint of extensive travels throughout the world, which he undertook either alone or in the company of naturalists such as Giambattista Brocchi or the English botanist Philip Barker-Webb, he amassed a varied collection of seeds and rare plants. The majority of these plants have survived and may be admired today. The gardens are laid out in the English style as parkland with lawns, borders and woodland.

The gardens were donated to the Commune of Bassano del Grappa in 1908 for use as a public park.

(*1*) *Apr–Oct: Daily 9–7*
(*2*) *Charge*
(*3*) *Kiosk*
(*5*) *Commune of Bassano del Grappa*

Bellagio

Lombardy

2. Villa Melzi d'Eril

The early 19th-cent villa in the Empire style, situated on the shores of Lake Como, was built by Signor Melzi, Vice President of the Italian Republic. Its present owner, Duke Tommaso Gallarati-Scotti, who was at one time Italian Ambassador to Great Britain, has amassed a collection of azaleas, rhododendrons and camellias and new varieties of rare shrubs and plants. The gardens run along the lakeside linked by paths shaded by plane trees.

On the upper terrace is an unusual Japanese water garden. The pools are edged with irises and lotuses and crossed at one point by an ornamental bamboo bridge festooned with wistaria.

Visit in April and May when the azaleas are in season, and also in autumn.

(*1*) *Week before Easter–Sep: Daily (except Sun and Public Holidays) 10–noon, 3–5*
(*2*) *Charge*
(*5*) *Duco Tommaso Gallarati-Scotti*

Bellagio

3. Villa Serbelloni

An extensive 18th-cent garden showing a marked English influence. The principal entrance is at the lowest level of the property which gradually rises to the majestic, curved terraces immediately below the villa. This lower area is arranged as informal parkland, planted with many olive trees and groups of fine specimen Italian cypress. It is traversed by a long, winding drive leading up to the house and upper garden which, beyond the villa, is mostly woodland with many fine old trees, a belvedere and superb views of the small Lake Lecco. The original foundations of the villa date from a castle destroyed by Galeazzo Visconti in 1375. The name derives from a former owner, Duke Alessandro Serbelloni. Apart from their beds and borders of multi-coloured annual plants, roses and flowering shrubs with a background of beautiful lawns, the three main terraces are embellished with many fine examples of topiary consisting of curiously shaped clipped conifers and other plants in geometrical forms. In a separate small garden there is a well-head and a fountain attributed to Cecilio Plinio.

The villa is used as a congress and cultural centre for international meetings sponsored by the Rockefeller Foundation.

(*1*) *By appointment with the owner or the local tourist agency*
(*2*) *Charge*
(*5*) *Rockefeller Foundation, New York*

Biella

Lombardy

4. Felice Piacenza Park of La Burcina

The Felice Piacenza Park is situated on La Burcina and overlooks the Lombardy Plains towards Turin. The summit is at approx 2,500 ft (833 m), while from its lowest to its highest point there is a difference of approx 750 ft (250 m). The total area covers approx 100 acres (40 ha), a small part of which is planted exclusively with rhododendrons in a natural setting.

Giovanni Piacenza bought La Burcina in 1855, but his first plantations date from 1848 and planting continued until 1860. In 1895 Piacenza's son, Felice, planted the first ornamental trees and in subsequent years the park assumed its present style. Felice Piacenza died in 1938, aged 95, and the Park passed to the town of Biella. The close connection of four generations of the Piacenza family has ensured a harmonious and effective programme of maintenance and development.

La Burcina is noted for the natural beauty of its views and its varied collection of native and exotic plants. On its slopes, its ridges and in its valleys it has been possible to create many different landscapes and find appropriate habitats for each species. The northern side of the hill is completely natural, with conifers, birch, and sweet chestnuts towering over an undergrowth of bracken, ferns, heathers, whortleberry and other indigenous plants. The southern and western slopes were transformed by introducing new flora, much of which has become naturalized and has assumed the luxurious growth associated with the favoured climate, all with a background extending to the horizon far below. The clear atmosphere makes normally brilliant colours still more vivid and the red and copper beech foliage contrasts with golden maples, while silver-leafed conifers contrast with the glaucous-blue foliage of *Cedrus atlantica glauca* and *Cupressus arizonica*.

Spring comes early, with deciduous magnolias in bloom together with the first rhododendrons and a profusion of cydonia, deutzia, *Choisya ternata* and the carefully protected local flora. The real glory, however, starts at the end of April, when over a thousand huge rhododendrons of many different varieties begin to bloom; the impressive show continues until June.

The rhododendrons are followed by masses of blue hydrangeas, with a purity of colour only found in such an acid soil. Later there are the genista and *Spartium junceum*, while autumn displays the colours of acers, liriodendrons, liquidambars.

(1) Daily Sunrise–Sunset
(2) Free
(5) City of Biella

Bisuschio, nr Varese, Lake Lugano

Lombardy

5. Villa Cicogna-Mozzone

The villa was formerly a hunting lodge of the Mozzone family. In the 16th cent the lodge was converted into a Renaissance villa built around a courtyard and the gardens were laid out around it. A fine belvedere terrace and a beautiful water staircase lined by cypresses descend the hillside.

At the base a waterfall flows into an ornamental pool flanked on either side by reclining statues and vases of brilliantly coloured flowers. The terrace overlooks the parterre gardens and the retaining wall descends to form the porticoes of a sunken garden loggia planted with maidenhair ferns.

There are fine views of the distant pre-Alps, while the lower zones of the adjoining park slope gently down to a wooded valley where, at one time, wild bears were hunted. In 1541 Mgr Bonaventura Castiglioni described the garden as 'a true gem of the Varese territory'.

(1) Mid-Apr–Oct 9–noon, 2–6
(2) Charge
(5) Family of the Conti Cicogna-Mozzoni

Cadenabbia, Lake Como

Lombardy

6. Villa Carlotta

The villa was built in 1745 by Marshal Giorgio Clerici, but derives its name from Carlotta, Duchess of Saxe-Meiningen, whose mother gave it to her as a birthday present. Elegant, 18th-cent terraced gardens slope down to the lake's edge in a series of small gardens planted with brilliant flowers

and high, clipped hedges. Pleached alleys running through a small grove of trees on the lowest terrace provide shade from the sun. Two symmetrical 'secret gardens' are laid out on either side of the house. In front lies the lemon terrace.

In the 19th cent an English garden was added with a romantic hollow planted with tree-ferns and exotic flowers while the rest of the garden was planted with a variety of flowers, trees and shrubs collected from all over the world. These include Himalayan, Brazilian and Mexican orchids, fifteen types of clematis, a giant sequoia and Japanese cryptomerias.

The greatest feature of the gardens is the vast number of azaleas which provide a glorious display in late spring, and for which Villa Carlotta is justly famous.

(1) Mar–Sep: Daily 8–6.30; Oct–mid-Nov:
*   Daily 9–noon, 2–4.30*
(2) Charge
(4) Villa (same times)
(5) Italian State

Cardano di Grandola, nr Menaggio

Lombardy

7. Villa Barone Bagatti Valsecchi

Created some 50 years ago by the late Barone Pasino Bagatti Valsecchi, formerly President of the Lombardy Horticultural Society, and now owned by the architect Barone Fausto Bagatti Valsecchi, this beautiful and unusual garden recalls the legendary 'hanging gardens'. It is situated at the edge of a deep valley surrounded by steep, pine-clad mountains, at an altitude of 1,200 ft (365 m), and only 15 miles (24 km) from the Swiss frontier, overlooking Lake Como. Parts of the garden are literally perpendicular and have never been walked upon. The only method of access for planting and maintenance is by means of rope ladders, grappling irons, and a type of bo'sun's chair.

There are, however, ample level areas linked by flights of rustic, floral steps planted with a variety of brightly coloured plants, from which there are views of Mt Grigne and Mt Legnone. There is a difference of approx 400 ft (122 m) between the highest and lowest parts of the garden. The level zones provide sites for many beautifully kept lawns, whose vivid green makes a perfect background for the masses of brilliantly coloured annuals, herbaceous perennials and alpine plants. Dominating the highest point is a fine group of the characteristic 'Italian cypress' (*Cupressus sempervirens* var. *pyramidalis*), whose dark green, pencil-like silhouettes are outlined against the distant Alps. In rocky crevices of the mountain side areas various garden escapes have naturalized, particularly berberis, buddleia, erica, solidago, deutzia, spiraea, *Spartium junceum*, etc. The gardens are also famous for their unique collection of all types of dahlias, which include numerous new hybrids raised at Cardano. Another speciality is the collection of Korean chrysanthemums used as pot plants and cultivated in the form of cascades.

(1) *By appointment with the owner*
(2) *Free*
(5) *Barone Fausto Bagatti Valsecchi*

Casalzuigno, nr Varese

Lombardy

8. Il Bozzolo

The 17th-cent villa of the Della Porta family is set in an isolated position in a valley of the Alpine foothills and the spectacular gardens are designed to be admired from the main road.

They form a series of balustraded terraces ascending the hillside and are placed on either side of a central staircase flanked by lemon trees in pots. This leads to the upper terrace and forms the main vista which disappears in true Baroque fashion into a thick wood. The upper terrace is laid out with an octagonal lawn and a colonnaded central fountain.

(1) *By appointment with the owner*
(2) *Free*
(5) *Della Porta family*

Cernobbio

Lombardy

9. Villa d'Este Hotel

Designed by Pellegrino Tibaldi and built in 1568 for Cardinal Gallio, the villa is now a luxury hotel. Little of the original garden has survived apart from a fine avenue of cypresses, but the monumental works carried out during the 17th and 18th cents still remain and are beautiful examples of that period. There are fine vistas, lawns, much mosaic work, terraces, areas developed as parkland, long flights of stone steps, all with a background of Lake Como. The villa was at one time the home of Queen Caroline, wife of George IV of England.

(1) *Daily*
(2) *Free*
(3) *Restaurant*
(5) *Villa d'Este Hotel*

Cogne, nr Aosta

Aosta

10. Parco Nazionale del Gran Paradiso – Giardino Alpino Paradisia

The property covers an area of 2·5 acres (1 ha) and was created in 1955 to mark the occasion of the Festa della Montagna. It is situated in the National Park of Gran Paradiso and contains approx 1,500 species of indigenous and exotic plants. The alpine gardens of Chanousia on the Col of the Little St Bernard (just over 7,111 ft, 2,188 m) were destroyed during World War II but are in the process of being restored.

(1) *Jun–mid-Sep: Daily Sunrise–Sunset*
(2) *Charge*
(5) *Trustees of the National Park of Gran Paradiso*

Colorno

Emilia

11. Giardino Ducale

The gardens surround the old castle which was converted into a palace for Ranuccio II by Ferdinando Galli-Bibiena in 1660. The garden was redesigned as an English romantic park by Maria Louise of Austria in 1816–20. In spite of the ravages of World War II, the park still contains many mature plants and a small lake encircled with weeping willows. Visit in spring.

(1) *Mon, Tue, Fri, Sat 9–12, 3.30–6.30; Sun 4–7.30. At other times by contacting the Keeper, Signor Mario Bonini, Via Mazzini 34, Colorno*
(2) *Free*
(3) *Restaurant*
(4) *Ducal Palace (same times)*
(5) *Commune of Colorno*

Garda

Veneto

12. Villa Idania

Situated above the small town of Garda which extends along the lakeside, this attractive modern garden was originally planned by the late A. Edwards of Manchester Parks and later developed by Henry Cocker – both previously at the Royal Botanic Gardens, Kew (qv) – for the present owner Contessa Ida Borletti. It combines English and Italian styles, with spacious lawns, olive trees, Lombardy cypress, an enormous herbaceous border, fine flowering cherries, including the infrequently seen yellow flowered *Prunus ukon*, excellent specimens of *Liriodendron tulipifera* and *Liquidambar styraciflua*, roses, and many flowering shrubs including the aptly named 'Beauty Bush' (*Kolkwitzia amabilis*).

The garden is on two levels, linked by a fine rock garden and a spectacular floral staircase. A dry stone wall is attractive at all seasons and flanks a long pergola covered with grape vines. There are superb views of mountains on one side and the vast expanse of Lake Garda on the other. The garden is of particular interest to those who garden on similarly calcareous soil.

(1) *By appointment with the owner*
(2) *Free*
(5) *Contessa Ida Borletti*

Gardone Riviera, Lake Garda

Veneto

13. Garden of Professor A. Hruska

From unpromising material consisting of a derelict vineyard, a knowledgeable and enthusiastic amateur established a superb collection of alpine plants in a natural setting. During a long and brilliant career in many parts of the world – from Lapland to Central Africa and the United States, as physician, dental surgeon, botanist, lecturer, explorer and garden lover – Professor Hruska was in 1911 appointed dental surgeon to the Tsar of Russia. Born in 1880 at Innsbruck, he eventually settled at Gardone Riviera.

The central part of the garden consists of a reproduction, in miniature, of a corner of the Dolomites with authentic rocks and faithfully duplicated contours which give the visitor an impression of being at a high altitude in those mountains. The rich collection of alpine plants has been gathered from all parts of the world, while there are also small lakes, mountain streams, grassy slopes, a fine collection of conifers and other interesting trees. Although Professor Hruska was an expert on alpine flora, he was fully aware of the value of other, more popular plants which extend the flowering period, range of colours and aesthetic appeal of the garden. It is this clever combination of rare and common plants which makes the garden so attractive at all seasons.

(1) Daily 8.30–5.30
(2) Charge
(5) Hruska family

Grezzana

Veneto

14. Villa Cuzzano

A 17th-cent villa built for the Allegri family which still retains its original design. It is something of a rarity for the Veneto, where the number of gardens maintaining a parterre lay-out is diminishing while the number of more informal, English-style gardens is increasing.

The long terrace running the full length of the villa offers superb views of the distant, lower levels and their renowned vineyards. While it is the magnificent parterre which is the dominant feature of the garden, there are also excellent vistas and fine specimens of cypresses and clipped yews. Villa Cuzzano has dovecots and an aviary.

(1) By appointment with the owner
(2) Free
(5) Arverdi family

Lake Maggiore

Piedmont

15. Isola Bella

The 17th-cent palace set on an island in the middle of Lake Maggiore was designed by Angelo Crivelli as a summer residence for the Borromeo family, who still use it as such. The palace contains a rich collection of paintings, furniture, famous tapestries and an enormous grotto.

The exotic Baroque gardens have trees and many tropical and rare plants. Inspired by the hanging gardens of Babylon, they are laid out as a pleasure ship on terraces and for this reason were originally thinly planted in order to emphasize their overall design. Each terrace is linked to the next by ornate stairways and contains its own separate garden with lawns and flowerbeds, pools, fountains and statues. They include an English garden, an azalea garden, an Italian garden, a grandiose Rococo amphitheatre ornamented with statues by Giorgio Vasari and a mosaic garden formed by yew topiary and roses.

The gardens are now more densely planted than when they were originally planted with the luxuriant foliage and flowers of breadfruit, tamarind, tea bushes, magnolias and orchids.

From the upper terraces there are panoramic views of the Alps and the Simplon Pass, the lake, Mt Mottarone, popular for skiing in winter, and the surrounding landscape. The gardens are particularly famous for their collection of camellia plants, many of a great age and size.

(1) Apr–Oct: Daily 8.30–noon, 2–5.30
(2) Charge
(3) Restaurant
(4) Palace (same times)
(5) Principe Borromeo

Lake Maggiore

16. Isola Madre

Isola Madre is situated in Lake Maggiore and has been in the possession of the Borromeo family since c 1200. The 16th-cent villa is surrounded by gardens which are famous for their collections of rare and exotic plants. The grounds are laid out in five long gardens with wooded areas to the north and west. Owing to the warm climate, their plants have grown to an enormous size and range from high Canadian redwoods and Himalayan weeping pines to a wistaria which has a breadth of 80 yds (73 m). The rhododendrons for which the island is renowned have trunks that are almost 12 in (30 cm) in diameter. The two most noteworthy plants on the island are *Jubaea spectabilis*, a giant palm 60 ft high (18·3 m), with a trunk 12 ft (3·6 m) in circumference, planted in 1858, and the largest specimen growing out of doors in Europe of the beautiful *Cupressus cashmeriana*, 100 ft (30 m) high and a glorious sight with its glaucous, silver-green, pendulous habit.

During the past few years renovation has taken place in the garden without in any way changing the basic lay-out. The enormous villa, closed and uninhabited for many years, is now being restored and furnished and will shortly be opened to the public.

Visit in May, when the azaleas, camellias and magnolias are in full bloom.

(1) *Apr–Oct: Daily 8.30–noon, 2–5.30*
(2) *Charge*
(3) *Restaurant*
(5) *Principe Borromeo*

Lonedo di Lugo, nr Thiene

Veneto

17. Villa Piovene

The villa, with later 17th- and 18th-cent additions, is believed to be the work of Andrea Palladio. Situated on the brow of a hill, it is reached by a great sweeping stairway designed by Muttoni, and overlooks the town of Lonedo and the plains below. The park which lies to the rear of the house was landscaped by Antonio Piovene in 1850. It contains natural grottoes deposited with stalactites and stalagmites and it is noted for its rare plants.

(1) *Daily 8–noon, 3–6*
(2) *Charge*
(5) *Contessa Caterina Piovene Vergnano di Villar*

Maser

Veneto

18. Villa Barbaro

This magnificent Palladian villa is, unlike many others, in superb condition thanks to the present owner, although the only remains of the splendid 16th-cent garden designed by Palladio are the interesting areas immediately in front of the villa and the exquisite 'secret garden'. Bounded on one side by the villa and on the other by the hillside, the garden is small in area, but the lavish use of water to provide reflections, and a massive, richly decorated wall at one end, help to create an imposing sense of space.

(1) *Tue, Fri and 1st Sun in each month 3–6. By appointment with the owner or the local tourist agency*
(2) *Charge*
(4) *Carriage Museum and Palladian Temple (same times)*
(5) *Contessa Anna Maria Volpi*

Milan

19. Castello Sforzesco and Milan Park

Originally built in 1368, the Castello was partially destroyed in 1447, but Francesco Sforza had it rebuilt. In 1521 the magnificent tower was struck by lightning,

causing 250,000 pounds of gunpowder to explode. Subsequently the castle passed through further periods of deterioration and restoration until it was finally rebuilt and restored to its present-day magnificence by Luca Beltrami in 1893–1904.

At the rear of the castle, and complementary to it, there is Milan's largest park, designed by the architect Alemagna in 1893. Its dimensions are on a grand scale, with roads, woods, streams, a lake, an artificial hill and a glorious vista linking the castle and the distance Peace Arch, completed in 1833 and inaugurated by the Emperor of Austria.

(1) *Daily Sunrise–Sunset*
(2) *Free*
(5) *City of Milan*

Milan, Piazza Cavour

20. Giardino Pubblico

Milan's oldest public park is situated almost in the centre of the city. Founded at the end of the 18th cent, it owes its present form to the modifications and extensions made by the architects Balzaretto in 1856 and Alemagna in 1881. There is a rich collection of mature specimen trees, many flowering shrubs and spacious lawns, a lake and a stream. There is also a small zoo.

(1) *Daily Sunrise–Sunset*
(2) *Free*
(3) *Café*
(4) *Zoo*
(5) *City of Milan*

Milan

21. Villa Belgioioso (Villa Reale, Villa Comunale)

The huge villa was constructed in 1790 for Conte Belgioioso from a design by the architect Pollack, with a vast garden in the romantic style which is the best example of its type in the area of Milan. This too was initiated by Pollack but completed by Villoresi. The serpentine lake is typical of the period and there are numerous fine trees, fountains and pools, the whole giving an impression of spaciousness in the centre of the city. Its history has been varied: after the death of Conte Belgioioso it was acquired by the State, and for a time used by the House of Savoy for receptions. It is now owned by the City of Milan and houses the Gallery of Modern Art.

(1) *Daily Sunrise–Sunset*
(2) *Free*
(4) *Gallery of Modern Art (Daily, except Mon 9.30–12.30, 2.30–4.30)*
(5) *City of Milan*

Montalto di Pavia

Lombardy

22. Castello Balduino

A medieval castle, originally a stronghold of

the Belcredi family of Pavia, dating from the 13th cent. The 18th-cent gardens were laid out by Giovanni Antonio Veneroni.

The present owner acquired the property in 1909 and commissioned the garden architect Giovanni Chevalley to complete and restore the gardens which had suffered from years of neglect.

The gardens are enclosed by one of the finest topiary hedges in Italy. The yew has been sculpted into circular or square bases and central domes which are interspersed with a parterre design of arabesques and diamonds filled with a variety of plants.

(1) By appointment with the owner
(2) Free
(5) Conte Balduino

Monte di Rovagnate

Lombardy

23. Villa Porlezza

A relatively modern garden of moderate size, noted for its extensive collections of shrubby potentillas, species of rose, its vast selection of aromatic, medicinal and culinary plants, and for the perfect state of upkeep, with its fine lawns and extensive plantings of flowering shrubs. The owner is an authority on aromatic plants and author of *Il Giardino degli Aromia* which not only describes over 300 species and varieties, but also gives recipes for their use, all of which he has personally sampled.

(1) By arrangement with the owner
(2) Free
(5) Dr Giampaolo Porlezza Taroni

Montegaldella

Veneto

24. Villa La Deliziosa

The original villa and gardens date back to 1622, but have been considerably modified over the years. Their main attraction is the many 18th-cent statues attributed to the workshop of Orazio Marinali. The most important of these is the series of figures representing characters from the Commedia dell'Arte, and at the rear of the house the great piece of sculpture known as *La Ruota* The Wheel, Orazio Marinali's allegorical conception of the Four Corners of the Earth.

(1) Thu and Sat 9–1
(2) Free
(5) Commune Tillio Campagnolo-Vicenza

Padua, Via Orto Botanico 15

Veneto

25. Botanical Gardens of the University of Padua

The gardens retain their original state and are the oldest botanical gardens in the world. They were founded in 1545 on the

instigation of the medical botanist, Francesco Bonafede. The walls surrounding the garden were constructed in 1551 and are 15 ft (4·5 m) high. In 1707 the tops of the walls were decorated with busts of former directors and curators. In 1700–4 the four iron gates were constructed and on their supporting pillars are inscribed in Latin and Italian the garden regulations of 1545, while the tops of the gates are decorated with iron Yucca plants in urns.

The gardens occupy an area of 4·9 acres (2 ha) and contain approx 6,000 species of plants. There is a fine arboretum which includes the famous Goethe palm commemorating the poet's visit there in 1786, and several other ancient trees; the chaste tree (*Vitex agnus-castus*) planted in 1550 and a *Ginkgo biloba* of 1750. Among the plants which have been collected from all over the world are those which are the first of their species to have been introduced into Europe. They were acclimatized here and then distributed elsewhere. These include: lilac (*Syringa vulgaris*, imported in 1565), sunflower (helianthus, 1568), the potato (*Solanum tuberosum*, 1590), jasmine (*Jasminum fruticans*, 1590), the tree of heaven (*Ailanthus glandulosa*, 1769), and the cultivated cyclamen (*Cyclamen persicum*, 1812). There is a display of over 50 species of iris, an ornamental garden, a collection of medieval plants, alpine and aquatic plants.

(1) Nov–Feb: Daily (except Public Holidays) 9–1; Mar–Oct: Daily 9–1; Public Holidays 10–1
(2) Charge
(5) University of Padua

Pallanza, Lake Maggiore

Piedmont

26. Villa Taranto

The French-style château, situated on the Castagnola promontory overlooking Lake Maggiore, was bought in 1931 by the late Capt Neil McEacharn. Inspired by the desire to create an Italian Kew and with the considerable help of Henry Cocker, who was appointed Superintendent in 1934, the property was laid out as a vast private botanical garden, combining both Italian and English styles. The gardens cover 50 acres (20.2 ha), with their highest point at 1,100 ft (335 m), and have an average annual rainfall of 90 in (2·3 m). The numerous water-lily ponds, vast nelumbium (lotus) pool with great pink and white flowers, fountains, waterfalls and swimming pool together with the garden, many glass-houses and several nurseries are all supplied from a reservoir constructed at the highest point and filled with water pumped from the lake. The area laid out in an Italian style consists of three vast terraces bisected by a wide canal of water and arranged in formal, rectangular, brick-edged beds planted with bulbs in spring and with annuals in summer.

In striking contrast to the formal design, there is a spectacular, artificial, but natural-looking valley, which traverses much of the garden from north to south and which is spanned by a graceful, single-arch stone bridge. This valley offers an ideal habitat for hemerocallis, hostas, primulas, astilbes, campanulas, irises, etc. Rhododendrons, azaleas and camellias are a speciality of Villa Taranto, especially in a birch and sweet chestnut wood, where the giant cardiocrinum (*Lilium giganteum*) is naturalized. The collection of rhododendron species and varieties is the finest in the country. Other features include a double herbaceous border divided by a long, narrow lawn providing a delightful vista leading from a mausoleum, where the founder was buried in 1964, to a fountain with the traditional putti beyond which is another vista filled with Australian tree-ferns.

At one side of the villa is a vast lawn with a central fountain, while much of the remaining area is laid out as parkland and planted with a rich collection of flowering shrubs, conifers and other trees, such as paulownia, melia, catalpa, liriodendron, etc. The collection of deciduous magnolias is particularly fine, while the many flowering cherries, many of which were imported direct from Japan, are a special feature in spring.

Although attractive at all seasons, the autumn colouring is particularly effective with acers, cornus, fothergilla, enkianthus, berberis, cotoneaster, liquidambar, rhus, scarlet oaks, etc. The total number of species and varieties of plants is approx 20,000, collected from all parts of the world. In a specially designed, heated glasshouse with a vast pool, the giant Amazon water-lily, *Victoria regia* (*Victoria amazonica*), is cultivated, with its floating leaves up to 6½ ft (1·9 m) in diameter. Other important features are an erica garden, a fine curved pergola with granite pillars, a bog garden, areas with naturalized bulbs, an octagonal piazza with a 17th-cent Italian well-head from a convent and an impressive staircase, adapted from a Portuguese garden, linking a terrace near the lotus pool to the formal garden. The estate was presented to the Italian State in 1940 and opened to the public in 1952. The garden has its own boat station served by the steamer service on the lake. The main entrance is on the inter-national Italian/Swiss highway.

(1) *Apr–Oct: Daily 8.30–Sunset*
(2) *Charge*
(3) *Café*
(4) *Chapel (mass is celebrated at 11 each Sun)*
(5) *Italian State managed by the Botanical Gardens of Villa Taranto Trust*

Parma, Strada Farini

Emilia

27. Botanical Gardens of the University of Parma

Traditional university physic garden founded in 1768 and ornamented with fountains and statues.

(1) *Apr–May: Sun 10–noon*
(2) *Free*
(5) *University of Parma*

Passariano

Friuli-Venezia Giulia

28. Villa Manin

16th-cent villa with 17th- and 18th-cent additions. It was built for the last doge of Venice, Ludovico Manin, and was at one time owned by Napoleon. After years of neglect it was restored by the Venetian Villas Association. Later the property was acquired by the Provincial Administration (1969), who opened it as a museum and public park.

The original gardens were designed as *un luogo do delizio*, 'a place of delights', and old records reveal that it contained arenas, mazes, theatres, fountains, baths, hanging gardens, astronomical clocks, aviaries and menageries.

The present lay-out still retains much of the attraction of its original design and there is an interesting collection of plants and trees including many rare species such as Himalayan weeping pines, the *Ginkgo biloba*, *Pinus strobus* the Virginian juniper and tulip-trees.

(1) *Thu and Sat 2.30–5; Sun 10–12.30, 2.30–5. By appointment with the Soprintendenza dei Monumenti at Friuli-Venezia Giulia, Via Aquileia 4, Udine*
(2) *Free*
(3) *Restaurant*
(4) *Villa (Daily, except Mon, 9.30–12.30, 3–6)*
(5) *Provincial Administration of Friuli-Venezia Giulia – Forestry Commission*

Pavia, Via S. Epifanio 14

Lombardy

29. Botanical Gardens of the University of Pavia

The original medicinal herb garden founded in 1558 was transformed into a botanical garden in 1773 and covers an area of 8·5 acres (3·5 ha). It specializes in roses, including botanical species, and is noted for its collection of *Bromeliaceae* and *Cactaceae*.

(1) *Spring–Autumn: Sun 9–noon, 3–7*
(2) *Free*
(5) *University of Pavia*

Pavia
30. Certosa di Pavia

The Carthusian Monastery was founded in
1396 by Gian Galeazzo Visconti of Milan
and the buildings date from the 15th and
16th cents. The small cloisters are planted
with flowers and evergreens around a
central Baroque fountain. The lawn is surrounded by a single trellis of roses and white
columns of Carrara marble. At one end are
23 monks' cells, each one comprising three
rooms and with its own enclosed flower
garden.

(1) *Jan–Apr, Sep–Dec: Daily (except Mon,
unless Public Holiday) 9–11.30, 2.30–
4.30; May–Aug: Daily (except Mon,
unless Public Holiday) 9–11.30, 2.30–6*
(2) *Mon–Sat: Charge; Sun: Free*
(4) *Certosa Museum (by appointment with
the Superintendent of Monuments,
Milan)*
(5) *Carthusian Order*

Rodano, nr Milan
Lombardy
31. Villa Invernizzi

This lovely villa on the outskirts of Milan is
in the Veneto style and has recently been
restored. The gardens, also recently restored, are an example of the successful
combination of the classical Italian and
English styles. There is the formally
designed garden, a lavish use of fountains,
streams and ponds together with what is
probably the largest and finest lawn in Italy,
flanked by long walks planted with hornbeam. There is a good collection of both
evergreen and deciduous trees and shrubs.

(1) *By appointment with the administrator*
(2) *Free*
(5) *Cav. del Lavoro Romeo Invernizzi*

Sala Baganza, nr Parma
Emilia
32. Carrega Woods

An 18th-cent hunting park with two fine
hunting lodges. The Villa Carino de Boschi
was designed by Petitot in 1775–89 for the
Duchess Maria Amalia of Bourbon. The
woods became a favourite haunt of Maria
Louise of Austria, who commissioned Gaz-
zola to design the Villa Casino del Ferlaro
in the 19th-cent neo-classical style. The
park contains water gardens, lakes, 18th-
cent baths, a swimming pool and a grotto.

There are plantations of Canadian firs,
beeches, chestnuts and pines; the area is
also rich in wildlife, and goats, wolves and
hares are among the animals to be found
there.

(1) *Mar–Oct: Sat and Sun 8.30–1*
(2) *Free*
(5) *Provincial Administration of Parma,
Communes of Collecchio, Felino, For-
nova, Parma and Sala Baganza*

Strà
Veneto
33. Villa Nazionale

The villa was built in 1735 for the Doge
Alvise Pisani, and designed by Girolamo
Frigizelica and Francesco Preti. At one time
owned by Napoleon's viceroy in Italy
Eugène de Beauharnais, the gardens, which
lie behind the villa, were probably refashioned as a grand park at this period.

It was customary for villas in the Veneto
to face directly on to the carriageway so
the ladies of the house could amuse
themselves by watching the arrival and
departure of visitors. This forcibly placed
the gardens at the back of the house. It
also meant that a central axis other than
the main driveway (so essential to
Renaissance landscape design) had to be
found. This puzzle was successfully solved
at the Villa Nazionale by using stable
buildings, suitably camouflaged with a
grand façade, rather than the villa as the
focal point.

(1) *Apr–Sep: Daily 9–noon, 3–5.30; Oct–
Mar: Daily 9–12.30, 2–5*
(2) *Free*
(5) *Italian State*

Stresa, Lake Maggiore
Piedmont
34. Alpinia

The gardens were created by Igino Am-
brosini and Giuseppe Rossi in 1934. They
occupy an area of 2½ acres (1 ha) and their
collections include over a thousand different species of alpine plants. Visit between
May and October.

(1) *Daily 9–noon, 2–5.30*
(2) *Free*
(5) *Commune of Stresa*

Stresa, Lake Maggiore
35. Villa Pallavicino

The upper zones of this 50 acre (20 ha)
garden, largely created by the Marchesa
Luisa Pallavicino, are relatively modern.
The early 18th-cent villa is one of the finest
on Lake Maggiore. Its immediate sur-
roundings are well furnished with many fine
old specimen trees. The style of the villa is
typical of Liguria, and reflects the Genoese
origin of the family. Apart from its rich collections of plants, the park and gardens
have animals such as deer, llama, ostriches,
pheasants and swans.

At the rear of the villa is a fine lawn and
the lower part of the estate is informal with
a large number of hydrangeas, woodland
plants, a stream with waterfalls, many
conifers, palms, naturalized bulbs, camellias,
rhododendrons and azaleas.

255

The newer, upper garden is more formal, with paved walks, spacious terraces, fountains, lawns, flowerbeds and borders with brilliant displays of annual and perennial plants, dahlias, many roses, and a delightful line of cypress trained in a series of arches which frame the superb views of the lake and distant mountains.

(1) *Late Mar–Oct: Daily 8.30–7*
(2) *Charge*
(5) *Commune of Stresa*

Thiene, nr Vicenza

Veneto

36. Castello Porto Colleoni Thiene

The present castle dates from the late 15th cent and was built on the site of an earlier construction. Two crenellated towers flank the main façade, which is decorated with faded 15th-cent frescoes and a five-arched Gothic window. An elegant portico below marks the entrance.

The gardens were probably laid out at the same time, but were entirely redesigned during the 19th cent when the fashion for romantic landscapes swept Italy. Of the original gardens two small 'secret', walled gardens at the sides of the palace, and the avenue of cedars along the north side of the boundary wall, remain. The garden is renowned for its magnolias.

(1) *Mid-Mar–Oct: Daily 9–noon, 3–6*
(2) *Charge*
(4) *Chapel*
(5) *Conte Gian Giacomo di Thiene*

Trieste, Via Marchesetti 2

Friuli-Venezia Giulia

37. Botanical Gardens of Trieste

The gardens were founded in 1872 by M. de Tommasini and specialize in local flora.

(1) *May–Sep: Daily (except Mon) 8–noon, 2–5*
(2) *Free*
(5) *Commune of Trieste*

Trieste

38. Miramare Park

The park which contains beautiful terraced gardens covers an area of approx 55 acres (22 ha) and is one of the largest in the Venetian provinces. It was laid out in 1860 by the Archduke Maximilian of Austria (brother of the Emperor Franz Josef) who was executed in Mexico in 1870.

(1) *Daily 9–Sunset*
(2) *Free*
(3) *Bar*

(4) *Castle (Summer: Daily 9–1, 2–5; Winter: Daily 9.30–4; Sun always 9.30–1.30)*
(5) *Italian State*

Trissino, nr Vicenza

Veneto

39. Villa Trissino (now Villa Marzotto)

The harmonious design of this garden with its green avenues flanked by statues by O. Marinali and G. Casetti, stairways, hanging gardens, fishpools and belvedere make it unique to Vicenza. Of note is the lower octagonal pool set on a grassy balustraded terrace overlooking the valley and hills beyond. Statues placed at each corner of the pool are reflected in the water and create an impression of a dance. The upper villa was refashioned in the 18th cent by G. dal Pozzo and stands on the site of an old fortress.

(1) *For further information and visiting hours contact the Vicenza Tourist Board*
(2) *Free*

Valeggio sul Mincio, nr Peschiera

Veneto

40. Parco Giardini Sigurtà

The 17th-cent Villa Maffei (now Sigurtà) was designed by Vincenzo Pallesino in 1693 and was for a short period used as Napoleon III's headquarters after the Battle of Solferino in 1859.

The adjoining farmland was converted by the present owner into an unusual modern garden noted for its lawns, displays of flowers and woodland walks. The recessed façade of the villa covered with bougainvillea overlooks the formal garden. To the back of the villa an avenue of fountains leads through wide borders of flowers to the topiary garden, where curious natural forms of *Buxus sempervirens* are accentuated by careful cutting into surrealistic shapes. From here the gardens sweep upwards to the Valley of the Water-lilies, where in the basin of a shallow valley lie several small lakes bordered by a mosaic of multicoloured flowers and threaded with water-lilies. A feature of this part of the garden is the wide expanse of green and the cypress trees which cover the slopes. Beyond this the garden rises to the Romeo and Juliet Esplanade, a clearing planted with shrubs, stone pines, cypresses and banks of flowers from which there are views of the Mincio Valley and Mt Baldo. To the left of the villa is the avenue of roses, a simple stone-paved track lined with a single row of red roses and tall cypresses, leading to the old crenellated castle of Scaligeri. Behind the castle is a secluded 'secret garden' with a deeply shaded lily-pond.

Other points of interest are the dog cemetery with its lily-pond and a small Gothic temple.

Among the trees of note are Japanese maples, an ancient beech and a magnificent dome-shaped oak.

(1) Sat, Sun and Public Holidays. Visitors must drive through the grounds without leaving their cars following a 4-mile one-way itinerary. Coach visits are allowed but should be booked in advance (Tel: 045-635203)
(2) Charge
(5) Dr G. C. Sigurtà

Valsanzibio di Galzignano, nr Padua

Veneto

41. Villa Barbarigo (now Villa Pizzoni Ardemani)

The garden of Villa Pizzoni Ardemani, which lies in the basin of a valley, was laid out in 1669 for Procurator Antonio Barbarigo and is one of the great gardens of the Veneto. Bordered by pleached alleys, the initial impression it gives is one of greenness, being almost totally created of formal and informal plantings of evergreens and deciduous trees and shrubs. It is remarkable for its size and its design, which is based on two clearly defined vistas. The central axis is created by the main approach to the villa and continues through it up to the crest of the hills beyond. The secondary axis is formed by the watergate which provides access for guests arriving by boat and directs the eye from the entrance through a series of glimmering fishpools on rising levels up into the hills beyond.

The intricate lay-out includes avenues, shaded walks, fountains, lemon trees in pots, statues, a maze, *jeux d'eau* hidden under the pavements in front of the house and a rabbit island.

(1) Mid-Mar–Nov: Daily 9–noon, 3–7
(2) Charge
(5) Dr Fabio Pizzoni Ardemani

Ventimiglia

Liguria

42. Villa Mortola and the Hanbury Botanical Gardens

This 17th-cent palace was originally owned by the Orengo family and was bought by Sir Thomas Hanbury on his return from China in 1867. The gardens were laid out as botanical gardens with the intention of forming a garden that combined old with new and tropical plants with indigenous plants. They were landscaped by the famous German botanist, Ludovico Winter. Their basic lay-out is that of an English flower garden with lawns, small hedges, herbaceous borders and a predominance of flowering scented verbena. The Villa Mor-

tola swiftly established itself as a centre for botanical research and in 1898 the first catalogue containing 7,600 entries was issued.

After the death of Thomas Hanbury, the upkeep of the gardens passed to his brother; and on his death to his son and daughter-in-law, Sir Cecil and Lady Hanbury, who created the Italian Garden with its white colonnaded pergola covered with vines and brightly coloured South American flowers. The most famous part of the garden is the olive grove which is planted with tropical flora, its deep green foliage and brilliant flowers offset by the delicate hues of the olive trees. Also of note are the avenue of *Cycadaceae*, the Australian forest and the collection of American aloes.

The gardens are also famous for their collections of cactus plants and of many varieties and species of orange, lemon, grapefruit, mandarins and other citrus trees. They are also traversed by the old Roman road, Via Aurelia, now much hidden and at a much lower level than the actual garden and crossed by a bridge. The 112 acres (45 ha), in this favoured position, ensure that the garden is never without flowers. The name La Mortola comes from the name *La Punta della Murtola*, where wild myrtle (*Myrtus communis*) grows on the rocky point washed by the waves of the Mediterranean, at the extremity of the property. La Mortola has also maintained the closest contact with Kew Botanic Gardens (qv) and for many years affected a student exchange system.

(1) Daily 8.30–5.30
(2) Charge
(3) Restaurant and bar
(4) Archaeological Museum (Daily 10–Sunset)
(5) Italian State

Verona

Veneto

43. Giardino Giusti

The gardens of the Palazzo Giusti have been famed for at least 350 years. They have been owned and developed by the Giusti family since c 1400, when they were known as Giusti del Giardino, a distinction which suggests they were pioneers of garden making in Verona at a time when the art was little practised in that area. The site is on the slope of a hill and thus appropriate for terracing, a feature still characteristic of the gardens, but later some levelling took place and the original design has been much modified and can only be guessed at. The present garden includes an imposing avenue of noble cypresses (*Cupressus sempervirens* var. *pyramidalis*) some of which are believed to be the largest and oldest in Italy. Even in 1611 a writer referred to the gardens as a paradise, after making an

257

extensive visit. Much emphasis is given to fountains, pools and rocks designed in many forms and decorated with shells and mosaics. The formal, terraced garden is typical of the early Italian style, with numerous temples, grottoes and statues.

(1) *Daily. For details apply to the administration*
(2) *Charge*
(5) *Giusti family*

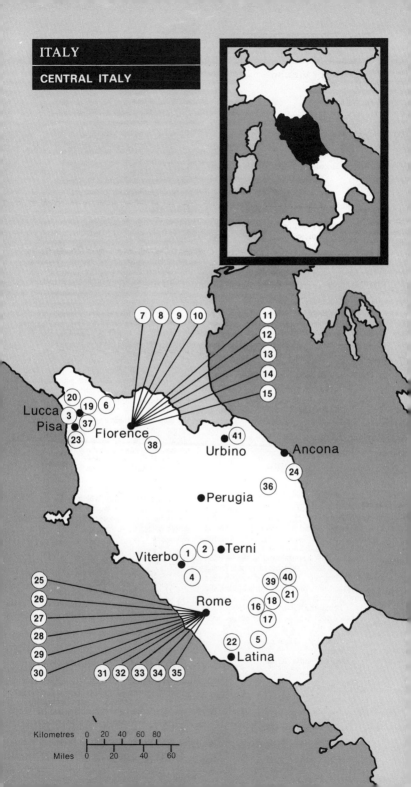

ITALY

Bagnaia, nr Viterbo
Latium
1. Villa Lante

Built as a summer residence on the slopes of the Cimini Hills, this modest palace is believed to have been designed by Giacomo Barozzio da Vignola for Cardinal Gambera.

The site is one of natural beauty and the gardens ascend the hillside in three terraces. There are crumbling statues of moss-covered stone and fountains fashioned as horses and river gods. Stone benches flank a long stone table which is bisected by a channel of smoothly flowing water in which bottles of wine could be cooled. The walls of the *al fresco* dining-room are of intricate trellis work, while one is open to a view of the parterre below and the roofs of the town of Bagnaia beyond. The chief feature of the garden is the balustraded fountain terrace which juts over the valley. Four simple parterres, each with a fountain at the crossing, lie on either side of the pool. Stone boats 'float' in the waters and in the centre is a fountain formed by the statues of four boys whose arms are outstretched to form mounts for a star of water.

Above is the Fountain of Lanterns and a stepped waterfall in the shape of an elongated crawfish taken from the Cardinal's coat of arms.

(1) Jun–Sep: Daily (except Mon) 9–noon, 3–6; Oct–May: Daily (except Mon) 9–noon, 2.30–5
(2) Charge
(5) Italian State

Bomarzo, nr Viterbo
Latium
2. Parco dei Mostri

The Villa Bomarzo was originally a medieval stronghold and was converted by Pirro Ligorio and Giacomo Barozzio de Vignola into a villa for Prince Orsini in the second half of the 16th cent.

The gardens were laid out in the wooded valley below the villa in the form of a sacred wood. They are famous for the strange monsters which have been carved out of the natural outcrops of stone, the most spectacular being the Giantess, the Giant, the Tortoise with a statue of Fame on his back and a group of two dragons.

(1) Daily Sunrise–Sunset
(2) Charge
(5) Signor Giovanni Bettini

Camigliano, nr Lucca
Tuscany
3. Villa Torrigiani

The original villa dates from the 16th cent but was completely redesigned in the 17th

cent by the diplomat Marchese Nicolao Santini.

The gardens are attributed to Le Nôtre. The grounds were restored at the beginning of the century by Marchese Cedro Lucca Torrigiano and escaped destruction during World War II. Of particular interest are the lemon gardens, the Temple of Flora, the Grotto of the Seven Winds, the Stalactite Walk, and the 18th-cent *jeux d'eau* concealed beneath pebbled mosaic.

(1) Easter–early Nov: Daily 10–noon, 3–6
(2) Charge
(4) Villa (same times); Chapel (on request)
(5) Simonetta Colonna Torrigiani

Caprarola
Latium
4. Villa Farnese

The villa was originally a fortress but was converted into a palace for Cardinal Alessandro Farnese in the 16th cent. Built in the shape of a pentagon, highly theatrical in design, it stands overlooking a series of terraces linked by a great 'horseshoe staircase. The gardens rise in slopes from the foot of the hill behind it and are cut off from the terrace by a deep ditch which originally formed part of the defence works of the old fortress; these are divided into two separate parts by trees. According to an 18th-cent print by V. Vasi, the square-shaped gardens were laid out with four main parterres also square in shape, and subdivided again into four sections containing a design in clipped box. Today the gardens to the south-west of the villa retain their original lay-out. In the spring the gardens to the other side are planted with wild orchids and the walls are covered with camellia blossom.

Deep in the woods above, an avenue bordered with pines opens on to the fountains and cascades of a 'secret garden'. Above this again is a flight of steps leading to the simple Casino garden which was originally designed as a secluded retreat. It is decorated with seahorse fountains and box hedge parterres surrounded by cypress and pine trees.

(1) May–Sep: Daily (except Mon) 9–12.30, 2.30–5.30; Oct–Apr: Daily (except Mon) 9–12.30, 2.30–5. By appointment with the Direzione Generale del Demanio
(2) Charge

Castel Gandolfo
Latium
5. Villa Barberini

The site of the famous villa of the Emperor Titus Flavius Domitianus (AD 51–96) was acquired in the 12th cent by the Gandolfi family, who erected a fortress there. In the 17th cent the property passed into the hands of Matteo Barberini, who became Pope in 1623. He converted the fortress into a Papal summer residence and laid out the gardens in terraces. The territory remained Papal property until the French Revolution. After the Lateran Agreement in 1925 the Estate was officially returned to the Holy See together with the neighbouring parkland of Cybo. In 1933 Pius XI commissioned Dr Emilio Bonomelli to redesign the gardens.

During the reterracing of the terrain, many of the ruins of the old Domitian villa were excavated and subsequently included in the garden's design. On the upper terraces avenues of *Quercus ilex* (evergreen oak), reputed to date from this period, may still be seen. Set back from the avenues is the small Pavilion of Repose, immediately below which lies the Garden of the Magnolia. This small and secluded 'secret garden' is laid out with parterres, fountains and lemon trees in pots. From the Garden of the Pavilion an avenue known as the Viale delle Pyramide continues with long vistas down paths set at right angles where ancient trees and marble statues form the only decorative relief. The central avenue eventually opens on to the Garden of the Madonna.

The most impressive part of the gardens is the belvedere which overlooks the spectacular Lemon Terraces. The simple raised pattern of the parterres is formed by low hedges of trimmed box filled with ageratum, salvia, thyme and dwarf coleus, the design for which was inspired by the moulded ceilings of Roman basilicas. By making the further terrace slightly longer than the first, an optical illusion of equal length to the nearest is created. The terraces are joined by flights of steps. Each terrace is laid out with four simple rectangular parterres intersected by paths. The outer lip of each terrace is lined by a hedge of cypress trees clipped into an arched hedge similar in design to an ancient aqueduct.

The gardens were considerably damaged during World War II but have been completely restored by Dr Bonomelli.

(1) *By appointment with the Direzione della Villa Pontificia de Castel Gandolfo. (Permission is not granted during the summer when the Pope is in residence)*
(2) *Free*
(4) *Villa (by appointment as above)*
(5) *Holy See*

Collodi, nr Pistoia
Tuscany
6. Villa Garzoni

This 17th-cent villa was built by the Marchese Romano Garzoni. The gardens are set apart from it on a steeply sloping hillside with views over the olive and cypress groves of the Nievola Valley.

Designed by the garden architect Diodati, they are renowned as one of the purest Tuscan examples of 17th-cent garden landscaping. Whilst retaining the Renaissance style of terracing, the transition from the parterre garden to the *bosco* is entirely Baroque in character.

ITALY

The formal parterre gardens lie on the lower esplanade beyond a semi-circle of box clipped to form curves. An ornamental balustraded stairway which forms the central axis of the gardens leads to the upper terrace, which is laid out with paths running through avenues of trees, oriental bamboo groves and a series of fountains and cascades. The upper gardens also contain a theatre, with statues representing Greek tragedy and comedy, and a maze.

The great allegorical statue of Fame dominates the water stairway. The statue is flanked on either side by the recumbent figures of Lucca and Florence, while below it small stone birds spill water from their beaks.

At the top of the gardens are the famous 18th-cent baths where men and women would bathe in separate enclosures and discreetly hidden orchestras played music for their amusement.

(1) *Apr–Oct: Daily 8–1, 2.30–Sunset; Nov–Mar: Daily 9–noon, 2.30–Sunset*
(2) *Charge*
(3) *Restaurant and kiosks*
(5) *Dilezza Bologna Society.*

Florence, Via P.A. Micheli 3
Tuscany
7. Botanical Gardens of the University of Forence

The 16th-cent medicinal herb garden derives from an earlier garden planted by the Grand Duke Cosimo I dei Medici. The gardens were laid out by Niccolò Tribolo and originally had a number of statues; the statue of Esculapio by Antonio Gino Lorenzo di Settignano still remains. They were looked after by Luca Ghini up to his death in 1556, after which they fell into decay until they were restored under the auspices of Cosimo III dei Medici. He handed them over to the care of the Botanical Society, whose founder Pier Antonio Micheli was responsible for enlarging the collections. In 1865 they came under the direction of the great botanist Teodoro Caruel, who installed the efficient and beautiful complex of glasshouses still in existence today. The herbarium and library were moved to the site in 1905 and it was given the name the Botanical Institute of Florence. The gardens consist of just under 6 acres (2·5 ha) composed of 9,000 species of herbaceous and arboreal plants, and are noted for their collection of palms, *Cycadaceae* and irises. Visit between May and September.

(1) *Mon, Wed, Fri 9–noon*
(2) *Charge*
(5) *University of Florence*

Florence, Piazzale Michelangelo

8. Giardino Iride

Founded in 1955 by Flamina G. Specht, it contains 1,000 different varieties of iris and includes specimens of 16th-cent strains. The rhizomes for these were specially imported from the Presby Gardens of Montclair, New Jersey. It is also the site of the International Annual Iris competition organized by The Italian Iris Society in order to select the best new varieties.

(1) Mid-May–early Jun. By appointment, the Iris Society, Piazzale Michelangelo, Florence
(2) Free
(5) Iris Society

Florence

9. Palazzo Pitti and Giardini di Boboli

The Boboli Gardens are thought to have been designed by Niccolò Tribolo in the 16th cent for the Grand Duke Cosimo I dei Medici and were originally purely Tuscan in character. A series of small symmetrical gardens of *boschi*, intersected by paths, covered the slopes; the geometrical parterre garden lay to the left. The central axis was created by the garden immediately behind the villa with a high central fountain.

The gardens were modified during the 17th cent and their whole function changed. Inspired by Ovid's *Metamorphoses* the garden became a place of entertainment rather than refreshment and the terraces, statues, fountains, *jeux d'eau* and even the paths with their tantalizing perspectives were intended to delight and surprise the visitor. The natural amphitheatre was accordingly encircled with tiered seats and formed a theatrical setting for the lavish spectacles and the sumptuous nuptials of the Grand Dukes.

The gardens also include a grotto, a fine avenue of cypress trees, a pointed pergola containing Giovanni da Bologna's statue of Venus, and the fountain of Oceanus with his allegorical figure of Euphrates.

(1) Jun, Jul, Nov, Feb: Daily 9–4.30; Mar, Apr, Sep: Daily 9–5.30; May, Aug: Daily 9–6.30
(2) Free
(4) Palatine Gallery (Mon, Wed, Thu, Fri and Sat, except 1 Jan, 2 Jun, 15 Aug, Easter and 25 Dec); Royal Apartments (Thu, Sat, first and third Sun in the month same times as gallery); Silver Museum (same times as gallery)
(5) Italian State

Florence, Via Pian de Guillari

10. Villa Capponi

The villa still maintains its 16th-cent gardens laid out on three terraces. The first terrace is grassed and runs the entire length of the back of the house with views over Florence and the Arno Valley and is divided from the second terrace, or lemon garden, by a hedge and an imposing gateway ornamented with griffins. There is a small 'secret garden' to the west end of this terrace.

(1) By appointment in spring with the Movimento Forestieri or the Comitate per La Visita ai Giardini delle più Belle Ville Fiorentine, Via Proconsolo 10, Florence
(2) Free
(4) Chapel
(5) Mr and Mrs Henry Clifford

Florence

11. Villa di Castello

The gardens were created for Cosimo I dei Medici, Duke of Tuscany, in c 1540, and surround the villa which was bought by two Medici brothers in the previous century. They are designed in the classical Tuscan style of three terraces with a garden room extension to the villa. The whole concept is still basically medieval. The central focus of the grounds is the large enclosed garden laid out with symmetrical flower-filled parterres and orange and lemon trees planted around a central fountain which was designed by Niccolò Tribolo. The original *bosco* of cypresses and bay trees surrounding it has disappeared, greatly lessening the overall effect of the garden.

The first terrace, originally the lemon terrace, leads off from the main courtyard and opens directly on to the famous grotto, which is decorated with shell mosaics, surprise fountains and animal statuary. The top terrace is laid out with a network of paths and pools and is dominated by Bartolomeo Ammanati's great allegorical statue of the Appenines. Two small 'secret gardens' lie to the side of the house. The one to the east originally contained a tree house where there was a musical surprise fountain; the other was once a medieval herb garden.

(1) Daily (except Mon). Jan, Feb, Nov, Dec: 10–noon, 1.30–4; Mar, Apr, Sep, Oct: 10–noon, 1.30–5; May, Aug: 10–noon, 2.30–6
(2) Charge
(5) Italian State

Florence, Via Pian de Guillari 8

12. Villa Il Guillarine

The villa was owned by the Bartolommeo family in the 15th cent. The property was then inherited by the Passerini family and acquired by Baron de Favrot in the 19th cent. It was later owned by an American,

Miss Daws, who sold it to the present owner in 1938.

The gardens are set on a steep slope and laid out in terraces. The date of the original lay-out is uncertain since it has evolved over the centuries. The avenue of cypress trees was planted in c 1900 and the wistaria pergola was erected in the late 1930s. The overall lay-out of the lemon garden, including the colour and design of the flowerbeds, is the work of the present owner. The terraced gardens descend in a series of small gardens blooming with a profusion of roses, flowering creepers and azaleas. There are also concentrations of scented flowers and displays of gladioli in terrace pots.

Visit during the spring and autumn.

(1) By appointment with the owner (Tel: 22-11-03)
(2) Charge
(5) Signor Cesarine Gualino Gurgo-Salice

Florence

13. Villa Medicea della Petraia

Originally a fortified castle surrounded by a moat and owned in the 14th cent by the Boccaccio family, it was converted by Bernardo Buontalenti into a Renaissance villa and laid out with gardens and a *bosco* of holm oaks and cypresses. The villa became the favourite residence of Vittorio Emanuele II when Florence was the capital of Italy.

The gardens which overlook rolling Tuscan countryside are planned with great simplicity as an extension of the villa and descend the terrain in front of the house in terraces. These gardens are among the most beautiful in Tuscany and contain a fine fountain by Niccolò Tribolo adorned with a statue of Venus by Giovanni da Bologna.

(1) Daily Sunrise–Sunset. By appointment with the custodian
(2) Free
(5) Italian State

Florence, Via Bolognese 120

14. Villa La Pietra

The villa dates from the 15th cent while the gardens were laid out in the 17th cent. They were greatly modified by the late Arthur Acton, amateur painter and designer, who bought the villa in 1902, and the fine work has been continued by his son with consistent imagination and attention to detail.

The garden is laid out in typical Tuscan style with a series of six terraces cut into the hillside, three garden rooms and a beautiful green theatre with 'footlights' clipped in box and delicate pieces of statuary modelled in the Meissen style by the 18th-cent Venetian sculptor, Francesco Bonazza. Its unusual character is derived from an intermingling of styles with carefully cut lawns, highly individual use of topiary, classical motifs and beautiful pieces of sculpture, many by Orazio Marinali.

ITALY

(1) Jan, Feb, Nov, Dec: Daily 10–noon, 1.30–4; Mar–May, Aug–Oct: Daily 10–noon, 2.30–6. By appointment with the Comitate per La Visita ai Giardini delle più Belle Ville Fiorentine, Via Proconsolo 10, Florence.
(2) Free
(5) La Pietra Corporation administered by Sir Harold Acton, CBE

Florence, Via di Vincigliata 26

15. Villa I Tatti: The Harvard University Center for Italian Renaissance Studies

The villa dates from 1020 or earlier and was owned in the 16th cent by the Zati family, who sold it in 1568 to the Del Caccias. The dilapidated villa and its neglected gardens were bought by the celebrated art critic and connoisseur, Bernard Berenson, in 1900. On his death the estate with its rich collection of fine art was bequeathed to the State. Bernard Berenson commissioned the architects Cecil Pinsent and Geoffrey Scott to re-landscape the drive and the oak wood, and to restore the terraced gardens to their former classical form with geometrically clipped box hedges, pebble mosaic paths and lemon trees in terracotta pots. Visit in May and June.

(1) Sep–Jul: Wed (except Public Holidays) 3–4. By appointment
(2) Free
(4) Villa and the Berenson Collection (scholars only by letter of introduction)
(5) Italian State managed by Harvard University

Frascati

Latium

16. Villa Aldobrandini

The Renaissance villa was designed by Giacomo della Porta for the Aldobrandini family in 1598–1603 and is still owned by them. It consists of a vast park and remarkable waterworks. The most magnificent of these is a great semi-circular water-theatre designed by Giacomo della Porta and executed by C. Mavierno, Giovanni Fontana and Olivieri. Cascades of water splash down into the water-theatre in the centre of which, encircled by columns and statues, is the figure of Atlas holding a terrestrial globe surrounded by a swirling waterfall. The groves and avenues of the park are planted with spreading ilexes and pines and there are ornamental box hedges and Baroque fountains, one of which is shaped like a galley.

(1) Daily 9–noon, 3–6 or 4 in winter. By appointment with the Tourist Information Centre

(2) *Free. A free entrance ticket must be obtained from the Corazza leather goods shop, Piazzale Roma. Outside shopping hours apply to the Tourist Information Centre (Azienda Autonoma di Soggiorno e Turismo del Tuscolo, Piazzale Marconi)*
(4) *Villa (by appointment with the owner)*
(5) *Principessa Aldobrandini*

Frascati, Via Giulia
17. Villa Falconieri

The villa was built in 1582 for Cardinal Rufini and was later acquired by the Falconieri family. Both the villa and gardens suffered greatly during World War II and have been partially restored. The grounds contain a fine mirror lake surrounded by some of the most magnificent cypresses in Italy.

(1) *Daily 9–noon, 3–6 or 4 in winter. By appointment with the Director of the Bureau of Central European Studies or to the doorkeeper in Frascati*
(2) *Free*
(5) *Bureau of Central European Studies*

Frascati
18. Villa Muti

Considered one of the most attractive relatively small gardens in Italy, this is essentially a green garden, with its basic charm depending on parterres of box and grass, surrounded by clipped hedges and trees. Originally designed in 1579, it was completed by Cardinal Arrigoni in 1595, since when it has remained virtually unchanged, although the parterre is possibly of a later date. The generous proportions of the parterre have permitted a more graceful design than is generally seen in such layouts, with elegant curves in the French style. At present the villa is unoccupied and the property is owned by a development company.

(1) *By appointment with the owners*
(2) *Free*
(5) *Società Immobiliare, Frascati or Rome*

Lucca
Tuscany
19. Municipal Botanic Gardens

The gardens were founded, together with a physics laboratory and an observatory, in 1820 by Maria Luisa of Bourbon, and formed part of an extensive programme of educational reform.

The first director was the medical botanist Paolo Volpi, who remained in charge until 1833. After World War I the gardens, which had been abandoned, were reopened as public gardens. The scientific and didactic tradition of the gardens was resumed for a short period during the years 1966–70, when Professor Lunardini took over the administration and enriched the collection. Since his resignation the future of the gardens as a scientific venture and botanical institute has been in question. The gardens contain 500 different species and cover an area of approx 5 acres (2 ha). They are laid out in two sections: one half is designed as a public park and the other half is devoted to the cultivation of plants. The grounds also include several glasshouses.

The park is noted for its collection of trees. Among those of interest are a cedar of Lebanon (*Cedrus libani*), planted in 1820, the *Sequoia gigantea, Cryptomeria japonica* (1890), *Taxodium distichum, Pinus strobus, Metasequoia glyptostroboides, Magnolia grandiflora* (1830), *Bluxus balaerica* (1880), *Sterculia platanifolia*.

In the garden section there is a fine specimen of *Cinnamomum camphora* (1888) which flowers annually, several examples of the *Ginkgo biloba* and an old lime. In the glasshouses are ornamental plants, including various varieties of croton, ficus, Dieffenbachia, Monstera, philodendron, fatsia, peperomia, sansevieria, scindapsus, spathiphyllum, dracaena, cyperus, coffea, and davallia.

(1) *Winter: Tue, Thu, Sat, Sun 10.30–12.30, 2–4; Summer: Tue, Thu, Sat, Sun 10–noon, 5–7; or by appointment daily (except Sun) 8–2*
(2) *Free*
(5) *Commune of Lucca*

Marlia
Tuscany
20. Villa Reale

The 17th-cent villa was built for the Orsetti family from Lucca and acquired by Napoleon's sister, Elisa Baciocchi, in 1806. She redesigned the villa in neo-classical style and modified the 17th-cent gardens.

The formal gardens are laid out in Tuscan style with a green esplanade in front of the house. A green theatre lies to the left formed out of clipped topiary work with grass seats and terracotta figurines of Columbine, Harlequin and Pulcinella.

Behind the house is a small parterre garden with a design of ageratum, geranium and coleus and a semi-circular pool, urns and fountains. The lemon garden with its flower-filled vases and statuary inspired the landscape painting by J. S. Sargent which was lent to the White House during Kennedy's presidency.

A narrow path leads through a thicket to a Baroque garden room. The grey stone is decorated with reclining gods and goddesses and the balustrades are capped with orange trees in ornamental terrace pots. The whole façade is reflected in the waters of the pool, at the far end of which is a fountain set in a small recess. A shaded alley on one side of the lake opens on to a circular fountain in a small clearing. The gardens continue with a delightful series of unexpected perspectives into the woods which stretch beyond. Within them is a simple wooden summer house with a loggia designed as an open-air dining-room.

(1) *Jul–Oct: Tue, Thu, Sun 9–11, 4–6; Oct–Jun: Tue, Thu, Sun 9–11, 4–6*
(2) *Charge*
(5) *Signor Eredi Pecci-Blunt*

Monte Porzio Catone

Latium

21. Villa Mondragone

The construction of the great villa of Mondragone was begun in 1567 by Cardinal Altemps, who commissioned Martino Lunghi to design it.

The garden is designed around a large courtyard where the landscape, in this case the splendid view from the main terrace over the plains of Latium, is incorporated into the overall plan. Typical of the period is the use of grandiose garden architecture. On the main semi-circular terrace is a three-tiered fountain by Giovanni Fontana and four strange stone carved columns known as the Pope's chimneys which conceal kitchen chimneys.

The focal point of the garden is the theatre in the 'secret garden' – a piece of semi-circular Baroque fantasy with seven arched niches containing statues; a *jeu d'eau* stands in front of it.

(1) *Daily 9–noon, 3–6 or 4 in winter*
(2) *Free*
(5) *Jesuit College*

Ninfa, nr Latina

Latium

22. Giardino Ninfa

Formerly the property of the Principessa Lelia Caetani, wife of the Hon Hubert Howard, and bequeathed to the Fondazione Caetani in 1977. It was built on the site of the city of Ninfa which was abandoned in the 16th cent and the ruins of this medieval city are still visible in the grounds. The gardens contain over 10,000 plants which have been collected from all over the world. Among the trees of note are sweet gums, crataegus, Japanese seaweed maples and loquat trees. Particularly impressive is the enclosed Italian lemon garden, threaded through with steams of water which derive from the source of the River Ninfa, and designed around an octagonal fountain. Symmetrical rows of orange and grapefruit trees are interlaced with loganberries and vines and lined with clipped box.

(1) *Apr–Oct: first Sat in the month 10–12, 2–5*
(2) *Charge*
(5) *Fondazione Caetani*

ITALY

Pisa, Via Luca Ghini 5

Tuscany

23. Botanical Gardens of the University of Pisa

Founded in 1543–4 by Luca Ghini, these university physic gardens are among the oldest of their kind. They cover an area of approx 7·5 acres (3 ha) and have a rainfall of 31–35 in (800–900 mm). Containing a rich and varied collection of plants from all over the world, they are noted for their *Liliaceae* and *Amaryllidaceae* (mainly Italian specimens).

(1) *Mon–Fri 8–noon, 3–5*
(2) *Free*
(4) *Laboratory; library; herbarium (same times)*
(5) *University of Pisa*

Potenza Picena

Marches

24. Giardini Buonaccorsi

The intrinsic charm of these 18th-cent gardens lies in the fact that the statuary, lemon trees in pots, fountains, the design of their parterres and even the espaliered lemon trees are still preserved almost entirely in their original state.

The gardens continue beyond the terraces, marked off from them by a wall, with an orangery, a walled orchard and vegetable garden. The grottoes are peopled with amusing Baroque automata which are among the few left in Italy in working order.

(1) *By appointment with the owner (Tel: 0733 671 21 0)*
(2) *Free*
(5) *Contessa Giuseppina Buonaccorsi*

Rome, Via Parisperna

25. Giardini Aldobrandini

The 16th-cent villa with its Baroque façade overlooking the Via Parisperna was originally designed by Lombardi for the Duke of Urbino, together with the gardens. It passed into the hands of the Aldobrandini family, who owned it until the end of the 18th cent. In 1929 there was a plan to use the villa and site for the construction of a large hotel, but the Italian Government intervened and purchased the property from the Principe Giuseppe Aldobrandini and destined it for use as a public park. Adaptations for this purpose, together with a new entrance in Via Mazzarino, were executed by the architect Marcello Piacintini.

The hanging gardens which are reached by a stairway carved into a Roman wall are planted with tall pine trees silhouetted against the skyline over colourful beds of camellias and azaleas. There is also a marble fountain and three pavilions, one of which housed the famous *Nozze Aldobrandini* fresco found in 1615 on the Esquilino.

(1) *By application to the custodian*
(2) *Free*
(5) *Italian State*

Rome, Piazza del Quirinale

26. Giardini del Palazzo Quirinale

The Quirinal Palace was built at the end of the 16th cent for Pope Gregory XIII. It was intended as a summer residence and constructed on the site of a former villa of Cardinal Ippolito d'Este who ceded it to the Vatican when he built his great villa at Tivoli (qv). In 1870 it became the residence of the King of Italy and in 1947 that of the President of the Italian Republic.

The great formal gardens were laid out by Carlo Maderna, one of the architects who was also involved in the design of the palace. Bounded on the one side by the Quirinal Palace and on the other by a precipitous hillside, they convey a sense of seclusion in keeping with their role as a Papal garden. The tall, severe hedges of clipped box give the gardens' simple rectangle an air of imposing dignity and splendour. The same geometrical motif is followed through in the interior of the gardens where shaded avenues are lined with high hedges of ilex, yew, cypress and bay and open off at right angles to each other. They lead into spacious courts and terraces.

The gardens were designed for Papal pageantry and were originally laid out with intricate parterres filled with *jeux d'eau* such as the water organ which in 1596 was housed in the small pavilion at the eastern end of the garden. These have all disappeared.

Essentially a green garden, the sombre tones of the umbrella pines, palms and evergreens are relieved by the brilliant colour of scarlet geraniums, ageratum and hydrangeas. The main flowerbeds lie in a small flower garden of annuals and also in the eastern section where there are plantations of crêpe myrtles (*Lagerstroemia indica*), magnolias and beds of canna.

(1) *Thur 2–5.30 or 4.30 in winter. By appointment with the Guardian*
(2) *Charge*
(4) *Palace (by appointment as above)*
(5) *Italian State*

Rome

27. Giardini della Villa Borghese

This vast complex of gardens and parks extends over 2,000 acres (8,092 ha) and, unlike other great estates, dominates the Villa and other buildings instead of the converse. The Villa Borghese itself, which is nonetheless enormous, was not originally intended as a dwelling place, and today it seems extraordinary that a private individual could create such an establishment for entertainment, and also to house an art gallery and library. In 1650, even before its completion, the boundaries exceeded 4 miles (7 km) in circumference, since when it has been much extended by the acquisition of other nearby parks and gardens. It is this vast area of greenery and trees which gives so much of Rome its feeling of spaciousness.

Originally started by Cardinal Camillo Borghese (later Pope Paul V) by the purchase of a modest vineyard, it was enlarged in 1620 by his nephew, Scipione Borghese, who also became a Cardinal. For many years his ideas were conserved on a marble block, since destroyed, placed on a wall of the villa. Written in Latin, it can be literally translated as follows:

> Whoever you are, enter here when you desire
> Here you are free to go where you will
> To ask what you wish
> This is a place of honest pleasures
> Made more for others than for the owner
> But do not abuse civilized rules
> If you do not want to be sent away

In 1885 this inscription became a vital piece of evidence in a curious law suit, when the then owner Principe Marcantonio Borghese was making contracts for the sale of the estate for building purposes, and closing it to the public. The City of Rome, through its Mayor Leopoldo Torlonia, and represented by the advocates Mancini and Meucci, took the case to court in the name of the public and their rights, so clearly defined by the famous *lapide*, and won the case, thus saving this park and garden from the developers.

The first plantings were made by Domenico Salvino de Montepulciano with 400 pine trees. Later development was by the architect Gerolamo Rainaldi, who made roads, woods, graceful slopes and contours, while the architect Giovanni Fontana projected fountains, grottoes, lakes, *jeux d'eau*, etc. Pietro Bernini added statues and groups of marble statuary. Further work was done under the supervision of Giulio Camporese and the Scottish artist Jacob More. The Flemish architect Ivan van Santen (Giovanni Vasanio) was commissioned to construct the Palazzina del'Orologio (little clock palace) while the church on a hill and the superintendent's house are the work of the architect Asprucci. Appropriately the latter is now the offices of the Director of Rome Public Parks.

Apart from its interesting history and architectural features, the park and gardens contain many superb specimens of palms, sub-tropical plants, deciduous and evergreen trees, water-lily ponds, lawns, formal gardens, cactus plants and a hippodrome.

(1) *Mon–Sat 9.30–4; Sun 9.30–12.30*

(2) *Free*
(3) *Bar*
(4) *Borghese Gallery (same times)*
(5) *City of Rome*

Rome, Via della Lungara

28. Parco della Villa Corsini

Villa Corsini was built in the 15th cent by Cardinal Girolano Riario and was at one time the residence of Queen Christina of Sweden. The palace was subsequently acquired by Cardinal Corsini, nephew of Pope Clement XII, who commissioned Ferdinand Fuga to redesign it in 1732–6. It became the property of the Italian State in 1884.

The grounds are laid out as botanical gardens at the foot of the Janiculum and now form part of the collection of the Institute of Botany, Rome. There is a fine herb garden and a collection of specimens under glass.

(1) *By appointment with the Director of the Institute of Botany, Via della Lungara*
(2) *Free*
(5) *Institute of Botany, University of Rome*

Rome, Via Santa Sabina

29. Park and Rose Garden of the Aventine

The rose garden is laid out in two separate sections in the shape of two amphitheatres. Only one half is open to the public and this is planted with roses interspersed with irises. 78 different species of rose are found here. Of particular interest is the collection of 149 types of climbing rose which includes 144 specimen plants illustrating the history of the rose over the last 150 years.

The other half of the garden is devoted to horticultural research and to the cultivation of prize-winning varieties for the Annual International Gold Medal.

Visit from May to September.

(1) *Daily throughout the year except in the height of summer*
(2) *Free*
(5) *Commune of Rome*

Rome

30. Vatican Gardens

The great formal garden dates from the 15th cent and was designed in 1506 by Donato Bramante, who completely refashioned the original medieval enclosed gardens. He constructed the Belvedere Terrace and landscaped the terrain in terraces linked by stairways. In so doing he revolutionized gardening design and set the pattern for all future Renaissance gardens across Europe. He died in 1514 leaving his work unfinished.

It was completed by Pirro Ligorio who designed the Villa d'Este at Tivoli (qv). Ligorio added the charming Casino of Pope Pius IV, a colonnaded building decorated with bas-reliefs and set in an oval courtyard.

The Fountain of the Galley, a small fountain by Carlo Maderno in the form of a model ship in full rig with a cannon as a fountain-piece shooting out spouts of water, also dates from this period.

(1) *Mornings only by appointment with the Secretariat of the Governor. For details enquire at the Ufficio Controllo on the left of St Peter's façade just beyond the Arco delle Campane*
(2) *Charge*
(5) *Holy See*

Rome, Via della Pilotta 17

31. Villa Colonna

The gardens rise in terraces from the Via della Pilotta to the Via XXIV Maggio. There is a magnificent 17th-cent Rococo entrance portal built by Filippo Colonna which is reached by a double ramp stairway with marble balustrades. Although this entrance is no longer used, it greatly adds to the overall decorative effect of the garden. The access to the gardens is now by a small door which opens on to an upper terrace with ancient pine trees and scattered with archaeological fragments, some of which are as much as 2,000 years old. The gardens descend by alleys lined with laurel and box through a series of terraces planted with flowering magnolias. In the middle of the garden is a tiered waterfall which flows into a lower basin designed in the shape of a boat – reminiscent of the *Navicella* of the Piazza di Spagna.

(1) *Sat 9–1*
(2) *Charge*
(4) *Colonna Gallery (same times)*
(5) *Colonna family*

Rome, Via Piazzale di Villa Giulia 9

32. Villa Giulia

The Villa di Papa Giulio or the Villa Giulia was built in 1551–3 by Pope Julius III, often regarded as the last Renaisance Pope.

The gardens are laid out in a symmetrical design of three small courtyards surrounding a central courtyard decorated with fountains and lily-ponds. The small courtyard on the east side contains a 16th-cent arrangement of parterres with clipped bay trees, oleanders and roses shaded by pines. Within the garden there is also a reproduction of the Etruscan Temple of Alatri, in the centre of which is a marble fountain designed by Bartolommeo Ammanati depicting the Arno and the Tiber.

(1) *Tue–Sat (except 1 Jan, 1 May, 2 Jun, 15 Aug, Easter and 25 Dec) 9.30–3; Sun and Public Holidays 9.30–1*
(2) *Charge*

ITALY

(4) *National Etruscan Museum* (*same times*)
(5) *Italian State*

Rome, Viale Trinità dei Monti

33. Villa Medici

This 16th-cent villa has a simple façade designed by Nanni di Baccio Bigio for Cardinal Ricco of Montepulciano. It was bought in the early 17th cent by Cardinal Alessandro dei Medici and in 1803 it became the property of the French Academy of Rome.

The gardens are some of the finest and most typical examples of urban gardening in Rome with flowerbeds, oleanders and paths hedged with trimmed box and ornamented with antique fragments.

They slope across from the Pincio up a hill planted with a wood of ilex trees and laurels, in the middle of which lies a small temple dedicated to Eros. From the summit of the hill are views over the city and beneath lies a terrace shaded by trees. In spring a flowering Judas tree forms a hedge of colour along the great wall which borders the Viale del Muro Torte.

(1) *Wed* (*except Public Holidays*) *9–11; or by appointment with the French Academy*
(2) *Free*
(5) *French Academy*

Rome, Vignanello

34. Villa Ruspoli

Now the property of Prince Ruspoli, this remarkable garden was designed and laid out between the end of the 16th and the beginning of the 17th cents, when a fortress castle was converted into a Renaissance villa. The garden contains one of the finest parterres in Italy, with the characteristic geometrical design of the period, the hedges of which are of box (*Buxus sempervirens*) although legend has it that they were originally made of another evergreen, rosemary (*Rosmarinus officinalis*). The garden also includes the almost obligatory 'secret garden' of the period; terraces and a pond of water-lilies. An interesting detail of the parterre of clipped box is the use of the initials O.O. in the design, recalling Ottavia Orsini, the original designer who in 1574 married into the Sforza family, the former name of the Ruspoli family.

(1) *By appointment with the Administration Ruspoli*
(2) *Free*
(5) *Principe Ruspoli*

Rome, Trastevere

35. Villa Sciarra

The Villa Sciarra, built in the 15th cent, was bequeathed to the Italian state in 1928 by the widow of the last owner, G. W. Wurtz, an American diplomat. The Italian Institute of Germanic studies was installed in the villa and the garden and extensive park were opened to the public.

The gardens are set on the side of a hill in Trastevere and are distinguished for their luxurious groves and flowers, topiary and strutting peacocks. There are long avenues lined by palms and an avenue of laurels whose vaulting branches interlace to form a dark tunnel. On either side of it are groups of shrub roses, hydrangeas and asphodels. A water-lily pond reflects an ornamental archway, three porticoes and the surrounding foliage; a casino, fountains and statues add to the picturesque charm of these gardens.

(1) *Daily Sunrise–Sunset*
(2) *Free*
(5) *Commune of Rome*

San Severino Marche, Via Settempeda 62027

Marches

36. Villa Collio

The original 18th-cent villa designed by Pietro da Cortona was destroyed by an earthquake in 1799. The present villa was rebuilt by Giambattista Collio in 1827 and designed by Giuseppe Lucatelli. The 18th-cent gardens are among the most beautiful in the area. They are conceived around a central garden enclosed by neo-classical colonnades and laid out with symmetrical parterres planted with myrtle which frame a circular fountain. The gardens are surrounded by English romantic parkland with statues and stone fragments.

(1) *By appointment with the owner*
(2) *Free*
(5) *Collio family*

Segromigno Monte, nr Lucca

Tuscany

37. Villa Mansi

The quadrangular villa is set against a backdrop of trees and mountains. It was built in the 16th cent and altered in 1634 by Muzio Oddi. The present 18th-cent façade with its recessed arches, coupled columns and balustraded staircase down to the front lawn, was designed by Filippo Juvarra.

The garden dates from the same period and was landscaped in the grand manner by Filippo Juvarra during the years 1725–32 with box hedges, fish ponds, statuary, fountains, cascades, a grotto known as the Bath of Diana, and a little Clock Palace or casino. The style and harmony of his basic design can still be admired but the central fishpool, the Bath of Diana and the Clock Palace are the only parts of his original Italian garden to have survived its transformation into 19th-cent romantic parkland.

(1) Mar–Nov: Daily 10–7; Dec–Feb: Daily 10–5
(2) Charge
(3) Bar and restaurant open Mar–Oct
(4) Villa (same times); Son et lumière
(5) Marino Salom

Settignano, Via del Rossellino

Tuscany
38. Villa Gamberaia

The villa was probably originally a farm-house and was owned by the Gamberelli family in the 16th cent. After 1717 it passed into the hands of the Capponi family. The present lay-out of the gardens, which are situated on the side of a hill, probably dates from this period. The property was ravaged during World War II and was restored by the present owner, Dr Marchi. A grassy terrace sometimes used as a bowling green is laid out in front of the house; it follows the length of the garden where it disappears into the *bosco* of cypress trees and eventually opens on to a monumental Baroque fountain set in a secret garden.

Half-way down the walk opposite the house is a grotto moulded with shells. Steps from it lead to the lemon garden with its clipped box parterres and wistaria. The central focus of the garden is the water parterre spread out in a mosaic of water and topiary. Stretching from the house to the end of the terrace on which it stands, it juts out over the Tuscan countryside. In spring the gardens are ablaze with tulips and in summer the pink oleanders and lotus flowers provide a magnificent display.

(1) Mon–Fri Sunrise–Sunset
(2) Free
(5) Dr Marcello Marchi: La Gamberaia Estate Trust

Tivoli

Latium
39. Hadrian's Villa

The villa was built between AD 118 and 138, and the gardens are believed to have been designed by the Emperor Hadrian himself, inspired by his travels throughout the Empire. In the gardens are replicas of the places which had particularly impressed him including the Greek Poikile, the Academy, Lyceum and Prytaneion.

Each part of the garden was designed as a separate entity and the whole is linked by fountains, cascades and water gardens. Of particular note in this respect is the Marine Theatre, situated on a small islet within a circular pool which was used as a swimming pool. It is reached by means of moveable bridges. On it was set a pavilion containing a portico which opened on to a courtyard

garden with a fountain and flowerbeds. This was surrounded by four rooms including a dining-room and a library. The most monumental construction in the garden is the Great Poikile, designed as a large swimming pool with shaded porticoes and a chariot race course. The gardens end with the Temple of Venus. The villa is set in the Vale of Tempe which was artificially landscaped to reproduce the famous beauty spot in Thessaly.

(1) Daily (except Public Holidays) 9–5
(2) Charge
(5) Italian State

Tivoli
40. Villa d'Este

The villa and gardens were designed by G. Alberti Galvani and Pirro Ligorio for the Cardinal Ippolito d'Este in the 16th cent and built on the site of a former Franciscan convent. The gardens, famous for the multiplicity of their fountains, were acquired by the State during World War I after an extensive period of decay. Although much of their former glory has disappeared, the fountains have been completely restored.

A quarter of the village was demolished to make way for the gardens, which were laid out on a slope in terraces, descending by paths and stairways to a large garden below. At the foot of the hill were placed an impressive series of fountains which at one time included a small fountain of singing birds who sang by means of a water mechanism until frightened by a mechanical owl. The principal fountains include the Rometta, a piece of architectural fantasy representing ancient Rome with a model reconstruction of the city and a network of fountains culminating in a small lake with an islet in the form of a galley and the Viale delle Cento Fontane, a stepped fountain on three tiers which forms the centre-piece of the garden and runs the whole length of the walk. Hundreds of small jets rise from the topmost tier which is decorated with obelisks, lilies, boats and eagles. Other fountains of note are the Oval Fountain and the Neptune Fountain. This is overlooked by the Baroque Organ Fountain, which once housed a water organ. The fountains are floodlit at night with music to accompany the sound of the water.

(1) Daily (except Mon and 1 Jan, 1 May, 2 Jun, 15 Aug, Easter and 25 Dec) 9–6
(2) Charge
(4) Son et lumière (Apr–Sep: Tue, Thu, Sun 8.30 pm–11.30)
(5) Italian State

Urbino, Via Bramante 28

Marches

41. Botanical Gardens of the University of Urbino

These gardens were founded in 1808 by Giovanni Brignoli di Brumnof di Gradisca. They specialize in indigenous and exotic plants and also have a fine collection of approx 4,000 medicinal plants.

Visit in May and June.

(1) Daily 10–noon, 3–5
(2) Free
(5) University of Urbino

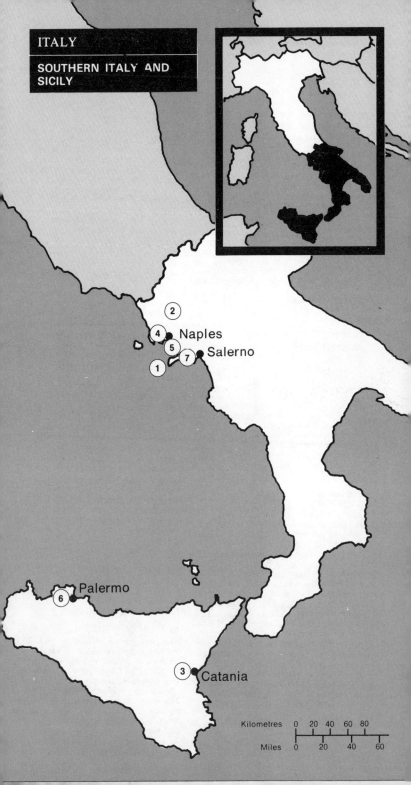

ITALY

SOUTHERN ITALY AND SICILY

② Naples
④
⑤ Salerno
① ⑦

⑥ Palermo

③ Catania

Kilometres 0 20 40 60 80
Miles 0 20 40 60

ITALY

Anacapri
Campania

1. Villa San Michele di Axel Munthe

The villa was designed in 1896 by the famous doctor and author Axel Munthe.

The gardens are renowned for their rare and exotic flowers and for the pergola of 37 columns which stretches from a beautiful white arched loggia with statues along the cliffs to the chapel. The walk towards the house leads through the gardens past an avenue of cypresses which have been transplanted from the Villa d'Este at Tivoli (qv).

(1) *Mar–Sep: Daily 9–6; Oct–Apr: Daily 9–4*
(2) *Charge*
(4) *Villa (same times); Chapel of San Michele (concerts in Jun and Jul); ruins of Tiberius' villa; Barbarossa Bird Sanctuary*
(5) *Swedish State, managed by the Foundation of Axel Munthe, Villa San Michele*

Caserta
Campania

2. La Reggia (The Royal Palace of Caserta)

Inspired by Versailles, La Reggia is the last of the Italian villas to be conceived on the grand scale. It was begun in 1752 by Luigi Vanvitelli for the Bourbon king, Charles III, and completed in 1774. From the rear of the monumental palace is a $\frac{3}{4}$-mile (1·25 km) vista down a rolling, stepped cascade. Its waters fall into a rocky pool overlooked by bronze statues of Diana and her nymphs fleeing from Actaeon and his hounds.

The park of 250 acres (100 ha) was conceived around this central axis which was designed to start with an elaborate parterre, although this was never executed. The water stairway is flanked by groves of trees crossed by avenues. Among the fountains of note are the Dolphin Fountain, the Ceres Fountain and the Venus and Adonis Fountain behind the great cascade.

To one side is the English Garden designed in 1782 by G. A. Graefer for Maria Caroline of the Two Sicilies. It is a picturesque garden surrounding a small lake and planted with tropical plants, cedars and cypresses. There is a children's park containing a miniature castle and glasshouses.

This palace was the headquarters of the Allied High Command in World War II and the scene of the unconditional German surrender in Italy in 1945.

(1) *Daily 9–1 hour before Sunset*
(2) *Charge*

272

(4) *Palace. (Daily, except 1 Jan, 1 May, 2 Jun, 15 Aug, Easter and 25 Dec, 9–2; Sun and Public Holidays 9–1)*
(5) *Italian State*

Catania, Via Etnea
Sicily

3. Giardino Bellini

The Bellini Garden of Catania was created by the Catanese Prince of Biscari who sold it to the Commune of Catania in 1854. The park and gardens evolved over several centuries. The original gardens were laid out by Gravina, the architect Sciute and the Frenchman Cusson, head gardener of the Tuileries. They were added to by Prof. Landolina towards the end of the 18th cent and the last alteration was made in 1932. They are filled with flowers and exotic plants and are noted for their floral configurations commemorating the composer Bellini.

(1) *Apr–May: Daily 6.30 am–9 pm; Jun: Daily 6.30 am–10 pm; Jul–Sep: Daily 6.30 am–11 pm; Oct–Nov: Daily 6.30 am–8 pm; Dec–Mar: Daily 7 am–8 pm*
(2) *Free*
(5) *Commune of Catania*

Naples, Via Foria 223
Campania

4. Botanical Gardens of the University of Naples

The gardens were founded in 1807 by Joseph Bonaparte, King of Naples, and now form part of the Faculty of Science of the University.

They were set out according to the systems of Linnaeus and Jussieu, but redesigned later according to more recent scientific principles and now consist of a wood, shrubs and rare plants. In 1928 the Ministry of Agriculture installed an experimental section containing collections of different species of potted, aquatic and hothouse plants.

(1) *By appointment*
(2) *Free*
(4) *Library and Herbarium (by appointment as above)*
(5) *University of Naples*

Naples, Via Cimarvia 77

5. Villa Floridiana

The great park is crossed by magnificent avenues and walks with a central driveway leading to the villa which was built by Ferdinand IV for the Princess Florida and now houses a collection of rare ceramics started by Don Placido di Sangro, Duke of Martina, which was bequeathed by his heirs to the Italian State. The grounds contain a small Doric temple, fountains, aviaries, glasshouses and an open-air theatre.

(1) *Daily 9.30–Sunset*
(2) *Free*
(4) *Museo Nazionale della Ceramica Duca di Martina (Daily Tue–Sat 9.30–4; Sun and Public Holidays 9.30–1.30; closed Mon)*
(5) *Italian State*

Palermo, Via A. Lincoln

Sicily

6. Botanical Garden of the University of Palermo

The gardens were founded on the instigation of Principe Caramanico, Viceroy of Sicily, in 1795.

They are planted with a fine display of outdoor tropical plants and a particularly comprehensive collection of *Cactaceae, Agavaceae, Aizoaceae, Crassulaceae, Euphorbiaceae, Asclepiadaceae, Moraceae, Liliaceae.*

(1) *Late Oct–mid-Jun: Daily 9–noon, 2–4; mid-Jul–late Oct: Daily 9–noon*
(2) *Free*
(5) *University of Palermo*

Ravello

Campania

7. Villa Rufolò

13th-cent castle with entrance tower, separate fortified tower and a chapel built by Niccolò Rufolò. The surrounding park and gardens, neglected after the Renaissance, were restored by the Scotsman, Francis Neville Reid, in 1851.

The gardens have literary and musical associations, having provided the setting for Boccaccio's *L'Amoroso Visione* and for the enchanted garden of Klingsor in Wagner's opera, *Parsifal*. They are laid out in terraces with an elaborate embroidery of flower-filled parterres and include a pleasure garden which is one of the rare surviving examples of a non-ecclesiastical medieval garden. It is constructed around a court-yard lined by two beautiful loggias in the Moorish style. The intricate architectural detail with which the porticoes are decorated is in the same style. There is also an unusual garden loggia which was probably used as an open-air dining-room.

(1) *Daily. Jun–Aug: 9.30–1, 2.30–7.40; Sep: 9.30–1, 2–7; Oct: 9.30–1, 2–6; Nov–Feb: 9.30–1, 2–5; Mar: 9.30–1, 2–5.40; Apr–May: 9.30–1, 2–6.40*
(2) *Charge (except Sat)*
(5) *Salerno Provincial Tourist Board*

MALTA

Valletta

⑦
⑤ ● ⑥
⑧
③
Floriana ●
②

①● Attard

④● St Venera

Kilometres 0 1 2 3 4
Miles 0 1 2

Attard, De Paule Avenue

1. San Anton

Built by Grand Master Antoine de Paule in 1625, the garden bears the name of his patron saint. The palace and its gardens, with flowerbeds and avenues of fine trees, were used by all succeeding Grand Masters and, when under British rule (1800–1964), by the Governors. The part that is open to visitors was first made public in 1882. Some of the rare trees were donated by other nations or planted by notable visitors. There are several ponds and a small zoo.

(1) Daily 7–Sunset
(2) Free
(5) Superintendent of Public Gardens

Floriana, St Calcedonius Street

2. Argotti Botanic Gardens

The garden was created in 1774 by the Bailiff Argote et Gusman, after whom it takes its name; part of his original villa still exists. It is the third oldest botanical garden in the British Commonwealth after those of Oxford and Edinburgh. The gardens are divided into three sections: the lower part, known as St Philip's, is noted for the beautiful and historic fountain which at one time stood in Valletta. In the enclosed part of the garden there is Professor Borg's famous collection of cacti and succulents as well as the ancient herbarium, a collection of Maltese flora and a collection of medicinal plants.

Various social activities are held in these gardens such as balls, fairs and exhibitions.

(1) Gardens. Daily 7–Sunset. Cactus Collection. On request Daily (except Sun)
(2) Free
(5) Superintendent of Public Gardens

Floriana, Duke of York Avenue

3. Kalkara Gardens

Officially opened by the Duke of York in 1927, the lower part of the gardens was redesigned and planted between 1974 and 1976. There is a rose garden and a terraced cactus and succulent garden, which is of particular interest. A number of rare trees and shrubs may be found here and the gardens afford a fine view of the Grand Harbour.

(1) Daily 7–Sunset
(2) Free
(5) Superintendent of Public Gardens

St. Venera, High Street

4. Romeo Romano

Early in the 18th cent the Grand Master Manoel de Vilhena built this for his own use. When under the British (1800–1964), the Baroque palace which stands at the upper part of the garden was the official residence of the Lt-Governor.

This garden is typical of 18th-cent Mediterranean gardens. Divided into three equal sections, the garden is terraced using the local stone. The surrounding high walls offer not only privacy but, more important, shelter from the winds which can destroy the citrus crop.

(1) Daily 7–Sunset
(2) Free
(5) Superintendent of Public Gardens

Valletta, Windmill and Pope Pius V Street

5. Hastings

Designed by Francesco Laparelli in 1566 as part of the overall design of Valletta as requested by the founder of the capital, Grand Master Jean de la Vallette.

At the upper part of the garden lies the monument dedicated to the Marquess of Hastings, after whom this garden is named. In the lower part is another monument, dedicated to Federico Cavendish Ponsonby (1838). A bird's-eye view of Floriana as well as a panoramic view of the Marsamxetto Harbour can be enjoyed from here.

(1) Daily 7 am–10 pm
(2) Free
(5) Dept of Agriculture

Valletta, East Street

6. Lower Barracca Gardens

Designed by Francesco Laparelli in 1566 as part of the overall design of Valletta. In the centre of the garden there is a neo-classical monument to Sir Alexander Ball, who served under Nelson and was later Governor of Malta, designed by Giorgio Pullicino.

(1) Daily 7 am–10 pm
(2) Free
(5) Dept of Agriculture

Valletta, Republic Street

7. The Palace

Designed by Girolomo Cassar as a garden within the palace built under the rule of Grand Master Le Cassière (1570–80). Tradition has it that the land upon which the palace and gardens stand was leased to the Grand Master by the noble family of Sciberras upon an annual payment of five grains of wheat and a tumbler of water from the palace's own well. This annual ceremony used to be held by the Grand Master at the hall of the Grand Council which today is known as the Hall of St Michael and St George. In the upper courtyard, Prince Alfred's Courtyard, there is the famous clock installed by Grand Master Pinto in 1745. Moorish figures strike the hours. In the lower courtyard, Neptune's Courtyard, among the hibiscus and palm trees there is a bronze sculpture of Neptune, a work by the Maltese artist Gafa which stood originally near the Fishmarket.

(*1*) *Daily 7 am–9 pm*
(*2*) *Free*
(*5*) *Dept of Agriculture*

Valletta, Castille Place

8. Upper Barracca Gardens

Designed by Francesco Laparelli in 1566. In the centre of the arcaded garden, built on a demi-bastion, there is a monument beneath which lie the remains of Sir Thomas Maitland, first Governor-General of Malta (1813–24). A monument dedicated to Lord Strickland, Prime Minister of Malta, lies close by. There is a sculpture in bronze by the Maltese artist Sciortino, Les Gavroches, and various plaques commemorating historical events or famous men. A panoramic view of the Grand Harbour can be seen from the long balcony.

(*1*) *Daily 7 am–11pm*
(*2*) *Free*
(*5*) *Dept of Agriculture*

La Coruña

● Lugo

⑲

⑱

Vit

● Burg

Segovia ●⑳

⑫

⑯

⑮ ● Madri

⑰

①

PORTUGAL

C

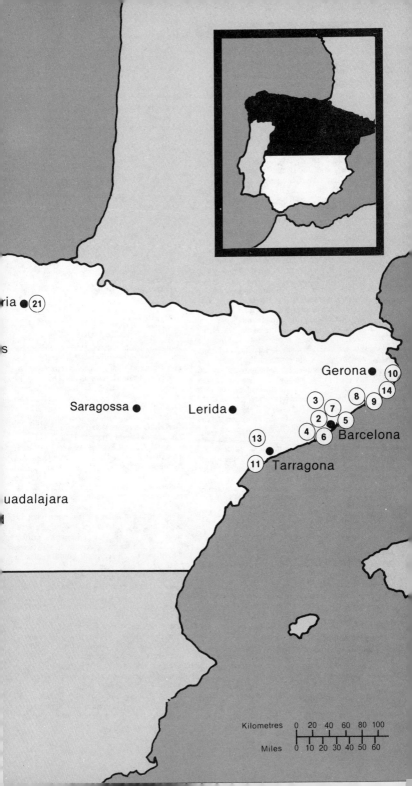

Aranjuez

Madrid

1. Palacio Real

The original palace dates back to the late 14th cent. It was later enlarged by Felipe II and in the 18th cent rebuilt to accommodate the court. It then became the summer residence of the Bourbons until the end of the 19th cent. The gardens underwent a succession of enlargements and changes.

On the east of the palace is the parterre. Crossing the river by two small bridges from the north-east corner of the palace the visitor reaches the Jardín de la Isla, designed by Juan Bautista de Toledo and remodelled by Sebastian Herrera in 1669. There are avenues – the Salon de los Reyes Católicos with its plane trees being one of the finest – walks and ornamental fountains. To the left on a small promontory is the Jardín de la Islita.

The advent of the Bourbons in the early 18th cent brought French landscape gardening to Spain and it was then that limes and horse chestnuts made their first appearance here. From the same era is the work of members of the Boutelou family, a distinguished French family of landscape designers. Esteban Boutelou the Second was gardener to the Queen and commuted between Aranjuez and La Granja de San Ildefonso (qv) and at the end of the 18th cent his son created two new gardens: the Jardín de la Primavera and the Jardín del Principe, the latter in the landscape style. Trees, shrubs and flowers were ordered from Europe and the Americas, and parterres were laid out. The gardens of Aranjuez still preserve some of their past glory, and the profuse foliage includes cedars, English elms introduced by Felipe II, cypresses, box, and there is a magnificent display of flowering plants.

(1) Daily (except 1 Jan, 18 Jul and 25 Dec) 10–Sunset
(2) Charge
(4) Aranjuez museums (Mar–May: Daily 10–1, 3–6; Jun–Sep: Daily, except 18 Jul, 10–1, 4–7; Oct–Feb: Daily, except 25 Dec and 1 Jan, 10–1, 4–5)
(5) Patrimonio Nacional

Barcelona

2. Botanical Gardens

Part of the Botanical Institute of Barcelona, these are situated in the Parque de Montjuic (qv). They were founded in 1930 by Prof. P. Font Quer, and the planting was started in the 1930s on territory previously used for the International Exhibition of 1928. The gardens are situated on the excavated site of an old quarry, and the south-facing slopes are favourable to Mediterranean and sub-tropical plants.

In the taxonomical garden are *Rumex lunaria* from the Canary Islands, the yellow-flowering *Sternbergia lutea*, *Cycas revoluta* and *Cinnamomum camphora* from the Far East. The Majorcan rock gardens contain interesting species from the Balearic Islands, including *Rhamnus ludovici salvatoris*, *Hypericum balearicum*, varieties of *Teucrium subspinosum* and *Digitalis dubia*.

From North Africa and the south Mediterranean come *Phlomis maroccana*, *Centaurea sempervirens*, *Ephedra altissima*, *Chamaerops humilis* and a plantation of *Cedrus atlantica*.

Species typical of northern and central Europe grow in the cooler low-lying areas. There is a wood of deciduous trees such as *Populus alba*, *Pterocarya fraxinifolia* from Transcaucasia, *Fraxinus ornus*, *Liriodendron tulipifera* and *Ostrya carpinifolia*. As well as ferns and the rare grass variety *Oplismenus undulatifolius*, there is a variety of Mediterranean plants. Visit in May and June.

(1) Tue–Sat 10–1
(2) Free
(5) Municipality of Barcelona

Barcelona

3. Laberinto de Horta

Situated on the hilly outskirts of Barcelona, this is the only neo-classical estate in the city that has not been surrounded by modern urban development. The summer retreat of the Marqués de Alfarrá was built in the 1790s by the Italian architect Domenico Bagutti and it has a markedly Italianate character. The municipality of Barcelona acquired and restored the property, opening it to the public in 1971.

A magnificent example of a late 18th-cent garden, it is spread over three terraces. On the upper level stands an elegant pink stucco summer house, reflected in the smooth waters of a large reservoir. This is surrounded on three sides by balustrades and is fed from a mountain stream; in its turn it waters the rest of the gardens, supplying the pools and fountains. On the middle level there are small temples with Tuscan columns and formal balustraded staircases, where pieces of sculpture stand against a background of foliage.

The main feature of the gardens is the cypress-hedge maze below the temple terrace, laid out on a square of level ground. At its entrance is a marble bas-relief of Ariadne and Theseus, and at the centre a statue of Daphnis or Cupid. On the higher level is a grotto with a statue of a reclining nymph and, lower down, a platform with a fine view of the Mediterranean.

The house itself, a large stucco structure painted in imitation of pinkish-grey marble, is of a Gothic-Arabic design which accorded well with the romantic garden constructed in the 19th cent at the same time as the house and now in a ruinous condition.

(1) Daily 10–Sunset

Barcelona
Monasterio de Pedralbes

In 1326 Elisenda de Montcada, wife of Jaime II of Aragon, founded a convent in a beautiful position remote from the city. Today modern buildings reach up to it, but the view over Barcelona and the sea is still remarkable.

Building took more than 100 years and the cloister was not finished until the 16th cent. The cloister garden has two paths which cross at the centre and the plants are irrigated by a system of canals supplied from the fountain in the Arabic manner.

In one corner is a fountain with 15th-cent sculpture, a 16th-cent cistern and benches with 18th-cent *azulejos*.

There are culinary herbs, fragrant shrubs, annuals, bulbs and orange and lemon trees, fruit trees and cypresses.

(1) *Sundays 1.30–2.30*
(2) *Charge*
(3) *Monastery rooms and chapels (same times)*
(5) *Real Monasterio de Santa Maria de Pedralbes*

Barcelona
5. Parque de la Ciudadela

Destroyed during the 1868 revolution, the citadel was turned into a public park between 1873 and 1888. The gardens were planned by José Fontseré, but the designs were modified to make way for the Universal Exhibition of 1888 and later replanted to accord with the taste of the early 20th cent.

The design combines classical and naturalistic features, and includes a great cascade, a lake, a music temple, and the Plaza de Armas designed by J. N. Forestier in 1919.

There are some good specimens of *Yucca elephantipes*, paulownia and Himalayan cedar, as well as magnolias and limes. The quantity and quality of sculptures by such artists as Mares, Arnau, Carbonell, Clará and Gargallo give the park something of the air of an outdoor museum.

(1) *Daily 10–Sunset*
(2) *Free*
(4) *Zoo (Daily 9–Sunset); Museum of Modern Art (Daily, except Mon and Public Holidays, 10–2); Natural History and Geological Museums (Daily, except Mon and Public Holidays, 10–2)*
(5) *Municipality of Barcelona*

Barcelona
6. Parque de Montjuic

Barcelona's most important park was developed for the 1929 Spanish-American Exhibition on a substantial hill, part of which was formerly a fortress. The ancient part of the gardens is one of the masterpieces of J. N. Forestier, the French architect and landscape gardener, who also founded the school of gardening at Montjuic. He initiated the neo-Arabic style, using tiles and ceramics. Here, at Montjuic, he skilfully modelled the different levels into terraces, rose gardens and pergolas.

The park also comprises several self-contained gardens, including the Mirador del Alcalde. Terraced and with abstract mosaic pavements, this garden has a fine view of the port. There are groups of yellow flowers, and trees from the tropics and the Canary Islands. The Jardines de Mossen Costa y Llobera specialize in exotic and tropical plants, particularly cacti. They also contain the 'Pal-lance' collection from Italy, which includes specimens of plants that are more than 200 years old.

The Jardines de Mossen Cinto specialize in bulbous and rhizomatous plants, especially from Mexico, California and South Africa, including hyacinths, irises, gladioli, narcissi, amaryllis, dahlias, anemones, lilies and water-lilies. The Jardines del Poeta Jóan Maragall surround the Palacete de Albéniz, the Royal Exhibition Pavilion of the Exhibition. They have fountains, statues, a parterre, a small temple and a variety of plants.

(1) *Main park and Mirador del Alcalde: Daily. Jardines de Mossen Costa y Llobera and Jardines de Mossen Cinto: Daily 10–Sunset. Jardines del Poeta Jóan Maragall. By appointment with the municipal authorities.*
(2) *Free*
(4) *Archaeological Museum, Ethnological Museum, National Museum, Pueblo Español (reproduction of houses and streets of the different Spanish regions arranged as a village)*
(5) *Municipality of Barcelona*

Barcelona
7. Parque Güell

Güell Park in the north-western part of Barcelona is the creation of the highly original Catalan architect Antonio Gaudi. It was laid out in the first decade of the 20th cent, and has several Art Nouveau characteristics. There are palm trees, pines and carob trees. It is not living plants but fossilized trees and the great mosaic at the entrance that are the focus of the park. In the words of the writer Aldous Huxley, it is 'fantastic; at once a fun-fair, a petrified forest, and the great temple of Amun at Karnak, itself drunk, and reeling in an eccentric earthquake'. The combination of multicoloured ceramic pieces is unique.

(1) *Daily 10–Sunset*
(2) *Free*
(5) *Municipality of Barcelona*

SPAIN

Blanes, nr Lloret de Mar

Gerona

8. Marimurtra Botanical Gardens

Situated on the slopes of the mountain of San Juan, the top of which is crowned by the ruins of an old castle and hermitage, the creation of these gardens dates from 1924. They constitute the life work of the German Karl Faust, who established the Fundación Carlos Faust, an international centre for Mediterranean biology. Since his death in 1952, it has been administered by a Board of Trustees of different nations, thus ensuring the Foundation's independent status.

There is an abundance of exotic plants, particularly of cacti and other succulents, palm trees and Australian plants, including an Australian eucalyptus that is 130 ft (40 m) high and 44 years old. There are more than 3,000 plant species in the gardens. A section for Mediterranean flora is now being created.

These gardens are not only delightful to visit, but offer a great deal of botanical information. There are well-equipped laboratories, where specialists and students sponsored by the foundation may work, and an up-to-date library. Scholarships are offered to students and graduates, and botanists from all over the world can study their subject *in situ*.

(1) *Daily (except 1 and 6 Jan and 25 Dec) 10—Sunset*
(2) *Charge*
(5) *Fundación Carlos Faust*

Blanes

9. Pinya de Rosa Botanical Gardens

Founded by Dr I. Fernando Riviere de Caralt in 1951, the gardens specialize in succulents, tropical and desert plants and contain one of the most important collections of cacti in the world.

There are more than 7,000 species of plants here, excluding the local flora. Among these is the collection of opuntia (prickly pear) which is regarded by some botanists as the most important in existence. Of the *Mesembryanthemaceae* group there are 780 species, and there are great numbers of agaves, aloes and yuccas.

Every year more than 1,500 plant species are sown, some of them new types. Hybrid plants are avoided, except for those botanically classified. All the plants have descriptive labels.

(1) *Summer: Daily 9–6; Winter: Daily 10–4*
(2) *Charge*
(5) *Dr Ing Fernando Riviere de Caralt*

Calella de Palafrugell

Gerona

10. Cap Roig Botanical Gardens

Designed in 1926 by Señor and Señora Woevodsky on the sheer rock above the sea at Palafrugell, the gardens blend well with the wild setting, with terraces built out of the rock. The garden contains Mediterranean shrubs, including 26 varities of mimosa, and rare plants, and a large collection of geraniums and lilies, as well as mesembryanthemums.

(1) *Apr–Sep: Daily 10–1, 4–8; Oct–Mar: Daily 10–1, 4–6. (Guided tours lasting ½ hr)*
(2) *Charge*
(5) *Señora Woevodsky*

Cambrils, nr Reus

Tarragona

11. Parque Samá

Established by Don Salvador Samá, Marqués de Marianao, this large garden was designed and carried out in 1881 by the architect Fontsere y Mestres. It had grottoes, an artificial lake and cascades. Today its main attraction is a fine collection of palm trees.

(1) *Mon–Fri (except Public Holidays) 10–6*
(2) *Free*
(5) *Marqués de Marianao*

El Escorial

Madrid

12. Monasterio

The royal monastery, a massive grey, granite building, was designed from 1559 by Juan Bautista de Toledo and Juan Herrera according to the specifications of Felipe II, who required 'a monastery, a temple and a tomb'. It was in the shape of a grid-iron, to commemorate the martyrdom of St Lawrence.

It is flanked on two sides by unadorned gardens, underlining the religious austerity of the king. Outside the monastery was the Jardín del Principe in which a pavilion was built for the man who was to become Carlos IV. He had a particular liking for small-scale houses and gardens. The pavilion was built by Juan de Villanueva at the end of the 18th cent. At about the same time the Casita del Infante was built, with a garden in the neo-classical style, two fountains and graceful terraces. In the early 18th cent large parterres were added to the north and south fronts.

Inside the monastery is the Patio de los Evangelistas. The severe styling of boxwood hedges without flowers is typical of a Spanish cloister garden of the Renaissance period.

(1) *Daily (except 1 Jan, 28 Feb and the afternoons of Good Friday, 18 July, 10 Aug and 25 Dec) 10–1, 3–6 or 7*

(2) *Charge*
(4) *Prince's pavilion, royal apartments, pantheon, chapter houses and library (same times); church (same days 7.30– 1, 3–6)*
(5) *Patrimonio Nacional*

Espluga de Francoli

Tarragona

13. Monasterio de Poblet

The Cistercian monastery is 44 miles (70 km) from Barcelona and 28 miles (45 km) from Tarragona. Founded in the 12th cent, the monastery was greatly helped by the kings of Catalonia and Aragon, some of whom were buried here. Abandoned from 1835 to 1930, the monks returned in 1940 after the buildings had been restored.

There are several gardens and orchards in the characteristic monastic style, the most important of which is the cloister garden, which is the centre of community life. In front of the refectory is a pavilion and for this reason the normal disposition of paths crossing at the centre is not maintained. There are culinary herbs, medicinal and fragrant shrubs, roses, box, laurels and cypresses.

(1) *Daily 10–1, 3–6*
(2) *Charge*
(4) *Monastery and Royal Palace (same times)*
(5) *Patrimonio Nacional*

Lloret de Mar

Gerona

14. Santa Clotilde

The Italian-style garden was designed in 1929 by N. M. Rubió, a student of J. N. Forestier, for the Marqués de Roviralta de Santa Clotilde.

The entrance is marked by two tall cypress trees. The gardens are laid out on the slope of the hill, with ramps and ivy-covered stairways converging on to small squares surrounded by Italian sculptures. They are very well tended, under the super-vision of the owner who lives here most of the year. Particularly attractive are the Escalera de las Sirenas (Sirens' Staircase) and a balcony looking out over the Boadella beach.

(1) *Apply to the administrator for per-mission to visit: D. Narciso Marti Carlio, Hotel Xaine, Lloret de Mar. (Tel. 33 50 12 or 33 50 08)*
(2) *Free*
(5) *Marqués de Roviralta*

Madrid

15. Parque del Oueste

Situated on the slopes overlooking the Manzanares river, the gardens were estab-lished at the beginning of the 20th cent, and replanted in 1940 and in succeeding years.

They form a fine landscaped park with winding paths and a fine display of roses.

(1) *Daily*
(2) *Free*
(5) *Municipality of Madrid*

Madrid

16. Parque del Retiro

The Retiro is Madrid's main park, close to the centre of the city and covering some 32 acres (13 ha). It is a small part of the original gardens of the Palacio del Buen Retiro, created during the rule of the last kings of the House of Austria. Once a retreat of the Conde-Duque de Olivares, it was given by him to Felipe IV in *c* 1631. At this time the construction of the palace was begun – the remaining part now used for museums – and the parterre known as the Jardin de las Flores.

The designer of the gardens was Cosme Lotti, who also contributed to the creation of the Boboli Gardens (qv) in Florence. One of the main entrances is through the imposing Puerta de la Coronela in the Calle de Alfonso XII. From this a wide avenue bordered by statues of the monarchs of Spain leads to a small lake. Here there are two matching fountains, a sunken garden, and a fine rose garden; also a beautiful specimen of *Taxodium distichum*.

(1) *Daily*
(2) *Free*
(5) *Municipality of Madrid*

Madrid

17. Royal Botanical Gardens

Situated next to the Prado, these gardens were founded by Ferdinand VI in 1755 and were moved by Carlos III to their present site in 1781. They were at that time one of the most celebrated botanical gardens in Europe, partly owing to their excellent botanical school, but mostly because of the large quantity of then-unknown tropical plants brought home from expeditions to the New World.

The original design is by the architect Juan de Villanueva, with 24 square beds divided by paths, and with stone fountains set in the centre of each bed, which contain specimens of all the botanical sexual classes listed by Linnaeus. This landscaping became less formal with the years and romantic elements were added in the mid-19th cent. De Candolle's plant classi-fication was applied to the planting, which still prevails today.

Improvements are being carried out by the Director, Prof Rivas-Martinez. The gardens are being restored to the original plan, and a collection of approx 1,000 dif-ferent specimens of Spanish indigenous plants is being brought together, as well as

600 types of roses. There is a rock garden and a herbarium.

(1) Research centre, including herbarium and library: Summer: Mon–Fri 8–2; Winter: Mon–Fri 9–2, 3–6. Gardens not yet reopened
(2) Free
(5) Patrimonio Nacional (Consejo Superior de Investigaciones Cientifidas, Instituto Botanico Cavanilles)

San Esteban de Oca

Pontevedra

18. Pazo de Oca

This is situated approx 15 miles (25 km) south of Santiago de Compostela, on the road to Orense, and is the most magnificent of the Galician palaces. The gardens were founded towards the end of the 18th cent by the Marqués de Camarasa. The overall harmony of design, the irrigation system, the balustrades, stone ornaments and profuse greenery combine to create an effect unique in Spain.

The palace has a crenellated tower. Past the entrance hall there is access to a patio-like garden, with an 18th-cent stone fountain at the centre surrounded by clipped box hedges in an unusual trefoil shape. In the background is a dramatic view of the Ulla valley. Another patio and fountain are reached from here and an arch leads through to lower lying gardens surrounding pools. A wide Baroque stone bridge separates a lily-pond from the lake beneath it, and in the centre of this is an unusual stone sculpture of a boat complete with cannons and sailors in 18th-cent dress. These waterways are skirted by wide avenues overhung by ancient box trees. There is a lime avenue where once horse races were held.

(1) Daily 10–1.30, 4–7.30
(2) Charge
(4) Palace (same times)
(5) Duque de Medinaceli

Santiago de Compostela

La Coruña

19. Monasterio de San Lorenzo de Trasouto

Situated ¾ mile (1 km) from Santiago de Compostela, the Franciscan monastery was founded in the 13th cent and reconstructed in the 17th cent. It was originally the property of the Condes de Altamira, ancestors of the present owner. Particularly striking in the cloister garden is the dense maze of clipped box. The intricate design comprises various symbolic devices. The park has a variety of fine trees, and the camellias are a particular feature.

(1) Summer: Daily 11–1, 4–8; Winter: Daily 11–1, 4–6

(2) Charge
(3) Monastery
(5) Duque de Soma

Segovia

20. La Granja de San Ildefonso

Situated 7 miles (11 km) outside Segovia at the foothills of the Sierra de Guadarrama on the road to Puerto de Navacerrada, at an altitude of 3,936 ft (1,200 m), and with a park of 358 acres (145 ha), this is known as the 'little Versailles'. Although royal connections with La Granja go back to the mid-15th cent, the present palace was completed for Felipe V in 1739. The first architect here was Theodore Ardemans and later the Italian architects Juvara and Sacchetti were employed on the garden front. The gardens were designed for Felipe by Esteban Boutelou, between 1727 and 1743.

The flowers, shrubs and trees serve as a backdrop to the monumental and complicated marble and lead fountains, the work of Thierry, Prémin, Dumandré and Pitué. There are 26 in all, making one of the most striking collections of fountains in Europe. Especially fine is the (47 m) high Fuente de la Fama, situated on a parterre opposite the south façade of the palace. To the west stands the extravagant Fuente Baños de Diana. With the fountain and parterre of Andromeda begins a vertical series of ponds called the Carrera de Caballos (Horse Race), and another sequence is known as the Gran Cascada. Flanking the east side of the palace are the Jardín de la Selva, a labyrinth and an apiary.

(1) Thu, Sat, Sun and Public Holidays 9–2
(2) Charge
(4) Palace and tapestry museum (late Apr–late Sep: Mon–Sat, except mid-Jul, 10–1, 2.30–6; late Sep–late Apr: Mon–Sat, except 25 Dec and 1 Jan, 10–1, 3–7)
(5) Patrimonio Nacional

Vitoria

Álava

21. La Florida

This is a garden in the 19th-cent romantic style, like the Laberinto de Horta (qv) in Barcelona. It was laid out in 1820 to designs by the architect Chavarri. In 1855 the gardens were enlarged to include the grounds previously owned by the convent of Santa Clara and they were landscaped by Velasco and the garden architect Zárraga.

With its central bandstand, lake and artificial mound, and planting of trees and shrubs, it is reminiscent of a French park.

(1) Daily
(2) Free
(5) Municipality of Vitoria

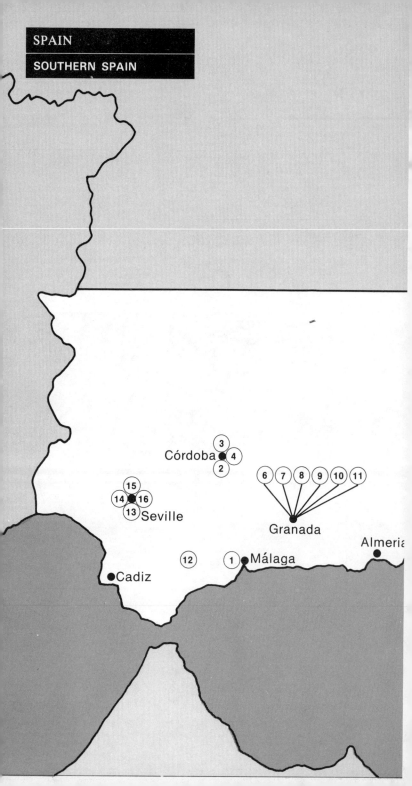

SPAIN

SOUTHERN SPAIN

Córdoba
③
④
②

⑥ ⑦ ⑧ ⑨ ⑩ ⑪
Granada

⑮
⑭ ⑯
⑬ Seville

Almeria

⑫ ① Málaga

Cadiz

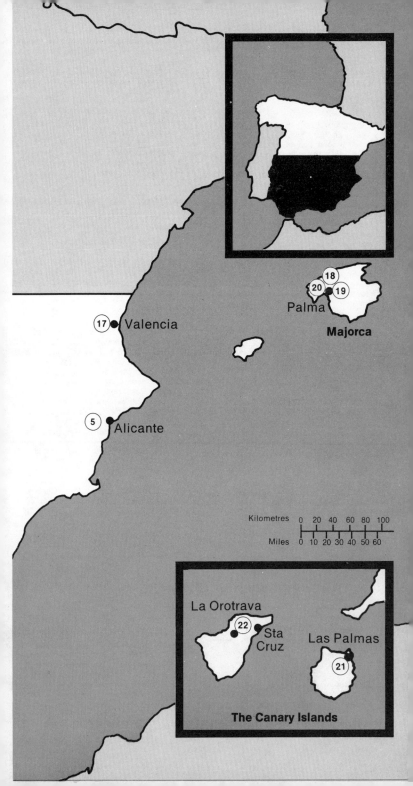

Kilometres 0 20 40 60 80 100

Miles 0 10 20 30 40 50 60

(17) Valencia

(5) Alicante

(18)
(20) (19)
Palma
Majorca

La Orotrava
(22) Sta
Cruz
Las Palmas
(21)
The Canary Islands

SPAIN

Churriana, nr Málaga

Málaga

1. Jardín del Retiro de Santo Tomás

The house was built and gardens laid out for Alonso de Santo Tomás, Bishop of Málaga, in the second half of the 17th cent, but almost all that remains of the original garden is a covered way, the vine arbour, to the right of the east front, and an upper garden with poplars, vegetable terraces and fruit trees, now very overgrown. Towards the end of the 18th cent the property passed to the Conde de Villalcázar de Sirga, who engaged the architect José Martin de Aldehuela to landscape the gardens. His first work was a garden in the classical French style, facing the main entrance of the house and centred on the marble Fuente de la Sirena (Siren Fountain). Its features are today somewhat dwarfed by the surrounding trees. This was followed by a Baroque garden, with a cascade, built on three levels. A long strip of water is bordered by walnut trees, and there are also jacaranda trees, a large variety of flowers, and an elaborate sundial, once part of the original garden.

(1) Daily
(2) Charge
(5) Duque de Aveyro

Córdoba

2. Alcázar

The Alcázar was erected for Alfonso XI in the early 14th cent. Inside are mosaics and other Roman antiquities.

The modern gardens laid out in Arab style can be entered from the south along a short walled approach. Steps lead down to a large pool and descend to further ornamental pools, fountains and trimmed box hedges. A large eucalyptus presides over a colourful mixture of geranium, veronica, bougainvillea, jasmine, cypress, oleander and fruit trees.

(1) May–Sep: Daily 9.30–1.30, 5–8; Oct–Apr: Daily 9.30–1.30, 4–7. In Summer the gardens are illuminated 10 pm–1 am
(2) Charge
(4) Alcázar (same times)
(5) Municipality of Córdoba

Córdoba

3. La Mezquita

The Patio de los Naranjos (Court of the Orange Trees) is perhaps one of the oldest existing walled gardens. It was begun towards the end of the 8th cent in the reign of Abd-al-Rahman I and enlarged 200 years later by Almanzor. It was formerly the Moorish court of ablutions, and, with its Baroque fountains and rows of olive, laurel and palm trees – later replaced by orange trees – extending the lines of arched columns within, it formed a fitting entrance to what was one of the largest and most ornate mosques.

Visit between mid-April and mid-May for the scent of the orange blossom.

(1) Apr–Sep: Mon—Fri 10.30–1.30, 4–8; Sat and Sun 10.30–1.30, 4–10; Oct–Mar: Mon–Fri 10.30–1.30, 3.30–6; Sat and Sun 10.30–1.30, 3.30–8
(2) Charge (except Sun)
(5) Cathedral Chapter

Córdoba

4. Palacio de las Rejas de Don Gome

The building is of 15th-cent origin and the garden is in the Moorish style. There is a succession of patios – large and small, sunny and shady – and a substantial garden with the house on one side and high whitewashed walls on the others.

One of the patios is planted entirely with box, and another has cypresses in the shape of a coronet as a centrepiece. The white walls of the house itself are very decorative, with the architectural detail painted a dark cobalt blue and heliotrope climbing to the eaves. The massive walls and intimate character of the last of the patios give it the apperance of an outdoor living-room. The lay-out is formal, centred on a fountain. The parterre is full of flowers at all seasons, including oleanders and standard roses. There are violets and stocks, and oranges and lemons are trained to grow almost flat against the walls.

On one side the garden wall is pierced by a series of wide openings like French windows which can be closed by substantial wooden shutters. At the end of one of the main paths a glorieta of cypresses provides a place to sit in the shade. The open runnels of water are a typically Moorish element.

(1) Apply to the owner for permission to visit
(2) Free
(5) Marqués de Viana

Elche

Alicante

5. Huerto del Cura

The old town of Elche is surrounded by orchards and gardens where half a million palm trees grow, in particular the species Phoenix dactylifera. Originating in Persia, they were acclimatized on the southern Mediterranean coast many centuries ago. During the Arab domination of Spain they were grown extensively on the Spanish coasts and, in the 18th and 19th cents, a number were planted in the orchards of Elche.

In the Huerto del Cura is an interesting palm known as the Imperial Palm, with seven satellite trunks growing from the main trunk. There are also sub-tropical plants such as cacti and bougainvillea, and orange, lemon, carob and pomegranate trees.

The garden was declared a Jardín Artístico Nacional in 1943.

(1) Apr–Oct: Daily 8–8; Nov–Mar: Daily 8–6
(2) Charge
(4) Plants for sale
(5) Hermanos Orts Serrano

Granada
6. Alhambra

The Moorish castle and royal residence was built mainly between 1340 and 1390, and partly destroyed to make way for the early 16th-cent Palacio Carlos V which adjoins it.

The Alhambra is entered by a footpath from the Puerta de las Granadas through trees and shrubbery to the Puerta de la Justicia. To the west lies the Alcazaba, the oldest (9th-cent) part, commanding from its watch tower a fine panorama. It is skirted by the Jardín de los Adarve, a battlement walk with box and myrtle hedges and jasmine and honeysuckle clothing the walls.

Next to the Mexuar – the council chamber – lies the most important of the patios, the Patio de los Arrayanes. This is an open court with a long, narrow pool at the centre, bordered by a myrtle hedge. To the east is the little Patio de la Reja, with a fountain and four cypresses, and the Patio de Daraxa, with cypresses, acacias, citrus trees and box hedges enclosing a partly Moorish fountain. To the south lies the famous Patio de los Leones (Court of Lions), once also full of vegetation, with its renowned massive grey fountain forming a contrast to the delicate arches and columns surrounding it.

Near the royal buildings lie the modern, terraced Jardines del Partal, descending to the porticoed Torre de las Damas set beside a pool whose waters reflect the buildings above.

(1) Summer: Daily 9–7.30; Winter: Daily 10–Sunset
(2) Charge
(3) Restaurant
(4) Alcázar, Palacio Carlos I (same times. Also May–Sep: Tue, Thu and Sun 9–midnight)
(5) Patrimonio Nacional

Granada
7. Carmen de los Mártires

A large cross of white stone on a mound commemorates the martyrs imprisoned and killed here by the Moors in the 14th cent, and a commemorative plaque indicates that in 1573 the Conde de Tendilla built a monastery here for the Discalced Carmelite Order. The celebrated mystic and poet St

John of the the Cross was prior here from 1582 to 1588 and a cedar in the garden is supposed to have been planted by the saint himself. In the 19th cent the land was sold to General Don Carlos Calderón, who built the house with its orchard and gardens. Today it is a public park.

As is customary in Granada, the gardens are laid out in terraces. Water is one of the principal elements, spilling from fountains and forming a wide canal in the upper part of the garden. In a wooded area to the north there is also a lake. Low box hedges frame the alleys of trees and the shrubs and climbing plants that grow in great profusion. The highest terrace has a circular pool surrounded by trees. Parallel to it and further down there is another garden with box hedges where there is a wall fountain. On the terrace leading to the house there are statues of the 18th-cent kings Ferdinand VI and his half-brother Carlos III.

(1) Summer: Daily 9–7.30; Winter: Daily 10–Sunset
(2) Free
(3) Restaurant (Summer)
(5) Municipality of Granada

Granada
8. Carmen de San Agustín

The original design of the carmen (Morisco garden villa) was probably 16th cent, and it has been rebuilt this century by the architect Gardia de Paredes in a style that blends with the oldest houses on the hillside. The present gardens were designed by the Catalan garden architect Beltrán in 1964.

The carmen is built on two levels. As is customary, access is at the higher-lying part, where there is a garden with rosemary and lavender and a variety of other plants, and numerous trees. On a level lower than the house there is a fishpond.

(1) Apply to the owner for permission to visit
(2) Free
(5) Don José Rodríguez Acosta

Granada
9. Casa del Chapiz

Two houses joined together, one of which belonged originally to the Morisco, Lorenzo el Chapiz. In the garden there is a central pool within an attractive lay-out of clipped hedges. There are pomegranates, cypress trees and myrtle.

(1) Apply to the administrator for permission to visit
(2) Free
(5) Escuela de Estudios Arabes de Granada

SPAIN

Granada

10. Fundación Rodríguez Acosta

Built by the painter Acosta in 1920, this modern *carmen* situated on the Alhambra hillside is today a centre for the arts and sciences, with living quarters for practising artists.

The gardens serve partly as an outdoor museum for the Classical Greek and Roman sculpture collected by Acosta on his travels. Laid out in terraces, they are set on the edge of a cliff with massive retaining walls and arcades offering beautiful views of the mountains and the *vega* (flat lowland).

The architectural setting is more Italian than Spanish. At one end a semicircular colonnade is reflected in the large pool sunk in the stone pavement. Cypresses and hedges of box and myrtle relieve the stern impression of stone and marble.

(1) Apply to the administrator for permission to visit
(2) Charge
(5) Fundación Rodríguez Acosta

Granada

11. Generalife

Summer palace of the kings of Granada, built in the 13th and 14th cents on the slopes of the Cerro del Sol overlooking the city and the Alhambra (qv). It may be approached along an imposing avenue of cypresses, planted in the 18th cent and reminiscent of Italian landscaping.

The first court inside the Generalife is the elongated Patio de la Acequia (Canal Court) which has fountains, shrubs, roses, clipped cypresses, a mirador and porticoes around a narrow rectangular pool which forms the central axis. A gateway to the north-east leads to the Patio de los Cipreses, with a U-shaped canal, fountain, roses, oleanders and three cypresses. From here a wide 19th-cent stairway leads to the upper garden, with ascending terraces in the Italian style. Here is the Camino de las Cascadas, a water stairway dating from Moorish times.

(1) Summer: Daily 9–7.30: Winter: Daily 10–Sunset
(2) Charge
(4) Generalife (same times)
(5) Patrimonio Nacional

Ronda

Málaga

12. Casa del Rey Moro

Clinging to the edge of the wild and rocky gorge at Ronda, this modern garden occupies the site of a Moorish palace, dating back to the mid-11th cent, of which scarcely a trace remains.

The French landscape gardener J. N.

Forestier was engaged to lay out a garden on the narrow piece of ground between the Calle Marqués de Paradas and the ravine. Turning the sloping ground to good advantage, he made three terraces, with a fourth narrow one on a ledge of the cliff beneath. There are fine vistas as well as Arab elements such as the use of tiles and waterways.

On the topmost terrace a fountain basin is sunk in the brick and tile pavement, from which the water is carried through open channels to a pool between a double stairway below. Pergolas against one of the outer walls are formed by ancient white marble columns supporting wooden trellis-work painted black. The flowerbeds are edged with box, the largest ones containing roses. Cypresses provide a contrast to the bright colours of mimosa and orange trees, and in the background is the glossy foliage of pittosporum.

Today, the gardens are somewhat neglected, but they command a fine view of the Tajo, and of the spectacular gorge of the River Guadalavín below.

(1) Apply to the owner for permission to visit: Cuesta de Santo Domingo, Ronda
(2) Free
(5) Señora Hernández

Seville

13. Alcázar

This is the most extensive example of a Mudéjar garden surviving in Spain. Although the origins of both the Alcázar and the gardens date back to the Almohade dynasty in the 12th cent, the present lay-out dates from the reign of Pedro I, 200 years later. Some patios, dating from the Almohade Alcázar (12th cent), are under excavation.

The gardens can be divided into four distinct areas: the Arab gardens adjoining the walls of the palace; the Renaissance gardens, in which myrtle and boxwood borders predominate; the modern flower gardens and the English-style gardens.

Features of special interest include a Renaissance fountain of Carrara marble in the eight-sectioned Jardin de las Damas, and the pavilion of Carlos V, which stands among lemon, lime and orange trees, and has a ceramic flagstone showing the lay-out of the former labyrinth garden. The pavilion has Cuenca *azulejos* and a fine cedar-wood coffered dome inside.

(1) Daily 10–1, 4–7
(2) Charge
(4) Alcázar Palace (same times)
(5) Patrimonio Nacional

Seville

14. Casa de Pilatos

The magnificent Renaissance mansion incorporating Moorish features was completed in the 16th cent by the first Marqués de Tarifa, who named it after the house of Pilate which he saw during a visit to Jerusalem, copying some of its features.

In the patio a handsome 17th-cent Italianate fountain of Carrara marble is surrounded by an elaborate arcade and an attractive pebble pavement. There is a domed grand staircase and, around the patio walls, polychrome *azulejos*. Large gardens extend beyond the patio, enclosed on two sides by walls ornamented by bas-reliefs brought here by Per Afán towards the end of the 16th cent. There are fountains and statuary among the trees and flowers. An orange tree, a giant magnolia and a lemon tree are survivors of the original garden.

The garden was redesigned in the romantic style in 1850 and was divided into eleven symmetrical squares around the fountain; four marble benches were added beneath a beautiful summer house that is covered with jasmine. In 1875 the Empress Eugenia planted a rose in the so-called modern or little garden and its pale pink blooms still flower every year.

(1) Daily 9–1, 3–7
(2) Charge
(5) Duque de Medinaceli

Seville

15. Palacio de las Dueñas

Built in the 15th cent by the Pineda family in the Moorish style, it was sold in 1484 by Doña Catalina de Riberato to raise the ransom needed to free a member of the family held prisoner by the Moors in Granada. The approach is open and sunny, unlike most Seville gardens which tend to be reached through dark entrance halls and shaded patios. An ample salon leads to the nobly proportioned central patio, with Moorish arches and tall palms. In the centre there is a small fountain. The patio leads through to the garden that surrounds the house which is made up of various enclosures, each laid out differently, with high box hedges, cypresses, pergolas and fountains. There is a profusion of flowers, especially in spring.

The gardens have the advantage of their own reservoir.

(1) Daily 10–1, 4–7
(2) Charge
(5) Duque de Alba

Seville

16. Parque de María Luisa

Praised by the writer Aldous Huxley as 'the most beautiful public park in Europe', the park was given to Seville in 1893 by María Luisa, widow of Louis Phillipe's son the Duc de Montpensier. It incorporates the smaller Jardines de las Delicias and part of the gardens of the 18th-cent Palacio de San Telmo, and it covers some 93 acres (38 ha).

In 1911 the French landscape gardener

J. N. Forestier was commissioned to re-design the gardens, and the result is considered one of his masterpieces. With Arab gardens as his inspiration, Forestier used local materials such as *azulejos*, and the park is delightfully laid out with shaded walks, open spaces and enclosed gardens. There are palms and orange trees, acacias, roses, cyclamen, and almond and jacaranda trees. Specially interesting are the Jardin de los Leones (Lion Garden), the Fuente de las Ranas (Frog Fountain), the Estanque de los Lotos (Lotus Pool), and the bowers named after illustrious Sevillian literary figures such as Bécquer and the Álvarez Quinteros. Several new pavilions were built for the Spanish-American Exhibition in 1929.

(1) Daily
(2) Free
(5) Municipality of Seville

Valencia

17. Botanical Gardens

The finest botanical gardens in Spain, they were founded in 1567 and transferred in *c* 1632 to the grounds of the leper colony hospital of San Lazaro. They were established in their present site in 1902.

Despite periods of decline and neglect in the past, a large number of trees and plants from all over the world have been successfully acclimatized here. Those from tropical and sub-tropical regions have done particularly well owing to the favourable climate.

Amongst the 300 specimens of trees and shrubs are massive oak trees, a large *Ginkgo biloba*, the Brazilian wool tree and the striking Chinese *Firmiana simplex*. There are also avocado pear trees, the tall Caucasian zelkova, and numerous types of palm tree including some of the valuable *Trachycarpus excelsa* group.

The gardens contain glasshouses, an umbraculum, nurseries, a library and herbariums. In 1968 an aviary and an aquarium were built. Between 1972 and 1976 a new School of Gardening and a Museum of the Environment were founded.

(1) Daily 9–7
(2) Charge
(5) University of Valencia

THE ISLANDS

Buñola

Majorca

18. La Alfabia

A patio is entered through an imposing archway with a marquetry ceiling – all that remains of the original 14th-cent Moorish house. Behind the building is a garden that has been allowed to grow wild, with winding paths providing shade from the sun. From

SPAIN

(1) Apply to local tourist office
(2) Charge

the patio with its central fountain another archway leads through a passage under the house to a small terrace. A path connects the house to a fine avenue of lime trees, ending in a tall stucco façade with a wall fountain in the centre and doors to either side. Here there is a long pergola with 32 octagonal stone columns in the Moorish style supporting a curved roof with vines. Small pavilions furnished with stone tables, and with stone jars between the columns, are part of an elaborate water display. Geraniums climb over the retaining walls, there are blue irises, clumps of pink stocks and yellow ixia. On the parapets are potted plants, and there are long rows of stone benches, a grove of pines, and a miniature lake approached by an ornamental flight of steps.

(1) Apr–Sep: Daily (except Sun afternoons) 9.30–12.30, 3–6.30; Oct–Mar: Daily (except Sun afternoons) 9.30–12.30, 3–5.30
(2) Charge
(4) House (same times)

Buñola

19. Raxa

This property on the road from Palma to Sóller occupies the site of what was a Moorish country estate. During the redistribution of Moorish lands it was given (in 1234) to the sacristan of the cathedral at Gerona, and in the 18th cent to Cardinal Don Antonio Despuig y Dameto. The cardinal owned land in Italy, and brought to the gardens a strong Italianate influence. He imported treasures from Rome, and quantities of exotic plants from Latin America, many of them provided by his contacts at the Royal Botanical Gardens, Madrid (qv).

A long stairway of soft grey stone, mottled by orange lichen, leads up from the house to a walled recess surmounted by six Tuscan columns and a statue, below which are stone benches and a fountain. In the background is a grove of Aleppo pines, probably first planted here by Arabian settlers. The great stairway is divided by seven narrow terraced gardens, clinging to the steep hillside with the support of retaining walls. With the upper terrace, these layers correspond to the eight paradises in the Koran – a typically Persian device. One of the terraces leads to a large pool and a balcony with a stone table, which makes an agreeable resting place with a beautiful view.

On the other side of the house is a patio, and beneath this a rectangular parterre with a central pergola, cypresses cut into arches, and a circular fountain in a shady grove of gnarled old olive trees.

The garden front of the house has the classical loggia typical of the Majorcan son.

Esporlas

Majorca

20. La Granja de Fortuny

This ancient Arabic farmstead is on the north-west of the island 3 miles (5 km) from Esporlas. During the division of land after the Conquest it was lent to the Cistercians for use as a monastery. It later belonged to the Vida family, and in 1665 it became the property of the present owners, the Fortuny family.

This is one of the most beautiful country houses to be found on the island of Majorca. It is built around a large patio, and on the side facing down the valley is a striking open gallery, with an arcade of marble columns supporting the roof. Behind the house is a small garden, laid out towards the end of the 18th cent in the romantic style. The paths are serpentine, and the beds irregular in shape. Behind the garden a high cliff forms a rockery, scaled by a succession of paths and stairways. Above is a pergola and a bath house.

(1) Apply to owner for permission to visit
(2) Charge
(5) Fortuny family

Tafira Alta, nr Las Palmas

Gran Canaria

21. Viera y Clavijo Botanical Gardens

This was one of the first botanical gardens to be established with plant conservation as its primary aim. Founded in 1952 by the administration of the Gran Canaria, it was designed and constructed by the Swedish botanist Eric Ragnar Svenson Sventenius.

It is primarily a collection of plants from the Macarones Islands – the Canaries, Madeira, Cape Verde Islands, Azores and Salvage Islands. The unique flora of this region is presented in a natural setting in the spectacular valley of Guiniguada.

There is a comprehensive collection of rare plants, some of them extinct in their natural habitat, such as the red-flowering *Lotus bertholetii*, *Limonium arborescens* and *Arbutus canariensis*. The modern administrative buildings are constructed of multi-coloured volcanic rock, and there is a striking memorial fountain. Besides a cool, shady area of laurel woodland (a type of vegetation exclusive to the Atlantic Islands, which has long been extinct in southern Europe and north Africa), there are large collections of Canarian plants such as sonchus, and tree-like *Rosaceae*. There are some magnificent cliff walks.

A small staff of botanists is engaged in research, and efforts are being made to develop the facilities into an institute of international status.

Puerto de la Cruz

Tenerife

22. Botanical Gardens of Orotava

Situated on the road between Puerto de la Cruz and la Orotava at Durazno, the gardens extend to 5 acres (2 ha). They were founded in 1788 by the Marqués de Villanueva del Prado on instructions from Carlos III. The intention was to acclimatize the new and useful plants being discovered by Spanish navigators in the Americas and Asia as attempts to grow these in Madrid and Aranjuez failed because of unfavourable climatic conditions.

There are now more than 200 species of plants in the gardens, both indigenous and imported. The constantly mild climate encourages luxuriant growth. There are Oriental-style orchid houses, and fine specimens of the Norfolk Island palm, Himalayan fig tree – growing red figs that taste like strawberries – Oriental plane – planted by the Marqués de Villanueva del Prado – and collections of plants of the genus plumeria and of the genus datura. All the plants are labelled.

(1) Spring and Summer: Mon–Sat 9–7; Sun and Public Holidays 11–7; Autumn and Winter: Mon–Sat 9–6; Sun and Public Holidays 11–6
(2) Charge
(5) Patrimonio Nacional (Instituto Nacional de Investigaciones Agrarias)

GIBRALTAR

Gibraltar

Alameda Gardens

Founded in 1816 by General Don, Governor of Gibraltar, the gardens are arranged as an informal park. Although the Rock covers an area of only 3 square miles (7·7 sq km), almost 600 species of flowering plants and ferns have been identified here, a good selection of which are to be found in the Alameda Gardens.

Abutilon, bougainvillea, plumbago and pelargoniums in profusion grow here, and in the sunken dell strelitzia and hibiscus. Fan palms (washingtonia) and dragon trees (dracaena) flourish among the pine trees. There are many gladioli, and wild freesias from South Africa have been naturalized in the gardens.

(1) Daily 8–8
(2) Free
(5) Government of Gibraltar

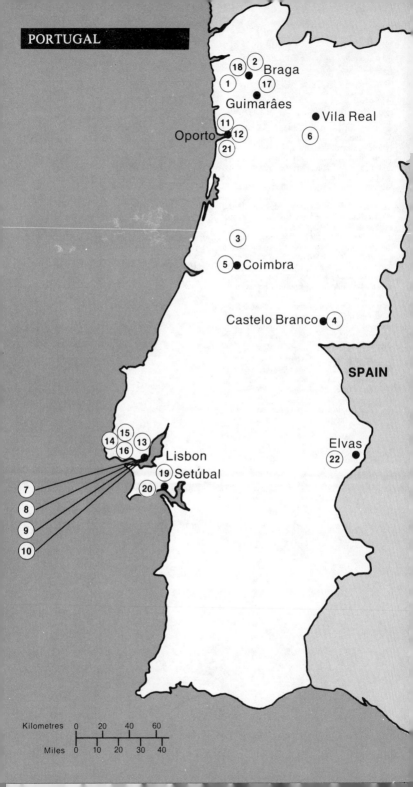

Barcelos

Minho

1. Municipal Gardens

Laid out in the 18th cent, there are flower-beds, obelisks of euonymus and yew. This is one of the most impressive – and gaudy – examples of municipal gardening in Portugal. The azaleas and camellias are clipped into circular clumps and there is a variety of bedding plants.

(1) Daily
(2) Free

Braga

Minho

2. Bom Jesus do Monte

Fine example of a staircase garden, leading up the side of a wooded hill outside Braga to the pilgrimage church of Bom Jesus. This is an uninteresting late 18th-cent building by Cruz Amarante. The Stairway of the Five Senses is a double staircase with orna-mental fountains, balustrades, obelisks and statues of Old Testament figures. The Stair-way of the Three Virtues has chapels to either side and fountains. The surrounding woods are full of mimosa and camellias.
There is an early 19th-cent lift beside the staircase.

(1) Daily
(2) Free

Bussaco

Beira Litoral

3. Tapada de Buçaco

This is Portugal's oldest and most famous forest preserve, extending over several thou-sand acres of the mountainside of the Serra de Buçaco, 40 miles (64 km) north-east of Coimbra. It was planted originally in 1778–81 by Carmelite monks, who had founded a monastery here in 1268. Some of the cells that they used still survive scattered throughout the forest. In 1643 Pope Urban VIII published a Papal Bull containing the threat of excommunication to anyone who entered and cut or caused damage to the trees, and at one time women were pro-hibited from entering the forest.

Among the trees are Mexican cypresses (*Cupressus lusitanica*) that are 100 ft (30 m) tall. The seeds are said to have been sent to the monks from Mexico in the 16th cent to be used for fuel and for cabinet-making. There are also magnificent specimens of *Platanus acerifolia* and *P. orientalis*, *Pinus montezumae*, the Monte-zuma pine, *Pinus pinaster*, *Quercus ilex*, *Q. suber*, the cork oak, *Quercus lusitanica* and a number of tilia species.

Azaleas, rhododendrons, hydrangeas and camellias grow in the valley of tree ferns, and near the northern entrance to the forest is a long staircase leading to a rock garden with fountains and pools. The remains of

PORTUGAL

the Carmelite monastery now form part of a hotel and this is surrounded by formal gardens and a good collection of camellias.

There are entrances to the forest at Penacova and at Luso.

(1) Daily
(2) Free
(3) Hotel restaurant
(5) Portuguese State

Castelo Branco

Beira Baixa

4. Episcopal Palace Gardens

The formal garden with topiary, flowers in pots, a large pool with flowers in ara-besque-shaped containers and Baroque statuary was laid out in the early 18th cent. There is a water tank with walls covered in *azulejos*, surrounded by ornamental sculpture, and an alley ending in two flights of steps is lined by balustrades surmounted by statues of Portuguese kings.

(1) Daily Sunrise–Sunset
(2) Charge

Coimbra

Beira Litoral

5. Botanical Garden

Covering approx 50 acres (20 ha), the garden was founded by Pombal in 1774–94 and is Portugal's largest and oldest botanical garden. The present plan is due to Julio Henriques, director from 1873 to 1918, and comprises six terraces connected by paths and steps. On the upper levels there are herbaceous plants and shrubs, box hedges, palms and conifers; the lower levels have a collection of bamboos, succulents on the open slopes and an adjoining arboretum.

A notable architectural feature is the formal sunken garden, which comprises box-bordered flowerbeds, roses, a fountain and decorative tiles. Nearby is the glass-house complex with a good collection of tropical plants. An aqueduct of 1570 passes over part of the garden.

(1) Daily 8–Sunset
(2) Free
(5) Portuguese State

Lamego

Beira Alta

6. Santuário Nossa Senhora dos Remédios

Perhaps one of the most inspiring approaches to a church in the world, 600 steps lead up the hill to the Baroque sanctuary. It is a double staircase with nine terraces, whitewashed and decorated with *azulejos*, balustrades, sculptures and foun-tains. In front of the church is a circular courtyard surrounded by obelisks, arches and pillars, surmounted by fine stone sculptures. In the centre is a 19th-cent fountain in the form of a merman riding a dolphin. The octagonal chapel bears the date 1783. A wide avenue crosses the staircase leading into the woodland on either side.

(1) *Daily*
(2) *Free*

Lisbon, Calçada da Ajuda

7. Botanical Gardens of Ajuda

A formal garden on a wide terrace in the shadow of the Palace of Ajuda, overlooking the Tagus. The parterres have low box hedges, and there are three fountains and water-lily ponds. Water spouts from the heads of cobras in the basin of the central fountain, watched by fish, frogs, ducks, sea lions and sea horses. Four 20 ft (6 m) poinsettias grow around the fountain. On a narrow terrace above, and behind an avenue of acacias, are four late 19th-cent glasshouses, all empty but for a single large banana tree.

There is a 20 ft (6 m) dragon's blood tree (*Dracaena draco*), with a spread of more than 40 ft (12 m), and worth noting also are *Schotia latifolia*, *Acacia armata* and 70 ft (21 m) specimens of *Grevillea robusta*.

(1) *Summer: Daily 9–7; Winter: Daily 8–5. Foreign visitors should apply for permission from the Ministry of Agriculture building in the Tapada da Ajuda*
(2) *Free*
(4) *Palace of Ajuda (Daily, except Mon, 10–5)*
(5) *Ministry of Agriculture*

Lisbon, Rua da Escola Politécnica

8. Botanical Garden of the Faculty of Sciences

Recently damaged by fire, the garden and buildings are undergoing restoration. It was founded in 1874 and covers approx 10 acres (4 ha). Of particular interest are the avenues of Washington fan palms and Canary Island date palms, and there is a fine dragon's blood tree (*Dracaena draco*).

(1) *Temporarily closed but will re-open*
(2) *Free*
(5) *Lisbon University*

Lisbon, Parque Eduardo VII

9. Estufa Fria and Estufa Quente

The name of the park commemorates the visit of Edward VII of England to Lisbon in 1902. The Estufa Fria ('cool' glasshouse)

was built by Carapinha in 1910 on the site of a quarry, enlarged in 1926 and opened to the public in 1930. The sunlight is filtered through a slatted roof supported on columns of rusticated masonry. The Estufa Quente ('hot' glasshouse) has a glass roof. Together they house a large collection of tropical and sub-tropical plants.

The plants in the Estufa Fria are comprehensively labelled and include ferns and tree ferns, banana trees, rattan and Howe Island palms, Brazilian plants, including *Jacobinia carnea*, and crinums. The filtered light on the foliage and the sound of running water, the vast leaves of the banana trees and the cheese plant (*Monstera deliciosa*) provide the visitor with the impression of being in the jungle.

In the Estufa Quente nothing is labelled. There is a large collection of agaves, a teak tree and a pool in the centre inhabited by flamingos. At the top of a series of steep paths and terraces there is a small collection of cacti.

(1) *Daily (except at Christmas) 10–6*
(2) *Charge (children under 10 free)*
(5) *Camara Municipal de Lisboa*

Lisbon

10. Jardim do Ultramar

To the east of the monastery of S. Jeronimos are the colonial gardens: most of the trees and plants are from countries that were once Portuguese colonies. At one time the gardens were linked with the Institute of Hygiene and Tropical Medicine.

An avenue of king palms leads from the gate past a small lake with an island on which banana trees grow. There are some fine Australian banyans (*Ficus macrophylla*), a specimen of *Ficus sycomorus*, with clusters of short aerial roots on its branches, several ginkgos and various types of cedar. Two further avenues of palms lead from the central avenue, one of Canary date palms and the other of queen palms and *Chorisia speciosa*, the trunk of this Brazilian tree covered with thorns.

At the top of the garden is a large pink house which has a small box-bordered parterre and is approached by white stone steps flanked by large rectangular tanks of water. This is now the Agricultural Museum and Herbarium. To the left of the main gate, up an avenue of coral trees (erythrina), there is a Chinese arch bearing the legend 'Macau'. This and the small garden behind, which contains several varieties of bamboo, *Fatsia japonica* and hibiscus, are the remnants of an exhibition held here in 1940.

(1) *Garden and Agricultural Museum and Herbarium: Daily (except Tue and Public Holidays) 11–noon, 2–5*
(2) *Free*
(5) *Portuguese State*

Oporto, Rua do Campo Alegre

Minho

11. Botanical Garden 'Dr Gonçalo Sampaio'

Founded in 1951 by Dr Américo Pires de Lima, the garden covers 10 acres (4·5 ha). There are several small sections, one of which is a box-edged parterre. The surrounding hedges are of clipped camellia. The small modern water garden has three circular pools set on slightly different levels so that the water flows through them. The garden specializes in orchids, cacti and rhododendrons.

(1) *Mon–Fri 2–5*
(2) *Free*
(5) *Portuguese State*

Oporto, Rua Entre Quintas 219

12. Quinta da Meio

This is an 'English' garden, created by William Tait, who was at one time in correspondence with Darwin and sent him plants. Some of the camellias survive from before he came to live here in 1881. The tulip-tree (*Liriodendron tulipifera*) is classified as a Monumento Nacional. Before the crown was damaged in a gale in 1968, it grew to a height of 124 ft (37 m) and was said to be the tallest in Europe. There are notable specimens of *Magnolia grandiflora*, *Sassafras albidum*, *Eucalyptus ficifolia*, *Cercis siliquastrum*, *Ligistrum japonicum* and *Wisteria sinensis*. In the shaded upper part of the garden are tree ferns and mahonias. Ferns and bog plants grow beside the stream and there are watsonias and sheets of *Iris kaempferi* on the terraces.

(1) *By appointment with the owner*
(2) *Free*
(5) *Miss Murièl Tait*

Queluz

Estremadura

13. Palace of Queluz

A small royal summer palace built by Mateus Vicente in 1758. The gardens were laid out by the Frenchman J. B. Robillon and they reflect the Rococo exuberance of the pink and green façade of the palace. The main parterre at the front, the Garden of Neptune, has box borders and faience vases, and lead statuary surrounds the small pool with the figure of Neptune. On the east side is a topiary garden and at the end of the central avenue of unclipped box a tall rusticated Rococo cascade (now dry) is flanked by three ancient Judas trees.

To the west of the palace a fine staircase leads to what was the canal, the walls covered with blue and white, pale yellow and sepia *azulejos*. This is crossed by a double bridge, also covered in *azulejos*. There is a double avenue of cypresses, and to one side the figure of a dragon spouts

water into a large basin. Other fountains are in the forms of a basket of flowers and a pair of clothed monkeys, one of which plays a violin, and there is a shell cascade.

(1) *Daily (except Tue and 25 Dec) 10–6*
(2) *Charge*
(3) *Restaurant*
(4) *Palace (same times)*
(5) *Ministry of Public Works*

Sintra

Estremadura

14. Monserrate

2 miles (3 km) from Sintra town, Monserrate has long been associated with the English. In the early 18th cent an English merchant from Lisbon, Gerald de Visme, rented the property, already renowned for its ancient chestnut groves and cataract, from the family of the Portuguese governor of India. The house built by de Visme, which was possibly rented by the eccentric English writer William Beckford, later fell into ruin. In 1856–60 the estate was bought by Sir Francis Cook and the house was reconstructed in the Moorish style by John Knowles. The gardens were laid out at this time: the landscaping was done by William Stockdale, the Romantic artist, with botanical advice from William Nevill of the Royal Botanic Gardens at Kew (qv). From that time until 1924 the head gardener was an Englishman.

Covering 75 acres (30 ha), the plantings of sub-tropical trees are unparalleled in Europe. Conifers, especially from the southern hemisphere, are well represented, and there are approx 25 species of palm in the gardens. In the moist, nearly frost-free, climate Norfolk Island pines grow to a height of 120 ft (36 m).

From the west terrace of the house grass sweeps steeply down to the central ravine and to the Bog Garden. There is a magnificent view with the backdrop of the Sintra mountain, framed by clumps of New Zealand flax, monkey puzzles and two great bottle brush trees. In the Bog Garden agaves, swamp cypresses, geums, bananas and bamboos grow beside the pools. At the top of the gorge, along the banks of the cataract (a small stream in summer) and in the shade of huge plane trees, grows a large collection of ferns and tree ferns. A small ruined chapel, strangled by vines, can be reached by the path which winds down through the ferns. This continues through the natural forest of pittosporum, cork and arbutus and wattle, past an Etruscan sarcophagus, back to the Bog Garden.

Many of the paths are badly overgrown and it is advisable to follow the signs, omitting the Rose Garden, which is not worth visiting. Beside the old stables there is an interesting range of buildings made from smooth granite boulders from the neighbouring hillside with cork-covered Gothic doors and windows.

(1) Daily (except 25 Dec) 9–6
(2) Free
(5) Portuguese State

Sintra
15. Pena Palace and National Park

In 1840 Dom Ferdinando of Saxe-Coburg-Gotha, consort of Maria II (and cousin of Albert, consort of Queen Victoria of England), laid out the gardens and built a palace with yellow ceramic domes and minarets in a Manueline Scottish Baronial style on the site of an earlier convent.

Entering the gardens through the crenellated main gate (cars may go right up to the palace and round the gardens), there is a small formal garden with bedding plants and box hedges, a magnificent specimen of *Thuja dolobrata* in the centre, clipped yew and the agave-like *Cordyline australis*. Beside the steep road up to the palace there are several fine specimens of araucarias among the forest of cedars, beeches and planes, and rhododendrons.

To the south-east of the palace the roads lead to the Cruz Alta, a plain granite cross marking the highest point on the mountain, and the Miradouro de Santa Eufemia. Taking the road to the west the Jardim das Camelias is reached, passing a hexagonal Moorish pavilion and square water-tank on the way. The camellias grow between tree ferns, and ferns cover the ground beneath. At the bottom of this valley there is a pool and a clearing beneath the spread of a Monterey cypress and a Monterey pine. The path to the right leads past a vast tulip-tree to the Fonte dos Passarinhos, a tiled Moorish pavilion. Above is an area of flowerbeds, glasshouses and camellias; below a sweep of grass leads down to lakes shaded by cedars of Goa, cypresses, spruce, pine, wattle and eucalyptus. In the middle of the largest lake is a small castellated folly and stunted oak. A door for pedestrians leads out here to the main road from Sintra.

Several magnificent Western red cedars and Californian redwoods are to be seen on the road leading westwards to the Feiteira da Condessa, a fern garden laid out by Ferdinando for his mistress, the Condessa de Ó. Above the fern garden with its pergola and stream is the Condessa's rustic cottage and garden, surrounded by rhododendrons, palms, Japanese red cedars and cedars of Goa, and spruce.

(1) Daily 10–6 or Sunset
(2) Free
(4) Palace (Daily, except Tue, 10–3); Moorish Castle (Summer: Daily, except Tue, 9–6; Winter: Daily, except Tue, 10–Sunset); Capuchin Monastery (Daily, except Tue, 9–6 or Sunset)

(5) Dept of Forestry

Sintra
16. Seteais

The palace, $\frac{3}{4}$ mile (1 km) from Sintra on the road to Monserrate (qv), was built in the 18th cent by Gildemeester, the Dutch consul in Lisbon, who made a fortune from a monopoly in diamonds granted to him by Pombal. It is now a hotel.

There are two separate wings to the building linked by a triumphal arch of 1802, through which is a fine view of the Pena Palace (qv). An avenue of limes runs along the west side of the palace; in front is a rectangular lawn with trees and potted plants; and behind lies a small formal garden with box hedges and roses.

(1) By arrangement with the hotel manager
(2) Free or tip
(3) Hotel restaurant
(5) Hotel Palácio de Seteais

Taide, nr Guimarães
Minho
17. Santuário Nossa Senhora do Porto d'Ave

The sanctuary, near the river Ave, is in a remarkable setting. A series of granite terraces and stairways with trees, plants, fountains and running water, and statues lead down to the church situated on the lowest terrace, at the bottom of the valley. The church is also interesting, with painted ceilings and other decoration.

(1) Daily
(2) Free

Tibães, nr Braga
Minho
18. Convent of Tibães

Derelict formal garden with the remnants of topiary and a water staircase that was the inspiration for the great staircase of Bom Jesus do Monte (qv). Small chapels are let into the hillside to commemorate the Stations of the Cross and there are statues of the kings and queens of Portugal. The water was designed to fall from wall fountains into semi-circular basins at each level and to course from the top by way of a spiralling channel.

(1) Entry not restricted though not officially open
(2) Free

Vila Fresca de Azeitão
Estredamura
19. Quinta das Torres

16th-cent manor house, now a hotel. There is a small formal garden and a water-tank. In the dining-room are two large tile panels depicting the Flight of Aeneas and the Burning of Troy, and the Death of Dido and the Building of Carthage.

(1) *By arrangement with the hotel manager*
(2) *Free or tip*
(3) *Hotel restaurant*
(5) *Quinta das Torres Hotel*

Vila Nogueira de Azeitão

Estremadura

20. Quinta da Bacalhôa

The palace was built in 1480 for the Infanta Brites, perhaps to the design of the Italian architect Sansovino. The garden was begun after 1528, when the property was bought by the son of Afonso de Albuquerque and it was he who built the garden pavilion with its three towers. Here are some fine *azulejos*, including one depicting Suzannah and the Elders of 1565 that is the earliest dated tile picture in Portugal.

The *quinta* is approached along a tree-lined lane off the Azeitão to Setubal road, and the entrance to the garden is through a small door off a large, open courtyard. Near the palace is a box garden: a maze with low hedges and a central fountain of quatrefoil form. From this formal garden a wide path lined with tiled containers for plants leads past orange groves to the pavilion and to the large water-tank.

The property suffered two periods of neglect: between 1650 and 1890, when the Conde de Mesquitella inherited the *quinta*, and between 1910 and 1936. In 1936 it was bought by Mrs Herbert Scoville from Connecticut and patiently restored by her.

(1) *Mon–Sat 1–5 by arrangement with the caretaker*
(2) *Donation to charity or tip*
(5) *Family of Mrs Herbert Scoville*

Vila Nova de Gaia

Minho

21. Garden of the Conde de Campo Bello

The garden contains specimens of *Camellia japonica* that are almost certainly the oldest in cultivation in Europe. There is evidence in the archives of the family of the Conde de Campo Bello that three plants were brought from Japan to this garden in the mid-16th cent. The oldest trees are now approx 30 in (76 cm) in diameter at the base and approx 30 ft (9 m) in height. The rose-pink flowers appear in February and March. There is a dense hedge of *Camellia mathotiana* and other notable specimens in the garden include *Aesculus hippocastanum* and *Liriodendron tulipifera*.

(1) *By appointment with the owner*
(2) *Free*
(5) *Conde de Campo Bello*

PORTUGAL

Vila Viçosa

Alentejo

22. Palace of the Dukes of Bragança

The palace was the seat of the dukes of Bragança and, after 1640, a residence of the kings of Portugal. The present building was begun in 1501 by Dom Jaime I. The garden with its box hedges and canals lined with tiles is attractive and peaceful.

(1) *Summer: Daily 9–7; Winter: Daily 9–6. Guided tours*
(2) *Charge*
(4) *Palace (same times)*
(5) *Bragança Foundation*

Ainola

Oulu

1. Botanical Garden of the University of Oulu

The garden was founded in 1960 and in an area of 12½ acres (5 ha) contains approx 4,000 species. It specializes in indigenous and northern plants. In the early 1980s the collection will be transferred to Linnanmaa, the new university site.

(1) Garden. Daily Sunrise–Sunset. Glasshouses. Mon–Fri 8–4; Sat and Sun noon–3
(2) Free
(5) University of Oulu

Elimäki

Uusimaa

2. Arboretum Mustila

The first plantings of domestic and foreign species, mainly conifers, were made by A. F. Tigerstedt in 1902. Rare broad-leaved species have been cultivated in a small area of the arboretum on the southern slope of the granite plateau. Here the soil is better and the land sheltered from the north wind. Of the 300 acres (120 ha), only 150 acres (60 ha) were planted. Towards the end of the planned route is a woodland garden with rhododendrons and azaleas.

(1) Mon–Fri 7.30–4; Sat and Sun by appointment
(2) Free; Guided tour: Charge
(3) Café (Jun–Aug)
(4) Nursery (May: Mon–Sat 7.30–4; Jun–Nov: Mon–Fri 7.30–4)
(5) A. F. and P. M. Tigerstedt

Helsinki, Unioninkatu 44

3. Botanical Gardens of the University of Helsinki

The garden was founded in 1833 and the construction of the Great Palm House was completed in 1889. The glasshouses were damaged in World War II but soon rebuilt. The Great Palm House is the most notable feature of the garden and in the water-lily house the giant water-lily, *Victoria amazonica*, flowers in summer. There is a systematic garden of approx 1,000 species and fine trees, in particular a poplar and an elm.

(1) Garden. Daily 8 am–9 pm. Glasshouses. May–Sep: Daily (except Sat and Midsummer Day) noon–3; Oct–Apr: Sun, Tue, Fri (except 25 Dec and Good Friday) 1–3
(2) Garden: Free; Glasshouses: Charge
(5) University of Helsinki

Naantali

Turku Pori

4. Kaivopuisto Park

A public park planted at the end of the 19th cent with lawns, trees, flowers and a bandstand, where in summer there are three concerts a week.

(1) Daily
(2) Free
(3) Restaurants, café and kiosk

Naantali, Luonnonmaa Island

5. Kultaranta

The summer residence of the Finnish presidents reached by the 656 ft (200 m) long Ukko-Pekkås Bridge. The granite house was built in 1916 and the garden designed in 1915 by Paul and Svante Olsson. It combines a formal lay-out, with flower-filled parterres and a fountain, with woodland surrounding the house on the rocky promontory on which it is situated. There is a good view across the water to the Convent Church.

(1) Jun–Aug: Fri 6 pm–8 pm or by appointment
(2) Free
(5) Finnish Government

Ruissalo, Turku

Turku Pori

6. Botanical Garden of the University of Turku

Founded in 1924, the garden has occupied its present site on the island of Ruissalo since 1956. The most interesting collections are of plants indigenous to Finland and of orchids, cacti and other succulents.

(1) Mon–Fri 8–3; Sat 10–noon; Sun 11–3
(2) Charge
(5) University of Turku

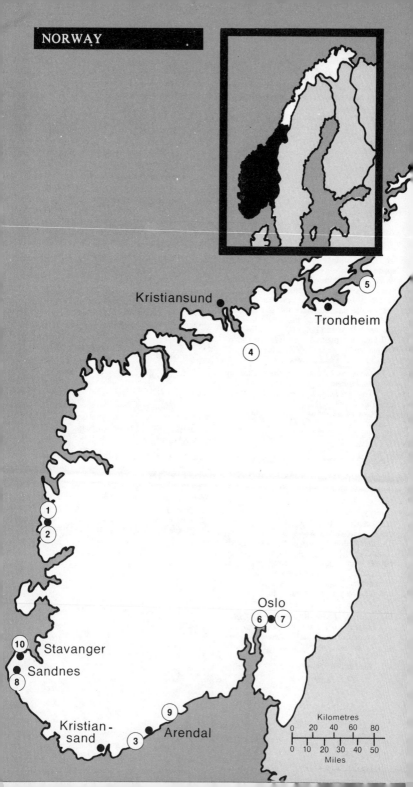

NORWAY

Kristiansund

Trondheim

4

5

Oslo

6 7

1

2

Stavanger

10

Sandnes

8

Kristian-
sand

3

Arendal

9

Kilometres
0   20   40   60   80
0 10 20 30 40 50
Miles

Bergen

1. The Norwegian Arboretum

Founded in 1971, the arboretum covers an area of 125 acres (51 ha) comprising hill ground, rocky gorges, a small lake and a long shoreline. All the plants are labelled.

(1) Daily
(2) Free
(5) University of Bergen

Bergen

2. University Botanical Garden

Founded in 1897–9. The glasshouse was erected in 1900–1901 and the lay-out of the garden was substantially altered in the 1930s. It is a small garden, covering an area of only 2 acres (0·8 ha), but it contains approx 5,000 species. There is an alpine rock garden and an economic plant garden, and of particular interest is the rhododendron collection. This includes specimens of the Tower Court collection, principally of F. Kingdon Ward origin, and specimens collected by Harry Smith in China and Tor Nitzelius in Japan. Orchids are a speciality in the glasshouse and among them are Ugandan species, some of which are rare in cultivation. Visit between March and June.

(1) Garden. Daily 8–8. Glasshouse. Mon–Sat 9–3; Sun noon–2
(2) Free
(5) University of Bergen

Dömmesmoen, nr Grimstad

Aust-Agder

3. Dömmesmoen State Horticultural College

The College was founded in 1923 and the garden was begun in the same year by a member of the staff, Ola Nordal. There is a wide range of shrubs and one of the largest oaks in Norway. Although intended primarily for the instruction of the students, the garden is of general interest.

(1) Daily
(2) Free
(5) Ministry of Agriculture administered by the State Horticultural College

Kvanne

Møre og Romsdal

4. Anne and Halvor Svinviks Arboretum

Started in 1941, the arboretum was planted and maintained by the owner, Halvor Svinvik, and his wife, Anne. Until it was given to the Royal Norwegian Society of Sciences and Letters in 1972, this was the largest privately owned collection of trees and shrubs in Norway, noted for its rhododendrons. The best months for a visit are June and July.

(1) By appointment (Telephone 073-63580 or Det Kongelige Norske Vitenskapers Selskab, The Museum of Trondheim, 7000 Trondheim)
(2) Charge
(5) Royal Norwegian Society of Sciences and Letters

Levanger

Nord Trøndelag

5. Staup State School of Horticulture

The school was founded in 1918. In the park of approx 12 acres (5 ha) there are various plants, trees and shrubs, and there is a vegetable garden, an orchard, a nursery garden and glasshouses.

(1) Mon–Fri 8–4
(2) Free
(5) Norwegian Government

Oslo, Trondheimsvn 23

6. Botanical Garden of the University of Oslo

In 1812 King Frederick VI presented his large estate at Tøyen to the university and in 1814 the Botanical Garden was founded, with Christen Smith as the first director. The glasshouses were built by Schübeler in 1868 and 1876. In 1913 the University Botanical Museum was erected in the eastern part of the garden, the greater part of which is laid out as an arboretum and park. Of particular interest are the systematic and economic sections and the alpine rock garden.

(1) May–mid-Aug: Daily 7 am–8 pm; mid-Aug–Sep: Daily 7–7; Oct–Mar: Daily 7–5; Apr: Daily 7–6
(2) Free
(5) University of Oslo

Oslo, Austliveien 29

7. Erling Dall-Larsen Garden

5 miles (8 km) from the centre of Oslo, this is a private garden which was begun in 1941. At first only vegetables were grown, but after World War II it was laid out as a rock garden and with shrubs and trees. There are a number of interesting perennials and it is remarkable that some of the plants survive so far north, at Latitude 60°.

(1) Summer: noon–3; 6–8 pm by appointment (Telephone 02-243556, 8–3; 6–10 pm)
(2) Free
(5) Mr Erling Dall-Larsen

303

Sandnes
Rogaland
8. Rogaland Arboretum

In 1970 the area that now includes the 111 acres (45 ha) of the arboretum was swept by fire and 95 per cent of the trees were destroyed. Although planting of the Rogaland Arboretum only began in 1972 and the trees are still small, it is already attracting a large number of visitors.

(1) *Daily Sunrise–Sunset*
(2) *Free*
(5) *Mr Bjørn A. Stangebye*

Songe
Aust-Agder
9. Solbakkens Herb Garden

The garden was laid out in 1914 by Christine Wüller with fruit trees, shrubs, perennials, vegetables and herbs, plants that are particularly attractive to bees and those used as dyes. Natural woods surround the garden and there is a *Krydderbua*, a room where the herbs are dried. The Norwegian Garden Association hold their courses on herbs here in August. The nearby Elvebakken guest house has herb tea and herb dishes on the menu.

(1) *Jul: Tue, Wed, Thu 11–5*
(5) *Mr Ansof Wüller Christopherson*

Stavanger
10. Ullandhaughagen

Founded and designed by Mrs Ingjerd Höie in collaboration with the Rogaland Folk Museum and Archaeological Museum in Stavanger in 1977, the garden now contains approx 200 species. These are principally herbs and plants that are useful to man: spices, plants used as dyes and a small collection of vegetables and cereals.

(1) *Daily Sunrise–Sunset*
(2) *Free*
(4) *Ullandhauggården, the Iron Age Farm at Ullandhaug (same times)*
(5) *Rogaland Folk Museum and Mrs Ingjerd Höie*

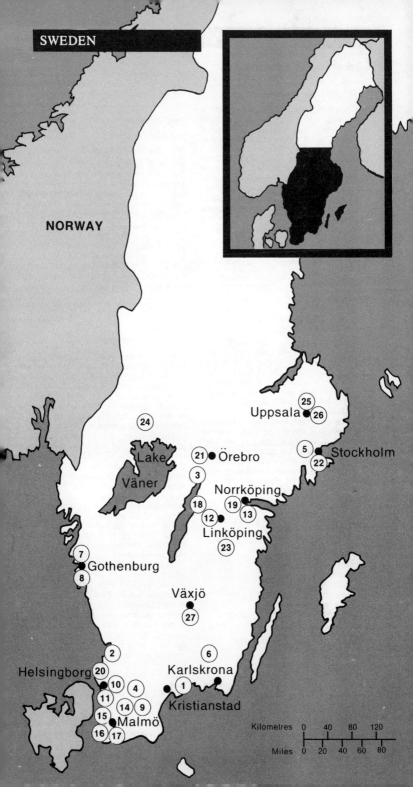

SWEDEN

Bäckaskog, nr Kristianstad

Kristianstad

1. Bäckaskog Castle

The kitchen garden and herb garden at Bäckaskog, which was originally a monastery, retain the character of medieval gardens. There is a rose and dahlia garden, a glasshouse built by King Charles XV and an islet known as the Island of the Refusals (*Korgholmen*), where the last governor of Skåne, Johan Ch. Toll, planted 12 trees to commemorate the times that he was turned down by a lady. There is also a collection of plants that are labelled with appropriate quotations from the Bible. The castle is a hotel.

(1) Mid-Apr–Oct: Daily 10–7
(2) Charge
(3) Restaurant and café
(5) Swedish State

Båstad

Kristianstad

2. Gardens of Norrviken

The gardens spread over the slopes of the Bjäre peninsula, descending to the Kattegatt. They were created by the landscape gardener Rudolf Abelin in 1906 and opened to the public in 1920. The original intention was to grow fruit and nut trees and more than 11,000 trees were planted. Some of these survive.

At the same time Abelin was working on a scheme of simplifying and adapting historical styles of gardening to suit conditions in Sweden. The result is a series of gardens which includes the Baroque garden, with a formal lay-out and topiary; the Japanese garden; the flower garden, with geometrical flowerbeds; the Renaissance garden; the rose garden; the King's Ravine, a woodland walk with flowering shrubs; the oriental terraces; the water garden in front of the villa; and the romantic garden, a glade with pools of water and shrubs, overhung by trees

(1) May–Sep: Daily 9.30–6
(2) Charge
(3) Restaurant
(4) Heated swimming pool; gardening demonstrations
(5) Stiftelsen Norrvikens Trädgårdar

Bastedalen, nr Askersund

Örebro

3. China Park

The park was established in 1961 by Ebbe Johnson in a disused limestone quarry near Lake Vättern. Illustrating both Chinese culture and horticulture, there are museums of Chinese art and costume, with examples of 18th-cent Mandarin dress, as well as a typical Chinese garden. This has five pavilions, streams and bridges and specimens of oriental trees and plants.

(1) Mid-May–Aug: Daily noon–5
(2) Charge
(3) Café
(5) Mr Tryggve Johnson

Bosjökloster

Malmöhus

4. Bosjökloster Castle

The castle dates back to 1080, the year that the Benedictine convent was founded here. Terraces descend to the lake, and there is a rose garden and a herb garden. In the park, part of which is a wild animal reserve, is a remarkable 1,000-year-old oak.

(1) Daily (except 15 Sep) 9–5.30; end Apr–beginning Oct: Sun 9–6
(2) Charge
(3) Restaurant and café
(4) Tower chamber and refectory; children's zoo and playground (same times)
(5) Count Thor Bonde

Drottningholm

Stockholm

5. Drottningholm

The palace was built for Queen Hedvig Eleonora between 1662 and 1686 to designs by Nicodemus Tessin the Elder and completed by his son. The upper storeys of the wings were added in the 1740s for Crown Princess Lovisa Ulrika, and the Rococo theatre was designed by Carl Fredrik Adelcrantz and opened in 1766.

The Baroque garden, composed of parterres, hedges and bosquets, basins, fountains and cascades, covers a rectangular area stretching away from the façade of the palace and confined on each side by lime alleys. This also was begun by the elder Tessin and continued by the son. The inspiration was Vaux-le-Vicomte (qv) and other gardens in France designed by Le Nôtre. It was completed in 1787 and restored according to the original designs in the 1950s. The English park that surrounds the formal garden was laid out in 1787.

The Chinese Pavilion was built for Lovisa Ulrika, as Queen, in 1763–9 by Adelcrantz, assisted by Jean Erik Rehn, replacing an earlier and similar *Lust Palais*. It is typical of the Chinoiserie that was a manifestation of the spirit of the Rococo throughout Europe at that time. The interiors were restored in 1960–7. There are four small pavilions, erected between 1760 and 1769, forming a forecourt to the principal building.

The bronze sculptures on the steps leading from the terrace to the formal garden are by Adriaen de Vries and stood originally in the grounds of Fredriksborg Castle (qv) in Denmark. The marble sculptures, copies of antique originals, are by the Italian Bartolomeo Cavaseppi and they were bought by King Gustav III in 1783.

Interesting features in the park are the Gothic Tower designed by L. J. Desprez, the two jousting arenas and the stone cairn on the Monument Island with lime trees radiating from it erected in honour of King Gustav III. A statue of the king was supposed to be erected on the cairn, hence the name of the island.

(1) *Daily*
(2) *Free*
(3) *Café*
(4) *Palace and Chinese Pavilion (Apr, Sep, Oct: Daily 1–3.30; May–Aug: Mon–Sat 11–4.30; Sun noon–4.30)*
(5) *Drottningholms Slottsförvaltning*

Eringsboda

Blekinge

6. Flower Garden

Founded by Verner Svensson in 1929, the garden was opened to the public in 1949. Covering 10 acres (4 ha), it comprises a series of gardens, some of them illustrating a theme or well-known subject: Lilliput Country has more than 100 dwarf species of trees and plants; Sleeping Beauty's castle is surrounded by a collection of roses. The museum, called 'The Arabian Nights', contains a diversity of objects from all over the world.

(1) *May and Sep: Daily 9–4; Jun and Aug: Daily 9–5; Jul: Daily 9–6*
(2) *Charge*
(3) *Café*
(5) *Mr Verner Svensson*

Gothenburg, Carl Skottsbergsgatan 22

Bohus

7. Botanical Gardens

Due to a generous donation by C. F. Lindberg, the first trees and shrubs were planted in 1916. The gardens were opened to the public in 1923. Covering 422 acres (175 ha), the principal features are a rhododendron valley, Japanese valley, bamboo grove and rock garden. In the hothouses there are good collections of orchids, cacti and begonias; and there is also an arboretum and a nature reserve.

(1) *Garden. Daily 9–Sunset. Hothouses. Mon–Sat 9.30–4; Sep–Jul: Sun noon–3*
(2) *Free*
(3) *Café*
(5) *Town of Gothenburg*

Gothenburg

8. Trädgårdsföreningen

The hothouse (*Palmhuset*), constructed in 1878 and containing a great number of interesting tropical plants, is the largest of

SWEDEN

its kind in Scandinavia. The park, which is in the middle of the city, was opened in 1842.

(1) *Park. Apr–Sep: Daily 7 am–9 pm; Oct–Mar: Daily 7–4. Hothouse. Mon–Fri 9–3.30; Sat, Sun and Public Holidays 10–3*
(2) *Free*
(3) *Restaurant*
(5) *Town of Gothenburg*

Harlösa

Malmöhus

9. Ovedskloster

Situated by Lake Vomb, there was a Premonstratensian monastery here as early as the 12th cent. There are magnificent avenues of limes and an 18th-cent grand avenue leading to the church of Oved. The formal French garden with parterres, terraces and fountains was laid out in 1768 after designs by Carl Hårleman.

(1) *May–Sep: Daily 10–5*
(2) *Free*
(5) *Ramel family*

Helsingborg

Malmöhus

10. Helsingborg Museum Botanical Garden

The garden, founded in 1936, specializes in the indigenous plants of Skåne, with sections for the study of taxonomy, economic herbs, agricultural botany and heredity and evolution material, including a gene bank for Scanian junipers.

(1) *Apr: Daily 10–5; May–Aug: Daily 10–7; Sep: Daily 10–6; Oct: Daily 10–4*
(2) *Charge*
(3) *Café*
(4) *Fredriksdal mansion (same times)*
(5) *Town of Helsingborg*

Helsingborg

11. Sofiero

In the 19th cent this was the summer residence of King Oscar II and the gardens were redesigned for Princess Margaret of Connaught, wife of King Gustav VI Adolf. When he died in 1973 the castle and park, which lie to the north of the town, were acquired by the Municipality of Helsingborg. A notable feature of Sofiero is the rhododendron ravine.

(1) *May–Jun and Aug–mid-Sep: Daily 10–6; Jul: Daily 10–8*
(2) *Charge*
(3) *Café*
(5) *Park Administration, Municipality of Helsingborg*

Linköping
Östergötland
12. Trädgårdsföreningen
Situated in the centre of Linköping, this is a public garden with an assortment of bedding plants, founded in 1859. Of particular interest is the specimen of *Metasequoia glyptostroboides*, the most recently identified pine.

(1) Daily
(2) Free

Lofstad, nr Norrköping
Östergötland
13. Lofstad Manor
6 miles (10 km) south of Norrköping is the manor house, now a museum, built in the mid-17th cent, with wooded grounds laid out by Countess Sophie Piper at the beginning of the 19th cent.

(1) Daily Sunrise–Sunset
(2) Free
(4) Museum (Mid-May–Sep: Daily 1–4)
(5) Länsmuseet, Linköping

Lund, Ostra Vallgatan 20
Malmöhus
14. Botanical Garden of the University of Lund
Situated in the centre of the city, the botanical garden has occupied this site since 1865 although it originated at least 100 years earlier. A distinctive feature, as designed by Professor Agardh, is the collection of shrub magnolias. There is a medicinal herb garden and a rock garden, and the glasshouses, in 12 sections, have 2,000 plants. The garden covers an area of 19 acres (8 ha).

(1) Garden. Daily 6 am–9.30 pm. Glass-houses. Daily 1–3
(2) Free
(5) University of Lund

Malmö
Malmöhus
15. Castle Park
Public park with long avenues of lime trees, a garden in the Japanese manner and children's zoo laid out in 1898 by the landscape designer Edward Glaesel.

(1) Daily
(2) Free
(5) Municipality of the City of Malmö

Malmö
16. King's Park
The official inauguration of the Park took place in 1872 and the pavilion was opened by King Oscar at a later date. Plans for the park, a flower garden and fruit garden were made by the landscape gardner Ove Höeg-Hansen.

(1) Daily
(2) Free
(3) Restaurant
(5) Municipality of the City of Malmö

Malmö
17. Pildamsparken
After the Baltic Exhibition of 1914 it was decided to create a forest park on the site. The war intervened and the plans of E. Erstad-Jörgenssen were set aside. In 1928 the park was opened to the public, the planting of the trees having followed the plans of Erstad-Jörgenssen, revised by the town engineer Erik Bülow-Hübes. There are today more than 20,000 trees in the park, and there is a lake, a pavilion (Margareta-paviljongen) and a children's zoo.

(1) Daily
(2) Free
(3) Café and Restaurant
(5) Municipality of the City of Malmö

Motala
Östergötland
18. Norra Freberga
The garden of the manor house was begun by the present owner in 1953 and designed by the garden architect Ulla Bodorff. The roses are a particular feature and the 10 acres (4 ha) also contain fine specimens of the mulberry, walnut, acacia and thuja.

(1) Daily
(2) Free
(5) Mr Ulf Ribers

Norrköping
Östergötland
19. Carl Johan Park Cactus Garden
A cactus garden with approx 25,000 plants, the lay-out of which is changed every year. It forms part of the 19th-cent municipal park, restored in 1964.

(1) Daily
(2) Free
(5) City Parks Dept

Nyhamnsläge, nr Helsingborg
Malmöhus
20. Krapperup Castle
The castle, dating from the 11th cent, belonged to the Krognos family. It is sur-

rounded by a moat and the gardens lie to each side. On the south is a Renaissance garden. An imposing park lies beyond.

(1) May–Sep: Daily 10–5
(2) Free
(5) Gyllenstierna Krapperupsstifelsen

Örebro
21. Municipal Park

A particular feature of the park, situated near the centre of the town, is the rose garden, and it is also noted for its herbaceous borders in summer. There is a sculpture, Resonance, by Arne Jones and an open-air theatre. A boat crosses to Stora Holmen, a small island in the River Svartån with a miniature railway.

(1) Daily
(2) Free
(3) Café (Summer)
(5) Commune of Örebro

Stockholm
22. Bergius Botanic Garden

The garden owes its origin to the brothers Peter Jonas and Bengt Bergius, who bequeathed to the Royal Swedish Academy of Sciences their entire estate, including their botanical collections. J. P. Bergius was a pupil of Linnaeus and specimens were procured for him by fellow pupils and by serving officers in the Swedish East India Company who travelled to the Far East. The Academy took possession in 1791, moving the collections to their present site at Frescati in 1880.

There are 36 open-air sections containing approx 9,000 trees, shrubs and perennial herbs and 1,000 annuals. They are arranged in systematic order or, as in the rock garden, according to their geographical origin. There are glasshouses for the collections of orchids, palms, begonias, succulents and some economic plants; and the Victoria House has aquatic plants including exotic water-lilies.

(1) Garden. Daily Sunrise–Sunset. Glasshouses. March–Oct: Daily (except Public Holidays) 1–4; Nov–Feb: Daily (except Public Holidays) 1–3. Victoria House closed Oct–May.
(2) Garden: Free; Glasshouses: Charge
(3) Café
(5) University of Stockholm and Bergius Foundation of the Royal Swedish Academy of Sciences

Sturefors, nr Linköping
Östergötland
23. Sturefors Castle

In front of the castle, built in 1704, is a formal garden with a rectangular pool, paths and low clipped hedges. The estate also includes an English park.

SWEDEN

(1) Daily Sunrise–Sunset
(2) Free
(5) Count Nils Bielke

Sunne
Älvs
24. Rottneros Park

The park with its famous collection of sculpture was created by Dr Svante Påhlson between 1938 and 1959. Påhlson, the manager of the wood-pulp factory and power station at Rottneros, enlarged the park gradually. It now covers approx 100 acres (40 ha) and comprises one of the most magnificent collections of rhododendrons in Northern Europe and parkland and formal gardens that serve as a setting for more than 100 sculptures – representative works by Swedish and other Scandinavian sculptors active during his lifetime, such as Carl Eldh and Carl Milles, and casts of some of the most influential European works of art, such as the Victory of Samothrace.

The iron foundries that were formerly here and the appearance of the country were described by the Swedish authoress Selma Lagerlöf in Memories of My Childhood and immortalized by her as Ekeby in The Story of Gösta Berling.

The manor house, destroyed by fire in 1939, was rebuilt by Georges von Dardel. Before it lies a mirror pool, which reflects in its waters the fine pedimented building, and beyond are the Cavaliers' Wings, built as guesthouses. There is a flower garden, the park lake and bird sanctuary connected by natural parkland and, to the south of the house, a series of small formal gardens containing sculptures: a rose garden, the Sculpture Court and the King's Garden. From the east side of the house there is a beautiful view over lawns and flowerbeds to Lake Fryken.

(1) Mid-May–Jun and Aug–mid-Sep: Daily 9–7; Jul: Daily 8–8
(2) Charge
(3) Café
(5) H. B. Rottneros Park

Uppsala, Villavägen 8
25. Botanical Garden of Uppsala University

In 1787 King Gustav III, following repeated requests by Linnaeus for a new site for the university's collections, gave the gardens of the royal castle of Uppsala for a botanical garden. The glasshouses contain some plants from the time of Linnaeus. The rock garden, which dates from 1873, now has a collection of Scandinavian alpines, and there are special collections of clematis, sorbus and old-fashioned roses.

(1) Garden. Summer: Daily 9–7; Winter: Daily 9–3. Glasshouses. Daily 10–noon

(2) *Free*
(5) *University of Uppsala*

Uppsala, Svartbäcksgatan 27

26. Linnaeus's Garden and Museum

The site of the original Botanical Garden of Uppsala University (qv) until the collections were moved in 1787. Laid out originally by Olof Rudbeck the Elder in the 17th cent, they were remodelled by Linnaeus with the help of the architect Carl Hårleman to resemble a miniature Baroque garden.

The garden was restored by the Swedish Linnean Society soon after 1917 following the description and drawings in Linnaeus's *Hortus Upsaliensis* of 1745. The plants are arranged and labelled according to his classifications. On one side of the wide central path are the annuals; on the other the perennials. In front of the orangery are the river pool, lake pool and bog pool with appropriate plants, and to each side are beds of spring and autumn flowers.

The house, rebuilt by Linnaeus in 1742–3, is a museum containing Linnaeus's household effects and possessions. There is a first edition of his *Systema naturae*, 1735, and a copy of *Genera plantarum*, 1753, in which he introduced the use of double names in botany.

(1) *May, Jun, Sep: Daily (except Mon) 2–4; Jul–Aug: Daily (except Mon) 2–5*
(2) *Charge*
(5) *Swedish Linnean Society*

Växjö

Kronoberg

27. Linnaeus Park

Named after the famous Swedish botanist, who attended the high school in Växjö which is close to the park. It contains a statue of Linnaeus, and there is a good cactus collection and displays of spring and summer flowers.

(1) *Daily*
(2) *Free*
(5) *Town of Växjö*

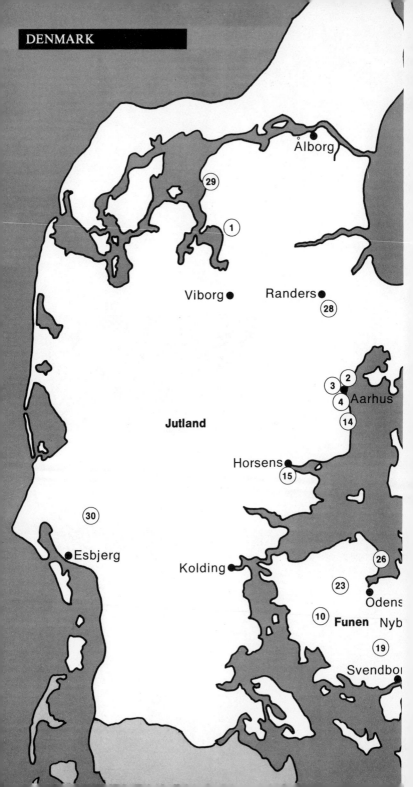

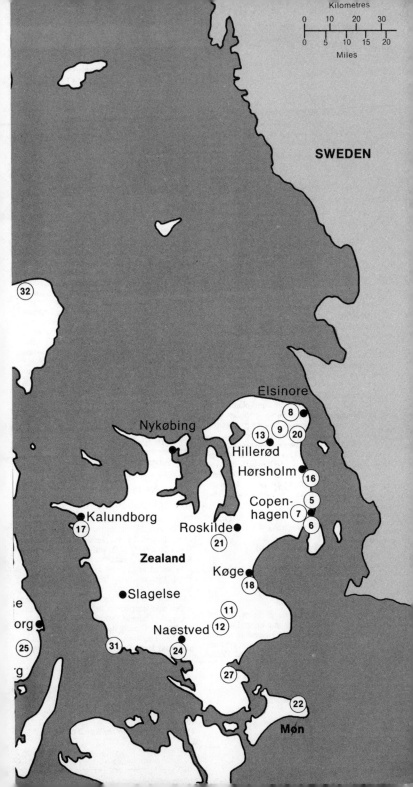

DENMARK

Aalestrup
Jutland
1. Rose Garden of Jutland
This modern rose garden was laid out on the banks of the River Simested in 1967. 15,000 roses are planted in beds terraced out of the slope of the river bank.

(1) End Jun–mid-Sep: Daily 9–Sunset
(2) Free
(3) Café
(5) Rose Garden of Jutland

Aarhus
Jutland
2. Botanical Garden
The original area of approx 11 acres (4.5 ha) was from 1870 to 1911 sublet as a demonstration garden to the Jutland Horticultural Society. It was then taken over by the City and extended in 1922, 1927 and 1943. Today it contains approx 7,300 plant species and regular exchanges of seed take place with botanical gardens all over the world.

A stream which flows through the garden is dammed to form four ponds. In the south-eastern part is the Flower Valley, a saucer-shaped area with terraces planted with a Danish border (for Danish plants), a botanical perennial border, a biological border (for medicinal plants and plants used for dyeing, etc) and a nursery border; also with roses, summer-flowering plants, botanical annuals and garden perennials.

Den gamle By (The Old Town) occupies part of the garden. This consists of houses moved from all parts of Denmark and re-erected and also shops and small industries. The glasshouses of the Botanical Institute (qv) are situated in another area of the garden.

(1) Mon–Sat 1.30–4; Sun and Public Holidays 10–noon, 1.30–4
(2) Free
(4) Den gamle By (same times)
(5) City of Aarhus

Aarhus, Mollevejen 10
3. Botanical Institute
Built in 1968 within the perimeter of the Botanical Garden (qv) and opened to the public in 1970, the most interesting of the glasshouses is the Monsoon House with its collection of plants from Thailand. Visit from mid-May to mid-September.

(1) Mon–Sat 1.30–3.30; Sun 10–noon
(2) Free
(5) University of Aarhus

Aarhus, Marselisborg
4. Forest Botanical Garden
The castle of Marselisborg on the outskirts of Aarhus has been a royal residence since 1902. In the woods that surround it an arboretum was established in c 1920. Today it contains 1,200 trees and shrubs from different parts of the world, as well as a wide variety of wild woodland flowers. In spring the wood anemones are a particular feature.

(1) Daily
(2) Free
(5) Commune of Aarhus

Copenhagen, Gothersgade 126
5. Botanic Garden of the University of Copenhagen
Moved to its present site on the old city ramparts in 1874 and laid out within a network of curving paths by the landscape architect H. Flindt, the garden covers an area of 24 acres (10 ha) and contains approx 25,000 species. All plants, including the trees in the arboretum, are arranged in groups according to principles of systematic botany. Amongst others there are sections devoted to annuals, biennials, perennials, roses and rock plants. There is also a section devoted to native Danish species. There is an extensive range of glasshouses, in one of which the giant water-lily, *Victoria regia (amazonica)* is a particular attraction. On account of the large number of ligneous species the garden is quite park-like, although several genera have not reached the age of a hundred years due to the clayey subsoil in parts of the garden and to a succession of severe gales.

(1) Daily 10–3
(2) Free
(5) University of Copenhagen

Copenhagen
6. Frederiksberg Castle
The slope below the castle was terraced in c 1700 and laid out in the Baroque manner after designs by the landscape architects Hans Henrik Scheel and Johan Cornelius Krieger. This great formal garden was naturalized at the end of the 18th cent by Peter Petersen. An Ionic temple is sited against a backdrop of fine trees in the Claudian manner. There is much serpentine water and astride it at one point is an exquisite Chinese bridge crowned by a pagoda roof hung with bells at the eave corners. This exotic confection in red, blue and gold leads to an island, where among the trees is a Chinese teahouse in the same manner. The whole park is dignified by fine forest trees planted to form glades in the manner recommended by contemporary English gardening writers and theorists.

(1) Daily 6–half an hour before Sunset
(2) Free
(5) Inspectorate for the Royal Gardens

Copenhagen

7. Rosenborg Castle

Close to the early 17th-cent red brick castle of King Christian IV is a parterre of dwarf box, yellow roses and heliotrope. It is enclosed by hornbeam hedges clipped to form bays in which seats are set. The framework of Johan Cornelius Krieger's Baroque garden of 1750 can still be discerned in the lime avenues and large grass 'platts', but today the general impression is of a natural park-like garden. In one corner is a fine double herbaceous border, which is related to a neo-classical temple.

(1) *Daily 6–half an hour before Sunset*
(2) *Free*
(4) *Castle (May–mid-Oct: Daily 11–3; Mid-Oct–Apr: Tue and Fri 11–1; Sun 11–2)*
(5) *Inspectorate for the Royal Gardens*

Elsinore

Zealand

8. Marienlyst

Charming neo-classical *trianon* built in the late 18th cent by the powerful Count Möltke for his wife Marie, from whom it takes its name. House and garden occupy the site of the former castle of Lundehave, built and provided with a garden by King Frederick II in 1587. This royal garden also served his nearby fortress of Kronberg, whose restricted site and military function left no space for gardening within its walls. The simple parterre of dwarf box and lime and two lines of rhododendrons, aligned on the principal elevation of the building, date from 1920. Trees and shrubs, informally planted, clothe the steep slope behind.

(1) *Daily*
(2) *Free*
(4) *House, which forms part of the Municipal Museum of Elsinore (mid-May–mid-Sep: Daily 1–4; mid-Sep–mid-May: Wed and Fri 1–3)*
(5) *City of Elsinore*

Fredensborg, nr Copenhagen

Zealand

9. Fredensborg Palace

The early 18th-cent palace is a summer residence of the Danish Royal Family. It lies at the centre of a Baroque lay-out of radiating avenues and at the end of the principal street of the little town of Fredensborg. Beyond the palace is a great lawn with some formal planting of heliotrope and other bedding plants. To the left is a dell encircled by pollarded limes; complementary to it on the right is a circular mound. From the lawn long allées of pollarded limes fan out, giving glimpses of a natural lake in the far distance. Between them the original bosquets have grown up into mature beechwoods. There is much sculpture in the French taste by Johannes

Wiedewelt and the whole composition was the work of the landscape designer, Johan Cornelius Krieger for King Frederick IV in c 1720. It was altered in 1759 for Frederick V by N. H. Jardin. The royal private garden, known as the *Marmorhave* (Marble Garden), is an enclosed parterre, quite independent of the larger design, with much Baroque sculpture by Wiedewelt, roses, hydrangeas and bedding plants.

(1) *Garden. Daily 6–half an hour before Sunset. Marmorhave. Jul and when Royal Family are not in residence 8–4*
(2) *Free*
(4) *Part of the Palace and Chapel Royal (Jul: Daily 1–5. Tour every half hour)*
(5) *Inspectorate for the Royal Gardens*

Glamsbjerg, nr Odense

Funen

10. Krengerup

This large 18th-cent house in a remote and beautiful part of the island of Funen is approached on a central axis through a great courtyard surrounded by service buildings – barns, cowsheds, stables and retainers' dwellings. On the garden side of the house the original formality has been softened and naturalized; there is a lake, a collection of hardy rhododendrons and a wooded park with rides cut through beechwoods.

(1) *Summer: Daily 7–9; Winter: Daily 9–5*
(2) *Free*
(5) *Countess Lily Knuth*

Haslev

Zealand

11. Bregentved

The estate of Bregentved is one of the largest in Denmark. It was bought in 1746 by Count A. G. Möltke, the powerful minister of King Frederick V, and the white-stuccoed mansion house in the Rococo taste dates from the same decade. It was enlarged and given an idiosyncratic copper-sheathed spire in 1891.

The framework of the original formal garden by N. H. Jardin can still be detected in the fine lime avenues that survive in their maturity. This garden was naturalized in c 1830 under the direction of Rudolf Rothe and extended in the 1890s. It now extends to approx 49 acres (20 ha) and is notable for its many fine specimen trees. Hans Christian Andersen was a frequent guest of the Möltke family and is believed to have drawn on the grounds of Bregentved and the surrounding countryside for the inspiration for several of his stories.

(1) *Sun and Wed 9–8*
(2) *Free*
(5) *Count H. H. Möltke*

DENMARK

Haslev, nr Naestved

Zealand

12. Gisselfeld

An extensive park in the English landscape manner was laid out towards the end of the 19th cent by an English garden designer named Milner as the setting for the large moated 18th-cent castle of red brick. It incorporates a series of lakes and fine trees. Near the entrance are formal beds, but elsewhere mostly shrubs and permanent planting. There is a spring garden, a fountain garden, a bamboo alley and a small picturesquely thatched and half-timbered watchman's house set up as a museum of local farming and garden implements. The hothouses contain banana, orange, coffee and cotton trees, as well as orchids and a group of insectivorous plants. Nearby is the Paradise Garden (separate entrance fee), an arboretum founded in 1814. The swans at Gisselfeld were the inspiration of one of Hans Christian Andersen's best-known stories, *The Ugly Duckling.*

(1) Apr: Daily (except Sat and Public Holidays) 10–5; Sat and Public Holidays 10–5.30; May: Daily (except Sat and Public Holidays) 10–6; Sat and Public Holidays 10–6.30; Jun–mid-Aug: Daily 10–7; mid-Aug–end of autumn vacation: Daily 11–5
(2) Charge
(3) Café
(5) Count Eric Danneskiold-Samsee

Hillerød, nr Copenhagen

Zealand

13. Frederiksborg Castle

The great red brick castle built for King Christian IV in the early 17th cent stands on an island in the lake. The garden originally consisted of a small vegetable, fruit and flower garden to the north and west of the castle. In *c* 1720 the landscape designer Johan Cornelius Krieger laid out an immense Baroque garden terraced out of the hillside opposite the principal façade of the castle to the north. The terraces are articulated by clipped box and pollarded limes. At the top is a circular sheet of water, enclosed by limes, with a fountain in the centre. This artificial pond supplies a series of cascades, which fall eventually into the lake at the foot of the hillside. To the east the hillside is laid out as parkland and to the west on level ground is a large park with an irregularly shaped lake and a 16th-cent bath house. Krieger's grand design survives unaltered and it is, consequently, one of the most historically important gardens in Denmark.

(1) Daily 6–half an hour before Sunset
(2) Free

(4) Castle (May–Sep: Daily 10–5; Oct and Apr: Daily 11–4; Nov–Mar: Daily 11–3)
(5) Inspectorate for the Royal Gardens

Højbbjerg, nr Aarhus

Jutland

14. Moesgaard

The neo-classical house was built in 1776 for Baron Gülcrone by the architect Zuber, who was also responsible for the design of the garden. It was originally in two parts: formality in the French manner around the house and, beyond, an English landscape garden. This was the first landscape garden in Denmark and an artificial ruin was a prominent feature of it. It has been greatly extended since the 18th cent and today provides a setting for a collection of Danish prehistoric monuments and reconstructions of ancient buildings, most of which have been moved from their original sites to make way for new roads and buildings.

(1) Daily
(2) Free
(3) Restaurant and café
(4) Moesgaard Museum of Archaeology and Ethnography (Daily, except Mon, 10–5)
(5) Prehistoric Museum of Moesgaard

Horsens

Jutland

15. Vitus Bering's Park

Rhododendron and azalea park with sculpture commemorating the explorer Vitus Bering (1681–1741), opened in 1957. Visit in May or June.

(1) Daily
(2) Free
(5) City Gardener's Office

Hørsholm

Zealand

16. Arboretum of the Royal Veterinary and Agricultural University

This collection of trees covering 37 acres (15·6 ha) was established in 1936 by the Royal Veterinary and Agricultural University as an extension to the Forest Botanical Garden. The first director was Dr Syrach-Larsen. 1,700 species and variations are represented, based for the most part on material from natural populations. There are many conifers from North America and from China, where seed was collected by Joseph Rock during his expeditions in the 1920s. The Arboretum at Charlottenlund, founded in 1838, is administered by the Hørsholm Arboretum.

(1) Mon–Fri 8.30–4.30 (visitors should apply to the office near the entrance); Sat and Sun by appointment

Kalundborg

Zealand

17. Lerchenborg

As a general rule in Denmark the relationship between a country house and the estate that supports it is emphasized by the close proximity of house and farm buildings. At Lerchenborg the latter are on an unusually impressive scale, arranged round an immense courtyard on an axis that passes through the centre of the principal façade of the stuccoed 18th cent house.

In the garden beyond there is much formal planting of clipped yew, box and lime, with an avenue continuing on the axis of the approach through the farmyard. To one side lies a modern rose garden, the largest in Scandinavia. Beyond are fine beechwoods.

(1) *Mid-Jun–Aug: Mon–Sat 11–5; Sun 10–6*
(2) *Free*
(3) *Café*
(5) *Count Levche-Levchenborg*

Køge

Zealand

18. Vallø

This vast Renaissance castle of fierce red brick was extensively remodelled in the 19th cent. Since 1738 it has been occupied as a residential institution for unmarried daughters of the Danish nobility. Beyond the moat is an extensive landscaped park with some areas formally planted, in particular a rose garden and borders of herbaceous plants. The mount surmounted by a group of four limes is a survival from an earlier garden. Near the house, and somewhat overpowered by it, is a parterre of dwarf box and roses.

(1) *Park and courtyard: Daily during daylight hours*
(2) *Free*
(5) *Vallø Foundation*

Kvaerndrup

Funen

19. Egeskov

The gardens at Egeskov are the most elaborate and the best known in Denmark. The walls of the red-brick castle, completed in 1554, rise sheer from the surface of the lake which serves it as a moat. The picturesque roof-line of conical towers and stepped gables is an embellishment of the 19th cent.

Around the lake lie 30 acres (12 ha) of garden. To the east is a formal Baroque layout dating from c 1730. It comprises a series of large 'open-air rooms' separated from one another by hedges of beech and horn-beam that are remarkable for their great age. Bisecting these enclosures and running parallel to the principal façade of the castle is an avenue of pollarded limes. This breaks as it passes in front of the castle to allow space for a Renaissance parterre of clipped box and red gravel, a reconstruction of 1962. The enclosures flanking the parterre are known as the Baron's and the Baroness's Gardens. Another is a spring garden planted with tulips; from June to October these are replaced by a large and notable collection of standard fuchsias. A further enclosure is planted as a traditional manor house kitchen garden: pergolas of espaliered pear trees and old-fashioned roses divide it into four triangles, one for herbs and hops, the others for fruit, vegetables and flowers for picking. There is an ancient maze of clipped beech and nearby a charming 18th-cent octagonal gazebo flanked by pleached limes. To the south-west is a new informal garden with shrubs and evergreen trees, perennials, a heather garden, a circular sunken garden devoted to roses, lavender and lilies and another to grey and silver plants. Traditional cottage flowers grow around the outbuildings. Visit from June to September.

(1) *Daily during daylight hours*
(2) *Free*
(3) *Café and restaurant*
(4) *Museum of Veteran and Vintage Vehicles (Palm Sun–mid-May: Daily 9–5; mid-May–Sep: Daily 9–6; Oct: Sat and Sun 9–5)*
(5) *Count and Countess Ahlefeldt-Laurvig-Bille*

Kvistgaard, nr Elsinore

Zealand

20. D. T. Poulsens Planteskole

This is a commercial enterprise specializing in roses. There is a rose garden, designed by Morten Klint and laid out in 1967, an arboretum and a large nursery garden. The nursery dates from 1878.

(1) *Rose garden. Daily*
(2) *Free*
(5) *D. T. Poulsens Planteskole*

Lejre, nr Roskilde

Zealand

21. Ledreborg

This grand Baroque house dating from the 1740s is approached at right angles to the main façade by an impressive avenue of mature limes nearly a mile (1·6 km) long. This culminates in a great forecourt, flanked by pavilions with a chapel on the central axis. Below the house on the garden side a succession of terraces with clipped box hedges descends steeply to a T-shaped formal water and a fountain in the bottom of a ravine. Beyond, the greensward sweeps up again to woods divided in the centre to give a glimpse of sky. This dramatic composition in the formal manner is a restoration of 1906, recently modified for ease of upkeep.

(1) *Daily*
(2) *Free*
(5) *Count Holstein-Ledreborg*

Magleby

Møn

22. Liselund

The house and garden date from the last decade of the 18th cent and were the creation, over 20 years, of Antoine and Lisa de la Calmette. The garden lies on either side of a stream that runs down through a cleft in the chalk cliffs towards the sea. Here and there the stream is dammed to form pools, a waterfall and a lake, and the paths that wind through the beechwoods give sudden glimpses of the sea below. Features of the park are the Swiss Cottage, Norwegian Hut, Chinese Tent and Necessary House, disguised as a log store. Liselund and its garden landscape are a charming latter-day expression of Rococo taste.

(1) *Daily*
(2) *Free*
(3) *Café*
(5) *Baron Niels Rosenkrantz*

Morud, nr Odense

Funen

23. Langesø Bulb Park

Within the grounds of an elegant manor house built in 1778 a modern bulb garden was established in 1957. Tulips are the particular speciality. They are planted informally in clumps according to colour and type on the edge of a mature beechwood and near a lake. The garden is managed by a consortium of commercial bulb growers. There are good walks in the surrounding woods.

(1) *Mid-Apr–mid-Jun: Daily 10–6*
(2) *Charge*
(5) *Baron G. Berner Schilden Holsten*

Naestved

Zealand

24. Gavnø

Otto Thott and his wife bought the estate of Gavnø in 1735. Twenty years later they began to re-model the ancient house that had occupied this beautiful site on the edge of a creek since the Middle Ages and the result was the handsome Rococo mansion that survives unaltered today.

The garden is one of the best known in Denmark. It is in the nature of a well-mani-

cured park, with lawns and fine trees, a pond and a summer house in the form of a *cottage orné* put up in 1843 for the pleasure of the children of the house. There is also a lime avenue, the trees given to Otto Thott in 1765 by King Frederick V because, in their original position in Copenhagen, they had begun to obscure an equestrian statue of the king.

Into this historical matrix a modern bulb garden has been woven to great effect. Everywhere in the garden are informally shaped beds, which in May are ablaze with thousands of tulips, narcissi, hyacinths, crocuses and other bulbous plants. The bulbs are a commercial enterprise and most of the plants seen in the garden can be ordered from the catalogue.

(1) *May–mid-Aug: Daily 10–5*
(2) *Free*
(3) *Restaurant*
(4) *Chapel and part of the house (same times)*
(5) *Gavnø Foundation*

Nyborg

Funen

25. Glorup

Glorup is little more than a Rococo *pavillon* of one storey with a deep mansard roof set round a courtyard. Unlike most 18th-cent country houses in Denmark, it has no adjacent complex of estate buildings, but its park is one of the most beautiful essays in Baroque design in the country. By contrast with the house, it is conceived on a grand scale that is truly French. With the passage of time, however, its severe geometry has been gradually softened by the natural growth of trees and turf, so that in its present state it is a rare synthesis of the formal and the natural schools of landscape design. Two parallel avenues of limes, about half a mile (0·8 km) long form the sides of a great rectangle that at one end is closed by the façade of the house (which dictates its width) and at the other by the horizon.

In front of the house and close to it is a parterre of clipped box and bedding plants; a great square pool separates the parterre from a long prospect of sheep-cropped turf, punctuated at intervals by pairs of fine urns on pedestals and fading eventually into a deciduous wood which masks the horizon. The avenue on the right leads from the entrance forecourt to a gate, beyond which it becomes a track through a cornfield and vanishes over the horizon. The left-hand avenue terminates with a fine circular temple with its statue intact beneath a shallow dome. Elsewhere the grounds are consciously informal with the remains of a Gothic bridge across a wooded ravine, lightly wooded parkland, more water and a mount surmounted by a large stone table beneath trees.

(1) *Thurs noon–6; Sun 9–6*
(2) *Free*

Otterup, nr Odense

Funen

26. Hofmansgave

The history of the gardens that form the setting of this small Rococo manor house (1784) can be traced back to the early 18th cent. The surviving garden in the French taste dates from c 1740. The seed for many of the trees in the English landscape garden (c 1810), designed by Flindt, was collected by the Danish botanist and owner of Hofmansgave, Niels Hofman Bang. The wooden Norwegian mountain house was the gift of Jacob Aall. A German romantic garden was laid out in c 1860 and the complex was further extended in 1920 and 1970.

The gardens contain a number of fine and rare trees, notably *Lonicera quinquelocularis, Caragana frutex,* a fine specimen of *Alnus cordata* planted in 1836, perhaps the oldest specimen in Denmark of *Pseudotsuga menziesii,* planted in 1862, and a *Morus nigra* that is approx 230 years old.

(*1*) *Summer: Daily 9–5; Winter: Daily during daylight hours*
(*2*) *Free*
(*5*) *Hofmansgave Foundation*

Praestø

Zealand

27. Nysø

An attractive late 17th-cent country house (1673) set in a contemporary Baroque garden in the French manner with avenues of limes and a lake. Nysø is known principally for its associations with the great Danish neo-classical sculptor, Bertel Thorvaldsen, who was a frequent visitor and had his own studio in a wing of the house.

(*1*) *Daily*
(*2*) *Free*
(*4*) *Thorvaldsen Museum (Apr–Sep: Wed and Sat 2–5; Sun 10–5)*
(*5*) *Mr P. Stampe Holst*

Randers

Jutland

28. Clausholm Castle

Castle, stable buildings and formal garden date from the 1690s. Together they comprise one of the earliest Baroque layouts in Denmark. The garden lies to the south of the castle and was probably designed by Nicodemus Tessin the Younger. The gardens were greatly extended in c 1760 by the planting of a park in the natural romantic manner to the west of the original Baroque composition. An impressive fountain in the Italian style has recently been erected on a terrace in the formal garden in accordance with a proposal in the original design.

(*1*) *Daily 9–6*
(*2*) *Free*

(*3*) *Café*
(*4*) *Castle (Palm Sun–mid-May and Oct: Sat and Sun 10–noon, 2–5.30; mid-May –Sep: Daily 10–noon, 2–5.30)*
(*5*) *Mr Henrik Berner*

Ranum

Jutland

29. Vitskøl Kloster

Re-creation of a monastic herb garden inspired by the finding of plants from the original Cistercian monastery garden, founded in 1158. In the 1940s Magna and Verner Leth took as their model the 9th-cent herb garden of the Diocesan Library at St Gallen, Switzerland. To this was added a 7-section medicinal garden in 1963 and in 1976 the small Fragrant Garden for the Blind, based on the one in San Francisco's Golden Gate Park.

(*1*) *Jun–mid-Sep: Daily 10–5*
(*2*) *Charge*
(*4*) *Ruins of the monastery and church; plants for sale*
(*5*) *Board of Supervisors of Vitskøl Kloster*

Sig, nr Varde

Jutland

30. Tambour's Garden

A modern garden, founded in 1940 by Gerhardt Tambour, containing a wide selection of plants from all over the world.

(*1*) *May–mid-Sep: Daily Sunrise–Sunset*
(*2*) *Charge*
(*5*) *Mr Gerhardt Tambour*

Skaelskør

Zealand

31. Borreby

Only the park and part of the garden at Borreby are open to visitors, but it is worth visiting for the views they afford of the gaunt red-brick castle (built 1556) with its moat and the picturesque jumble of cottages and service buildings over which it presides. Hard beneath the walls and within the moat is a tree-lined lawn which was once the kitchen garden. There are old lime avenues and in one place a large group of rhododendrons. House and garden are enclosed by a well-wooded park.

(*1*) *Daily during daylight hours*
(*2*) *Free*
(*5*) *Mr C. H. Castenschiold*

Tranehuse, nr Grenå

Jutland

32. Meilgaard

The 16th-cent castle of Meilgaard was

319

extensively altered in the 19th cent. Its four-square bulk is relieved by the ogee-capped entrance tower and the strong contrast between white plastered walls and red pantiled roofs. There is a moat, wide expanses of grass, closely mown in the Danish fashion, and fine mature lime trees. The principal attractions are the display of tulips and other bulbous plants in spring and early summer, planted in island beds in the grass, and an exhibition of summer houses.

(1) Daily
(2) Free
(3) Restaurant
(5) Mr N. Tuil

England

The National Trust
42 Queen Anne's Gate,
London SW1H 9AS

National Gardens Scheme
57 Lower Be grave St,
London SW1W 0LR

Gardeners' Sunday Organisation
White Witches,
Claygate Rd,
Dorking,
Surrey

The Royal Horticultural Society
Vincent Square,
London SW1P 2PE

The Northern Horticultural Society
Harlow Car,
Harrogate,
North Yorkshire

Scotland

The National Trust for Scotland
5 Charlotte Square,
Edinburgh EH2 4DU

Scotland's Garden Scheme
26 Castle Terrace,
Edinburgh EH1 2EL

Royal Caledonian Horticultural Society
44 Melville St,
Edinburgh 3

Northern Ireland

Ulster Gardens Scheme
c/o The National Trust,
Rowallane,
Saintfield,
Co. Down

France

Société Nationale d'Horticulture de France
84 rue de Grenelle,
75007 Paris

Caisse Nationale des Monuments Histor-
iques
62 rue Saint Antoine,
75004 Paris

Belgium

Espaces Verts et Art des Jardins
rue du Châtelain 20,
B-1050 Brussels

Italy

Comitato Visita Giardini Fiorentino
Via Proconsolo 10,
Florence

Spain

Institudo de Estudias de Jardineria y Art
Paisajista
San Mateo 13,
Madrid

USEFUL ADDRESSES

West Germany

Zentralverband Gartenbau e.V. und
Deutsche Gartenbau Gesellschaft e.V.
Kölnerstrasse 142–148,
5300 Bonn-Bad Godesberg 1

Zentralverband des Deutschen Gemüse-,
Obst- und Gartenbaues
Koblenzerstrasse 33,
Bonn

Austria

Oesterreichische Gartenbauvereinigung
Parkring 12,
Vienna 1

Switzerland

Gärtnermeisterverband Schweiz
Forchstrasse 287,
Zürich

Verband Deutschweizerischer Gartenbau-
vereine
Mensingen, Berne

Norway

Norsk Hagetidend
Motzfeldsgt. 1,
Oslo

INDEX

INDEX

INDEX

INDEX

If you have found this book useful, you may want to obtain these guides:

EUROPE'S WONDERFUL LITTLE HOTELS AND INNS (REVISED EDITION)
edited by Hilary Rubinstein

> 500 entries, 200 of them brand new

Written especially for discerning travelers who shun the brassy tourist establishments and seek out charming little hotels and inns, places with special character and personal service.

AMERICA'S WONDERFUL LITTLE HOTELS AND INNS
edited by Barbara Crossette

Three hundred charming places to stay—in every state in the Union and in most Canadian provinces. (Available January 1980)

THE WINETASTER'S GUIDE TO EUROPE
by Anthony Hogg

A country-by-country, region-by-region guide to on-the-spot visits, tours, and wine-tastings at vineyards, cellars, and distilleries throughout Europe. Over 300 establishments, with addresses, phone numbers, and names of contacts. (Available January 1980)